PRAISE FOR *DAN RICE*

"Rice has turned out to be the most modern of figures, a man who embodied many of today's obsessions: the fascination with celebrity, the blurring of high brow and low, the appropriation of African-American culture by whites, the intersection of popular culture and politics."
—*New York Times*

"It is a great story that Carlyon has chosen to tell . . . There is much to admire in this work. The writing is lively . . . and the stories are fresh . . . *Dan Rice* helps recover not only popular entertainment itself, but the whole of 19th Century show business."—*Chicago Tribune*

"Wonderfully appealing and constantly fascinating . . . Carlyon has produced a masterful work of cultural and theater criticism that advances the literature as well as it entertains."—*Publishers Weekly* (starred review)

"David Carlyon has produced an exhaustively detailed history of Rice's colorful career . . . Carlyon seems ideally suited to write a biography of Rice."—*New York Times*

"Not just a biography of a unique and colorful man, but a portrait of a fragile America being played out on the stage of Dan Rice's Great Show."—*Providence Journal*

"A most extraordinary contribution to the field . . . Eminently readable, scholarly study [with] remarkable insight, sophisticated analysis, and unblemished research."—*Theatre History Studies*

"If anyone can write Dan Rice's biography, it is David Carlyon and he does not disappoint the dedicated reader of American humor and its rich tradition. His learning is deep, his knowledge of the American 19th Century thick with instance and detail, yet his narration moves along swiftly and efficiently."—*Buffalo News*

"A compassionate and moving biography and an incisive look at a neglected aspect of American popular culture."—*Booklist*

"A well-researched and informative study that will delight connoisseurs of American theater and entertainment."—*Library Journal*

"In this well-written and fascinating biography, Carlyon paints a vivid picture of a simpler, rougher time in America, when the roots of our popular culture were just being formed."—*Book Magazine*

"Well-researched and witty . . . thanks to David Carlyon, Rice may find a new audience here in the 21st century."—*Time Out NY*

DAN RICE

DAN RICE
THE ORIGINAL HUMORIST AS HE APPEAR'D IN HIS
GREAT UNION SPEECH.
Before the MEDICAL STUDENTS. Philada. Dec. 20th 1859

DAN RICE

THE MOST FAMOUS MAN YOU'VE NEVER HEARD OF

DAVID CARLYON

PUBLICAFFAIRS
NEW YORK

To Barbara, Daniel, and Will

Published in the United States by PublicAffairs™, a member of the Perseus Books Group.

Printed in the United States of America.

Book Design by Nina D'Amario.

Library of Congress Cataloging-in-Publication data

Carlyon, David.

Dan Rice: the most famous man you've never heard of / David Carlyon.—1st ed.

p. cm.

Includes index.

ISBN-10 1-58648-239-4 (pbk)
ISBN-13 978-1-58648-239-8 (pbk)

1. Rice, Dan, 1823-1900. 2. Clowns—United States—Biography. I. Title.

GV1811.R4 C37 2001

791.3'3'092—dc21

[B]

2001041869

CONTENTS

PART 3

The Great American Humorist: 1853—1856

PART 4

"Something Higher": 1856—1860

PART 5

The People's Candidate: 1860—1867

PART 6

Reverse of Success: 1868—1883

PART 7

Old Uncle Dan: 1884—1900

FOREWORD

by Ken Emerson

"I am clowning and also my nigero singing and dancing is drawing good houses."

When Dan Rice wrote this in 1843, American popular culture was off to the races, where shortly it would whistle Stephen Foster's "doo-dah!" and eventually Dan Emmett's "Dixie." Dan was friends with both men and in town when "Dixie" and Foster's first hit song, "Oh! Susanna," premiered publicly, in New York and Pittsburgh, respectively.

It was during Dan Rice's heyday that America put the "pop" in popular culture. The steamboat, the locomotive, the telegraph, and inexpensive, rapid-fire printing presses knit together a nation. These revolutions in transportation and communications created the mass that made mass entertainment possible. A century and a half later, 1850 is only yesterday.

P. T. Barnum, Rice's occasional competitor, pioneered modern publicity and advertising. His "humbug" is today's hype; his Jenny Lind our Three Tenors. In the miscegenation of blackface minstrelsy—Rice's "nigero singing"—lie the origins of much if not most of American popular music, from Irving Berlin to Eminem. The penny press spawned tabloid journalism.

America before the Civil War witnessed the birth of the notion and phenomenon of celebrity, which depended on mass communications to create a mass of celebrants. Later in the century, Henry James recognized celebrity's American provenance when he observed of France's most famous actress that "Mlle. Sarah Bernhardt is not, to my sense, a celebrity because she is an artist. She is a celebrity because, apparently, she desires with an intensity that has rarely been equaled to be one. . . . She is too American not to succeed in America."

Not everyone considered America's "modern improvements" to be progress. Retreating to Walden Pond, Thoreau scoffed, "We are in great haste to construct a magnetic telegraph from Maine to Texas; but Maine and Texas, it may be, have nothing important to communicate."

It was Dan Rice's genius that he gave Maine and Texas—and the rest of a nation that was expanding territorially and compressing technologically—something to talk about. Americans shared a laugh at his jokes; a leer at his ladies in tights; amazement at Excelsior, the horse that climbed stairs, and Lalla Rookh, the tightrope-walking elephant; controversy over Rice's political and regional sympathies; and suspense as Rice's roller-coaster career hurtled off and on the tracks. His celebrity united the nation at water troughs and watering holes before there was a water cooler or Starbuck's.

Among Rice's many roles in "the show business"—minstrel song-and-dance man, Shakespearean jester, circus showman—his most modern was stand-up comedian or "American Humorist." Rice's "hits" on current affairs and his flirtations with running for office blurred the boundaries between political and popular culture long before Leno, Letterman, and *Saturday Night Live* became stops as obligatory as Iowa and New Hampshire on presidential candidates' itineraries.

Rice possessed to an uncommon degree an entertainer's urge to be all things to all people. This, his quick wits, his indomitability, and his ambivalence, torn as he was between roguery and respectability, enabled him to bridge temporarily the growing divisions of race, region, class, and "high" and "low" culture that sundered the nation in and after the Civil War. These great divides proved Rice's ultimate undoing, however, and no popular artist overcame them until Mark Twain.

Twain remembered Rice fondly in *Huckleberry Finn*, re-creating his childhood excitement when the circus came to Hannibal. More than nostalgia is at play in Twain's adult recollection, however. I suspect he also recognized Rice as a co-conspirator in popular culture and his predecessor as American Humorist.

Ken Emerson is the author of *Doo-dah!: Stephen Foster and the Rise of American Popular Culture.*

PREFACE

Dan Rice and I were both clowns. When I began writing about him, I assumed that label was all we shared.

I had been one of Ringling Brothers and Barnum & Bailey Circus's cavorting crew, anonymous, low paid, and apparently interchangeable. Decked out in baggy pants and a big red nose, I flung gags into the three-ring spectacle. Rice, in stark contrast, was a rich, glittering star—the Johnny Carson of the nineteenth century—standing alone in the center of his own show's single ring. The spitting image of Uncle Sam in stripes, a top hat, and the most recognized goatee of the age, Rice was a talking clown, quipping spontaneously, booming out Shakespeare, singing about bloomers, feuding with Horace Greeley—and running for president. He was Will Rogers, Robin Williams, and John McCain rolled into one.

The gap between Rice and me seemed even larger as I studied antebellum performance. In the 1850s, the circus overlapped with theater, minstrelsy, and lectures in a bubbling stew of adult fare, full of near-nudity and racy jokes, of violence, and public affairs. Increasing the excitement, audiences of all classes and interests voiced their opinions in a noisy public conversation across the footlights as they talked to each other and to the performers.

When I was a clown myself, I had not heard of Dan Rice. He had long faded from cultural memory, and even in the circus, no one mentioned him. But even knowing, I would have found little in common with him as I changed into costumes as a chaps-wearing cowboy with no pants, as Mercury delivering flowers in winged spats and winged helmet, as a ballerina with an inner-tube bustle. If someone had told me about the once-famous clown, I might have jabbered about the eternal nature of comedy, but circus had become children's fare and innocuous, worlds away from Rice's performances.

That was especially true in my early days on the circus.

Clowning is hard work. That's a self-mocking joke that clowns pass around, teasing their own pretensions, but it is also true. After the fun of performing in college musicals with crazy-leg clowning, and the sheltered attempts of the two-month Ringling/Barnum Clown College, professional clowning felt like being doused in ice water. I struggled to be funny through thirteen shows a week, three on Saturday, while running in and out continually. Sometimes the cold water was literal: In Atlanta, when Clown Alley—the clown dressing area—was near the backdoor, winter rain blew in. Sometimes we were wet from heat: In St. Louis in August, the arena was not air-conditioned, so we had to drag on costumes still sopping from the sweat of the previous show.

Emotionally, it was tougher yet. I knew hard work. I had fought forest fires, served as a military policeman, labored in a factory, graduated from law school. I had even been a substitute teacher. Conventional wisdom says that clown makeup is a mask, but I felt vulnerable, my inadequacies as a clown laid bare. I would try a gag and it fell flat, leaden. I ran through the seats in Come-In, the clown pre-show, trying to think of something funny to say, but sounding stupid. I felt like a fraud. In the huge arenas Ringling plays, thousands of people watched my failures. On weekday afternoons, those same arenas were comparatively vacant, making the whole enterprise feel empty. Ahead stretched forty towns in fifty weeks.

Good clowning is hard because laughs are easy. There will always be someone to giggle if you slap on makeup, throw on mismatched clothes, and make a stupid face. People responded to my makeup and costume as if I were a clown, but I had gathered enough experience in performing to know that it was because they expected so little from circus clowns. Worst were the polite laughs. They were pity laughs, which meant that those watching believed I was such a bad performer that they had to encourage me. Believing myself worldly wise, I had assumed that I had no romantic illusions about circus life. Warnings about its difficulties seemed like stories for scaring the younger ones, inapplicable to me. I was wrong. Alone, weary, repeatedly sick and having no time to recuperate, my illusions crashed down on me. I saw nothing but relentless, thankless work. I was wallowing in self-pity. I didn't care.

Gradually, though, I found my (crazy) legs. There was no moment of epiphany, and I still often floundered. But I discovered the audience, and with it, renewed and renewable energy. Earlier as an actor, I had picked up the article of faith that playing to an audience is pandering. But as a clown, I had to turn from that faith and become a heretic. Show after show, week after week taught me that pandering is what happens when you pander, because you ignore your own standards or have lousy standards in the first place. Playing to an audience, by contrast, is dancing. You lead because someone has to lead; you try to please because that's what partners do. As you move, they move you. Challenge, insight, or amusement are possible, but only between equals. Like Fred Astaire with Ginger Rogers, playing to an audience is a constant attempt to match your steps, your strengths, your standards to theirs. As I learned to clown, my aim matured: I tried to connect.

As I explored Dan Rice's life, I rediscovered the lessons I had learned in performance, and realized why, despite the enormous differences between his clowning and mine, he fascinated me. Though I never accomplished his monumental success, I began to thrive as a clown when I learned that I was not performing *for* the audience, but *with* them. Rice rose to dazzling fame by singing and joking to people who responded in a continual creative cycle. Before me, Dan Rice had grown to supreme fame because he connected supremely.

ACKNOWLEDGMENTS

One great pleasure of writing this book has been the generosity of those who have offered their time, expertise, information, documents, and encouragement.

Those who write about circus history have helped me immensely, beginning with Stuart Thayer, who provided a foundation for this work in his own comprehensive research, and advised me. Bill Slout was similarly invaluable. Fred Dahlinger, Jr., Director of Collections and Research of the Robert L. Parkinson Library at Circus World Museum, gave me on-site assistance and a steady stream of information and documents. Fred Pfening III allowed me access to his reels of the *New York Clipper*, and, with Fred Pfening, Jr., suggested contacts, ideas and advice. Robert F. Houston, Orin C. King, Tom Parkinson, John Polacsek, Richard J. Reynolds III, Robert F. Sabia, and George Speaight also provided valuable assistance.

I am indebted to those responsible for collections of circus holdings: Fred Dahlinger, Jr., Meg Allen, and Erin Foley at Circus World Museum; Annette Fern and the staff at the Harvard Theatre Collection; Joan Barborak and staff at the Hertzberg, San Antonio Public Library; Howard Tibbals of Oneida, Tennessee; Terry Ariano at the Somers (N.Y.) Historical Society; Marty Jacobs and staff at the Museum of the City of New York.

For family information, I want to thank Ruth D. Debruin, West Long Branch, New Jersey; Brenda Lincke Fisseler of the French Simpson Memorial Library, Hallettsville, Texas; and in Erie County, Pennsylvania,

Caroline Veith and Russell Wood of the Girard Historical Society and its Hazel Kibler Museum, Tim Rohrbach, and especially Sabina Shields Freeman, for sharing her hospitality and research on Rice's family in Girard, and Sister Mary Lawrence Franklin at Mercyhurst College, for providing help with Rice family scrapbooks. I appreciate the perspective shared by Rice's descendants, Jeannie Celli, Tim Connolly, Betty Gardner, Elton R. Petersen, and especially John Anderson, who not only gave me insight into Rice's last years but also entrusted me with Rice's surviving papers.

This book developed out of a dissertation nurtured by Karen Halttunen, Les Hinderyckx, Chuck Kleinhans, Joe Roach, and Bill Worthen, and supported by Northwestern University's School of Speech Alumni Fund Dissertation Year Grant. I am indebted to many in the academic community for their advice and encouragement, including Rosemarie Bank, Marvin Carlson, John Frick, Hendrik Hartog, David Mayer, Bruce McConachie, Brooks McNamara, and Don Wilmeth.

As a practical matter, this book would not have been complete without the patient assistance of Northwestern's Interlibrary Loan Office, and Jacqui Anderson and the staff at the Larchmont, N.Y. Public Library.

Among the innumerable others who provided advice, ideas and information, I want to thank Earl Adams, the Honorable Phyllis W. Beck of the Pennsylvania Supreme Court, Charles M. Knoll, Jane Kunzog, and Dr. Jane Nicholson; for insight into animal training, I am indebted to Dawnita Bale, Dean Chambers, and Barbara and Buckles Woodcock; and for introducing me to Dan Rice, I thank my fellow actor and friend, Michael Preston.

My debt, like Dan Rice's financial obligations, can never be fully repaid to the innumerable people who helped me at state and local historical societies, public libraries and private collections, city, county and borough offices, historical exhibits, churches, manuscript collections, law courts, medical offices, university libraries, archives and collections, and museums from Sarasota to Salt Lake to Spokane, from Keokuk, Iowa, to Rochester, New York. I particularly want to thank John Hoffman, University Library, University of Illinois at Urbana-Champaign; Steve Gossard, Illinois State University Milner Library-Special Collections; Ellen B.

Thomasson, Missouri Historical Society, St. Louis; Madelyn Kent, Seymour B. Durst Collection, City University of New York Graduate Center; Jessica Silver, Trinity Church, New York City; Norman P. Carlson, Fenton History Center, Jamestown, N.Y.; Deane L. Root and the staff of the Foster Hall Collection, University of Pittsburgh; and Audrey Iacone of the Carnegie Library of Pittsburgh.

I want to thank Ken Emerson, Stuart Thayer, and my mother Betty Carlyon for wading through the massive original draft; Peter Osnos for his faith in this book; Jennifer Blakebrough-Raeburn for her extraordinary thoroughness in copy-editing it; and especially my editor, Kate Darnton, for her sensitivity, grit, and encouragement.

The generous help I have received has strengthened this book beyond my powers; the errors are mine.

My greatest thanks go to my magnificent sons, Daniel and Will, bouying me with great senses of humor, and to my wife, my partner, my friend, Barbara. I am grateful that her patience was long; I am also grateful that it was finite, or I would never have escaped the gravitational pull of the fascinating Dan Rice.

PROLOGUE

Across a grassy field stood the tent, white canvas under skies so blue that all later skies seemed pale. Flaming red and yellow heralds had popped up on fences like mushrooms on a midsummer morning, and today was the day. The circus was in town. Not just any circus, but Dan Rice's Great Show!

The night before, for miles around, folks had hitched up by lantern glow, bedding down excited children in the wagon, telling them to hush and get to sleep. Others saddled up horse or mule, and some set out walking. As stars made their slow circle in the sky, the countryside made its way to town, a few miles an hour in the dark, to see Dan Rice. A talking clown, Rice was the best circus clown the United States has known. He had a quick wit that kept the country laughing, a lightning spontaneity that made his words always fresh, and a powerful voice that reached thousands at a time. People passed his jokes around like the molasses candy sold at his show. In the years between his visits, people repeated his songs over their quilting, or at the blacksmith's, to "Oh, Susanna" and other popular tunes. Stocking up at the dry goods store, they chuckled again at the stories he had told about his feuds. On this summer night, Pa in his broad-brimmed hat shook the reins and whispered a Rice joke to Ma in her bonnet. She giggled, then smacked his arm and shushed him. Don't wake the little 'uns. Up ahead another leather harness creaked, and another axle groaned over bumps on the dirt road. Trickles of travelers became streams as the sky began to glow in the east, not yet light, no longer dark.

In town, kids woke early and rushed through their chores so they could get over to the field. Some locals huffed about immorality, and puffed about wasted time and money, but mostly folks agreed that Rice was a whole team and a hoss to let. The most famous performer in the history of American circus, he was "the demigod of the sawdust. . . . Add to a splendid physique, a sonorous and far-reaching voice, fair vocal powers, a talent for impromptu localizing, self-possession under all circumstances, natural gifts of oratory, individual magnetism to hold the largest audience, unchallenged and graceful mastery over the horse, dauntless courage and reckless liberality, and you have the secret of his popularity." When $5 was good weekly wages, he made $1,000 a week, roughly $20,000 a century and a half later. His top hat and trademark goatee were known around the country. If he was not intimate friends with all the famous people he claimed, he knew more of them than most, enjoying a prominence few could match. His circus titles resonated through the century, his early "One-Horse Show" epitomizing a small enterprise, and his "Great Show" still echoing in the slogan made famous by Ringling Brothers and Barnum & Bailey, "The Greatest Show on Earth."[1]

The string of circus wagons and riders rolled onto the lot. Traveling themselves since a 2:00 A.M. breakfast at the last town's inn, they climbed down, stretching off the night chill, yawning themselves awake. Nostalgia sees circus through a rosy glow, but troupers were as rough and rowdy as their critics complained. That was especially true on an outfit led by pugnacious Rice. With fists and words, he waded into the teeming nineteenth-century throng. A public figure roaming the shared territory of civic issues and entertainment, the great clown tartly commented on events of the day in summer tents and winter theaters. People fidgeted about the new fad of bloomers, so Dan joked about it. He sang to Washington audiences about Buchanan's cabinet when uncertainty about the president-elect's choices had pundits in a tizzy. Everyone came eager to hear his latest about P. T. Barnum, the local sheriff, or Stephen Douglas. If something was on American minds, Dan was *thar*, as his era liked to say.

The canvas was unrolled, then spread out, and soon it began to rise. Dusty from a season's travel, it still gleamed in the morning sun. Sunday-go-to-meeting clothes mingled with linsey-woolsey, all streaming toward the tent in a holiday mood. It *was* a holiday, as big as elections and the

Fourth of July. People were howdyin' and civilizin', catching up with gossip about a dress or a horse or a neighbor, joking about a politician, recalling Rice's last trip to town. Some children were held tight by nervous parents; others, hats flying, chased through the growing crowd. Older boys noticed the older girls, who noticed back. People wandered to booths outside the tent, to finger the ready-made clothes, or to buy whiskey. A few took a chance on a game of chance and hoped they had a chance, which they didn't. As the streams became a flood rolling up to the tent's grand entrance, a pickpocket plied his unobtrusive trade. A child in hand tugged toward the ticket seller. Four bits for a chair, two bits to perch on a narrow bleacher plank.

Inside, a year's fantasies became flesh. The band brassily accompanied rollicking clowns and pretty equestriennes and muscled acrobats. The sights settled in memory to the taste of peanuts and lemonade, and the rich smell of sawdust, sweat, and horse manure.

Mark Twain wrote about just such "a real bully circus" in *Huckleberry Finn*. Rice's show visited Hannibal, Missouri when Twain was young Sam Clemens, and the writer would have remembered. His young narrator, Huck, called the circus "the splendidest sight that ever was," the handsome men riding easy and the ladies "looking just like a gang of sure-enough queens, and dressed in clothes that cost millions of dollars, and just littered with diamonds. It was a powerful fine sight; I never see anything so lovely."[2] As for the clown, Twain could have been describing Rice:

> all the time the clown carried on so it most killed the people. The ring-master couldn't ever say a word to him but he was back at him quick as a wink with the funniest things a body ever said; and how he ever could think of so many of them, and so sudden and so pat, was what I couldn't noway understand.

Rice *was* quick as a wink. His "hits" on the times kept people laughing throughout the country. Would he trot out another song about his famous feud, lambasting his one-time friend, the circus manager, Doc Spalding? Had a newspaper sniffed that Rice's language wasn't pure? He would get down on that editor like the Mississippi on a sand bar. When Davy Crockett bragged, "I can outspeak anyone," he had not met Rice. Folkloric cousins, Davy and Dan could outshout thunder; they lived lives that spun off tall tales like sparks off flint. In the twentieth century, Richard Pryor's comic volatility and Robin Williams's antic spontaneity hint at Rice's talent, and Babe Ruth, Elvis, or Michael Jordan provide a sense of his national stature. The *Cincinnati Daily Enquirer* stated the case: "His humors are adapted to the times, his hits local, his satire telling, his wit pointed. . . . He is the great master-spirit of the nineteenth century . . . the most amusing man of modern times."[3]

Yet while Rice stood astride the antebellum world, an American colossus of roads and rivers, it has become difficult to see him clearly. He donned makeup and motley, but he also dressed like a gentleman for performance, nothing decorating his face but his famous goatee. He ran for office three times, including a bid for president in 1868; but those legitimate campaigns have been dismissed as publicity gimmicks, and his fiercely anti-Republican views have dissolved into the appealing fantasy that he and Abraham Lincoln were fast friends. Rice's brawls have descended to chuckles about "dustups," as if they were few and inconsequential. Profound laughter rolling deep in the culture at Rice's quips has dwindled now to small grins at circus clowns, or to indulgent smiles at giggling kiddies. Even those who know about Rice have unwittingly relied on derivative fictions originally generated by his publicity, repeated so often they became treated as fact.

Why the diminishment, the obscurity?

Part of an answer lies in changes in circus itself. It would become very different from what it was in antebellum days, primarily an adult entertainment, full of sex and violence. The rural one-day stands, memorialized in nostalgia as transitory spectacles for the naive, were balanced by months-long winter engagements in city theaters, when Rice and other circus stars competed with plays and minstrelsy for sophisticated public attention, and all the shows included politics. (To emphasize the experience of that seasonal rhythm, this book will take a chronological path through Rice's unfolding career, summers and winters shaping new themes.)

More broadly, the rowdy participation of antebellum America that fueled Rice's fame has been forgotten, scorned by later standards, or reduced to narrow class terms. Rice flourished at a time when performers talked to mixed audiences, who talked back. These populist patrons energetically insisted on their views as much as French kings a century before, or critics and grant-giving foundations a century later. Performance was a public conversation in which the broad culture thought out loud about what it believed, feared, and hoped for. Sometimes, matters went too far. Fights were as common at the circus as in the country generally. The Astor Place Riot of 1849 left over twenty dead, shocking a nation. Yet still antebellum Americans gathered at political rallies and theaters and minstrel shows and circuses to think out loud together, like diplomats huddled in marble corridors, or gossips gaggled at work. In this pulsing civic discourse, no one engaged audiences better than Dan Rice. Articulating inchoate thoughts rumbling across the cultural landscape, he sparked his lightning wit through the age's thunder. When he spoke directly to people, he also spoke for them, providing a kind of a laughing, working draft as they struggled to figure out what they thought. Rice expanded his remarkable life into dazzling tales that fed larger stories Americans told themselves about who they were as Americans. It is no coincidence that the age in which Rice reached the height of his interactive powers was also the time of great political involvement. Energized by torchlight rallies, speeches that lasted hours, and highly partisan newspapers, 80 percent of those eligible voted for president in 1856 and 1860.[4]

Rice's rise and fall parallels that pinnacle of participation, and its decline. The transformation of America's older market economy to a larger and corporate society of industrial capitalism created massive social anxiety. The corresponding emergence of a middle class made that anxiety worse as it fostered uncertainty about status in the officially classless society. People desperate to pull through the age's confusion latched on to the idea of aspiration. To "aspire to something higher" became the era's slogan. That was especially true of the new middle class, which used aspiration to stake a claim above the lower orders without violating democratic ideology by calling them lower. Given the conflicted nature of aspiration, it is not surprising that it remained vague. Without ever naming a particular goal, people in editorials, plays, magazines, conversations, politics, and performance endlessly repeated that they aspired to "something higher."

Rice alertly made aspiration his guiding principle. Performance had traditionally defended itself from attacks on its morality by insisting on its respectability: "All will be unobjectionable." Rice turned that ancient defense on its head, claiming the high road himself. *He* aspired to something higher. In that, he joined the cultural movement that was splitting amusements into "entertainment" and "art." (Those were new concepts, the former originally referring to room and board, as innkeepers entertained their customers; and the latter meaning a craft, like the art of animal husbandry.) So Rice declared that he was creating a "higher" enterprise. He removed "clown" and "circus" from his ads, presenting himself as the Great American Humorist in Dan Rice's Great Show. His new stance increased his great popularity, and that popularity helped propel the new idea in performance, that Art and Entertainment, highbrow and lowbrow, were not just different ends of a performance spectrum but distinct and inevitably opposed categories. Increasingly, he defined the audience's very attendance as an act of refinement.

During and after the Civil War, however, the emerging middle class became more secure about its place in society. Internalizing aspiration, it no longer needed to parade it. To boast of being genteel was no longer genteel. In the world of performance, it came to seem in the very nature of things that some forms were high and others low. Once, ballet had been disreputable as a leg show, opera arias had mingled with street ditties, and Shakespeare's plays were wildly popular, but they all rose in the emerging cultural hierarchy. Rice might have raised circus, too, or at least his own show, but the diminished participation cut off his greatest strength. In the stark stratification that ignores ancient overlap, circus, with its smells and spectacle and jokes, slid low, and the Great American Humorist fell to being merely clownish.

Rice could not stem the tide because participatory audiences became redefined as boorish. Even if someone had come along with his comic talent, quick mind, and powerful voice, there would be no "Rice" school, no influence on later performers, because the engagement of audiences that had been his great strength was no longer possible. Audiences that had felt comfortable in boisterous opinions about circus feats and acting skills grew tamer, quieter, polite. The theater-going habit began its long decline as audiences were cut out of a conversation increasingly relegated to experts. Rice did not lose his voice as much as audiences lost theirs. Now uncertain, they deferred to critics. Or to undefined and undefinable categories: High is worthier than low, tragedy worthier than comedy, "serious" worthier than "fluff."

Just as Rice's influential insistence on "something higher" helped create standards that pushed circus low, in a similar irony, his fame contributed to his obscurity. The potent partnership he enjoyed with crowds became perceived as a danger. America has long worried over the potential threat of celebrity as it draws attention and exerts influence. Celebrity is deemed worse in the political realm, a platform for manipulating presumably benighted masses. Observers historically repeat the dire warning that American morals are in jeopardy as the counsel of the best and the brightest, that is, those same observers, is swept away by "claptrap"—a trap to snare clapping. When Manhattan tumultuously welcomed Andrew Jackson in 1833, the "better sort" fussed that a demagogue's popularity surpassed George Washington's. Popular Rice was eventually seen a threat to the body politic, both for his politics and his popularity.

Abraham Lincoln knew the boisterous world of manual labor and full-throated singing, fights, and dirty jokes. Twain knew it, too. So did Walt Whitman, who reviewed Rice's circus. Each of them, like Rice, participated in that rambunctiousness, and it fed their work. As society changed, Rice's contemporaries evolved into sentimental icons: Lincoln as the Sainted Martyr, Twain as America's Humorist, and Whitman as the Great Grey Poet. Rice had been more popular than Lincoln, he was the Great American Humorist before Twain, and his fame exceeded Whitman's. However, as the other three icons grew, Rice shrunk to Old Uncle Dan, sanitized as a children's favorite, his hard edges softened into second childishness, and mere oblivion.

The traditional image of a circus audience laughing at a hilarious clown in a tent on an open field suggests infinite horizons, not only of the circus but of America. Yet, glorying in that image, collective memory constricts the raw and rowdy original to threadbare nostalgia. By the time Rice's death ushered in the twentieth century, Americans could no longer comprehend his funny, combative, sometimes vulgar, and often political words as those of a circus clown. But in a nineteenth-century tent under a summer-blue sky or on a winter's night in a fashionable, filigreed theater, that was what people expected from Dan Rice, circus clown. His hits on the times, rendered in his powerful voice, made him what Whitman yearned to be, the singer of America's song.

PART 1

A PERFECT RUSH

1823 ☛ 1847

1

HOME, SWEET HOME

The adored daughter of a New Jersey country preacher charms her way past his strict principles and flies off to a "merry-making" at the Monmouth races. There she spies a sport from Manhattan, who turns out to be an important importer-exporter, Aaron Burr's friend, and law clerk to Martin Van Buren. They elope to a justice of the peace, and then to his home across the Hudson. After a son is born, the preacher tracks down his impetuous daughter and forces an annulment, with $1,000 damages for seduction.[1]

As with other tales Dan Rice would tell, some of this one was true.

The young woman, Rice's mother, was Elizabeth Crum, born on March 4, 1803, the tenth of thirteen children of Elizabeth and Richard D. Crum. The Crums had been colonists from Holland, possibly Teutonic knights before that. In 1690, Floris Crom was High Sheriff of Orange County, New York. A family story marries Floris's son, Cornelius, to a woman of the Six Nations. If true, that made Cornelius's great-grandson, Dan Rice, one-eighth Mohawk, Oneida, Onondaga, Cuyuga, Seneca, or Tuscarora. The other side of Elizabeth's family were Gardners, from Nantucket. By 1823, the Crums lived in Ocean Township, New Jersey, near Long Branch, which was on its way to becoming a fashionable seaside resort for the urban *bon ton*. The Crums were of a different ton. Besides being country folks, they were Methodists. Barely large enough to be a trivial cult in 1800, the Methodist Church was becoming the largest denomination in the United States through its appeal to democratic, some would say vulgar, tastes. John Wesley's church had achieved its explosive growth by celebrating the religious impulses of common people and eliminating pew fees, a denial of social distinctions that incurred the disdain of more established denominations. Exuberance confirmed Methodism's low status. It was a church on fire, spiritually and emotionally; a jumping, singing, clapping church. Reinforcing the idea that worshippers bowed to no supremacy but God's, ministers chosen from the congregation, lay preachers like Crum, outnumbered the ordained three to one. Preacher Crum lived a fervent distrust of authority that would be the family heritage. Nor was he a shy country mouse outside church. He had served as a "matross," or gunner's mate, in the Revolution. (The family boasted that he had started as a drummer boy with General Washington.)[2]

Elizabeth had inherited the family fervor. Her son remembered her as a "shouting Methodist."[3] When she met her man, she did not wait dutifully for permission but grabbed her freedom.

The "important importer-exporter" was Daniel McLaren Jr., a Manhattan grocer following in the footsteps of his Scottish father. In 1790, when the nation's first president moved in to 39 Broadway, McLaren Sr. owned a grocery a few doors down, at number 30. He moved farther up Broadway in 1795, the year his son was born. His wife died when the boy was twelve. McLaren Jr. clerked for his father as they switched locations regularly, each time moving on May 1, Manhattan's notorious Moving Day. Following Dutch colonial custom, leases expired on May Day, when the noisy, crowded streets became noisier with people, and more crowded with tables and chairs, beds and bed pans in every cart or dray or wagon that could be found, plunging "hapless Gotham" into pandemonium, like a giant game of musical houses. In 1820, McLaren Jr. set up shop on Chatham Street, now Park Row. (He dropped the "Jr." in 1829, four years after his father died.) It was a block south of the intersection of five streets, then called "The Collect," after the Fresh Water Pond, source of the city's water until it became so polluted that it had to be filled in. Soon came a new name, the Five Points, internationally infamous for degradation. During his visit to America in 1842, Charles Dickens was allowed to tour the Five Points only with an armed escort. But in McLaren's day, the area—later to become Chinatown—was an ordinary slum of native whites, Irish immigrants, free blacks, and slaves (freed by New York proclamation in 1827). Craftsmen's shops abutted brothels, and the first city tenements bumped up against slaughterhouses. Grocers frequently sold liquor and many grocer-grog shop proprietors traded in stolen goods. None of that made McLaren's shop a dive. Though economic forces were starting to segregate neighborhoods by class, the city's vibrant mix persisted. A few blocks west of McLaren's store lay City Hall, and a little to the east, where Manhattan bulges into the East River, Corlear's Hook gave its name to local workers, the "hookers."[4]

Elizabeth's belly grew with the full moon in January 1823. She knew the bloody facts ahead, and the danger. Countless headstones commemorating mother and child still bear mute testimony to the risks of childbirth in the nineteenth century. Sweating in the damp chill as winter rain rattled the windows, her hair matted to her head, she labored. Labor. Usage has worn the word smooth, but it still hints at severe exertion, through surges of pain, ebbing and spiking again, hour after long hour. On January 25, Elizabeth gave birth to a boy. She named him Daniel after his father; but that same father gave the name Daniel McLaren to a later son, suggesting that this first baby was an "engagement child." Or illegitimate: No record has been found of the Crum-McLaren marriage, and the family story included the contradictory claim of $1,000 in damages for seduction. Premarital pregnancy was not unusual. Though rates had dropped from a Revolutionary-era high, over 20 percent of the women who married in the 1820s were pregnant.[5]

As the mother returned with her baby to Long Branch, the father turned to other ventures. In 1824, McLaren obtained a charter for the New Jersey Protection and Lombard Bank in Jersey City, a ferry commute across the Hudson from his grocery. The bank started strong, selling $128,000 in insurance, but warning signals went up in June when McLaren delayed payment of a required $25,000 to the state's School Fund. He finally paid, but immediately borrowed the money back for himself, using the bank's stock as security. When McLaren stalled repayment and then asked for a larger loan in the fall, he sparked a run on the bank. In November 1825, less than a year after starting, business was suspended. The failure shocked the state. Investigating, the legislature discovered that the insurance policies were worthless and the bank's initial capital, supposed to be $400,000, had amounted to only $50,000. That was less than McLaren paid himself for his services. He had also paid a lobbyist for help in "explaining principles" of his enterprise, which moved the investigating committee to the startling conclusion that "legislation may be subverted by interested persons." Unnerved by the fiasco, New Jersey approved no more bank charters for three years. The state tried to sue McLaren in New York, but, despite what a later study of New Jersey banking called "his remarkably artistic handiwork," he had done nothing illegal. The Newark *Centennial* summed up McLaren's scheme with words that could apply to his son's life; it was "so much like a fairy tale as to be almost incredible, and more like romance than real history."[6]

Little Dandy was growing into a lively toddler among the dusty country lanes, but it was not the life his mother wanted. Elizabeth was not content under her father's strict régime, she returned to the city with her son, perhaps bringing a new husband along. On March 19, 1825, she married a Jersey dairyman, Hugh Manahan, in a Methodist ceremony in Manhattan. At twenty-one, Manahan was a year younger than his strong-willed bride. Family lore says they met over milk on Mulberry Street, on his route delivering to Elizabeth's sister, Catherine, married to a painter, Hugh Reed, also from Long Branch. Manahan worked for others until 1827, when he got a farm on the Bowery near Art Street—now the site of Cooper Union. He supplemented his milk route by supplying the Harlem Railroad with cordwood. A later photograph shows Manahan with the hint of a grin, unusual for portraits of the time; Rice recalled a man who drank, chased women, and took him to the races. The small family lived on Mulberry, perhaps with the Reeds.[7]

Around the corner, on Chatham, was McLaren's store. It is not clear whether Dan knew then that McLaren was his father. When he did find out, he idealized the absent father, conjuring a grander parent than his genial companion of the streets and the tracks, Manahan. The difference can be seen in Rice's corresponding stories of each man with a prostitute.

New York was rife with brothels and "nymphs du pavé." Prostitution, catering to a rowdy male culture, was an open secret all over Manhattan. Whitman claimed that 95 percent of men, including "the best classes," visited brothels. Some community leaders, such as George Lorillard, in whose tobacco factory Rice claimed he had worked, made money from "parlor houses" in respectable neighborhoods. As for the women, it has been estimated that up to 10 percent between the ages of fifteen and thirty engaged in the trade, a proportion that rose in hard times. A woman who would normally earn $3 or $4 a week could pull down $10, sometimes much more, as a "Venus Pedestris." Against that backdrop, Rice paired each of his fathers with a famous prostitute. Though both purported amours were probably fiction, the disparity in the women he chose reveals a stark difference in his image of the two men. He coupled Manahan with a symbol of degradation, the famously murdered Helen Jewett, whose probable killer got off because he was from a "good family." Meanwhile, Rice matched McLaren with Madame Jumel, who managed her prostitution so well that she became rich, then sufficiently proper to wed Aaron Burr. Rice claimed that his father was Jumel's advisor and that McLaren proposed marriage to her after she had divorced Burr; but the prospective union crashed on the rocks of his ugly snaggle teeth, which he wouldn't fix for fear of dentists.[8]

Rice later blamed his mother and her "exacting Methodism" for pushing Manahan into Jewett's arms. The names of his siblings show Elizabeth's strong hand. In 1827, she gave birth to a second baby, whom she named William Crum Manahan after her younger brother. (Though William was her husband's first name, he went by Hugh.) When her third child was born, in 1831, she again looked to her side of the family and named her daughter Elizabeth after herself and her own mother, who died that year. Two years later, she used her sister's name, Catherine, for another baby. The girls were nicknamed Libbie and Kate.

Dan probably chafed under his mother's strict régime as well. He was a buster, gregarious and pugnacious, a blend of his mother's fire, his father's audacity, and his stepfather's geniality. He was apparently "the terror of orderly schools," including the Kellogg Seminary of Orson Shubael Kellogg, at Broadway and Prince. One fanciful tale put Dan back in New Jersey, as a boy attending Princeton University. With "burlesque constructions of the ancient classic," he dazzled the learned faculty, just as the boy Jesus had confounded the temple elders. No matter which school Dan attended, the spelling in his early letters shows that he was not a diligent student. Mostly, he drove a milk wagon for Manahan.[9]

Dan's true education lay in the turbulent medley of early Manhattan. Even before the opening in 1825, the Erie Canal, which sent grains and hides flowing east, and goods and people west, was transforming New York into a metropolitan city. A seaport swagger overflowed from the wharves, where squat canal boats now joined tall sailing ships, with bowsprits jutting over the docks, and webs of masts, spars and rigging towering above. Immigration boosted the population past 100,000 in 1820 and double that through the decade. Expansion pushed Manahan north, to a farm on Fifth Avenue near 14th Street in 1829, and up to 26th a few years later. Yet most of the island remained woods or pasture. The Bowery of Manahan's first farm was, in Whitman's words, still a "shrubby,

Rice's boyhood playground, Broadway, New York (1836).

viny, orchardy, cabbagey road," and Dan remembered picking blackberries on Chatham Street. Running barefoot, he climbed trees and splashed through brooks, a homespun shirt flopping in the breeze. He could have been Huck Finn.[10]

Manhattan's rural Eden overlapped urban bustle, which included animals. With dogs always underfoot, rabies scares were common. In the hot summer when Dan was eight, panicky authorities ordered the killing of unleashed dogs and set off a massacre. Pigs wandered freely, squealing, rooting, copulating, and defecating; periodic attempts at regulation led to hog riots, in which hundreds of black and white women attacked the authorities to free their porkers. Bull baiting had mostly disappeared, but cockfighting and rat fighting—terriers slaughtering collected rats—were still treats. Then there were horses, and horse manure. Plodding horses pulled drays, while barouches clattered behind frisky mares, and racing took over city streets. Third Avenue was a favorite stretch, starting near Manahan's farm, "straight, nearly level for a long distance, macadamized and kept in good condition." It is easy to envision Dan on his stepfather's horse, flinging a challenge to another rider.[11]

Foremost in Dan's education was the human menagerie. The streets were symphonic with yells, singing, and oaths. Swaggering Bowery boys—infamous as "b'hoys"—jostled open-mouthed bumpkins while immigrants from all over crisscrossed staid old Knickerbockers, proud to be as stodgy as they fancied the original Dutch settlers had been. Dan's voice, growing from childish treble to solid baritone, rose over the cacophony. With an eye for clothes, he would pause at a vendue—a street auction—or under the awnings that covered the sidewalks, looking in at turbans and dresses of copper-colored satin, trimmed in white satin and black velvet. Street vendors offered a movable feast: strawberries, hot corn, pineapples, "Albany beef"—sturgeon from the Hudson—and "saltwater vegetables"—clams and oysters. Dan later pictured himself bedeviling a young Cornelius Vanderbilt peddling clams from Rockaway. Nighttime had its own delights, including bright lights. The year Dan was born, the city awarded the first gas franchise. Though working-class neighborhoods continued to rely on the feeble flicker of whale-oil lamps, and theaters were mostly lit by candles, gaslight began to make Broadway the great white way.[12]

Public life offered its amusements. Christmas was still only a modest religious holiday, but New Year's filled the streets with people; the well-to-do paid social calls during the day, and nighttime revelers, like the "Callithumpians," beat on pans and confronted the gentry. The Fourth of July was the country's grand holiday, its hours of speeches followed by the drinking and iced cream of "pic-nics." Elections were also public celebrations. Rallies under the hot sun blended into torch-lit meetings, the speeches punctuated by cheering and chanting, stomping and jeering, and more drinking. Violence flared often. When Dan was eleven, the first popular election for mayor sparked demonstrations against the propertied classes, with the militia called out to restore order. Strikes similarly combined political action and group celebrations. Tailoresses went on strike in 1825, and in 1836 tailors condemned the local aristocracy in one of the largest mass meetings the city had known. Special occasions added to the exciting brew. When the city welcomed Andrew Jackson in 1833, the whole city seemed to be a party, with Old Hickory cheered "three times three" and serenaded at his hotel. Fires were another civic amusement. "Connoisseurs of conflagrations," rich and poor alike ran to fires, bounding in the wake of the volunteer fire companies. The bucket brigades of the colonial past, anchored by merchants and masters, had been replaced in 1820 by private companies of journeymen and apprentices eager to enjoy swagger sanctioned by public service. Rival companies fought often, sometimes on the way to fires, to the point of letting a building burn while they battled.[13]

Fighting was a major component of civic amusements. On a small scale, there were simple fisticuffs, always a favorite activity for Dan. Combatants peeled off cumbersome clothes and earrings for battle. Gangs, overlapping with fire companies, organized the violence. Five Points gangs such as the Plug Uglies, the Roach Guards in blue-striped pantaloons, and the red-suspendered Dead Rabbits battled crews from other parts of the city, the Bowery Boys, the East Side Buckaroos, and the Slaughterhouse Gang. Black men banded together, too, though their gangs were blamed on abolitionists. The educated and high-born had their own feuds, fights, and duels. That included newspapermen. William Cullen Bryant, editor of the *Evening Post*, whipped a fellow newspaperman; and James Gordon Bennett, editor of the *Herald*, sold papers by printing the details of attacks on himself. Fighting sometimes escalated: 1834 became known as the "Year of Riots," and in one 1839 fight, over 1,000 men battled. A disturbance in the Bowery Theater jumped to the street, where white abolitionists and black citizens were attacked.[14]

Like street fare, theaters were intensely participatory. In November 1832, when Junius Brutus Booth—father of Edwin and John Wilkes—performed Richard III at the Bowery Theatre, management oversold the house; so people sat on the stage, fingering the props and refereeing the Battle of Bosworth Field as if it were a street fight, and boys ran for coins thrown by the characters. Later ages see it as outrageous behavior, but the *New York Mirror* was bemused by the "avalanche of spectators," including "jolly tars, and a number of apple-munching urchins. The scene was indescribably ludicrous. Booth played in his best style, and was really anxious to make a hit, but the confusion . . . occasioned constant and most humorous interruptions." It was "all done in perfect good humor, and with no intention to make a row."[15]

Dan was part of the exuberant crew, cheering at the circus, heckling mistakes at wild-animal shows, hissing bad actors. One story puts him on a dark street alone after a play about graveyards and ghosts at the Bowery Theatre. Spying a shape behind him, he decided it was the Devil and ran home in a fright—chased all the way by a black dog. Dan might have attended the opera. In the 1830s, opera audiences were still mixed, and popular music "was simply whatever sold the most copies and was known to the most people, whether it be simple, strophic English song or an adaptation of music from Italian opera."[16]

The rambunctious Manhattan mix was perilous. People were knifed, gored, burned, maimed by faulty equipment, smothered in cave-ins. Rice twice narrowly escaped drowning in the Hudson, and joked about another, near suffocation, cracking that he had matured so early because he was manured so early when he fell into a vat of "stable earth," saved only when Manahan spotted his red shoes. Winter added the hazard of sleighs, which were muffled on the snow, often running people down. Sleigh bells were not decoration but a safety measure to warn of onrushing danger. Disease was rampant. Cholera hit New York in 1832, in the world's first global epidemic. The disease killed thousands of New Yorkers that year and during a resurgence in 1834. In one day, eight people died on Mulberry Street, including one at 27 Mulberry, where Dan had lived with the Reeds. No one knew the cause, but cholera was worse in cities; those who could afford to flee did so. Others, including Manahan with his milk routes, stayed and prayed and worried.[17]

Women endured their own hazard, childbirth. Late in the fall of 1835, Elizabeth took to her bed to deliver another baby. Public and private mingled in the antebellum world, spilling through thin walls, under ill-fitting doors, out of open windows. A gasp of pain in the night that jabbed Elizabeth from a fitful doze would waken Dan, too. As December began, the baby struggled out of her womb, through the birth canal, into the air. Mother and child, little Hugh, named for his father, were weak.

Midway through the month, as the ordeal in the Manahan home continued in growing cold, fire broke out in the city. Hoses froze to ice, so people watched helplessly while the conflagration spread, blazing from Wall Street south. Firefighters in Philadelphia turned out because they thought the glow to the north was a fire of their own. The year of 1835 would be called the Year of the Great Fire; the blaze was the most destructive in the city's history, its losses estimated as high as $40,000,000. Philip Hone, one of the city's first mayors, called it "the most awful calamity which has ever visited these United States." The next day, crowds wandered through the smoking ruins, as looters fought with shopkeepers, tourists of their own devastation. Then came snow, and more snow, piling up for weeks, turning the streets into canyons. Pedestrians risked avalanches crashing from the roofs. Deep holes in the streets made sleighing just as dangerous. Walls of ice looked like black marble.[18]

In the midst of these public troubles came a small, domestic one, the death of Elizabeth Crum Manahan on January 31, 1836. Soon her baby died too. The family arranged a plot in the cemetery attached to St. John's Chapel, an Episcopal church at Hudson and Carmine. Church policy restricted burial to Episcopalians, but maybe the great snow created an exception for this Methodist. Yet another storm delayed the funeral. Dan later exalted his mother, fitting the age's taste for maternal saintliness, but an emotional undertow tugged at his stories about her. None depicted a lighthearted moment, or loving behavior. The anecdotes mostly portrayed Elizabeth as a severe woman. Showing more ambivalence, the longest story told of her death. Rice put his father dramatically in the shadows at the cemetery, a Romeo mourning his Juliet, but did not place himself there. It is not logical to blame a dead parent for leaving, but children have felt abandoned by less.[19]

Soon after Dan's mother died, Manahan married a woman named Elizabeth Tapscott. Dan and his siblings remembered her as a hardhearted stepmother who beat them when their father was out. To be fair, a headstrong teenager who had lost his mother could not have been easy to cope with. In any case, Dan moved out. He remained close to the Manahans, but had nothing more to do with Tapscott or her three children.[20]

The year Dan was born saw the debut of the opera *Clari*, which included "Home, Sweet Home." That song was destined to become the most popular of the century, touching a rootless country's yearning for stability.[21] The lyrics may have been mawkish, but as Dan struck out on his own he had reason to look for "peace of mind, dearer than all." To hope for a sweet home.

2

GO WEST, YOUNG MAN

"Hello, the fire!"

Dan warned of his approach from the path along the Erie Canal. Travelers from the bullnose boat tied up at the water watched him, a muscular boy of medium height, with a thick neck and broad shoulders. As he moved into the circle of light, they saw alert eyes under wavy hair stringy from a long time on the tramp, a grin framed by a prominent nose and solid cheekbones. A panther screeched in the dark forest. Dan was watching them too, as he eased his way around their suspicion with friendly words and jokes. By the time he had tied up his horse and hunkered down at their fire, he was welcome.

Dan's stepmother may have been cruel, but it was wanderlust sending him into the world, with hard times adding extra incentive. A nationwide bubble of investment, speculation, and building had collapsed into the Panic of 1837, a depression that staggered the country. The spiral of inflation ruined merchants and "manufactories." Banks failed, and those that didn't called in loans. Gold and silver was hoarded. Stores and hotels printed their own paper money, or scrip—called "shinplasters" because it was good only for plastering wounded shins—and theaters gave change in IOUs. Whigs blamed Andrew Jackson because he destroyed the Bank of the United States, Jackson blamed Whigs for their speculations, and both blamed London for manipulating America's finances. In the bitter cold of 1837, 5,000 New Yorkers, gathering to condemn greedy merchants, turned into a mob, wrecking warehouses and hurling flour into the streets.[1]

"Go West, young man." Horace Greeley's famous phrase referred to the opportunities opened by the Erie Canal rather than to cowboys, to Buffalo, not buffaloes. Late in 1837, Dan traveled up the Hudson River to Albany. One of the nation's major cities, an Atlantic seaport by way of the deep Hudson River, Albany had become a gateway to the West thanks to the new canal. As Dan traveled, he would sing when someone brought out a fiddle. He had discovered a talent for singing and dancing when he shouted hymns at his mother's church, did jigs in the stables, and joined in choruses sung by an audience. Now, he put his talents to use. As the fiddle music crackled by the fire, the notes rising with the smoke, he kicked up dust performing a jig in triple time, then switched to the jerky syncopation of a hornpipe, on the verge of tap dancing.

As he lay down to rest, the bordering forest made a stripe of the stars above, a reminder of the laborers who had felled trees, dug roots, cut rock, and plowed through marshes, making the way straight for the canal through irregular nature. Across that strip of starry night rode the autumn constellations. There was Perseus, the hero, and the winged horse Pegasus. Dan's path in 1837 formed a kind of terrestrial constellation, a horsey stick figure across the map. The Hudson River traced the front leg, the canal to Buffalo was a horse's neck, and a swing south to Pittsburgh made the long equine head. Just as the ancients saw heroes and horses in their night sky, this stick figure tells of Rice's fortunes, and of the horses that carried them. Horses were central to American life, in work and play, like the race meeting where his parents met. Theaters presented plays featuring horses, and the circus was founded on horses. A stampede of phrases—horse of a different color, from the horse's mouth, to beat a dead horse, horse sense—testified to the animal's importance. Steam ruled the rivers, but horses were the four-legged engines of progress on land, crucial for travel or transport or plow. The horse, not the dog, was man's best friend.

Dan may have headed west simply on hope, but he consistently said that he had been taking a horse to Pittsburgh. As usual, he embellished. He later said he was a celebrated jockey transporting Dusty Foot, which he had ridden to triumph on Long Island's Union Course, for John C. Stevens. These were glittering associations. Dusty Foot was a famous trotter—not ridden by a jockey—and Stevens was a leading sportsman, who founded the New York Yacht Club and won the first America's Cup, named after his schooner. There were other fictions. Rice also said that he had made his way west in high steamboat style with Henry Clay, who fiddled while he danced. Rice spun other tales of his early Western days. He depicted himself as a cabin boy who had caused the death of William Henry Harrison by holding the president's coattails too high, leading to fatal pneumonia. Rice said he was a riverboat gambler who had won a steamboat from her captain but, ruled by an "instinctive principle of justice," gave it back. He concluded the Dusty Foot story by hitching the horse to one of the major disasters of the steamboat era. In 1838, the *Moselle* exploded near Cincinnati, shooting bits of timber, boiler, and bodies to the Kentucky shore, and killing over a hundred people. Rice put himself on the *Moselle*, pushing Dusty Foot into the water just before the blast.[2]

Young Dan's early travels were much less grand. He was a child loose in a harsh, violent world. Moving from his stepfather's milk route to this westering course, Dan embodied the country's changing economic system. Children traditionally worked on farms, in stores—and on milk routes—when the family formed an economic unit. With the rise of industrialism, child workers, younger even than Dan, were needed to feed the engine of progress. Children, small and inexperienced, had to compete with adults for work, shelter, and food. Boys and girls were kicked, beaten, abused for fun or sex, and murdered, often unmourned. An 1848 study of the Erie Canal found that many of the 10,000 boys working on the "Big Ditch of Iniquity" were cheated of their meager wages, while malnutrition and overwork pushed the mortality rate "horrendously high."[3] Perhaps worst of all for the ragged girls and boys on the streets and in the theaters, the "better sort" saw them only as noisy, thieving nuisances, isolating them further in their defiant misery. Yet none of those horrors made their way into Rice's memoirs. By the time he told the tales, he had steeled himself against whatever he had been forced to endure.

Dan turned south from Buffalo. He told of sympathetic Indians near the Cattaraugus Swamp who helped him get through the snow. Trudging down Lake Erie into Pennsylvania, and then along the shores of the Allegheny River, he wouldn't have seen Pittsburgh among the steep hills of western Pennsylvania until he was almost upon it. Even on arrival he would not enjoy a clear view. Pittsburgh's manufactories, the ubiquitous use of coal for home fires, and the barrier of those hills filled the air with smoke. Long before the steel industry got rolling, Pittsburgh was the Smoky City.

Crossing the St. Clair Street (later 6th Street) Bridge, Dan entered a city ready for action. Starting as a French trading post, Fort Duquesne, and then Fort Pitt, after the English prime minister, William Pitt, Pittsburgh was proud of its growth from sleepy village to smoky chimneys. The main streets had just been equipped with gas lighting, and the city wards had recently been numbered. The dark now echoed with the tapping sticks of night watchmen. Of course, becoming a city meant city woes. The unpaved streets became seas of mud in the rain, and were rolling clouds of dust otherwise, alive with rats, dogs, and the usual savage pigs. When Charles Dickens wrote about his famous American tour, he typified Pittsburgh by its waterfront, an "ugly confusion of backs of buildings and crazy galleries and stairs."[4] But it was an important city, a staging point for the South and the West. The Allegheny and Monongahela Rivers met in the sharp wedge of Pittsburgh, blending to become the Ohio River, the country's major route inland from the East. Cut by a hundred-foot hill at its eastern border, the city was like an arrowhead pointing west. Like Manhattan, Pittsburgh was bordered by rivers bouncing urban energy back on itself, concentrating it.

Later, Rice said that a fight welcomed him to Pittsburgh. That could well be true. Dan was as contentious as the two-fisted city, always a fighter. Even his nose was aggressive, a broad prow pushing him forward into the world. The way he told it, he had draped his coat over Dusty

Foot against the cold, a ridiculous sight that prompted local urchins to chuck coal at him. Chasing them down, he "impressed his personality upon them in well-directed blows." He related other fights, including an epic Pittsburgh battle with Devil Jack, the Bully of Bayardstown. Rice fondly recalled this early belligerency, when "we used to fight and frolic together. Pittsburghers, my son, are renowned to this day for their fighting propensities, but they are lambs now, perfect lambs to what they were at the time."[5]

Dan joined the rollicking crew dancing and singing in the stables.

Fortunately for Dan, his knack with horses got him work even in hard times. Life in a stable suited him perfectly. Besides horses and their companionable whinnies, there was camaraderie. The stable was a kind of worker's club of jokes, gossip, and music; Dan's voice rose over the rest in sentimental ballads such as "Home, Sweet Home" and racier fare that wouldn't be heard in a parlor. He was industrious and "worked at anything he could get to do, from exercising horses at the race-track to driving a hack." While everyone knew horses, professionals were rare. Fewer than 1 percent of Manhattan's workers were drivers, coachmen, or hackmen. Draymen like Dan, who drove the low, heavy wagons used for cartage, were an even more rarified group. A newspaper, using the most stalwart image available, joked about a storm making "a drayman acknowledge himself nervous." Dan later said he owned a stable with an Englishman named Massingham. More likely, he worked at Edmund Massingham's stable on Front and Ferry, a block off the Monongahela. He was "embracing every opportunity to better his condition."[6]

Some Saturday nights, Dan danced in James Wilson's kitchen. Wilson was a local impresario, whose Shakespeare House on St. Clair Street stood on the route from the north, and whose Shakespeare pleasure garden in East Liberty was a stop for wagons on the Philadelphia turnpike from the east. The 1837 city directory listed East Liberty as a suburb where the respectable could "live happily, retired from the bustle of the city business." Wilson hired Dan to drive a carriage; that meant picking up Wilson's daughter and her friends from school on weekends. It must have been a rollicking ride, the girls giggling at Dan's teasing as over the fields they'd go, laughing all the way. "Jingle Bells" became an image of placid Victoriana, but it records the joyride of sleighing and all its frenzied races and crashes. Sleigh rides also provided a chance for young women and men to be alone, bundled up and enjoying the same independence that cars would provide in the next century. Not for nothing was sleighing called "an orgasm of locomotion." On Saturday nights, the girls called Dan into the kitchen to entertain around the warm stove. So he sang and whirled, a fine clog dancer making temperatures rise and faces flush.[7]

Rice translated another driving job, at the Allegheny Arsenal, into a story about Charles Dickens. Pittsburgh greeted the lionized writer in 1842 with parties and balls. That was a new word, "lionized," fitting the emerging sense of celebrity in which a writer, as well as a politician or an actor, inspired popular enthusiasm. But celebrities did not always return the enthusiasm. In his *American Notes*, Dickens flung criticisms freely. When it wasn't decay he saw, it was mob rule, or money-grubbing in "that vast counting-house which lies beyond the Atlantic." Boston ladies "rather desire to be thought superior than to be so." The state of Ohio was a "miserable waste of sodden grass, and dull trees, and squalid huts," and the Mississippi was an "intolerable river dragging its slimy length and ugly freight." Dickens saw America's morals, degraded by newspapers, forcing the better sort from public service. His disdain for Pittsburgh's waterfront, though, was balanced by praise for the "pretty arsenal." More factory than fort, surrounded by an imposing stone wall for looks, it turned out bullets, small arms, and cannons, hauled by drayman like Dan. Like Harper's Ferry, the Allegheny Arsenal was an important federal depository. Rice claimed that he had driven Dickens from the arsenal and given him a lecture on manners: "When you next assist a lady to alight from the carriage don't squeeze their hands so hard, or one day she will give you the Dickens."[8]

Late in 1839, Dan steamed downriver to Marietta, Ohio. A room on a steamboat cost $5, too extravagant for a stable hand. He could barely afford deck passage at $1.25, the "very undesirable way of traveling." Outside town, he went to work on a farm. Rice was a gregarious man, and he may have known the prominent Pittsburghers he later claimed as friends, such as Congressman Harmon Denny; Judge Wilkins, ambassador to Russia; and the arsenal's commander, Capt. Edward Harding. But the Ohio winter of 1839 featured a humble German immigrant, George Reppert. Dan was still young, on his own in the world, and that "good old gentleman" and "dear old Mother Reppert" and all the boisterous Reppert cousins and grandchildren became a second family. Dan recalled them warmly, devoting pages in his memoirs to the "continual round of enjoyment." The 1840 census recorded the Repperts, and it also noted a "Male/15–20 years"—perhaps the first recorded glimpse of young Dan. When Annie Reppert married, the countryside turned out to celebrate, bringing food till the table groaned under the weight. Suddenly the boys ran in, crying "Murder!" People recoiled at the red streaming down Dan's head. But it wasn't blood, it was a cherry pie, thrown in his face for effect. "Oh, mein Gott," laughed Mother Reppert, "Dan, you be such a teufel." Like a first love, these memories stayed with him, adorned by a clownish pie-in-the-face.[9]

Rice's jockey stories began to make sense. While New York tales had him as a boy riding impromptu contests on Sixth Avenue or on Tucker's Lane in Harlem, in Pittsburgh he grew into the strength needed to handle a half ton of horse as it bumped against other horses, legs driving, muscles straining beneath the glistening hide. A publicity biography, *Sketches from the Life of Dan Rice*, boasted that he raced horses as the "Idol of the West," but less grandly he was one of the "catch riders" wandering the West, drawn to wherever there were horses or horsemen. In the racing-mad West, the turbulent scene at the tracks matched the circus lot. There were "booths as at a fair, where everything was said, and done, and sold, and eaten or drunk—where every fifteen or twenty minutes there was a rush to some part, to witness a *fisticuff*—where dogs barked and bit, and horses trod on men's toes, and booths fell down on people's heads!"[10]

America's first professional songwriter, Stephen Foster, memorialized the racing fever in "Camptown Races," its apt original title being "Gwine to Run All Night." Foster knew that fever well from his Pittsburgh home. He also knew Dan, one of those riders and fighters, as the lyrics said, who had his "hat caved in." Dan was becoming fast friends with Stephen's older brother, Morrison, and wherever "Mit" and his friends went, Stephen was sure to follow. The friendship may have started when Mit moved into Pittsburgh in 1839 to work for a relative, Cadwallader Evans, who owned a mill at Ferry and Water Streets, a block from Dan at Massingham's stable. Mit and Dan were also buddies with Cadwallader's son, George, who must have worked at the mill, too. For errands on Mit's next job as a clerk at a cotton factory, he acquired "a fine little Poney," which he could have stabled at Massingham's.[11]

The boys paraded the urban playground of a booming city, which topped 80,000 by 1840, half of them immigrants. They swaggered, serenaded, and teased the young scholars at Western University, later the University of Pittsburgh. Feasting on oysters, they made the city their oyster. At the Foster home, always open to lively sparks, Dan's baritone would have been a welcome addition when Mit's family and friends got together to sing. It was all part of Stephen's musical education and Dan's social education. Pittsburgh evenings saw concerts, circuses, plays, dioramas, and temperance rallies. Fourth of July picnics lolled in America's abundance: peach, gooseberry, and apple tarts, rose ice cream, sponge cake, coconut drops, strawberries and cream, fruit jellies. Mit's parents worried about indulgence. His father warned, "Don't eat so much meat and strong food. Above all, let me entreat of you, not to be led out after night to those eating houses, where Oysters and all manner of food is gormandized, and the system loaded with bile, by which disease and death soon follow." Social life means social distinctions. After Mit and George—and possibly Dan—were snubbed by a rich friend, Mit's mother consoled him by letter. "Now, my dear son, be content with your humble lot, and bear yourself with dignity. . . . Avoid huge talkers who have a contempt for religion and poor persons. . . . Your levity is corrected by your not being too well off, and your actions are govern'd by your not being able to draw too freely of the draft of plenty, which can only create a fever of which we are sure to die."[12]

Dan had no one to write him comforting words, nor to advise him to curb his voracious appetites. Perhaps he found consolation with women. In a world in which men often forged their strongest bonds with other men, Rice emphasized that he was "extravagantly fond of female society." He regaled later listeners with his romantic escapades in Pittsburgh, when "poor innocent me" carried notes to his girl from his rival, believing they were about business.[13]

When Dan was about seventeen, he married Margaret Ann Curran. Church records and municipal files tell nothing of Maggie, or about her meeting Dan. The 1840 census showed the Felix Curran farm across the Monongahela from Pittsburgh. Pittsburgh directories refer to other Currans, but this farm in Lower St. Clair township had the only entry showing a young woman who might have been Maggie, like that boy on the Reppert farm, "15–20 years." The census noted that Felix and his wife could read, suggesting that the young woman could, too. Rice did say that Maggie had been on the stage; otherwise he, too, offered little about his wife. He gave a one-sentence account of their courtship and wedding: "I met her one evening and we went around the corner and were married." Maggie had no known contact with her family after she left home, and parental disapproval peeks through Dan's implication that they snuck off, just as his parents had. Dan sent Maggie back home while they waited an opportunity to leave together.[14] To elope, then stay apart is unusual, but not unknown.

But if the historical record is slight, the play of imagination conjures a picture of Dan's meeting Maggie: He wanders down to the river to see George at Evans's mill. The sun feels good after a winter of dark and dank quarters. Mit comes along, settling in to help them watch steamboats on the water and the people parading by. Then a farmer plods up, his horse loaded with grain, his family trailing behind. Dan notices the short girl. Though not as homely as a hedge fence, she isn't pretty either, with a square jaw on a plain, square face. But something draws Dan just the same. Maybe he sees his mother's face in the girl. Maggie has his attention, and now he gets hers as he fixes her with his bright eyes. "Lovier" was a vulgar version of "lover." Vulgar it may have been, but its three syllables captured the active flirtation of fresh love.

3

LEARNED PIG, LEARNING DAN

"Oh! Anybody can tell time by looking at the watch." Dan was talking to a pig.

Ambitious to do more than drive drays, Dan found a job in 1841 presenting C. L. Kise's learned pig, Sybil. Just as the vocations of theology, medicine, and law were boosting their images by becoming "learned professions," so too did pigs trained to do tricks become "learned." In eighteenth-century London, Samuel Johnson, Mary Wollstonecraft, and William Blake had waxed enthusiastic about a learned porker, and an 1817 pig ostensibly joined their writerly ranks with an "autobiography," *The Life and Adventures of Toby, the Sapient Pig.*[1]

While Rice and Kise were later depicted as a partnership, Dan was a hired hand, and not well paid, either. In 1849, the publicity biography, *Sketches*, blithely declared that he toured with the pig only to "indulge an itinerant disposition"; an account half a century later said the tour furnished "a monetary benefit in the case of Mr. Kise, but merely a name for Dan Rice." Dan glorified his associate by saying that Kise sold P. T. Barnum his first humbug attraction, Joice Heth, presented as George Washington's 161-year-old nurse.[2]

Dan filled out the pig performance by singing duets with Maggie. They had set out in the spring, after the annual flooding over the point of Pittsburgh had subsided. Roads through the hills and hollows of Pennsylvania had become passable again, the mud hardening in the warming sun. *Sketches* aptly called it a tour of "Porky and presumption." Dan's native cockiness grew in the stables as friends clamored for his singing and stories. Now self-assurance was also a performance necessity. Stars can afford to be humble; their admirers supply the oxygen for their fire. But an unknown performer has to provide his own fire, fuel, and oxygen to coax an audience into a connection they don't yet know they want. That requires real confidence, to buoy the performer, and apparent confidence, to buoy the audience; then they can relax, like guests at a well-run party. Dan learned that even when he bungled a performance, he still had to swagger into the next town as if he had been cheered to the echo.

Rice later pictured grand triumph and ennobled Sybil as "Lord Byron," but it was a humble tour. The ability to impress friends is vastly different from professional proficiency in what was called "the show business." He was a beginner, with many lessons to learn. At first, walking into town and approaching men lounging outside a hole-in-the-wall tavern, Dan probably rushed to boast of all the Learned Pig's wonders, but he gradually realized that his beginner's nervous eagerness pushed people away rather than drew them in. Necessity taught him that people's curiosity would do part of his work. Sybil can waltz, he might say, then pause to let them chew that over before modestly boasting that she could calculate figures, too. Meanwhile, his voice was a double-edged sword, majestic but overwhelming until he began to modulate it. The performance, he could thunder, will be more instructive than a menagerie of exotic beasts and—then undercutting the bombast—more entertaining than a menagerie of politicians. Piquing people's interest further, Dan learned to whisper to the pig and pretend to listen to the answer.

Sometimes he did a poor job of tickling curiosity, or a storm blew, and he got no crowds. That meant a hungry road to the next town and Dan's few pennies would go for the pig's fodder. That was not affection, but necessity; a drooping pig would perform poorly. When Dan was lucky, he got the "ball room over the bar room" mentioned in *Sketches*. Otherwise he, Maggie, and the pig performed in a stable lit by a few flickering lanterns, people paying a few cents or a bartered potato to shoulder a cow out of the way and lean against a rough-hewn wall. Rain added the dank smell of wet, dirty clothes to the pungent mix of animals, hay, and the sweat of hard labor. How many people gathered? Ten some places, fewer in others, more in a village hall. If there weren't any women, the men swore, belched, and laughed about a fart while they waited. When Dan judged the audience was ready, some mysterious place between initial excitement and impatience—and he would judge wrong many times—he entered with his pig, a wig tied to its head, a bow on its neck. He squeezed to the front, brushing past grimy jackets and grubby shirts. The small group watched, a little nervous about being humbugged. They would look like fools if they appeared to believe the outlandish claim that this bacon-on-the-hoof could tell time, yet the young performer appeared so sure of himself. Now he was refusing to show the watch. Was it really a battle of wills with a pig?

"I suppose you must have your way—here it is." Dan seemed to relent, holding the watch out as Sybil seemed to consult it. Then she scratched once, twice, seven times with her right hoof! Seven o'clock! Ten times with her left. 7:10! As a later report put it, the pig "tickled their bumps of marvellousness."[3] How could a pig tell time?!

Of course, it was a trick. Pigs learn in days what might take a horse two or three years; sometimes pigs even waddle into the next trick without waiting for their cue. That cue can be a cough, a shift in body position, two steps forward, or holding the whip in a certain way, all without the audience's realizing. If Sybil squealed when Dan held up his watch, it wouldn't have been porcine curiosity about the time but a response to the cue of the watch held high. Pigs also have acute hearing, so Dan clicked his thumbnail on a fingernail as a signal. Seven clicks, then ten clicks, and the pig scratched out 7:10. Rice revealed another technique. By ending a question with the word "now," he gave the cue for an affirmative response. "Is Tyler president now?" A grunt for Yes. "Was our last audience as clever as this one?" A vigorous head shake for No.[4]

Dan was finding his way as a performer. If a quip worked, and the watching strangers relaxed into it, becoming that curious creature called an "audience," he would offer up another one. But if the joke lay lifeless, he could patch over the awkward pause with another pig feat. Dan was doing more than alternating jokes and tricks; he was learning to craft a performance. A pig scratching in the dirt holds little interest for an audience. It helps, but only slightly, to claim that the animal is telling time or adding figures. Dan discovered the need for drama, and that meant opposition. His pretend exasperation and the pig's apparent hesitation endowed Sybil with a stubborn personality, creating a battle of wills like the conflict in a good play. Dan needed to learn to plot that opposition without letting the plotting show, making the artificial sequence—or artifice, later called "art"—appear "natural."

Dan's progress was not smooth. Small steps of improvement were followed by abject mistakes that seemed worse than the first blunders. But intermittently, then increasingly, smooth moments flowed. A quip that had never worked before drew a laugh; inspiration yoked two small bits of comic business into a new, better one; an impulse sparkled. Gradually, luck and skill combined in increased control, not in the crude sense of manipulating an audience but in the growing ability of give and take with an audience, like riding a wave.

Dan learned the old trick of incorporating local events into his performance. *Sketches* recorded it as his "method"—the newly scientific age cherished systems—to enter town in disguise and gather gossip to use when he performed. In central Pennsylvania, Dan heard a rumor about the culprit who had burned a barn. When the victim, Hans Jaacks, attended the performance, Rice created a sensation when he cued Sybil to nose out the suspected arsonist. (*Sketches* alluded to a more extravagant version heard on Western steamboats: Jaacks won a conviction on the pig's evidence.) Dan's audience did not have to believe in pig magic. It was enough that Dan did what a good performer does; that is, he persuaded them that they had seen something special. Half a century later, he was still calling the Farmer Jaacks episode "my first hit."[5]

"Who's the biggest fool here?"

Dan Rice's Learned Pig telling Hans Jaack's fortune.

A dandified view of Dan's start in "the show business."

This was one of Dan's best bits. He waved his arm, a common orator's flourish in that oratorical age, so that his audience did not realize the wave was a signal. The pig began shuffling back and forth, apparently about to pick one man, then another. People, unaware, held their breath. It was an old routine that had been used by Richard Tarleton, who first acted the clown parts in Shakespeare's plays. Performing with the trained horse Marocco, "the most mentioned entertainer of Elizabethan times," Tarleton asked for the "verriest fool in the company." He used a variation that Dan may have employed: "Who here is the verriest whoremaster?"[6]

Performance at its beginning levels was like the era's prostitution, not necessarily a permanent situation but a sporadic vocation, entered into easily, and just as easily abandoned if better-paying propositions came along, or if indignity began to outweigh rewards. Dan may have set out with the pig because it was the path of least resistance or a chance for adventure beyond Pittsburgh's wharves. Performance also provided human connection. Conventional wisdom sees that as an embarrassing hunger for approval, a kind of emotional prostitution, but that explains too much and too little. Too much because any occupation beyond menial labor can be a search for love and approval; too little because people perform for a multitude of reasons, including ideas, talent, the need for expression, and pleasure. In the best circumstances, the performer and the audience join to form that paradoxical creature, an intimate community of strangers.

"Who's the biggest fool?" Dan repeated. Another paradox of performance is that the performer leads the audience by following them, paying heed to what interests and amuses them. The thread between Dan and his audiences was sometimes taut enough for the instant of performance to vibrate, alive and sparkling, but other times it grew slack, lifeless, even dangerous with ominous grumbling. Dan, twenty years old, was feeling his way, gaining the experience that would allow him to tell the difference, and crucially, to adjust his performance. As another small crowd wondered who the pig would pick for the butt of the joke, he sent another small signal. Maybe he crossed his arms or raised a heel. Then Sybil ran right to him, as if judging him the biggest fool. Laughs exploded! The fooler had been fooled! An animal simply seeking the food it has learned it will get for doing a specific action looked like a vehement accuser, aroused and relentless. As Sybil continued to squeal, nuzzling at his leg, the audience realized that Dan had set up the joke; but first, if he got it right, they would laugh, instantaneously, viscerally. He was learning the subtle alchemy of blending a disparate group of people into an audience and convincing them that his aggregation of skills, jokes, and tricks was gold. He was learning to perform.

4

"CIRCUS"

Grown to 180 pounds on a 5' 8" frame, Rice strutted into the historical record on March 9, 1843. A Pittsburgh circus advertisement commanded:

> LOVERS OF FUN, LOOK HERE!
>
> Dan Rice takes a benefit at the Amphitheatre this evening. He's the genuine, as all can testify who ever witnessed him. We expect a crowded house to-night and therefore advise all to go early.

Circus seems eternal, but in 1843 it was less than seventy-five years old. Though its elements—riding, variety acts, and clowning—are older than history, Philip Astley gets credit for bringing them together regularly in his circular arena. He was giving riding lessons in London when he decided in 1768 that people would pay to see him perform tricks on horseback. That made circus the "child to the riding school," a development that followed the changing nature of warfare. As monarchs no longer relied on mounted aristocracy for protection, aristocrats no longer needed to be taught riding, which put cavalry officers out of work. Some became riding masters like Astley, giving lessons to the rising middle class and, for advertisement, offering exhibitions. Make circus, not war.[1]

John Bill Ricketts, who had ridden for Astley's rival, Charles Hughes, sailed to America to start his own show. In Philadelphia on April 3, 1793, he presented the first American circus, a neat half-century before Rice joined on. Again, the elements were not new in the New World. In Mexico, "circus-type diversions" had enlivened Montezuma's court. The Quaker City had already seen equestrian exhibitions, and Thomas Poole added a clown to his trick riding in the 1750s. Nevertheless, like Astley, Ricketts gets credit for regularly combining riding, acrobatics, and clowning, all within a 42' circle, circumscribed by a low wooden fence. From the saddle, Ricketts leapt over a "Riband," caught an orange on the point of his sword, danced a hornpipe, hung by one leg while sweeping the plume of his hat on the ground, and balanced on his head. Standing on two running horses, he put "a GLASS of WINE in a HOOP, turning it round rapidly." He concluded by supporting an apprentice on his shoulders as he rode.[2]

Despite Ricketts's feats and George Washington in attendance, circus remained a fragile enterprise. It was not even clear what this embryonic form was. A letter writer confessed, "I might as well attempt to describe a piece of music or painting by language, as to express a full representation of the exhibition of the circus." Then in 1799, Ricketts's building burned, and the next year he was lost at sea. A decade after the first American circus, there was no American circus. Still, managers tried again. A French circus troupe sailed to Plymouth, Massachusetts, in 1807. The following year, an equestrian exhibition lured people from the Harvard commencement. These years of struggle included an outlandish prediction in 1811: "Some accidental turn of fashion, or that insatiable thirst for novelty which constitutes a predominant feature in our national character may make the (circus) popular and lucrative."[3]

Three major events around the time of Dan's birth shaped this new business. First came bareback riding. Originally, riders had performed their feats in the saddle or, later, on a pad. In England, Andrew Ducrow had created the "Poses Plastique Equestrianism," in which he imitated classic statues and national types—gladiator, British tar, Moorish warrior, Neapolitan fisherman—while riding. This scenic riding extended into story lines, like plotted ballet. Most extravagant were "hippodramas," plays featuring a rider or with a horse as the lead actor. Then in 1822, James Hunter rode a horse "in the rude state of nature"—without saddle or bridle. Scenic riding continued but the most acrobatic riders now performed their feats standing on the slick, sweaty back of a galloping, leaning horse. The split between scenic and bareback riding resembles the twentieth-century split between rhythmic gymnastics and traditional gymnastics—itself a descendent of circus, especially in high bar, floor exercise, and pommel horse.[4]

Also shifting was the word "circus." The first circus had not used that label. Astley called his arena "Amphitheatre," a word that signaled the mixed nature of his venture, which slid between drama and feats as an amphibian slides between land and water. Astley's title might have become a generic label, just as the title of an early London performance space, "Theatre," came to stand for plays. Then Astley's rival, Charles Hughes, looked to the performance circle for inspiration and called his building "Circus." Though he sought Roman grandeur, Hughes' Royal Circus echoed such commonplace traffic circles as Piccadilly Circus. In the Philadelphia of 1811, a similar urge for classical associations brought forth the "Olympic" arena. Meanwhile, simply advertising an arenic exhibition drew people. Then in 1824, James W. Bancker, perhaps the first American-born circus proprietor, transferred the word "circus" from arenas to the enterprise itself. Touring along the Erie Canal, he applied the name of his building, the New York Circus, to his traveling troupe, "Bancker's New York Circus." The usage caught on, becoming standard within a year.[5]

The third major innovation came in 1825 when J. Purdy Brown erected his "pavilion"—a canvas tent. Circus had been presented in the open air, in buildings like Ricketts's, and in makeshift affairs like Astley's first venture, with canvas walls blocking the view of those who did not pay. Because tents had been used for rehearsals as early as 1807, it was not remarkable that Brown set the tent up, but that he took it down to move on. That changed everything. Now shows traveled whenever they needed a fresh audience, daily if necessary. The push of technology, a new method of weaving canvas in a lighter weight, responded to the pull of audiences, as new settlements scattered across the country. Circus continued to use city theaters in winter, but now proprietors could be flexible on tour, and income rose. So did expenses. Previously, proprietors had paid for little more than performers' salaries and horse feed. Now, they had to provide food and lodging for the performers and for the workers who set up, pulled down, and transported the tents.[6]

Circus remained a work in progress. In 1829, a company was arrested for "enchantment and sorcery" in Pennsylvania, the bill of charges simply copying the show's offering. From 1793 through 1830, fewer than four hundred people filled American circus rosters. The menagerie, later an adjunct to circus, was a separate enterprise for years, and powerful competition, too. Not until 1826 did a menagerie and circus combine, and it was another decade before that combination become commonplace. Meanwhile, acts moved freely among theater, circus, menagerie, and minstrelsy. Whiteface and blackface clowns jostled in the circus ring. Some performers with circus skills—half a dozen rope-walkers, the "Antipodean Whirligig" who spun on his head—never appeared in one. The quintessential image of the circus strongman first appeared in a circus strongwoman, Madame Jansen, in 1811. A cord hanging from two ends for swinging evolved into three acts: the "corde volante," or cloud swing; the flying trapeze; and the slack rope. Meanwhile, some acts disappeared. One was almost literally a dead end: A circus performer's act consisted of hanging himself by the neck.[7]

Rice joined the growing business when he was twenty, signing on with Samuel H. Nichols's Circus and Theatre. Nichols was an innovative manager. One of the first to combine circus and menagerie, he pioneered the bright display that would become identified with circus, adopting a red canvas tent in 1840, using elaborate wagons, and giving a street parade with the band members mounted on horses sporting brass bells. He had built an amphitheater in Albany, a 3,000-seat brick octagon. When he arrived in Pittsburgh, he erected another arena for the winter of 1842–1843. Putting up a building for a season still made sense when labor and wood cost little. Nichols kept people coming during this long winter stand by reducing ticket prices, engaging "three Indian Chiefs" to dance and make speeches, and hiring this local favorite, Dan, now "Rice."[8]

Taking a benefit meant that Dan had risen quickly in the show business. A performer's benefit, unlike a benefit for charity, was compensation, the proceeds from ticket sales for the benefit performance added to salary. Leading performers "took" one benefit, or more, the star usually taking the last one of an engagement; others—performers, treasurers, managers—split a benefit, or got none. Like stock options for executives, the benefit was theoretically based on results, people presumably filling the seats for their favorites, who received the revenue. At the benefit for the strongman Mons. Guillot, he hoisted three men on a platform by his teeth, lifted two hundred pounds with his hair, and pulled against horses. The *Post* referred to him when Rice's turn came. "Why is Dan Rice like Mons. Guillot? Because he *draws* more than the horses."[9]

Rice was probably a strongman, perhaps a singer. Whatever his role, he later minimized it in this, his first circus, perhaps because of retrospective embarrassment. He said that he had been a stable hand learning tricks from Guillot when he was persuaded to dance the Camptown Hornpipe at a performance. The audience begged for a "negro song," but the only one Rice knew was coarse, and "would not bear repeating." When he sang it anyway, disapproving looks told him that he had gone too far.[10] Better to blame humiliation on amateur inexperience than on a professional blunder.

Dan's path to the circus was not a direct one. In that, he was similar to P. T. Barnum. Barnum's name would become a synonym for circus a half-century later, though he had little to do with circus until then. In 1836, Barnum had worked for a traveling circus as a ticket seller and treasurer; but then he steered into other amusements, making his name famous as an impresario, producing and presenting a variety of attractions, especially the exotic and odd in his American Museum in New York. A story connected the two men there, Rice as a strongman attraction in Barnum's museum. Another story sailed strongman Dan on a European tour, giving a private exhibition for Prussia's King "William," and escaping the Spanish Queen Isabella's "wily intrigues" of seduction. (She would have been ten.)[11]

Rice did perform as a strongman in Philadelphia after the Learned Pig tour had ended in southeastern Pennsylvania. He later claimed that he had his first paid professional engagement there, singing and lifting weights at the Masonic Hall, followed by work at the Chinese Museum. The following summer, Dan retraced the Learned Pig route with feats of strength. Other accounts have him starting in a contest of "old-fashioned negro dancing," $50 first prize, or performing with the minstrel pioneer, Sam Sanford, at Palmo's Opera House in 1843. The variety continued in Nichols's circus. Rice might have been clown, singer, actor, lecturer, or comic monologist, all roles he later took on. Rice, embodying the American faith in new starts, also echoed performance history. The Romans had combined actors, clowns, jugglers, and dancers under the label "histriones," and the medieval minstrel was a performer of many parts.[12]

After Nichols's show, Dan and Maggie went on tour again. From central Pennsylvania, Dan wrote to his friend, Mit Foster:

Harrisburgh, June 17, 1843

My Dear Met

I take my pen in hand to informe you that I am Well an A doing Well and I hope that this Letter Will Finde you in the same Way.
I have had A long jorney of it an am most tirde out. I rote to gorge A Bout to Weekes A go an tolde him to direct his Letter to Carlisle P. A. But I did not go thare. An so I rote to the Postmaster At that place to direct the letter to Reading P. A. an you tell gorge that if he dont heare frome me in A Bout A Weeke he must right to me at Reading fore I expect to Be there the forth of July an you must right to me as soone as you can We are doing A Big Bisiness. I am making money pretty fast I am getting tow salerreys A Bout a twenty five dollars A Weeke I am clowning an also my nigero singing and dancing is drawing good houses I think that Weel Be Back With the show in the fall give my Best respect to all of my friends and tell them that I am A going it With a perfect rush

I Remane yours

I expect that gorge is maried tell me if he hase got ths congude

Rice is alive in the letter, full of bravado and allegiance to his friends. Like a homesick kid in the army, he devoted much of the letter to instructions about mail. Though Rice, like most in his era, spelled poorly, "Met" may have been Mit's name pronounced in a Western drawl, just as "nigero" spoken lies halfway between "Negro" and the word that would grow offensive over the years, "nigger." Mit and Dan both missed the wedding of their pal, "gorge" Evans, on June 1. The postscript—"hase got ths congude"—could have been a bawdy joke about George's relations.[13]

The show enjoying Rice's "perfect rush" is not clear, a reminder of the small enterprises lost to history. Though two accounts put Dan with the showman Hugh Lindsay, one as a $4-a-week puppeteer, the other on a blackface troupe, nothing links either to this summer show. Dan may have been with the Philadelphia Zoological Gardens, a menagerie on tour near Harrisburg about the time Dan wrote from there; but the traveling Zoo stayed in Pennsylvania through July, while Dan moved on to New Jersey. Whiteface and blackface clowning suggest a circus, but Nichols had taken his red tent west, and Aaron Turner's circus, moving east from Pittsburgh in June, had no Rice on its bills—though he might have been on an "outside show" trailing along.[14]

Rice did not make the claimed $25 a week. Half that would have been extraordinarily good pay for a novice. The claim of two salaries is another exaggeration. Circus performers usually did more than one job, making themselves, in the contractual language, "generally useful." When that second task was playing in the show's brass band, it meant "doubling in brass." Rice magnified his role more in a second letter to Mit, from Trenton on July 24. Mentioning a trip into New York probably on an errand for the show, perhaps visiting his sisters, Libbie and Kate—he wrote that the company "has to lay still until I come back." In a business where each day's performance provided the only income, a troupe could not afford to stop simply because one of their number was absent. "The show must go on" did not testify to performers' courage but to economic necessity.[15]

The former Danny McLaren, then Manahan, declared his independence with a JohnHancock flourish.

The most significant aspect of the letter is the signature. Dan Rice had literally made a name for himself.

Rice lived a life full of fiction, and uncertainty about his name is fitting. He may have come into the world as Daniel McLaren III, after his father. He could have been Daniel Crum. On Elizabeth's marriage to Hugh, her little Dandy likely became Daniel Manahan. In Pittsburgh, "the boys" called him Dan Dusty Foot. He may have adopted his show business moniker during the pig tour, which provided money to Kise "but merely a name for Dan Rice." But why Rice? Over the years, dubious explanations popped up: His father dubbed him in honor of a famous Irish clown; Rice was his mother's middle name; and Grandpa Crum named the boy after a relative—but Scottish McLaren's "famous" clown remains unknown, Dan's mother was not "Rice," and the good reverend would not increase suspicions of illegitimacy by giving his grandson a different name from either parent. A twentieth-century tale depicts Dan picking the name because he liked rice pudding.[16] Meanwhile, the most likely explanation has lain simultaneously obscure and obvious.

Dan appropriated "Rice" from the most popular performer of his youth, T. D. Rice. Thomas Dartmouth Rice had become a national sensation in blackface, performing his celebrated Jump Jim Crow, a jerky dance that he said faithfully imitated a Negro stable hand he had seen, and whose ragged clothes he had bought. As a boy, Dan could have seen T. D. in New York "dance and turn about and jump just so, ev'r'time he jump Jim Crow." Imitators multiplied, embedding "Jim Crow" in American consciousness. An early historian of blackface wrote truer than he knew about T. D.: "Not only on the stage, but in the sawdust ring of the circus, Rice had many imitators."[17]

Dan's adoption of T. D.'s name has remained virtually invisible because of something else obvious and obscure: his "nigero singing and dancing."

America was crazy for blackface. To the twanging thwang of the banjo, and the clatter of tambo and bones—tambourine and bone castanets—white men smeared burnt cork on their faces to sing, waggle their legs in imitation of blacks dancing, and tell jokes in "negro" dialect. Between 1750 and 1843, over 5,000 theater and circus productions included blackface. Though blackface tends to be studied apart from other forms, it emerged significantly out of circus. Gottlieb Graupner, known as "the father of American orchestral music" for his role in founding the Boston Symphony, blacked up for an 1809 circus. Credit for first jumping Jim Crow in a circus was given both to T. D. and to Dan's boss, Nichols. Many performers, like Dan, slid from the shiny greasepaint of whiteface to the flat black of burnt cork, with its pungent smell of burned popcorn. So common was "negro pantomime" in circuses that proprietors who had none advertised the absence.[18]

This year of Dan's "nigero" impersonation was especially significant. On February 6, 1843, four circus performers between summer seasons, Frank Brower, Dan Emmett, Frank Pelham, and Billy Whitlock, gathered in a New York hotel room for what might later be called a jam session. They then crossed to the Bowery Circus to serenade the proprietor, Nathan Howes, sitting by a stove at the door. A hit, they appeared on stage in blackface as the Virginia Minstrels and launched a national craze. "Parties organized all over the country, and no circus that season was complete" without its band of Ethiopian "delineators." Through the growing craze, it made sense for an ambitious beginner to appropriate the name of the most famous practitioner of the popular form, T. D. Rice, who continued as a solo act. It was also sensible to hide that debt. One article in 1846 did volunteer that Dan's "negro characters" put him "close on the heels of his illustrious name-sake"; otherwise the subject was avoided. Even the fact that Dan changed his name was barely acknowledged. Because mentioning Rice and blackface together would remind people of T. D., Dan steered clear of any hint of his last name's origin.[19]

(A different motive continued obfuscation into the twentieth century. Slavery is America's original sin, a shame that shivers down the centuries in awkwardness between whites and blacks. As Dan's appropriation of T. D.'s name might call blackface to mind, later accounts mostly hid it.)[20]

Dan and Maggie returned to Pittsburgh late in 1843. Over the winter, Dan worked at whatever he could get as the depression lingered. Conditions in Western theaters were "perhaps the most grievous in the history of the American stage." It was the same story in New York, where the 1840–1841 season had been "one of the most depressing in the history of American theatricals," and the following was worse. The number of American circus companies fell to ten in 1843, the lowest since the early days. Rice would say that his first song-writing effort, assisted by his "gifted chum," Stephen Foster, had been "Hard Times."[21]

Meanwhile, Maggie was expecting. When a new baby girl survived the dangerous process in February 1844, the new parents named her Elizabeth, after Dan's mother and his sister. Like her aunt, she was called Libby.[22]

Farmers make hay while the sun shines; performers make tracks. As roads dried in another spring and ice broke up on the rivers, Rice headed west. Reaching Iowa by March 1844, where elders remembered struggles with Sac Indians and amusements still included wolf hunts, Dan performed in hall shows, singing, dancing, spinning comic tales, and playing strongman. In Davenport, he performed in the Le Claire House, with its bad acoustics. He told a story about dodging the license in Davenport (avoiding the municipal fee for performance), drawing a crowd in rival Rock Island to hear of that escapade, and then sneaking out without paying there. Downriver in Muscatine, Dan rented space in the tavern of good-hearted Capt. Jim Palmer, who was on the door and declined to charge any of his friends, which left Rice with little.[23]

Rice frequently had trouble with money. *Sketches* admitted to his "many expensive tastes, the indulgence of which he could not deny himself when he had the means." One story suggests that financial predicaments landed him in jail: Rice said that his friend's mother, Mrs. Cadwallader Evans, offered to loan him bail after a mistaken arrest for theft.[24]

Rice's informal apprenticeship in these early days peeks through his fables like glimpses through a river fog. He allegedly carried mail from Chicago to St. Louis, and claimed an acting debut as a demon in *Sleeping Beauty* at the St. Louis Museum. One of Rice's more extensive and frequently repeated fictions coupled him with the Mormon leader, Joseph Smith. Smith had been hounded from upstate New York to Ohio, then to Nauvoo, Illinois, on the Mississippi, where a mob lynched him in 1844. Relying on the age's anti-Mormon prejudice, Rice wove a tale of joining Smith to develop his own humbugging skill. He would pretend his strongman tricks were divinely aided, Smith would preach to the attracted crowd, and they would split the offerings. But Joe, jealous of Dan's influence, sent him across the river to proselytize in Iowa. There, when passing St. Louis merchants "exposed the pretended Mormon's miracles" and the outraged Hawkeyes pressed ominously close, Dan improvised a song and won over the crowd, which sang the choruses. Back in Nauvoo, cheated of his share, he convinced Joe to pretend to walk on water, using a platform hidden just below the Mississippi's surface. The night before the "miracle," Dan rowed out to remove planks. The next morning, the Mormon prophet splashed in, losing his composure and his reputation. (The water-walk story was fifteen years old, told on Smith in his Ohio days.) Rice threw in a titillating hint at Mormon polygamy: The ladies, eyeing manly Dan, wondered "whether he had yet made his selection of the usual spiritual comforts just introduced by Joe."[25]

Though a fabrication, the Mormon story nevertheless highlights the age's violence. Dealing with querulous or corrupt locals, trying to persuade money from the pockets of those who had little, confronting rowdies intent on combat, Rice constantly moved on the border of safety, with little protection but his fists and his budding ability to sense an audience's mood. Dan knew he had quelled the Iowa crowd's anger because he "could read their faces better." He would make mistakes. When he pushed a joke about a local too far, he would sweat to breathe life back into the performance, trying to reconnect. Sometimes he failed, and that elusive creature called an "audience"shied away, and they would be strangers. That meant more than disapproval; it could be dangerous. Mark Twain bundled his boyhood memories along the Mississippi into *Huckleberry Finn*, in which his fictional Duke and Dauphin, scratching out a living like Dan, flee for their lives. Hot tar on a body stripped naked, with feathers for insult, could lay a body up for weeks. It could be fatal. The crowd in the Mormon story stood for the mobs Dan faced on the frontier, alone, frightened, hoping to escape without a broken bone, or tar burning his flesh.[26]

On November 18, 1844, Rice tried circus again, as a comic singer in Albany with the North American Circus of Gilbert R. Spalding. Later ignoring Nichols, Rice claimed that he had started in circus with Spalding. He said it was in the spring of 1844 among the "Diggers" of Galena, miners in western Illinois.[27] He gave a sprightly account of his interview with Spalding:

SPALDING: "You say you can sing comic songs?"
RICE: "Yes."
SPALDING: "And do negro songs and dances?"
RICE: "Yes."
SPALDING: "And pull against horses?"
RICE: "Yes."
SPALDING: "And climb the fireman's ladder?"
RICE: "Yes."
SPALDING: "Can you drive a team?"
RICE: "Yes."
SPALDING: "Can you learn to ride, and figure in the Grand Entry?"
RICE: "Yes."
SPALDING: "Can you play clown?"
RICE: "I can try."
SPALDING: "Well if you can do all those things, and whip three men a day in addition, I'll board you and give you $15 a month."[28]

Rice rarely worried about consistency: Here, the allegedly famous jockey agrees to learn to ride for the show's opening parade; the brash comic performer who boasted of a $25 weekly salary modestly allows that he will try to play clown for $15 a month.

5

CLOWN TO THE RING

Even as Rice was explicitly billed as a circus clown for the first time in June 1845, his role remained ambiguous. The ads for Nathan Howes's circus promoted him as one of the show's blackface "Ethiopean Serenaders," with "Songs, Glees, Choruses and Extravaganzas" of slaves . . . "at the south." Nathan Howes built shows and launched careers for decades with his brother, Seth Howes, himself eventually called "father of the American circus." Now Nathan hired Rice to lead the Serenaders with his "Congo Tambo"—tambourine—touring with the New York Bowery Circus through New York, Massachusetts, and Rhode Island. Rice's leadership was all the more notable because he joined Dan Emmett, an original Virginia Minstrel, who would later write the quintessential minstrel song, "Dixie." The two Dans continued with Howes in New York in the fall. Rice was still no star, billed as a modest "D. Rice, clown."[1]

Maggie may have joined Dan in the strolling display of fashion on Broadway, a place for shopping and flirting, "kind looks and *billet doux*." Nine months later, their second child was born.[2]

The most prominent feature in this exhibition, next to HERVIO NANO, and the boy WALTER AYMAR, is the famous
BAND OF ETHIOPEAN SERENADERS!
Led by Mr. D. RICE, as follows:
Mr. D. EMMIT,....................BANJO MELODIST.
" FREDERICKS,....................VIOLIN.
" D. RICE,....................CONGO TAMBO.
MASTER STICKNEY,....................BONE CASTANETS.
Nothing can excel the popularity of these inimitable Melodists, in the various Songs, Glees, Choruses and Extravaganzas, given in imitation of the slaves upon the different plantations at the south. Mr. EMMIT and Mr. RICE have many of their own composition, which have never been sung at any other establishment

Rice and Dan Emmett, author of "Dixie," played to America's craze for blackface performers.

Howes took his company to Baltimore's Front Street Theater, opening mid-December in the face of a gale. The *Sun* joked that the wind roamed "the streets like a herd of huge elemental mammoths," flinging a sign for "Mangling" (clothes pressing) against a surgeon's house, and "Shaving" at the door of a money broker's. Rice made his own jokes about the weather.

RICE: "Can you tell me what mathematical wind is?"
RING MASTER: "I give it up."
RICE: "A wind that extracts roots from the earth."[3]

Rice returned to New York in February. Though his travels down the Mississippi had not taken him beyond Cairo, Illinois, he was billed as "a great favorite from the South" to make his minstrelsy seem plantation-genuine. A lithograph of Rice showed whiteface clowns in four routines: one dancing; another grabbing his shin after a blow from the ringmaster's whip; a third standing with legs apart and holding a sword, point to the ground; and the fourth with dogs biting his bottom. Though they represented Rice "as he appeared in Howes' & Co. Circus, Palmo's Opera House, New York, Feb. 23d, 1846," the images were stock cuts, used for other performers, too. The central image showed Rice out of the ring, elegantly dressed and posed fashionably; he held white gloves in one hand,

The variously spelled "Shaksperian" clown was a popular variation on the talking clown.

which he rested on a pedestal, and a top hat in the other. His hair rolled to a bob framing a clean-shaven face. He had not yet grown a goatee.[4]

Back in Baltimore again, as the "best comic vocalist in the United States," he was crowned by ancient and modern similes: He could make people "grin the edge off [Time's] scythe, as Davy Crockett did the bark from the hickory"; and he was "a perfect galvanic battery of humor, evolving the electric sparks of native wit."[5]

As Rice began his circus career, it was not still clear what "clown" meant. Perhaps deriving from "clod," the word originally referred to a country clown, or rube. The transition from clown-rube to clown-performer can be seen in Shakespeare's *As You Like It*, when Touchstone, the court fool, hails a rube as a clown, only to be admonished by Rosalind: "Peace, fool, he's not thy kinsman." Even as the performing clown emerged, the older usage continued. Walt Whitman complained of "clowns and country bumpkins," and the weekly *Spirit of the Times*, the country's major show-business periodical, mocked a rustic in Boston in 1842 as a "clown *veritable*, dressed like a clown of the Ring." Meanwhile, the rustic became a performance type himself, his red wig and ruddy cheeks later adopted by some clowns.[6]

While the pretend ineptitude of comic riding produced the first circus comedy, the clown embodied its variety. That variety could be seen in Rice at this Baltimore stand as he sang in blackface and whiteface, joked, danced, acted, and performed feats of strength. Earlier, in 1817, a "clown to the rope" had assisted a tightrope walker. Five years later, a circus at New York's Park Theatre first designated a "clown to the equestrian acts." This clown to the ring was a kind of property man, handing the rider props, setting up hurdles, holding the "garter" or ribbon over which the rider leapt, and hoisting the "balloons"—paper-covered hoops—through which he jumped. His comic business also provided a rest for the rider.[7]

With the revolution of bareback riding, the clown rose from humble adjunct to become part of the new triumvirate at the core of the circus: rider, ringmaster, clown. The rider had literally given up the reins, so the ringmaster controlled the horse, setting its pace and stopping it. The master of the ring adopted the outfit of the master of the hunt: riding boots, white breeches, and bright red coat. His whip, originally a necessary tool for the job, became a symbol of authority. Then the ringmaster and clown re-created the ancient partnership of straight man and comic. Clown antics can be funny alone but, as Rice discovered with his pig, conflict is more interesting. Now, the ringmaster appeared to struggle to control the clown, an opponent seemingly too stupid or too sly to behave properly.[8]

RING MASTER: "You are rude, and I feel that all my instruction is lost upon you."

RICE: "What have I done?"

RING MASTER: "You appear better fed than taught."

RICE: "Yes, I feed myself, and you teach me." (Rice began to exit, when the ringmaster pulled him back.)

RING MASTER: "Remember, sir, I never follow a fool."

RICE: "All right, Master, I'm not so particular about it. I will."[9]

The circus clown and ringmaster resembled the stage clown and his partner, Pantaloon, in looks and repartee.

(Too much can be made of the opposition. A romance was growing of the clown as truth-teller, flinging challenge to authority, a romance augmented by literary examples, such as the Fool in *King Lear*, but the circus clown was a performer in a carefully structured routine. The ringmaster did literally hold the whip hand, and the clown did mock him, but both were pretending. While Hamlet's admonition is often invoked, "And let those that play your clowns speak no more than is set down for them," clowns usually do speak mostly what is set down in their preparation—though the most effective bits are often those designed to look like improvisation.)

From the antebellum opposition of ringmaster and clown emerged the talking clown. While knockabout clowns continued to provide physical comedy, this new type perfectly suited an age enthralled by oratory. Here Rice's talents converged. His agile wit and powerful voice combined to make him the exemplary talking clown.

Almost immediately, he began to incorporate a variation: the Shakespearean clown. In Baltimore, Rice's burlesque readings of "Shakspeare" were "perhaps the most amusing feature in his performances." Shakespeare's plays were the most popular works on the stage, attracting the genteel and the million, bankers and bootblacks, prudes and prostitutes—though prudes preferred bowdlerized versions, the naughty bits excised by Thomas Bowdler. If plays reveal themselves best in performance, then the nineteenth-century mechanic, who attended more often than a twentieth-century English professor, knew his Shakespeare well. Shakespearean clowns fit that interest as they varied their usage from brief, mangled quotations to astute parodies. To introduce equestrian acts, for instance, clowns would bellow Richard III's "My kingdom for a horse!"[10]

Rice's "Shakespearianism" centered on two burlesques, "Dan Rice's Version of Othello" and "Dan Rice's Multifarious Account of Shakespeare's Hamlet." Despite the titles, he did not write them. The "Othello" had appeared in print before his career began, and he surely borrowed the "Hamlet" as well. Nevertheless, they were his, just as singers have signature songs written by others. Rice introduced his burlesques into the ring and became known for them. Nor were they stray doggerel. Their rhymed couplets of iambic pentameter and clear synopses of the plays show a sophisticated capacity. Dan's "Othello" was barely a burlesque, beyond the mockery in the first couplet—"In Venice once there lived a sooty fellow, / By trade a soldier, and by name Othello"—and the joke in the final one—"This tale is writ in Shakspeare's lyric finis, / But his account is not as good as mine is." Rice could have broadened the performance by using "nigero" dialect, but as the script itself was not comic, he may have played it straight. Before a performance of his Hamlet, a newspaper warned, "You that have tears, prepare to shed them now."[11]

Shakespearean clowns are another reminder that antebellum amusements intertwined significantly. Theater and circus competed for the same audiences, both using concluding farces, offering scripted narratives that starred horses, and presenting dramatic spectacles, often on the same stages. "Museum" and "lecture hall" were euphemisms for theater that allowed those opposed to entertainment to attend "educational" plays. The overlap can be seen in a twentieth-century complaint that happened to encompass Rice's varied talents. In his fifteen-volume history of the New York stage, George C. D. Odell wrote, "The reader may recall my constant lament over the limpets of the theatrical body—those dances, songs, wrestling bouts, feats of strength and juggling, rope-walking, etc. . . . stuck like a leech to the regular plays."[12]

While he was touring Canada with Howes in the summer, Dan learned that Maggie had given birth to a daughter, Catherine Anne Rice, on August 3. Maggie was in Long Branch, with the Manahans. The baby was named after her aunt, Dan's spitfire sister, Kate. Family lore had Dan's stepfather, Hugh Manahan, moving to a Long Branch farm soon after his wife's death. The 1850 census showed him as a fish carter by then, married a third time, and owning property worth $2,000. Dan's brother, William, also a fisherman, married a local in 1849. (The seventeen-year-old "Caroline" Manahan listed working for a neighbor may have been Dan's sister, Catherine.)[13]

Dan did not hurry home to see his new child. The trouping life did not allow that luxury, but there may have been another reason. A month later, he was in Rochester when the *Daily Democrat* commented that he had recently been subject to "ills that flesh is heir to," his "wits sharpened by adversity." The report could have meant his health; Dan was often laid up from fighting or illness. But the paper was casting a wry eye on Rice's roving eye. In the ring, he described the effect of his kiss on a woman, who "felt as if something was running through her nerves on the foot of diamonds escorted by angels, shaded by honeysuckles, and the whole spread with the melted rainbow. Jerusalem! what power there is in a full-breasted kiss."[14]

He practiced what he preached. On August 28 the sheriff of Buffalo offered a $50 reward for Rice's capture on charges of assault on an aggrieved husband and criminal conversation—legal language for adultery. Rice had been arrested but given leg bail: He escaped. The road's combination of loneliness and temptation is potent, but Dan's promotional biography, *Sketches*, remolded the story with a heroic Rice. Seeing the abused wife of on horseback between towns, exposed to the elements by a thoughtless husband, Dan gave her a seat in his carriage. When the husband threatened brutality, Rice "would interpose his arm," and then arranged a room for the wife in his hotel. Hearing violent noises that night, he broke in to save her. "The facility with which his sympathies are aroused is a weakness which can be worked upon with the shallowest pretexts." The valiant clown dashed the bully-husband "against the wall with one hand, while with the other he placed the fainting lady upon a sofa," her clothes in disarray. However, the same details allowed a less innocent interpretation, perhaps with a knowing wink to the reader about Dan's offering a ride, an arm, a room, and his "aroused" feelings. Instead of breaking in on the husband, it would fit the facts the other way around.

On August 31, Rice was captured on the *DeWitt Clinton*, a steamer carrying Lake Erie freight between Buffalo and Sandusky, Ohio. Rice had probably gone west when Howes's circus went east, but got caught sneaking back. The charges were dropped, one story says because Howes paid the $100 fine and the husband, in Howes's band, was not around to press charges.[15]

Sketches continued Rice's version: When Sheriff Pierce comes for the arrest during a performance, the audience forces him to let Dan finish, and the clown promises to surrender during the last act. Changing into street clothes, he walks arm-in-arm with Pierce into the ring. Suddenly, he bolts. While the sheriff farcically stumbles against the actors in the show's farce, Dan dodges out the front. The narrative interrupts itself briefly for a showman's complaint about the congested entrance, "where people always will stand, no matter how many seats may be vacant or how incommodious it may be to others." Dan dives under the ticket-wagon, where the sheriff bumps his head. The clown then hides in a peddler's cake wagon and rides away covered with dough, resting on gingerbread. Returning to Buffalo and jail, Rice bides his time by making speeches from his cell window, on "the Rights of Man, *Habeas Corpus*, Democracy, Progressive Principles, Woman, Chivalry, and matters and things in general."[16]

Word of the arrest reached Maggie, who was caring for their two little girls. News traveled slowly in the 1840s, but it traveled. Visitors, newspapers, gossip among those in the show business—somehow she would hear. Dan's relatives, whether they thought him guilty or innocent, would have sympathized with Maggie, but sympathy can be hard to take, jabbing at suspicion like a tongue flicking a toothache.

In October 1846, Rice joined another leading circus figure, "General" Rufus Welch. The eight-month stand at Philadelphia's National Theatre was the longest Rice would ever play in one town. Adding a four-month summer tour with Welch's National Circus made it the longest stretch that Rice would work for one man. In Welch, Rice found a congenial role model. Nichols had gone broke; Spalding was methodical and close with money; and Howes focused on his family. Meanwhile, no circus man was better liked or more admired than Rufus. Spending expansively and loaning easily, he was never wealthy. For this Philadelphia date, he decorated the theater in burnished gold, cream, and pale white under the "rich classic light" of a chandelier. Rice saw in the open-hearted, open-handed General a man who matched his own expansive character.[17]

Welch began in the show business with menageries. In the early 1800s, wild animal displays stood distinct from circus. Touting its educational value, menagerie posed as morally superior to clown vulgarity and circus display of the human form. Menagerie owners promised an education, even a biblical lesson, in their display of exotic animals. At Sunday meeting, people heard about the camel; at the menagerie they could see one. As this publicity advantage held sway in the 1820s, menagerie outdrew circus. In a pamphlet published by the new American Sunday-School Union, two brothers are enticed by a smooth-talking circus man until their father urges them to a menagerie, saying that circus animals are whipped and the performers "are generally idle and worthless people," who take money from those who can't afford it. He warns that circus tempts boys to run away, "and then there is no hope of their making useful men." But circus was more dynamic, and menageries countered by adding performance. Still, within a few years of Rice's circus debut, most menageries had become parts of circuses.[18]

Rice's perfect rush had propelled him to the front ranks of circus in barely five years. Working for Welch, he joined the best clowns then working, some of the best America has known; he shared the ring with Joe Gossin and William Kemp, then with John May, who had clowned for Nichols in Pittsburgh, and Joe Pentland. (Rice would one day eulogize another clown, Joseph Blackburn, deceased in 1841, as the best he ever met.) Welch opened with "First Clown by the celebrated Dan Rice, a Mimic and Buffo of the first and highest reputation," and newspapers praised Gossin and Rice as "the funniest fellows imaginable."[19]

Rice later published a lecture that he said he had delivered at the city's new medical school, on invitation of Doctors Goddard and Pancoast. Goddard was president of the new Franklin Medical College (and in the 1880s, Philadelphia's Jefferson Medical College had a Prof. Pancoast), but an invitation was unlikely. The medical business was striving to become accepted as a profession, and inviting a clown to speak would have undercut that effort. But students and doctors do attend amusements. Addressing the audience as if it were a class, Rice lectured on chemistry as applied to human greatness, concluding in a cascade of nonsense. "Chemistry, gentlemen, in brief, embraces the nature and qualities of the mind, kites, soap bubbles, thunder, lightning, bed-bugs, fleas, mosquitoes, parasites, adulterated teas, coffees, sugar and drinks, music and perfumery, besides many other ingredients which, if I am again called to preside over this learned assembly, I shall take occasion to notice more particularly."[20]

Yet for all his success, Dan was still a young man, still learning a difficult craft. He was not prominent enough, for instance, for anyone to correct the typo in the advertising, "John Gossin and John Rice, Clowns." He was too proud to ask his celebrated clown colleagues for advice, but he would be watching. Just as he had learned in his first years to watch the audience, gauging the effect of his words and action, he would observe his compatriots to see what went over well. One practical lesson was the advantage of offering another attraction than clowning. Pentland had a riding act, Kemp ran on barrels and on stilts, and handsome Gossin with his black ringlets did a bit of everything. So Rice used his skill with animals to train and present a dog, "Seth Howes." It was named after the showman, perhaps in mockery of the tightfisted Howes. Like the Learned Pig, Rice's dog could "add, subtract, multiply, divide, tell how many persons there are present, distinguish colors, tell the time by any person's watch, name all the prominent and distinguished characters of our country, and answer any reasonable questions asked by the audience." Again, Rice multiplied a few tricks by a few situations to suggest an infinite range of animal intelligence. The marvels, earlier porcine, now canine, rested in Rice's ability to structure the presentation.[21]

Welch varied his offerings over the eight months to keep his appeal fresh against major stars. After Edwin Forrest, the preeminent American actor, presented *Damon and Pythias* for his benefit, Rice burlesqued it with his own version. Rice and his blackface performers also competed against three troupes, including other Ethiopian Serenaders and the Sable Harmonists at Peale's Philadelphia Museum and Gallery of Fine Arts. Because sleighing was always tough competition, Welch countered after a snowstorm by advertising only "Clown, Dan Rice, 'Verbum Sat.'" That's short for the Latin, "A word to the wise is sufficient." (From November 20 into January, Richard Sands and Lewis B. Lent replaced Welch in the ads. Since the performers remained the same, it is not clear whether Sands & Lent took over the building under their own management or in partnership with Welch.) By the end of the run, Rice had become the show's preeminent performer, given the honor of the season's last benefit.[22]

Rice headed out that summer with Welch's National Circus into Quebec. In September 1847, the show hauled up in Pittsburgh. This stand put Rice in Pittsburgh for what Ken Emerson, in his biography of Stephen Foster, calls "the birth of pop music." On Saturday, September 11, the Eagle Ice Cream Saloon saw the first performance of Foster's "Oh! Susanna." After Rice's own show, he could have joined the crowd to hear his friend's new song repeated. (Rice used the melody for many of his own songs.)[23]

Rice was growing important enough that critics felt obliged to give him advice. A local paper, the *Daily Morning Post*, heaped the usual praise for "the great favorite" on his benefit, but cautioned that his "jokes are in some respects objectionable. Dan, however, is a young man, and years will improve him." The next day, he met the paper's editor and turned on the charm, which led to a reconsideration. "We like him the better the more we see him. He is, without doubt, one of the best clowns in the country. There is more originality in his 'system of amusement' than is generally exhibited by the wags of the ring. We were yesterday introduced to him, and judge from his appearance and conversation that he is every inch a gentleman."[24]

At the end of October 1847, Rice returned as a star to New York. It must have been gratifying for the poor boy from Mulberry Street to read James Gordon Bennett's *Herald.* "Dan Rice, the great Shaksperian clown, is drawing houses commensurate with his fame . . . on dropping in there last night whilst he was letting off some of his jovialities, we found the audience in a perfect roar of delight. The fact is, Dan Rice is a great clown, and the patrons of the circus know it." The writer, Park Benjamin, contributed a sketch to the *New World*, calling Rice highly distinguished and comparing him to the great English stage clown Joseph Grimaldi. Rice had "so capital and quick an apprehension of the humorous, with a more certain power of controlling his hearers, as if by the influence of animal magnetism. If he goes on as he has begun, studying his art and endeavoring to excel in it, the biography of the stage or circus will present us no more successful Jester."[25]

For his benefit, Rice's first in New York, he went the whole hog. He appeared in his burlesque of the Battle of Buena Vista, lectured on Phreno-Magnetism, gave his great War Speech, imitated the well-known actors, Junius Brutus Booth, Forrest, and Macready, sang original comic songs, and presented "HIS GREAT EQUESTRIAN ACT." (This was a rare notice of Rice performing on horseback.) Now important enough for New York to claim him as a native, he was "the jester of all jesters, whose ready and pointed wit has obtained for him the title of the Shakesperian Jester, as, indeed, his effusions are as much superior to that of the usual run of clowns, as the undying Will's writings are to those of the veriest Grub street poet."[26]

PART 2

ONE-HORSE SHOW

1848 ☛ 1852

6

SPALDING AND SPICY RICE

Gilbert Spalding was an Albany druggist who sold supplies to Sam Nichols for his circus, mixing paints and providing whale oil for the "chandeliers"—the round, spoked platform of lamps or candles pulled up over the circus ring. It was on that circus, duly painted and brightly lit, that Rice performed in Pittsburgh. After Nichols fell behind on payment, Spalding met him on the road in February 1844, planning to sell off the show's equipment to recoup what he could. But as Spalding directed the circus back to Albany, he discovered that he had a knack for the business. The show began to make money. So in April, he revived an old Albany title, the North American Circus, and remade himself as a circus proprietor, "Doc" Spalding.[1]

It was odd for the quiet thirty-two-year-old druggist with the Van Dyke beard to join this boisterous world. Vastly unlike Rice, Spalding was "not one of the many who are willing to be talked to at all times." Nevertheless, like other proprietors who had established themselves first in other lines of work, he brought more method than romance to the task. Doc Spalding was sharp and shrewd, "ready for anything that had money in it." Reserved personally, he was bold in business. Rather than shutting down his show for the winter, he sent it South; he wasn't the first but he made it pay. He hired Edward Kendall, the country's most famous Kent bugle player, to lead his band. (Kent, or keyed, bugles, with holes and stoppers, were a historical flourish soon swept away by technology, succumbing to the easier-to-play valve cornet.) Another bold decision was to fix on Rice as one of the show's two stars. The other star, Charles J. Rogers, was a safer choice. He had made his debut the year before Rice was born, and by 1848, Rogers may have been the best scenic rider in America.[2]

In the North, Rice had been the "great favorite from the South"; now he went there billed as a Northern luminary. Spalding opened a stand in Mobile in January 1848, advertising that Rice could "readily command $50 a night" and was "probably the most extraordinary man in his line that has ever existed." The exaggerations showed that Rice's star was rising. With his "stentorian" voice, the "size and muscle of a giant and the agility of a gymnast," he drew thousands. The Western theater managers, Noah Ludlow and Sol Smith, were forced to close their Mobile season early when the circus drew 2,000 the same night they had 18 people.[3]

Rice's offerings included his "Multifarious" Hamlet. Perhaps entering the ring at a lugubrious pace, draped in black and clutching a skull, he launched into his poem's one hundred lines in mock declamation: "Hamlet, the Dane, of him just deign to hear." Who was "so dismal and unhappy? / It was, my eyes! the ghost of Hamlet's pappy." The piece allowed Rice to parody actors, including the British star William Macready, who did a handkerchief-waving frolic to demonstrate Hamlet's madness: "Gracious, how he did fly around and prance— / Just in this place Macready makes him dance." (The stage comedian Dan Marble similarly joked about Macready's handkerchief dance—his "pas de muchoir"—as part of his "pile-up-the-agony-talent.") The parodies worked because people knew actors the way later ages know the batting stances of favorite baseball players or the private lives of movie stars. Because audiences knew performers well, they deeply enjoyed Rice's satire of a death scene: "But ah! alas! ho, oh. ha, hi, he, hum." His piece rattled to its conclusion like a vaudeville sketch:

> . . . and so they all did die,

Which is so dismal that it makes me cry—
Hububaluh—boo—boo—boo—a first-rate story
Some die for love, some they die for glory.

(Decades later, Rice dismissed his Shakespearean clowning as bastardized misuse. Fitting later assumptions about clowns, he claimed he did little more than alter Hamlet's "Is this a dagger I see before me," into "Is that a beefsteak I see before me / With the burnt side toward my hand? / Let me clutch thee! I have thee not, / And yet I see thee still in form as palpable / As that I ate for breakfast this morning.")[4]

Rice was an affable star who hobnobbed with prominent locals. A spree with Mayor J.W.L. Childress and Judge Alexander McKinstry grew into a Western yarn about Mayor C and Judge M, "the poet laureate of the State," bundling him off for song and spirits, then staggering to M's bachelor apartments to sleep. In the single bed, when C and M squabbled over the blanket, Dan kicked them both on the floor. His dignity offended, Judge M insisted on a trial then and there, in their nightshirts, "guiltless of coat and pants." Dan argued for the defense so energetically that he broke a water pitcher; this attracted a watchman, the typical Irishman of fiction, drunk and with a brogue. So "that drunken baste Pat Riley" burst in and hauled them off to jail. Mayor C, annoyed that Dan foiled his attempt to escape, resumed his official capacity to fine the clown $15. Though this may have begun in fiction—an earlier story made Lewis Cass, the Michigan politician, and Martin Van Buren similarly argumentative bedfellows—a spree of Rice's seems likely. If it had been a complete fabrication, the real mayor and judge could have made their displeasure official by preventing the circus from showing.[5]

New Orleans, the next stop, was the major city of the South and one of the largest in the country. Spanish influence, its French past, and international trade made it a worldly metropolis. Steamboats, inbound or out for Bayou Sara and Belize, Albany and Antwerp, belched smoke over squat rafts and pirogues. Foreign visitors and immigrants mingled with boatmen; plantation owners and free blacks wove around lines of slaves toting boxes and lifting bales. New Orleans, a human bouillabaisse (to use a word new at the time), enjoyed its pleasures, including circuses. After a major brawl between keelboatmen and Creoles had sprawled out of a circus and into the street, New Orleans jauntily named it Circus Street (now South Rampart).[6]

Spalding set up on St. Charles Street, then moved to Congo Square, favored for public gatherings. Like a tourist bureau offering its inhabitants for viewing, the *Picayune* urged people to visit the square "to be amused by the peculiarities of the negro race." Circus sought whites and blacks alike, but segregated the latter into "Colored Boxes." For Rice's February 5 benefit, Rogers impersonated Shakespearean characters such as fat Falstaff, vengeful Shylock, and crook-backed Richard II without dismounting. Rogers's Shakespearean characters for Rice's benefit hints at rivalry: Rice was being touted as "the original who first made the Bard of Avon minister to the amusements of the circle."[7]

Rice took another benefit on the show's last day in town, March 5. His admirers presented him with a gold bearing the inscription "Filius Momi—Son of Momus"—classical mythology's god of ridicule. Appearing in Mobile and New Orleans before 17,000 people, Rice was on his way to becoming what the bills had proclaimed, a Southern favorite.[8]

Spalding's show steamed north, flags flapping. Because most of the country's roads were still back roads, transportation flowed mostly by boat, as did the population that provided an audience. Circuses went only downriver until 1822, when Victor Pepin first used a steamboat to transport a circus back up the Mississippi. Shows traveling by steamboat had to be small, but they got a jump on wagon shows, which had to wait into the spring until the roads were dry.

The troupe reached Cincinnati on April 9, a Sunday. Managers piously promised that their performers observed God's day but since they traveled on Sundays, what they mostly observed was God's handiwork from the deck of a boat, or on a plodding horse. The burghers of Cincinnati had added their own footnote to God's creation, a kind of 11th Commandment of order with tidy red-and-white houses, well-paved roads, and tile footways. Along the waterfront, the irregularities of land were overshadowed by the steady grid of windows in the four-floor warehouses and offices, accented by the paired smokestacks of steamboats along the river. Church spires cracked the square geometry, and the arch of the paddle-wheel on the boats hinted at bending river and rolling land but otherwise, visual order matched the civic order imposed on this wild West.[9]

Rice was eclipsing Rogers. In Cincinnati, though hoarse on opening night he built up a following through that week that filled the 2,000-seat tent for his benefit on Saturday, with hundreds turned away. In St. Louis, all was "Rice Rampant!" Rogers presented characters from Dickens's *Pickwick Papers*, but Spalding's Monster Circus featured its star clown in "new Burlesques of Shakspeare!—Comic Improvisations!—Original Conundrums!—Comical Speeches!—and a whole store of Quirks, Pranks, and Facetia." The *St. Louis Reveille* waxed classical, "impatient to see the Democritus of the sawdust," referring to the Greek philosopher who espoused an infinity of worlds, like Rice's infinity of talent. Plaudits rolled daily in the *Reveille*, *Union*, and *Missouri Republican*. Performers, while taking benefits for themselves, also gave them for charitable causes. Tendering benefits for rifle companies and fire companies, Rice was not merely "occupied with the vanities and follies of life [but] the philosophy of the most thoughtful philanthropist. Dan is a whole-souled fellow." Woven through the praise was the refrain of originality. The *Reveille* saw "something new and spicy" in Rice every evening, with his brain "a perfect storehouse of wit and humor, which no sooner sends off a stock of fancy articles than it receives a new consignment."[10]

As Rice played to large crowds, he counted the people in the seats, calculating the take. They had come to see him. Why accept a portion in salary when he could get it all?

Rice had the ego and the ambition for ownership. Now he and Doc Spalding joined as "projectors." That was a mid-century term for community leaders, especially businessmen, who "projected" an idea into the future. America saw projectors—more visionary than entrepreneurs, more practical than visionaries—propelling the advancement of society. Rice's plans may have begun in March, when Spalding bought a steamboat, the *Allegheny Mail*, in Nashville. Doc kept the North American Circus as a wagon show while joining as partners on a boat show with Dan. Spalding would not need persuading to hitch hosses and pull together. He could make money on this second show, and, with Rice away, Rogers could shine. Even better for Doc, he did not have to advance any cash. He owed

Dan $1,500. By investing that amount in the show, he got a partnership while erasing the debt. Though self-interest is obvious, tapping Rice as partner reflected one of Spalding's strengths as proprietor, his ability to delegate.[11]

It is difficult to know how Spalding owed Rice that much money. At a time when stars made $25 a week—the Mobile boast of $50 a night notwithstanding—the clown's salary would have had to be $100 a week, with none paid out since January. Spalding may have owed Rice from the 1845 engagement, yet to carry a large debt for so long seems unlikely for the methodical proprietor. Nevertheless, even when they argued, both sides agreed on the amount.

At any rate, $1,500 was plausible as half the capital. A thirty-person circus like Spalding's North American could be started for $4,000–8,000, about the cost of a two-hundred-acre farm, and Rice's was smaller. Competition was few on the ground in the South and the West, so shows could be smaller, and costs lower. Records of an 1839 outfit, June, Titus and Angevine, offer perspective. Predictably, the major investment was equine, $5,000 for ten ring horses and twenty-two baggage horses. Horses for the ring were more valuable because they had to be trained to keep a steady pace while riders jumped on their backs, the band blared, and people cheered. Eight wagons, bill printing, and the tent and poles came to $1,800. In the early years, a new center pole could be cut daily in the woods, or bought for a buck. But with the center pole roughly half as high as the diameter of the tent it supported, forty-foot poles were hard to find when tents grew to eighty feet across, so shows now carried their own. Side poles held up the side walls. A Spalding innovation, quarter poles in between the center and sides, made it possible to support a larger top and higher side walls, accommodating more rows, up from eight to eleven, and thus more income. Total daily expenses were $120 here, salaries and room and board in local inns constituting the bulk of it. As for revenue, tickets cost 25¢ for a seat on the narrow boards of the bleachers and 50¢ for "reserved seats"—chairs by the ring—so that Dan, with a tent holding 3,000, could cover daily expenses easily. One report put his receipts at $1,000 for four shows.[12]

Rice's new manager was Spalding's twenty-seven-year-old brother-in-law, Wessel Ten Broeck Van Orden, Jr. The son of a doctor, Van Orden

Most sitters frowned for a daguerreotype portrait, but Rice, in his fashionable best, couldn't resist an impish smile.

was descended from two venerable Dutch families. He had gone to Maryland to practice law before returning to Albany, where he married Spalding's sister, Caroline. She died three years later, in 1845. Having Van Orden on the show to watch Spalding's interests made business sense, but Rice knew that the older man was reserving judgment. He was also saddling Dan with an incompatible companion. Touring is hard enough when people are congenial, and long-legged Wessel and stocky Dan were a mismatched pair, body and soul. Van Orden, with little discernible sense of humor, held himself aloof, and Rice was a sociable man. Worse, Van Orden would have been defensive as he struggled to learn his job with a show he considered Spalding's, and Rice saw as his own.[13]

Rice opened his first circus with the St. Louis performance on May 25, 1848, of Dan Rice & Co.'s Metropolitan and Hippo-Dramatic Circus. Spalding's show had left town. "Metropolitan" signaled urban sophistication, on the strength of five performers who had "hitherto been confined to those centres of refinement and luxury"—that is, Brooklyn, where Van Orden hired them. "Hippo-Dramatic"—"hippo" for horse—referred to the two scenic riders, one who performed scenes of England, Ireland and Scotland, and Henry P. Madigan, the "personater of Indian and Sailor characters." The *Reveille* was curious to see Rice "in the new aspect of proprietor and manager, and watch the effect his new relations may have upon his witty lucubrations"—his learned discourse. To create fresh interest, Rice pushed the local angle, emphasizing that all properties and paraphernalia had been constructed in St. Louis. The paper picked up the theme and urged its readers to patronize Rice both for the compliment he paid local mechanics and the financial benefit his show brought to the city, including his plan to construct an arena "worthy so important a city as St. Louis is destined to become." But though Rice, with Glenroy, still found praise as "the greatest clown and greatest equestrian in Christendom," Spalding's circus had exhausted the local market. Rice left after three days.[14]

Heralding his way was a herald, a narrow poster nine inches wide and two feet tall. A handbill, meant to be passed around, it could also be stuck on barns and walls along with the larger circus advertising. This herald featured the "*Hero of the Day, The World's Jester, The great Shakspearean Clown, The Gentleman, The Scholar, The Poet, The Tragedian, The Orator,*

Reveille.

ORNING, MAY 25, 1848. NUMBER 1250.

Regular Packets.

Regular Weekly Packet for Peoria and Peru, Illinois River.

The splendid, fast-running and double-engine steamer PRAIRIE BIRD, O. H. Pratt, master, having been thoroughly repaired, painted and fitted up, will commence her regular trips on the opening of navigation, to the above and all intermediate ports, leaving St. Louis every SATURDAY AFTERNOON, at 4 o'clock. Her speed and comfort for the accommodation of passengers, cannot be surpassed by any boat in the trade; and passengers and shippers may rely upon her continuing in the trade during the whole season. For freight or passage apply to R. F. SASS,
11 Commercial street.

Fort Madison, Burlington, Oquawka, New Boston and Bloomington Weekly Packet.

The new, staunch-built steamer ELIZA STEWART, Captain Edds, will commence her regular trips as a packet between St. Louis and the above-named ports, on the opening of navigation—leaving St. Louis every FRIDAY EVENING, at 5 o'clock, and arrive at Bloomington the following MONDAY MORNING;—returning, will leave Bloomington the same day, and arrive at St. Louis the following WEDNESDAY MORNING.

The Eliza Stewart is entirely new, of light draught, and, as a comfortable passenger boat, is not surpassed by any boat in the trade.

For freight or passage apply on board.

Regular Packet to Louisville.

THE MOUNTAINEER; Henry, master, has commenced her trips as a Packet, between St. Louis and Louisville, and will leave the former city regularly every Saturday afternoon, at 4 o'clock.

St. Louis, May 14, 1848. my14

1848.—REGULAR SATURDAY PACKET—1848.
For Peoria and Peru, Illinois River.

The new and fast-running passenger packet HIGHLAND MARY, F. A. Burke, master; and J. B. Woods, Clerk.

This new, light-draught double engine steamer, will commence her regular trips in March, leaving St. Louis every SATURDAY AFTERNOON, at 4 o'clock.

Returning, will leave Peru every TUESDAY MORNING, at 8 o'clock, and Peoria, at 4 o'clock, P. M., same day, and stopping at all the intermediate landings below.

For freight or passage apply on board, or to
T. H. CAVANAUGH, Agent,
Commercial street.

N. B.—Passengers and shippers can depend upon the HIGHLAND MARY making regular trips throughout the season, as *she draws only eighteen inches water, and was built expressly for the trade.*

1848.] NORTHERN LAKE LINE. [1848.

Via St. Louis, Chicago, and Buffalo, to New York and Boston—No more Staging—Water Communication Through!

THE following magnificent steamers and packets compose the line:

From St. Louis to La Salle:

Steamer Herald, P. Devinney, master, Monday.

DAN. RICE & CO.'S
Metropolitan and Hippo-Dramatic Circus.

Proprietors, Dan. Rice & G. R. Spalding; Immediate Superintendent, Dan. Rice; Mastre de Cirque, F. Rosteni; Clown, Dan. Rice.

It is respectfully announced to the citizens of St. Louis, that this establishment will be opened in this city, under the beautiful new Pavilion,

Corner of Third and Pine streets,

On Thursday Night, May 25th, 1848,

and continue open *for three nights only, positively.*

On Saturday Afternoon, at 3 o'clock, a performance will be given, for the accommodation of Ladies and Families.

The Troupe and Properties being, with scarcely an exception, composed of new *materiel* (many of the former recently arrived, or to arrive,) precludes the possibility of giving a detailed account of the entertainments. The salary list will be the highest paid in any Circus, and several members of the troupe unquestionably the best the country affords. Still, every thing is as yet untried—discordant *materiel* to be harmonized, and people and horses to become accustomed to each other. No means will be left untried to render the incipient performances of the establishment worthy of the reputation that the company is bound to win when every thing shall have become matured.

That department of the establishment which is not dependent on practice, the *comforts and beauty of the Pavilion,* the *courtesy of the attachees,* the *method, order, and decorum* pervading every thing, cannot fail to render this a model Circus. A deep sense of the obligations already incurred by the proprietors of this establishment, for the unlimited patronage they have heretofore received from the citizens of St. Louis, will be the best assurance of their sincerity in promising an entertainment worthy of patronage.

my23 DAN. RICE & CO.

Notary Public, Clerks of Courts, Societies, &c.

C. H. RIGIMIN, corner of Morgan and Second streets, is now prepared to furnish, at the shortest notice, SEALS and PRESSES, which he warrants to give satisfaction, both in price and durability.

N. B.—Brands and Stamps cut, and all kinds of small machinery furnished. Freight and other small Steam Engines, Turning Lathes, Copying Presses, and Card Presses. Printing Presses repaired at the shortest notice. apl tf

Saint Louis Reveille.

From the French of Lamartine.
THE HOLY LAND.

BY JOHN G. WHITTIER.

I have not felt o'er seas of sand
The rocking of the desert bark;
Nor laved at Hebron's fount my hand,
By Hebron's palm-tree covered and dark;
Nor pitched my tent, at even-fall,
On dust where Job of old has lain,
Nor dreamed beneath its canvass wall
The dream of Jacob o'er again.

One vast world page remains unread,
How shine the stars in Chaldea's sky!
How sounds the reverent pilgrim's tread!
How beats the heart with God so nigh!—
How round gray arch and column lone
The spirit of the old time broods,
And sighs on all the winds which moan
Along the sandy solitudes!

In thy tall cedars, Lebanon,
I have not heard the nations' cries,
Nor seen thy eagles stooping down
Where buried Tyre in ruin lies.
The Christian's prayer I have not said
In Tadmor's temples of decay,
Nor startled with my dreary tread
The waste where Memnon's empire lay.

Nor have I from thy hallowed tide,
Oh, Jordan! heard the low lament,
Like that sad wail along thy side,
Which Israel's mournful Prophet sent!
Nor thrilled within that grotto lone,
Where, deep in night, the Bard of Kings
Felt hands of fire direct his own,
And sweep for God the conscious strings!

I have not climbed to Olivet,
Nor laid me where my Saviour lay,
And left His trace of tears, as yet
By angel eyes unwept away;
Nor watched at midnight's solemn time,
The garden where His prayer and groan,
Wrung by His sorrow and our crime,
Rose to one listening ear alone!

I have not kissed the rock-hewn grot
Where in His Mother's arms he lay,
Nor knelt upon the sacred spot
Where last His footsteps pressed the clay;
Nor looked on that sad mountain head,
Nor smote my sinful breast, where wide
His arms to fold the world He spread,
And bowed His head to bless, and died!

[*National Era.*

AN INCIDENT AT WALLAWALLA.

[*From the Oregon Spectator.*]

Fort Wallawalla was one among the earliest posts established west of the Rocky Moun-

The first circus bearing Rice's name.

and whilom Preacher, DAN RICE!" The cut of the clown-with-sword used on the 1846 Howes lithograph appeared here, with images of minstrels and the *Allegheny Mail* on the other side. As agent, Van Orden wrote the lush copy describing the "Sovereigns of the Circle" in Rice's show. Getting almost as much ink as Rice was ten-year-old "M'lle Rosa" Madigan, who leapt her little horse over barricades, hooves kicking up sawdust. Prof. Muller was "Director de Orchestre." With a trumpet and probably a clarinet, the musicians played virtually nonstop as they mingled sentimental ballads, popular tunes, and what would now be considered classical music. The "Maitre de Cirque, F. Rosteni"—elsewhere "Rosestein"—was nineteen-year-old Frank Rosston (who might have earlier performed blackface with Rice).[15]

Even as Van Orden mocked the "exploded clap-trap" of typical circus advertising, he exploded some over "spicy and racy" Rice in "the noonday refulgence of whose wit, the facetious attempts of all other clowns pale and glimmer with a feeble and uncertain light." The herald announced that Rice was preparing three books for publication, his memoirs, the "Reminiscences" of Joe Smith, and "Shakespeare travestied." It then quoted a long piece from the *New Orleans Delta* that laid out Rice's fictional biography: He had disputed with the faculty at Princeton, danced for the Diggers around Galena, disseminated Mormon doctrine for $50 a month, exposed a humbug mesmerizer, and trouped with actors, all "to keep the ball in motion." This first circus of his own may have inspired other stories he told. Setting up outside Davenport to avoid a large $20 license could have prompted his early tale of dodging the license. In Nauvoo, Smith's widow joined Rice for supper on the *Allegheny Mail*; perhaps she told him the story of Smith's walk-on-water.[16]

Not everyone was pleased with Rice. In Hannibal, Missouri, where twelve-year-old Sam Clemens could have watched Rice's show on June 26, the *Hannibal Journal* printed one of the most excessive attacks Rice would ever face.

> This motley gang of bacchanalian mountebanks about which so much noise has been made by some of the presses of our neighboring cities, lately exhibited, or rather exposed themselves in our town . . . this miscalled circus taken all together is one of the most contemptibly obscene things of the kind that has ever disgraced our city. . . . As to Dan Rice,

> the "great Shakspearian clown," we think the title Shakspearian blackguard would suit him much better. He is as perfectly devoid of true wit as he is of the principles of common decency, and every attempt he makes at anything of the kind is a mere slang drawling of the most repulsive obscenity. It is perfectly sickening to hear the most beautiful language and sublime ideas of the immortal "Bard of Avon" prostituted and mingled up with the most commonplace dram-shop slang by the sacriligious [*sic*] tongue of this brazen faced traducer who, leper like, turns every thing he touches to moral filth and uncleanliness.

The laughable excess could be dismissed as backwater crankiness, as many in big cities who enjoyed Rice surely thought. The *St. Louis Reveille* was one: "He is never forced to descend to a coarse jest to provoke the laugh of the vulgar. Some of his new readings of Shakspeare are inimitable, and he gives that *touching* one called Hamlet, to-night."[17]

However, this was more than dueling opinions. Increasingly concerned that their rambunctious country was growing too rambunctious, people looked for representative heroes or villains. To many, the new Jacksonian democracy of large-scale participation and reduced elite control threatened the republic of the Founding Fathers. To those who worried, the changes wrought by and represented in Jackson increased the risk of mob rule. A fundamental American question asked whether a people could safely be sovereign, controlling the conflicting forces and special interests tugging in disparate directions. The broadening of popularity from a few military heroes to an assortment of public figures focused the issue, and Rice's growing renown made him representative. Attuned to the cultural currents, Rice advertised that "while we cater for *The Million*, we do not forget to select the viands that experience has taught us, are most palatable to the '*Upper Ten Thousand*.'"[18]

Suspicion of mass opinion was becoming a mass opinion. Increasingly, the fact that many people liked something was itself becoming suspect. A Mobile newspaper, commenting on Rice, noted that it was "no wonder that the audience are involuntarily carried along at his will, and that they become apparently unconscious puppets in his hands." At the time, that was hyperbole to emphasize his command of the situation. Gradually, that praise would curdle as Rice's charismatic influence came to mean the manipulation of the mob. Rowdiness in performance venues was being redefined as poor manners, rather than an esthetic taste, held by right. Later that season, the *Pittsburgh Morning Post* reflected the conflict when Rice doubled prices for his benefit to 50¢. On one hand, the *Post* anticipated "such an assemblage of the beauty and fashion of the city as is seldom witnessed"; on the other, "this change in price will secure quiet, and probably preclude such perfect jams as have so far thronged the circus." Dan would not relish less of a jam, but he did appreciate being depicted as the favorite of a small elite.[19]

So when the *Hannibal Journal* attacked, it joined a larger battle. In the paper's heated words, Rice appealed to "the vilest passions of the human heart." It was not sufficient to critique Rice's performance: He had to be attacked because others applauded.

> And yet, strange to tell, this misnomer of a circus, pandering as it does to some of the vilest passions of the human heart, is tolerated, nay, even largely encouraged by people who under other circumstances arrogate to themselves the title of a moral and even religious community.

Like other criticism, this was less about Rice's performance than his popularity. Whatever he actually said disappeared in the Missouri paper's tirade that he was "pandering," a code word that damns both performer and appreciative audience. The *Journal*, hugging a secret pride of its lonely battle against the "noise" of benighted opinion, damned a brazen-faced traducer.

Rice took his next step as a manager on August 10, 1848, in Pomeroy, Ohio. He split from Spalding, paying off most of his partner's half and taking a mortgage for the rest. Rice declared independence in his choice of color: He painted over Spalding's red-and-white with purple, accented by yellow and gold. He further asserted his independence in ads that dryly teased the typical grounds of praise: This new management was young enough to escape the follies of youth and experienced enough to avoid the stale habits of long experience. Rice's strongest urge was not away from Spalding, but from Van Orden. The ancient antagonism between performers and people of business rankled in their daily contact on the road. Van Orden's lawyerly precision gave him little sympathy for Rice's financial and emotional extravagance. Even if Van Orden had been a competent manager—and the fact that Spalding used him only twice, and briefly, suggests otherwise—Rice despised supervision. Making things worse, neither man was clearly in charge. Van Orden stood over Rice's shoulder, reminding him what he owed Spalding, raising an eyebrow at personal expenditures. Van Orden may have treaded further and given his opinion of Rice in the ring.[20]

Travelling down the Ohio and up the Cumberland, Dan played Evansville, Louisville, Clarksville, and every *ville* big enough to generate a crowd. Maggie was now before the public as Madame Rice. No act was listed, so she was an auxiliary. Circuses have room for spouses, who stand to the side and grace an act or add bodies to fill out group numbers such as the opening Grand Entry, in which well-trained show horses follow their weaving paths regardless of rider. Maggie was described as "delicate in form," which meant short, not fragile.[21] Circus women had to be strong in muscle, constitution, and will. Popular imagination conjured the shy Victorian flower of easily shocked delicacy, but Maggie did not get the vapors. She had borne two daughters, raised them on the road, endured the same hardships as Dan, and nursed him when he was sick.

The other new name on the bills was "E. Rice"—four-year-old Libby. She did little more than ride her pony around the ring, but in the calculus of performing, a small child has large appeal.

After the boat rounded into the muddy sweep of the Mississippi at Cairo, Rice may have literally played in "Dixie land." Glenroy later recalled a stand at Dixie's Landing, Tennessee. His memory may have conflated some river stop with the "Dixie land," written by Rice's friend, Dan Emmett. Yet, the source for that enormously popular 1859 song is still uncertain, so perhaps a particularly hospitable Dixie ran a landing above Memphis, remembered by Glenroy and immortalized by Emmett.[22]

As Rice floated downriver, General Zachary Taylor was on his Whig campaign for president. His victories in the Mexican War assured that he would beat Cass, the Democrat, and Van Buren, of the tiny Free Soil party. Rice had capitalized on the war fever in the winter of 1846–1847, singing "Rough and Ready, or the Campaign of 1846." A year later in New Orleans, as veterans were mustered out, he presented "Dan Rice in Mexico," a burlesque on the Battle of Buena Vista. Now, on November 1 in Baton Rouge, with Taylor watching, Rice dusted off the old Mexican War numbers. After the show, Old Rough and Ready visited backstage. Out of this backstage handshake Dan's fertile imagination grew a crop of stories: He had campaigned for Taylor in Louisiana; he was a delegate at the Whig national convention; he stood as a pallbearer for the General. Later, Rice declared that Taylor had made him an honorary colonel out of political gratitude. Eventually, it would be told that Rice paraded Old Rough and Ready on his bandwagon, inspiring the political phrase, "on the bandwagon," though that phrase did not appear until the 1880s. The first Taylor tale came when Rice survived yellow fever in 1848; he then claimed that the general, using battlefield experience, had nursed him. Though blessed with a powerful body, Rice's constitution was worn down by relentless travel. His recurring illnesses gave him what his family called a "healthy abhorrence" of doctors. He made a joke of it, declaring that he avoided them because he had been a fake medicine man himself and knew their tricks. During this bout of yellow fever, Maggie nursed him, as usual.[23]

Rice's declaration of independence had been premature. Whatever money came in, more went out. As the assets of the show leaked to creditors, Rice turned to Spalding again. The world saw the same Dan Rice show, but Dan and Doc recapitalized it as a new venture. This was not generosity. Spalding knew that he could still make money from Dan's appeal. This time, he protected his interest with liens, so that no one else could attach the show. Anyone with claims—horse dealers, printers, wagon makers, tavern keepers—would be subordinate to his interest, preventing the show from being broken up piecemeal.[24]

Despite the setback, Rice had reason for hope as he settled into New Orleans, his tent pitched on Poydras near St. Charles. The papers forecast renewed kudos for the "King of Clowns metamorphosed into the Prince of Circus proprietors." He leapt on every passing fancy. When the Phoenix Fire Company burned, Rice offered a benefit for the company. The New Orleans racing season began in late November, and within days he was presenting burlesque Pony Races. His scenic rider, achieved a "*beau ideal* of dramatic equitation" by miming, on galloping horseback, a dalliance with maidens. Rice capitalized on the good notices to open a riding school during the day. The *Delta* speculated that many ladies enrolled "partly out of curiosity to see the great clown in citizen's dress." Rice added a new feature, the pony, Aroostook, named after a river in Maine. The horse could race in one direction, turn the other way, suddenly stop in a docile bow with forelegs stretched forward, daintily pull a handkerchief from the trainer's pocket, and dramatically rear on its hind legs. Rice later recalled a battle of wills with the spirited horse in training. In honor of Rice's skill at training, admiring locals gave him a gold-headed cane.[25]

Rice's appeal, generating what the *Delta* considered "the most crowded houses we have ever seen in this city," hurt the business of the St. Charles Theatre run by Ludlow and Smith across the street. Rice added insult to injury, blaring the music of his band in concerts on a platform directly across from the St. Charles. He was copying Spalding's concerts; now Rice had the resources to present a musical force to rival Spalding's "magic bugler" Kendall with his own "wizzard bugler," Almon Menter. Drums, clarinet, and bugle were more to Rice than noise to attract attention, though like the country, he reveled in music. Throughout the century, brass bands provided the country's musical entertainment, with marches, hymns, ballads, spirituals, and classical music.

The *Delta* took a lively interest in the conflict between the circus and the St. Charles. As far as it was concerned, Rice "placed the illegitimate far ahead of the legitimate drama," especially the pitiful fare at Smith and Ludlow, who "will have to put on more steam to keep pace in the regards of the people, with such admirably conducted establishments as those of Dan Rice." Smith and Ludlow could not get up that head of steam. The *Delta* complained of hackneyed plots, with "a young man of good natural heart and . . . a heroic wife, who is always ready to sacrifice everything for him, but honor," and actors "so far below mediocrity that no plummet or line of criticism can ever reach them." With Zachary Taylor in town, it was the "old story—crowded houses, and 'horse opera' in the ascendant." Meanwhile, the "theatre was so miserably lighted, that the audience had more the aspect of a funeral assemblage than of a company assembled for amusement." In that era, lighting shone on both sides of the footlights equally, but no one was lit at the St. Charles, which was "so dark that you could not recognize a person in the next row of seats."[26]

Failing in their natural venue, the court of public opinion, Smith and Ludlow turned to the law, petitioning the General Council to shut down Rice as a public nuisance. They cited the condition of Rice's building and the noise of Menter's band. The *Delta* adopted mock outrage. "Oh conscience! Have Ludlow and Smith . . . no consideration for the tastes and partialities of the enlightened mass of all colors, who still cling to the barbarism of the 'Horse Theatre,' and too often find in it more real amusement than in the maudlin sentimentalities of the legitimate drama!" The council rejected the petition, finding the music "to be a source of pleasure and refined gratification to the citizens." The *Delta* continued in low-comedy high dudgeon. "Oh, Jerushy!" Smith, looking down on "weather-beaten canvas, sawdust, rough-planed and backless plank seats, with most perilous gaps between, as remnants of a barbarous and benighted age," had set himself up "as a Judge in Israel, and informs the respectable families of our city that their taste and preference are for a nuisance, rather than for a true, legitimate Temple of Thespis—one in which the deficiency of gas in the circle is made up by the abundance of it on the stage." The *Delta* approved. "Daniel and Solomon, of old, could not have rendered a wiser judgment. There let it rest. Let Dan have his music and crowded houses, and let Sol enjoy the consciousness of unappreciated genius." Buoyed by success, Rice petitioned the Council himself, requesting abatement of the daily $10 tax, suggesting that the $230 he had already contributed to city coffers ought to be sufficient. His request was denied. New Orleans enjoyed his circus, but not enough to forgo revenue.[27]

Rice brought the rivalry into his ring. Despite his waterproof pavilion to "protect the sovereigns," a soggy night had watered down his audience. A few hundred in a three-hundred-seat house is exhilarating; the same few among thousands of empty seats is depressing. Rice shook off the disappointment, again finding material in what the world offered. He surprised the tiny crowd by appearing in street clothes.

> Ladies and gentlemen. . . I have for several days contemplated giving my people a holiday. . and no better opportunity will probably occur than now, when you know there are not enough of you to enjoy yourselves. Old Momus himself, or Sol . . . would have to come here to make you laugh with so much elbow room. It's "agin natur" to be entertained, with no more people to help one to laugh, than one sees in the theatres—therefore, gentlemen, you will please call upon Mr. Weld at the office, and get your money. I am going to invest a dollar upon the St. Charles Theatre, and recommend you, if your bowels of compassion can

be moved by a contemplation of a "manager in distress," to go and do likewise.

A voice from the crowd objected: "No, you don't. You and Sol are in cahoot, and you divide the profits."

Rice's response reveals a detail of his improvisational method. He did not reply to the substance of the objection immediately, but said, "On my honor," and made a "deferential bow he learned while preaching." The theatrical expression "to wing it," meaning to improvise, originated in forgetful actors who edged toward the wings, where a prompter whispered their words from the script. Once Rice had made it to the center of ring and stage, he never voluntarily moved away, but his method relied on the evolved sense of winging it. He was the "prince of waggery."[28] That New Orleans night, Rice was buying time to craft a response in his mind. It is the same delay tactic that lawyers use when they chant "incompetent, irrelevant, and immaterial," which means nothing by itself but allows time to search the memory for a reason why something is incompetent, etc.

Live performance is never perfect. Sometimes spontaneity fails. That is the risk and simultaneously part of the glory of live performance. The failed bits make it human, giving a context to the striving for perfection, and to the rare moments when it happens. The rest of the glory lies in the interaction, in the mutual awareness that audience and performer depend on each other. "You had to be there" is not only an apology for a joke that suffers in the re-telling. It is also a fact of life of humor: Comedy exists in a shared moment. Suddenly, Rice realized that he could combine two things on people's minds, this taunt that he would share profits with Sol, and the rumor that the St. Charles was in collusion with another theater to reduce competition.

"On my honor, no!" Repeating the phrase as he slowly rose from his bow, Rice bought himself a moment more to shape his response. "That would involve the necessity of sharing the losses, and the American Theatre relieves me of so undesirable a duty."

In that moment, on that spot and day, nothing other than Rice's words would have hit so well. Live performance is never perfect, but, paradoxically, sometimes it is.[29]

7

READING, NOT ACTING CLOWN

In antebellum America, performance and politics were public conversations, and the people played a voluble role in those overlapping realms. Just as crowds peppered political rallies with their opinions, audiences hissed actors off the stage, or stopped plays to insist that a soliloquy be repeated. The *Spirit of the Times* had editorialized about "The Right to Hiss." Performers in turn addressed their citizen-patrons directly. The system of benefits, in which actors' salaries depended on how many people bought tickets in support, reinforced reliance on the audience. In England, theaters required licenses issued by the government, but in America, according to the *Clipper*, only "THE PEOPLE" conferred license to theater. Lighting's subtle but powerful effect contributed to this exchange. Because technology could not yet focus lights on the stage, performers and audiences were equally lit, equally regarded. The opera impresario, Max Maretzek, said of the Astor Place Opera House that "everybody could see, and what is of greater consequence, could be seen. Never, perhaps, was any theatre built that afforded a better opportunity for the display of dress." Public patronage was no metaphor, but an antebellum fact of life.[1]

However, just as Jackson's bond with the broader democracy worried his political opponents, a worry increased by European uprisings such as the Paris Commune of 1848, rowdy interaction in performance caused anxiety. Decorum—passive and quiet spectators—was touted as a solution to this newly conceived "problem" of participation. Some even deemed actors' inescapable physicality a hindrance to the proper appreciation of plays. The English writer Charles Lamb had famously claimed that the plays of Shakespeare were better read than acted; the French philosopher Diderot reputedly stuck his fingers in his ears at a performance so that, free of the actors' voices, he could "enter strongly into the fine pathetic conceptions of the author." The *Spirit of the Times* echoed the sentiment: "Midsummer-Night's Dream, we confess, gives us far more pleasure in the quiet of our room. . . . We prayed only that it might not be utterly spoiled of its charms in the hands of the actors." Though antebellum audiences continued to make noise, those who had more money, education, or determination to see themselves as culturally higher began to favor "decorum." Increasingly, the "man of taste and discrimination will not be seen in the theatre, but will prefer 'To read his Shakspeare o'er at home.'"[2]

Like the culture wars that would erupt in the United States a century and a half later, this society-wide struggle became focused in individuals, in this case, the two leading actors of the day, the American, Edwin Forrest, and his English counterpart, William Macready. Their friendly rivalry had turned bitter during Forrest's British tour in 1846 when he hissed Macready's performance of *Hamlet* in Edinburgh. Some attributed the notorious hiss to jealousy, but Forrest said he had expressed displeasure for reasons of taste, complaining that Macready's handkerchief-waving dance, the one Rice had parodied, defiled a noble play. The two actors seemed to fit a neat opposition. Forrest, with legs like tree trunks and a booming voice that his critics scorned as "rant," embodied concerns that a crude country was growing cruder. (Forrest's brawny build made it plausible that he nearly became a circus acrobat.) By contrast, Macready symbolized Old World sophistication as he declared that he aimed to elevate the theatre, and bragged of his scholarship in researching his roles. However, this dichotomy, originally esthetic but increasingly political, ran roughshod over details. Forrest also researched his roles, and also claimed that he aimed to elevate theatre. The chauvinism attributed to the energetically American Forrest was more than matched by Macready's notorious disdain for foreign performers on London stages. Perhaps most crucially, those who were determined to raise Macready as a symbol of refinement had to ignore that he was on the downside of his career, and that his "refined" gestures were mere quirkiness to many observers. His last season in London had been a "sad failure," critically and financially; the theatre manager, Noah Ludlow, expressed the scorn of many for Macready's "affected, inflexible and angular" acting.[3]

Rice's rising prominence, based on his direct connection, shot him into the middle of this culture war. It became manifest during an engagement at the Alhambra Theatre in New York. Cholera had chased Rice from New Orleans. His plans for a grand winter season there had disappeared in the often fatal scourge he remembered from his Manhattan youth. In New Orleans, it had been business as usual on December 22 as he received a gold-headed cane at the afternoon performance, flush with the holiday crowds and ads promising greater glories to come. Yet by 5:00 P.M., as winter darkness fell, he was on the *Grand Turk* swinging out into the current, headed north. In the era's phrase, he had "absquatulated." He kept a small "Dan Rice" circus traveling Mississippi bayous, but he was gone. After stopping in St. Louis to boast to a local editor on New Year's Eve, Dan traveled to brief starring engagements at Cincinnati's Eagle Circus, Philadelphia's American Circus, and Sands & Lent in New York.[4]

There on February 10, 1849, the *Spirit of the Times* gave him one of the most remarkable notices of his career when it yoked him to the Forrest–Macready feud and the cultural contention beneath it. At the Alhambra, Rice was giving "inimitable Shakspearean readings," while Forrest was playing Macbeth at the Astor Place Opera House in the first benefit for the new American Dramatic Fund for actors. Though Forrest presented "a drama as it should be acted,"

> Rice was much more modest. He stepped into the saw dust without any preliminary flourish. . . . Dan belongs to a new race, not the clown of

> the stage, the pantomime, nor even the ring, but the pure American clown—in fact, you may call him the Macready of the circle, he is a profoundly intellectual and scholar like specimen of a clown. Instead of relying upon the somersaults and tricks of his predecessors, he strikes into a quieter, anti-physical, school of performance—indeed he is the reading, not acting edition of the clown.[5]

It was a resounding endorsement, aligning Rice with Macready's anti-physical school. That was not surprising, for all Rice's physicality. A talking clown, he ranged widely and skillfully, commenting on events of the day. Rice could be solemn, sensible, even wise. His clowning was "profoundly intellectual and scholar like"—just as Macready's acting elsewhere was described as "most scholar-like in conception—most artistic in execution."[6] So the *Spirit of the Times* distinguished this "pure American clown" from those of stage, pantomime, and even circus: He was the "reading, not acting edition of the clown."

Rice was planning a wagon show for the summer. Short of money for wagons and horses, he turned again to Spalding. Doc put up the cost because he knew the potential for success with Dan, but he was not willing to be partners again. Spalding preferred those like him, sober and steady. Recognizing that a balance of business and performance expertise could produce a formidable team, he turned instead to his star rider, Charles Rogers. Rogers was older than Rice, and calmer. He was also willing to defer to Spalding's ego. The older man's name came first in their title and stayed there: Spalding & Rogers North American Circus. If Rice minded that Rogers took the spot that might have been his, he never mentioned it. He knew his own character enough to realize that it would suit him better to head his own outfit, however mixed the results, than to be subordinate in another's.[7]

Plans bore fruit at about the time Rice reached Cincinnati, near Spalding's winter quarters, in a bit of national publicity. "Scraps from the Diary of Dan Rice," written by Van Orden and placed in the *Spirit of the Times*, recounted Rice's carouse in Mobile. That episode became a chapter in *Sketches from the Life of Dan Rice*, a souvenir book sold on the show and available at a Cincinnati bookstore for 25¢. A hundred pages of glorifying biography, *Sketches* was filled with exaggeration, fancy, and fiction, all shaped by the theme of respectability. That trait was not presented as an additional attribute. Instead, the stories insisted that Rice was a hero *because* he was a gentleman. He gathered "*materiel* for amusing reflections" for both a public audience and for "the social circle." Though accustomed to the "the appliances of wealth with which his father is surrounded," he was a self-made man: "To early influences Mr. Rice is scarcely indebted for his present station and prosperity. He is emphatically the 'architect of his own fortunes.'" Rice could honestly make that boast, having been on his own since he was thirteen, yet that fact mattered less than his staking a claim to the American ideal of self-advancement, in which ability trumps connections. At the core of the myth of the self-made man lay middle-class faith in industry, sobriety, and frugality, tenets emphasized in *Sketches*. The biography offered the sentimental detail that Rice had never been happier than in the simple labor of delivering milk; it pictured his "strict habits of sobriety" in foiling a scheme to get him drunk and cheat him; and his youthful extravagance became a cautionary tale, his financial mistakes maturing him. Emphasizing Rice's self-control, *Sketches* alluded to no merely neutral characteristic but what a historian called "the moral imperative around which the northern middle class became a class." As *Harper's* professed, "Above everything else, . . . success in life is vitally connected with your own moral growth and improvement, by means of patient, faithful self-culture."[8]

The theme continued as the book set escapades in the context of refinement, like artifacts in a plush box. Rice did not simply best humbugs such as Barnum, he withstood the pressures of life that made others crumble to vulgarity or worse, for he "has embarked in nearly every project within the range of an enterprising Yankee, and experienced success and reverses in each that would upset a man of ordinary fortitude." As far as *Sketches* was concerned, those who complained about Rice were not higher morally, as they postured, but lower, since a "fondness for equestrian and gymnastic exercises pervades the highest and the best in the land." Even the claim of success as a jockey argued Rice's social elevation because he impressed gentleman-owners with his inner qualities. That fit the nineteenth century's growing belief that the inward and outward person were not simply different but opposed. That belief in reality versus appearance grew from the Romantic movement, and ironically gained momentum from Romanticism's rival, science, which discovered layers beneath apparently solid surfaces. The ideas of Darwin, Freud, and Marx took root in that fertilized ground, propelling the belief that what a person says and does is somehow distinct from another, more real part of that person. In a potent characterization, which is still used to praise the latest movie star or politician but was new then, Rice's strength lay "in his always being original, natural and easy."[9]

Publicized as the President's Jester "by the grace of Zachary Taylor," while also claiming commission from "a discriminating public," Rice prepared for the summer in Cincinnati. His new show featured a pair of eleven-year-olds, Jean Johnson, picked up in New Orleans, and Rose Madigan, advertised in womanly terms as a "Venus de Medicia [*sic*] in face and figure." Her father, Henry, a general performer in gymnastic tricks and riding, was "Directeur de Cirque," and twenty-year-old John Glenroy was "Glenn Roi." Circus was already using French to seem "deluxe." Still, it remained a small-time operation: "Maitre de Cirque" Rosston was also the costumer. Mesdames Rice, Madigan, Thrift and Nash made the spectacles seem grander and the roster larger. Though the show would be called the "Dan Rice Circus," it was Spalding's, for the $2,300 he had put up, until Rice paid him off. Rice featured a grand display of horses and wagons, "regal and republican," lavishly described in the appendix of *Sketches*. The wagons may have been Spalding's idea. He was featuring his own wagon, the $5,000 Apollonicon, a giant pipe organ built on a twenty-foot wagon drawn by a forty-horse hitch, a parade in itself and a substitute for a band in performance. Rice's "regal" wagons included the "Court and State Equipage of Louis Philippe, Ex-King of the French," inspiring this puckish speech to his ringmaster, published playfully:

> Louis Philip was xtravagantly xtolled, xceedingly xecrated. He xhibited xtraordinary xcellence in xigency; he was xemplary in xternals, xtrinsic on xamination. He was xtatic under xhortation, xtreme in xcitement and xtraordinary in xtempore xpressions. He was xpatriated for xcesses, and to xpiate his xtravagance, xists in xile.[10]

Rice xtended the phrase he had used for his stud of ponies, applying "Democratic Poneyantum" to the republican wagon he drove himself.[11]

Rice's "equipage" figured in a story told about a meeting in the Finger Lakes of upstate New York one July midnight. Gardner Crum, a part-time Methodist preacher like his father, got out of bed to answer a knock on the door. A call that late would have been surprising enough in a village where everyone kept farmer's hours. More startling, the visitor addressed Crum as Uncle. He said he was Elizabeth's son, the one they had called Dandy. As much as his peripatetic life allowed, Dan remained connected to his relatives. His splintered past never let him forget how fragile the family bond can be, nor how easily broken. Now, with money in his pocket, his name on his show, and that show worth as much as Crum's farm, he had taken a personal detour to reacquaint himself with his mother's people. Hoping for surprise, he accomplished the effect he wanted: Uncle Crum did not believe that Dan was his nephew.

This was the story told thirty years later by W. C. Crum, a newspaperman and circus publicist, but that night he was just William, a teenager dazzled by a view of the world not seen over the south end of a mule plowing north. Generations of plain-style Methodist Crums had grown up in modest circumstances, yet here was a stranger not only claiming to be a relative but cutting a dash in smart clothes and diamonds that sparkled in the candlelight. Behind him in the road stood a coach in lustrous red, its gold trim catching the small light. At last seeing touches of Elizabeth in the sturdy young man's face, Gardner embraced his sister's child. Dan, at that moment both a boy eager to please and a man of parts, returned the hug with force. Late into the night, by the light of the restoked fire, Dan regaled the Crums with stories about places he had gone, people he had seen, things he had done. His sleepy cousins were alternately shy and excited by this remarkable stranger. Uncle Gardner and Aunt Nancy, like Dan's circus audiences, swung between doubt and amazement at the stories. Their flinty scruples against show—both in performance and personal flash—softened in that midsummer night. Though these hardshell Methodists would have been chagrined to admit such a superficial standard, Dan was famous in his world. Arriving to vague memories of Elizabeth's little Dandy, perhaps with the secret shame of bastardy, he left in the morning wreathed in glory. It was only local glory, family glory, but it was enough for the dawning day.[12]

Earlier, as Rice had been making final preparations to move his wagons to Pittsburgh for the summer tour, the Forrest–Macready feud boiled over. It happened on May 7, when both actors were playing *Macbeth* in New York, Macready at the Astor Place Opera House, Forrest at the Broadway Theatre. Predictably, subsequent accounts emphasized antithesis, Forrest's rowdy supporters against the elite associations of Macready's venue. But the Broadway was just as refined, or more, since the Astor Place had abandoned grand plans for subscription-based opera and was now simply another of the city's theatres.[13]

At the Astor Place, hisses, hooting, and groans greeted Macready. He continued performing, even though the remainder of the play became a dumb show, his lines unheard over the noise. After the performance, he decided to leave town, a decision that alarmed the elite. They cared little about another night of Macready, but they were determined to hold fast in their culture war. His premature departure would be a lost battle over theatre behavior. So, a committee led by Washington Irving called on him, imploring him to continue the run, guaranteeing a quiet audience. Macready yielded to their pressure and to his ego. He would lead their struggle to tame the masses.

On Thursday, May 10, Macready's performance began at 7:30. At first, it seemed that the committee had won. Tight security at the doors screened out known troublemakers. Police were on duty outside, and the militia was on alert in Washington Square, a few blocks away. But only a few ladies attended, a sign that trouble was expected. Scattered hisses in the seats blended with the noise from outside, where the crowd grew to 10,000. Macready supporters believed that they were upholding standards, but so did the crowd in the street, outraged that their opinions were being tyrannically overridden. Both sides, agreeing that an elite sought to squelch theater noise, were pushing to a showdown. A few street lamps were torn down and a few paving bricks were thrown through the windows. Though there were probably only five hundred active protestors, half of them boys, the throng made everybody bold. Inside, a few were arrested and expelled. That was at 8:30. So far, it was not unlike other disturbances New York had known, and Macready continued.

Then things turned ugly. When stones hit the police, they were brought inside the theater, and the crowd outside was read the Riot Act, formal notice that action would be taken if they did not disperse. Then the troops were called in, men on horseback, and infantry with bayonets fixed. The crowd surged; the cavalry drove them back; they surged again. It was 9:15. The abbreviated performance was concluding, but the streets remained clamorous, and the militia became increasingly nervous. "At last the awful word was given to fire—there was a gleam of sulphurous light, a sharp quick rattle, and here and there in the crowd a man sank upon the pavement with a deep groan or a death rattle." Then another volley, and a third. Over twenty people were killed.[14]

The Astor Place Riot frightened many people into the conviction that the best audience was a quiet audience.

The Astor Place Riot shocked the country. Arguments over public conduct had rocked back and forth for years, but this changed everything. What had been a metaphorical battle became literal. Many, like Walt Whitman, abandoned their enthusiasm for the brash energy of theater.[15] Others tried to diminish the riot into a farcical feud turned tragically bad. Still others, seeking larger meanings, lamented the excesses of patriotism. A few decided that the riot revealed what the country had always tried to deny: the existence of social classes in the United States. Ego, chauvinism, and class did play a part, but the cause of the riot was foremost an extension of the struggle over the public conversation of performance, just as war is an extension of politics by other means. What had been a gradual shift in attitude over crowd participation crystallized with the riot, as opinions gravitated to opposite poles. Even those who sniffed at a "mere actors' quarrel" were taking sides, implicitly arguing that the judgment of the million, who were interested, did not matter.

The tempest blew into Pittsburgh when Rice arrived on a 285-ton side-wheeler, the *James Millingar*. As usual, Rice met acclaim. He was "a host in himself, and if he makes as many dollars here, as he nightly utters witty sayings, he will almost be a millionaire before he leaves Pittsburgh." As was also usual, he met friction. America was a violent place, fights breaking out wherever people gathered, even at church. Pittsburgh rowdies were notoriously tough on traveling shows. An altercation popped up outside Rice's tent on Front Street, rough enough that it even frightened the police away. But with the Astor Place riot still fresh, the police returned in force the next night, clamping down hard. Rice, defending audience enthusiasm, published a handbill criticizing the force. The *Gazette* objected, claiming that it had never heard any complaints against the police, except among drunks. The *Post* disagreed. The initial incident had been "harmless," the participants merely scamps: "O, boys! what a public nuisance you are, all of you!" The paper concluded that the police had been drunk and made things worse. They did get so rough with boys hanging around Rice's tent on his last night that they nearly killed one.[16]

Of course Rice kept trouping. Violence was an occupational hazard of circus.

In mid-August, Rice brought his circus to Saratoga Springs, where his father lived. After the New Jersey bank had "exflunctificated," as the age put it, Daniel McLaren had made his way to Saratoga, the home of racing and summer elites. In 1832 he bought the Pavilion Hotel, built in 1819 as an elegant establishment, the first floor partitioned so that it could be opened into one grand ballroom the 150-foot length of the building. Painted white, it was trimmed in green to match the ivy twining up the porch columns along the expansive front. Once one of Saratoga's leading hotels, "in its palmy days the abode of fashion and elegance," the Pavilion increasingly served those who were not the fashionable trade but visited to witness it. A boast Rice made for his father, that Madame Jumel stayed at the Pavilion, bore out its secondary status. Despite her wealth and marriage to Burr, Jumel would not be welcomed by the "American aristocracy" at the Longacre and the Congress, or by the nouveau riche at the United States Hotel.

McLaren was still capable of causing a stir. Just as his bank had rocked New Jersey, he roiled the waters of Saratoga. In 1839, he decided to tap a mineral spring. Though workers quit because of the danger of digging in the swampy, gassy area, and costs rose, McLaren persisted, creating the Pavilion Fountain. In 1840, he bottled water for the Albany and Boston markets, opened an office in Manhattan, wrote a book extolling the Fountain's virtues, and planned a garden for outdoor amusements, like Niblo's Garden in New York. But his plans foundered when he charged locals for access, sparking what became known as Saratoga's Stamp Act. A public meeting adopted a resolution "requesting the boys not to break down the fixtures of the fountain that night." Naturally, the boys did just that, and torched the bottling plant, too. McLaren dropped the local charge. Though he continued to sell water and published a second edition of his book, he lost money. The following year, he sold the hotel for $18,000; shortly afterwards, the Pavilion Hotel burned down.[17]

Did father and son meet? Rice said nothing. There is another mystery. The 1850 census that recorded McLaren, fifty-five, property $5,000, also showed a son, Daniel McLaren, Jr., eighteen. If Rice's parents were married, as he loyally maintained, he would have been Daniel McLaren Jr. himself, making the Saratoga boy Daniel McLaren Jr. II. No account mentions this half-brother of Rice's.

In some ways, the father remained as invisible as the mystery son. *Sketches* had made a virtue of separation, saying that Rice could not reconcile with his father "without humiliating concessions." Now, bejeweled, he would have to make none. He had his own pavilion, to match his father's Pavilion Hotel. Still, Rice jangled with ambivalence about his father. He did boast of McLaren's wealth, cleverness, and important associates, setting the stage for his own glory; nevertheless, Rice remained resolutely silent about encounters with his father. Absence is powerful evidence, and in his own story, Rice made his father disappear.

After ending the touring season in mid-August in Albany, Rice bought a farm south of there, on the Hudson River near New Baltimore, Greene County. Van Orden used his lawyerly skills to arrange the details. It was not only a winter quarters for Rice's outfit, it would be his home. Like Spalding, like McLaren, he now had a place in the world.

8

FORECLOSURE

A young man took his best girl, himself, and his new beaver hat to Rice's circus. Rice pointed out the hat to the assembled multitude, and made it a running gag, contriving lyrics on the spot to the tune of "Oh, Where Did You Get That Hat?" As Rice sang verse after newly minted verse, the crowd joined the choruses, rising in their seats to point at the beaver hat and pound home the musical question. The embarrassed young man left the tent and stamped his hat flat, cured of "all my aspirations to be an exquisite."[1]

Rice had his own trouble with a hat. Maggie was watching the show on October 20, in Baltimore at the Front Street Theatre with their friends, Dr. William Leonard and his wife. Leonard, a prominent local doctor, had helped plan the new city hospital. After the performance, the trio made their way outside. As they waited for Dan, Leonard was accosted by George Appleby, a compositor at the *Baltimore Sun,* who was angry about a debt. Appleby hit Leonard in the face and called him a "damned thieving son of a bitch." Coats flapped, oaths burned the air, and hats flew. Arriving on the scene, Rice jumped into the fight. When watchmen ran up to quiet things down, they arrested Appleby. That would have ended things except that the newspaperman managed to sneak Rice's hat away. The headgear itself did not matter; if it was damaged, Rice would buy a new one. He was never shabby when he could afford better. But he would not tolerate the affront. The next morning, he stalked into the offices of the *Sun*. There sat Appleby on a stool amid tables piled with newspapers and cases of type, his workspace lit through ink-splattered windows. Rice spotted his hat. Whether the hat was shoved underfoot, splotched by tobacco that had missed the spittoon, or cocked on Appleby's head in triumph, the sight of it made Rice mad as an old radish. He knocked Appleby off his perch and pummeled him. The *Sun,* already irked by the clown's jokes at its expense, now had its chance for revenge. It depicted Rice clubbing a weak, old man in a "stealthy" and "disgraceful" attack. Exaggeration overflowed when the newspaper reported that Rice had to post $5,000 bail, for it was only $300. The trials—Appleby's for assault on Leonard, and Rice's for assault on Appleby—were postponed when Rice had to leave town with the show. The *Spirit of the Times* was probably teasing Rice when it vowed that if anyone watching him "is not amused and made joyous, he can take our hat."[2]

The fight was about more than Rice's prickly honor. He was under pressure, being squeezed for payment by Spalding. Business was bad for everyone in 1849, and circus managers were cutting salaries. Spalding similarly tightened the screws.[3] A good manager is attentive, almost without thought, to what is coming in and going out; the balance sheet confirms what is already in mind. That was not Rice's mind. Focused on himself and his audiences, he paid little attention to daily expenses or long-term obligations. When he had the tin, he lived well, ate well, dressed well. He was generous, loaning even when he owed money himself. In neither spending nor lending did he give much thought for the next day. Despite the testimony in *Sketches*, he had not grown up with the habits of thrift and planning, those cornerstones of the new middle class. In his old convivial realm of the stable, when someone was flush, everybody joined the party; the rest of the time, they all did without. Some react to youthful poverty by becoming miserly. Rice went the opposite direction, into extravagance.

As the season closed, Spalding reasserted ownership of Rice's show. It was a grinding setback. Three times Rice had set out to dazzle the country with a circus, just as he dazzled it with his clowning, and each time he had come up short. After trying to become a showman like Doc, and a projector like his father, he again limped to the end of the run owing money. He pleaded for a delay, assuring Spalding that better times were ahead, but he had been saying the same thing for two years. Spalding was adamant. It was his dough and his show. What was due is unclear. Van Orden claimed that the debt had reached $23,000, though $15,000 of that was the horses, surely an inflated amount for a small show. When Spalding reclaimed the show, he gave Rice $750. It might have been payment to Rice for tending the horses over the coming winter at the farm, though that was steep for stabling and care. It might have been for back wages. Or perhaps Spalding sought to clear the books, to quiet any claims Rice might make to the show.

After Rice and Spalding argued, Van Orden retaliated by going to Greene County to reassert Spalding's rights to Rice's farm.[4] Dan and his family were allowed to stay, just as he remained caretaker of the circus that was no longer his. Van Orden would later claim that he had intervened to help an impecunious Rice in the purchase of the farm, paying off the original debt and taking a bond for the deed as security. Rice disputed that, maintaining that the clever lawyer had misused his power as agent to get the farm into his name. Though Van Orden's version was probably closer to true, he did make $1,000 from the maneuver, a great deal for simple helpfulness. Beyond this particular argument lay a new financial world. As America struggled through the birth pains of capitalism, Rice tried a variety of financial tools: loans, pawnbrokers, purchase and labor contracts, liens, mortgages, endorsed notes, drafts, bonds for deed, and letters of credit. In this new world, objective standards continued to mingle with old-fashioned subjective biases. This unpredictable blend of business and personal motives, in an atmosphere of rampant bankruptcies, made anxiety over the financial system worse. A friend might have his debts carried on the books for years, while a stranger—or enemy—would face swift foreclosure. Van Orden's claim on Rice's farm was prompted as much by animosity as by business necessity.

Rice particularly blamed Spalding's brother-in-law for his troubles, with mutual animosity dating from their forced march together on tour. Even as Van Orden had composed Rice's publicity, his low regard for the clown peeked through. In his introduction to the episode with the Mobile mayor and judge, Wessel figuratively shrugged at Rice's role as a master storyteller, claiming that he had to fill out the mere "skeletons" of stories that Rice provided. Dismissing Rice's ability to convulse audiences, he apologized that the Mobile tale "by no means furnishes the greatest *material* for a laugh." Rice had been forced to endure Van Orden's condescension. Now he had to watch helplessly as Van Orden foreclosed on the farm. Even if Doc had instigated the action, Dan got his dander up for Wessel. For years, he blamed Van Orden for old debts, and a decade later he was still placing responsibility for the split on Wessel's "malign influence."[5]

The clown turned to work. Supporting his wife and girls required it; his energy and his personality demanded it. In a need that went down to the bone, he had to prove his importance to all who had slighted him: Spalding, his father, hated Van Orden. In December, he left his family and the animals at the farm, and took Rose Madigan with him to New York to the Astor Place Circus, in a tent outside the opera house. Rice followed William F. Wallett, the preeminent English clown, on his first American tour. At first, the English clown was deemed smoother, but soon the *Morning Star* declared, "No clown has ever appeared here who so soon became a general favorite as Dan Rice—not excepting even the great Wallett, who sent an immense reputation in advance of his appearance in this country."[6]

On January 1, 1850, Rice went to Philadelphia, where he checked into the Jones Hotel, a leading establishment. This was more than extravagance. Rice had learned on the pig tour the importance of appearing prosperous, especially when poor. Two days later, he wrote to Spalding, "Circumstances ar such that I cant feed them horses any more."[7] The horses were a large part of what remained of the show, still at the Greene County farm. They could form the base of a circus for the summer season, if Rice came up with the money. Despite three failures and more arguments, Spalding was planning to invest in Rice again. He could still make money with the clown. Predictably, he limited his risk. Keeping the horses on the farm over the winter shifted the burden of care to Rice, who had to raise his share for a summer show. If he did not, Spalding suffered no loss, simply taking the horses for his own circus. In the letter, Rice claimed that Spalding had purchased the circus for that $750 payment. Regardless, that money had gone, too. Rice wrote that he now had enough for his family only; nothing was left to keep the horses and he could not borrow because his credit had been ruined by "that god dam vanorden." He demanded that Spalding retake possession, but he really wanted more money. He offered to stable the horses for a price and to board the men with Mrs. Rice. He promised that it "shant cost you mutch," though it was not supposed to have cost anything. The horses had belonged to Spalding since November, but Rice had probably seen them as half his in anticipation of profits from the circus-to-be. Now, with no circus in prospect, they were useless to him. Worse than useless. Rice was paying to feed them, and to feed the hands who came with them.

Rice went to Baltimore, where he was to open on January 7, and waited to hear from his former partner. Spalding's reply can be inferred from Rice's next letter, sent from the Exchange Hotel. Spalding insisted that Rice fulfill their original deal and tend the horses through the winter. Rice answered on January 10, apologizing but declaring the situation unpreventable. As far as he was concerned, he was simply being honest, with no "humbugin about it." He asked for more time to come up with the money so that he could pay for the farm. He had high hopes in pending lawsuits, he wrote, and he also had prospects for loans. One of those prospects was a promise of money by April from his father. That could have meant McLaren or Manahan, probably the latter. McLaren was a businessman who would have expected a cut of the show; Hugh would simply have loaned the money. But Rice could not have picked a worse time to ask. Though Manahan was a fish carter and owned a farm, Fresh Pond, fishing and farming were seasonal. In the dead of winter he would have little ready cash.[8]

Rice was trying to bridge the growing gap between Doc and himself. At the end of his first letter, he implored Doc to "let the past be forgoten and you and me will try to be Better in the future." More than ingratiation for financial favors, it was a personal appeal. "I shall be most anxious and

Gilbert "Doc" Spalding was one of the century's premier circus managers.

happy to heare from you." Rice had in effect lost two fathers: McLaren left, and Manahan married a new wife. In Spalding, a steady older man, Rice may have found some paternal comfort. Even if Dan could not bow to Doc's authority and, like a rebellious son, struggled against it in these alternately pleading and swaggering letters, he was trying to avoid an irrevocable break. Rice wrote that he asked that Maggie and the girls be allowed to stay on the farm through the summer, and that his stepbrother, William, be given a wagon and team to work the farm, only because there was "some genrosity about you." He picked up the thread a few sentences later, writing that Doc "must act a little generous with me." Promising to pay everything back by April, he entreated Spalding to "recollect one thing that poor dan Rice hase worked harde for you at menny a place and made you monny and hase nothing himselfe."

Spalding said no.

Confidence had fueled Rice's perfect rush. It had enabled him to wrest himself out of the common run of stable hands, transforming insignificant Daniel Manahan into rousing Dan Rice, his new name on everyone's lips. But with the circus gone, the farm foreclosed, a home for Maggie and the girls lost, and the showcase for his respectability vanished, Rice's confidence faltered. Poverty was worse now. To be poor when starting out has a certain nobility. Show business has a long tradition of struggling beginners; since that tradition is known best through the few who succeed, success is inherent in the tradition. But things are different once a name has been made. Romantic images evaporate in the stench of failure. Debt pressed down on Rice, a silent reminder accompanying every dollar he earned, a tap on the shoulder with every dime he spent. Having moved for a moment in the world of proprietors, Rice fell again into the million. As the prosperous said, he "couldn't come it."

Rice also fell into self-pity. Now, "it seems that all and everything that I do or undertake turns out bad," he wrote to Spalding, "and I only can say take and do as you please with me." Circus histories usually depict Spalding as the calm, steady opposite to Rice's tirades but, in their fights, the older man gave as good as he got. Van Orden and Spalding were models of the new capitalist age, applying business-like rigor to the haphazard world of circus; but their severity, reinforced by Van Orden's enmity, pressed on Rice's buoyant spirit. He was emphatically *not* a model showing off the age's calculated method and balance sheets. Rice's perfect rush slowed almost to a halt.

Knowing that he was losing the farm, Rice moved Maggie and the girls out. Just as Rice had passed off his duty for the horses Spalding had entrusted to him, he shuffled off responsibility for the farm once he saw that he could not keep it. The Greene County home of his hopes was now just land, wooden buildings and fences that belonged to someone else. The circumstances explain why Rice later complained bitterly that Van Orden had forced his family out, while Van Orden insisted that Rice had abandoned the farm. Van Orden may not have literally forced Maggie and the girls into the cold winter, but that picture held a psychological truth for Rice.

Rice moved his family to Long Branch, back among the Manahans, and once again turned to a winter show. He made his way to Charleston, South Carolina, for the Great Western Circus of Thomas McCollum, a four-horse rider, and Dennison Stone, brother of the company's riding star, Eaton Stone. Stone and McCollum had once promised to protect their audiences from the impurities of Shakespearean clowns, meaning they had none; now they hired Rice for his Shakespearean clowning. Five weeks running in the national *Spirit of the Times,* they advertised a $5,000 challenge that no one could match their roster, plus another $1,000 on Rice's horse—now "Aristook" rather than Aroostook, perhaps for the hint of "aristocrat." In Charleston, the young cream of Southern society threw Rice a dinner. At the end of the meal, they settled back in the hazy glow of gaslight and cigar smoke to listen. Rice probably began with a joke compounding the local money crop of rice and his name. Then he told a story dazzling in its virtuosity. Even with editorial smoothing, it showed Rice's facility. He said that the rascal Scaramouch, a stock figure from commedia dell'arte, searched for a lost bottle by divination. Rice listed sixty-seven varieties, from divination by air, or Aeromancy, through Hydromancy (water), Lampodomancy (lamps), and Zoomancy (living creatures). Unable to find the bottle, Scaramouch cried "hullaballiboowhoohooyoosee" and went to sleep. In a verbal tour de force, Rice concluded allegedly in Hebrew, Syrian, Chaldee, Persian, and Armenian.[9]

In mid-March, Rice left the tour to return to Baltimore for his trial. The judge fined Appleby $20 for the assault on Leonard, aggravated by rudeness before ladies. Rice had to pay $50 because his attack was more violent, it took place on a Sunday, and it was a "gross trespass on the social rights of the proprietors of the Sun."[10]

As summer began, Rice mustered his scant resources to start his own show again. The offerings began with the traditional Full Dress Entrée, followed by Jean Johnson, Rice's pupil, somersaulting on horseback, Aristook's tricks; Rose Madigan; Johnson on the tightrope; Osborne and Glenroy in scenic riding, "Animated Pictures on Horseback"; La Thorne performing "Sports with Cannon Balls"; Henry Madigan impersonating Indians in "Aboriginal Sports"; and Harper in "Corpuscular Feats," probably acrobatic clowning. The rest was Rice: a Macready imitation, songs, speeches, and burlesques, and his "multifarious account of Shakspeare's Hamlet!" With scant offerings, there was no intermission. The performance finished with a "Sentimental Pastoral Equestrian Ballet" by Mademoiselle Rosa and Master Jean.[11]

Rice repeated the Metropolitan & Hippodramatic title but omitted his name to shield his assets from his creditors. The advertisements listed his young ringmaster, Rosston, as proprietor. Rice had tried this dodge on Spalding in a letter. Even while admitting that he had forfeited the show, Rice asserted that his star horse had not been part of the deal, but belonged to Rosston. He warned, "You better not trouble yourselfe about aristook, as you cant get him. I did not sell him to you and if you starte me in the show I can rent him or at least hire him frome frank." This was no small issue. Ordinary ring horses ran to $300, but this highly trained steed was a major draw, worth many times that.

Like a good politician, Rice knew how to play on local sympathies when he reached Baltimore. Referring to "the lying *Sun*," he joked about the recent dustup over his hat—and bought only one day's advertisement for the week. To the tune of his friend Foster's "Susanna," Rice sang "Good Old Baltimore," declaring that "I'm sure I'll settle here." Zachary Taylor's visit the year before, and his noted fondness for the ladies, inspired other lyrics: "And if he ain't an 'ultra Whig,' / Of truth I am a misser, / If he didn't prove in Baltimore / He was an *ultra kisser.*" In "Song of Baltimore," Rice admitted his fondness for the ladies, adding a sentiment that could stray from innocence if accompanied by a leer: "And with the magic charm of witches, / They'll melt your heart down in your breeches."[12]

Rice put his name back in the title when "Dan Rice's Circus" swung down to Washington for a week in early June. Passions were running high on the bedeviling problem of slavery. The North grasped at opportunities to establish, once and for all, that the Founding Fathers had intended to limit slavery until it died naturally; the South insisted that any restriction on their "peculiar institution" violated the original intent of those same Fathers. Meanwhile, each side saw conspiracy, with devious plots threatening their own beleaguered virtue. When California sought admission as a free state, which would swing the Senate's voting balance to the North, fervent oratory rang out. Heating matters more, there was a push to abolish the slave trade in the District of Columbia, a move advocated earlier by an obscure Illinois congressman, Abraham Lincoln. Rice jumped into the excitement. To the tune of Foster's "Oh, Susanna," he sang "A Peep at Washington," working puns on the leaders in the struggle. Foote footed the bill, Webb wove a web, Cass had a Cobb (pipe) to chew. Cobb had been elected Speaker of the House after sixty-three ballots, and Rice sang about that, too. He warned about abolitionists, who advocated disunion as they raged against the Constitution that allowed slavery: "But let them speak with all their might / This union they cannot sever."[13]

With his political hits and convivial nature, Rice certainly attracted senators and congressmen to his audience, and he might even have been friends with a few; but the way he told it, Webster, Douglas, and the rest adjourned Congress so that they could join President Taylor in Rice's audience. Even if he didn't befriend the nation's leaders, he could satirize their well-known quirks. Salmon Chase's lisp and precise way of speaking would have been easy to mimic, as would Charles Sumner's Boston accent and Sam Houston's Texas drawl. The deep-voiced clown would have been particularly adept at Stephen Douglas's thundering, foot-stomping, fist-waving style. He might have edged into the Little Giant's notorious vulgarities; Douglas's public "God damns" and "by Gods" and "farts" and "bastards" caused some to turn in embarrassment, but for others they made Douglas a plain speaker and a perfect brick. So, too, with Rice.[14]

Important friends or not, Rice remained a small dog in tall grass. His circus barely raised any notice in the papers. On July 24 in Camden, New

Jersey, he could not pay the license so, to avoid regulations of professional amusement, he showed without charging admission. The Genius of Mirth was reduced to passing the hat. Making his way through upstate New York, he increasingly blamed his troubles on Spalding and especially Van Orden. Rice added a verse to his "Hard Times":

> A man named Van Orden, I had almost forgot—
> He is the worst one there is in the lot;
> He will swear, lie, and swindle, he will cheat, and he'll write,
> And, for sixpence a head, he'll take sheep in the night."

Then there was "The Devil and His Agent," a Faust parody in a Scottish accent, in which Van Orden gets caught stealing, then as a lawyer, embezzling from clients. The lyrics concluded with an "Anticipatory Epitaph, For One To Whom It Applies":

> Friend, at this spot a moment dwell,
> Van's body's here — his soul's in hell;
> He robbed, while living, friend and foe,
> And now he's gone to rob below.

The *Syracuse Standard* warned of "bad taste in so long a recital of his private griefs"—though it admitted that the denunciations were fun.[15]

Finally, Van Orden had enough. On September 12, he had Rice thrown in jail for slander, in Pittsford, near Rochester. Some people would be chastened by the experience. Not Rice. Released after a week, he walked into Spalding and Van Orden again, and the sheriff, too, with a newspaper notice "To the Citizens of Rochester." He claimed that friends from Albany had tried to pay his bail, pledging three times the amount required, but that the sheriff had colluded with Van Orden to refuse it. The jail, rechristened by Rice as "The Blue Eagle Jail" for the match factory sign outside his cell window, became the subject of more songs. Rice capitalized on the furor. His ads promised "full Revelations of the Mysterious Knocking Lock-ins," and named Van Orden conspirator with "Old Dot and Go One," the sheriff's nickname because of his wooden leg. The Rochester paper enjoyed the public quarrel, and reported that Rice's circus was crammed with people eager to hear "The Great Delivered." His denunciations were so strong that they "would make anyone wince who was not encased in the hide of a *Rhinoceros.*" The sensation reached to Buffalo, with the *Express* there reporting that Rice "gives harder slaps than ever."[16]

Rice moved on to Pittsburgh, where he borrowed money from Mit Foster, and then to Cincinnati. There the *Enquirer* decided that his wit "flashes with a brighter, steadier and purer light than was its wont in days gone by—while even then it dazzled and delighted, now it also edifies." As Rice prepared to "pack up his 'slanging fakements'" and steam south on the *Summit,* Spalding's North American Circus came to town.[17] Rice's former partners heard what he had been saying, not the sanitized version in the papers, but everything in juicy, offensive detail. Spalding decided to stifle his rival once and for all.

On November 12, as Rice played Covington, Kentucky, Spalding had the sheriff seize Rice's horses. It is not clear whether Spalding claimed them based on their original deal or because he bought them from W. B. Carroll, who reportedly replaced Madigan but had been fired by Rice. Another possibility was that Rosston, whom Rice considered a boy he "had raised, and who, I thought, was bound to me by so many ties of gratitude," had sold out to Van Orden. Rice wrote Mit from Louisville that he could not pay him back, "owing to new difficulties presented by my friends Van Orden & Spalding." Mit would have understood. His brother Stephen was having his own money troubles as he tried to do something new in American culture: make a living as a songwriter. Dan must have been embarrassed to beg off paying. The letter is formal, addressed to "Dear Sir," and he had someone else write it.[18]

This was worse than losing his farm. The first had been a private loss, however painful. Now, a failed showman four times over, Rice had no circus. Without a stud of horses, without money for performers' salaries, his career was in jeopardy. Rice was often counted "a host himself," but audiences expected more. Maggie could fill out a scene, but she had no act of her own. That left Rice with his young apprentice, Jean Johnson; the tattooed man, James F. O'Connell; and a single horse, which may have been Aristook. Later, Rice said that it was and, alternately, that Spalding had taken that animal, too. (It was gone from Rice's ads by December, and Spalding later advertised it himself.)[19]

With his one horse, Rice kept on because he always kept on. He boarded his tiny band on a boat, either paying his little cash or sweet-talking the captain with a promise of receipts from the next town. Charm alone could not carry the day; he also borrowed on his wife's jewels. He sent his agent ahead, on a steamer when he could afford that, otherwise floating down the river in a skiff. Sometimes Rice may have had to revert to the early clown role of advance man entering town ahead of the show and taking to a stump to extol the acts.[20]

Letting gravity take him south, Rice saw turbulent waters hemmed in by the silent forest. The Mississippi River descends in collective memory to panoramas of dreamy Tom Sawyer days and sweeping lawns of graceful plantations, but it was and is a force of nature, haunting the heart of America. As an 1826 traveler observed with a shiver, the "face of the Mississippi is always turbid; the current everywhere sweeping and rapid; and it is full of singular boils, where the water, for a quarter of an acre, rises with a strong circular motion, and a kind of hissing noise, forming a convex mass of waters above the common level, which roll down and are incessantly renewed. The river seems always in wrath."[21]

Early in the morning the boat steamed up to another dock, jolting everyone fully awake as it pulled taut against its lines. Then while it bumped against the water-soaked pilings, thick with mossy green except where rubbing had worn them smooth and shiny, hands would unload the show. It was a wet world of rain and rivers, musty wool, and cotton clothes soaking to the skin. Winter was worse. The first frosts made the world glisten, as water numbed fingers. One trouper remembered cold water splashing through the hull in the night and freezing his blanket, so he had to crack it to get up; yet even with the whole troupe shaking from fever, they performed because it was "play or starve."[22] In many ways the age was close to the twenty-first century; speed and science were revealing their marvels, and attitudes were forming that would resonate into the millennium. But in brutish nature, 1850 was ancient. It had less in common with the snug houses and weatherproof clothing 150 years later than it did with the wet and cold world 1,500 years earlier.

Cold, warm, wet, or dry, Rice set up, re-creating the world all over again. A baker does not build the bakery each morning, but a circus starts from scratch every time, remaking an empty lot, transfiguring weary men lugging canvas into sparkling performers framed by a tent, bleachers, and ring. Rice augmented his apprentice's acrobatic feats by announcing that the boy was Jean Lafitte Johnson, great-grandson of the French pirate of the Gulf, Jean Lafitte. As for O'Connell, although tattooed men had been displayed since 1818, he appears to have been the first on a circus, starting in 1836. In later years, his tattoos would have made him a circus "freak," those who displayed some natural or developed body oddity. In 1850, display was insufficient, so O'Connell sang and performed "unique and spirited dances," apparently with talent. The primary appeal, though, lay in his blue tattoos and accompanying stories of the "habits and customs of the savages" who had captured him on the Caroline Islands, south of Hawaii. He described the torturous process of tattooing, told of romance with the chief's daughter, and related his stirring escape from cannibals by canoe. It might all have been true, but his tales of the South Seas tales repeated the lyrics in the popular "King of the Tongo Islands" (a tune Rice used), with a chorus of "ho-kee po-kee."[23] As for the one horse, Aristook or a hastily trained replacement, it would have to do. Without it, Rice would not have had a circus but a hall show, barely more than his early solo ventures.

The little band took what crowds they could get, putting on a brave face each time, and then moving on. They loosed the mooring and swung out into the current. When there was no money, Rice begged a ride on the next boat. They augmented their diet by shaking pecan trees in the daytime and making chowder at night, after the show. Days were bleak, nights were hungry, but they kept going. A favorite joke of the era made light of the ubiquitous steamboat explosions: "The last time I saw him was when the biler burst, and I was going up, I met him and the smoke pipe comin' down."[24] As the explosion of Rice's talent flung him skyward, he ran into the wreck of his early hopes comin' down. His circus and farm were foreclosed. Would his hopes be too?

9

ONE-HORSE STORY

"Ladies and gentlemen, introducing Dan Rice and his one-horse show."

As Rice told it, he was presenting Aristook when a bearded gentleman stepped up to the ring, swept off his hat, and made his mocking announcement, to which Rice shot a quick retort: "After all, Dr. Spalding, the taking of Troy was strictly a one-horse show!"[1]

In the tradition of the Greeks' Trojan horse, Rice's "One-Horse Show" was a founding myth, transforming the bleak days with a single horse into glorious legend. He did not call it a "one-horse show" when he had only one horse. It was hard enough to gather a crowd in those struggling days without broadcasting the deficiency. A one-horse town was an insignificant place; a one-horse show was even more negligible. But as he fought his way back, Rice converted "one-horse" into a boast of quality over quantity.

In the process, Rice discovered a subject and a method. The subject was the feud with Spalding and Van Orden. Like rip-roaring Davy Crockett wrasslin' a bear, Rice dragged the quarrel into the ring. Crucially, he kept it funny. Later ages would sigh over the comic artist transmuting pain into laughter, but the work of clowning has little to do with that soupy literary conceit, and audiences have little patience for anguishing. As Rice warbled "Rochester Song No. 3" about his arrest, he looked into eyes in the crowd, assessing each smile and cough and silence. The attention to detail that failed in his finances snapped into focus in the ring, as he learned on the laughs that Spalding and Van Orden stood for more than his private quarrel. The new capitalism raised inchoate fears of oppression by mysterious forces. The country personalized that anxiety in the form of the confidence man. Swindlers were ancient, but a new incarnation emerged from the original confidence man, a charlatan who approached victims on the streets of New York in 1849 and, after spinning a yarn, asked, "Have you confidence in me to trust me with your watch until to-morrow?" Worse than this one man stealing a few purses, the Confidence Man seemed to threaten American innocence itself. Accordingly, Rice shaped stories and songs to depict Spalding and Van Orden as con men. Rice sang a lyric about Van Orden that made it explicit: "That 'friend' my confidence did get," before he swindled and "sloped." Similarly, in a routine colloquy with the ringmaster, Rice spoke of the six signs of a fool, the sixth being an inability to distinguish friend from foe.

Ring Master: "I take issue with you, Mr. Rice, on the sixth point. He must be a brainless fool not to know his friend from his foe."

Rice: "Yes, but people can live without brains."

Ring Master: "Well, you are so very sharp, tell me how long a man can live without brains."

Rice: "If anyone will tell me how old you are, I'll tell them how long a man has lived without them."

Ring Master: "Oh, sir, you are a fool indeed."

Rice: "Shakespeare says, 'Call me not a fool till heaven has sent me fortune.' Master, heaven has not been very kind to me. It sent me a fortune at one time, and then sent a man to fool me out of it."[2]

As Rice expanded his private fight into a public morality tale, he also found a new method. He had begun his circus career in the opposition of clown and ringmaster. For the ancient pairing of authority and transgression to work, the ringmaster must appear powerful, the clown seemingly subordinate. As Rice's stature increased, especially when he became an owner, that symbolic dichotomy wavered. Now Dan tapped Doc and Van as unwilling partners in an implicit colloquy. While continuing the traditional exchange with the ringmaster, Rice figuratively turned full front, allying himself with the audience. He said what his audience would have said had they been in the ring—and possessed his mercurial wit. More than direct address, the technique employed personal involvement. Making his concerns theirs, he made their concerns his. They faced cheats and liars; he faced cheats and liars. He rose; they rose—or planned to. Dan's charm made his focus on himself palatable but he also stood for his audience. On his arrival in New Orleans, the *Picayune* proclaimed his representative stature:

> He has met with reverses such as would have destroyed any other man, but there is that principle of elasticity about him that the tighter the strings are drawn upon him the greater the rebound. . . . himself the cynosure of all eyes and the magnet that draws around him all that is agreeable or profitable in his line. Such men must succeed and cannot be destroyed.[3]

Young in his career, he was already seen as a symbolic figure who "must succeed" as he carried the bright hopes—against the dark fears—of the times.

Rice's "little circus" loomed large in the Crescent City, his band brassily playing outside fifteen minutes before each show, and the great rider, Levi North, performing on his horse, Tammany (which Rice may have joined to the one-horse story). Crowds poured into Dan's tent, and praise tumbled out. "How many of our readers will confess to themselves their silent preference of the good old fashioned Circus to the Italian Opera?" Disdaining the antique jokes perpetrated by most clowns, Dan "can see something ludicrous in every passing event, and he has the genius and tact to turn it to account."[4]

That particularly meant the feud. Like an artist who has found his muse, Rice spun song after One-Horse song, a dozen set in New Orleans. He reserved special scorn for that "long-legged man . . . well known as thieving Van." At some point on the contested farm, Van Orden must have been surrounded by fluttering hens, because Rice kept conjuring the image of Wessel stealing chickens. That was the focus of "The Lost Chickens," a parody of a sentimental ballad, "The Lost Child"—complete with off-stage squawks. In this one, Van Orden also stole a pelican, the Louisiana state bird. The polka being a lewd new dance craze, Rice sang "The Polka" about "Dark and melting quarteroons," then added, again, that Van Orden "stole my last chicken" while clumsily trying the polka. In "Pills and Quills"—ex-druggist Spalding and writerly Van Orden—Rice sang forty-seven verses of denunciation. The length did not deter audiences used to hours of oratory at the theater and at church, and at "stem-winders," political speeches so long that watch stems had to be rewound. In the chorus, with the audience joining heartily, Rice yoked his old boss, Sam Nichols, into the fight:

> Then go it Nicholas—go it Rice,
> They've robbed you both very nice;
> Your shows they've got, so let them sweat,
> For Satan is not ready yet.

Now "these artful dodgers" would rob a new partner, "poor doom'd Charley Rogers." Sharing a performance bond with Rogers, Rice never pulled him into the feud. The chickens squawked again, with Rice imitating the frenzied birds, and Van Orden stumbling in a "chicken-fit." Illicit sex spiced up the brew as Rice sang that married Pills was having an affair with Francelia Delsmore, a rider. Like the penny papers retailing scandalous tales of orgies and debauched innocents, Rice simultaneously deplored and reveled with his grinning audience as he sang that Spalding "practiced the Delsmorean art." (Rice was on to something. His rivals publicly denied every accusation except this one, and after Delsmore married, becoming Margaret Frances Ormand, Spalding gave her property in Indiana.)[5]

After Spalding & Rogers' North American Circus arrived in New Orleans on January 11, Rice added the great two-horse rider, Thomas McCollum, then another, Sam Stickney. It stretched his budget to pay three premier equestrians, but Rice wanted to counteract Spalding's star, Rogers. As his foes moved into the American Theatre, near Rice's tent, he increased his attacks on Spalding, not yet arrived himself, and especially on "goddam van orden." Some attacks were solemn:

> Ladies and Gentlemen: A strange fate has been mine since I last had the honor of appearing before you, and I learn that those who were the instruments of that fate have been most busy in attempts to poison the minds of the citizens of this place against me, otherwise I should not intrude my private affairs upon your notice. These people say they started me in business. So they did, and it was a most disastrous business, for I was called by them from a very profitable engagement in Baltimore to New Orleans, to play for them. I went; when I got there, they first tried to cajole me into less favorite terms than they had offered me, but finally, finding that I was more important to them than they were to me, they came to terms, by which their shattered fortune was redeemed, as the good people of the South were pleased to favor me with their smiles, and money flowed to the coffers of the managers.

The speech laid out Rice's version of events: He was forced into partnership when they could not pay him; Van Orden, who had controlled his affairs, gave notes instead of paying the bills, putting him $3,000 in debt; they determined to plunder the little money he had left, so while he thought he had bought his farm, they put it into Van Orden's father's name, and convinced Rice to mortgage personal property to Spalding besides. Next, while he was on tour making them money, they took his circus and forced his family out. He went out again under the name of Rosston, but Spalding's money turned the "boy whom I had raised" against him. Then they sent out a circus specifically to destroy his. He said he did not seek sympathy, "and as far as this quarrel is concerned, I wish your motto to be that of the ancient lawgiver, *fiat justitia ruat caelum.*" Let there be justice though the heavens fall. Rice may have employed a writer's words but the sentiments were stoutly his.[6]

Van Orden had been advised to ignore the clown. Spalding, in New York tending his ailing father, would have said the same, knowing that a response would give Rice more publicity. But Van Orden was excitable and, like Rice, unable to let things rest. So he published a handbill, "DAN RICE AND VAN ORDEN! THE OTHER SIDE OF THE QUESTION!" Much in his litany of transactions and amounts was probably true; Rice denied few details. Here is the tale of the three circuses Spalding put money into, and the proposed fourth one. Here are the figures, albeit not always clear in the welter of loans and leases and letters of credit. But Van Orden repeated Rice's mistake of overstatement. He gloated that he had rescued a "ragged and penniless" clown, his family in the almshouse. He blamed the failure of their joint circuses on Rice's dishonesty. Further straining credibility, Van Orden claimed that Rice had encouraged "a chivalrous fire-eater of Baltimore to travel several hundred miles expressly to shoot me." Van Orden also denounced as beneath contempt the rumors that he and Spalding were abolitionists. Finally, he characterized the clown's financial setbacks as moral failure. Van Orden applied the stereotype flung at successive immigrant groups, of a lazy lout avoiding work and frittering away money.[7]

Offended that Rice did not know his place, Van Orden carried that condescension into his attitude toward the audience. "If his auditors choose to have his private grievances thrust upon them, as a substitute for wit, very good." He implied that they enjoyed Rice's sallies only because the clown pandered to base tendencies. "And yet a morbid taste for slander is so prevalent, that I am satisfied his employer has only to announce that he will answer this card in the Ring, and his canvas will be thronged." Appealing instead to the "influential and discriminate portion of the public," Van Orden wanted it both ways, approving audiences when they agreed with him and scorning them as a mob when they didn't. Van Orden reprinted the two pleading letters that Rice had written in January 1850, ostensibly to support his claims but actually to ensure that the "influential and discriminate" saw Rice's poor spelling and grammar, a sign of the uneducated lower orders. Rice's writing would improve, but in 1850 Van Orden signaled to the growing middle class that Rice was not someone to be taken seriously by people of importance. Similarly, patrician John Quincy Adams had condemned Andrew Jackson for being "a barbarian who could not write a sentence of grammar and hardly could spell his own name."[8] Tone-deaf to humor, Van Orden did not realize that he was reinforcing Rice's jokes. "Of course his scene in the pastry shop, as well as the description of the removal of the poultry from the farm, which I am told he renders very amusing, are unfortunately pure fabrications." Rice would happily acknowledge one charge, that he had cried, "I wish to God Van Orden would have me arrested." It would give him even more material.

Rice's plight sank into the feelings of Orleaners like a snagged boat into the Mississippi. The *Crescent* advised him to give up personal speeches, but was only half serious, teasing that audiences "won't let him descend to be an orator. They want his jokes, not his complaints. He talks about persecution, when his immense tent is filled to its utmost capacity. May he always find such persecutors as nightly punish him by their presence." The *Picayune* similarly decided that "Dan's circus, like the rolling snow ball is continually growing larger, and at the present time, numbers more performers of merit than has before been concentrated within one establishment in this city for many years." These accolades may have been planted by Rice's agents, but Van Orden could get no more than a single laconic line, that they gave a day performance. Even the *Delta,* which inclined toward Spalding, could not ignore Rice's advantage. In a classic rationalization for empty seats, it reported that Spalding offered a show "without the chance of being crowded to death."[9]

Responding to Van Orden's handbill, Rice published his own, "Dan Rice's Bulletin! Number One!" He quibbled over some of the financial claims, but mostly repeated the accusation he had made in the ring, that the nefarious pair had schemed to rob him of circus and home. "The fiendish exultation with which he charges me with being penniless and in debt will find no response in the feelings of a generous community, and comes with a bad grace from one who has been the cause of my misfortunes." Tellingly, he focused on Van Orden's condescension. Complaining of the "ungenerous exposure" of the letters, Rice pointed out that Van Orden was using them not for their substance, but to make him appear bad. Rice turned Van Orden's sneer around. The letters prove "nothing more, than that with a limited education I was thrown into the hands of designing men, whose naturally bad dispositions were rendered more dangerous by the floss of a college career; and it will be readily conceded that my chance of coping with them was hopeless, with all the advantages which they held against me." It was an effective rebuttal in an era when formal education was mostly limited to the children of the few who could afford it. Rice emphasized that Van Orden was also sneering at audiences: "The enlightened community of this city must feel grateful to this accomplished scribbler, for the high estimation he has of their taste."

Van Orden shot back with "Crucible!", another handbill in which he repeated his original attack, and on the reverse side threw in more scorn. Dan and Van were like cartoon characters bashing each other. Whack! We gave you your start! Thud! My clowning made you rich! Splat! You were destitute, and you're illiterate besides! Crack! Spalding's an adulterer, and you're an awkward excuse for a man! Van Orden quoted Rice in a letter absolving the lawyer of fault. A judge might accept that as evidence, but the court of public opinion would see it for what it was, concessions forced from Rice when he was vulnerable. Van Orden's pretense of generosity disappeared in legalisms: "The 'Bulletin,' then, resolves itself into this, (even assuming, for a moment, that every word of it is true) that I have been shrewder than himself, and have exacted the full conditions of the bond."[10]

Blind to the reference to Shylock, Van Orden reinforced it, sneering that he would have his bond. He made it easy for Rice to cast him as the era's mustache-twirling, mortgage-foreclosing villain. The symbol of the confidence man reflected the age's anxiety about trust. Business and society both posed trust as an ideal. Financial affairs increasingly conducted between strangers at a distance implicitly required confidence in the other's sincerity, as did the new notion of companionate marriage, love exalted above arranged or economically convenient unions. Both spheres insisted that one should be able to judge what is in another's heart; that is, have confidence in each other's sincerity. But, since human nature had not changed, and trust remained a leaky vessel, anxiety increased. Rice articulated the dark side of this new faith when he spoke of the bitter lesson he had learned from Van Orden: "Never trust too much to a friend."[11] The paradoxical insistence on dishonesty to protect against dishonesty went deeper.

I've Circus truck enough,
With other useless worldly stuff,
To cancel every honest debt
That ever I contracted yet.

Anxiety over this new financial world was rarely expressed as blatantly, yet it was common.

Rice had topics other than the feud. Spalding had pioneered circus use of the Drummond light, a new, brighter light created by burning a piece of calcium oxide, or "lime." In "Spaulding and Rogers' Circus," Rice mocked this innovation—known as "limelight"—as a trap for greenhorns, whose sap-full heads are like jack-o-lanterns, in turn like Spalding's empty head. Despite his sneer, Rice used the Drummond light himself until he replaced it with an electric light so bright that "it pained the eye" and caused such a crush that ticket sales had to be stopped. Rice also performed a minstrel turn with his old friend, Dan Emmett, on the day Spalding and Rogers left. Then, when his show concluded for the evening, Rice washed off the blackface and scooted across the street to the St. Charles Theatre, where he performed Act V of *Richard III* on horseback for an actor's benefit. After one of his riders, Horace Smith, shot a man over "domestic matters of a delicate nature," audiences gathered to hear what Rice would say in the ring. Then there was the Jackson Monument. For years people had talked of honoring the hero of the Battle of New Orleans, but little had been collected. Rice decided to move things along with a benefit. The papers applauded and the Monument Committee, headed by the mayor, sent thanks. For the patriotic occasion, Rice wrote a song about the battle that touched the pride of New Orleans.[12]

Masonic records curiously interrupt Rice's season. Like many circus managers, Rice was a Mason, but a confusion of dates between this New Orleans engagement and his New York lodge creates a puzzle. Rice should have been in New York on February 24, when he joined New York's Holland Lodge #8, because a Mason must attend his own initiation; yet the New Orleans advertising promised him in the ring on February 22. Of course, circus advertising has been known to stray from accuracy, so Rice might have been in New York despite the ads. But he wouldn't have missed his own benefit in the Crescent City, which was on the same March 10 that he was raised to Master Mason in New York. Rice's growing stature must have enabled him to circumvent normal Masonic procedures.[13]

As Rice was settling into his third month, P. T. Barnum arrived, Jenny Lind in tow.

Lind was a Swedish soprano celebrated in Europe. Barnum, looking for something to present that was more refined than his early frauds and freaks, had signed her for an American tour. Turning her into a national sensation, he founded his publicity on Lind's purity. But in the continuing paradox of public concern about private virtue, virtue doesn't sell tickets unless it is made public; and so the showman publicized her charities and donations. In the process, Barnum kept himself in the forefront of her publicity. At the conclusion of Swedish Nightingale's first concert in the Crescent City, Barnum himself took a bow.[14]

This later picture shows the genteel image Barnum was beginning to present.

Having made Spalding and Van Orden into comic subject matter, Rice now did the same with Lind, offering Lind songs and a burlesque opera, "Lindiana."[15] But he had to tread lightly. It was one thing to battle rival businessmen who acknowledged doing him harm, but it was another to criticize a woman who stood for pious refinement. Rice finessed the issue by adopting a jokingly avuncular attitude, as if he were Lind's selfless adviser. That worked because of people's uncertainty about Barnum. As Barnum's reputation grew, he tried to sidestep his old reputation as a humbug, but he was still suspected of blithely pushing exaggeration into lies. And despite his new pose of refinement, Barnum still paraded his name like a brass band.

The mixed feelings about Barnum shadowed his latest project. Was Lind genuinely magnificent or was she another humbug? That conflict showed in reviewers' uncertainty. The *Delta* praised her "brilliant" opening performance in New Orleans, but hesitated: "That she is a faultless singer will not be pretended, and that some of her notes are a little hard may be conceded." Rice played with the ambivalence. In "Ode to Jenny Lind," he included a verse that slid from praise into an implication of sharp dealing: "You're a maid with a good heart, / And well you play your part, / Humbug or no your [*sic*] smart." Another song took a fling at the many Lind articles for sale. "Everything now is called Jenny, / For the purpose of making an honest penny." Barnum had pumped up interest in Lind's first concert by holding an auction for tickets; Rice deplored the speculators who made money from the auction, teased the hat maker who displayed the first ticket with a Lind hat at his shop, and mocked Barnum himself: "The Crescent, Delta and Picayune, / Are filled with news both morning and noon; / How boats do sink, and Jenny Lind, / How Barnum sucks the people in."[16]

Barnum did not deign to notice Rice directly. His new pose as purveyor of refined culture required that he ignore a circus owner. No sweaty acrobats or narrow plank seats or defecating animals for him, not with the saintly Lind to peddle. (She had apparently refused to appear in one theater because the smell from circus horses lingered.) But Barnum was a showman, and he knew that Rice posed formidable competition. The same day that Barnum arranged for Lind to meet the Apostle of Temperance, Father Mathew, Rice sent a contribution of $500 to the charismatic temperance leader. Barnum followed Rice's donation with his own, for the same amount—and made sure the newspapers knew about it. When Rice caused a stir with a benefit for the Jackson Monument, Barnum countered by publishing the list of Lind's total contributions to charity, down to $100 for "Poor Blind Man."[17]

Though Rice had been in town for months, his appeal held strong against the Prince of Humbug and his Swedish singer, as the *Picayune* noted:

> The excitement which the advent of Jenny Lind has caused does not seem to affect the prosperity of [Rice's] establishment, on the contrary, the pavilion appears to be more densely crowded every night. . . . Every available novelty worth having is seized upon by him with avidity, and a continual excitement is thus kept up which has not flagged since he first appeared.

Similarly, the *New Orleans News-Letter* claimed that Rice outdrew Lind. Seats could be had for her performances, but Dan was forced to turn away thousands. "In fact, if will take some two or three nights to admit those who purchased tickets for his benefit."[18]

Meanwhile, Spalding & Rogers lagged behind. In the war of handbills, Van Orden had bragged that their show was "drawing larger and more respectable audiences" than any circus in New Orleans in years. Rice demurred, singing in "The Polka" that Van Orden could claim "his Circus full, / But the people here he cannot gull." The papers agreed. When the *Crescent* likened Rice's appeal to Lind's, and reported his show "equal to any thing we have ever seen in the Circus line," it sprinkled faint praise on Spalding, whose performances "appear to please the audiences but we would suggest a little more attention to the dress of the supernumeraries. We have never heard of an Arab wearing brogans and pantaloons 'forty inches round the bottom.'"[19]

10

LIKE A PHOENIX

The wharves in Pittsburgh were bustling in the heat. As clerks grappled with bills of lading and carters with barrels, boatmen shouldered past all to the nonstop accompaniment of rantankerous chatter.

"Sa – a – a – a – y what!? By the piper that played before Moses, if yer spilin' fer a fight, I reckon you'll find me an owdacious scrounger."

"Aw, don't be a crosspatch."

"She slung the nastiest ankle in Kentuck and she had a right smart chance o' leg too."

"I swow!"

Amid the noise came another one, faintly at first, over the water. It floated from the *Hudson,* steaming up. On the deck under flapping flags played Rice's ripsnitious brass band, led by Joe Messemer.

Rice had left New Orleans in March, riding his One-Horse story up the Mississippi. To keep his performers together, he had sent them out as the Phoenix Circus; meanwhile, Rice split off to perform for a week with a circus in St. Louis to make money to bankroll his summer show. As he dug away at Spalding, the response from his audiences told him that he had struck performing gold. The wrangle perfectly fit the Jacksonian message that men could rise, and that wealth, education, and position did not equal respectability. Dan splattered jokes over Doc's carefully cultivated image of aloof reserve. More galling for Spalding, he and Van Orden kept giving the clown opportunities to depict them as lascivious Pills and diabolical Quills. Throwing Rice in jail provided him with material. Taking away his horses cast him an underdog. Counterattacking reinforced his appeal. The title of Rice's small show carried implicit reproach: Like a phoenix from the fire, he rose from the ruin.

When Rice reunited with his troupe, he brought along his daughters. Though young for the rigors of the road, they joined the family trade, a circus tradition and a nineteenth-century practice. "La Jeune Kate," not yet five, and her older sister, "La Petite Elizabeth"—"Libly" in one ad—were the "Infant Prodigies." They did little more than sit on ponies guided by an adult hand, but when Kate and Libby rode in mad dashes around the ring, crowds cheered. Meanwhile, Dan was teaching his girls poise. They learned to move with grace and to stand as if bestowing a gift on the audience.[1]

In June, Rice made a key addition to the roster. He had pitched his tent in Hawesville, Kentucky, under the river bank near a spring. That afternoon, a barefoot boy came by to water his snow-white horse. Knowing the showman's weakness for smart horses, the boy rode his mount up a cordwood pile to show off. A circus man was always on the lookout for likely horseflesh. Horses that pulled the wagons wore down over a season, and smart ones were valuable in the ring. This one was clearly special, with a quick intelligence, and Rice decided he had to have it. Following the boy home, he met the father, the local doctor, who knew what he had and wasn't going to let the animal go cheap. After serious horse trading, they traded horses. For a horse and $200, Rice got this white one, which he named Excelsior. He began presenting as if it were the original "One Horse."[2]

Child performers were very popular.

This month also saw the first appearance of "one-horse show" in print, when the *Cincinnati Enquirer* quoted Rice that "he has 'no one horse show any longer.'" Separated by five hundred miles of river, the Cincinnati and Pittsburgh papers now enlisted in the battle between Spalding and Rice.[3]

Pittsburgh favored its hometown boy, an affection he returned as it had "welcomed me with a mother's fondness." Circuses usually advertised a week or two in advance, but Rice fired his opening salvo five weeks early. Not due to arrive until July, he began his advertising on May 26, which happened to be the day Spalding started his Pittsburgh engagement. Rice's ads flung defiance. He had been struggling, and Pittsburghers knew that, especially Mit, who had only recently gotten back the $50 Dan had long owed. But he was back on his perfect rush. When Rice advertised that "DAN IS HIMSELF AGAIN!"—no adjunct, no protégé, no employee—Spalding knew that the announcement was directed as much at him as to the citizens of Pittsburgh. Dan had not folded his tents, nor given up when he had no tent to fold. Now he presented "THE DAN RICE CIRCUS TRIUMPHANT!"[4]

Nineteenth-century performance commentary must be read with caution. Showmen often paid for complimentary articles, called "puffs." An Illinois editor declined Rice's offer of free tickets in exchange for a positive notice—though he gave one anyway. Rice had hired a new agent, Charles H. Castle, who was known as "Old Roughhead" because he had been a canal boatman. A good storyteller like Rice, and a fair singer and jig dancer, too, Castle was one of the best advance agents of the century. Yet even if a piece was a puff from Old Roughhead's pen, it was not indiscriminate praise. Paid or not, the age's opinionated newspapers did not yield editorial independence. They made their own judgments, and they criticized freely. It was like the barter system that developed in the twentieth century, when news organizations traded articles for access and story ideas. For weeks, the local papers, especially the *Daily Morning Post,* cheered the hometown boy in print. It passed on a report about Rice's months-old donation for Natchez orphans, putting it not in the amusement column but in "City Intelligence," the section devoted to items of civic interest. Going back even further to boost Dan, the *Post* printed the text of his previous year's farewell address. Every performer tried for rapturous publicity. Dan got it.[5]

The day Dan opened his tent across from the American Hotel, a sultry June had vanished into bright July skies. The hometown crowds cheered, and praise festooned his way. He was "the great and glorious Dan," whose path from New Orleans had been "a series of triumphs more brilliant than were ever before achieved." As he rose "into the highest regions of poetry," his spacious pavilion was crowded "almost to suffocation," and the enthusiastic crowd "were laughing almost continually."

Live performance at its best is a collaboration of the willing and eager with the talented and inspired. Energy meets energy. In Rice, one strong body, one pair of lungs, and one set of vocal cords all worked together in the service of one human imagination to boom out words and ideas and jokes and songs, while thousands of human imaginations bounced them back. On the Fourth of July, when Penn Street was blocked by people jostling to get tickets, Rice made the partnership explicit. He had formerly been an actor for the audience, he said, but now he stood with them as a "participator"; they were all equal participants in the public conversation of performance. The *Post* doubly endorsed that stance, printing two items on the speech, one printing it in full. As he "blends the artist with the clown, and pleases the refined and distinguished, as well as the million," he gave a "Fourth of July speech, as is a speech." He spoke nobly of noble founders, groaned with the oppressed under the tyrant's sway, ranged freely on political, religious, and intellectual freedom, and expanded on the country's vast geographical scope, which had created an equally vast intellectual scope in the new democratic soul. Rice was sounding the same notes that Daniel Webster used on the Senate floor or Henry Ward Beecher propounded from the pulpit. When Ralph Waldo Emerson urged American self-reliance, he wrote what Rice was saying (just as Emerson's insistence that "imitation is suicide" matched claims for Rice's originality).[6]

As is often true of patriotism, it was political. Rice cautioned against "wicked demagogues" brewing the "storm of fanaticism." That meant the abolitionists, who were vastly unpopular. Van Orden had denounced rumors that he and Spalding favored abolition; so did Barnum in defense of Lind, who "prizes too dearly the glorious institutions of our country to lend the slightest sanction to any attack upon the Union of these States." Rice concluded his speech by consigning those who would endanger the Union to "everlasting infamy."[7]

Meanwhile, downriver, Cincinnati at first preferred Spalding, whose winter preparations bolstered the local economy. The *Enquirer* decided that the faint praise Spalding had received in its upriver rival meant that he was "taking Pittsburgh by storm." Predictably, Rice received a lukewarm welcome but Cincinnati warmed to Rice as the week wore on. Familiarity bred respect for Rice. The Rochester *Daily Democrat* had sniffed that those "who admire this kind of amusement will here find such as will please them"; but before the clown left, the newspaper was singing his praises.[8] He was different in person than expected. Hearing about a marvelous clown, people based their expectations on clowns they had seen. But Rice was not simply a funnier clown than others; he was different, mingling jokes, solemn thoughts, civic observations, and songs. Other clowns turned serious at times, but it was non-comic relief, as if their comic work and real selves were distinct. Rice's solemn moments did not stand opposed to his quips. Amusement overlapped political discourse, gravitas blended seamlessly with levitas.

Rice's public role swept through the informal network in which newspapers copied each other's items. When he came to Buffalo, the *Express* reprinted his patriotic speech from Pittsburgh, adding its own introductory homage. Rice "stands alone in the profession he has adopted, and which he has raised far above what it formerly was." He was jester to the "sovereign people." A week later, the *Rochester Daily Democrat* copied the Buffalo paper, adding Rice's public morality tale, casting Spalding and Van Orden as villains.

> They thought him completely ruined, and their exultation was great. But they reckoned without their host. Dan's indomitable perseverance and energy were aroused by his character. He struggled manfully against the tide of adversity, and he has lived to see the machinations of his enemies fail in all points, and like a Phoenix, he has risen from the ashes.

The *Spirit of the Times* copied the praise from Buffalo, making it a national story. "As the fancy takes him, he changes from gay to grave, and passes from the ludicrous to the sublime in a manner that stamps him as a genius and an artist of the first order." By September, the *Syracuse Standard* was repeating the political theme as it cheered Rice's performances: "He has gained more applause than all the statesmen of the country put together, and tickled the sides of more people than ever voted for President."[9]

Not all were enthralled. The church especially deplored amusements. Beecher railed against circus and theater for making "honest business" seem boring, and the American Sunday-School Union similarly disapproved. *Sketches* told of Rice's "Crusade against Bigotry and Superstition," assailing a preacher who had called his troupe immodest, naked, and depraved. This summer in Weedsport, New York, Rice launched another crusade. A Methodist minister was thundering against Rice's circus. In response, the clown announced that on Sunday he would make his tent a church and preach a sermon. According to Rice's account, a crowd arrived expecting jokes and was instead amazed by his theological discourse on divine love. Stirred by the sermon, a Presbyterian preacher, who had attended out of curiosity, spontaneously pronounced a benediction. Rice declared that being attacked from the pulpit was his best publicity.[10]

Rice floated his circus over the rivers and canals of New York, Pennsylvania, and Ohio. It had become a fair-sized venture. Rice billed himself as the Prince of Clowns; but with his role changing, he hired Thomas Burgess as clown, probably of the singing variety, and Charley Brown as "comical clown," or knockabout. Late in August, James Robinson's company stopped for a visit. One of the pleasures of a nomadic existence is the chance encounter with other nomads. A few days later, when Rice's route went past Utica, his company returned the visit, and the two troupes had a lively party through the night.

At Buffalo, Rice hired a steamboat, the *Empire State,* to carry them across Lake Erie to Cleveland. Rice asked the captain to tow the show's bullheads, too. The captain was reluctant because the sky looked ominous. The usually placid Great Lakes can blow up powerful storms. While Rice's pet, a bull terrier, scampered around their feet, the captain resisted, but few could match wills with Rice. So the canal boats, with Rice's men aboard, were tied aft. Off the watery parade chugged, like a momma duck with her ducklings tagging along behind. But Lake Erie was no pond. A tempest blew up, awesome and wild. Rain whipped across the deck of the steamboat, which struggled to make headway. Suddenly, the hawser snapped. As the boats flapped on the heavy swells, scudding backwards, those on them could do nothing but watch through sheets of rain as the steamboat, laboring in the heavy waters, turned back to help. Catastrophe on land crashes quickly, but disaster on the water can unfold with time to contemplate a haven just out of reach. Even as the steamboat neared, the men on the bullheads knew that their unwieldy crafts could suddenly flip and that they would be lost, dead in sight of safety. The captain maneuvered in the jarring, irregular waves of the

Great Lakes blow, working his boat alongside the smaller ones. Ropes flew, fingers smashed, wood crashed into wood. The men, frightened, breathless, scrambled over the side of the steamboat. The captain let the canal boats go, and turned for Cleveland. For twenty hours, they drove through the raging storm. Reaching the harbor, it took five men at the wheel to get the *Empire State* safely in, even as they watched a schooner founder. Rice's boats were discovered the next day, beached forty-five miles from Buffalo. The only loss of life was the bull terrier. Rice wanted to erect a headstone, but couldn't decide where to put it. As a man who worked in the world of animals, Rice had been fond of his pet.[11]

11

ALTERNATING RINGMASTERS

Snow in New Orleans! Flaky puffs floated into the Mississippi River and piled white mounds on the boats. Snow swirled around Spanish moss like a lacy dream, draping a blanket of white on Lafayette Square and layering frosting over the black iron filigree of the balconies. It settled like a dusting of sugar on the arms of people out walking in wonder. Eight inches of snow in New Orleans.[1] What could top that?

Rice could, literally. On January 13, 1852, he drove over the surprising snow on a makeshift sleigh, bells ringing. Grinning smartly, his cheeks rosy, he clucked the horses along, nodding at the people as they pointed and waved. One who saw him was Noah Ludlow. Though Rice had been stiff competition for Ludlow and Smith's St. Charles Theatre, there were no hard feelings. Rice would perform at the benefit of Sol Smith's son, and on this wintry day, Ludlow appreciated his fellow showman's allure.

> Passing down St. Charles Street I beheld Dan Rice, the celebrated equestrian manager, in a sleigh, with a fine span of horses with bells. . . . I will venture to say it was a sight that no man living in that city had ever seen there before. The sleigh was composed of a large dry-goods box on a pair of temporary runners made of a two-inch plank. This was not a splendid turn-out, but it produced as great a sensation as would the lord mayor's carriage driven through the streets of New Orleans.

Others tried to sleigh on this snowy day, yet Ludlow looked back through Rice's expanding celebrity and remembered him alone. In a carousel of mutually reinforcing impressions, a celebrity is celebrated.[2]

Rice had regrouped after the Lake Erie storm, buying three new boats for the canals of Ohio, then spending $7,000 on a steamer, the *Zachary Taylor,* for the trip downriver. Back in the Crescent City, Rice's Circus & Great Hippodrome opened a four-month stand on St. Charles Street. Just as Broadway would later stand for American theater, St. Charles was the amusement capital of the South. The rollicking street included a "cloud of nonsense and rant" at the St. Charles Theatre, the St. Charles Hotel billiard room, and, next to the offices of the *Crescent,* the saloon of Dan Hickok, who owned the pelican that Van Orden allegedly stole. At the Veranda Hotel, where Barnum had stayed, one could experience "the acme of human bliss" by jumping "from a bath into the chair tonsorial." Other pleasures could be found at the brothels, the doggeries for drinking, and a "shiny house . . . where all sorts of dancing was done." On the street, an organ-grinder vied for attention with a who would scientifically measure the lungs with his "Respirometer." The *Crescent* later versified about the "Street Music" outside the window.

> All day the Museum doth send forth its strains;
> While Dan Rice's band all the live-long night reins.
> . . .
> Then, moreover, we have, all the while, from the street,
> A concert of sounds the most liquid and sweet:
> The carts keep a roaring, the carriages rattle,
> Like the mixed notes of small arms and cannon in battle.
> With these, at due intervals, mingles the rout
> Of folks who, being drunk, find it pleasant to shout;
> And now and then rises to vary the play,

The bellow of crowds looking on at a fray.
On our left is bawled forth a most maudlin tune;
On our right there's a rumbling bowling saloon;
Before us two orchestras rave to the wind;
We've the shriek and the roar of a railroad behind.
Now pray, let me ask you, and asking it weep,
Do the folks in this town ever need any sleep?

What the French Quarter came to signify, a perpetual Mardi Gras, started in earnest a few blocks over, on rambunctious St. Charles.[3]

Rice's circus thrived in the competition. Teaming up with the Southern favorite, Little Jimmy Reynolds, his clown "duplicate," Rice burlesqued an 1849 boxing match that had been an international sensation. He also presented the Four Hungarian Brothers in a posing act; the Creole Dancers with "negro" specialties; and "the Mexicans," probably precursors to Wild West riding. A man who won the show's lottery for a pony got so excited that Rice repeated the feature. One transparent but effective boost for attendance was a silver trumpet awarded to whichever fire company attended in the greatest number.[4]

Still presenting minstrels, Rice sometimes took the lead, though "not hiding the brightness of his humor by placing it under a black face." Minstrelsy had leapt from the circus to become one of the most popular forms America would know; its topicality was like Rice's. A description of minstrelsy's stump speech, the "high spot in the evening's entertainment," fit Rice: "Clever lines and comic material of the more traditional sort were skillfully interwoven with pungent comments on local celebrities and public affairs, local, national, and international. Politics, of course, was a specially fruitful field, and much of the success of the monologue depended on impromptu sallies in which real blackface stars excelled." A big, booming voice was required to put it over, and Rice possessed that as well.[5]

Benefits for charities, on top of benefits for stars, added to the draw. The *Crescent* applauded that Rice gave so generously when he had his own money troubles. One recipient of Rice's largesse, a priest at St. Anne's, thanked him for giving away $90,000 in New Orleans over the years. The *Picayune* waxed eloquent in gratitude.

> Mr. Rice has distinguished himself . . . throughout the whole length and breadth of the union, by his manifold donations to charitable institutions. Himself, comparatively speaking, a poor man, depending upon his own exertions for the support of himself and family, he nevertheless, unsolicited, spares a large proportion of his earnings towards mitigating and alleviating the wants of others. What he gives is with no niggard hand; he does not in his charitable benefits retain expenses, but hands the gross receipts to the recipients of his bounty. Such conduct is noble, and fully entitles him to the lasting respect and esteem of every admirer of philanthropy. [6]

Performers' and managers' benefits also drew people, with special features added to the appeal. For Little Jimmy's benefit, there was an exhibition of jewelry; Castle, in his "first and only appearance on any stage," rode the comic mule; and "Twenty Amateurs" volunteered a benefit for the manager, Harry Whitbeck. The *Picayune* applauded the enthusiasm, if not the skill of these amateurs, "well known respectable citizens" all.[7]

Rice had ambitious plans. A few years earlier, he had advertised in Galveston that he would bring his show there. This season, Texas saw a reputed Rice circus, alternately called Maltby's New York Circus and the Star State Circus, but the *Crescent* scoffed at word that it was Rice's. It called that report a humbug, like trying to convince "the children of Israel to cross the Red Sea on a railroad but it won't do." Rice was looking further than the Lone Star State. He advertised for a ship for a world tour to South America, up to San Francisco, and across the Pacific to Asia, concluding with stops in European ports. Rice proposed to take one hundred people, thirty horses, and thirty tons of freight. It would have been one of the circus's most remarkable tours, but the project never materialized.[8]

When Rice was in Cincinnati, Spalding had stopped to buy a boat but left immediately, avoiding head-to-head competition with Rice. Now, however, as Spalding & Rogers followed Rice into the Crescent City, they brought added ammunition, walrus-mustached William F. Wallett, England's leading circus clown. Calling himself the Queen's Jester after a command performance before Queen Victoria, Wallett, like Macready, made great claims for his erudition. He told of a triumph in Cambridge, when the university had tried to shut down a circus by using an ancient law, until he did research and discovered a loophole in the original act of

Parliament. In distinguishing between the fool and the jester, an honorable position "filled by an educated gentleman," Wallett proposed that the jester had a kind of license to speak the truth. "Like the wearers of other professional costumes, legal and clerical, jesters are privileged to say and do many things which would not be kindly received from laymen." Industrializing society was beginning to venerate the truth-telling iconoclast but the underlying model had flaws. It was implausible because authority was unlikely to welcome criticism even from those in motley costumes, and it ignored the fact that mockery upholds authority as easily as it subverts it. Finally, most of the examples offered, like Wallett's, turned out to be apocryphal or literary. Nevertheless, the idea was gaining strength. Physically or mentally impaired people, some of them jesters, had been called "naturals" because, in a rude state of nature, they were ill-adapted to function in society; as the Romantic era decided that society itself was ill-adapted, "natural" came to mean an inner, freer, and theoretically more "real" self.[9]

Presenting Wallett was a coup for Spalding & Rogers, who set up within hailing distance of Rice's tent. Here was a clown to rival Rice, and he enjoyed an elegant reputation besides. Welcoming "the distinguished European commedian," the *Picayune* as a matter of course equated talent and social status: "Mr. Wallet's reputation at home, and his intimate association with the nobility and gentry of England, as well as his wide-spread fame over Europe, is *prima facie* evidence of his extraordinary genius."[10]

Spalding and Van Orden tried to enlist Wallett in their feud against Rice but the English clown declined. The craving to beat Rice down seemed excessive to him. So, "I one night ran out in my dress into the ring where Rice was performing. There we fraternized, and he introduced me to his patrons." The audience loved it. From that moment, recalled Wallett,

> I became a great favourite with the frequenters of both circuses. For Dan was a sort of martyr in the eyes of the New Orleans people; and it was believed that our proprietors, who were rich and powerful, had come on purpose to crush his company. In fact, the feeling rose to such a height that it was dangerous for our managers or any of their company to be recognized by the populace after dark.

Making friends with Rice did not endear Wallett to his employers, however. Their show could not attract an audience so they left for Mobile, "where I found to my cost, that the conduct of the managers was entirely changed, and they took every opportunity of showing their ill will." Here was confirmation of what Rice had been saying of his rivals. He asserted that they acted maliciously; Wallett, with no ax to grind, agreed. Rice had offered Wallett a job. Now, chafing under Van Orden, Wallett telegraphed to ask if the offer was still open. Rice wired back, "Come immediately; we have announced you." (Rosston was back from Spalding, too. Either Rice forgave him for selling out to Van Orden, or Rosston forgave Rice for a false accusation.)[11]

On February 2, 1852, Rice stood in the center of his gaslit tent, letting anticipation build until he strode to the curtain, flinging it aside to reveal Wallett. Rice did not shy from the contrast. "Dan will bring merit forth, and knows no jealousy," said the *Picayune.* The response to Wallett's appearance with Rice was, to use a then-vulgar word, "amazing." The crowd erupted in cheers. Walking arm-in-arm to the center of the ring, the two clowns were dressed in the "garb of their respective nationalities," Wallett's costume like a British flag and Rice probably sporting stars and stripes. It was a dazzling stroke.

Belying suspicions that their egos would clash, the two "celebrities" worked well together. Wallett took a farewell benefit on the seventeenth, but returned a week later for another run. Like John Gielgud and Lawrence Olivier trading the roles of Romeo and Mercutio eighty years later, Rice and Wallett alternated. Rice took the part of the ringmaster to Wallett's clown, and then Rice clowned to Wallett's ringmaster. The feat had tremendous appeal. It made each of the stars seem gracious, yielding attention to the other. It also gave both clowns more material. A joke told one night could be answered the next, and the alternation itself invited quips. The strategy had another advantage for the clowns: Ostensibly competing for the crown of "cap and bells," Rice and Wallett did not have to top each other nightly. For Wallett's final farewell, on March 5, the bills promised they would switch back and forth one more time, in "Shakesperean lectures, lectures on Mesmerism, on women's rights, &c." At the performance, Rice spoke movingly about their friendship, then presented Wallett with a large, engraved silver vase, concluding, "So long

Rice's English compatriot, the "Queen's Jester," William F. Wallett.

as he lives, he will never go hungry for a lack of Rice." Wallett responded in similar respect and word play: "While I live, Rice will always have a 'Wallett' at his disposal." Later, Rice would depict himself as a bumptious clown contrasted to the elegant Queen's Jester, but in 1852, they were gentlemanly compatriots.[12]

Meanwhile Spalding, Rogers & Van Orden's American and European Amphitheatre avoided Rice. Returning from Mobile, they could have stopped in New Orleans again but Pills and Quills showed across the river in Algiers and then headed up the Missisippi.

Rice took his farewell benefit on March 25 in a new tent holding 5,000. The performance lasted five hours but—accommodating the short attention span of that modern age—"so arranged that visitors can come and go to suit themselves." Then he took Dan Rice's Hippodrome north. At the same time, he left another "Dan Rice's Circus" behind. It is not clear what stake he had in it. Whitbeck managed this new attraction, which had the same performers of Maltby's earlier Star State Circus. After a week, Whitbeck switched to Swiss Bell Ringers, followed by a final flare of circus activity, a one-day "Dan Rice's Circus" on April 18. It included "Rice, the old clown." As for the genuine article, he was fondly remembered, even having a race horse named for him. Dan Rice had played so long in the Crescent City "that he was regarded as a fixture, a some thing that was attached to the soil."[13]

12

CURSES, FOILED AGAIN!

Rice's show heaved up in New Madrid, Missouri, where Kentucky and Tennessee jam into the big toe of Missouri. Among the curious gathered to watch the boat unloading was one derelict specimen who stuck his nose into everything until Rice ordered him away. When the offender refused to leave, Rice pushed him off. A little later, another man came running down to the landing. That had been no tramp but the local justice of the peace, who was returning with a pistol and "a little whiskey aboard," looking for Rice. The clown boarded his boat to hide just before the justice stomped back on the scene, yelling and waving his pistol. Jiminy Crickets! He was fixin' to bodiacerously split that circus snollygoster open down the middle! After a while, weary of confinement, Rice tiptoed down the plank to sneak up behind the rampageous JP. He snatched the pistol, fired it in the air, and handed it back. "Here, judge, here's your pistol. I am Dan Rice." The two men made up and drank champagne through the night.[1]

Even as master of a huge establishment, advertised at two hundred horses and performers, his largest roster, Rice continued his gregarious ways. He called everyone on the lot by name, and everyone called him "Dan." The show was Dan Rice's Hippodrome, borrowing its title from Franconi's Hippodrome. Henri Franconi had combined "hippo" for the horse of circus, and "drome," meaning track; he had presented the show first in Paris in 1845, then in an English version in 1851, drawing crowds at the Great London Exposition with its Crystal Palace. Rice's was the first Hippodrome without a track. He used the name to suggest Franconi's other feature: grand spectacles. Rice expanded his old tournament idea into a glorious pageant featuring knights, squires, heralds, "the Queen of Love and Beauty, and her Maids of Honor, and Lords and Ladies in waiting, with appointments, trappings, and wardrobe of most gorgeous style." The subtitle of his spectacle, "Rice's Dream of Chivalry," suggests its dramatic structure, Dan pretending to fall asleep in the ring and waking to "the days of chivalry and knight-errantry, . . . with strict regard to costume and all the accompaniments of the mimic war." Twain would use the same conceit for *A Connecticut Yankee in King Arthur's Court.*[2]

The ads announced that performances would begin precisely at 8:00 P.M., and there would have been some urgency each night to start, finish, and pack up for the trip to the next town. However, "precisely" was rarely precise. Throughout human existence, work had focused on tasks, not time. Harvesting corn, digging clams, building bridges—all were tasks that took the time they took. It was the same with sports. Horse races and "pedestrianism" lasted till the racers finished, and boxing and baseball went their full course, too. At work, the flexible time included time out. Work was a convivial affair; workers took breaks to rest, to chat, to have a drink. Domestic chores—what became known as "woman's work"—continued to combine labor and sociability. However, the notion of time was in transition. Increasingly, manual tasks were set to the clock. The new industrial system accelerated that change because factory work—women's and men's work—required regularity, uniformity, punctuality. Standard time zones were adopted in 1884, to make railroad scheduling easier. So, too, with sports: new ones, such as football, begun in 1869, and basketball, 1891, were set to a time.

Family remained a touchstone for Rice. Three years after Dan's late-night visit to his relatives, young Will Crum was doubly seduced by Dan's dazzling words, into the world of show, and into its showiest aspect, publicity, as W. C. Crum, circus agent. As for Maggie, Dan told of playing all-night, no-limit poker with riverboat gamblers, Pettibone and Canada Bill. With the pot growing, he returned to his room at 4:00 A.M., waking Maggie as he got the rest of their money. He said it was $25,000. "My wife—good woman, my wife"—objected:

> "Where you goin' with that money?"
> "Going to bet it."
> "No, you ain't," she says.
> "Yes, I am," I says, and I slammed the door.

Back at the table, he threw down the cash, calling and raising. At that point, Canada Bill and his pal pulled out bowie knives, the 1850s weapon of choice. "Yes, sir, bowie knives—great big long fellers. I whispers to Fowler: 'Swipe the swag and sherry your nibs.' That's slang, you know. Then I says to Bill and Pettibone: 'Hold on, hold on; don't let's have any trouble,' and while I was sayin' that I picks up a chair and hit 'em both. I slammed 'em good. Lord, I was a strong young feller then. Later, I handed my wife a big diamond ring. That shut her up. Then I promised her I'd never gamble any more and I never have." That was Dan's version, looking back. He may have quit gambling for the only indications of it after that were the lottery tickets he bought. But the detail that he shut Maggie up was likely the other way around, that he himself shut up after misreading the danger so badly.[3]

Life on the river was usually less dramatic, mostly passing peacefully. The shore slipped by, slow upriver, quicker down. Green masses of branch and bush seemed too dense for movement, but deer crashed along and a wolf stole noiselessly down the bank toward a rabbit watching a watching traveler. High above, a hawk made lazy circles in the sky. The boat aimed for a green wall of woods before slowly turning a twist in the river to face another green wall, then another twist. The rivers were like contorted snakes on the landscape, wiggling in every direction. Fish splashed. Mosquitoes buzzed past the ear. A traveler rode time on the water.

In 1852, Doc Spalding pioneered again. Rather than simply traveling by boat, he commissioned Cincinnati craftsmen to build the *Floating Palace*, which accommodated performances aboard. It a rectangular box two stories tall, bowed out in the front, with a roof swooping up fore and aft to fit the 2,500 seats inside. Roof and hull were chained together for safety. The length accommodated a foredeck, seats, a ring—though probably less than the standard 42'—a box office, dressing rooms, and stables. It also boasted "saloons for refreshment," leased out as a privilege for $5,200 yearly. There was no room for an engine, so the *Palace* was pushed by a tug. Soon Spalding added his own propulsion, a 274-ton side-wheeler, the *North River.* "Capt. Van Orden," no longer entrusted with management, led the publicity crew aboard another companion boat, the *Hummingbird,* seven feet wide. With no tent to set up, tear down, and

Interior of Spalding's *Floating Palace*, with a view of the exterior at the bottom.

transport, Spalding could show three times a day, selling many more tickets. He claimed he had put $45,000 into his vessel, making it a draw itself this first season. No music lover like Rice, Spalding kept looking for ways to eliminate the band, this time with a "Cathedral Organ" and twenty bells played "as perfectly as the Keys of a Pianoforte." The piano, which, unlike a harpsichord, could be played softly and loudly—"piano" and "forte"—was an accessory of the new middle class, so this comparison underlined a major selling point of the craft, its gentility. Spalding had outfitted the boat with carpeting, plush armchairs, draperies, carvings, and large polished mirrors, all that could be found in the best theaters and in the parlors of the most genteel.[4]

Rice kept narratively flogging Pills and Quills. Customers cheered his song telling how those dastardly foes had persuaded "Oh! Bill Spriggins, [to] heave that last brick bat, / It didn't hit Dan Rice's head, It only smashed his hat!" Word had reached the South in April that Rice had lost a libel suit in New York and now faced a whopping $1,558 fine. Legally, libel refers to writing, and slander to spoken defamation, suggesting that Rice got into trouble more for publishing his animosity than for what he said in the ring. Van Orden spread rumors that the clown was dead, but he was hitting his head against the bulwark of Rice's appeal.[5] Frustrated, Spalding and Van Orden would have been tempted to say what fit the tales he told of them: "Curses, foiled again!"

When Rice's boat nearly crashed, he had a new story to tell. The captain had mistakenly steered the *Zachary Taylor* away from the river channel. Spotting the error just in time, he reversed engines with shouted commands and a wild clanging of bells. Water churned over the paddles as the boat slowly, slowly backed into the channel. Adrenaline carried them through, but it was a near thing. If the captain had not acted quickly, they would have run hard aground, the bottom ripped or people killed if the boilers exploded. Rice blamed Spalding and Van Orden. In song, he called the *Floating Palace* of those those "New York sharps" a floating firetrap, which, in a fire-prone age, hit a nerve. When Spalding's ads assured that everyone could exit in fifty seconds if necessary, everyone knew what that necessity might be. The focus of the song was Rice's accusation that Spalding and Van Orden had deliberately shifted the buoys to run him aground. While "All dirty tricks we shun," his opponents on the "floating scow" were trying to destroy his show. To move buoys was not a tactic beneath either side. The agent, T. F. Taylor, traveling ahead of Rice's show, treated "the boys to a circus ticket and something else that was very cheap then—only twenty-two cents a gallon." Liquored up, they waited for Spalding's boat and threw "a shower of Black Diamonds, now called Pittsburgh coal. Some of the boys on the *Palace* said they dare not stand on the bow of the boat when it landed at towns on the river, so desperate was opposition." At Wheeling, when Spalding day-and-dated Rice—showed at the same place at the same time—the absence of a fight made news.[6]

It was one of the great rivalries of the American circus: Spalding and Rice, with a side order of Van Orden. For years along the Mississippi, saying the name of one automatically conjured the others. Even as Rice complained, he prized the feud. Spalding and Van Orden were matchless foils: They allowed him to perfect the message of personal advancement he had been developing from the days of the Learned Pig. When Rice sang of "wealthy men," it was not a neutral description but a clear message to his audiences that these were representative men of power, "New York sharps," arrayed in might against "the Innocent." The notoriety of the feud fed into a struggle over performance: Would circus continue to be led by performers like Ricketts in that first American show, and Rice, whose appeal was based on involvement with the audience, or would businessmen like Spalding rule? Beyond lay a larger issue: Would the work of the world proceed as it had for centuries, among those who knew each other, artisans and farmers and crafts workers, or would larger, impersonal forces dominate? The dichotomy is artificial: Larger social forces have always influenced apparently unique dealings between individuals; at the same time, seemingly cold-blooded business has always had a personal component. Nevertheless, the ground was shifting.

Buoyed by his success, Rice began to rely more on impulse, to "catch folly on the fly." Now "better than ever," he was "much less studied than formerly."[7] On April 23, celebrated as Shakespeare's birthday, Rice paid tribute in a poem asking how the "lowly" born Bard rose to be "the brightest and the best." The democratic answer was clear: "Our Shakespeare"—the populist possessive—had made his way with native genius rather than wealth or position. Like the American ideal. Like Rice.[8]

Four years after the *Hannibal Journal* had blasted him as a blackguard, the *Hannibal Tri-Weekly Messenger* admitted that he had been an "incorrible [*sic*] wretch . . . but then he was young and verdant—now, since he has cut his 'wisdom teeth,' a more modest clown never convulsed his audiences with laughter." In that Mississippi town, Rice bragged that his tent seated 10,000 and that his establishment had cost $50,000, the latter exaggeration beating Spalding's boast for the $45,000 *Palace.* A poem advertising his Hippodrome extolled the show's knights, Bedouins, Roman slaves, Indian braves, and dancers "with steps elastic, / [who] trip the toe light and fantastic." Tripping this light fantastic were Rice's "Creole Ballet Troupe," forty strong in the ads. The word "Creole" lay along a fault line in the constructed idea of race. It originally referred to those of French or Spanish extraction, proudly white in the day's racial politics; however, meaning was shifting, to stand for people of mixed race, perhaps after the slaves of the original Creoles adopted their masters' fierce pride. Creole slaves, for instance, never permitted other slaves to join in their weekend revels in Congo Square. Rice offered "Colored Boxes" in New Orleans, but it was "Creole Boxes" in Mobile. Calling his dancers "Creole," Rice suggested exotic European allure, with a dash of Southern heat, just as he sang elsewhere of "dark and melting quateroons."[9]

In Memphis, Glenroy quit the show after an argument with Rice. The rider had agreed to continue after his contract ended on August 3, but he would no longer take part in the street parade. Performers are jealous of their time. When Whitbeck asked him to turn out for the parade anyway, he refused. Rice, happening along, told Glenroy to turn out or leave. The rider did leave, retiring to the hotel. The next day, Rice had cooled down and invited him back, but when Glenroy declined and asked for his pay, they parted friends. Glenroy later worked for Spalding but, thirty-five years after his split with Rice, he wrote that "our friendship still remains perfect."[10] Except for Van Orden, Rice held no grudges.

PART 3

THE GREAT AMERICAN HUMORIST

1853 ☛ 1856

13

THE BARNUM OF NEW ORLEANS

A kaleidoscope of activity through the winter of 1852–1853 embedded Rice deeper in the life of New Orleans. Arriving to cheers for the "veritable, original, indomitable, immortal Dan," the showman performed in a brief November stand, took his company to Mobile, and returned, on a kind of Southern amusement circuit. He also set up an alternate Rice troupe in one city when he was in the other; and he established the first large-scale museum in the South.[1]

Maggie now appeared in the ring with a featured act. It was a manage act, a variation of *haute école,* or high school riding, the kind of thing seen in performances by the Lippizaner stallions, in which a rider guides the horse through movements with little apparent direction. "Mrs. Rice, although delicate in form, by great skill and practice, manages a powerful and spirited horse." (In American circus, it is pronounced "manage," rather than the French *mènage.*) It was more practice, with Dan, than

Maggie, finally a performer, in her riding habit.

skill. Maggie was not a natural at riding, or she would have developed the act earlier, especially in the one-horse days when Dan needed acts badly.[2]

The couple stayed at the City Hotel. Most hostelries offered the American plan, that is, room and meals combined; but the City's European plan of charging only for the room suited show people, whose schedule did not fit regular meal times. Practicality mattered little to Rice, though. The luxurious City Hotel was the latest in hotel design, having wide hallways, a withdrawing room for ladies, and a gentlemen's parlor, where Dan could settle into a morocco-leather armchair, amid a swirl of cigar smoke and conviviality, to scan the papers from around the country or gossip about Spalding. [3]

In a flurry of five days, Rice performed in the "old style," next missed performances due to illness, then returned in his now "usual style." In the ring, Rice's old style—the traditional colloquy with the ringmaster, full of bold jokes and bald puns—overlapped with his new style of refined jesting, but he increasingly emphasized the latter. So did his publicity.

Rice next sailed his Hippodrome circus across the Gulf to Mobile. There, expectation was on tip-toe. "Mere circuses bear as little relation" to Rice's "as amateur performances do to professional dramatic efforts." He arrived to the worst rain Mobile had seen in a quarter century, yet still opened on November 18 in a building jammed with people.

> "Dan" was here some five years ago, and then established a reputation which has not been forgotten or equaled since that time. We have had the "Queen's Jester," Wallett, and any number of other harlequins, but for real *artistic merit*—for the power of producing the broad and irresistable laugh—none have approached Dan Rice. . . . He is the unquestioned Yorick of his tribe![4]

Rice had to compete with the twentieth century in the form of "Chloroform, or Mobile a Century Hence," a play predicting that 1952 would see air transportation, theaters on electric ships, and kisses sent by lightning. Next to those wonders, asked the *Register,* what were "the Hippodrome of Rice, the Floating Palace of Spalding, or the Railroad to Ohio"? Rice was fined when he did not get a license, which inspired the *Register* to word play: "In fine, Dan got mulct in a fine. . . . Dan may be fined, or refined, easier than we can find another Dan like him." However, he was now well known for turning adversity to advantage. "But Dan is rich—rich in pelf—and richer still in humor, and we have not the slightest doubt that he will make more jokes out of the trial than it cost him in dollars."[5]

Mid-December, Spalding's elegant *Floating Palace* bobbed into view. The feud was fading. Spalding had seen the mistake of directly challenging Rice, who himself muted his tone, in part because he could not afford to continue the battle. Glenroy estimated that the feud cost his former boss $100,000 in legal fees and damages. A man who sued Rice got poetic advice the clown himself might have heeded:

> If life's all sugar and honey,
> And fortune has always been sunny,
> If you wish to get rid of your money,
> I'd have you go to law.[6]

Van Orden as usual overplayed Spalding's hand, inflating the pitch of middle-class refinement in the *Floating Palace* into the "luxurious tastes of the aristocracy." Spalding had his own license problems. Every town charged for a license to exhibit, usually $10 to $20 daily (though New Orleans required theaters and amphitheaters to pay $950 for the winter season in state, city, and Charity Hospital tax). He had planned to avoid the daily expense by asserting that the navigation license for his waterborne *Palace* was sufficient. Baton Rouge authorities were not persuaded; they impounded his boat and took him to court. Spalding's lawyers argued that the federal navigation license superseded local fees, but national authority was a weak argument in 1853 and Spalding had to pay.[7]

After offering a $100 Dan Rice's Purse for a pacing race at the Mobile track, and taking his final benefit, Rice shipped out January 10 on the *California,* its fresh paint glistening in the sun, and its wharf and deck both crowded. All Mobile, it seemed, turned out to send "Capt. Dan" off in style." He set his orchestra on the upper deck, "where they did, indeed, 'discourse most eloquent music.'" His horses were stabled below. "We know not how many horse power the California had in her engine, but she had a mortal quantity of horse power on her forward deck."[8]

Another troupe, which may have been Rice's, replaced him in Mobile. Led by his manager, Whitbeck, it had a roster featuring those who had worked for Rice, including Jean Johnson, O'Connell—boasting a "an enormous beaver of the Western Texas style"—and Messemer on the cornet-a-piston, the new invention with keys. This troupe had performed in New Orleans before Rice set up his tent there, preceded him to Mobile with the old Star State Circus title, then returned to New Orleans without that title. Now they were back in Mobile again, in the building that Rice had left behind, labeled, like his own troupe, "Dan Rice's Hippodrome." Rice was an "untiring caterer in the amusement line, who sought to excel Barnum in the rapid production of novelties."[9]

His major venture of the season, Dan Rice's Museum, opened in New Orleans on November 26. Precursors of today's specialized edifices, museums developed from random accumulations of unusual items. Paintings, fossils, freaks of nature—anything fit as long as people would pay two bits to see it. "Museum" and "amusement" each had root in the Muses. Just so, the projectors of these jumbles—Moses Kimball in Boston, John Scudder and Rubens Peale in New York, then Barnum and his American Museum, and now—proclaimed that they simultaneously amused and instructed. New Orleans had seen small collections, but nothing on the scale of Rice's museum, reported to have cost $75,000. Information on daily operations comes from a Rice ledger, the surviving scraps of which cover the first month. Items included $170 to Whitbeck, running the amphitheater across the way while Rice was in Mobile. On opening day in the rented four-story building on St. Charles, the *Crescent* writer enjoyed a two-hour ramble through "50,000 Antique and Natural Curiosities," but only a hundred others showed up; meanwhile, expenses piled up. Advertisements cost $3–$6 each week in the *Crescent, Picayune, Delta, Bee, Republican,* and French-language *Orleanium.* Another major expense was lighting. Rice paid for candles, limelight, and gas; one-third of the daily receipts went to the gas man—a supplier's way of ensuring payment. More exotic charges included 75¢ for a blacksmith to shoe the wooly mare, a supposedly new species, and $4 for "cosmorama glasses." The cosmorama, invented in 1808, was a glorified peepshow, a room with lenses—"glasses"—in a wall to make the panoramas behind them, of ancient ruins, Niagara Falls, or ships at sea, look realistic. The cosmorama had fallen into low repute in the United States, and special scorn was heaped on Barnum's at the American Museum; but the cosmorama was revived when Hubert Sattler arrived from Europe in 1850 with an elaborate collection of images and the transforming idea to remake the viewing space into a middle-class parlor.[10]

Another ledger entry gives a glimpse of Rice's character while solving a small mystery. His boss with the Learned Pig, C. L. Kise, had dropped from the historical record, but the ledger records payments to a C. L. Kys. The money, a few bits here and there, and $3 on Christmas Eve, suggest a handout for a friend down on his luck. Similarly, Rice hired John Gossin, who had been what Rice was becoming, the "Grimaldi of America," a special favorite in New Orleans and New York. Though blessed with talent and looks, his long black hair worn in ringlets, and well liked by everybody, Gossin had long been a drunk. Nevertheless, Rice hired the broken man. This February 1853 engagement was Gossin's last. Rice always bragged about his solitary start in life to emphasize the distance he had traveled, but that was for public consumption. Privately, he remained loyal to the companions he made on his way.[11]

Back from Mobile in January, Rice returned to a museum seemingly about to expire. Receipts had not run far ahead of expenses. Daily attendance sunk as low as a paltry five or six. Barnum had made $1,500 a week in the early days of his American Museum; Rice was bringing in about $200.[12] Barnum had become a museum manager on site, figuring out what worked through his mistakes, just as Dan had learned performance through his own early mistakes. By contrast, Rice had been trying to learn how to run a museum from miles away, while managing his circus business, and performing, too. Empire building is not easy. A final ledger page dribbled away in random items: corn meal 25¢, apples 10¢, milk 20¢, alcohol 20¢. This grocery list evokes the picture of a caretaker in an empty hall, apple cores at his feet, eating mush and getting drunk.

But Rice did not give up. He hired his friend from Baltimore, Dr. William T. Leonard, as manager. (Whitbeck left for Havana with a troupe.) A legitimate doctor, Leonard had also been editor of the *Southern Ladies' Book,* a monthly. Now he turned his attention to the Museum.[13]

Boldly, Rice and Leonard did not retrench, but rented a larger building, a brick one at 107 St. Charles. New ads claimed 100,000 curiosities, double the original boast. They promised wild animals; the two largest "Mosaic Paintings" in the world; the country's most extensive collection of birds; a model of every building in San Francisco; and a painting of Belshazzar's Feast. The painting was a joke referring to Dan which the Bible-reading age would enjoy: Belshazzar was the biblical king at whose feast the prophet Daniel read the writing on the wall. The projectors added a lecture room. Rice's fondness for music came into play, as a band now held forth on the balcony, floating tunes over the heads of St. Charles amusement seekers. Boldly, Rice and Leonard raised the admission to 50¢ to create snob appeal. Barnum later testified to the value of this strategy when he quoted Seth Howes in a letter about a venture in England: High prices "would fill our tents with royalty, nobility & gentry—whereas if we charged *less,* those classes would not attend at all & mix with the rabble." Similarly grandly, Rice's rocks, bugs, and shells became specimens of "MINERALOGY, ENTOMOLOGY, and CONCHOLOGY." The snob appeal appealed to the snobbish *Delta.* "Mr. Rice has laid the foundation of a most instructive and agreeable resort, and we do hope he will meet with the encouragement from the citizens of New Orleans that his institution and his enterprise deserve. In establishing a Museum of natural and historical curiosities, Mr. Rice is filling a hiatus severely felt in this city." By mid-February, the ads boasted a million curiosities. As an indication of rejuvenation, a year later Rice declared this January 25 re-opening the start of the Museum.[14]

Meanwhile, Rice and his circus company had steamed back to New Orleans on January 13 on a flood tide of praise copied from Mobile. Rice would "witch the world with wondrous horsemanship." Despite Spalding's show, "No circus, past or present can produce greater variety, or produces more winning skill." Rice "certainly has the golden-egg goose." The Crescent City added its own encomiums. "From the 'One Horse Show,' as in derision his enemies were wont to denominate his Circus, he has built up the most magnificent establishment of the kind in the country," it was a "manufactory of fun." As for Rice, whether "as the clown, as the refined jester or as the broad negro, he is equally good." He could keep the audience enthralled even when, on a private bet, he did not say anything throughout a performance. He was a "genius," a "wizard."

When words failed, they made up new ones: He introduced new traits of "clownism"; crowds thronged to his "funniements."[15]

This season repeatedly saw Rice linked to Barnum. In Mobile, Rice "determines to excel Barnum." Rice's Hippodrome was so great that the *Crescent* knew "not what to call Dan Rice, a Barnum, or an Astley or Franconi, or whether we shall at once acknowledge that he combines the prominent traits of character of all of them." By mid-February, Rice's agent, Castle, was in town, helping push the idea that Rice, "like Barnum, figuratively speaking, is always getting up something new" at his Hippodrome. As a manager, Rice was the "Barnum of New Orleans."[16]

Celebrity is the talent for social appeal, whether in jokes or writing, singing or parties, politics or seduction. Of course, publicity plays a role, but it is more than that, or Barnum would have rendered all his attractions as popular as Lind. Castle could have done little had Rice not filled the bill. As a talking clown, he delivered hits on the times "red hot and still heating." The *Delta* used his Museum as springboard for a jab at politics and Barnum.

> A Desideratum.—Wanted immediately, for Dan Rice's museum, a person who can bring reliable proof that he ever read a President's message, all through . . . It is supposed that after a short and profitable engagement with Rice, he can make a most lucrative engagement with Barnum, in New York, who has still left the bouquets and carpet used on the arrival of Jenny Lind.

Similarly suited for the Museum, thought the *Crescent*, was the fiery Speaker of the Louisiana House, E. Warren Moise. "Can't Dan Rice cage this celebrated wild animal?" Then there was the "Finale of the Senatorial Farce," in which a handful of Democrats had blustered about unseating a Whig, only to have their effort fizzle. "Our democratic friends must get up their dramas better, or they will cease to draw in competition with such ingenious caterers for public amusement as Dan Rice."[17]

Rice was no passive symbol, though, on which others expatiated. Hamlet calls acting a mirror to nature, and that metaphor of reflection has become embedded in cultural memory. Yet Hamlet's creator, Shakespeare, showed a more comprehensive understanding of performance as both a reaction to the world—the mirror metaphor—and a creation adding to it, a new proposition for the audience to consider. As Rice expanded his scope through the feud, he came to the same knowledge as he mirrored cultural themes and proposed them. In Mobile, his Hippodrome ad had promised important information on the mayoral election that week. Back in New Orleans, he announced that he had news from California to pass on to his audience. For "Dan Rice's Valedictory," he sang of his One-Horse Show—a "candy stand" compared to his current Hippodrome—and of state legislators complaining how hard they worked, while sipping sherry cobblers. The governor could fuss that a new law intruded on his powers, but "such change is all the rage, / And we behindhand must not be, / In this progressive age." With a close race for the state supreme court, Rice added verses criticizing the negative campaigns, with "party tricks" and "running t'other down." Rice then latched on to an old joke: To avoid partisan wrangle, Louisiana could turn to him as a compromise candidate, for "as precedents must rule, / That man the best Chief Justice makes / Who is the greatest fool." As the *Crescent* saw it, there was little that escaped "Rice's quick perception and sagacious appreciation. In the ring, he always gives the last joke, and, whether it be trade in cotton or diplomacy concerning Nicaragua, he has his comical idea and coins his gold, and political and commercial speculators may thank their stars if they fare half as well."[18]

Next Rice joined prominent citizens, including the mayor, in endorsing a "scheme"—the word then not suggesting disreputable practice—for a lottery. The featured prizes were $1,000 and a special edition of *Ornithology,* by the former New Orleans drawing teacher, James Audubon. An ad for the lottery recorded a dialogue between Rice and his ringmaster, who announced that he had just bought a chance in the lottery.

> **DAN:** —Well, why did you do so? Did you not know that I had done so before you, and picked out the very number that is going to win the big prize? You know very well that I am the luckiest man in the world, and that I always win. Don't you recollect our one-horse show? Everybody thought at the time that we had a full troupe of horses, and were, consequently, as well satisfied as if they had seen them all in operation. Everything depends on how matters are managed, and by whom. Now, if the chances should be against me, and I should not win anything great in Spear & Co.'s Lottery, I will still have gratification in knowing

> that I have assisted in carrying out a good purpose. Don't you perceive that this scheme will be the means of disseminating a vast amount of knowledge throughout this great and growing community? . . . That Spear is a whole team, and hard to beat.

Rice's refined jester was a civic booster. Still, the older comic traditions asserted themselves as the ringmaster called Rice an artificial fool, the clown objected, and the ringmaster cracked his whip at him.

> DAN: —Now, ladies and gentlemen, old and young, black and colored! [Ha! Ha! Ha! From a darkey in the pit] What are you?—Molasses-colored gentleman? [Laughter and cries of Go on! Go on!] Well, as I was going to say, I want you, one and all, to go to Spear & Co.'s and give them a benefit.

The casual racism of the day included confused racial categories, with the "darkey" neither white, black, nor colored.[19]

Spring blew new breezes. On March 1, Rice's Museum became the Great Southern Museum. The press continued to use the old name, and Rice was listed as proprietor, but Leonard's stake probably increased. Rice would not have allowed his name to be taken off the Museum without financial persuasion, probably debt to Leonard. The papers took new notice. There were now "pictures in oil, painted pictures, printed pictures and pictures done with plaster of Paris." The *Picayune* mentioned curiosities from Africa, China, and—cracking a joke on their backwater neighbor—"at least one from Texas." There were the Soirees Magiques of Professor Jocko, a minstrel troupe, and the Wild Boy of Ceylon. Rice and Leonard made an explicit appeal to respectability: "A Lady is always present to give polite attention to Ladies and Families." An important element of the Museum was the lecture room, which made the claim of education manifest. The "Zeugladon," a one-hundred-foot "Great Sea Monster" fossil discovered in Alabama in 1848, was fascinating by itself, but the experience became richer—and more respectable—with the lecture of a Dr. Koch. Though the jumble of attractions at the Museum seems unscientific, it was not frivolous. Louis Agassiz, the famous naturalist and Harvard professor, came to New Orleans the same season for the same reasons as Rice's Dr. Koch, to lecture on natural history to inquisitive citizens.[20] The Wild Men of Borneo may have been slaves, as many such exhibited "natives" were, and the Zeugladon might have been a fake, but, as people turned their gaze to the Pacific seas or into prehistory, the ground was being prepared for the work of anthropologists, and for the ideas of Darwin. Though antebellum Americans were often narrow-minded, they also grappled with topics beyond their habitual world.

For a reputed $4,000 wager at the end of March, the Museum pitted its grizzly, General Jackson, in a fight against a bull, Santa Anna. For publicity, "his huge Bearship" was paraded through the streets. The battle in a cage twenty feet square was to be held across the river in Gretna, out of reach of city authorities, just as Shakespeare's Globe, bear baitings, and houses of prostitution stood safely across the Thames from London's law. Crescent City feelings were mixed. The *Picayune* approved, but the *Delta* called it shameful, more suited to Madrid than to genteel New Orleans. "If this encounter is regarded by any sane person in the light of 'sport,' we would like to know what their notion of brutality is." However, as ferries carried 3,000 people to the spectacle, including political candidates, the *Delta* devoted a full column to excited description. Just as sensationalist press peddled sex and gore while declaiming piously about public service, the *Delta* excused its extensive coverage: "We do not think that the recital is calculated to give much encouragement" to such an amusement.[21]

Wirh mint juleps in season as April began, Rice concluded his long run. First, though, he hosted a grand entertainment for the press at his hotel. He had no need of publicity at that point. His benefit performance for the firemen was now so customary that the *Delta* regarded it as an annual event, and his own benefit on April 1 would be filled by a simple mention in the bills. Yet he was looking to seasons ahead, building goodwill. He also sent the *Delta* a basket of champagne, which yielded its longest item on him, "In Vino Veritas." Still, it did not name him, perhaps worried that its status as arbiter of esthetic tastes would be compromised by too close an association. Nevertheless, the omission showed that it expected its readers to know who Rice was. Meanwhile, the *Picayune* called him the "king of clowns, the most pushing, persevering, unconquered and unconquerable fellow that ever made a stand up fight with misfortune." At his establishment, all is "superior to any circus appointments that have ever been in the South."[22]

Leonard's energy kept the Southern Museum humming after Rice left. To call attention to a changed function, advertisements said the lecture room would open in May, even though it had been part of the operation since January. Leonard presented plays under the guise of "lectures," providing an excuse for those who considered themselves too moral to attend theater. After months of barely noticing the Museum except to complain, the prim *Delta* drizzled praise: "Mr. Rice, who has, with commendable zeal, established a Museum in this city . . . has built a Lecture Room in connection with the Museum, in which dramatic entertainments will be given *a la* Barnum, in New York."[23]

Like Barnum, Rice tried to become an institution himself, his name representative of a constellation of enterprises. As a clown, Rice was unsurpassed. Yet as a showman, though he had the know-how to present exhibitions well, he did not achieve Barnum's deft touch. Of all Rice's ventures that winter—the circus he brought to New Orleans, the Museum he established, the Amphitheater troupe in which he may have had a hand, the Hippodrome troupe he took to Mobile, and the Hippodrome arena he left behind there—the ones that flourished were those that featured him. Always a sufficient condition for drawing crowds, Rice continued to be a necessary one.

14

SEE THE ELEPHANT

Rice was proud of his 5,000-seat tent. Scorning expense, he had a large lithograph made, "The Newly Constructed Pavilion for Dan Rice's Great Hippodrome & Menagerie." Like a heaping custard pie rising to the sky, the big top is crowned by four American flags. The sidewall sections stretch into the distance, as if covering acres of ground. People clustered at the ticket tent off to one side, and at the main tent, all show the tip-top of respectability: women in bonnets and men in top hats, bumpkins and rowdies nowhere to be seen. The sidewall is pulled open to reveal four acts performing for an audience in a semicircular hint of the ring. The central figure is the central image of the circus: a running horse and a rider. The rider, carrying a girl on his shoulder and wearing a flowing top and plumed beret, is performing a scenic act, with a rescue in the Romantic vein. To the left, a woman rears on her horse, and to the right, a minstrel in striped pants and curly wig plays a banjo. Further right, two clowns play leapfrog, one with the phallic hint of a stick between his legs. Rice

A view of the tent on the lot, idealized to omit the "outside" shows, games of chance, pickpockets, and local rowdies.

does not appear in the scene, probably because the lithographer created an image that could be used for another circus if Dan didn't pay.

Two other omissions are more telling. Few children appear in the lithograph, reflecting the adult nature of the antebellum circus. Youngsters did attend when the advent of the circus in a country town created a holiday; and in cities, circuses were starting to present family matinees. Meanwhile, footloose boys—bootblacks, messengers, stable hands—frequented theaters and circuses. But mostly circus focused on grownups eager for the risqué jokes, the horsemanship and physical prowess, and the titillation of legs in tights. Even the "pea-nuts" and sweets were for adults, who rarely got treats. Also mostly omitted from the lithograph were black people, only two showing. This absence did not reflect fact as much as hide it. Blacks attended in the North, while shows in the South could barely have survived without their patronage. The lithograph's virtual erasure of blacks sent a reassuring message to anxious whites that they would be comfortably in a majority.[1]

On tour, caged animals and curiosities from Rice's museum were set up on one side in the tent for viewing before the performance. Fifty cents—higher than city prices—bought a view of a "Brazilian Tiger," the grizzly, an ostrich and an "ourang outang." Macaws screeched in a flutter of feathers, monkeys scolded a mongoose, and a pair of alligators stared impassively at the passing world. Rice was one of the first to exhibit many of these wild animals along the Mississippi. There were also wax figures, including one of Lajos Kossuth, a Hungarian revolutionary who had received a hero's welcome in New Orleans during Rice's 1851–1852 run. The living human exhibits included the Wild Boy of Ceylon, a "lusus naturae," or joke of nature. A Chinese family, playing their native long-necked banjos and gongs, featured the "most beautiful creature of her high class who ever escaped from the celestial empire," teenage Princess Pwan Yeko—and her feet. Foot binding had stunted them to 2½", said the advertising.[2]

Rice claimed 1,000 features, in a song, "Dan Rice's Welcome," fifty-seven verses long. "My show of horses had but one, / I've now 'E Pluribus Unum.'" Not letting go of the feud yet, he still made jabs at the hog-napping confidence man, Van Orden. He sang of his lump of California gold, of the Happy Family, a mixture of small animals and birds, and of his own family, "Dame Rice" and Katey and Libby, "two chips from the old block." He also sang of his comic mules. He had used a single one the previous winter, but this was the first time anyone had presented a pair. The highlight of the act was simple. After a performer trotted around the ring on the apparently docile mule, customers were invited to try but, once mounted, were bucked off. Rice concluded forty verses after singing "Before I close" by apologizing for the long song that his extensive roster required, but he knew that his listeners would pay another 50¢ to see it again.[3]

The lyrics offer a glimpse of Rice's engagement of the audience. As he sang from the ring of "that little shaver, / Who, grinning, sits in that front seat," or of "Yon lady, too," who has a smile for him, Rice was doing more than dealing with the audience collectively, but playing to individuals. Rice also referred to his own presence: "So come we'll lead you to a seat." He did not adopt the performer's usual pose above the audience, akin to the third-person omniscience in a novel. Instead, he was simultaneously the storied Rice and a human being like them, assailed by misfortune and impelled by pluck. He teased his own grandness. "Now pardon, though a modest man / (And sure I hide it all I can)." Referring to the audience and to himself, he joined them to him: "First, as I am a ladies' man" was simultaneously a joke on himself and on whatever woman caught his flirtatious eye; a joke enlarging direct address in ever-widening circles to her companions, then to people in the close vicinity, and ultimately to the whole audience.

With a Hippodrome and a Menagerie, Rice was riding two popular waves. Richard Sands and his partners Avery Smith, John J. Nathans, and Seth B. Howes purchased Franconi's Hippodrome in London, built an arena for it in New York on Broadway, and transported it over in 1853. For months before the May 2 opening, papers breathlessly reported that it held over 10,000 people, and cost hundreds of thousands of dollars. So extensive was the publicity that designers and artisans were mentioned by name.[4]

Some huffed about all the puffery. A new amusement weekly, the *New York Clipper,* pointed out how much this French enterprise was homegrown and of middling talent, sprinkled with exotic associations to be "nibbled by the American gullibles after foreignisms." Because Franconi bowed to the $1 boxes but ignored the 25¢ pits, those "pitites . . . are beginning to recognize this want of true American gentility in this true representation of 'foreign airs.'" Still, the show's size, dazzle, and novelty ensured its success. It ran for seven triumphant months. In October, it was still pulling in $1,500 nightly, much better than the $500 at Barnum's American Museum and $1,000 at the Bowery Theater. In 1854, after stands in Washington, Baltimore, and Philadelphia, the show returned to New York for four more months.

Though he was no innovator, Rice had a powerful sense of contemporary excitements and astutely anticipated this one. When the drumbeat for Franconi's began, his own Hippodrome was well established. He had toured with it in the summer of 1852, and brought it south for his winter season. There, the *Crescent* had labeled his show "a new era in Circus business." As a small herd of hippodromes followed the next few years, the *Cincinnati Enquirer* complained that recently "there has not been a circus started, but was heralded and advertised as a Hippodrome. Such things as a matter of course, give the public much dissatisfaction." The word, which "should be a signal of splendor, began to be regarded as a humbug."[5]

The hippodrome's big lure was racing, an old circus feature now enlarged to include new contests, such as chariot races and monkeys riding horseback as jockeys. Franconi's had a larger arena, but on the road circus ponies dashing around the tight 42' circle offered the same excitement as the tight turns of rodeo barrel-racing. Circus races were often rigged so that the star would win, and the *Spirit of the Times* complained about a "Hippodrome humbug race." Nevertheless, even contests with a predetermined winner can be exciting, as professional wrestling shows. Glenroy recalled one race that kept going because Rice did not drop the flag to stop it after its three laps. Here was another glimpse of Rice in performance, ignoring the riders to watch the crowd, gauging the effect. Just as he would stretch a joke to the right tension until he sensed the perfect time to pop it with the punch line, he let the race continue beyond the scripted end, building the excitement. (Glenroy recalled this one because he fell and was knocked unconscious.)[6]

As for the other half of Rice's title, Menagerie, the touring world was experiencing a curious reversion. In the 1830s, menagerie and circus had competed for patrons, with animal displays ascendant, but the dynamic circus eventually took over, and menageries mostly faded away. But in 1852, for no apparent reason, menageries made a comeback. Half a dozen combined with circuses that year, followed by four in 1853, including Rice's, and three more in 1854.[7] Perhaps Rice and the other owners piggybacked on the "moral" reputation of menageries in response to some subtle religious revival, powerful but little noted, like a current surging under the apparently calm surface of the Mississippi. If not strictly religious, an impulse of reform was spreading throughout the country. Temperance advocates harangued the public. The Seneca Falls convention in 1848 made women's rights an issue. Agitation over slavery was growing. Horace Greeley was one of the more visible manifestations of reform as he used the platform of his *New York Tribune* to leap on every passing fancy. Even the vast majority who considered such causes misguided, and Greeley foolish, felt the same urge to betterment. A circus could tap into that public righteousness by presenting a menagerie. When Rice advertised that "Persons can visit the Menagerie without visiting the Hippodrome," he was stating the obvious. Of course people could enter the tent to view the animals and then leave before the performance, as people now can avoid objectionable movies. But just as campaigns today against excess in movies are part of a larger political landscape, objections to nineteenth-century performance included a desire for fellow feeling. Rice recognized that yearning for the comfort of agreement. In announcing the obvious, that people could visit the menagerie but avoid the performance, this showman was signaling his sympathy with those who objected to "show."

Another, practical reason encouraged the flurry of circus-menagerie combinations. In 1851, Seth Howes combined his touring expertise with Barnum's name and knowledge of exhibition to send out P. T. Barnum's Asiatic Caravan, Museum and Menagerie. The two showmen toured the spectacle for four years, to great profits and critical scorn. Newspapers from big-city Brooklyn to small-town Illinois considered the Caravan a shabby affair. When Rice played Cincinnati in July 1852, he got little press, while the Asiatic Caravan received plenty, though it was regarded as a low-rate affair, and Barnum the "humbugger of humbugs." But money talks, and it told circus owners that people would pay for variety, especially under the label of morality. Rice recognized trends, and was quick to leap to the front of them.[8]

In June, Rice brought his Hippodrome & Menagerie to Cincinnati. When he offered a benefit for any purpose the mayor chose, the *Enquirer* insisted that Rice "should be held in high estimation by those who reap the benefit of his charitable deeds. When here with his one-horse show (as he calls it) last week, he gave the whole receipts of one performance to the poor." The piece concluded with words that were music to any showman's ears: "We would, therefore, recommend DAN'S establishment to the public and to the press wherever he may go."[9]

Rice reaped another benefit from his benefits: They became weapons against Spalding, as the feud simmered down to a rivalry. When the fight had raged hot, Rice had aimed his animosity at Van Orden. Increasingly though, Rice shoved Van Orden off the stage and instead depicted a struggle between two equals, Spalding and himself. One peaceful way to carry on the contest was through charity, a battle of nice. On August 27, back in Cincinnati, Rice and Spalding held dueling benefits for New Orleans cholera sufferers. But Spalding upstaged himself by giving himself a complimentary benefit. The *Enquirer* mentioned that event in the same issue that it announced that Rice had raised $371 for New Orleans relief, with nary a word about Spalding's contribution.[10]

Though long past his struggles with a single horse, Rice would place the story of his One-Horse Show in 1853. He also set two important fictions in this year. Rice said that his father became a bank president in 1853, though it had been a quarter century earlier; and the clown bragged that he had been sent by President Pierce to carry dispatches to Queen Victoria and had shaken her hand, saying, "My dear Madame, this is the American fashion." That he set these three fictions in 1853 suggests the importance the year had for him: It was the year he acquired permanent winter quarters.[11]

Midsummer, Rice brought his circus to Girard, Pennsylvania, 120 miles north of Pittsburgh. A small village in the far northwestern corner of the state, where it bumps up to meet Lake Erie, like a chimney on the state's roof, Girard was on the rise. Northwestern Pennsylvania's major east–west road was Girard's Main Street, and north–south traffic increased in 1845 when a canal on the borough's western border connected Lake Erie to rivers down to Pittsburgh. Seeing itself ripe for a boom, the village of four hundred incorporated in 1846, naming itself for the township in which it sat, in turn named for the Philadelphia millionaire, Stephen Girard. (He was honored for having helped finance the War of 1812, which saw a major naval battle on nearby Lake Erie.) When Rice was playing New Orleans over the winter of 1852–1853, he would have read of the completion of the Erie railroad past Girard, which cut the time between Buffalo and Cleveland from two days to eight hours.[12]

A year earlier, Agrippa Martin, an animal trainer, had invited Rice to consider the area, but Dan already knew it, ever since his original trek west. Also, a dozen miles northeast lay Erie, where he had hidden from the adultery charge. The South was cozy for Rice, with mutual affinity and great success, but he had grown to manhood in the North, felt its habits, its ways of thinking and speaking. He knew in his bones the dramatic changes of Northern seasons that occasional Crescent City snow could not duplicate. He had come of age tramping the thick forests of oak, maple, and elm, and knew them better than the trailing vines and thick mists of the bayous. More practically, he must have realized the importance of a Northern base if he was to expand beyond regional prominence. Girard afforded plenty of land and access for his circus East or South in the summer, and himself to the Northeast for winter circuses.

Looking back, a local remembered when the clown came to Girard:

> Myself and the boy who was with me were waiting for the arrival of the circus on the bridge that spanned Main street. . . . About noon time we saw a boat coming north and knew it must be the circus. I ran down the towpath to meet the boat and saw a man standing on the hurricane deck who I recognized from the picture on the billboards as Dan Rice. He was a fine looking man with no facial adornment. At that time he was about thirty years old. A fine specimen of physical manhood. I have heard it said that when armed with a wagon spoke he could lick a dozen men, which he often did in a circus fight.

(Rice had not yet grown his goatee.)[13]

When Rice made $3,000 in Pittsburgh on the Fourth of July, receipts "never before equaled in the Western country," he didn't spend it on jewels this time. After playing Girard on July 21, he bought land on the north side of Girard's public square, paying Col. John McClure $18,000. Leery of creditors, he put the property in Maggie's name. Though poverty had stopped knocking on the door, Rice remained ill adept financially. In Memphis, he had been forced to sell his steamboat, the *James Laughlin,* for $10,000 to pay salaries. In May, he had been demitted from the Masons; lodge records do not explain why his membership was revoked, but the usual reason is failure to pay dues. (He later ignored that awkward detail and claimed that he had been a Mason most of his life.)[14]

The season of 1853 was notable for Rice for another reason: He completed a trio of animal acts that would form a fundamental part of his reputation. He already owned the comic mules and Excelsior, which was garnering singular attention as the "Pearl of the Euphrates."[15] Now he would "see the elephant." That antebellum phrase, probably originating in literal usage some time after the first elephant was brought to America in 1812, connoted wisdom gained through experience, often painful.

The elephant Rice saw was a small one. Originally called Jenny Lind from 1848 to 1851, she was then Juliet, paired with a pachyderm Romeo at Franconi's Hippodrome. Rice bought the elephant and renamed her Lalla Rookh. The name resonated for antebellum audiences. In 1817, the Irish poet, Thomas Moore, the most popular songwriter in the English-speaking world before Stephen Foster, had used that title for a poem, telling of an exotic Eastern princess—Moore said "Lalla Rookh" meant "tulip cheek"—torn between duty in an arranged marriage and love for the troubadour escorting her to that marriage, before she discovers that he is her betrothed in disguise. Passages in his poem, perhaps the most translated of the time, were favorites of "romantic school girls and love sick boys." When Moore died, one obituary praised him over Alexander Pope, and his contemporaries were sure that "Lalla Rookh" assured him literary immortality.[16]

Rice often said that he had trained Lalla Rookh, but his 1857 *Pictorial* credited Charles Noyes. Only twenty-one, Noyes was already one of the age's best animal men. In 1853, he was working for Franconi when he left with the elephant and a white camel for Columbus, Ohio, where Rice was playing. The transfer seems suspicious; Franconi was unlikely to give up such a talented elephant easily. The story is told that Noyes had trained her on the sly; but he told only of the trip west, the first instance, he said, of an elephant's being transported by rail, during which she mischievously pulled the bell signaling a stop.[17]

Noyes arrived with Lalla Rookh in mid-August, and two days later Rice advertised her as "recently imported." It is not clear what her initial skills were, but other elephants were walking on hind and fore knees, standing on two feet, and walking over the trainer, without a word as a signal. Rice also offered customers the chance to "SEE AND RIDE THE ELEPHANT" around the ring. Lalla Rookh was valuable for publicity: An article in the *Crescent,* "Seeing the Real Elephant," told of a pachyderm promenade in the Crescent City. A gentleman walking home one evening felt a tap on his shoulder and turned, indignant at the familiarity. But it was not a stranger's hand, it was the raised trunk of Rice's elephant. As was Lalla Rookh's custom, explained the writer, "he carried his trunk with him." (The story changed the elephant's gender: A woman approaching a man on the street at night conveys a different meaning.) Though not intending to frighten the man, and only "careless in handling his baggage," the elephant was so mortified that the paper considered it unlikely that he (she) would appear again that season.[18]

Before his annual turn downriver, Rice played St. Louis, where the *News* declared that "the great hippodrome man" introduced a "never-to-be-forgotten era in the affairs of the universal Puke nation"—Missouri. He had been touring a Great Hippodrome for the past two seasons, so a turn to the superlative was natural. In November, he promised more than the ordinary circus performance, and instead "the greatest show that ever traveled." Decades before other circuses used the phrase, an Arkansas paper praised Rice's as "the greatest show on earth."[19]

15

PEOPLE'S CHOICE

The public conversations of performance and politics both increasingly engaged America's abiding dilemma, slavery. On January 23, 1854, Stephen Douglas introduced the Kansas-Nebraska Bill in the Senate. His attempt to solve the problem, the bill would in effect repeal the Missouri Compromise, which prohibited the extension of slavery into the Northern territories. Though that compromise had become nearly sacrosanct, Douglas judged that continuing squabbles made a change necessary. Popular sovereignty, his notion that each territory be allowed to choose slavery or not, seemed an obviously democratic solution. Power to the people. In part, he based his judgment on a belief that slavery concerned few people—if you discounted the views of slaves, and nearly everybody but slaves did. Because abolition was still a fringe idea, an "abominable fanaticism," as Whitman put it, pragmatists believed that slavery was a veil over the real issue of power politics, each section convinced that the other was seeking national domination. Economics exacerbated the struggle. The South considered the emerging industries of the

North a threat to "nearly equally distributed" wealth across regions, though Louisiana and South Carolina had more than double the national average of $356 a person.[1] Each side, cloaking itself in the Constitution, sniffed conspiracy in the other side. Complicating matters, both sides were racist, which meant that few people, even abolitionists, could see a place for Negroes in the civic life of the United States. The country would be fine, thought a majority North and South, if only white Southern fire-eaters would return to their duels, and Northern white reformers to their Free Love or socialistic Fourierism.

The Constitution sanctioned slavery, but many hoped that the "peculiar institution" would die a natural death, a hope that grew as it became hemmed into the Southeast. Even Southerners considered the possibility of freed slaves. In 1851, the *Crescent* contemplated a reported decrease in slavery in Virginia and Maryland: "At this rate both of these states will, in ten years, be ready for abolition." Three years later, the *Delta* interrupted its attacks on abolitionists to quote, without comment, an English journal predicting the likely end of "barbarous and obsolete" slavery. However, Douglas's bill, by making slavery theoretically legal everywhere, rubbed the North's face in it, driving many closer to abolition, or at least to a fear that a Slave Power did control national affairs. In response to the abolitionists—and to guilt—the South was shifting from apology to self-righteous bluster: Slaves were like family in the South, contented and cared for, and slavery was good for the country. In "Abolitionism Vs. Republicanism," the *Mobile Register* argued that the South's paternalistic slavery was a republican bulwark against the raging torrent of democratic liberty that had flooded revolution across Europe.[2]

About the time Douglas introduced the Kansas-Nebraska Bill, Rice picked up the issue. He brought Joseph Field's dramatic company from Mobile to New Orleans and presented their *Uncle Tom's Cabin,* "by Mrs. Harriet Screecher Blow." Harriet Beecher Stowe's 1852 novel, *Uncle Tom's Cabin,* a scathing attack on slavery, had become became an international sensation, extended by many dramatizations. Though some thought the play adaptations simply presented a good story, others saw their political ramifications. The *Clipper* objected to one 1853 version as "calculated to open afresh the breach which has just been closed between the different sections of the Union." The version Rice presented, though full of jokes, had a serious side, indicated in the subtitle, "Life in The South As It Is." The *Delta* gave its readers an excerpt, repeating the point made on Southern editorial pages, in Northern songs, and in Congress: Slaves were happy in the South, and did not need Northerner's ignorant concern.

> Uncle Tom's Cabin.—(Scene—Uncle Tom, shivering and forlorn, amid the inclemencies of a Canadian winter. A Philanthropist approaches.)
>
> **PHIL.** —Well, Uncle Tom, you seem to be in trouble? What do you want?
> **TOM.** —Dunno, Massa.
> **PHIL.** —Do you want a home?
> **TOM.** —No, Massa.
> **PHIL.** —Do you want money?
> **TOM.** —No, Massa.
> **PHIL.** —Do you want clothes?
> **TOM.** —No, Massa.
> **PHIL.** —Well, what do you want?
>
> (In the distance, the strains of 'Old Folks at Home' are indistinctly heard, and Uncle Tom, listening with tears in his eyes, breaks out, saying—'Massa—that's what I want!')

Like this song of Foster's, better known as "Swanee River," the play argued that slaves preferred warmth to freedom. Dan and the Foster boys came of age in the Democratic politics of western Pennsylvania, where sympathy for the workingman did not extend to the slave.[3]

The show was a hit. Houses overflowed, and the papers raved that it was true to life. The *Crescent* found the play artistic, full of "drollery, with something of the pathos and experience of negro life." The *Picayune* offered its opinion: "great run at Dan's . . . well got up . . . well acted." The colloquy with Uncle Tom, declared the *Delta*, "brought tears into the eyes of almost every one present, in the same manner as other points produced irresistible laughter." The *Delta* expanded its usually minimal coverage of Rice to call the play "pathetic," meaning poignant, and "ludicrous," funny. "The Canadian snow scene, where amid old pines bending under waves of snow and glittering with ice, the fugitives long to get home, and sing the popular song, 'Carry me back to Old Virginny,' is quite melodramatic and also exceedingly correct." ("Melo-dramatic" referred to a harmonious blend of music and drama.) Topping it all, the *Spirit of the Times* made Dan's nightly throng into national news.[4]

Settling into a pattern of winters in the South and summers in the North, Rice had returned to New Orleans to open "Dan Rice's Amphitheatre" on December 3. Under construction since the summer, the 2,000-seat building opposite Perdido Street stood two doors down from the St. Charles Theatre. Though accounts called Rice the owner, it belonged to the builder, George Lawrason. The dress circle formed a horseshoe around the ring, sweeping up in "Amphitheatrical form" so that everybody could see over the row in front; above the dress circle was a balcony, labeled the "Parquette." Behind the ring stood the stage, with doors on either side to the dressing rooms underneath and to the stables out back. Elegant saloons offered space for promenades, conversation, and liquor. Though impressive, the structure had flaws. Too many of the seats were far back, and the balcony obstructed views on the main floor.[5]

Joining the praise, the *Delta* dipped into nostalgia: "Early memories . . . the old brook, the quiet old horse. . . . Who cannot recollect the first time he ever went to the circus show?" When crowds at the Amphitheatre blocked St. Charles Street, the paper returned to the exciting present: Dan "goes ahead with more vigor, the greater the competition he has. He is emphatically a People's man." (The paper had made the same point earlier, in what was praise in 1848 but would not be so in later years, that Rice led a troupe of "Red Republicans of the histrionic school," referring to a socialist movement in England, and to its newspaper, which published the first English translation of the *Communist Manifesto.*)[6]

Rice had planned to take his company to Mobile after a short run, to be replaced while he was away by Madame Tourniaire and her family, but when that French troupe was delayed getting downriver from St. Louis, he stayed on. He couldn't allow his new Amphitheatre to go dark immediately after opening. He continued through the Christmas rowdiness, such as those throwing "torpedoes"—firecrackers. On January 3, Louise Tourniaire arrived with her troupe. "Fat, not very fair, but forty," she was the most graceful equestrienne of the day, performing in ordinary riding dress as she rode both bareback and saddled. The *Delta* saw "more grace displayed . . . than we ever witnessed in the most fashionable ball rooms,"

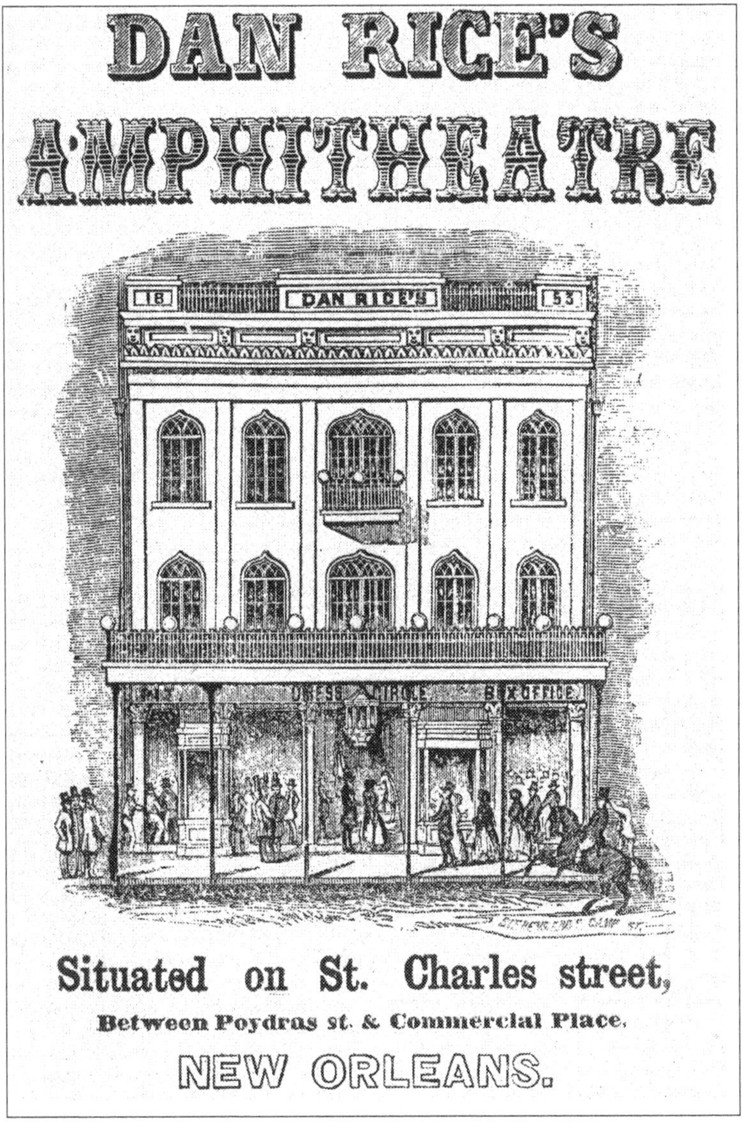

Rice's name stood high over New Orleans's vibrant St. Charles Street, with his Amphitheatre and the Dan Rice Museum.

and the *Picayune* discerned evidence of the good taste of the one who had hired her, Rice.[7]

When he did take a troupe to Mobile, he left Lalla Rookh, his "Dwarf Elephant," behind at the Southern Museum, now a pair of four-story brick buildings, at 107 and 109 St. Charles. The prices had been reduced to their original levels. Two bits, children 15¢, bought a look at a horned chicken said to be a cross between a barnyard bantam and a bull. Three special attractions heightened interest: A magician, Professor Joseph Warner; the Mysterious Lady, who allegedly inhabited a six-inch brass ball, and could answer any question or sing; and the Fat Lady, Mrs. Graham, weighing eight hundred pounds.[8]

Dan's troupe returned from Mobile at the end of January, swapping places with the Tourniaires. He vied for audiences with Louis Gottschalk's symphony for ten pianos, "Bunker Hill;" the acrobatic Ravels at the St. Charles; and Van Amburgh's menagerie, now showing on the *Floating Palace.* Spalding's barge had not worked as a circus arena, so he rented it out. The editor of the *Crescent,* declaring that more people went to Rice's show than to both theaters combined, told of hearing "the shouts of applause ringing from Dan Rice's even while we write." The paper's fondness for Rice was so pronounced that when three ropes were stretched from its office to the Museum roof, the *Delta* teased that Dan was "obliged to have two or three *lines from the Crescent before he can hoist his flag.*" Some of the plaudits were for Maggie, greater this once than for Dan. "Mrs. Rice's riding is always much admired for the grace and intrepidity it displays, and Dan's jesting in the ring is very amusing."[9]

Rice lost two friends this winter. The tattooed stalwart of the one-horse show, James F. O'Connell, died on January 29. Jimmy had remained loyal to Dan, who stayed faithful in turn, carrying him when he grew sick. As O'Connell lay dying, he asked Jean Johnson, the other one-horse show veteran, to dance at his funeral. So late on a chilly January afternoon, as they laid their friend to rest on the banks of the Mississippi, the circus band played a lively tune while Jean danced a hornpipe. Another old compatriot, John Gossin, the clown, also passed on. Rice, "a man who never forgets his friends, and has more friends to remember than falls to the lot of all men in this world," paid for a marble headstone.[10]

On March 6, two days after the Senate passed Douglas's Kansas-Nebraska Bill, Rice presented *Uncle Tom's Cabin in Louisiana,* a new version written by Leonard, leaning more toward comedy. It especially mocked the North: Mrs. Convention Sympathy, a Higher Law Expounder and a Bloomer of First Class; Mrs. Harriet Bleacher Straw, a milliner authoress; Mr. Universal Freedom; and Young America, A Fast Young Gentleman from Down East. The play also presented a mob, which the South expected of the riotous North. Ages and genders were crossed, and the black characters were played by whites, including Rice as blackface Uncle Tom.[11] He added a song, to the popular tune of "Wait for the Wagon," its lyrics repeating the familiar Southern charge that Northerners did not treat slaves well—simultaneously a cynical rationalization and a telling point.

> I trable'd round de country and felt dat I was free,
> For I was cold and starvin' from de elbow to de knee,
> But Massa hab forgib me, and I know dat all am right,
> Though if (to audience) it givs you pleasure I'll run off eb'ry night.[12]

Rice had another hit. The *Crescent* was particularly enthusiastic. He played the part "as though he had been born and bred on the stage. The audiences were convulsed with laughter." Drawing all classes, Rice was showing "a great deal more histrionic merit than we had given him credit for, and is even better as a low comedian than as a clown." It advised strangers to attend, for we "have never seen a better representative of negro character nor a more effective representation of domestic slavery as it is." On March 22, it went further:

> We confess that we had never before seen negro comedy upon the stage in that perfection in which we have often seen it at its proper home, the merry plantation, when, on some occasional jollity, Cuffy gave loose to himself in all his boundless hilarity and was the inimitable, the native-born Jack-pudding. As for Dan, he shines the very chief of this as of almost everything else, whether the droll or the man of sense, the parson, the lawyer, or the horse-jockey. Of the ebony Dan stands the very Garrick . . . of sooty performers, the true Black Prince . . . He was well sustained, and the whole piece is the only genuine presentment of negro life and manners that we have ever seen.

Demand kept the play running eighteen straight performances, in an age when two in a row was unusual. The *Picayune* called it "the most popular drama ever produced in New Orleans." Since Rice's early days, the *Picayune* and *Delta* had shifted their coverage away from circus to what were becoming considered refined entertainments: theater, opera, and classical music. Now, though, the *Delta, Crescent,* and *Picayune* all noticed, praised, endorsed. Even the St. Charles Theatre bowed before the storm of Rice's success, flattering by imitation in its new drama, "The Old Plantation, or Uncle Tom As He Is."[13]

The season concluded with the regular roll of benefits for the stars. Maggie now warranted one of her own, on April 6. Though the benefit was labeled "A Family Affair," Dan did not appear, keeping up interest in his own benefit. "Citizens! To the Box Office!" urged his ads, for the "Country is in Danger!" of growing grim without the jester's jokes. In the "High Court of Momus" and "For the District of New Orleans, the individual and collective community is hereby summoned to appear at Dan Rice's Complimentary Benefit, Wednesday Night, April, 12, and show cause, if any there be, why they should not laugh at the Numerous Funny Scenes then and there to be presented." That day, Rice led his company on a parade through the streets to excite attention. When he reached the Amphitheatre, fireworks were set off from the balcony to the accompaniment of the band.[14]

New Orleans was enraptured. Here was a man, convulsing audiences, who made abundant Southern sense. He identified himself as a resident of the city to, registering at the City Hotel as "Dan Rice, N. O." Hundreds were unable to get into his benefit, and the crowd who did overflowed the stage until none of the dramatic pieces could be presented. Rice's departure prompted a comic show of dismay that was not completely a joke. "Dan Rice is going! Tell it not in Lafayette or Carrollton, or down about Esplanade street. Let the children remain in ignorance, and let the moments of his stay be improved." Dan rehearsed acts in the ring during performances as he prepared "to enchant hundreds upon hundreds of thousands of people elsewhere during the coming months. The superb trappings which have been carefully laid aside during the winter, are now brought out," refurbished in new purple, yellow, and gold paint.[15]

The Southern Museum would remain open for another month, and the Amphitheatre would have a brief dramatic season in June, but here was a last opportunity for those "who wish to see equestrianism in its highest and most attractive phase.[16]

Before Rice left came an incident not on the bills. "Not on the bills" referred to a change or interruption to the proprietor's roster of features.

On Good Friday, two days after his benefit, Rice was attending to the details of closing his winter season and making final preparations for the summer tour. It was quiet on St. Charles. A storm was coming, settling a sultry blanket over the city; suddenly, a man named Robinson came stomping up the street. He had been fired and vowed to get Rice. Drunkenness on the job was always a problem, resulting in fines or dismissal. When Rice appeared, Robinson denounced him with ugly curses and bloody threats. Dan "finally laid himself alongside the menacing calumniator and supplied him with a sock-dologer right in the middle of his angry countenance." Scrambling to his feet, Robinson pulled out "a sort of compromise between a bowie-knife and a cleaver," declaring that he would split Dan in two. Rice ran inside to get a pistol. He had been described as someone who sent forth "bullets of the brain." Now he made things literal as he came out, shooting when Robinson lunged at him. The shots shocked everybody into stunned peace. Robinson disappeared. A boy who had taken a ball in the foot hobbled off for care. Dan presented himself to the authorities, but no charges were pressed. Soon he was on his way upriver.[17]

16

$100,000

"China!"

It was the circus version of "Land ho!" a trouper's cry on catching the first glimpse of a church steeple, the highest point in town. To circus hands, sluggish with lack of sleep after a jarring night ride, it seemed as if they had traveled to China.[1]

Performance was only half of circus. As soon as the evening show finished, the heavy work began. Pine knots, or torch balls, cotton soaked in alcohol and stuck on an iron stake, gave off an unsteady light as canvas men tore down the tent, rolled up the sections, and packed them in the wagons. Then they dismantled and loaded the bleachers, named after racks for bleaching. The men might smooth down the plowed ring bank, introduced by John Robinson in 1852 as an improvement over the wooden fence, but they sometimes skipped that task. It was a long night of work, and they did what they must, no more. (An Iowa town council in 1864 noted that Rice's men had failed to level the mound.) When done, the roughnecks joined the performers at the hotel or, too tired to walk

On the lot, with the town's church steeple the highest landmark around.

into town, spread straw under a wagon. A night's sleep was brief, lasting only until it was time to move on. That might be three in the morning, or earlier. A surviving hotel ledger noted that breakfast had to be prepared for Rice's troupe at 1:00 A.M. Then, warm night or cold rain, it was time to hitch up in the dark and get on the road.[2]

"Sleep was the dragon which pursued me then with a relentless and irresistible power." Those were the words of W. C. Coup, who would be one of the century's leading showmen. "There was scarcely a moment when I was not under its spell, at least to some degree. It was like a vampire that took the zest and vitality out of my very life sources and I went about almost as one walking in a dream." Even in good weather sleep was rare and after a "stretch of hard travelling I was for weeks like a person drugged." Adding special torment were the age's roads. "No other human being can realize like the showman the volume of dread hardship and disaster held by those two small words, 'bad roads.'" The "hubby"—ribbed roads—jarred the wagons, and rain that chilled the bones converted roads to rivers of mud, sinking the heavy wagons to their hubs and stopping the whole train. Nor was that the worst.

> Perhaps the most disheartening of all bad-road experiences is that of losing the way—a thing which happened with perverse frequency. Just imagine yourself a member of such a caravan. You have slept four hours out of sixteen and are crawling along in the face of a drenching, blinding rainstorm—soaked, hungry and dazed. The caravan has halted a dozen times in the forepart of the night to pull out wagons and repair breakdowns. But it halts again, and the word "lost" is passed back along the line of wagons. That means retracing the route back to the forks of the road miles in the rear. Many an old circus man has wished himself dead on hearing the word "lost."

Wretchedness could turn dangerous. Another showman told of a driver who jerked awake and saved himself just as his lead horse went over a precipice.[3]

Yet for all that, performers daily performed awesome feats of skill, strength, and dexterity. And remained mentally alert enough, like Rice, to catch folly on the fly.

The world of performance joined the participatory spirit abroad in the land, where people demanded a voice. For a speaker with "a golden tongue was not enough. An orator entered the new institutional mesh only if he persuaded his audience that he and they held a common stake in a common cause." So to reach an ever-widening audience, those who addressed an audience—actors, musicians, scientists, photographers, painters—borrowed techniques from each other. That included a clown like Rice, and prominent preachers, like Henry Ward Beecher. A word portrait of Beecher fit Rice: "He is what one might call instinctively popular, feeling the public sentiment, and always keeping just ahead of his people, and on the top of the wave. No one could make more of an excitement while it lasted, or quicker scent a coming reaction." Beecher courted the same popularity that Rice enjoyed, using the same energetic performance style. When Beecher's Plymouth Church burned down in 1849, his new design resembled a circus arena. "I want the audience to surround me so that I shall be in the centre of the crowd, and have the people surge all around me." Perhaps his animosity toward amusements reflected a competitor's jealousy. Politicians jumped in, too. Off in wild Illinois, Douglas and Lincoln both sought election by using a folksy style, common before the Civil War, that mingled crude daily speech and airy oratory. Rice joined that slang-whanging crew as he combined elegant allusions and suggestive jokes in partnership with his audiences.[4]

That included bloomers, loose trousers gathered at the ankle and worn under a shortened skirt. Their inventor, Amelia Jenks Bloomer, intended the pantaloons as a clothing reform, a practical solution to the difficulties of skirts, but caused a sensation. In retrospect, bloomers seem tame. After all, Hiram Powers's *Greek Slave* had recently been shown in the country's first major exhibition of the life-sized statue of a female nude. Nonetheless, bloomers, shocking both for the hint of leg they allowed and for their suggestion of pants, became a fixation for men. The *Crescent* had breathlessly reported on the arrest of one Emma Snodgrass, "encased in horrid unmentionables" in Boston. Considering that she was respectable—her father was a New York police chief—and pretty, there could be only one explanation: "She must be insane." Rice joined in the jokes. In "The Bloomer Song," published in sheet music and sold for a dime, he informed men that women cut their skirts short to avoid spit tobacco, so the ladies "will lengthen their habits when you mend your own." In another song, "The Bloomer Polka," Rice suggested the prurient element of the controversy when he sang about the sight of legs and urged women to ignore the prudes and dress as they please.[5]

When Rice toured in 1854, the *Kentucky Statesman* reported "roars upon roars of laughter," with thousands turned away. Other circus performers enjoyed similar tributes. What was increasingly different about Rice was that newspapers praised not simply his talent and popularity but his new approach. The *Rochester Union,* reinforcing the praise, repeated the Buffalo *Post*: "What is it about Dan which causes him to command so much larger space in the public eye than any others of his class? This is a query that is not hard to answer. The rest form a class, and each *one* has the character of every *one*. While Dan, though nominally of the class, is as unlike any one of them as can be imagined, so, also, is his exhibition." Dan was "the inspiring genius of the whole." A key part of that genius was his command of the crowd. As newspapers declared about him, *"Vox populi, vox Dei"*—the voice of the people is the voice of God. Later ages would grow suspicious of that populist refrain, but at the time it was "sacred to every nation. It is an infallible motto, an unconquerable war cry; and if there be virtue in it, the great Dan must still fulfill his destiny, conquering and to conquer."[6]

For the summer tour, Rice published a courier—a booklet—*Dan Rice's Amphitheatre.* Engravings of his Amphitheatre and his Museum were wrapped in eight pages of praise for his increasingly promoted respectability. He had burst "the fetters of a lowly fortune" to become a "juvenile cosmopolite," and then "the greatest wit since the days of Sheridan." Rice was growing more sophisticated in his publicity. Though depicting his life to be as full of "melo-dramatic point as the most ardent lover of romance could wish it to be," the courier shrewdly avoided doubt-inducing details. There were no tales of tricking the Mormon Smith or out-humbugging Barnum here. Instead, Rice's inner worth attained for him "a celebrity for not only rare genius but for gentility, high-toned sentiment, and sterling worth."[7]

It would not be a touring season without troubles. Complaints bubbled up in the Buckeye state. To the *Ohio Independent,* Rice's circus was a "traveling pestilence," with worn-out wagons, swayback horses, and hard, dirty men. The *Chillicothe Advertiser* reported that Rice, caught in a drunken brawl, brandished a pitchfork trying to avoid arrest. Then he got into a scrape with an Ohio landlord about not paying his bill. And there were the usual troubles of touring, including blowdowns. In Rochester, New York, a gale tore the canvas down and broke the center pole, forcing cancellation of the afternoon show. A new pole was cut and the canvas was patched in time for the evening performance, but another storm thundered through, lifting the tent and splintering the wooden seats. In the sudden dark, the canvas whipped in the drenching rain like sails in a storm. The tent had to be slashed to free the thousands trapped underneath.[8]

Rice would later say that he made $100,000 in 1854. The claim must be taken with a grain of salt. That round number clearly appealed to him, because he regularly repeated that amount in his memoirs: His father had been left $100,000 in a will; his father had owed $100,000 on his death; the feud with Spalding had cost Rice $100,000; Howes had offered Rice $100,000 for Excelsior. Nonetheless, Rice was making money. He told of taking in so much that they fell asleep in the ticket wagon as they counted into the night.[9] A rough estimate nudges him toward that grand amount. He presented approximately 330 shows: nine a week in New Orleans, or 150, and six a week on the summer tour, for another 180. If he cleared $300 a show, achievable with the 2,000-seat Amphitheatre and a 5,000-capacity tent, and earned more money from the Southern Museum, he would be approaching $100,000.

17

BEARDED IN HIS DEN

As Rice shifted his presentation of himself as a gentleman in the ring, he made the shift visual, adopting the dignity of a beard by growing a goatee. While a beard tucked down at the bottom of the face could accommodate whiteface or blackface makeup, it was not traditional for a clown. Rice had sported one in the late 1840s, but then went clean-shaven again, at least through the 1853–1854 winter season. Otherwise the *Delta* would have been mentioned a goatee on Rice, for it elsewhere teased the goatee as "that caricature of a beard" and its "hirsute foppery." Rice's goatee was distinctive because it had no accompanying mustache. It complemented his friend Mit's, whose moustache and side whiskers covered everywhere except the chin; it was as if they were completing two halves of the same hirsute face.[1] If cartooning styles of the time had used the abstraction of later ages, the drawing of a goatee and a top hat cocked to the side would have been enough to tell a reader that Rice was meant. Looking like a goat's beard, the chin hair waggled like a goat's tail as Rice told his tales.

November 1854 found Rice in a swirl of business activity. In Cincinnati, he arranged a boat, the *U.S. Aid,* for a circus to tour the South. This troupe included the Franconis. They had been the talk of both sides of the Atlantic since their Hippodrome, so hiring them was a coup for Rice. He advertised this show as "Rosston's Circus" in the Queen City, but as the "New Orleans Hippoforean" the rest of the time. In his ledger, he gave it yet another name, the "Crescent City Circus."[2] In 1850, Rice had omitted his name from the title because hard times forced him to shield himself from creditors. Now he did so because times were good. His success meant that more and more people would expect to see him in a Dan Rice circus.

Meanwhile, Dr. Leonard had gone ahead to New Orleans, to re-open Dan Rice's Amphitheatre with plays featuring New Orleans's star actress, Charlotte Crampton. Leonard experimented with an innovation, starting, rather than ending, the evening with a farce. Flipping the usual order of things meant that people would straggle in during the farce and not interrupt the play; public rambunctiousness was starting to dissolve. Suddenly, in mid-December, "a vacuum in the manager's chest" closed Rice's Amphitheatre. After a shuttered weekend, when Rice may have sent promises from upriver, the Amphitheatre re-opened with a new lessee and manager, Captain J. Mann.[3]

On Saturday, December 23, the day Dan and Maggie arrived at the City Hotel, during a stretch of "Indian summerish" weather, Rice's Amphitheatre began offering plays in the afternoon. Circuses had been presenting matinees in New Orleans, but the city had never seen daylight drama before.[4]

Rice was credited with another innovation this winter, the introduction of peanuts to the American circus. However, they were already an established staple at amusements. In 1852, the *Delta* joked about "pea nuts," cracking an indelicate pun on "afflatus," or inspiration, and "flatus," intestinal gas.

> There seems to be, in the minds of a certain class of people, an indefinable connection between poetry and pea nuts. They are not able to enjoy

> Shakespeare, at the theatre, unless under the afflatus, or perhaps, in flatus of this odorous and inspiring nut. . . . The odor is a sort of compound between our roasted coffee and stinking fish, and the noise more disagreeable than the squeaking of an ungreased axletree. We wish the managers of our public places of amusement would erect a pea nut gallery for the express accommodation of those who choose to crack their nuts at the expense of the comforts of others.

This may have been the first appearance of "peanut gallery."[5]

But nothing helped, not starting with farces, nor introducing matinees, nor peddling peanuts. Foreclosure hit Dan Rice's Amphitheatre. On Christmas Eve day, Rice published a notice to all creditors. Little was left of 1854's $100,000 but the boast, like a damp patch on dry sand after a splash. The Amphitheatre would soon reopen as the Pelican Theatre, in honor of Louisiana, the Pelican State. (Adding insult to Rice's injured pride, Spalding leased it the following season.)[6]

Then, two days after Rice's last benefit, and the same day the international star Agnes Robertson arrived from England to play his ex-Amphitheatre, the contents of Dan Rice's Museum were put up for sale. Once proudly advertised with the city's other amusements, the Museum now jostled for attention in the auction columns against Irish linen, figs from Sicily, St. Bernards, and of course, slaves. (Sixty-six human beings could be purchased on "Very Liberal Terms," one-quarter down, with a mortgage at the Bank of Louisiana.) Proceeds from the Museum sale were estimated around $40,000, although the *Picayune* understood that "this is but barely half of their original cost."[7]

Rice did not stay to watch his empire crumble. Only a month after arriving, he stood on the deck above another paddlewheel splashing north. Leaning at the railing, smoking a cigar, Rice saw a study in shades of brown—muddy, scudding water, spidery tree branches, dirt, dead leaves and empty bushes—as if a giant had carved the landscape from the same piece of dismal wood. Above his head, smoke flowered out of the double smokestack and rolled back down the river, where his Hippoforean was wandering to Vicksburg and other points on the Southern compass.[8] His name no longer graced the cityscape, four stories high on the Amphitheatre over St. Charles. The Museum had dwindled to lines on a balance sheet, no more to represent Rice as the American Museum stood for Barnum, nor to provide a steady stream of profits.

As his fledgling Southern empire showed, Rice's appeal remained tied to what audiences heard him say in performance. That was both strength and weakness. Any clown—anyone in clown makeup—can raise a few laughs, even if they're paltry ones, like leaves scattering down an empty street. With good clowns, good comedians, the jokes are better, the moves clearer, so the laughs are deeper. Rice, a great clown, made even ordinary jokes seem funny through his extraordinary ability to forge a bond with and among the strangers who made up each successive audience. Hilarity flowed less from repeatable punch lines than from a sense of shared humanity in the immediate moment. But his ability to create fellow feeling rendered him less able to see the larger picture. His world was that immediate moment, with no overall strategy, other than following where success seemed to beckon. He had become a circus clown not because of a driving inevitability but because it fit his abilities. Similarly, he had become a man of New Orleans simply because each winter season brought greater success. He was able to build a career on his remarkable talent but, other than a home in Girard, he could perfect no establishments. Vibrant immediacy was a potent foundation, but a risky one.

However, this was no repeat of the dark days of his show with one horse. As the boat steamed upriver, past Live Oak Plantation and Bonnet Quarre Creek, Water Proof, Hard Times, and Duckport, he could calmly cast his mind back to New Orleans. His career had flourished there, and the cosmopolitan city still delighted in him. There, he had bested Spalding and, in the opinion of many, beaten the great humbug Barnum to a draw. There, he had introduced the South to the large-scale museum, and in doing so he had helped propel the growth of those institutions. The grand arena he had constructed for his circus was the gem of the city's theatrical venues, soon called the Academy of Music. On this trip north, in the steamboat's saloon at night, as the rings on his fingers glimmered in the glow of kerosene and candles, Rice similarly dazzled in the gleam of attention. On deck again in the morning light, wrapped against the growing cold, Rice watched Hardin's Wood Yard and Devil's Elbow slide past. Being a regional favorite had been gratifying, but it was not enough. No matter what memories crowded his mind as the brown water slapped against the downstream drift of logs, he also thought ahead. Deciding to let Southern field lie fallow, he turned his attention northward.

Back in Girard, he had set mechanics to work constructing winter quarters for his wagons and animals, and also a grand place to live. Ultimately, magnolias and dripping moss weren't his style, nor was the primary model of Southern gentility, the plantation. He would be a country squire, not snoozing up a sleepy bayou, but in a town, surrounded by people and winter bustle. A story tells of Rice's giving an elaborate reception on his arrival. Dan and Maggie would have wanted to meet their neighbors and stake a social claim. They did not intend Girard to be an impersonal resting place between seasons, a private version of the winter hotels frequented by show people. It was to be their home, with their girls in school there, apparently their first full-time schooling. Not all the locals were thrilled sharing their town with the great clown; a showman does not slot easily into the social scale of small-town gentility. Nevertheless, no one could fault his house, a middle-class showcase. Cut-glass chandeliers reflected the tiny flares of gas flame. There were overstuffed sofas decorated with lace, and carpeting to cushion life's hard shocks. To display their good taste, Dan and Maggie hung paintings, lithographs, and the new technological marvel, "stereotype," prints of images from metal plates. Having lived humbly, Dan and Maggie were proud to show how they could make a home comfortable and beautiful. Rice's success would grow, yet he later called this year he moved to Girard his "most successful season. Money mattered to Rice. Home was more important.[9]

Because Girard lay on a convenient east–west path, showmen stopped to visit, welcomed at Dan's open door. He was always part of the convivial crowd, swapping stories, trading tips, telling the dirty jokes that would offend audiences. Two who might have come through were Rufus Welch and Lewis Lent, to talk contract. They had hired Rice for his longest run, in the winter of 1846–1847. Now he traveled to Philadelphia at the end of March 1855 to join them again. Presenting his comic mules at Welch's stand on Walnut Street, Rice brought along his newest apprentice, Charley Reed, to give him experience. When Rice starred in a Saturday matinee for juveniles, the ads announced him as "the Children's Clown," a special point needing be made or people would assume that he was presenting the usual adult fare. Announced for one week, he was "Re-

Rice was presenting himself as a respectable businessman, with a country estate, a newspaper, and a refined image.

engaged" for a second. Like farewell tours, "final" performances were not always final. The *Picayune* teased about shows that announced imminent departures but didn't leave. In the bills "of a circus, concert or cock fight, there are as many 'lasts' as in a cobbler's shop." A man jollied his friend, glum because the circus was leaving.

> "Oh! there's plenty o' time. Come along, Jack."
> "No! you see it says, 'Last night of the circus.'"
> "Come along, I tell you! Plenty of time. There's pos-i-tively and abso-lute-ly to come yet."[10]

Though Rice played only two weeks of Welch & Lent's months-long winter season, his stature had risen enough to give him the privilege of the benefit on the show's last night in town. He was joined by his old comrade, William Wallett, for another exchange of quips and compliments in the ring. Even as he got his accustomed praise, though, Rice faced the risk that his Southern popularity was constricting his career. That risk glimmers through an extended joke in the *Philadelphia Sunday Dispatch*:

> As Forrest is to the legitimate drama so is Dan to the sawdust, and throughout the entire South and West the universal cry is "Hurra! for Dan Rice!" Children are named after him in Indiana. New towns are christened Riceville; and itinerant missionaries, who wish to stir up the "dry-bones" and wake the faithful, can always have a full congregation when they preach about *Daniel* in the lion's den. Some wag says that the passage in the "Merchant of Venice" about a "Daniel coming to judgment," is the only thing that gave Shakspere a literary reputation in Arkansas.[11]

Lumped with places the East considered backwaters, Rice knew he had to pull himself above that chauvinistic presumption.

18

DAN RICE'S GREAT SHOW

Changes were revitalizing the circus business. The hippodrome movement raced along, Spalding's Floating Palace made a big splash, and circus expanded to the upper Midwest, into Texas, and across the continent to the Pacific. There were new acts, such as the perch act, in which one person supported a pole climbed by another. When Herr Cline, an Englishman, walked a rope to the peak of Rice's arena in New Orleans in 1852, he joined the daredevils in the first ascension acts, inside the tent and out. Circus advertising boomed with the advent of cheaper printing and the introduction of paste, instead of tacks, to post bills. A noisy novelty would soon split the air, the steam calliope (CAL-ee-ope to circus people), becoming "the nearest approach to realizing the idea of 'music for the million.'"[1]

The mid–1850s were also significant for Rice. As he swung round what he called the "Cereal Circle"—"the wheat lands of the frigid North to the *Rice* fields of the Sunny south"—he engaged in a kind of harvest of features. He now had Maggie, Rosston, Noyes, Johnson, and Castle, his show agent supreme. Early in 1854, Rice had hired Jacob Showles, a twenty-eight-year-old New Orleans "posturer and equilibrist." That summer season, he got a new apprentice, thirteen-year-old Charles Reed of Kentucky. A year later, he hired James L. Thayer. Twenty-three-year-old Thayer had started as a circus "chandelier man" in 1846, filling the tin lamps with whale or lard oil, and then became a tinsmith. Next, he was a boss hostler, handling horses and driving, until he joined Rice. Rice's sister, Libbie Manahan, was now also along for the ride. She said that Dan brought her on the road because he wanted her companionship. Perhaps he did not find it with Maggie; if marriage gets hard, the enforced intimacy of trouping makes it worse. Maggie and Libbie became close themselves, like sisters, but Libbie's statement hangs like a cloud over the marital sun.[2]

The elements contributing to Rice's success included his potent trio of animal acts. Excelsior, one of the most remarkable circus horses ever, followed subtle cues so well that there seemed to be no cues; it was the Learned Pig on a grand scale. Rice encouraged the notion that his great horse did not simply mimic human intelligence but actually possessed it. When Dan whispered, the horse leaned his head down, as if the two were huddled in conversation. To questions, the white steed shook his head yes or no. Excelsior could also limp as if lame, jump rope "with the precision of a school girl," and shoot a pistol tugging a rope with his teeth to pull the trigger, despite the explosion. In the climax of the act, Excelsior walked up and down stairs. The stair walk, with hooves clattering an awkward rhythm up, then down the wooden steps, was risky. One slip meant a broken leg, and then Rice's great horse would have to be destroyed. The entrance was stunning: The striking white animal stood rock-steady on a platform carried on the shoulders of ten men. Even on that less-than-stable base, a right front hoof poised on a short post, the horse made no movement other than the quiver of a muscle under the skin and the light swish of his tail. It was a living statues act, a remarkable feat of training and equine poise.[3]

Lalla Rookh was another amazing feature, intelligence and warm mammal eyes making her an anthropomorphic marvel. Though not yet

The name of his horse, its stair-climbing, and its platform entrance all expressed Rice's aim of refinement: Excelsior, ever higher.

performing a headstand consistently, she would be the first elephant in America to accomplish the feat. Rice said that he was hauled into court after she failed to do the trick as advertised, but he turned trouble into triumph, joking that while Lalla Rookh could stand on her head, her feminine modesty precluded the indelicate display. Much more remarkably, Lalla Rookh walked a tightrope. It remains one of the most amazing feats that an animal has ever accomplished. Rice's ads pictured the "Tight-Rope Walking Elephant" on a rope slung a few feet off the ground, strung between two pairs of crossed beams. The story goes that Noyes promised Rice that he could train the elephant to do it or he would pay for the specially manufactured rope, which cost the considerable sum of $180.[4]

Rice's great tightrope-walking elephant, Lalla Rookh.

The claim of a tightrope-walking elephant remains suspect. Some have said it would have been impossible to rig a rope strong enough to support an elephant, especially in a sawdust ring at each town. And because all tightropes sway a little, it would seem similarly impossible to persuade an elephant to step onto such an unstable path, much less often enough to learn how to balance on it. Rice's elephant may have walked on a plank, itself an impressive feat, perhaps with a rope on it to make the boast acceptable. Despite all doubts, though, Lalla Rookh apparently did walk a hemp rope six inches in diameter. Newspapers repeatedly testified to seeing the remarkable trick. The *Philadelphia Sunday Mirror* declared that the elephant "not only dances, rings bells, and fires pistols, but actually walks a tight rope, like a true born sailor." More evidence lies in the absence of complaints. The claim and image of Lalla Rookh on the slung rope ran in ads for years, yet no objection about a humbug surfaced. Nor was a plank ever mentioned. Even those who criticized everything else about Rice did not challenge this claim of an elephantine rope-walk.[5]

With work still being done in Girard, Rice had ended the 1854 season near Albany and sent his show into winter quarters in Schenectady. There, he hired a local wagon maker, Ebenezer Brinton, to build wagons for the next season. Over the winter, he gave his Girard neighbor, Grip Martin, a small interest in his new show as part payment for horses and equipment. In mid-April, his family joined him in Schenectady. Rice probably had presents for Maggie and the girls. Eight years old, Kate would still be playing with dolls, but what about Libby, who had turned eleven in February? Maybe he bought a dress for her, or kid gloves from a fancy shop.

On May 1, Rice played Albany, Spalding's old stamping ground, to start his summer season. Circus hands would later call a rookie a "first of May." Some speculate that it referred to the date when beginners quit, chased away by the hard work. Others, reversing that reasoning, believe the phrase applied to those who started on May 1, when shows began the touring season. All the theories embrace the spring-like sense of new beginnings. But "first of May" was not simply a romantic symbol to the old-time circus; it signaled a time when money could be made again, after months stuck in the ice and snow of winter quarters, with feed bills for the stock and expenses for upkeep on the wagons, and no income on either. If every baseball team used to envision the World Series in spring training, then every circus started out in the green of spring with high hopes for blue skies, grass lots, and a bulging treasury.

Rice headed out with another key element, a new circus title. He had tried a variety of names: Metropolitan, Hippodramatic, Hippodrome, Menagerie, and plain Circus. It was as if he had been trying on each title for size. The "One-Horse Show" had punch, but it was a slogan for making a point rather than a title representing his risen glory. In 1855, hacking through grandiloquent thickets, he found it: Dan Rice's Great Show. The title was rich with meaning. "Circus" was absent from his circus, but "Dan Rice" effectively said the same thing. It was not his ego that added his name but sound business. By now, little in a title could trump the appeal of the ineffable Dan. He remained the "observed of all observers"; he *was* his circus. With "Show," Rice once again transformed vilification, defying those who preached from the pulpit and murmured in the parlor against "show" as superficial display. ("Spectacle" is the twentieth-century equivalent, description sliding into slur.) If all was vanity in this earthly realm, then the "mere show" of amusements was worst for the prim and oh-so-proper. Facing sneers that "show" had no substance, Rice would prove them wrong. "Dan Rice's Great Show" was a potent four words in five quick syllables.[6]

Crossing to Pennsylvania, back on the same ground he had traveled with the Learned Pig, Rice retold that tour's story with a new twist for the locals: The pig had not drawn in Reading, and Dan was stuck until Judge Heidenreich lent him a horse and wagon. When luck again ran against Dan in Allentown, matters were worse, as "a crisis in his wife's health was approaching." She was pregnant, due soon. Rice sold the horse and wagon so that he could send his wife home to "prepare for the stern realities of married life." The punch line of the story led to this season fourteen years later, when Rice surprised the judge by presenting him with a new carriage and pony, a $500 outfit to replace the original $50 horse and wagon. Many would consider Rice's selling the original team a theft, but the story displayed the replacement as proof that he was an "honest man, and a man of honor." This tale reads like the kind of fiction found in *Sketches,* yet Rice told the story in 1855 in Reading, when the still-active Judge Heidenreich would readily denounce it if it were a fraud. Rice always assessed whether he had left a "good name" in a town, to ensure a welcome on the next visit. He would not risk that reputation for an anecdote.[7]

Rice's rise had been transformed into a representative story. Audiences would know the arc and end of a piece that Castle put in the papers once they read that Dan had started life "with no capital but his native genius and strong determination to succeed in the world." He had risen "from comparative obscurity," as heroes must rise in America's recurring cultural myth.

> Fond hopes and bright anticipations of the future, thus suddenly and cruelly blasted, would have utterly crushed a disposition less resolute and determined than his; but misfortune served only to arouse him to new and more zealous efforts. He lost no time in brooding over wrongs he had not the power to right, but again launched out into the world, resolved to deserve, if he did not win success. . . . he commenced ascending the rugged hills of fortune; but with no very bright prospects to cheer him on, but with a consciousness of right and his own integrity, and an unbending determination to rise like the Phoenix, from his ashes; step by step having to contend with numerous unforeseen and gigantic difficulties, he fought his way up and to his credit be it said, he is once more on the high road to fortune.

From the ashes, he rose to gain a "position before the world more brilliant, except in one instance [Barnum], than was ever attained by any member of his profession." His publicity resonated when it said that, self-taught and self-made like many illustrious men, he was "most essentially a man of the age."

That was not the end of the story. Achieving worldly success was insufficient, everyone nodded sagely. In a culture that honored material success, anxiety about the social price of that success burst out in repeated insistence that other things were more important than money. What made Rice's triumph complete for the public were his "high toned gentlemanly qualities," and reassurance that his success flow from the "taste and delicacy" in what he presented. He was worthy of public attention because of his "correct appreciation of the refinement of the better classes of society," enabling him to do "more than any man living to elevate the character of arenic amusements to a standard of respectability, worthy of the patronage and countenance of all." This was Rice's story, and it resonated because it was the story his culture kept telling itself about itself.[8]

19

SERVIS RENDERD

Rice was busy over the winter of 1855–1856, shuttling between his new home and his circuses. In November, his schedule would have been hectic even for an airplane traveler, as he went from Girard to New Jersey, back to Girard, downriver to Mississippi to drop in on his Crescent City Circus, then north to Chicago and Cleveland, and back home again. He allotted himself $1,000 for "Servis Renderd."[1]

The Crescent City Circus was a family affair. His sister Libbie was a performer now, and married to Jacob Showles. The same intimacy of the road that was shivering a gap between Dan and Maggie had brought Libbie and Jacob together. Dan and Libbie's brother, William C. Manahan, was manager. He had no circus experience, but he was family. The troupe was waiting for wagons in October, so Rice sent a message to Ebenezer Brinton, urging haste. Then in November, Rice changed his tune from hurry to patience, writing the wagon maker that he had put all his funds into "paper"—publicity material. Shows needed a steady supply of paper, and Rice bought from the leading printers in the business, Farwell in Boston, Sarony & Co. in New York, and Strobridge in Cincinnati. He often lagged on those bills, too. Frank Farwell, who, on a weekend holiday in 1851, had ridden on Rice's boat, turned up another time to raise some on account. Rice, "never any too prompt in paying at any stage of his career," declined to pay, so Farwell telegraphed his shop with instructions to stop shipments. Castle, who happened to be visiting Farwell's, spotted the wire, put it in his pocket, ordered more printing, saw it shipped, returned to his hotel, and then had the telegram delivered again. Rice was not abashed by debt. "Now I am very sorry about that," he wrote in his second letter to Brinton, but, as if the wagon maker were the one who owed the money, "Until then Do the best you can, it will all come Right." After attending to a lawsuit in New Jersey and checking posters at Sarony's in New York, Rice ventured to Schenectady to see Brinton. Whatever Rice said was persuasive, for he got his wagons.[2]

In mid-December, Rice played Baltimore for the first time in half a decade. The trouble between Rice and the *Sun* was "all O.K. now." He brought Excelsior and the mules to Delavan & Stickney's Great Southern Circus at the Front Street Theater.[3] (William Delavan, out of the business since 1850, needed money and borrowed $25 from the clown.) At nights, Rice performed, and during the days he tended to business, telegraphing his show in Natchez, contacting Rosston in Pittsburgh, wiring money to Castle in Girard to bring animals along, and sending more money to Sarony and to Farwell. He bought a 50¢ lock for his dressing room, purchased two chances for $20 in a raffle from the gymnastic leaper, Tom King, and gave $20 to "poor pepol for wood & coal." As a visiting star, Rice paid the properties man—"props"—and the gas man, for lighting, for his act. On December 28, Rice lavished $30 on holiday presents for his girls.

Rice also paid a five-year-old debt to a tailor. He did it so that he could then buy more clothes, "that I gave to Mrs Hopper [Hope?] for Early favors." Because Rice recorded these "Early favors" openly, they were probably innocent; yet the possibility of services of a personal kind cannot be ignored. Dan always doted on the ladies, and he did have one adultery charge to his credit. His cryptic scrawl in the ledger entry is like an old-fashioned striptease, mostly respectable, yet suggesting more.

Sex was a ripe part of public life. As embodiments of life and death, sex and violence are understandable human preoccupations, making them perfect subjects for the era's circus. Newspapers openly reported on circus affairs and elopements. As the antebellum equivalent of Las Vegas, circus displayed showgirls and boys in revealing wear. Even the nickname for tights, "symmetricals," suggesting two lines off a common axis, carried a lascivious wink. Many people were convinced that circus, ballet, and theater aimed mostly to show off women's legs, which was often true. A favorite play of the day, *Mazeppa,* based on a poem by Byron, thrilled audiences when the hero was tied to the back of a horse clattering in close proximity over the canvas-and-wood "mountain passes" of the stage. That thrill increased when Adah Isaacs Menken took the male role. Seeming virtually nude in flesh-colored tights and a ragged, revealing top, she created a scandal that was both the rage and outrage of the age. Later ages, inured to the sight of human flesh, see modesty in old pictures of thick, flesh-colored tights, but intent was then as now: Display the maximum allowed by society's standards while hinting at what is not quite seen. (Circus still parades sexuality beneath its family-fare image, G-strings with a G-rating.) The era's turbulent sexuality erupted in a diarist's heavy breathing over a woman on the trapeze: "The only clothing she had on was a blue satin doublet fitting close to her body and having very scanty trunk hose below it. Her arms were all bare; her leg, cased in fleshings, were as good as bare up to the hip." During her act, men "held her upside down in the air, her limbs all sprawling apart." Then, "half nude as she was," with "her fair young face all crimson with heat and wet with perspiration," she stood at the climax of her act "perched up there, naked and unprotected, with no one to help her."[4]

Clowns' jokes added to the sexually heated atmosphere. Newspapers never printed the stronger stuff, but Rice hinted at Mormon polygamy and teased Henry Ward Beecher about adultery. The clown could also fling at a favorite target, a couple flirting, with titillating insinuation, "There he is! I would rather be that young man up there with his arm around his girl than to be President." As the crowd laughed at the pair's discomfort, Rice pretended to sympathize. "That's all right, young uns; just go on like you was, and we won't say any more about it. I had no idea these people would be so unmannerly as to laugh." Mildly amusing in

Sex, with an unabashed display of bodies, contributed greatly to the appeal of the circus.

print, Rice's joke could become laughably salacious with a wink or a leer. Spicier fare can be inferred from newspaper complaints about clowns using hackneyed jokes from *Joe Miller's Joke Book.* Originally published in 1739, the book was so popular in the nineteenth century that it grew tenfold in succeeding editions, with earthy jests like the one about the new wife who suggested that her husband stay in bed and rest a little. "No," he replied, "I'll get up and rest a little." Other jokes were not so discreetly monogamous. It was said of a wench who spent time around the law courts, "if she had as much law in her head, as she had in her tail, she would be one of the ablest counsels" in town.[5]

Rice played Baltimore through January 1. Though historians traditionally equate theaters' box-pit-and-gallery structure to class divisions, managers did not split things for the convenience of historians. Delavan & Stickney charged the same 50¢ for their pit that they charged for the boxes. (The "Boy's" and "Colored" galleries cost one bit, 12½¢.) Rice earned $100 a show the first week, $50 the second, and got the proceeds of two benefits for an engagement total of nearly $1,200, an extraordinary amount in the mid-1850s. Nevertheless, word reached Cincinnati that the stand was a flop. It may have been more than bad weather that prompted Rice to call that holiday week "the most unplesant I ever knew."[6]

News from Louisiana made New Year worse for Rice. A fire had killed fifteen of the Crescent City Circus's horses. The *Opelousas Courier* deemed it arson, noting that the same stable had burned a year earlier when a menagerie was there. Rice wrote to Brinton again, saying that he couldn't pay on the wagons now because he had to replace the stock from the fire. He was exaggerating, though, when he added that his loss had been about ten thousand dollars.[7]

Despite the loss, Rice had cash, lots and gobs and mortal slathers of the stuff, as they said. He could have paid off Brinton or Farwell, or sent money to buoy his show in the South. Instead he took his family on an extravagant vacation. Dan, Maggie, and the girls caught the train to Philadelphia on January 6, putting up at the elegant Girard House. The next day, a wintry Monday, they frolicked from shop to shop—"shopping," in a recently coined word. Dan bought cloaks for his girls, silk for a basket, and bonnets for their dolls. He got a purse for Maggie, as well as material for another joke:

> "I went shopping to-day for my wife."
> "What did you get?"
> "I bought a new hat. Oh, it was a tiresome job."
> "Why so?"

"After I bought it I ran all the way back to the hotel with it."
"Why so?"
"For fear the fashion would change before I reached there."

The same day, he paid a tailor $50, perhaps for more fashion for Maggie, but he was the sartorial star of the family. As Rice had crossed from the Mississippi to the Ohio, Cairo had noted his fancy clothes and gold jewelry.

> Dan was dressed to kill, and Frenchified nearly to death. He stood up straighter than a bean pole, and had nearly all California on his fingers. By the way he carried himself, we presume that some country paper has nominated him for next President. Spangles are looking up. Long may they shine! [8]

Rice continued the family vacation in New York City, arriving the day after the worst storm the city had seen in years. It was miserable traversing the streets, standing in wet straw in hundred-passenger sleighs, feet frozen and noses bitten by bitter wind, or slogging through snowdrifts, trying to dodge the small fast-moving sleighs. Watch where you're going! Aw, tell it to the marines! Dan hired a sleigh to speed his family to the Astor House. With its central dome and Corinthian colonnade overlooking fashionable Park Row, the hotel cost $10 a day, double Baltimore prices and more than many a daily wage.

Dan didn't spend much time with his family, except on the road. Back in Girard Rice stayed only four days before leaving to star at the National Theatre in Boston with Col. Joseph Cushing's New York Circus. During his first two weeks, he again earned $100 a night, sending Maggie $300 of it. At his second benefit, he mixed religion and science: He was the "High Priest of Momus" presiding at the "Funeral Obsequies of Dull Care," and a scientist dissecting Hamlet's "Psycolhological" state. He also sang comic duets with Rose Madigan, whose father, Henry, had just settled with Rice for back pay from 1849. The herald offered the unusual feature of money back if anyone was dissatisfied with the performance. Monday, February 4, saw Rice's "re-engagement." Audiences grew smaller over a run, so Rice's salary dropped again to $50 a show. Circus-savvy audiences knew that his first Farewell a week earlier was not final, for they turned out in greater numbers this time.[9]

On February 12, Rice tallied up his winter finances: $4,270 income, expenses of $3,380. No more money would come in until the summer season, but Rice continued his extravagant ways. Preparing to leave Boston, he gave a tip to all forty of the Revere House staff. The night before he left, he also threw a party that cost $27, a third the size of his hotel bill. In a final flourish, he tossed $2.50 to the boy who fetched him a sleigh that cost $1.50, the equivalent of tipping a doorman $50 for a $30 cab ride. Farwell came to see Rice off, and to tap his friend for more on account.

While lavish living cost Rice, he was also generous. He was sending money to Jean Johnson from the One-Horse Show days, apparently for old times' sake. Back in New York, Dan loaned his stepfather, Hugh Manahan, $150. His brother, William, was in town too, and Rice paid for all three to stay at the Florence House. (Rice saved the Astor prices for Maggie and the girls.) On February 14, the three men took the train to Erie, Dan paying again. It was a short visit. Two days after arriving at his son's new home, Hugh returned to New York. The spare ledger entries do not reveal what Dan felt in his stepfather's presence, but he noted in his ledger that for the loan to Hugh, "I took his note on Demand." That might have simply been legal language signifying the kind of note, but Rice did not use the phrase to record any other loan.

Rice turned to the business of his new estate. He bought more land, including a nineteen-acre plot for $2,000 from Grip Martin.[10] Rice paid for horses' keep and housekeeping. He disbursed money to the gardener, butcher, druggist, and grocer, and even donated $5 to the Universalist Church. He was having his liquor shipped in, a lot of it, with $31.50 due at the express office.

His new title, Dan Rice's Great Show, clearly resonated, for he prepared to use it again for the 1856 season. Others adopted "Great Show" too, including James Myers, who had worked with Rice in Boston. To the *Cincinnati Enquirer,* it appeared "that all circus companies traveling are now called 'great.'" Nevertheless, Rice's financial health remained tenuous, even though his show was worth $30,000. He recorded an $1,100 payment at the end of May to "G. Martin In full for Grate Show." Rice had given Martin a part interest in the show a year before, in lieu of payment. He was able to pay it off now only because he swapped part of the Great Show again for more money, this time to Farwell. Over the winter, Rice had paid the printer $1,000, but owed more, and his promises had worn thin. So on May 1, Farwell took a one-third interest in Rice's circus in exchange for $4,000 to $5,000 in cash—the pile of debts made the amount indefinite—and the promise of another $5,000. (This was an old way of joining the circus world. The druggist Spalding, a horse dealer named Adam Forepaugh, and other printers did the same when payments stopped.) Farwell installed twenty-five-year-old Charles Warner, a hotel barkeeper, as treasurer.[11]

Meanwhile, Rice's Crescent City Circus was not doing well as it meandered through Mississippi, Tennessee, and Louisiana, having little luck separating people from their coins. On April 23, a week before the Great Show was due out in the North, Rice calculated that his Southern circus was worth $4,000, and had lost $5,000. Still, Rice was sending money to Jacob and Libbie to ensure that they got paid, and he kept his brother as manager. The small circus tramped on, through Alabama, Georgia, and the Carolinas, before meeting up with the Great Show in Virginia.[12]

Despite Rice's casual attitude toward money, there is a kind of nobility in his refusal to hoard. He continued to fall short at Spalding's game of sending out a show as a manager and seeing it come back a success. Performers who managed on their own rarely had the success of a business man such as Barnum or of a manager–performer partnership such as Spalding had with Rogers.[13] Still, Rice kept risking his money to the vagaries of audiences, trying year after year to build and sustain his circus. As another first of May rolled around, Rice had work to do, and Servis to Render.

20

HEY, RUBE!

"A stilled whirlpool of human faces." That's how Walt Whitman described the crowd in Rice's tent one August afternoon. In Brooklyn's heat, Whitman had come as a newspaper writer, squeezing his bulk onto a narrow plank seat and joining the "compressed mass of human beings melting under the tent," to watch one of his favorite themes enacted, the vigorous combination of mind and body. Fretting that the new craving for refinement put Americans at risk of becoming effete, Whitman believed circus was a healthy alternative. "A circus performer is the other half of a college professor. The perfect Man has more than the professor's brain, and a good deal of the performer's legs." He was not alone in his worry, or in his proposed solution. "We love the circus," intoned the *Cincinnati Enquirer,* "because it teaches a truth, that in our too intellectual age we are not a little apt to forget—'No sound mind without a sound body.'"[1]

However, Whitman's pleasure was mixed. He was glad that circus had become an American institution, for "Something very good may come of it, by-and-by." He also deemed Rice's troupe excellent, and enjoyed another of his passions: oratory. He could have been describing Rice in *Leaves of Grass:* "To inflate the chest, to roll the thunder of the voice out from the ribs and throat, / To make people rage, weep, hate, desire with yourself, / To lead America—to quell America with a great tongue." But the poet-reviewer complained of Rice's double entendres, and his pronunciation "in a 'stupen-jew-ous' manner." When the clown proclaimed that "Cuby" would one day be part of the United States, Whitman informed his readers that it was a "gag." That was "something which comic men fall back upon when their resources for making legitimate fun are exhausted. Most allusions to the American flag are gag; such are always applauded. A compliment to lovely woman is gag; it never fails to bring down the tent. A moral maxim is gag; it is certain to be audibly approved."[2]

However, Whitman was not immune to such claptraps himself. When Rice condemned hitting a man from behind, adding that they "do so in Congress, but that isn't the way with the Brooklyn boys," Whitman applauded editorially. Here was something to "illustrate the moral tone of the Ring."

This gag referred to an incident in the United States Senate. On May 22, a man named Pickens Butler decided that his cousin, South Carolina Senator Preston Brooks, had been insulted by Charles Sumner, the senator from Massachusetts. So Butler approached Sumner at his desk on the floor of the Senate, and beat him senseless with a cane. The next day John Brown and his abolitionist followers killed settlers in Lawrence, Kansas. One day later, May 23, Rice and his troupe got into a melee in Batavia, New York. The three outbursts were not equally weighty, but all were blows to the body politic. While Whitman enjoyed posing as a rough, celebrating the country's "barbaric yawp," the would-be b'hoy worried that the yawp had grown too barbaric. Internalizing the paradox of American democracy between individual assertion and community adhesion, he worried about that violence in the Senate, about the abolitionists, about rowdy crowds. He had once reveled in the participatory dynamic of performance, but the Astor Place Riot frightened him away. Now he was warning himself, "Be bold! be bold! be bold! Be not too bold!" So a manager like Rice, who "amuses a million persons a year, should regard himself somewhat in the light of a public instructor." Rice did, and Whitman approved. "The mere seating of this vast concourse was a moral lesson. . . . The care taken of the ladies, the perfect order that prevailed everywhere, the universal *right feeling* of the audience, the manly civility of the attendants, were all admirable to watch." (When he said that no policemen were necessary, Whitman stretched the point. As Rice noted of his Bedford, Massachusetts stop, most towns assigned police to preserve order at the circus.)[3]

Violence was one of America's favorite sports. Fueled by alcohol, any public gathering could generate fights, and circus was in the thick of the battle. Half a century after a worker on the first American circus, Ricketts's, put a man's eye out in Montreal, violence was still going strong. In 1848, Gossin had been on a carouse that resulted in a killing. The next year, John Robinson kicked a man to death. In 1850, a Spalding employee cracked a man's skull with a slung shot—a blackjack. In 1852, four years after Levi North pulled a knife on a driver, he was stabbed himself. In Ohio in 1853, Welch's troupe fought a two-day "Hippodrome War." It was not just men: Joe Pentland's wife horsewhipped a man who had gossiped about her.[4] Meanwhile, fighting was so common that it made no news. W. C. Coup remembered the stark risk:

> If the showmen were rough, so also were our patrons. The sturdy sons of toil came to the show eager to resent any imagined insult; and failing to fight with the showmen, would often fight among themselves. . . . In other words, "fighting was in the air.". . . Not once a month, or even once a week, but almost daily, would these fights occur, and so desperately were they entered into that they resembled pitched battles more than anything else.[5]

When a "majority of the towns were rough towns," a circus had to be an "efficient fighting unit." Mining and river areas were especially notorious. So were college towns. Rice recalled that Yale men required "unnumerable thumpings" before they learned to let circuses alone, and those at the University of Michigan were late imbibing that "salutary lesson." Alcohol made things worse. At Huntington, Massachusetts, in June, Rice noted "everybody drunk." Many tried to push their way into the show, or sometimes just picked a fight. Then, if one of them was hurt, tent ropes might be cut, a stable burned, or the show followed to the next town, to be attacked anew. Nor would circuses garner much local sympathy. An Illinois paper gave two sides to a whiskey-fueled fight, the locals' and the circus's, as "it is no more than right for us to give both versions—and we trust our readers will not believe a word of the last one."[6] So common was violence at the circus that Rice noted its absence in Salem, Lynn, and Charleston, Massachusetts: "good order no fights."

Circuses provided plenty of provocation. In Rochester, Rice admitted more people than there were seats, so few of the thousands went away satisfied. When the civic-minded showman, in tune with other circus proprietors, added after-show concerts in 1857, he picked up extra money charging for it but also generated antagonism as some balked at paying another quarter to stay in their seats. Circus hyperbole set up inevitable disappointment; the *Cincinnati Enquirer* joked that "Dan always had the faculty of humbugging the people a little stronger than anybody else—Barnum excepted." Mockery, at which Rice excelled, would provoke more anger. After "a Red headed theife" of a constable gave him trouble, Rice re-enacted the squabble in the ring. He could boast that the people became incensed against the constable as a result, but that man and his friends would be angry themselves. People were cheated as well. A skilled ticket seller could shortchange, unnoticed. Like birds in the wake of a boat, rigged games of chance abounded. Then there were pickpockets, who popped up wherever crowds gathered. A Baltimore paper told of one at church, and a Philadelphia paper reported a jolly tale of a policeman, stationed at the theater to watch out for the light-fingered gentry, who had his own pocket picked. Pickpockets were a major problem for circuses. Because some shows harbored the thieves for a share of the booty, all were blamed.[7]

Wherever fault lay, the "Hey Rube" exploded regularly. That is circus slang memorializing the good old days of violence. When a circus worker was attacked, he yelled "Hey, Rube!" and the troupe rushed to join the fight. Biting, gouging, kicking—no holds were barred, for who could have barred them in the melee? Rice called it "a terrible cry, [meaning] as no other expression in the language does, that a fierce deadly fight is on, that men who are far away from home must band together in a struggle that means life or death to them." The rallying cry of "Hey, Rube"—later transformed into a noun—seems likely to have been a challenge flung at a local Reuben, but circus stories say otherwise. Glenroy provided the first attribution, recalling that in 1848, a member of Rice's troupe was attacked at a New Orleans dance house. That man yelled to his friend, Reuben, and the whole company rushed to help.[8]

It is appropriate that Rice was part of this first "Hey, Rube" tale. If he had not become famous for his clowning, circus history would have to include him for his fighting. He fought to protect his circus; he fought in contentious pride; sometimes, he fought just for fun. Rice was a genial man, but he could deliver a "New York kiss" with the best of them. While calling him the "most remarkable clown this country has produced," Charles Stow, one of the century's great circus agents, maintained that the glory of defeating Rice forced him to face every local bully, placing him "in more personal encounters than any other living man." Coup made a similar double boast for his fellow showman: "Perhaps the greatest clown America ever saw," Rice was also a natural fighter who "would face a mob at anytime and under any circumstances." Even a joke about his prominent nose, so big it "speaks his talent," expanded to a celebration of this "fine specimen of athletic manliness." Rice recalled one incident, with his boss canvasman, "an ugly, surly fellow . . . who knew he could whip an average man with one of his hands tied behind him. So he thought he could whip Dan Rice." One night, when his crew refused to work and retired to a bar, Rice found them:

> Now, Tom Hurley, you and your men—these fellows who are now trying to hide behind the bar—have been making your boasts that you were going to stick this show; that you were not going to pull a stack, and that we would play h—l getting to the next town. Now, I want to say to you, you ____! ____! ____! ____!, you and these other fellows with you get back to that lot as quick as you can. Take down every tent there; load all of them, and be ready to start by 1 o'clock.[9]

The story is representative. A "man of the most supreme bravery, [Rice] did not care whether it was a barroom fight or a battle with 'natives' who were bent on breaking up the show; he did not care whether it was with pistols, knives or brass knuckles—he was always there." To "be there" in antebellum lingo was no mere location; it was emphatic assertion. Even Rice's ads swaggered: His show "can DEFY THE WORLD!" He warned "base imitators" that they "will soon find out, should they ever cross his track with their spurious concerns." The ad did not specify what they would find out, but notice was served.[10]

Disputes and performing co-existed on all circuses; Rice made them virtually identical. It was not merely coincidence that the *Rochester Daily Advertiser* declared, just before Rice's show arrived, that riot and circus had "become synonymous terms." When Oswego declined to give him a license on the grounds of immorality, the Oswego *Times and Journal* complained of those who wanted to ban the pleasures of circus and drink in "this work-a-day world," only to swell the "fund of the 'Kickapoo amelioration society.'" Forty miles down the canal, the *Syracuse Standard* warned that "Dan has got his spunk up, and says he'll be d—d if he don't perform all he advertises, whether the old Dads of Oswego like it or not." With police on alert and Rice on his way, trouble was brewing. While some saw a challenge to civic order, the *Standard* believed that the "starched aristocracy" was trying to impose on the people, perpetrating "ridiculous 'old fogy' notions." Ultimately, calm prevailed.[11]

Rice did not win all his fights. In mid-August, he was in Hudson, New York, one of the perennially troublesome river towns. Butcher Metcalf had been tossed out of the tent for causing a drunken disturbance. Rantankerous, he got together a "posse" of his chums and found Rice outside his hotel, where they insulted him. When they shoved the boy holding Rice's horse, the showman chased them. Outdistancing his friends, he caught up to two men, leveling one and hitting the other, but then Butcher's men pounced, giving him "a most unmerciful flogging—John H. Best knocking him down and stamping upon him until he pled for life." After his men had assisted Rice back to the hotel, they went to Best's saloon and wreaked havoc, using everything "from a slung-shot, to paving stones." In his ledger for the 1856 season, Rice mentioned fights but not his beating.[12]

Rice's ledger noted the usual array of incidents, large and small, good and bad. In July, Maggie's horse fell on the road into Rhode Island and she lost a diamond breastpin; Libby and Kate, twelve and ten, rode back the next day to retrieve it. On July 24, the center pole fell, dropping the tent and breaking a boy's shoulder; Rice paid $25 for a doctor, and gave $5 to the boy. Rice paid $12,000 over the season on circus accounts, Girard bills, and personal items, and another $5,000 for land. His accounts included a September splurge in Philadelphia, when he purchased a hat, gloves, a dozen shirts, a blue jacket, a suit for $60, more than the cost of Maggie's dresses, and a gold watch and chain for $130. He also paid the last installment on a mortgage on the 1850 circus led by Rosston, bought a lion and lioness for $150, and gave "an old Sharpe" the balance due on a patent for some kind of fluid that had turned out to be worthless.

When the summer began its turn to fall, Rice went to Virginia to visit the Crescent City Circus. He planned to combine his companies, but he was also going to check on his brother, who had been stabbed in North Carolina. Then, after a stand in Baltimore—where he was given a new label, "popular artist"—Rice rolled west into Ohio.[13] On October 21, heading north toward Lake Erie and home, his show traveled up a grass road to Windsor. There, his "little pupil," Charles Reed, spotted a pickpocket.

Rice waited to catch the scoundrel in action, then pounced. He recorded the action in his ledger as if writing for the movies, complete with dialogue and a fade-out:

> I said, "Never let me see you near this show again or following it. If you dare do it, I will proclaim it who and what you are."
> "Well," said he, "what am I?"
> "You are a pickpocket."
> Said he, "You are a liar!"
> "Leave this ground!"
> "I will when it suits my convenience!"
> "You must and I will make you."
> Says he, "If you touch me, I will kill you!"

The showman had his men hold the thief and sent for local officials. Instead of beating the man, Rice determined to law it.

Meanwhile, the audience, having heard the commotion, was streaming out of the tent. They decided that this sparring beat the scheduled performance all hollow. In *Huckleberry Finn,* Twain depicted his circus as an island of calm in the antebellum sea of violence and fraud. A mob and a killing precede the circus scene, and tar-&-feathers follow. Yet even in the idealized calm, Twain hints at the circus violence he knew. When a drunk climbs into the ring to ride, "a lot of men begin to pile down off the benches and swarm towards the ring, saying 'Knock him down! throw him out!' and one or two women begun to scream." But the ringmaster quiets them, and it is revealed to be an act, the Flying Wardrobe, with the pretend drunk stumbling into the ring to ride comically and then expertly, shedding costume after costume until they "kind of clogged up the air."[14] Like Twain's fictional crowd, the real one at Rice's circus became incensed. "Some said kill him but I made them cool down." Taking the situation in hand, Rice had his men march the thief off to the local justice of the peace, the curious parading along. Suddenly the pickpocket whirled and hit Rice in the eye. "Still I offered no resistance determined that the law should have its course and not to allow myself to be provoked to strike another man while I lived—as I had made a promise that I never would as it cost me a fortune." Presumably he meant fines, such as the one due the "Red headed theife" of a constable or the $100 for fighting in Batavia.

The whooping crowd elbowed its way up the narrow stairs and into the office of "Squire Thomas, a slow Justice of the Piece, as Rotten a piece of Justice and very small at that." People pushed and jostled for the best vantage point. A circus with Rice was fun; a trial with the clown on the bill was even better. He was losing business, but his fighting spirit overwhelmed practicality, as usual.

The wheels of justice ground slowly. Rice wrote that an hour was wasted getting lights and finding paper, ink, and law books. As the old Squire botched several attempts to make out a writ, people's comments befuddled him even more. Meanwhile, the pickpocket continued to abuse Rice, becoming "almost ungovernable Still I said men do not touch this vile creature." At last, all was ready. Lights were lit, ink and paper marshaled, the writ written. The crowd settled down and the thief shut up. The small justice assumed his grand position.

The first trial concerned the assault on Rice. Only one man in "this god forsaken place" knew the pickpocket, Johnson. At least "that is the name he gave in." The acquaintance—"his name (a novel one) Smith"—became the defense lawyer, his expertise stemming from his own arrests for passing counterfeit money. As the judge lingered over every detail, the crowd grew impatient. "Some said let us take him out & tar & feather him." In antebellum America, group action had nearly the stature of law. Rice, the most commanding presence in the room, could have let the mob take the crook. "Still I persisted and talkd them out of it." Finally, the legal system rumbled in deliberative majesty to a decision: Guilty, with a $10 fine, plus costs.

Rice was shocked. The "most deep dyde villian that ever ran unhung" had been charged with intent to kill, and had to pay only $10!? Adding insult to injury, "the man all at once began to have friends." Rice was "thunder struck" by that development, but he "was not long in discovering the cause of this magic change of feeling in said honest community." Unfortunately, what Rice discovered remains a mystery, shrouded in his poor penmanship. Even as his use of language improved, Rice became a byword for illegibility: It was said of a local doctor and Rice "that when they write to anyone unacquainted with their hieroglyphics it is usual to send it back for a translation."[15] Whatever caused the change in community feeling, it had something to do with money: "It was reported by his wise Shylock attorney that the unknown thiefe a one or two thousand dollars." *Had* a thousand dollars? Whatever Rice meant precisely, the pickpocket had managed to make allies through that universal friend, money.

As Rice pushed for the robbery trial, a man warned that the floor was about to crash in, and offered his store, conveniently down the stairs, for part II. The Squire immediately fled, followed by the turbulent crowd, which bumped against Rice's men at the top of the stairs, where they held "Johnson." They were the guards, either because no one else had taken up the task or because they had overawed the local constabulary. If nineteenth-century circuses were efficient fighting units, Rice would have had an especially efficient one. Johnson continued to threaten Rice, swearing that "he would kill me the first chance he had—I was in much pain with my Eye coverd over and being such a crowd around him and me—I thought it ok to have my men protect me as the court could not do so." The crowd shuffled and shoved its way down the stairs and into the store below.

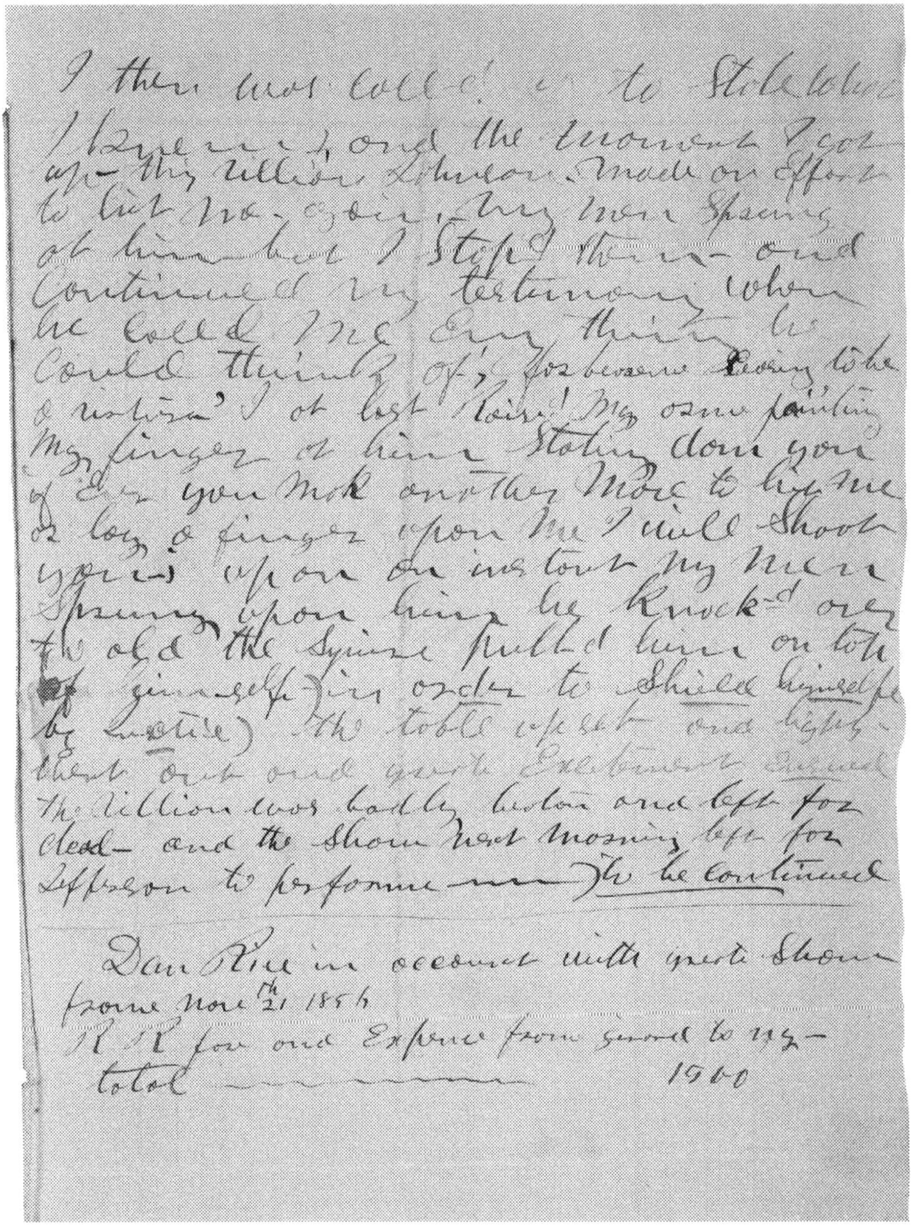
I then was called on to state what
I knew, and the moment I got
up the villian Johnson made an effort
to hit me again, my men sprang
at him but I stopped them and
continued my testimony when
he called me every thing he
could think of; forbearance ceasing to be
a virtue I at last raised my arm pointing
my finger at him stating done you
if ever you make another move to hit me
or lay a finger upon me I will shoot
you in upon an instant my men
sprung upon him he knocked over
the old the squire pulled him on top
of himself in order to shield himself
by justice) the table upset and lights
went out and great excitement ensued
the villian was badly beaten and left for
dead— and the show next morning left for
Jefferson to perform — To be continued

Dan Rice in account with great show
from Nov 21th 1856
R R fare and expence from ... to ...
total 1500

Rice recorded the capture of a pickpocket, the incompetence and local bias of a justice of the peace, and a fight.

> well time Rolled on and we began to discover that there was a disposition on the part of many to let him go but some sevral of the element who were honest men interfened in getting the old Justice into Court once we commencd the examination of the Second charge for Robbery.

After the man whose pocket had been picked gave his evidence, it was Rice's turn. The "moment I got up this villian Johnson made an effort to hit me again. My men sprung at him but I stopd them and continued my testimony when he called me every thing he could think of, 'forbearance ceasing to be a virtue' I at last Raisd my arme pointing my finger at him"—Rice's sturdy arm held it steady, a ring gleaming in the candlelight—"Stating dam you if ever you mak another move to hit me or lay a finger upon me I will shoot you." The farce continued: "upon an instant my men sprung upon him he knockd over the old Squire pulled him on top of himself in *order* to Shield himselfe by Justice) the table upset and lights went out and great Excitement ensued."

Farce turned solemn again, as the villian was badly beaten and left for dead. He did not die, so Rice was not hauled back for trial. Or perhaps the Squire could not find the right writ. Rice's account of the fight and the season concluded quietly: "and the show next morning left for Jefferson to performe)to be continued."

PART 4

"SOMETHING HIGHER"

1856 ☛ 1860

21

CABINET OF CURIOSITIES

Girard was quietly busy in winter: wagons were repaired, costumes sewn, animals fed, new tricks rehearsed. At the same time, the Rices carried on their middle-class life. To help them, they bought *Mackenzie's Five Thousand Receipts in All the Useful and Domestic Arts,* an 1856 alphabet of recipes, from brewing and calico printing to enameling, perfumery, silk-worms, and wine making. Advice manuals, how-to tomes, and recipe books were immensely popular as the growing middle class simultaneously paraded its refinement and anxiously sought to figure out what refinement was, including the domestic arts. ("Art" still mostly meant "craft," and was only starting to be applied to performance.) The winter's cozy geniality was perfect for Rice, who always had something new for "the boys." One story, set in the local carriage shop, told of a salesman asking for Rice just as the showman walked in the door. The carriage maker's mouth was full of tobacco, so he pointed at Dan with the red-hot tire he was working at his forge. Dan heard the question, saw the glowing piece of metal, and immediately said, "Give me a dollar and I'll lick it!" The salesman was thrilled. He would witness one of Rice's amazing feats! He pulled out a silver dollar. Dan took the coin, licked that, put it in his pocket, and walked out.[1]

The peace may have been ruffled through the winter of 1856–1857. Years later, Dan said that he and Maggie divorced in 1857. That wasn't true, but he may have been recalling a season of trouble with his wife. His land deals have left a possible clue. Maggie's name had been on the deeds since his first Girard purchase, but when Dan bought twenty-five acres this January, his name alone was "of the second part" on the contract. He and Maggie were entering a new stage in their lives. No longer struggling together to build a show, they were also past whatever bloom had been on the rose. The girls were older, Libby thirteen, Kate nearly eleven, and off at school. (Kate later donated a scrapbook of clippings of her parents' careers from 1856; perhaps she started it prompted by homesickness.) Neither girl was on the show now. Too old to be childishly adorable, they had not yet developed the skill or womanly strength for an adult act. At the table now it was Mother and old Dad, alone together.[2]

After a month home, Rice took the train to New York. He put off Brinton again from there, writing that he would have no money until spring, though if "unforeseen circumstance should put the availability into my bones, the pecuniary result shall be made known and the agreeable dollar be at once forthcoming from yours most truly." Dan may have had someone else write the letter but, an intelligent man, he had been soaking up self-education; flowery expression was not beyond him. (Fancy words did not always work; three years later, Brinton hauled Rice into court for $570.) Then, after a brief return to Girard to buy more land, Rice traveled to the nation's capital, to open February 18 with the Washington Circus, which also featured the rising star rider, James Robinson.[3]

The capital was buzzing. James Buchanan's inauguration was a public holiday and Washington was awash with celebrating "Buchaneers" seeking office with the new administration. Rice had a room at the Marble Front Hotel, but not everyone was so lucky in what was essentially a small Southern town. So in the days leading up to the grand event, Rice advertised that 2,000 people could sleep in the tent on Pennsylvania Avenue, for 50¢ extra. (The ads noted an exception: "After the performance all colored people will be excluded, as no provisions are made.")[4]

Older countries might look down their noses at the raw country, but here was a peaceful change of government that few others had accomplished. The country carried a palpable pride: At least it did this right, even as belligerent words flew between Southern fire-eaters and Northern radicals. A solid Northern man, Buchanan calmed many fears when he promised that the South's "peculiar institution" of slavery would not be disturbed. Still, curiosity about his cabinet increased the excitement. With campaign promises past, Buchanan's choices would tell much about his intentions. As he kept his state secret, the *Evening Star* joined the ancient tradition of political pundits flip-flopping authoritatively. The day after the new president was sworn in, the paper speculated about his possible choices. The following day, it professed itself "amused . . . with the different speculation and theories mooted in this connection." Buchanan "fairly bagged the wondermongers" by keeping his cabinet a secret. A day later, the paper boasted that its original speculations had been accurate.[5]

Rice sang about the mystery to 20,000 over his three-week run. His song, "Captain Dan Rice, The Nation's Humorist, on Buchanan's Cabinet," had a different verse for each member. The tune he used was from a song, "Root, Hog, or Die," that had become a national cry of action: Get-food-or-perish. The song began with a plug for Rice's hotel and its proprietors, the brothers Brown, who "feed me mighty well." This could have been a trade, like product placement in a movie. Rice put himself in the first chorus:

> Though I'm chief cook, bottle washer, captain of the waiters,
> Takes old "Buck" to strip the jackets from the taters;
> They say about his Cabinet he's acted very sly,
> But I've found out all about it—"it's Root Hog or Die."

Verses followed on Buck's picks. There was the Michigan man, Lewis Cass, able to handle tricky foreign diplomats as secretary of state, for he will "strip off their disguises, like peelings off of taters." James Floyd of Virginia was secretary of the Army. Though few expected war between the regions, it concerned some Northerners that a Southerner would de-

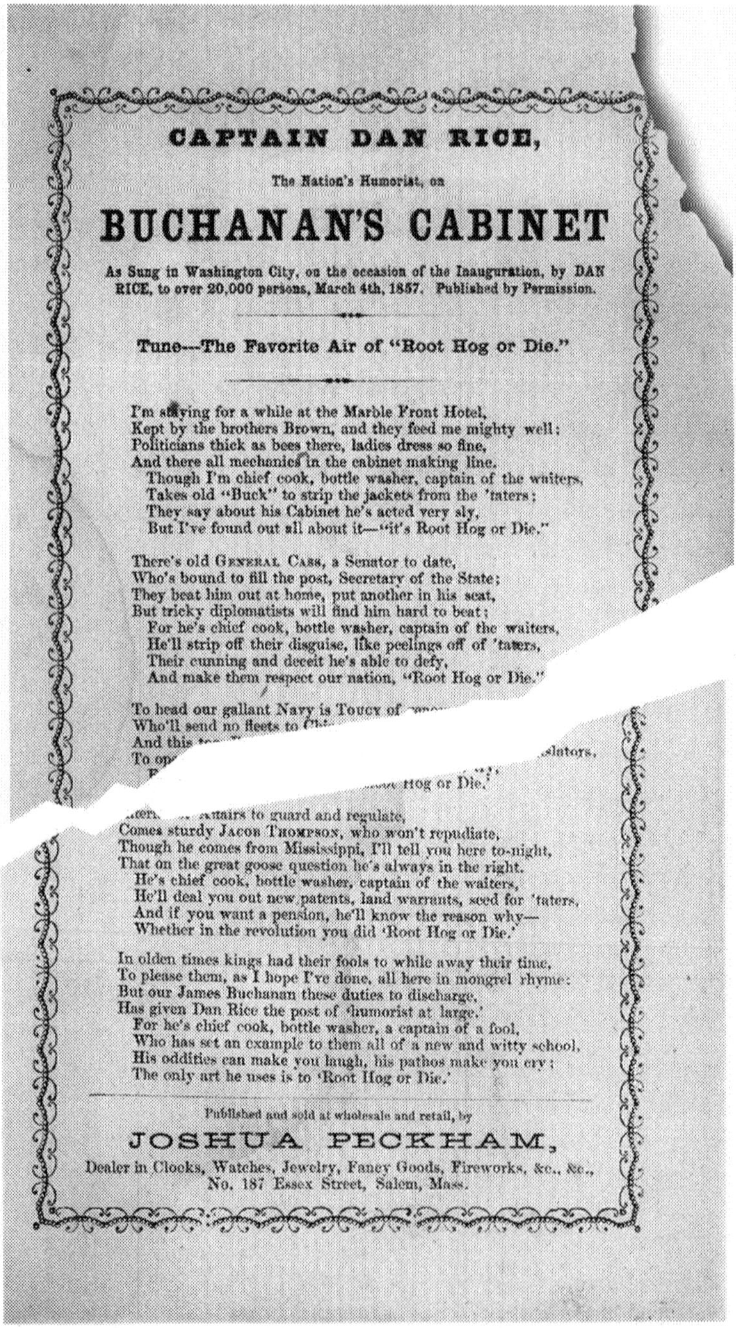

Increasingly political in performance, Rice sang about Buchanan's cabinet.

termine where in the "line of battle the troops will be deployed." Buchanan himself was "captain of a fool," as he made Rice "humorist at large."[6]

Yet other than this song, Rice never made much of Buchanan. That is curious because, of all the presidents Rice claimed to have befriended, Old Buck was the most directly connected. Dan's friends, the Fosters, were part of the same Pennsylvania Democratic machine, and Buchanan's in-laws besides. Stephen and Mit Foster's sister had married the president's brother. Rice conjured links out of less, yet he never added Buchanan to his cabinet of stories. This curious gap must have flowed from loyalty to the Fosters.[7] As Buchanan kept himself distant from his impecunious in-laws, their friend Rice kept his distance from Buchanan. Later, when history rendered this president an inconsequential preliminary to the Civil War, Rice had little incentive to invent stories.

Following the usual re-engagement after a usual "last week," Rice went to Philadelphia to join Lent's Winter Show at the National Theatre. The bills declared that Rice "carefully avoids all Personal Allusions calculated either to wound private feelings, or to offend." As Rice's Personal Allusions continued unabated, that notice suggested he was using more topical material. Rice rarely rode, but he performed the "veritable Pete Jenkins," a new name for the old Flying Wardrobe act described by Twain. Next, in Baltimore for a two-week stand, Rice played Don Juan, "Or, The Libertine Destroyed!" at his first benefit. For his second one, he pulled out all the stops. He presented a burlesque, "The Mule Traders," and offered $10 to anybody who could ride his mules. He offered another $100 to anyone who could run a mile around the ring in under five minutes, a fast clip considering that the race was all turns. Finally, he spun "Mississippi River Yarns, Dutch Stories, Irish Anecdotes, and Yankee Peculiarities."[8]

In its comic types, performance was addressing the longest-running question in American history: What is a true American? The b'hoy, the sly Yankee, the backwoodsman, the grinning Irishman, even the blackface "nigger," isolated by the horror of slavery and the abomination of racism, showed America thinking out loud about itself. Rice appeared at a benefit with Eph Horn, "The Greatest Living Delineator of Negro Character." That billing meant that Rice was presented as less than the greatest blackface, but he wouldn't have minded. That was partly because Baltimore was a Southern town, where blackface didn't go over as well. Minstrelsy, created and mostly performed by men of the North, fed the conflicted needs in the antebellum North to feel superior while having a good laugh. The South, where whites enjoyed a social structure enforcing racial superiority, had less need for blackface. Rice had another motive for avoiding blackface. Just as he pursued his campaign to depict himself as no regional creature but a man of the whole nation, he was no longer a specialist restricted to what had become a narrow, if popular genre. As American Humorist, he did not simply seek to add another type to the comedian's lexicon; instead, he was reaching for a grand synthesis. His "original character" knew the North, the West, and the South, knew planters and plowmen and poets, draymen and dandies, the city slicker and the country rube. Rice offered "Wit so Whimsical! Jokes so Jocular! Puns so Pointed! Satire so Severe! Remarks so Ready! That all will say he is truly entitled to the rank of the Great American Jester."[9]

22

A GENIUS FOR FUN

Rice settled an account with a three-dollar bill, but the money was returned with the message: "This note is counterfeit, please send another." Replying a few months later, Rice

> apologized for the delay, saying he had been unable till now to find another counterfeit three-dollar bill, but he hoped the one he now enclosed would suit, professing at the same time his inability to discover what the objection was to the other, which he thought as good a counterfeit as he ever saw.

It must be admitted, thought the *Cincinnati Enquirer,* that Dan swept that board.[1]

Counterfeits were a recurring risk, especially because local banks issued their own currency of varying denominations and reliability. Particularly susceptible were traveling shows. A person who got bad money would be reluctant to pass it on to a neighbor, but a traveling circus ticket window was tempting. As *Sketches* complained, "Hundreds of spurious dollars are offered to the Treasurer during the season by persons who sustain an unblemished reputation amongst their townsmen." When he bought a book about history of coins from a Boston professor, Rice was probably seeking to protect himself. Charley Warner, the show's new treasurer, was given unusual prominence for someone in that position when he was introduced with a warning: He was sharp as a steel trap and would not take bad bills, so "our friends must bring us good ones."[2]

Rice's critics would call his taller tales counterfeit, but they were true in a mythic sense. Later portraits of Lincoln as a backwoods hick, of Barnum as wisely dignified, of robber barons as benevolent, were no more accurate than Rice's tales. As the showman's prominence grew, America relished his stories of the boy rising to fame.

By popular conception, clowning is a kind of counterfeit, too, the makeup a mask hiding true feelings. Similarly with performing generally. That had not been the case historically. Despite a suspicion dating from Plato, who deemed performers liars to be expelled from the ideal state, most people across time and across cultures have been eager to embrace the real pretend of performance. Public behavior was seen as a kind of performance, too, a way of presenting yourself to others. The country had been founded on, and the Constitution created in, the Enlightenment view that what people did in public—the performance of their civic duties—mattered more than the complex blend of motives, impulses, and goals that lived in their unknowable hearts. By their actions, you shall know them. But things changed in the nineteenth century. Influenced by Romantic-era notions and reacting to an increasingly complex world, people sought something that felt like genuine truth beneath confusing appearance. Authenticity became a kind of trump card. Products sold better if they were pitched as unadulterated; a social bungler was "at least being honest"; politicians competed to prove their sincerity. Performance joined this shift. Spectacle now came with assurances that a representation was historically accurate. Forrest, Macready, and Wallett gained stature by publicizing the research they did for accuracy, and actors who desired not to be hissed off the stage should "dress properly, according to the age and occupation of the individual represented, and the epoch and county he lived in." Romanticism's insistence on universal truth behind appearances was preparing the ground for Sigmund Freud to seek psychological truth beneath polite appearances, for Charles Darwin to dig out biological truth hidden in the ages, and for Karl Marx to spy economic truth under the machinery of capitalism. Once discovered, the x-ray reinforced the urge to see deeper.[3]

Just so, in declaring a new kind of clown, Rice said that he stood before his audience as genuinely himself. He advertised his Dream of Chivalry as historically accurate. He presented his hits on the times as wise, personal observations, like a newspaper editor's. He increasingly matched his pitch to the culture's lust for authenticity.

Authenticity, as a component of respectability, infused *Dan Rice's Pictorial,* a four-page, newspaper-sized publication—called a courier—filled with act descriptions, pictures, and jokes. (Rice apparently purchased a local paper, the *Conneautville Crisis,* to do the printing.) Instead of the usual alliterative assortment of awesomely amazing adjectives about the circus, the *Pictorial* focused on refinement. The front page pictured Rice as a solid citizen in a coat and cravat, and the text staked less claim for talent or humor than for propriety. Like a high-toned gentleman, Rice offered reforms, "the first great causes of revolution," which have "launched new faiths—established liberal governments, peopled new countries—crushed out feudal systems in the old world—and destroyed illiberal prejudices in this new." The beneficial effects of reform, having spread to theology, law, medicine, literature, and politics, now reached to amusements, which were "necessary institutions—affording a healthy relaxation for the masses." Dickens made the same point in the mid-1850s in his novel, *Hard Times,* which posed the oppression of industrialism and its regimented educational system against life-affirming circus. Dickens put his theme into the mouth of a circus proprietor, Sleary, giving him an infantile lisp: "People must be amuthed, Thquire, thomehow . . . they can't alwayth be a working, nor yet they can't be alwayth a learning." Those watching Rice's show agreed, considering it a "safety valve for overworked humanity." He went further. His Great Show, not merely escapist entertainment for the masses, was supported by the elite, "thousands of well-educated, intelligent people" who sought "splendor, refinement, training, novelty and true wit." Half a century later, George Bernard Shaw declared that he wanted a theater to which he could take intellectuals without embarrassment; Rice anticipated Shaw when he proclaimed his determination "to make Equestrian exhibition worthy of the countenance of the intellectual and refined." No reformer has done more than Rice, insisted the *Pictorial*: He has "rendered the arena like it was in olden times, a place of classic resort. The groveling babbler in spotted dress, and the low buffoon he has driven from the ring, and now in his 'Great Show,' stands out proudly as the acknowledged humorist of the day."[4]

Demonstrating the advance of Rice's stature, the *Cincinnati Enquirer* copied the *Pictorial* for the start of its annual circus preview. Copying was a practical convenience for an editor who had less to write to fill the daily quota—but it was also an endorsement. The *Enquirer* reinforced that endorsement by adding a preface. "Of Dan we can say," it began,

> he has a genius for fun. His humors are adapted to the times, his hits local, his satire telling, his wit pointed, his jokes harmless, and his conversational powers unlimited. . . . He is the great master-spirit of the nineteenth century—the man who, above all, the people most admire. With an enviable reputation for integrity of character, and a universal fame as the most amusing man of modern times, his name is a tower of strength. Among the upper circles . . . Dan Rice is the magnet of attraction.[5]

He insisted that his Great Show was not merely inoffensively acceptable, it was a positive force for reform. He boasted of his stars' "Refinement and Originality." Thomas Canham's Keystone Orchestra did not simply play the usual polkas, marches, and patriotic airs, but also selections from Verdi and Mendelssohn. Rice's talent for engaging audiences rose to its greatest strength just as audiences were most eager for what he offered: authenticity, respectability, especially refinement. [6]

Rice even presented his rhinoceros as refined. The Living Unicorn, it had been exhibited on the Barnum & Howes Asiatic Caravan in 1854, was sold or loaned to Cushing the next year, and then not exhibited in 1856, perhaps because it was a poor draw. A rhinoceros could not do much. Comparing the animal's horn and the clown's prominent nose, the *Clipper* joked that "Rice" was short for rhinoceros. (The word had not yet been trimmed to "rhino," which was still slang for money, suggesting a folk source for "pay through the nose.") When Cushing and Howes prepared to present a circus in England in 1856, they wondered what to do with their hog-in-armor. It was troublesome to transport, and the English might not take to it. Meanwhile, Rice had demonstrated that comic mules drew audiences. So Howes and Cushing offered to buy Rice's pair. He was willing, because he could train more. He put the price at $5,000, but when he was offered $1,000 and the rhinoceros, Rice swapped. Though he asserted the rhino was worth $4,000, making the deal a good one, to the show world he had been "sold." What could he do with a rhinoceros?[7]

He could train it. One day in Girard, leaning against the animal's pen, he lit his cigar with a red-hot poker. The rhinoceros nudged him at that moment, so Rice jabbed back, forcing a retreat. The next day, the animal backed up when it saw the showman holding the poker. That told Rice it could learn, so he set to work. Or he set Noyes to work. As with Lalla Rookh, Rice took credit for the training, but he also acknowledged Noyes's contribution. In May 1857, Rice presented the first trained rhinoceros in the United States, and perhaps the first performing rhinoceros since the days of ancient Rome. Rice named it Old Put, for Israel Putnam,

Rice's rare performing rhinoceros, "Old Put."

the general who had defended West Point during the Revolution. The tricks were simple. Old Put climbed steps, "spoke," lay down, and sat back on its haunches. Differences in its "trot, gambol, and run" depended on the music played by the band. Rice did create a small drama by yelling "Fire!" so that the animal could hit a bell with its horn, as if raising the alarm. Otherwise the limited range of actions posed a publicity problem, as Howes and Cushing had discovered. After proclaiming that Rice exercised his will over "the most obdurate disposition of animal nature," what else could be said? One tactic was to change the subject. In an article on the rhinoceros in the 1858 *Pictorial,* the publicity agent wrote about his astonishment at the animal's description, about the greatness of Rice, and the grandness of Excelsior. A trip to see the critter left him discussing the trip, not the critter. Finally, the one-horned "machine" made an appearance in a few lines at the end of the account. It was "the largest one ever captured," a claim difficult to assess because Old Put was also "the only Rhinoceros in America." The more important publicity tactic was respectability; against a backdrop of columns and drapery, the animal was pictured with one foot on a pedestal like a middle-class gent posing in a portrait gallery. [8]

Barely two weeks into the 1857 season, breaking his vow never to hit a man again, Rice was arrested in Rochester for assault and battery. In June, he was beaten up himself, this time by a machinist in Syracuse. (He then missed shows, which led to complaints in Oswego: His replacement was dull, Excelsior was not presented, and the rhinoceros was "unanimously voted a humbug and a bore.") At Attica in August, another "general knocking down and dragging out" made the news. Officers sent to quell matters were themselves beaten away. The citizens then "took hold of the matter in earnest," fetching guns from the local arsenal. A well-regulated militia being necessary to the security of a free state, the right of the people to keep and bear arms against a circus was not infringed, so Rice's company surrendered a few men to arrests. As for Rice, just before a flying visit to his family in Girard, he was horned by his rhino. His publicity joked about the "uncivil 'hist'" [hoist], but it was serious. The animal was reputed to have killed one keeper, and Rice did not fully recover until the following spring.[9]

Rice toured Canada through the summer of 1857, including stops in Montreal and Toronto. His publicity employed a new way to announce his circus, the ads in the *Toronto Daily Globe* exhorting "Wait for the Carnival!!" Moving south through new York, Rice reached Brooklyn, where his tent was "crowded to suffocation" with 5,000 people. In the *Daily Eagle,* Rice touted the $75,000 his circus had cost.

Announcing he would winter in Philadelphia, Rice ended the season in Pittsburgh. Smoky City papers loyally cheered. A "*protégé* of Pittsburgh," he had become the "leading showman of the age," with an "outfit better and more extensive than any ever owned by man individually." His "success in life is a pattern for the rising generation." He summarized the appeal of his show as it reached its fullest form:.

1st. THE TIGHT ROPE ELEPHANT.
2d. THE TAME RHINOCEROS.
3d. THE TRICK CAMEL.
4th. THE TALKING HORSE.
5th. THE COMIC MULES.
6th. THE TANDEM MANAGE MARES.
7th. THE only ORIGINAL HUMORIST, DAN RICE !

Some of the praise came because he brought money into the local economy, more "we are informed, . . . than any merchant in the city." (When Spalding closed in Cincinnati, he paid accumulated salaries of $15,000, and much of that went into the stores.) Part of it, too, was local pride. Presenting his "Comic Positions on Horseback"—another rare riding appearance—Rice was a Pittsburgh boy who "has won the race." As had become typical, the *Post* was especially pleased by the class of people who patronized his show. "One of our oldest and most valued subscribers told us that he was glad to find that the circus was so modified, that it was worthy of the support of those who viewed refinement as one of the best claims that could be put forward for public patronage. Who says that Dan Rice is not a man of uncommon intellectual acumen."[10]

The backwoods Rice had been traveling for years had long been regarded as an empty wasteland to be overwhelmed. The later image of Africa as a trackless, forbidding jungle was originally applied to the

American interior, where Michigan was considered impenetrable forest, and Nebraska a desert. But a new vision was growing. Increasingly, Americans saw value in the sweep of the continent. The United States, it was said, had a "manifest destiny" to rule from the Atlantic to the Pacific, and beyond, as Dan's jokes about annexing Cuba attest.[11] About the time that the doctrine of Manifest Destiny acquired its name, in 1846, that vision was finding expression in the landscapes of the painters known as the Hudson River School. Capturing the country's awesome beauty, they painted craggy mountains and sheltered meadows, waterfalls, and wide vistas that their fellow citizens had never seen or, seeing, had scorned. These painterly images sometimes served a more practical purpose. In 1852, the Baltimore & Ohio Railroad sought to increase the value of its land by hiring William Louis Sonntag to paint pleasing pictures that might persuade people to settle along its tracks. America's first major school of painting was also a marketing tool.

The Hudson River School was reaching its prime along with Rice. At first glance, that is a mere coincidence of time. The painters ignored the clamorous and growing cities, which had the greatest concentration for audiences, to create a prettified image of sparsely populated, mostly tranquil vastness. A scholar pointed out that the peacefulness of the paintings constituted "an essential denial of the grim conflagration of Civil War." Before that denial came a denial of the massed energy and confusion of the growing antebellum republic. The painterly vision of peace, rendered in delicate shades and subtle light, obscured the cold, dirty, and wet world that Americans lived—and in which Rice labored. For him, Hudson River meant river towns and their constant fights. That rawness extended to the energy out of which Rice created his comedy. Yet his participation in the same urge to transcend coarseness, to drape a pretty veil over crude life, made him an intellectual kin to the Hudson River School. Both the clown and the painters were responding to and helping further a culture-wide urge of elevation. Like them, Rice was creating an elevated image, though his subject was himself, and his canvas was the circus ring. The *Cincinnati Enquirer* was not being ironic when it called him a "genius for fun."[12]

23

EXCELSIOR!

Men and women shivered against the chill as they made their way up Broadway. At Prince Street, they entered the elegant Metropolitan Hotel and passed through the brightly lit lobby to Niblo's pleasure palace. The first arrivals bustled into the chilly theater at the 6:30 P.M. call of "Doors." Empty rows gave way to pairs and pockets of people, chatting, yelling to friends. Outside was cold and dark; here, conviviality reigned. As more made their way up the narrow stairs, noise increased. Anticipation grew. Individuals were becoming an audience.

Rice was now a major figure in amusements. With all the options that Manhattan offered, including the American Museum, promised by Barnum to be comparable to eating "hasheesh," multitudes chose Rice. The Broadway Theatre had dropped *Mazeppa,* "fearful that Rice's show might diminish their receipts." His Great Show averaged receipts of $500 a night through February. With tickets ranging from the ironically labeled "aristocratic price" of 25¢, up to a plebeian $1 for a seat in a private box, that meant 1,000 people a show, probably more. His benefit garnered over $800. (Overall through the winter of 1857–1858, at Baltimore's

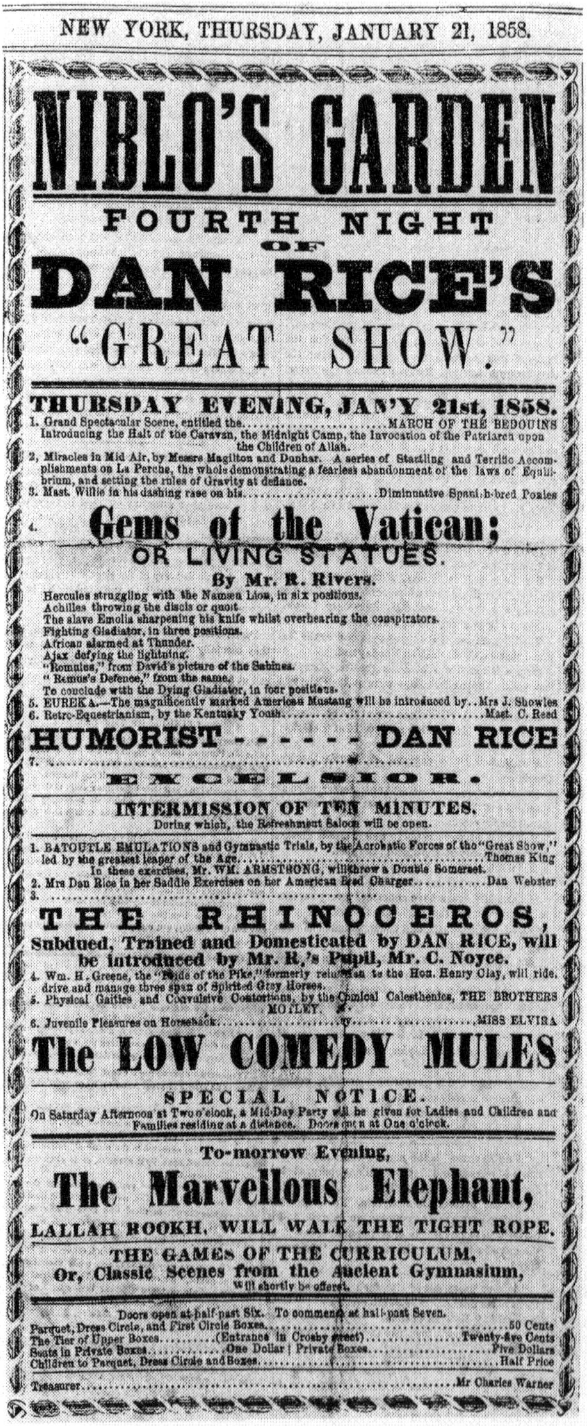

NEW YORK, THURSDAY, JANUARY 21, 1858.

NIBLO'S GARDEN

FOURTH NIGHT

OF

DAN RICE'S

"GREAT SHOW."

THURSDAY EVENING, JAN'Y 21st, 1858.

1. Grand Spectacular Scene, entitled the............MARCH OF THE BEDOUINS
Introducing the Halt of the Caravan, the Midnight Camp, the Invocation of the Patriarch upon the Children of Allah.
2, Miracles in Mid Air, by Messrs Magilton and Dunbar. A series of Startling and Terrific Accomplishments on La Perche, the whole demonstrating a fearless abandonment of the laws of Equilibrium, and setting the rules of Gravity at defiance.
3. Mast. Willie in his dashing rase on his............Diminutive Spani.h-bred Ponies

4. Gems of the Vatican;

OR LIVING STATUES.

By Mr. R. Rivers.

Hercules struggling with the Namean Lion, in six positions.
Achilles throwing the discis or quoit.
The slave Emolia sharpening his knife whilst overhearing the conspirators.
Fighting Gladiator, in three positions.
African alarmed at Thunder.
Ajax defying the lightning.
"Romulus," from David's picture of the Sabines.
"Remus's Defence," from the same.
To conclude with the Dying Gladiator, in four positions.

5. EUREKA.—The magnificently marked American Mustang will be introduced by..Mrs J. Showles
6. Retro-Equestrianism, by the Kentucky Youth............Mast. C. Reed

HUMORIST - - - - - - DAN RICE

7. ....

EXCELSIOR.

INTERMISSION OF TEN MINUTES.

During which, the Refreshment Saloon will be open.

1. BATOUTLE EMULATIONS and Gymnastic Trials, by the Acrobatic Forces of the "Great Show," led by the greatest leaper of the Age............Thomas King
In these exercises, Mr. WM. ARMSTRONG, will throw a Double Somerset.
2. Mrs Dan Rice in her Saddle Exercises on her American Bred Charger............Dan Webster
3. ....

THE RHINOCEROS,

Subdued, Trained and Domesticated by DAN RICE, will be introduced by Mr. R.'s Pupil, Mr. C. Noyce.

4. Wm. H. Greene, the "Pride of the Pike," formerly reinsman to the Hon. Henry Clay, will ride, drive and manage three span of Spirited Gray Horses.
5. Physical Gaities and Convulsive Contortions, by the Comical Calesthenics, THE BROTHERS MOTLEY.
6. Juvenile Pleasures on Horseback............MISS ELVIRA

The LOW COMEDY MULES

SPECIAL NOTICE.

On Saturday Afternoon at Two o'clock, a Mid-Day Party will be given for Ladies and Children and Families residing at a distance. Doors open at One o'clock.

To-morrow Evening,

The Marvellous Elephant,

LALLAH ROOKH, WILL WALK THE TIGHT ROPE.

THE GAMES OF THE CURRICULUM,
Or, Classic Scenes from the Ancient Gymnasium,
Will shortly be offered.

Doors open at half-past Six. To commence at half-past Seven.

Parquet, Dress Circle, and First Circle Boxes............50 Cents
The Tier of Upper Boxes..........(Entrance in Crosby street)............Twenty-five Cents
Seats in Private Boxes............One Dollar | Private Boxes............Five Dollars
Children to Parquet, Dress Circle and Boxes............Half Price

Treasurer............Mr Charles Warner

The advertisement for Rice's show in Philadelphia in January 1858, as he was reaching the height of his appeal.

Front Street in December, at Niblo's the next two months, and at Philadelphia's National into April Rice's show averaged $300 a night.) Yet for all the appeal of circus, the word was vanishing from his ads. His enterprise was simply, grandly, Dan Rice's Great Show.[1]

"Circus," for instance, did not appear in the daily *Programme*, a proto-*Playbill*. Rice paid $15 a week to cover half the front page of the periodical with his offerings. For his fourth performance in town, January 21, 1858, it listed the fourteen acts in that night's show.[2]

1. Grand Spectacular Scene, entitled MARCH OF THE BEDOUINS

A clang of the ringmaster's bell got the show underway, shortly after 7:30. In later ages, the house lights would dim to signal the start, while lights on stage would focus attention, but here gaslight and candles continued to glow over all. Performers had to grab attention, becoming more interesting than the hubbub in the seats. Rice's company marched into the ring in strength, "Bedouins" by dint of the $8 he had paid for costumes, plus another $1 for the "Heigh Priest" robes. It was a good opening number, an exotic but vague parade, giving stragglers time to settle in.[3]

2. Miracles in Mid Air, by Messrs Magilton and Dunbar.
A series of Startling and Terrific Accomplishments on La Perche.

As the Bedouins decamped, Dunbar—George Nice—and Harry Magilton strode into the ring. Dunbar held the perch pole while Magilton scampered up to balance himself upside down and hold himself out horizontally. Acrobats soon faced a higher bar. In Paris a year later, Jean Léotard became the first person to fly from trapeze to trapeze. Eventually, a performer's status would reflect the degree of danger in an act, which meant either height or wild animals.[4]

Léotard made another contribution. A major appeal of the circus, and cause for complaint, was its display of bodies. Like ballet, the circus provided a chance to ogle in the name of esthetics. Whitman made the case, calling the male members of Rice's company "all perfect in their several ways. . . . It can do no harm to boys to see a set of limbs display all their agility." Léotard enhanced the display with the tight-fitting body suit that bore his name. A London music hall song about "the daring young man on the flying trapeze" focused on the allure—"all the girls he does please"—and the threat—"my love he has purloined away."[5]

3. Mast. Willie in his dashing race on his SPANISH-BRED PONIES

After the stillness of a perch act, the next offering needed to re-energize the audience. Rice assigned the task to an apprentice, Henry Whitby. The band played loudly as young Whitby sped around the ring on ponies leaping over bars and gates, their hooves kicking up sawdust.

4. Gems of the Vatican; OR LIVING STATUES

Richard Rivers, standing on his cantering horse, posed as famous statues in the Vatican Museum. Though that was a papal museum, "Vatican" then referred to its location on the Vatican Hill, one of the famed seven hills of Rome, and not yet to the papacy itself. Rivers's impersonations included Hercules struggling with a lion, a Roman slave sharpening his knife while overhearing conspirators, the blackface joke of "African alarmed at Thunder," Ajax defying the lightning, and the Dying Gladiator in four poses.

5. EUREKA.—The magnificently marked American Mustang will be introduced by Mrs. J. Showles

Libbie Showles had been taught by her brother, Dan, and her husband, Jacob, to break horses as well as to perform on them. As she became an integral part of the roster, the family circle wound tighter. Maggie called Libbie "sister," and Dan called Jacob, now a trusted associate, "brother." Jacob's specialty was the "Grotesque Gymnast," his "crotchety positions" inspiring press agents to verbal contortions: In his flexible body, "cartilaginous structures exist where the osseous system ought to predominate," while his "muscles are as elastic as the conscience of a member of the legal fraternity." Showles's versatility was valuable. He also did pantomime, performed on horseback, rings, and slack rope, and employed the perch pole in imitation of "Persian Dervishes" sitting on air.

Showles may have even replaced his brother-in-law on occasion. A January ad promised the "American Humorist" without naming Rice, and during the summer, publicity labeled Showles a "talker in the Ring."[6]

6. Retro-Equestrianism, by the Kentucky Youth Mast. C. Reed

Dan treated Charley Reed as family, too. He added Charley's expenses to the family's, and Dan's genuine delight in his apprentice shone through the *Pictorial* puffery. Charley's "rapid improvement became a matter of surprise to his friend and guardian," leading within a year to a principal act. The *Pictorial* explained that Reed's skill at riding backwards was the result of a health cure for a sickly boy: Study had broken his health so his parents bought him a pony, and he recovered by emulating feats he had seen at the circus. The story conveyed a message of refinement. Any urchin could be strong; here was recovered strength in a good family. Charley's refined parents hired ballet masters who taught the boy "symmetry of form, . . . graceful movements, . . . apt conception of classical style." The *Pictorial* illustrated that grace, picturing Charley atop a horse galloping inside a ring fence, the boy turning a pirouette, toes pointed, arms elegantly extended.[7]

7. Humorist – – – – – – – Dan Rice

Rice was engaged in a remarkable evolution. Just as he dropped "circus" from his ads, so did the most famous American circus clown shed "clown" from his publicity. He "has entirely discarded clowning and comes before the public as a dispensator of the humors of American character." He now performed in the coat, trousers, and tie of a gentleman, the daily costume of the middle class. It became so routine that when he did revert to the clown's traditional white paint and body suit, comment was required.[8]

Why did Rice drop the clown pants? Answers suggest themselves: The clown always wants to play Hamlet; like Barnum and Stephen Foster, Rice was trying to expand his audiences by drawing those who considered themselves refined; his flair for fashion prompted him to dress well in the ring. But Rice's scope was broader than desire for esteem, cash, or style.

Americans were worried. Many believed that old-time values were disintegrating. The world moved faster. Politicians seemed smaller than they had been, inept if not liars and crooks in a degenerate popularity contest. Morals appeared in decline and the decay of parental discipline made children "more unmanageable than they used to be." Little of the anxiety was new. John Adams had bristled that Washington was one of the "great masters of the theatrical exhibitions of politics," the "best actor of Presidency we have ever had." But Jacksonian democracy had altered the old social and political equations, shifting decision making from a gentry elite to a broader mass of people. While some considered that an expansion of America's brave experiment, others worried about mob rule. Many people saw evidence of that threat come to life, like a powerful river flooding its banks, in the lurid penny presses, in the rowdy torchlight parades and exuberant excess of elections, in the "saturnalia" of drunken rowdiness that still characterized New Years and Christmas. They saw it in the fights at performances, especially following the Astor Place riot. The people, once neutrally "the million," were increasingly characterized as a raw mob blindly following demagogues. Performance itself was seen as fallen from grace, with actors less able and audiences log-stupid. But blaming parents or politicians or performance, while comforting, mostly missed the point. America, a small, agrarian republic of disparate parts, was enduring massive growing pains as it transformed itself into a large, industrialized, interconnected democracy. In the half-century leading up to the Civil War, the population of the United States grew six times faster than the world's, and its cities expanded even more rapidly. The Civil War changed much, but it also made manifest the powerful changes already in progress.[9]

Socially and economically, the older bifurcation—the "lower orders" and an elite—now had a mediating middle, the increasingly influential but also anxious middle class. Because the United States was officially classless, this new middle could not acknowledge itself as a class. At the same time, it *needed* to distinguish itself from those below and above, like a teenager determined to be neither a child nor a stuffy grownup. The old Revolutionary clichés could at least rhetorically dispatch those above: They were undemocratic snobs who put on airs; their money-power-position didn't make them happy; they were ineffectual experts who had less common sense in their entire bodies than the average American had in his little finger. Those below, however, presented a more difficult quandary. To dismiss the lower orders as low raised the risk that you were being elitist yourself.

The solution was elegance itself: People said that they aspired to something higher. That claim of aspiration put the middle on a par with the presumptive elite *and* provided separation from the lower orders, all without mentioning class. In his poem "Excelsior," Longfellow gave people words with which they could think about their lives, as the poem's hero knows not why he ascends the mountain but keeps striving onward and upward. The poet made his intent explicit in a letter: His hero was "filled with aspirations" for "something higher." Rice used the same words when he announced that he sought to raise the circus above what it had formerly been. He was not simply invoking the antique defense of respectability but saying what could now be heard in songs, sermons, and Fourth of July speeches, in editorials and the ubiquitous advice manuals, on the streets and in Congress. Professionalism, an apparently neutral adoption of standards for doctors, lawyers, and professors, swam in the same upward stream of "elevation."[10]

Profoundly influential, "something higher" was also profoundly vague. This ubiquitous cultural aspiration had no ultimate destination, but only the urge, the direction "up." The lack of definition might seem to have been a problem. The aspiring middle could not prevent anyone from staking an aspirational claim: A clerk who stood behind the counter might call himself a "gentleman," and a prostitute could "act like a lady." Verbally at least, hierarchy became democratized. Nevertheless, the inherently vague criteria made aspiration particularly effective for discrimination. "Not our kind of people" carried a wealth of exclusionary meaning, without another word spoken. As a novelist later wrote about Old Money, they "knew precisely where this refined essence was to be found; it was in themselves and all that pertained to them." It was an exclusive system masquerading as inclusive, seen in the mockery of those who did not fit. The *Brooklyn Daily Eagle* made a mock defense of ladies who were insulted by being called women: "Here is true gentility. Why should a lady, necessitated by pecuniary pressure to vend bonnets and ribbons, be insulted by being called a sales-*woman*. It is to be hoped that . . . the laundress shall no longer be irreverently alluded to as a washer-*woman*." With everything uncertain, anything could be criticized: Calling an actor's part a "role" was considered by some to be "in miserable taste."[11]

A few days after Rice opened, the country's largest circulation paper, the *Herald,* which did some of Rice's printing, endorsed his expanded stature in a piece comparing "The Oratory of the Forum and the Ring." Like Congress, Rice at Niblo's "resolves himself into a committee of the whole every evening, and addresses the audience upon the topics of the day." As he made Greeley a target, he "incurred the wrath of the philosophers of the *Tribune*." Rice hoped to ignore the scurrilous paper, but

> as it might get into some decent man's house, and create a false impression against me, I am bound to say that, though I am a fool by profession, I have some regard to consistency. Now I don't think that a newspaper which is continually preaching about hot corn, vegetable diet, and so forth, should object to the Celestial grain and South Carolina staple—Rice.

Rice then hinted that Horace was a drunk, and concluded with a staple of New York humor, the New Jersey joke: If he were as bad as the *Tribune* believed, he would "desert the United States and go live in Jersey." The *Herald* approved "this specimen of the oratory of the ring [as] not inferior to the average of Congressional speeches." The "professional jokers of Congress" should summon Rice "and extract his jokes under oath. It will serve to enliven the debates, and in due time some of the members may fit themselves for the cap and bells they seem so anxious to wear."[12]

Aspiration now drove Rice's career. It had appeared early, in his publicity and endorsing comments. In 1848, the *Cincinnati Enquirer* had called Rice great because "the gentleman sits upon him as naturally as does the clown garb in the ring." The theme quickened through the 1850s. *Dan Rice's Amphitheatre* in 1854 contained little about the building but much about Rice's "genuine refinement" as he achieved a "celebrity for not only rare genius but for gentility, high-toned sentiment, and sterling worth." By 1858, Rice stood as a middle-class gentleman who dispensed wit and wisdom. Actually, even wit was suspect. As *Harper's* explained, "Wit is only the foam on the surface of the soul; wisdom is in the depths below. . . . There is a 'time to laugh'; but there are more times to be sober, thoughtful, serious, and he is a fool, not a wit, who is always on a grin." Just so, Rice "is not witty; neither does he aspire to be; and he has frequently laughed at criticisms that have styled him as such."[13]

Making popularity respectable, Rice was helping make respectability popular.

EXCELSIOR

Rice named his horse perfectly. With aspiration the urge, "excelsior" was the motto of the age, applied to songs and omnibus lines, opera companies and photographers, "base ball" clubs and minstrels. The word would become generic for packing material, probably derived from some Excelsior company. That packing material became symbolic, as later ages saw the word "excelsior," like "aspiration," as mere stuffing, purple prose packed around the real stuff of life. But "excelsior" was the real stuff itself, or at least the prism through which people looked at life. So Rice elevated his pitch for Excelsior: not simply a well-trained animal, it was the "animal with a soul." Excelsior embodied elevation in his two most impressive feats. The first was the stair climb. Clambering up steps, Excelsior was literally climbing to "something higher." The horse's entrance told the same tale of elevation: He was carried into the ring standing on a platform on the shoulders of ten men. Rice paid supernumeraries to tote the horse but his publicity said that local gentlemen vied for the honor. Art usually imitated nature, said the *Pictorial*, but in this "quintessence of animated beauty," nature performed the harder trick of imitating art as Excelsior re-created "Bonheur's celebrated equestrian statue." The reference was to Rosa Bonheur, whose naturalistic depictions of animals made her the most famous woman artist of her time and raised French painting's popularity in America. Rice's horse brought the statue act to an apotheosis, honoring the trainer for his skill, the beast for near human-like intelligence, and the audience for being sophisticated enough to appreciate what they were seeing. Excelsior.[14]

INTERMISSION OF TEN MINUTES.

The Refreshment Saloon here contributed heavily to a proprietor's treasury.

1. BATOUTLE EMULATIONS and Gymnastic Trials, by the Acrobatic Forces of the "Great Show"

The second act needed a rousing start to lure people back to their seats. Fitting that bill were all the company's men in energetic group acrobatics, leaping off a "battoute" springboard, wooden precursor of the mini-trampoline. A reviewer anticipated later complaints that there was too much to see: The act "tires the eye by the necessity which compels it to travel over the mixed and confused mass of the various games." That "confused mass" represented most of Rice's payroll. Armstrong, featured in a double "somerset," earned only $15 a week. Rivers, Dunbar, and Magilton, stars of the show, made $25; and King, "the greatest leaper of the Age"—still peddling a lottery, Rice still buying tickets—earned $20. (Most of them put up at a boarding house, while Rice stayed at a hotel. In Philadelphia, he again resorted to the Jones Hotel, where "ye jollie hoste" treated a crowd who came to serenade Rice.)[15]

2. Mrs. Dan Rice on her American Bred Charger, Dan Webster

Rice presented all his performers as refined. The most crucial to his aims though, other than himself, was Maggie. He was a projector forging an aspirational project; she was its heart. As the middle class increasingly restricted women to the domestic hearth, it made a virtue of that restriction, venerating them as the family's moral guide. In antebellum America,

> the woman ruled; as wife, mother, or sister; the home was the cradle of affection, the woman molded the character of the child, and tempered that of the man, for which "A domestic woman of her husband seen / To be at once both subject and the Queen, / Whilst he, the ruler of their wide domains, / She sitting at his foot-stool reigns."

This hearth was idealized as a refuge against the extremes of poverty and elitism. A diarist wrote "of domestic happiness, love, and confidence, not in the upper crust of society, nor indeed in the lower, but right in the middle, where all the good things are."[16]

This image of women as the moral center of the family had flaws. Among other things, it turned history on its head, for women traditionally had been considered less moral than men. With a few saintly exceptions, Woman was Eve, a temptress luring man into sin. Morality aside, the new ideal ignored the legions of women who worked beyond the hearth, on farms, in shops and factories, and on the streets, selling goods or themselves. It also concealed how much domestics made domesticity possible. Nevertheless, the ideal of the woman presiding over the family hearth held a powerful grip on the age's imagination. Divorced from public life, where her husband might be forced to act less than honorably, his "better half"—a nineteenth-century term—protected him by her greater spirituality. Redefined as the embodiment of purity, she "molded the character of the child, and tempered that of the man." A curious kind of privacy settled over the public world, where the man did and said things that his wife must not know about. Thus protected, she soothed him on his return from economic battle and, more important, cleansed him. Respectability and morality tumbled together.

Rice had picked up the theme of the idealized woman early in his career. *Sketches* detailed a footloose boy, sheltered by the influence of a saintly mother. "Doubtless in all the temptations through which he has passed . . . the remembrance of home and maternal advice protected him." Pages of praise for him in *Rice's Amphitheatre* resolved to one point, that the nobility of his nature was revealed best when he sat at "his own fireside, enjoying the society of his excellent lady, and the innocent prattle of his lovely children."[17]

Presenting his wife as respectability incarnate was not inevitable. Though Maggie's personal morals were high, as a performer she was doubly suspect, for she displayed herself in public, which many still considered vulgar in women, and she did not stay at home. When money woes forced Anna Cora Mowatt, a woman of high society, onto the stage, a poem defended her respectability: "Ne'er heed them, Cora, dear, / The carping few, who say / Thou leavest woman's holier sphere / For light and vain display."[18] Dan addressed the problem by turning his publicity from

Maggie's skill, which was probably limited anyway, to her character as the epitome of womanly modesty.

Beyond Maggie's personal respectability, Rice applied the theme of the idealized woman as a guarantee of order. Whitman wrote about more than Rice's show when he commented that the "presence of ladies (in thousands) has tended no doubt to the purification of the circus." It was precisely the pitch Barnum made for Lind, which Emerson repeated, rhapsodizing that Lind "needs no police. Her voice is worth a hundred constables, and instantly silenced the uproar of the mob." Similarly, Mrs. Rice's "virtue has the effect of keeping vice in check."[19]

Then, more than a performer, she was preceptor of an "elegant school of Lady Equestrianism." At Niblo's, Mrs. Dan Rice offered no riding tricks but "Instructive Illustrations of Horsemanship, arranged for and dedicated to the Ladies of New York." Her "Saddle Exercises" provided a healthful model that "the whole sex should emulate."

> Dauntless, though graceful, dashing, though chaste, impulsive, though modest, she diffuses fascination in the road exercises that charms all beholders. . . . by her example she has induced many a sentimental miss who was pining with *ennui* in the boudoir, to seize the rein, direct the sporting palfry and dash over the plain, thus dispelling all the ill results of an idle life.[20]

Later ages would cluck about passive Victorian ladies but another, more active image was stirring. Whitman, concerned about "frail-constitutioned" women, urged the same solution as Rice, athleticism and exercise. This sturdier model was offered in plays and novels as the True Woman.[21] Rice capitalized on that avatar to challenge the suspicion of female performers as painted women. If ladies learned "the natural science of riding" from Maggie, "the bloom of health would appear on their cheeks, and cosmetics and carmine would never be resorted to." That echoed middle-class *Harper's,* which observed that riding gave a lady a "flush of health" and "full development of figure." Maggie also offered spirituality. In her horse, White Surrey, could be seen "Etherialized Poetical Motions truly Vivifical to the Connoisseurs of the Modern Equestrian School." In all, she "exerts a silent influence of sanctity on all around her . . . the tendencies of the place all turn to purity and self-respect." (Beyond publicity persiflage, she held sway backstage. The old minstrel, Brower, led the company in presenting her with a fancy bridle, in thanks for "the womanly attention" she paid to a sick member of the company.)[22]

On May Day 1858, an admirer sent Maggie a "philo-poem." He framed it in antebellum authenticity as "a simple gift, with the heart's pure prayer." The writer held her in high regard not only because she was married to Dan "but also for her own merit as a true woman—'Heaven's last, but best gift to Man.'"[23]

3. THE RHINOCEROS

Excelsior was not the only animal Rice adorned with gentility. Lalla Rookh was sagacious, the mules were "educated," and the Waltzing Camel followed "the votaries of Terpsichore." Yet Rice could tease his own aspirations, as he labeled the rhinoceros "unfashionably gross." (Similarly, scoring off an old friend, Rice named the awkward camel "Van Orden.") When the rhinoceros got out of its pen and encountered the proprietor, William Niblo, the episode prompted mock politesse reminiscent of the tale of Lalla Rookh's nocturnal stroll.

> "Niblo's Interview With A New Actor."—A few evenings since, as the popular and successful manager of "The Garden" was taking his evening's round, to see that all was right about the house—the gas turned off and the fires out—he encountered suddenly, in the middle of the stage, a new actor upon his boards. It was nothing less that the rhinoceros of Dan Rice,.... Niblo, with his usual courtesy, said "Good evening," and the rhinoceros snorted, which was as much as to say, Will you take a horn? The manager incontinently declined the invitation, making the best of his way behind the scenes to get some one to put his new friend out.[24]

4. Wm. H. Greene, the "Pride of the Pike," formerly reinsman to the Hon. Henry Clay, will ride, drive and manage three span of Spirited Grey Horses.

Attention wavers at performances. Later audiences, trained to the idea that attention must be paid, blame themselves. Nineteenth-century crowds assumed that if they were bored, it was because the performance was boring. After all, regular attendance made them experts. So audiences recognized an act that merely filled out the program. The "Driver of Old Kentucky" did little more in the winter ring than he did overland in the summer, which was to drive horses. The value of the act lay in the fact that Rice could tell a story: Henry Clay took the reins from Greene, but the team got out of control until Greene restored order, allowing as how Clay should stick to guiding the chariot of State.[25]

5. Physical Gaities and Convulsive Contortions, by the Comical Calisthenics, THE BROTHERS MOTLEY.

Magilton and Dunbar returned to the ring, their acrobatics transformed to a comedy turn in motley. A flip-flap that landed cleanly in the first act could be done with fake dizziness in the second, or a stagger into a surprise somersault.

6. Juvenile Pleasures on Horseback by MISS ELVIRA

In exchange for labor, apprentices got food, shelter, and training. The romance of running away with the circus, already a cliché, ignored the reality that shows needed a steady supply of adept youngsters, small and light to take the top spots in acrobatic or riding feats. Plucked from the streets or taken from a farm, they lived in a nether world, neither offspring nor paid employee, with beating always a threat. Glenroy recalled a "pleasant apprenticeship," even though he risked flogging when he missed a trick. Of course, beatings were standard for sons and daughters too. And, like Rice after his mother died, many youngsters were on their own in the world, treated like miniature adults. The *Clipper* was outraged when meddling politicians decreed that children, a significant portion of theater audiences, could not attend alone. The "moral gentry up in Albany" were abrogating the liberty of children to choose their pleasures, an affront in a free country![26]

One apprentice recalled a "uniformly kind and patient" Rice, who took "pleasure in lightening my tasks whenever it was possible." Nevertheless, the work was hard, sometimes risky. Reed was still angry seventy years later that Rice had made him ride the "vicious and high mettled, dangerous" Excelsior between towns.[27] A few apprentices, such as James Robinson and Reed, became stars, just as a few emerged from the thousands in twentieth-century gymnastic or tennis schools to become stars. Some, like nine-year-old Elvira, got a trade and steady work, a partner for life when she married a rider, and a traveling community. Others, like eight-year-old Willie Whitby, vanished, fate unknown. This ominous prospect paled in comparison to the systematic exploitation of children in factories and mines, but circus apprentices were more visible. After the Stickney family replaced the Whitbys on Rice's show, bad publicity followed twelve-year-old Robert Stickney's fall from his horse.

> The poor little fellow was sorely hurt. But Circus boys are taught to suffer in silence, and so he did not cry or moan. His face only turned white as chalk and a strange light shone in his eyes. He was made to mount the horse again and finish the act, though he fell off hard twice, from sheer weakness and pain. Was it not brutal and barbaric in Stickney, the father, to compel Stickney, the son, to go through his performance in agony acute, simply to satisfy a parcel of noisy spectators?[28]

Learning any physical skill leads to accidents. Often the best way to surmount them is to try again. To get back on the horse. So a teaching practice that seems cruel to an observer might be the best way to learn. Robert became a star, while nothing else in the career of the father, Sam, condemns him. Of course, the reproach in the Philadelphia paper was less concern for the boy than a device to flog the crude tastes of the masses, that "parcel of noisy spectators."

The Low Comedy Mules

Rice knew that people still enjoyed broad comedy, though it diverted his aspirational message. He offered $25 to anyone who could ride one of his mules. Meanwhile, the *Philadelphia Evening Journal* warned Reynolds that gentlemen do not spit in their hats before putting them on. Still the same paper advised its readers, "If you are cobwebbed about the heart, if your nether jaw hangs idly, if your faith in the existence of fun is enfeebled," hurry to the Great Show.[29]

24

DANIEL McLAREN

Rice's father, Daniel McLaren, became associated with the show in 1858, but it was no sentimental reunion. Rice needed money.

The *Spirit of the Times* passed on the rumor that Rice had made $12,000 in New York, and the *Philadelphia Evening Journal* announced that the crush of people in the Quaker City might force his show to adjourn to Independence Square, but the *Clipper* was closer to the mark: The "Quakers don't exactly as yet see into the great 'respectability' of the thing." So it came as no surprise at the end of Rice's winter season when he recorded himself $6,500 in the hole. Still, like a farmer, regardless of debt, he had to seed the ground for the spring. Preparing for a 3,000-mile tour of 125 towns, he spent another $9,000. (That included $200 to Maggie on the Great Show account for boarding the grooms over the winter, plus a little more to buy ostrich feathers for fashion's sake.)[1]

The printer, Frank Farwell, already owned a one-third interest in the show. In April 1858, Rice transferred the remainder to Farwell and to his

About the time Rice adopted the name Daniel McLaren, his father, of the same name, re-entered his life.

father, McLaren. Soon the *Clipper* was assuring its readers that Rice was still alive. While assurance could be explained by his recurring absences, another reason loomed large.[2]

Rice had begun using "McLaren" himself. He adopted it as early as February in Philadelphia, when he made out a circus pass for his friend Mit Foster on the back of a calling card engraved "Dan'l M'Laren." He also paid $10 for a woodcut of a coat of arms that showed him in a costume of stripes and stars, wielding a club against a skeleton, while Excelsior joins in the attack. The caption, "Filius Momi," reinforced the meaning: Death would be conquered by this son of Momus, Greek god of ridicule.[3]

The bills, and especially his show title, continued to use "Rice." It would have been foolhardy to drop it. Dan Rice was now probably better known than any other performer of the day, and people wanted to see him. His continued popularity—and prosperity—depended on what is now called name recognition. But if he did not risk losing his audience by putting "McLaren" in his title, Rice used the name to appeal to a culture suffused with anxiety about identity. Just as he had discarded the "mask" of his clown makeup, Rice became genuinely, authentically, sincerely "Daniel McLaren."

Elevation was ascendant. In a new issue of *Dan Rice's Pictorial,* now listing McLaren and Farwell as publishers, the absence of "clown" continued. The sole reference was this: "We then heard of Dan Rice, a clown—then of Dan Rice the Manager of the 'One Horse Show.'" Only eight words in the four newspaper-sized pages mentioned the role that had made him famous. Rice was depicted instead as an "artiste," in "the new style of arenic amusements he has recently (that is, within a year or two) introduced. He has repudiated 'Clowning' of the O. S. [old style] School, and comes out in the position of Humorist, giving the people a series of serio-comical and semi-philosophical conversations." Suspicion of the crowd surfaced: Despite Rice's "rare faculty of gaining the sympathy and support of the masses," he "never makes a personal effort for popularity." A gentleman does not pander. The *Pictorial* made Rice's claim of elevation explicit:

> As a man we admire him for the many good qualities of his head and heart, and particularly for the great efforts he is constantly making to elevate his profession. Persons of low or immoral character can never become attachés, and his constant care is to engage only those who are a credit to the art in which they labor.

As Rice presented it, his every aim was higher.

The *New York Times* had called Rice's show a "provincial attraction" early in the winter but, as often happened, Rice changed minds. Within a month, the *Times* reconsidered: "In everything Mr. Rice aims to go beyond the traditions of the circus, and really succeeds in producing something new."[4] Like other newspapers across the country that covered Rice, the *Times* intended something larger than performance detail. Endorsing his aspirational stance, these papers were staking their own claims to aspiration. The *Times*, for instance, was now attracting readers by its dedication to "higher" journalistic standards. As the aspirational ideal spread through the country, it rode on a necessary mutuality. For a claim to higher things to be effective, it had to be acknowledged by those who considered themselves similarly sensitive to higher things. Elevation must meet elevation.

> For polite ladies and gentlemen were not simply performers on the social stage of the parlor; they were members of an audience watching the genteel performances of one another. The function of the laws of tact was to ensure that members of the polite audience would assist, encourage, and honor a genteel performer's claims to gentility.

In just that way, the newspapers were assisting, encouraging, and honoring Rice's claims to gentility. Critiques were social responses in dialogue with the performances themselves. The great French actress Rachel and her New York audience were, decided *Harper's,* equally refined, "equally worthy." Puffs, though often unreliable in their details, nevertheless provide potent evidence of this mutuality, as they were copied from ads and repeated in other newspapers, winding mutuality tighter. A report on Rice's fashionable houses affirmed the aspirations of Rice, of the audience, and of the newspaper making the report. Increasingly, simply being an audience became a test: Were you elevated enough to appreciate elevation? In Chicago, his audiences were "equally as respectable as they were numerous," and Rice had "abundant reason to be proud of the classes" he drew.[5]

While everyone spoke of aspiration, not all agreed on its dividing line. As Rice ventured into Wisconsin, the *Kenosha Times* emphatically denied that he qualified. The editor wrote that a circus in town made life and property unsafe. Blackleg swindlers, pickpockets, and cutthroats followed a circus, "whose only possible means of subsistence is plunder." Rice's troupe was "a worse evil to the country than pestilence and famine." When Rice missed a show, he was not simply sick, he was "rabid with rage," and when he returned in motley again, he was dressed in "scraps of old red and white petticoats" to make himself a baboon for the boys.

> This class of characters are a nuisance and a pest. . . . As a rule they are constituted of the very dregs of American population. They have neither

> character, principle or position. They live by false pretences and by appeals to the most vulgar passions of the race. They steal away the very substance of our local prosperity, that they may spend it in debauchery. They shear us of our moral and pecuniary strength, as Samson was sheared of his hair. There is a contamination in their very presence anywhere.

Citizens would be doing their civic duty if they would hang Rice's troupers "by their rascally necks till they were dead, and then pitch them into Lake Michigan; and Dan Rice himself should . . . swing from the highest tree of them all." Behind the venom lurked frustration: People liked the circus. They liked Rice. Worst of all for the *Kenosha Times*, they ignored the advice of such journalistic dragons of respectability. So it was not surprising that the paper concluded its attack on Rice by sneering at the people. It declared that its opinion about the clown was "honestly entertained and frankly expressed"—sincerity again—so those "who don't like it 'can lump it.'" People who attended Rice's circus would "have simply to suffer the consequences."[6]

As he swung down through Illinois in mid-summer, Rice faced another challenge. He had to go head-to-head with politics.

Performance and politics had long overlapped. Rice was playing New York in 1848 when the *Spirit of the Times* observed that in "consequence of the election, little attention has been paid to theatricals." During Buchanan's campaign against the Republican's first national candidate, John Fremont, the *Clipper* joked about the rivalry "between the Drama and the presidential campaign. Many people argue that there is no occasion to spend or break a dollar for amusement in the theatre when so much of the real article can be had for nothing outside."[7]

Rice embodied the overlap. If a controversy was brewing, people went to catch Rice's opinion on it, the way people would later watch television comics joking about a political blunder. The *Boston Herald* announced its impatience "to hear Dan give his political view, remarks upon social reforms and his general exposition of the philosophy of life."[8]

Now he had to compete for attention with the Lincoln–Douglas campaign. On July 17, Rice and Douglas both arrived in Lincoln, Illinois. The crowd that gathered at the train station to greet Douglas had half an eye cocked for the arrival of Rice's circus. Reports don't say whether the two men met, though it would have been a natural opportunity for both to increase their publicity. Rice did become an ardent advocate for the Little Giant. In any case, Rice drew the same rowdy, involved audiences and used the same oratorical techniques as the Little Giant and his challenger, the little-known local lawyer. Both politicians used the same slangwhanging style that Rice employed, and both also told ribald jokes. Lincoln had studied classical speeches, but a description of him on the stump also fit Rice in the ring: He employed a "free-wheeling, raucous brand of personal oratory. In the seven debates, Lincoln and Douglas gave alternating speeches punctuated by humor and stories while surrounded by enthusiastic crowds that hung on their every word and interjected constantly with cries of 'That is so!' or 'Hit him again!'"[9]

(That fall, politics in a circus tent became even more literal. On September 4, the Spalding & Rogers show was in Lincoln, Illinois. Douglas was scheduled to speak there, so the managers invited him to make his oration in their tent, and tendered the same offer to Lincoln. A circus tent was one of the largest structures in the United States, much bigger than the churches, schools, and lecture halls used for public meetings in rural areas, bigger than anything but a few city theaters and halls. So after the performance, the Little Giant spoke to thousands in Spalding's tent, from the stage used for the after-show concert. Though Lincoln had planned to speak on the same stage, Republicans mocked Douglas as a circus performer, a contortionist who came down on all sides of every issue. Unsurprisingly, Lincoln changed his plan, skipped the tent, and spoke another day in a grove half a mile away. The circus added a postscript to the story: Lincoln was supposed to finish by 2:00 P.M., after which the circus would get the crowd. But he kept plowing his rhetorical field, so the circus managers gathered the parade at the edge of the grove, struck up the band, and marched to the tent, the crowd trailing behind; only a few friends lingered to hear Lincoln to the end.)[10]

As the summer turned to August heat, Rice's show was traveling overnight from Brazil, Indiana. The elephant and the camel were chained together, as usual. As they walked through the darkness, harnesses creaking, wagon axles squeaking, and the chain clanking between them, Lalla Rookh rolled out her trunk along the ground, like a ribbon in slow motion, searching for food, while "Van Orden" jerked its neck in that awkwardly graceful cadence of the camel. The long train of wagons and riders roused from its half-doze as the first rider reached a bridge, the soft clop on the dirt road changing to a hollow drumming. The steady horse beat on the bridge changed to the syncopation of camel hooves and the muffled bass of elephant feet. Suddenly, with a crack, the bridge crashed into the creek. Men shouted and horses neighed in fright. Lalla Rookh trumpeted in surprise, then clambered back into view. The camel was not so lucky. It hung on the chain, its neck broken. It was a major loss for Rice.[11]

Meanwhile, rumors floated that Excelsior had died, too, which would have been much worse. Few attractions in mid-century America had the appeal of Rice's remarkable horse. The rumors may have started because Rice kept Excelsior out of the show when he himself was sick. One local editor made a joke of being unable to hear the Talking Horse because he sat far back, because children were crying, and because the horse "did not make his appearance previous to the close of the performance." But there may have been more to it. Earlier, in Wisconsin, as Excelsior reached the top of his stairs, a man stood up and yelled that he bet $100 that the horse could not jump down. Rice said that he refused to risk the life of such a valuable animal on such a small amount, but would go for $500. The man sat down. Then, as Excelsior was halfway down the steps, the man stood again, saying he bet $100 that the horse couldn't jump from there. Rice summoned the man into the ring, where they conferred while the audience buzzed and Excelsior obediently waited, halfway down the stairs. Then Dan gave the command and Excelsior jumped, falling with a groan. Panic ran through the stands. The audience knew that a broken leg meant the horse would have to be put down. But Excelsior scrambled to his feet. Rice grandly spurned the $100 to ringing cheers.[12]

The rumors of Excelsior's death prompted sympathy at first. The *Cincinnati Enquirer* regretted to hear of the passing of "probably the best trained horse that ever stepped foot in the arena." Then the *Clipper* discovered that the horse was still alive. "Perhaps it was one of those advertising dodges. Who knows?" A month later, in August 1858, on hearing of the camel's death, the *Clipper* was suspicious. "Now, this may be correct, but Dan is so given to gags that we should not be surprised if this turned out to be one of the latest."[13]

A curious detail rumpled the usual flow of hyperbole in Rice's publicity, like a bump in bed linen. An ad in Marietta, Ohio made the usual boasts: The famous Conversationalist led a Company of Artists of Superior Merit! A 20-Horse Carriage carried Canham's Brass and String Bands!! Boldface bravado promised 7 Features Which Can Be Seen In No Other Exhibition In the World. (That included the now-dead camel, though the bills assured that Rice's show Performs All It Advertises.) It was business as usual as the ad, contrasting itself to the gasconade of other circuses, sent its own volleys gasconading across the countryside. Yet two words, in large letters, were not usual: The agent would like to "Quietly Remark" on the show's features.[14] Quietly Remark? Why would a circus lower the volume at all, much less brag about doing so in large, loud letters?

Aspiration increasingly meant a quiet and subdued style. To be a gentleman was to be undemonstrative. Anything that smacked of excess violated this new sense of decorum. As Robert Browning had written vaguely in a poem a few years before, "less is more." Meanwhile, the True Woman kept the domestic realm a serene bastion, protected from the din of people in public. When on the street, respectable women "deflected rather than drew attention" to their dress and demeanor, in a deliberate contrast to the bold manner of working women. It was the same impulse that persuaded a writer in 1872 to claim that respectable and educated New Yorkers had abstained from voting because their "refined taste made them shrink from the coarse rabble that surrounded the voting places." Working-class sociability was increasingly demonized as out-of-control rowdiness, contrasted to the emerging middle class's "purposive play," which had a goal, just as in business. Even laughing became vulgar. A century after Lord Chesterfield wrote a famous series of letters to his son, the American middle class was reading them and seeking to lead "proper" lives by following their aristocratic precepts, including this one about laughing:

> I must particularly warn you against it: and I could heartily wish, that you may often be seen to smile, but never heard to laugh, while you live. Frequent and loud laughter is the characteristic of folly and ill manners: it is the manner in which the mob express their silly joy, at silly things,

> and they call it being merry. In my mind, there is nothing so illiberal, and so ill-bred as audible laughter.

Prevented by democratic ideology from labeling the lower orders "lower," one could point out that they laughed vulgarly aloud. Praise from early in the 1850s that "everybody laughed immoderately" at Rice's jests was turning into a criticism.[15] The bias against robust behavior extended to slaves and succeeding groups of Irish, Italian, and Jewish immigrants: They were loud, they waved their hands when talking, they were pushy.

Performance adopted decorum as an ideal. Ever since the first actor, people have wondered how much actors enter into the emotions of their characters. That is, do actors really feel or do they pretend to feel? Middle-class Americans decided that they could finally answer that ancient question. The socialite-turned-actress Mowatt described "two distinct schools of acting." Sincerity, in which an actor "abandons himself to all the absorbing emotions that belong to the character he interprets," stood against "the grand and passionless school," against "rant."[16] It was the same cultural impulse that held Rice up as the reading, not acting, clown in his "quieter, anti-physical, school of performance."

Rice leapt (quietly) on the (moderate) bandwagon. He published the Rules of the Great Show, not because anyone beyond his circus needed to know them, but to demonstrate his allegience to "the moral laws which govern all well regulated societies." Predictably, refined women led the way. There was Maggie, of course, and after her, Sallie Stickney. A star rider from a circus family—her brother, Robert, was the boy in the story of the fall—Sallie was presented as the epitome of propriety. Rice's publicity treated her engagement like a debutante's coming-out party, fitting "the social position her family enjoys, and the care and attention bestowed upon her moral and physical education." Rice declared that he hesitated to make principal riders of women because they might be inclined "to make efforts not in the slightest degree compatible with the ordinary rules of decorum," but he made an exception in her case because a committee of gentlemen entreated for her. By contrast, "stars of the Ballet are notoriously liberal in their display of personal charm, and the majority of equestriennes . . . never allowed too much drapery to interfere" with their exertions. The comment is a reminder that ballet dancers were then despised as immoral. As if a "different order of beings" from proper women, they were seen as doing little more than showing off their bodies for pay, like strippers in later ages, and worse. In 1860, a writer deplored the "*nude* style of dressing that now prevails at the circus." Any suspicion that men might be watching more of Sallie than her "quiet pictures and classic positions" was allayed by assurance that ladies of Philadelphia were her patrons.[17]

Illness kept Rice out of shows over the winter, and then periodically through the summer of 1858. That fall, word reached New York that he was dangerously ill in Zanesville, Ohio, with "affection of the lungs," possibly pneumonia. (On a different show that winter, Thayer advertised that he had played in place of Rice for six months, but Rice was too well known to be replaced without complaint or comment.) Now, however, incapacitation was his ally. Instead of Dan Rice the performer, he could depict his absences as Daniel McLaren's gentlemanly withdrawal from vulgar performance.[18]

25

GRAMMATICAL ASSASSIN?

Early in 1858, the *New York Tribune* labeled Rice "a grammatical assassin," jeering that "the King's English nightly dies a hundred deaths under his tender mercies." But the *Tribune* was not the only paper in town, and Rice returned to New York a year later to more success at Niblo's Garden. (The Philharmonic Society was presenting concerts at Niblo's too, apparently in the Saloon.) As Rice, the new American icon, bumped against an old one, Rip Van Winkle in an operatic incarnation at the Academy of Music, genteel praise rolled along. Rice "converses with the fashionable audiences before him like a man accustomed to good society," throwing off "*bon mots* . . . in the most courteous manner possible." His friends could be found "in the highest ranks of fashion and opulence." Among Senators, Congressmen, and other political characters" such as Sam Houston and Stephen Douglas, Rice shone as one "whose eloquence has held spellbound more inhabitants of this Universal Yankee Nation than all the others put together." Still, the *Tribune* took aim again. It wished the managers would stop the "threadbare inanities of Mr. Merryman," either by padlocking his jaw or cutting out his tongue. Of course, Greeley's principles did not prevent him from taking Rice's money for front-page ads, which invited a "REFINED AND INTELLECTUAL COMMUNITY" to performances.[1]

There were also differences of opinion about the editor of the *Tribune.* Though influential nationally, the neck-whiskered, piping-voiced Horace Greeley was often considered a cracked pot. He self-righteously bubbled over every new intellectual current, whether free love, abolition, or spirit rapping (séances), and the *Clipper* labeled his attacks on Rice "shallow bigotry." In any case, Rice reached more people than Greeley: Thousands upon thousands heard him in the ring and even more read the newspapers cheering Rice. [2]

The *Clipper* was endorsing respectability. "Dan Rice (Dan McLaren) . . . has accumulated a large fortune, which he distributes with a liberal hand. He enjoys his *otium cum dig* [leisure with dignity] in the village of Girard, Penn., on a princely estate which reaches across the heart of Pennsylvania." Rice kept on adding property, buying land at the end of winter seasons when he was flush. He landscaped around his large frame house and a conservatory with shade trees and lawns sporting statues, the whole enclosed by a brick wall. The estate was said to cost $60,000; a brick barn cost another $26,000.[3]

Rice joked about those who took a high moral stance against him. In one of his speeches, after referring to the city's new reservoir (present site of the New York Public Library), and punning on the *press* of everyday life, including the "terrors of the *Tribune,*" he told of a man who opposed all shows but sneaked into the circus tent. Caught laughing at the mules till he cried, old Broadbrim asserted that the tears flowed from grief at seeing so much talent perverted. "Whether he meant in my person or in the mules, I never knew."[4]

Rice's supporters bantered back. The *New York Herald* teased that he has begun "to pay the penalties incident to fame by having a Presidential nomination at the hands of some newspaper editor down South." The joke juxtaposing performance and politics also appeared in the *Clipper,*

The apotheosis of how Rice now wanted to present himself: calm, wise, respectable.

"Rice on the Presidential Course" at Niblo's, where "he will 'define his position.'" A month later, the paper warned to "Clear the track for Dan Rice in 1860! His platform is now before the people. . . . Other candidates may get up mass meetings, but Dan Rice can get up mass benefits, and the great masses respond heartily." Similarly, the *New York Atlas* promised that Rice would convene "to define his position on the Cuba question, and to give his opinion on Presidential aspirants. It will be rich." For his benefit mid-February, Rice promised to lecture on American politics.[5]

Yet it was not completely a joke. Rice pushed the overlap of politics and performance further than anyone else. Other clowns were funny and original, other performers were popular, and other public figures wielded influence, but it would have been difficult to find another American in any field who matched Rice's reach and prominence. On Washington's Birthday, the clown combined patriotism, politics, and aspiration in a speech to a "select [and] distinguished" audience at the Metropolitan Hotel. "There was no unnecessary display at this re-union, no noisy ostentation that, with a prelude of puffing, would mark such a meeting. . . . There was an appropriate modesty about the whole affair, at once characteristic of those who were the hosts, and of the unpretending career of the recipient." Rice's speech displayed his quiet good taste.

> There is an every-day patriotism, which men . . . ostentatiously parade whenever an allusion made to our dear native land will permit—a noisy and proscriptive enthusiasm that is more like galvanized metal than true gold. I do not like the mouthy patriotism of the bar room. There is a deeper feeling inwrought into the very nature of man, and one that, while it can never be quenched yet never burns in fitful flames. It is in the very life of his inner soul.[6]

Though Rice's words resonated at the core of middle-class aspiration, the *Tribune* remained sourly unconvinced. The newspaper acknowledged crowded houses for the circus, but it could not abide Rice.

> There is but one objection to the manner in which everything is done, but that objection is a chronic one; it can never be removed by any mild remedies; heroic surgery and the actual cautery is the only treatment. Of

> course we mean the talking clown. Everybody knows that, and everybody who goes to the circus wonders why the infatuated managers permit a fine performance to be marred, and the enjoyment of hundreds of persons to be spoiled, by the intolerable dullness and inane stupidity of a star-spangled clown.

The paper theorized that managers who wanted Excelsior and the mules were forced to take Rice. But it had "a bright thought, a coruscating idea! Perhaps $50 a night or so will induce Mr. Dan to perform the other donkeys and keep his own mouth shut. . . . Try it, Mr. Manager, try it for Charity's sweet sake."[7]

Greeley led the way, but the words came from the pen of Mortimer Thompson, a short, mustached man who wrote comic pieces under the name "Philander Q. Doesticks." A graduate of the University of Michigan who began his career writing for his brother's Detroit paper, Thompson/Doesticks had become prominent enough to be described in Rice's 1856 *Pictorial* as the "Dickens of America." Despite the complaints in the *Tribune* about Rice's English, Doesticks used the same slangwhanging technique. Just as Rice flipped between calling Excelsior a "harse" and waxing poetical, Doesticks alternated between pieces displaying uneducated slang and others that read like early Mark Twain. (At a séance, Doesticks learns that "Samson and Hercules have gone into partnership in the millinery business. Julius Caesar is peddling apples and molasses candy . . . [and] John Bunyan is clown in a circus.") It was understandable then that some attributed the attacks on Rice to professional jealousy.[8] But there was more to the attacks in the *Tribune* than that, an excess that poured out like boiling pitch from the ramparts. The *Hannibal Journal* had declared Rice a "brazen faced traducer" who turns all to "moral filth and uncleanliness." Kenosha thundered that circuses were worse than "pestilence and famine," and that Rice should be lynched. The *Tribune* joined the parade of invective. "Everybody knows" that Rice was a disgrace, and he should have his tongue cut out.

Why the excess? Like its predecessor finger-waggers, the *Tribune* made it a personal grievance: Rice "continues to afflict us and the public."

In part it *was* personal. Responding to attacks, "Mr. Rice walked into St. Horace with a refreshing coolness." Rice's response may have included a prank in which his partisans pasted his picture over Greeley's on posters for the latter's lectures. Rice also held a mock funeral for Doesticks's dead wit, the ceremony complete with a dirge played by the band, a coffin pulled slowly into the ring, and a skull representing Philander.[9] Understandably, editors shot back. Rice's mockery of them confirmed their belief that he held nothing sacred.

The responses were also political. When Rice wasn't skewering Greeley, he was making high fun of the bewhiskered editor's Whig politics. Rice had grown to manhood among Pennsylvania Democrats like the Foster family. The extreme positions of an ultra-Whig like Greeley made irresistible targets.

Beyond the personal or political, society was waging a war over respectability, larger than the late twentieth-century culture wars, and Rice's popularity made him a central figure in the contest. The difference in opinion about Rice depended on whether defenders of middle-class values were willing to accept him as aspirational. Greeley clearly was not. A self-appointed cultural arbiter, he was desperate to guard the ranks of respectability from slangy Rice. (Greely nurtured similar misgivings about Abe Lincoln, who faced the same criticism: "Fashionable exquisites sneer at his manners. Dilettante scholars criticize his speech.") Another would-be arbiter decreed that a good manager ought to be honest, knowledgeable about human nature, "forcible in his remarks to blackguards," and charitable with benefits. That much fit Rice. But the full list of proposed traits had little to do with amusements and a great deal to do with a narrow strata of society. A manager, in this edict, should be married, a strict temperance man and an abolitionist, a member of a "respectable church," and he should cultivate only "respectable members of the press." Most important, he should "not be a floating vagabond, who can pack his trunks in an hour's notice." Since that described every manager who led a traveling show, the only ones who qualified were those who were politically agreeable and had settled down. Rice, to the contrary, embodied the traits of the teeming street that the emerging bourgeoisie was pitting itself against: "muscular prowess, masculine honor, swaggering bravado, and colorful display."[10]

Rice was a phenomenon of nature. His effect was palpable, physical. Bodies unconsciously leaned forward. Unaware, their mouths opened in anticipation, people felt what he said as if it were what they were about to say themselves. Beyond popularity, beyond laughter, audiences yearned *toward* Rice; they felt his whirlwind of human energy, and were swept up in it. His critics though saw that energy, and the corresponding popularity, as proof of harm. Praise for his "power of controlling his hearers, as if by . . . animal magnetism," was being transformed into a uneasiness about mobs and manipulation.[11]

That meant that the millions who knew of Rice, and had seen or hoped to see him, had to be explained away. Greeley simply denied their existence, deciding against all evidence that people attended Rice's performances only for the mules. *Porter's Spirit of the Times* had taken a similar slant a few years earlier, depicting a bemused audience tolerating an inept Rice: He makes "unintentionally ludicrous speeches, and his un-grammatical sentences and improper pronunciation sometimes create a great laugh, of which he is not aware." Others, like the *Kenosha Times,* derided Rice's fame by turning on the audience itself, scorning popularity by attacking the populace. Rice's critics recast his great strength, his ability to bond with an audience, as a great fault. "Dan Rice. Who has not heard of him? And who has not heard of the Devil.—And yet he is still the same old Devil."[12]

Along with Rice, the audience was being demonized. Worry about mob rule inevitably extended to audiences. In theaters and circuses, participation was customary, with conversation common and rowdy enthusiasm running across classes. Audiences were not simply expressing an opinion, they were exercising the duty of "THE PEOPLE" in a republic. That was not empty theory but a practical matter of performance. Performers can be self-indulgent, whipping their grand speeches into grandiosity or underplaying so subtly that they are unheard and unfelt. Experienced antebellum audiences would not stand for it, and kept actors honest. Newspapers supported audience comment. "Why then should we not have a right to express our impatience by stamping, or our dissatisfaction by hissing, when their recess is too long, or the acting too bad?" Even when the *Delta* clucked about conversation in the theater, it championed hissing. Whitman had reveled in the rowdiness. "Yes," he wrote, "the place of the orator and his hearers is truly an agonistic arena. There he wrestles and contends with them—he suffers, sweats, undergoes his great toil and extasy."[13]

But times were changing. Whitman's enthusiasm disappeared in his warning against "melodramatic, Methodist Preacher, half-inebriated, political spouter, splurging modes of oratory." The would-be b'hoy now complained that all the entertainments of the "nearly grown and just grown lads, about Brooklyn and New York, are injurious," and by 1863 he would declare that opera was the only amusement that satisfied him. As the *Times* put it in 1858, the "very stability of good government" depended on "the refining and conservative influence" of the arts.[14]

What effect did its proponents want from that refining influence? What was the alternative to audience involvement? Sniffing that "no human being can endure" Rice, *Porter's Spirit of the Times* articulated its ideal: "A THEATRE FOR THE CRITICS." Later ages would accept as natural what audiences were then starting to decide, that they were not patrons or partners but spectators who should follow the lead of experts to watch with quiet good taste. The infinite variety of audience behavior was diminishing to a single, middle-class imperative: To behave. When the French star Rachel came to New York in 1855, her audience, according to the middle-class journal *Harper's,* "behaved well. . . . There was no hooting, no whistling, no tumult of any kind. One indiscreet brother tried to yelp, and was instantly suppressed." Seating similarly played a part. Originally, patrons wandered among benches and bleacher planks, for a better view or to chat. Individual seats, introduced as a luxury for an extra charge, became routine. By the time Rice advertised "seats, for Everybody" within a few years, that luxury had become a command: Sit down and shut up.[15]

But the war for decorum was not yet won, so the *Tribune* continued to rage, decrying the "inane vulgarisms" of Rice. "However, he subsides after this week. May his shadow never be seen here again!" Again the *Clipper* took notice.

> A WAR OF WITS—DOESTICKS VS. DAN RICE—Two well known public characters, . . . both noted for their ambition and faculty for making the public laugh—*with* not at them—have lately taken it into their heads to pitch into each other, and see if they cannot make each other cry, while the public still laugh. Mr. Thompson, of the *Tribune,* . . . not liking the style, stuff, prolixity or pronunciation of Dan Rice, of Nixon & Co.'s Circus, recently criticized that humorist and conversationalist in a

> rather tart and testy manner; said he was too tedious in his talk, wrong in his pronunciation, and wholly guiltless of fun or other merit as a clown. In return for which public notice, bestowed through the columns of the *Tribune,* Mr. Rice, very naturally retorted, in his province in the ring, and said several severe things of Mr. Philander Doesticks.

The *Clipper* made clear that it was an even match.

> Both these fun-makers are professional men, each in his line. Both are reporters, and can give a good or bad report of any one, at any time, with the advantage of a large circulation. Thus, it is caustic pen against caustic tongue.
>
> Whether the war will continue, or when it will end, none can judge, save those who have had experience in the business of bandying personalities, and can calculate the amount of pleasure and profit in such a game of public give-and-take. The *Tribune* has a large circulation, and Doesticks drives a glittering pen. But on the other hand, . . . Dan Rice, with a large audience, has been known to wield a tremendous influence in the South and West, swaying them pretty much as he pleased. . . . For our part, we are generally advocates of peace; but in this case we don't care how long the fight lasts. It is a free fight. The pair are well matched. And what with the eccentricities of Dan and the gall of Doesticks, there is plenty of sport for the readers of the *Tribune* and the patrons of Niblo's.

The battle between these "reporters" was a grand episode in the raucous life of antebellum America. As the *Spirit of the Times* put it, "A public man, like friend Dan, hardly knows what thousands of friends he has, until he has been saluted with the abuse of the *Tribune.*"[16]

Rice's reputation continued to flourish. Before the New York engagement, he played with Nixon's Circus at the Howard Atheneum in Boston, where the *Herald* declared itself eager "to hear Dan give his political views, remarks upon social reforms and his general exposition of the philosophy of life." (It also reported that he had declined an offer of $50,000 for a season in California.) In Philadelphia, the *City Item* changed its preference for Wallett, deciding that Rice "is quite as polished as the former, and far more original." Rice's nine days in Baltimore rendered the Front Street Theatre "crowded with our most respectable citizens," who delighted to see the unusual feature of Rice "On Horseback! On Horseback! On Horseback!" The *Cincinnati Enquirer* had earlier made the case grandly for Rice, who possessed "indomitable force of character and genius . . . Few men have seen more vicissitudes, encountered more difficulties, met more reverses, and experienced more triumphs, been more abused or more praised than this self-same Dan Rice." [17]

Comic mules became routine circus fare after Rice introduced his first pair, Pete and Barney.

Rice now announced that the summer season would be his Farewell Tour. It figured in his April 11 benefit. Those tendering the benefit, including the preeminent American actor, Edwin Forrest, published a letter repeating Rice's aspirational message. Expressing their personal friendship, they wished to endorse "the elevated style of humor in the arena which you have originated, and which, while it has a tendency to a reform, rather seeks to please by its innate merit than by buffoonery of the clown."[18]

Still, he could not shake criticism. *Porter's Spirit of the Times* ran a long piece objecting to circus treatment of its animals and children; the article presented a thinly disguised depiction of Rice as "Buggins, the excruciating jester." In Philadelphia, his critics found more ammunition for complaint in a squabble with the manager Lent. They should have been paired harmoniously; Rice had worked for Lent the previous five winters. But Rice was missing his great animal attractions, Excelsior and "them mu-els," being held in New York pending payment of debts. Then, after Excelsior arrived, the horse broke down and had to be withdrawn. In turn, Lent withheld salary. When Rice didn't get his money, he vilified Lent in the ring. Lent responded in print, including a note of the "amount overpaid D. Rice, $133.99." The politically influential Col. John Forney of the *Press* joined Lent's side, declaring like Greeley that he preferred the mules to Dan's jokes.[19]

Doesticks and Greeley, having been catawamtiously chawed up by Rice, were more circumspect when Rice returned for a brief re-engagement at Niblo's. Only as the circus was closing did the *Tribune* venture a contrary word. Niblo's would be shut for repairs that the paper labeled "purification." Greeley remained avid to deny Rice credit in the undeniable fact of crowded houses. The "patronage thus far bestowed has been prompted by personal regard for 'Niblo's,' rather than by any real countenance" of circus. Meanwhile, respectability's ostensible focus on the character of an amusement dropped to reveal concern about the character of the patrons: "The coming week will bring back the old faces to the dress circle." It was a club, and Rice was not welcome.[20]

26

THE END?

What Rice *said* and *did* was growing less important than what he *was,* covered by the silt of celebrity. He remade himself into "Daniel McLaren," boasting—modestly—of his respectability, and establishing an estate fit for a gentleman. No longer clowning, he was the American Humorist. His circus that *"IS NOT A CIRCUS!"* was free from features now "considered so objectionable in many exhibitions by the refined and educated classes."[1] What more could he do to fit the ideals of the modern middle class?

He could announce his retirement.

The farewell tour is a time-honored tactic for attracting business, and Rice had been indulging since 1852. The two-cent *Clipper* put in its two cents worth: "Rice's farewell tour seems to put the cap-sheaf on his usual popularity. . . . No Doesticks (or any other chop sticks) can eclipse the fun Dan makes . . . as long as he can wag his wag's tongue."[2]

But this 1859 farewell was more than an advertising dodge; it was a declaration of respectability. In 1854, *Rice's Amphitheatre* had made the case: "Mr. Rice will e'er long leave a profession which has long been distasteful to him, and we may yet look to see him famous in another career." The same year, the actress-socialite Mowatt used the same language, observing that to "declare that the stage is distasteful is looked upon as a sign of professional aristocracy." Rice had become one of amusement's aristocrats; he was presenting this farewell tour as an aspirational culmination before finally escaping the suspicion of vulgarity that clung to performance. He elevated so high that he nearly floated above the circus: The *Clipper* announced that he "plays clown, now-and-then, to keep his hand in." He would be a gentleman deigning to gratify requests for his appearance rather than a performer currying public favor, for as the *Pictorial* insisted, "he never makes a personal effort for popularity." It was one of the paradoxes of the middle class that how one appeared to others was both beneath notice and an obsession. Performance in its exhibitionistic splendor pivoted on that paradox, as performers—like politicians—insisted on their desire for privacy in continuing public display.[3]

Yet even as Rice suggested that noblesse oblige prompted him to appear a few, final times, another reason surfaced. He was broke again. He was even still paying Van Orden. To the *Cincinnati Enquirer,* he was "McLaren, (formerly Dan Rice, who is bankrupt)." When he announced that his father was now sole proprietor, "successor to Dan Rice," it was not clear whether he had sold to McLaren, Sr., or used him to hide from creditors. Rice announced that he had given up two-thirds interest in the Great Show for $25,000 and 17,744 acres in Texas, his declared intention being to settle poor families there. But a letter Maggie wrote to their "dear Dauters" at boarding school put human faces in the picture. She warned them not to expect to visit home in April, since "it mabee that your pa cante aford it."[4]

In her letter, Maggie was full of maternal concern—asking Libby to take her younger sister when she went walking—and homey chat about the apprentices and a bird Aunt Libbie had sent. She urged the girls to "im prove you time while at Shool for my Dears : mother knows the wante of Some one to Teach hir when young." Maggie was embarrassed by that lack: "Libbe you muste not lette my letters bee Seen by enione of girles for the will make fun of it."

When she wrote that Kate's picture was hanging in "my" bedroom, that could have reflected Dan's absence on winter engagements, but it also could have meant separate rooms. Physically separated in the winter when she stayed in Girard, and on the summer tours when he was absent, they were becoming emotionally separated too. Maggie found comfort in her close relationship with the company, such as the show's young treasurer, Charles Warner. He added his name as witness when she signed her season's contract with Daniel McLaren, proprietor, to perform her two horses for $100 a week, and to provide the services of her pupils, Julien Kent, Charles Reed, Estelle Barclay, and Fred Barclay for $85 a week. If any were unable to perform, the salary stopped. Business is business. In the meantime, Dan included curious lyrics in an 1859 collection of his songs, a songster titled *Dan Rice's Original Comic and Sentimental Poetic Effusions.* One effusion came from that year's benefit in Baltimore. The song included the usual topicality, about a streetcar tax veto and a new invention, a ship that could sail underwater. Yet this time, Rice added precautionary words to wives: "Beware of sly attachments and flirtations on your lives."[5]

Rice led his show to upstate New York as he had in 1855 and 1857, alternating years so that he would not wear out his welcome. The season preview of the *Cincinnati Enquirer* put Rice's forty performers at the high end of medium-sized circuses, with average daily expenses of $250. (There were twenty small outfits, with $150 expenses, and a few big shows like Spalding's, with over two hundred horses, one hundred people and expenses of $500 a day.) Making explicit his claim to the Universal American Character, Rice encompassed "Irish Reminiscences, Negro Eccentricities, Northern Drollery, Southern Chivalry, Eastern Acuteness, Western Adventure," all of them "Master Pieces of the Master Mind." Heading into New England, Rice pushed himself into the middle of a controversy, offering to pay for the Fourth of July cannon salute in Lowell, Massachusetts after the aldermen and the council had locked horns over the issue. As the *Clipper* put it, he "emphatically fired himself off at Lowell, and has had spread eagle times ever since, so that the Great Show makes louder reports than ever. Excelsior!" Elevation continued to weave through his publicity, which presented Mrs. Rice's horses as so cultivated that they could keep time to the music. (It was the other way around, Canham's Keystone Brass Band adjusting its tempo to the horses' movements.) In Connecticut, notorious as a poor show state, he nudged his elevation pitch into religion. Dan "sows broadcast and yet gathers his crops as he goes along" there, outdoing

> Peter the Hermit, or any of those famous equestrian missionaries in the Holy Land during the Middle Ages. . . . St. Paythrick himself did not start the snakes out of Ireland quicker than Dan Rice has dispelled the prejudices of our Connecticut friends in regard to traveling exhibitions. Let the good work go on. The ladies, the children, the newspapers, and the clergy, are all "full of show," as soon as Dan's Great Show arrives.

He bolstered that success by distributing tracts for a clergyman on entering Hartford.[6]

Sunday was usually a day of rest for a circus, one of the rare opportunities during a touring season to laze for a few minutes, to wash clothes, to write letters, or to catch a fish, but one Sunday Rice marched his company into a quiet village church. That must have set the small congregation buzzing as last night's barely dressed stars entered in modest apparel, walking across the rough floor to take their places on the hard wooden benches. In "the jarsies," Rice continued as the "great apostle of philosophy." The *Clipper,* now reporting on him in nearly every issue, teased about this new religiosity: "Much joking used to be made about Dan having designs on the next presidency, but it is certain now that Dan has the religious classes on his side, in addition to his general popularity." But just as Rice's farewell tour was more than an advertising dodge, his pitch of religion was more than what the *Clipper* called a "pious dodge." He was staking a claim among the moral. He insisted "that not one in twenty of the business men in New York pay as much attention to the moral and religious instruction of their apprentices as I pay to the children whom I educate to appear in the arena!"[7]

At the end of May, Dan and Maggie visited their own children, now attending the Utica Female Seminary. The seminary, originally housed in a theater, had grown in reputation, with former (and future) governor, Horatio Seymour, among the trustees. Libby and Kate—"Kitty" in the class list—took a wide variety of subjects, including meteorology, philosophy, and chemistry, with emphasis on "moral advancement." Semester tuition averaged $26; Latin, French, and drawing cost extra, and a whopping $16 was charged for lessons in the piano-forte. There were personal expenses too. Budding young ladies at fifteen and thirteen, the girls were still young enough to ask, "What did you bring us?" Kate wrote requesting bottles of cologne, material for doll clothes, and a gold ring as a present for a friend. One of Rice's jokes compares grown women, who desire one birthday every two years, to a young girl at school, who wishes she could have two birthdays a year for the presents.[8]

A large blow landed over the summer. Rice lost Excelsior. Stories stretching over months of the horse's death make it unclear when he finally died. Spring rumors of his death were matched by credible reports of his appearance. In Utica, Excelsior—"Who is NOT Dead!"—proved himself the "great Artiste-Horse of America." But dead he was, of lockjaw, sometime in the summer. Rice never announced the demise, and he kept advertising Excelsior as part of the show. Still the *Clipper* scoffed. That "horse so well named (Excelsior) after the motto of New York's state arms, . . . keeps rising (especially up stairs) after every time he dies a newspaper death." It could have been a business catastrophe for Rice to lose a draw like Excelsior. Somewhat assuaging the loss was a replacement Rice had picked up around 1856, another white horse to be called "Excelsior, Jr." Rice did not finally acknowledge the change until March 1860, when he referred to the "celebrated Excelsior, the predecessor of the Excelsior now included in the stud."[9]

It would not be a circus season without violence, and Rice had more than his share in 1859. His doorkeeper clubbed a fourteen-year-old to death as the boy crawled under the canvas in Albany. In Coxsackie, another turbulent Hudson River town, two Rice men were sent to Sing Sing for manslaughter, though a third employee, acquitted, blamed it on locals' "bad fighting rum, which is the cause of nearly all such rows, and for which the showmen are blamed." Rice recalled that the legal proceedings cost him $13,000.[10]

More trouble came in September. Maggie wrote the girls from Trenton, admonishing them to study hard and cheering them with the reminder that winter would bring "Slariding." They were troupers enough to know that it was "Strang in getting a letter from this place this the third day for us," but their Pa was sick again, suffering from an old complaint, "indjestie," and a large blister on his side. The show had gone on to Easton, Pennsylvania. After the evening performance and a brief night's rest, the company began to stir at around four in the morning to grab a quick breakfast before the run. A hand in the stables put his lantern on a board sticking out of the wall, but suddenly the board fell and the lantern exploded into flames. As horses jerked at their ropes fire licked up the walls and crackled through the hay. Fighting their way through the smoke, hands reached Lalla Rookh, trumpeting in fright, her trunk waving wildly, and got her out, but a dozen of the horses were not so lucky. Spirited animals that had stepped nimbly around the ring were now a sad sight to greet the morning. Rice estimated the loss at $5,000. He arrived to look at the carcasses, gather his company, and move onto Allentown, where they would once again be cheery for the folks in the seats.[11]

To publicize his Farewell Tour, Rice chose an image he had used in 1856, showing him in a coat and vest, a high shirt collar, and a cravat knotted like a black rose around his neck. The first impression is, predictably, of a respectable public figure. But human faces are rarely precisely symmetrical: Covering half of a picture shows a certain look, while covering the other half gives a different impression of the eye and mouth. So it is with this picture. The right side of the picture, the left side of Dan's face, displays a man at the height of his powers; it is a strong, calm face, prepared for anything. Yet if the left of Dan's face shows a man at the full tide of his power, whether the issue is wits or fists, the right hints at an ebb. Fights had not scarred him, though they had broadened his nose, but the fun of fighting had clearly passed. This half of the face, in the shadow of that generous nose, looks uncertain, as if seeking a peace it did not expect to find.

The country faced the same split between robust optimism and anxiety. In Baltimore, Rice's competition included a play called *Extremes.* In it, Caroline Richings sang an old song occasionally used on civic occasions, "The Star Spangled Banner!" (It would not become the national anthem until the next century.) The "extremes" of the play were undoubtedly rabid abolitionists—Whitman denounced them as an "angry voiced and silly set"—and Southern fire-eaters who vowed to fight. For decades,

DAN RICE,
ON HIS
Farewell Tour as a Humourist,
WITH THE GREAT SHOW,
THROUGHOUT THE UNITED STATES.

Rice announced his farewell not because he planned to retire, but to proclaim that he stood above the vulgarities associated with performance.

Cassandras had been predicting that wrangling over slavery would doom the great American experiment. So far, the predictions had been laughed away, often in Rice's arena, as the country continued its brawny, apparently boundless ascent. There had been fights and riots over slavery, but America was accustomed to violence, and after each crisis things settled down.[12]

One strength of the American political system is that continuity seems inevitable, yet that is also a weakness, making it easy to forget how delicately things are balanced. Balance is less a noun than a verb, a dynamic action, as a baby learns when trying to stand, or as Lalla Rookh on a rope knew in her body. As Rice moved out of Baltimore, America was losing its balance. John Brown had attacked the federal arsenal at nearby Harper's Ferry, raising dizzying alarm throughout the country. Here was proof of the dire predictions by Southerners and conservative Northerners that abolitionists meant it when they said that they would destroy the country to free the slaves. Hotheads screeched that the great American experiment was ending; the rest began to worry.

27

RING CYCLE

In Europe, Richard Wagner was writing musical pieces with action revolving around a magic ring. In Philadelphia, Dan Rice was presenting the same thing. Though his Great Show remained very much a circus, despite the absence of that word into the winter of 1859–1860, Rice made musical drama a major part of the entertainment. The music of Wagner—who had completed two of the four operas in his Ring Cycle—would have suited Rice's spectacle of *The Magic Ring* perfectly.

Rice was at the height of his career, "a progressive in business, conservative in politics." Even Rice's horses enjoyed better grooming than many "a man who calls himself well-bred." Mrs. Rice exerted "a silent influence of sanctity on all around her." To underline that point, Rice excluded visitors from backstage, without having to add that the rule kept men from the common practice of seeking sex there; because a full "Corps de Ballet" filled out his *Magic Ring,* the suspicion of prostitution was especially strong.[1]

Starting at 7:00 P.M. to accommodate the three-and-a-half-hour length, Rice's *Magic Ring* offered scenes forged by modern stagecraft. His father, having purchased the National Theatre, on Walnut, had fitted up scenery, wardrobe, and "appointments" reportedly costing $25,000.[2] This "melodrama"—literally, music drama—presented thirty-three actors, the ballet corps, and one hundred auxiliaries, for a total of three hundred, plus the horses. A description of the first act conclusion gives a taste of Rice's *Ring*:

> THE REALMS OF FIRE. The lovely Princess Eveline and her faithful attendant, Leela, fast in the power of the mighty Godah . . . bound within the bosom of *Etna's Burning Mountain*—King Cupid, quick descending, arrives with Herbert, Franco, and Whirliburg to the rescue of the distressed damsels—Herbert takes from the Princess' finger the FIRST of the rings which gives the Wizard power over the Four Elements—Sets her free and they ascend on *The Dragon Car over a Rolling Sea of Liquid Fire.*

Next follow scenes set in the elements of water, earth, and air: Niagara Falls, and the "RISING OF THE WATERS!—*Ascent of the Lovers on the Bosom of the Deep*"; Mexican silver mines, then an earthquake swerve to a Sicilian vineyard for a fight with the Black Knight; and the Palace of Rainbows, where Herbert seeks his bride. Finally, hero and heroine triumphantly ride a chariot into the Hall of the Hundred Knights, as the performance surges to an "Ascent of the Spirit of the Ring—Fame, Victory, and the Spirits of the Air—SUPERB TABLEAU." The evening concluded with circus acts.[3]

Rice had other spectacles. There was his standby, the *Dream of Chivalry,* and a new one, his *Great English Steeple Chase,* conveying "a fair idea of the dress and *modus operandi* of the British steeple chaser. . . . 'Tis a manly pastime.'" Resembling *The Magic Ring, The Elephant of Siam* had a dying sultan, a usurper, a fire fiend, a rightful prince, a fair maid, and assassins, and Lalla Rookh, which still walked a tightrope "without the use of a balance-pole!" Another new work was *Ward's Mission to China,* following the visit of diplomat John Ward to China in 1859. The visit sparked Western interest in an exotic East, just as Commodore Matthew Perry's trip to Japan had in 1854. Rice promised an accurate "re-

Rice presented grand spectacles of music, mythic stories, and elaborate scenery.

alization of the Costumes, Ceremonies, Peculiarities, Sports and Pastimes of 'The Central Flowery Kingdom,'" and the *Sunday Dispatch* decided that it knew enough about China to assure its readers that the "properties were all correct, and the costumes faithful." (Ironically, for all the interest generated, the mission had failed, a fact Rice used to compare a "quadris-tupid critter" to Ward in the land of "Bamboodledom.")[4]

These spectacles spoke to Rice's age in many ways. Long before electricity was harnessed for special effects, before the development of flameproof synthetics, and certainly before computerized systems could coordinate intricate set and lighting changes, the National's stage launched thrilling ascensions, splashed with fire and water, that fit the contemporary love for modern technology and spectacular scenery. The exotic opportunities for dance—"A RUSTIC BALLET" of Sicilian peasants, an Evil Wizard, Chinese costumes, knights, water elves—matched those in ballets such as Tchaikovsky's *Swan Lake.* The mythical background in *The Magic Ring* flowed from the Romantic curiosity about other-worldly life. Foremost was the age's taste for a higher meaning or deeper truth or greater *something* than the workaday world. Rice's spectacles were more theatrical than his usual performances, but his pitch was the same one that Wagner was making in Europe, about aiming for a new, higher form of performance. With performers now hailed as "artistes," audiences were being told, genteelly, that quiet attention was respectable. When Wagner turned out the lights on the house to create a separation of audience from stage, what he called a "mystic gulf," it was less an innovation than the culmination of a long turn away from the audience. Rice's *Ring* rolled into Wagner's mystic gulf.

Rice played Philadelphia from November 1859 through March 1860, a five-month run that was his longest as a star, longer than his winter seasons in New Orleans. (New features included a clown, Tony Pastor, destined to become the preeminent vaudeville impresario.) He had opened, as usual, "to one of the largest and most fashionable audiences ever seen" at the National. He was, as usual, original, for "no living man knew him to rehearse anything whatever. His sallies of humor are as fresh to his own associates as they are to his audiences." The past and the future overlapped in this engagement. Rice gave a charitable benefit for James Bancker, the first to name his troupe a "circus," and now proprietor of the saloon attached to the theater. As Dan and Maggie took up residence again at the Jones Hotel, he made it known that Philadelphia was to be his home, "and the Great Show will hereafter be permanently located here." Taking out a Girard mortgage, Dan and Maggie listed themselves as being "of Philadelphia." Rice continued to buy land in Girard, but, needing money as usual, he began to mortgage his older plots. Perhaps, like those with weekend places, he now envisioned his "country estate" as a retreat.[5]

Early in the run, Rice traveled to Pittsburgh to testify in a lawsuit over horses seized the previous year from the Great Show. McLaren and Farwell had sued the sheriff for damages, claiming that, because they owned the show once Rice had sold his interest to them in April, his creditors couldn't seize the show's horses because of claims against him. To call a courtroom a circus was later derogatory; on November 16, 1859, it was description. For five hours on the stand, Rice held forth as he did in the ring. It was a perfect chance for lawyer jokes, like the one about the child who stubbed his toe, fell over a lawyer, and was never afterwards able to tell the truth. Reports pictured the courtroom in a roar of laughter, Rice delighting the crowd and flustering opposing counsel, who finally gave up. (The jury decided in favor of the Great Show and awarded heavy damages, $1,350.)[6]

More jokes appeared in a new publicity courier, *Dan Rice's Budget*: In modern chivalry, discussion is the better part of valor; Rice could reform Congress because he could handle mules; High Art was a painting of the Andes. While the jokes sound trite, Rice made them fresh. As "presiding genius," he talked to the audience "in his own off-hand manner—never twice alike"—while of course "good taste reigns over all." To his occasional ribaldry—he enjoyed women's dresses in the "Low and Behold Style"—Rice added jokes about a nagging wife. The "Eternal Scold" roars louder than tempests, trumpets, or hell itself. In "Trick for Trick," she stands over six feet tall high and throws pots at his head, while he must make her breakfast as she sleeps till noon. So "I must take care of number one; / I'll sell my traps, and cut my stick"—that is, leave. These antique jibes were curious from one publicizing his wife's aspirational importance.[7]

On February 27, Rice dazzled Philadelphia with a new feature, the elegant rider Ella Zoyara. The act included a graceful assortment of acrobatic tricks: standing on the horse's back, riding it over hurdles, jumping through "balloons." But neither tricks nor grace were the attraction. What got the Quaker City buzzing was a question: "Is she a boy or a girl?"[8]

Spencer Q. Stokes had started the Zoyara craze with his protégé, a young man named Omar Kingsley, of graceful figure and jet-black hair. Stokes had dressed Omar-Ella as a girl, allegedly for years, and then took him to Europe in 1852, where he performed before royalty in Berlin and Vienna. Upon returning to America, Stokes added the exotic last name, "Zoyara." Publicity for Stokes's stand at Niblo's early in 1860 insisted that European aristocracy had been totally fooled, lavishing flowers and love poems on "Ella," but the deception could not have been that complete. If the rider had been clearly a woman, people would have been impressed by her athleticism, but there would have been no sensation. Sensation grew from uncertainty. "Disputes nightly arise among the spectators on the subject of the fair equestrian's sex." The *Spirit of the Times* was not amused: "If the person *is* a man, the 'humbug' is a very dishonest one, and of questionable propriety. If a woman, for the sake of all parties the point should be settled." With talk of getting together a committee of women to inspect the performer, the counterfeit dispute rolled merrily on. The *Clipper* took a more light-hearted approach, alternating genders:

> He was unfortunate enough to lose her balance while performing his bare back act, and before she could recover himself, down she went, sustaining an injury to one of his feet, which incapacitated her from appearing for a short time. He is again on hand, however, or, at least, on foot, astonishing the spectators by her wonderful command over the horse.[9]

Rice threw his own Zoyara into the confusion. Ironically, since his *was* a woman, he built sensation not from a lie, but from the truth, disbelieved. Rice's Zoyara was probably Estelle Barclay, the apprentice he had presented in 1857 variously as Estella, Estrella, and Estello. The *North American* covered this Zoyara's first appearance on November 27.

> Considerable excitement was created at the National last evening by the debut of Mad'lle Ella Zoyara and so recorded on the books of the Continental Hotel. This is a very graceful and accomplished rider, very femininely pretty and winning; but the wonder is that this seemingly delicate and charming girl is really a boy! To all appearances the actions and looks are much those of a girl as ever were seen in a circus ring. And what is still more curious is that the jet black luxuriance of hair, so long

and beautiful, is not a wig, but the natural hair dressed after the fashion of females.

Like the original, this one sparked titillated curiosity. When Rice's Zoyara married his comic actor Frank Drew in St. Louis in 1860, the *Bulletin* speculated that confirmation of female gender would diminish "her attractive powers as an *artiste.*"[10]

Controversy sells, especially with the hint of sex, and Rice kept the pot boiling by pretending to be outraged by the other Zoyara, and by a third one who had cropped up. In Baltimore, where Zoyara's sex continued to be "a vexed question," Rice compounded uncertainty by exhibiting Zoyara's "mother" driving the band carriage team of a dozen black horses through the streets. This driver could have been a woman, a carefully disguised man, or an obvious man in a dress for a joke. These performers may have confused people, but there was no doubt about its presenter: "Dan *is* a showman, and understands his business better than Barnum ever did his." A "sell" was a humbug, like being sold a bill of goods. Rice now had, in this woman pretending to be a man pretending to be a woman, a "remarkable 'dam-sell.'"[11]

As usual now, Rice touched on politics. He urged members of Congress to shun "all Dissolute habits; there is too much Dissolution talked already." As the country's opinions became sharper, so did Rice's. He was "delighting the denizens of the Quaker City with Union speeches."[12] Now a local incident that made national news became a platform for his views.

Philadelphia's famed medical schools, including the first for women, attracted students from all over the country. In December, Southern students decided that they had enough of taunts and threats, so they prepared to leave. *Porter's Spirit of the Times* suggested that this might make Northern hotheads realize that they were pushing the South away. Locally, the *Sunday Dispatch* was less sympathetic, declaring that the students had been persuaded to depart by competing Southern schools, those "badly organized 'one-horse' colleges" jealous of the stature of Philadelphia's schools. ("One-horse" was now common currency.) In any case, for a final hurrah, on December 20 three hundred of the Southern medical students attended Rice's Great Show, where he gave a rousing Union speech. In 1860, that meant scorn for abolitionist zealots. "As a resident citizen of Philadelphia," Rice said that the city had more sense than to sympathize with those who supported the wild actions of John Brown and those like him. He urged the Southerners to avoid imagining that the fanatical principles broached by the few were the sentiments of the many who governed public opinion." A year later, the *Cliper* continued to allude to the stir Rice had created "by his great speech to the students . . . during the excitement among the John Brown-ites."[13]

Rice was so proud of the speech that he included it in *Dan Rice's Budget* and had a lithograph prepared showing him in mid-oration. In the speech, he deplored the absurdities wreaked by fanaticism throughout history; he reminisced about the kindness he had received in the South; and he emphasized his intimate knowledge of Southern life. He spoke of building a church for "his colored friends," while his "negro stories . . . seemed highly relished by the colored gallery." That was a section set apart for "RESPECTABLE COLORED PERSONS." One joke got a big laugh from both races, according to the account: "White folks were just as good as colored folks as long as they behaved themselves. (A sentiment which elicited much merriment, whilst his kindly allusions to the blacks were invariably received with tumultuous applause by the Southern students.)" Afterwards, the students made up a party to surprise Dan at his hotel, where they presented him with an inscribed, gold-headed cane.[14]

The applause for Rice's "kindly allusions to the blacks" serves as a reminder that Northerners, even abolitionists, were vulnerable to the Southern charge that they disliked black people. Racism was not solely a Southern disease. A biographer of Walt Whitman, for instance, excuses him for being in concert with "other Americans whose best-expressed ideals held great potential for freedom but whose attitudes or behavior sometimes conflicted with these ideals." That conflict included the popular belief expressed by Whitman that the "nigger, like the Injun, will be eliminated: it is the law of races."[15]

Rice's successive songsters displayed his greater involvement in politics. In his 1859 *Comic and Sentimental Poetic Effusions,* he focused mostly on local politics and those comic effusions. A year later, his second songster, *American Humorist and Shaksperian Jester Song and Joke Book,* repeated many of the earlier songs but began to emphasize his conservative Democratic principles, particularly in his mockery of abolitionists. He included his speech to the Southern medical students; "Hard Times This Side of Jordan," about "Maniacs" trying to force the sections apart; "Wait for the Wagon," the song from his version of *Uncle Tom's Cabin,* which mocked Northern hypocrisy over slavery; and "Dan Rice's Humors of the Day," warning that the country's pillars had been shaken by Harper's Ferry. In "Our Own Side of Jordan," North and South "are at war,

> With pens and mouth,—
> Whether slavery's a blessing or a burden;
> But let each one have her right,
> And stand up day and night,
> For the Union and her own side of Jordan.

To underline the conservative Union message, the cover showed Rice in a costume decorated with stars and stripes, a clown costume rather than his now usual gentlemanly clothes. Dan in the same costume illustrated the published version of the speech for the Southern medical students. Always a patriot, Rice literally embodied the American flag.[16]

PART 5

THE PEOPLE'S CANDIDATE

1860 ☛ 1867

28

HOUSE DIVIDED

In 1847, Rice had been in Pittsburgh for the debut of Stephen Foster's "Oh, Susanna." Twelve years later, the showman was in New York as another friend, Dan Emmett, introduced another song destined to become an enduring American favorite. Emmett was performing with Dan Bryant's Minstrels when he first sang his new song, "Dixie," on April 4, 1859. A Northern white man in blackened face before a Northern audience, Emmett wished he was in Dixie, hooray, hooray.

With a catchy tune wedded to lyrics feeding the country's lust for nostalgia, the song was an immediate sensation. It leapt from the stage to the streets to become "one of the most popular songs of the day, . . . sung, whistled, and played wherever the English language is 'prevalent.'" The song soon seemed authorless and timeless, passing into folklore as a favorite of Lincoln's, but Emmett could not have written "Dixie" at any other time, for it was a political song, ripe in the moment. It joined the campaign to prove that slaves were happy in their bondage, an anxiously defensive effort responding to the abolitionists' inescapable point that people should not be enslaved. Many such as Lincoln thought slaves should be freed but, with no constitutional way to eliminate slavery, they couldn't bring themselves to endorse abolition. In 1847, Calhoun estimated that two-thirds of Northerners believed that slavery was wrong, but only 5 percent of them supported abolition.[1] Meanwhile, apologists spluttered that slavery cushioned blacks from freedom they neither wanted nor could handle. But evasions, excuses, and constitutional explanations could not hide the fact that America stumbled badly with its original sin, from colonial New England's hypocrisy in scorning slavery while benefiting from the slave trade, through the Founding Fathers' compromises on slavery in the Constitution, to mental and spiritual antebellum contortions justifying slavery. Of course, that is hindsight. In 1860, argument raged in pulpits, plays, books, and newspapers, in Congress and in song. The apparently innocuous "Dixie" was as politically pointed in antebellum America as saying "comrade" was in the 1930s, or "peace" in the 1960s.

In 1860, Rice made a decision, also apparently neutral but just as politically charged. At the "full tide of his professional celebrity," he turned south. After a few performances in Washington, patronized by senators and representatives, Rice turned to Virginia and North Carolina. (Maggie headed home, making news when she lost her purse containing $600.) Rice's itinerary made business sense, for he had not been in the old South for a decade. It also made political sense. To cap the climax meant to surpass or outdo: While Rice's pro-Union, anti-abolition sentiments played well in the North, they capped the climax in the land of cotton. No one who had followed Rice's career would be surprised that Richmond found the show "unique," and the overflow audience "of high respectability." If anything, the South was keener than the North for Rice's aspiration. In Petersburg, the *Express* broke its habit of ignoring circuses, and the *Intelligencer* vowed that the city's largest crowd ever, 4,000, attended because "Dan has discarded the word 'Circus' as being unworthy of his exhibition."[2]

Meanwhile, in Chicago the Republicans nominated Lincoln for president. Two years earlier, his House Divided speech had brought him national celebrity. Now Rice picked up Lincoln's metaphor in singing "Things That I Like To See."

I would like North and South to leave slav'ry alone,
And stand by the Union unto the last stone:
To settle the question by war, blood and vice,
Is like burning your house to scare out a few mice.
. . .
I like to hear preachers preach peace and good-will,
Nor sectional hatred e'er strive to instill;
Let them teach the great truth, from the Great Book of all,
That States, like a house that's divided, must fall.
. . .
I'd like moderation all parties to sway,
And slavery would dry up and soon blow away.
Freeman's blood shed by Freemen would kill Freedom's tree;
And there'll be no shelter for you or for me.[3]

Though history shows Rice on the wrong side of the slavery issue, he was in the majority in 1860. More than that, he was standing on principle. Like Lincoln in the pre-war years, Rice based his stances on the Constitution's acceptance of slavery.

As in the enthusiastic North, Southern crowds cheered Rice's jibes at abolitionists. In Raleigh, with his show "evidently superior" to any before in North Carolina, his words made him "the greatest clown in the world."

> Rice himself, who seldom plays in the ring now, and is unquestionably the best humorist in the world, has always, in the Northern States, even when it has been against his own interests, manfully stood up for Southern rights, and brought the whole power of his acknowledged specialty of sarcasm to bear upon those, who, profiting by the wealth of the South, have vainly attempted by raising sectional issues, to sting the bosom which has fed them.[4]

This comment came at the end of May as Northern Democrats met in Baltimore. Their national convention in Charleston had disintegrated, so they convened at the Front Street Theatre, recently vacated by Rice, to nominate Douglas.

In 1860, no other performer, and perhaps no other American figure, had Rice's reach. In the first comprehensive American circus history, T.

Rice presented himself as an embodiment of the United States.

Allston Brown concluded with the era's pinnacle of circus excitement, the showman Rice: "His intellect is fine, his perceptive powers acute, his fancy fertile, his judgement sound, and his imitations great."[5]

Beyond circus, Rice's name had become one to conjure with. An Ethiopian troupe in Buffalo presented the satire "Daniel Rice." Bryant's Minstrels—hosts of Emmett's "Dixie"—transformed Rice's *Dreams of Chivalry* into a "Dream of Shovelry," and enjoyed its own five-month New York run. And after years of race horses named for him, another equine "Dan Rice" popped up in Minnesota as the star of *Mazeppa.* The *Clipper,* even while warning its readers that Dan and T. D. Rice were different men, gave Dan credit for T. D.'s wildly popular "Jump Jim Crow."[6] Dan's competition in Baltimore included Frank Chanfrau, who had created an indigenous stage type, Mose, the Bowery b'hoy, that had caused a sensation in 1848. However, by 1860, when Chanfrau's Mose had run out of steam, he satirized Edwin Forrest, *Camille, Il Trovatore,* Shakespeare, and—the highlight of the entertainment—Dan Rice's Circus. The flattery of imitation flew over the Atlantic. Circus Blennow in Germany advertised an "Entree comique par Mr. Dan Rice." His whole circus was imitated when the impresario John Wilson presented a "Dan Rice's Great Show" in San Francisco, and then in Hawaii. While Wilson was "coining money" with the name, he probably paid for the privilege, for Rice never complained, though he had warned earlier that "His name cannot be legally used by any other establishment." From Hawaii to Germany, from larceny to lampoon, Rice's name blazed.[7]

Now this singular Dan Rice became solitary. He and Maggie had shared two decades of traveling hardships, illnesses, lawsuits, and bankruptcy. They had raised two daughters. Despite his jokes about nagging wives and extramarital affairs, their partnership had endured. For twenty years, under trying conditions, the pair had balanced the push and pull of marriage. Now, it pulled apart.

The first overt indication of a split came at the end of June 1860. After years of only buying property in Girard, Dan and Maggie Rice—"of Philadelphia"—sold some of it to Dan's cousin, W. C. Crum, for $18,000. With Warner as witness, Maggie signed over her interest before the court clerk in Knoxville, Tennessee, where the Great Show was playing. The couple was making financial arrangements for the split. (Rice bought the property back for $20,000 in April 1861.) Then on August 1, 1860, Dan signed property over to Maggie, "in consideration of the love and affection which I have and bear for my wife." The apparent affection may have been contractual language to show "consideration," a legal requirement that each side give something of value. This contract referred to them as Margaret Ann McLaren and Daniel McLaren, again "of Philadelphia." Rice also transferred the 17,744 acres in Texas he said he had acquired for his share of the Great Show in 1858, and lots in Hickman, Kentucky, lying on the route down the Mississippi.[8]

The divorce was amicable, with no need for the family to take sides. Libbie and Jake Showles, for instance, would alternate tours with Dan and Maggie. Amicability was possible under the divorce laws, looser than they had been (or would be later), especially in the North. Grounds included adultery, but the couple could agree to the legal fiction of "constructive desertion," presenting "such indignities to her person, as to render her condition intolerable and life burdensome." Twenty years later, Dan explained to a reporter that their marriage had been pleasant but passionless, except for Maggie's occasional jealousy. He had decided to divorce her, he said, because they had been unable to have a son, but that may have been rationalization. Reports at the time show that the decision had not been his. Dan was in Philadelphia when the *Clipper* passed a rumor from the Quaker City that Maggie, who "has done much, very much to dispel the clouds of misfortune that have hovered over her husband's brow," obtained a divorce. Similarly, another paper alluded to but did not name the "causes that led the lady to legally disband the ties that bound her to the famous Daniel." A third paper was more pointed: The circumstances "are too well known to require comment, sufficient as they are to win for her the sympathy of the public, as well as the generous support of those who are intimately cognizant of all the details of the affair."[9]

Whatever steadying influence Maggie had provided was now gone. There was an aspirational cost, too. In culture's ongoing morality tale, her refinement had certified his aspiration, her goodness guaranteeing his. Now he had lost the moral shield of the "true woman." Though the loss was not a fatal blow to his aspirational project, it was damaging.

After a stop in Girard, he rejoined his "Monster Show" in Cincinnati. Rice heralded his Queen City opening on August 9 with a special feature: He announced that he would take Lalla Rookh for a swim in the Ohio River.

People thronged to the river on the sultry morning of the swim. The *Times* estimated that, despite weather as hot as an oven, 15,000 stood by the Cincinnati wharf, and another 3,000 waited on the Covington shore, where the swim was to start. In between, more people watched from steamers and skiffs. For the few bent on their normal business, perhaps carrying a load of Procter and Gamble's fancy soaps, police had to clear passage. Women wearing a fashionable mix of plaids, prints, and paisleys shaded themselves from the sun with the aid of striped parasols and bonnets swirled with ribbons and bunched with bows. Men, similarly colorful, sported a rainbow of vests and ties, while their hats made a mini-skyline at head level. Children kept the picture in constant motion, like flies around jars of honey. Calling crowds a "swarmery," Thomas Carlyle sneered but conveyed the vibrant energy.[10]

Skepticism rippled through the crowd as it neared 9:00 A.M., the announced start. People began to wonder whether they might be the victims of an elephantine humbug. Then Lalla Rookh appeared on the old Kentucky shore. Cincinnati could see her ears flapping and her trunk swinging along the ground. As she entered the river, many sweltering on shore must have wished that they could roll in the water, too. She frolicked until Noyes persuaded her that the show must go on, so she set out for the Ohio side. "Rice in person superintended the voyage of her Asiatic majesty," as he led in a skiff while Noyes brought up the rear in another boat. Lalla Rookh continued to play, spraying water. Sometimes only her trunk stuck out of the water. Then she would dive and stay down so long that people worried that she had drowned, until a surge carried her body half out of the water. As her "elephantship" neared Cincinnati, she became annoyed at the boats crowding her and turned on them. To escape, the rowers displayed speed "which would have put even the famous Harvard Boat Club to the blush." The chase carried her so far that Rice had to bring her back to Covington, where she set out again. Forty-five minutes after starting, Lalla Rookh landed in Cincinnati, at the foot of Race

Street. In the words of the *Commercial,* "many of our fast men . . . are generally supposed to have 'seen the Elephant' under nearly every possible aspect;—now that they have seen the *aquatic* animal, their education may be considered as complete." Both the *Clipper* and the *Spirit of the Times* carried long accounts of the event—though the *Spirit* snubbed Rice by not mentioning his name.[11]

Rice paid dearly for the triumph. A month later, Lalla Rookh died in Indiana, of "lung fever" reportedly brought on by her dip, a diagnosis influenced by the age's belief that baths were unhealthy. Rice reportedly had refused $20,000 for Lalla Rookh. By coincidence, the elephant on the West Coast Rice's Great Show also expired after a plunge into a river, tumbling over falls in northern California.[12]

Rice soldiered on. Without the draw of Lalla Rookh, he reverted to old strategies. In Madison, Indiana, he announced that he was in his favorite city; he admitted children free; he gave firemen a benefit; he alluded to the virtual endorsement of the authorities in waiving the license fee; and he invited praise for "banishing the clown altogether" from his circus. In Louisville, "Genial Dan" played the retirement card again, announcing that "the people's clown" might be giving his last performances, which drew the "most fashionable people" and the "most prominent clergymen in Louisville. . . . (This is a fact; no 'blowing' about it.)" The spirits of Excelsior and Lalla Rookh continued to hover over the show, at least in images in the ads.[13]

In St. Louis, Rice bought a steamboat, the *James Raymond,* named for the deceased menagerie man. Rice acquired the side-wheeler from Spalding, who had used it to push his *Floating Palace.* With their feud now history, business was business. Predictably, the St. Louis audience comprised "the *elite* of the community," and Rice was "unquestionably an original genius." After Carondelet, Cape Girardeau, and Cairo came a week in Memphis. Rice was able to exhibit for free because he gave a benefit yielding $2,000 to the Sons of Malta, a fraternal organization to which the mayor belonged. It was also in Memphis that Rice allowed a local marksman to test the boast that the rhinoceros's hide was impervious to bullets. Fortunately, they fell to the ground, flattened by the thick skin.[14]

On Rice's second day in Memphis, Lincoln was elected president. Angry voices screamed for war, shouting in the South that they would secede, in the North that they would force submission. The majority, including most of the minority who had voted for Lincoln in the four-way split, worried about the growing influence of the abolitionists. As things heated up and the sections drew further apart, Rice stuck to his plans. He continued "away, away, away down South in Dixie."

29

SOUTHERN SYMPATHY

Shouts and applause rolled like a battle cry on January 26, 1861, through Rice's old Amphitheatre, renamed the Academy of Music. That afternoon, when word reached New Orleans that a Louisiana convention had voted for secession from the Union, the tension of uncertainty had exploded into excitement. Cannons fired salutes, church bells rang at the "joyous tidings," and the *Daily Crescent* unfurled a newly designed Confederate flag outside its offices.[1] As night fell, half the city seemed to be squeezed into the arena. The throng knew just the man to help them outholler thunder.

Rice had come to town a returning hero. It was nearly biblical: seven years of triumph in the South, followed by six years away. On his return, "Old Dan" waxed nostalgic, fondly recalling the support he had enjoyed in the old One-Horse Show days. (The phrase had spread: The *Clipper* chided the malign influence of "one-horse politicians.") He emphasized, though, that those days were past. Called on to sing one of the old songs, he declined, saying they were "buried with the tomahawk of the war that once raged between himself and Dr. Spalding." He even ventured something like a good word for Van Orden, hoping he "would live to be a better and wiser man."[2]

THE WALTZING CAMEL.

Rice named the comically awkward camel after Van Orden. Notice the stars and stripes.

In any case, secession excitement gave Rice a larger topic. His opening parade on December 10 made his sympathies clear: His honorary marshals were from Southern states only. Having a representative for South Carolina was especially significant, as it was the leading Southern saber-rattler. Rice's inclinations also sang in his music. When the parade halted opposite the Clay statue on Canal Street, Rice's band played "The Marseilles Hymn." The South, seeing itself defying tyranny, had appropriated the great anthem of the French Revolution to make "The Southern Marseillaise." New lyrics were added, but the English translation by the poet Percy Bysshe Shelly aptly expressed Southern feelings: "Shall hateful tyrants mischief breeding. . . / Affright and desolate the land, / While peace and liberty lie bleeding?"[3]

So it continued in the ring. Rice joked about his presence in the South: "Hearing that the Union was about to be dissolved, he wished to be on the sunny side." The *Algiers Newsboy* quoted Rice on his opening night. Praising "one of the most chivalric of the Confederacy, the Palmetto State, South Carolina," he wielded Union as a weapon to attack Northern fanatics:

> The South has been aggrieved and she knows it, and the whole civilized world knows it; but none more seriously than those who have attempted to deprive her of her rights, those fanatical people who have violated those holy privileges of the ballot box by passing laws contrary to the Constitution. The folly of their ways they have already discovered, and that powerful comedy, good, sound, common sense, is already beginning to operate in those States, the citizens of which, it appears, did forget the eleventh commandment, "Mind your own business."

The *Delta,* a fiercely anti-Northern paper, forgot its old coolness toward Rice to embrace him as "a man who had endeared himself to the Southern people by the upright, manly course he has always pursued in regard to his expression of opinions relative to the rights of the South." Recalling Rice's speech to the Southern medical students in Philadelphia, it reminded readers of his advice to "meddling abolitionists to mind their own business." As for secession, "Rice glories in the movement of South Carolina, although he regrets the emergencies that drove her to it."[4]

As a Christmas treat, Rice announced that he would, to make "the Little Folks happy, appear in his old fashioned Striped Dress, as the Children's Clown." But he soon returned to his suit, adult humor, and politics, an irresistible combination. The 1,800-seat Academy of Music was "overcrowded every night, and if there were room enough for all creation, it is an open question whether all creation wouldn't insist on coming in," crowed the *Delta.* The paper forecast an "abstropulous" benefit for Rice, who could have been a product of South Carolina, as the Palmetto state was "well known to produce capital Rice."[5]

So, on January 26, secesh excitement reached its peak. In Rice's amphitheatre, raw emotion had people standing on the seats, waving arms and pounding each other's backs, their faces mobile with yells, some fierce, some laughing. Rice stood in their midst, waiting. When he began to speak, the hellaballoo drowned out his first words. Time drowned out the rest, for no one wrote them down. As the *Delta* commented about his opening night words, "were they not heard by a multitude such as precludes the necessity of repeating them?" Whatever he said, the paper approved. On the same page that it reported "The Last of the Union in Louisiana," the *Delta* testified that Rice had covered himself with glory, not only as clown, philosopher, and moralist, but as "politician and patriot of the combined Palmetto and Pelican school," referring to South Carolina and Louisiana. His speech that fateful night was consistent with what he, and many people, had been saying for years: The Union was threatened by abolitionists, what Whitman called "a few and foolish red-hot fanatics." Hadn't William Lloyd Garrison, one of their leaders, said, "Accursed be the American Union"? And what they proposed, that slaves should be freed immediately, without compensation, seemed preposterous to most. Even Lincoln declared that he would free no slave if that would save the Union. Yet this small interest group advocating abolition seemed to wield power disproportionate with their numbers, especially now that they had helped elect Lincoln. Those candidates who had tried to accommodate North and South had been surpassed by a politician avoiding straight answers, labeled by the *Clipper* "a sectional candidate to the Presidency of the heretofore United States."[6]

As Rice steamed away from New Orleans, the *Delta* and the *Picayune* both considered him "peculiarly well adapted, by association and sympathy, to please our people." That meant he was a "true Southerner," in the words of the *Natchez Daily Free Trader.* "Dan is Southern, feels it, talks, it, acts it."[7]

Hindsight sees the gathering storm, but the nation had barreled past many threats of dissolution, always finding some compromise. The *New York Times* in 1858 mocked the notion of a "Southern Confederacy" as the pipe dream of a fake aristocracy. As late as 1860, a businessman who believed that war was probable "was much laughed at, and . . . his reputation as a man of sense and judgement suffered seriously." More generally, "it was almost universally held in the North that the South never would secede, just as the South believed that in case of secession the North would not fight for the Union." Even at that, the country was not neatly split North and South but muddled, like the four-way presidential election. The election itself had not endorsed abolition but was a qualified judgment by a Northern plurality that Lincoln offered the best chance of keeping things patched up without giving away too much to the South. Well into 1861, an air of unreality prevailed, as if all the heated war talk were more performing. The *Clipper* blithely dismissed alarm: "Freedom of speech is guaranteed to every man in the North. . . . Go into any of our hotels, and you may hear secessionists boldly proclaim their sentiments, and no one attempts to interfere with them. So in our theatres." Even after Fort Sumter, the New York–based *Spirit of the Times* continued to defend the Confederacy, and the *Clipper* could still make light of Barnum "trying the patriotic dodge."[8] Rice's Southern sympathies fit into the chaotic jumble.

Meanwhile, the political excitement was interrupted by more financial troubles and by a domestic event.

In February, the week after Rice left New Orleans, the Great Show was sold at auction. It was not clear which "D. McLaren" had been proprietor. A clipping saved by Rice pronounced the show "owned by him and under his control," while the *Newsboy* of Algiers, across the river, reported the opposite, that Rice had been managing for McLaren. In any case, it was gone. Rice's dilemma was poetically considered in "Sonnet to a Famous Humorist," which observed "that the jests you break . . . Have left you . . . grandly *broke.*"[9]

The following month, Kate wrote to her mother from the Academy of Visitation in Georgetown, where she and Libby had transferred. Perhaps Dan felt Southern-inflected Washington would be more congenial for them than Utica, in upstate New York. Kate's letter reveals why, on the day Maggie had signed over interest in their Girard property, Dan had sold all the goods in a house in Philadelphia—beds and bedding, bureaus, washstands, books, pictures, silverware—to Charles Warner, and why Warner was no longer with Dan's show. In her letter, jauntily signed "O'Rice," Kate inquired about Charley, and asked her mother to "give him my love." Warner had evidently kept his eye on more than the books. Sometime this spring, Dan's former wife married his former treasurer, a younger man. Rice's later claims that there had been no love in his marriage may have been the face-saving bravado of a hurt man.[10]

When Fort Sumter was shelled on April 12, an old antagonist seized the opportunity to attack Rice. Greeley proclaimed that a "sharp look-out should now be kept up for the detection of spies" on Rice's show. The New York editor, referring to a speech Rice made to Girard volunteers in April, declared that the clown was trying to "pass himself off as a Union man." Worse, Greeley accused Rice of forming a secession military organization to spy for the rebels. That accusation bubbled out of confusion between performance and military politics. The original Zouaves were Algerians in a French infantry unit who were noted for bravery and colorful uniforms. The fame, flashy outfits, and unusual name made a perfect opportunity for spectacle, which circus had been exploiting since 1836. In 1856, Rice produced his own "Zouaves of Algeria," wheeling their mounts in military "evolutions." Now, when war still seemed mostly a grand pageant, Zouaves were everywhere, in military units displaying themselves in flowing red pants, and in professional performers showing off close-order drill. Troupes of both kinds, soldiers and performers, strutted in Cincinnati, St. Louis, New York, and New Orleans. Greeley's diatribe against Rice's Zouaves as soldiers ended with an attempted witticism: "This Rice may, after the manner of his class," ride horses well but "his attempt to perform a similar feat between two stools" will lead to a fall.[11]

Rice had been modifying what he said as he moved North, muting his talk of an aggrieved South. But what was most interesting in Greeley's at-

Rice began to picture himself defying Southern guns, though he ran no blockade at Memphis.

tack was that he left out: Rice's words. Greeley avoided quoting Rice because the humorist continued to sail in the main stream of Union politics. For a Northern majority, to "go it" for the Union meant disdain for both groups of fanatics, those "John-Brownites" who had forced the issue, and the secessionists who belligerently rose to the bait. Two days before the inauguration, the *Clipper* expressed a common thought: While opposed to Lincoln's election, it was willing to give him a chance; however, "We . . . detest the fire eaters and political traitors of the South as we do the Black Republicans of the North. Both are alike amenable to censure, and both should be alike condemned for the difficulties which now encompass us."[12] Greeley knew that quoting Rice would remind people that they agreed with Rice. It was more damning to take the innocuous fact of the clown's Zouaves and add the false hint of spying. The war was also a political campaign, a struggle over its meaning, and Greeley was a politician smearing an opponent.

Rice counterattacked in Cincinnati, where the *Enquirer* gave an account of his response from the ring. Touching Greeley "upon the raw" with spicy anecdotes, then pitching into Doesticks, Rice kept his audience laughing for half an hour, until he "closed his rattling volley amid a roar of applause. Rice pursued the matter in a published letter. He wrote that he was willing to be subject to criticisms of a free and honest press, which he respected, but the heart of things was not his unquestioned loyalty but Doesticks' jealousy.[13]

After a week in Covington, with its "proscriptive" license of $88 a day, and in Newport, Rice steamed back across the river late Saturday to Cincinnati. A "mischievous wag" told the police that Rice had concealed arms on his boat, so a posse hurried to the landing, "where Dan's boat lay quietly moored, the stars and stripes floating gracefully in the midnight breeze." Rice protested "the mobocracy," but submitted to a search. There were no arms on board, though the account joked that there were *legs,* including those of the fair equestrienne who had kicked a man invading her privacy. The whole affair was ridiculous, said the *Enquirer,* for "there is no more genuine lover of the Union than this same Dan Rice."[14]

Content that he had mastered the situation, Rice turned up the Ohio River. Citizens from Mason City, in western Virginia, asked him to speak on "the political aspect of the present crisis." Locally, that included the fear of invasion, against which prospect Rice volunteered his men. The rumor of arms to attack the Union transformed into its opposite, that he carried cannons to defend it. In his talk, Rice started with the assertion that he did not aspire to political office, a sign that he was beginning to think about it. Now, instead of sympathy for an aggrieved South, he expressed shock at secession. Men must have the moral courage to proclaim to the rebels, "Thus far shalt thou go, but no further." Mason City, he eloquently declared, had that moral courage.

> This evening, as the sun sets in his golden couch and your cannon proclaims the Union men's triumph, the hills and villages of your sister State, Ohio, will re-echo with joy, and before old Sol shall have arisen, the lightning conductor—that fleet courier, the telegraph—will make the whole country aware that the fires of liberty have not resolved themselves into ashes.

Rice repeated the warning he had given in Erie: Though Southern leaders were traitors, their soldiers would be worthy opponents. "But your cause is a holy one," and will prevail. Rice then begged off saying more. He was tired, having "labored hard for the last six months to save the Union."[15]

Regardless of Rice's Northern sentiments, the attacks on him continued. Greeley may have sincerely doubted Rice's loyalty, but the political charges dovetailed with his earlier attacks on Rice's respectability. The *Tribune* ostensibly meant circus performers when it complained of "men of his class," but the phrase conjured a broader, social complaint. To Rice's critics, a man who would appeal to a crowd in the North would appeal to a mob in the South, and one who poked fun at upstanding men of the community, such as Greeley, would tear that community down. Rumor, as constant in war as battle, became Rice's companion.

The *Clipper,* falling into the confusion of the times, roamed all over the lot on Rice. In its May 25 issue, the search of his boat mutated into a tale that he refused to hoist the American flag from his mast, trained a howitzer on the Cincinnati crowd, and escaped to the Kentucky shore. On June 15, the *Clipper* reversed itself. Implicitly accepting Rice's denial, it published a May 30 letter from Wellsville, Ohio, where he was playing. It was a stout defense written by "The Doctor," probably his agent, Dr. Richard Jones (who had attended the Philadelphia College of Medicine).

Ultimately—and accurately—"Any slander that Greeley can obtain against Rice is 'old pie' for Horace." Then the *Clipper* turned again, like another twist in the Mississippi, deploring Rice's "intense Southernism" (as well as his "sardonic fun over his debts"). Labeling Rice "A Chameleon Clown," the papers asserted the existence of a list *"of Minute Men, signed by Dan and his company, to defend the South unto the death!"* There was no list. Finally, in August, the *Clipper* didn't know what it thought, printing opposing views from Minnesota. "Squibob" complained that Rice was only "a sort of Union man," who called his kangaroo "Jeff Davis" but "very coolly stated that when in the South he called him 'Abe Lincoln.'" Another observer on the scene, "Chips," disagreed: "Rice was serenaded at his hotel, called out, and made as sensible a national speech as I ever listened to."[16]

Down the Ohio Rice went, and up the Mississippi. In St. Louis, he again declared that he did not aspire to politics. He no longer rode the *James Raymond.* Rice later said that General Fremont had confiscated it, though it was not pressed into service until 1863. Another source passed on a story that the Confederates used it for patrol duty, her calliope playing on moonlit nights. In Lyons City, Iowa, Rice said that he appeared in the ring to prove he wasn't dead, or if dead, he was only to save funeral expenses. He made his first venture to Wisconsin, though he said he had been there in his early days.[17]

Now Rice lost another animal. In La Crosse, he lampooned the town council as extortionists for their $50 license, and the *Tri-Weekly Democrat* complained on his behalf, pointing out that his company had spent $600 in town on clothing, jewelry, and supplies. Then, as Rice's troupe steamed north on the *Lucerne,* towing a barge carrying the rhinoceros cage, a fast Minnesota packet boat, the *Key City,* swept downriver around a bend, making waves that rocked the barge, plunging Old Put's cage into the water. The current prevented any rescue. Rice estimated the loss at $20,000, though his agent was able to milk the calamity for publicity by filling the local papers with fanciful details. The *Clipper* was not pleased by the fictions. "What motive the La Crosse *Democrat* can have had in misleading its readers, we are at a loss to conceive. We know that Dan Rice is up to such dodges, but an editor of a newspaper is supposed to have some respect for his patrons, be his own reputation good or bad." After the bloated, stinking carcass of the rhinoceros was hauled from the river, Rice sued the *Key City* for the loss.[18]

In two years, Rice had lost Excelsior, Lalla Rookh, and Old Put, three of the greatest draws of mid-century circus. Any one of them could attract a crowd; together they had made Rice a formidable manager.

In Chicago, site of the convention that had nominated Lincoln, Rice played to 50,000 people in September. He had been delivering his version of Union sentiments all over. When he passed through Cleveland, where "his 'voice is for war' to the last gasp," he said he had a plan to raise a cavalry unit of 1,000 circus riders, and had been contacted by a call from Washington to discuss the matter. In Girard, he gave another speech as he joined the local state senator, Morrow B. Lowry, in bidding Erie volunteers farewell. Rice again denied interest in politics, though he called himself a "disciple of principles" enunciated by Douglas. Rice admitted he had opposed the election of Lincoln as a sectional candidate, but claimed that Lincoln was following Douglas's doctrines. The question now, he announced, was not abolition, not Republicanism or "Democracy but that of actual war." The South must be beaten, no matter what the cost. "Fiat justitia, ruat caelum." Let justice be done though the heavens fall. In Chicago, the *Post* pronounced itself "anxious to listen to his adventures down south, and his ideas of things in Secessia," while the *Chicago Tribune* appreciated his "good sound political common sense," and promised soon to "show to the public that Rice, under the guise of Motley, has done the Federal cause much service."[19]

Then Rice led his Great Show home. The *Cincinnati Enquirer* reported that he was lying in clover after a profitable season, but the Utica paper painted a different picture. His politics continued, though the *Clipper* disapproved. "From the moment he enters the ring till the curtain falls on the last act, he endeavors to prove himself a union man; he pitches into everybody, with the exception of Abe Lincoln and his Cabinet. This will do very well on the Stump, but in the Ring it is out of place."[20] Those offended by his hits on the times were growing in number, and now even a show business paper had decided that they should not be part of the show business.

In Girard he talked again, fleshing out what was becoming his standard Union speech. He declared that his observations around the country made him no politician but simply for the Union, though he said that the surest way to lose the South would be the abolition folly. "Elect your strict partisans, place your rabid abolitionists in power, assert by your votes that the war is not constitutional, but sectional, and you will then drive millions from your support and sympathy." As for Old Abe Lincoln, he is honest, "adhering to a constitutional conduct, [dealing] heavy blows both upon abolitionism and secession." Rice endorsed the Democrat for state senate, and got in digs at the Republican, Lowry, who had shared the podium with him in August, but whose "odious and unconstitutional" abolitionism stood contrary to Lincoln. "Let the masses disregard the wants of political tricksters and assert their power at the polls in defense of the Union, the Constitution, and the Laws." The crowd yelled approval, and the *Erie Observer* concluded that Rice was sound. To the *Erie Gazette,* he was a "patriotic, true-hearted man," going "for the Union first, last and all the time." When the text of his speech reached Cincinnati, the *Enquirer* found much to cheer in his declaration that abolitionists are as "dangerous an enemy as the most hot headed Secessionist." Supported by "corrupt press" such as the *New York Tribune,* they encouraged secession by persuading the Southern man that "his home is to be invaded by a host of John Browns, who intend to set his slaves free and arm them against him." The *Enquirer* could not agree more. "True as preaching, and vastly more profound."[21]

Rice concluded on a personal note, confessing that the dream of his life had been to settle down in a favored spot like Girard. Thanking his neighbors for the privilege of their society, he assumed an unwonted modesty: "I have endeavored to deport myself with such propriety as my limited education would permit." Then, speaking to people who would have known the circumstances, he referred to his broken marriage: "But my fond dreams have been disturbed, for reasons to which I need not allude. That I have sometimes erred is probable—for I am but human—but I feel a consciousness of having intentionally wronged no one." He then expressed his "anticipations of building up and again enjoying a home in your midst."[22]

30

UNION, ALIAS PEACE

Rice tickled the scarlet-coated ringmaster, who whirled in outrage. "I don't suffer such familiarity," he barked, threatening Rice with the whip.

"Don't suffer? Well, now you are quite different in your views from a young lady I was sparking t'other night. I asked her if she would suffer a kiss. 'La,' says she, 'I should not suffer it; it would make me feel good.'"[1]

Experience formed the joke. On November 4, 1861, the showman married Charlotte Rebecca McConnell. He was thirty-eight, she was eighteen, the only child of Henry and Charlotte McConnell, among Girard's wealthiest and most prominent families. Henry McConnell owned the leading mercantile business, and he and his wife had helped found the local Presbyterian church. In 1860 Rice donated $1,000 he could ill afford to that church after a visit by its young ladies, presumably including Rebecca.[2]

The family was not pleased having a showman for a son-in-law. Rebecca's cousin lamented to her diary: "Monday. Cold and windy. Mother,

Dan's second wife, Rebecca McConnell, the flower of the Girard elite, was the same age as his daughter.

Ellen and I working at our house all day and evening. Water in the cellar. Rebecca went to Mrs. M's [H's?] house and married Dan Rice. How can it be that she has ruined herself and broken her parents' hearts."[3]

Part of the family's distress flowed from the difference in age. The wedding day was Rebecca's eighteenth birthday, perhaps chosen because she no longer required parental consent. Of course, thirty-eight was not old but Dan's daughter Libby was the same age as Rebecca. There was his worldliness, too. He had been everywhere and presumably done everything. Rebecca, by contrast, was a sheltered girl, trained to be "accomplished" so that she could take her place among the local elite. He had seen the elephant while she, so to speak, had barely heard of it. Beyond the disparity in age and experience, the McConnells simply looked down on Rice. He may have been the toast of New Orleans and lionized in New

York, but he was rungs down on the local social ladder, a newcomer, and a showman besides, who dressed loud and talked big. They could turn one of his sentiments on a woman's heart back on him: "The magic of the tongue is the most dangerous of all spells."[4]

Other neighbors were more hospitable. As "the representative of Girard throughout the world," Rice had put his adopted home on the map. When he lauded Girard during a Philadelphia stand, the local paper decided that exemplified "the proverb, True as Dan Rice!" While the McConnells' narrow horizons had schooled them to recoil from Rice's worldliness, others in Girard took him as he offered himself, a sophisticated and amiable man. He was "rated something of a philosopher and a wise men by the inhabitants. And such he was in no small degree, for he was a traveled man and had an observant mind."[5]

The parents' distress generated a story that made its way into a Pennsylvania state publication. A state school official was speaking at McConnell's church when he noticed men slipping out the back. He tried to be more ingratiating, adopting "our most melodious and winning tones," but one by one, they left. Worried that his talk had driven them away, he was assured afterwards that a local crisis had arisen. McConnell, holding Rebecca at home, was trying to prevent the marriage and had summoned reinforcements. At the same time, Rice's men were determined to reunite the couple. Battle was brewing until a compromise was reached, and Dan carried off his prize. Like the fiction of Rice's aiming a howitzer at Cincinnati crowds, or the new one that a Union force had seized Rice's menagerie, this one aimed mostly at putting the showman in a bad light. Rice's men and the local nobility surely bandied words, but this was not the Capulets and the Montagues, and there was no assault on the McConnell manse. The touring bureaucrat may have been told an embellished version to hide the fact that his speech was as boring as he had feared.[6]

For Rebecca and Dan, all was honey and hugs. In a Valentine's Day letter to Jacob Showles, Rice wrote, "I am in love up to my eyes." Their love match was an apt symbol for a changing age. The practical idea of marriage as an economic partnership was being overwhelmed by the romantic ideal of love, just as Dan had moved from sensible Maggie to this pretty daughter of Girard. Rice's ardor for his young bride was disconcerting to many. Advice manuals were counseling that "indulgence of human passions was threatening community life," and his own family had reservations. Decades later, Rice's former apprentice Charley Reed was still muttering that Dan and Maggie had both been foolish in marrying younger partners, especially Dan and his "young chit of a girl."[7]

The party after the wedding was a grand affair. In a village of six hundred people, three hundred turned out in style to celebrate the marriage of its famous son. They roamed over a house fitted up in "most admirable taste, dictated by Mr. Rice himself." He had recently paid $3,200 for a pair of Tuscany-crafted mosaic landscapes, vibrantly colored in red agate, lapis lazuli, and verde antique. A gallery on the second floor boasted works in nearly every "picture art": frescoes, paintings, engravings, and the work of the "photographist." The view from the windows offered more "artistry" in the landscaped grounds. Whatever reservations Dan's side of the family had, they came to celebrate. Both Libbies and Kates were there, his daughters and his married sisters elegantly gowned. After "wit and sentiment"—toasts and speeches—the chairs were cleared away and the band tuned up for dancing. A centerpiece was Rebecca's ensemble, included in an account because "Lady readers are always curious to know how a new bride is dressed." She wore white silk with a flowing train and a brocade flounce, trimmed with point lace and orange flowers. The McConnells did not stint for their only daughter. Opulent material was the equivalent of furs and jewels later. Some brides economically chose a print fabric so that the gown would later serve as their best dress, but Rebecca did not make that small economy, instead following the fashion set by Queen Victoria when she wore white at her wedding in 1840. Capping the McConnell climax was costly jewelry, including diamonds securing her lace veil.[8]

Reporting on the event, the *Clipper* merged politics and the personal. Rice is "trying to set himself right on the Union question," the most sensible step being the union with Rebecca. However,

> Dan's step no. 2 is, making what he wishes to have believed as union speeches, made up principally of denunciations of abolitionists, a set of men, in the extreme sense, that are so in the minority, that they can hardly be said to exist. Dan is shrewd enough to know this, and feels that

> he will make but few enemies on that side of the house; while by thus knuckling to the South, by playing one of their cards, he hopes to make and retain friends among them, so that he can show a "clean bill" with them when the war is over. That sort of Union, *alias* peace, *alias* "secesh" doctrine, won't stand.

By then Dan and Rebecca were in Cincinnati, having left Girard two days after their wedding. He opened a seven-week run at the National Theatre, the couple stayed at the fashionable Burnett House, patronized by railroad magnates and the governor. Dan gave his bride nothing but the best for her honeymoon. War fever was high. The theater was rumored to become an armory; General Halleck, about to gain command of the Union armies, was also at the Burnett; and Menter and his band, soon off to war, serenaded the happy couple at their hotel.[9]

Despite competing attractions—John Wilkes Booth, Adah Menken, *Hamlet* at Pike's Opera House, Donizetti's *L'Elisire D'Amore,* a lecture on the first days of the rebellion—Cincinnati was on the "tip-toe of expectation" for the Great Show. Dan added spectacles, including *St. George and the Dragon.* The mysterious Zoyara continued to tickle curiosity. Even though Dan "acknowledged the corn," admitting that his was a woman, she appeared at times in male attire, and was declared alternately to *be* Sallie Stickney and to be *married* to Sallie. Rice still had a great equine attraction, the replacement for the original Excelsior in the great white horse, Excelsior, Jr. It was blind but so remarkable that people wagered that it really could see. One "intelligent foreigner" swore that if Rice took the horse to Europe, it would constitute one of the most attractive features exhibited there; the *Enquirer* quickly added that Rice was too refined to do it for mere gain. Then there was the Great Daniel himself, whose genius and wit "must command admiration." Altogether, the Great Show was the best place the *Enquirer* knew to dispel the "blues."[10]

Rice had his own blues behind the habitual public optimism. He was sick again and faced another lawsuit, in Albany. His Valentine's Day letter to "My Dear Brother" was rife with low spirits. Jacob should feel "no Uneasiness about the future as I am and have been mindfull of your and my dear Sister's interest," yet Dan followed that assurance by admitting that these "are most Gloomy times indeed and it is hard to arrive at any con-

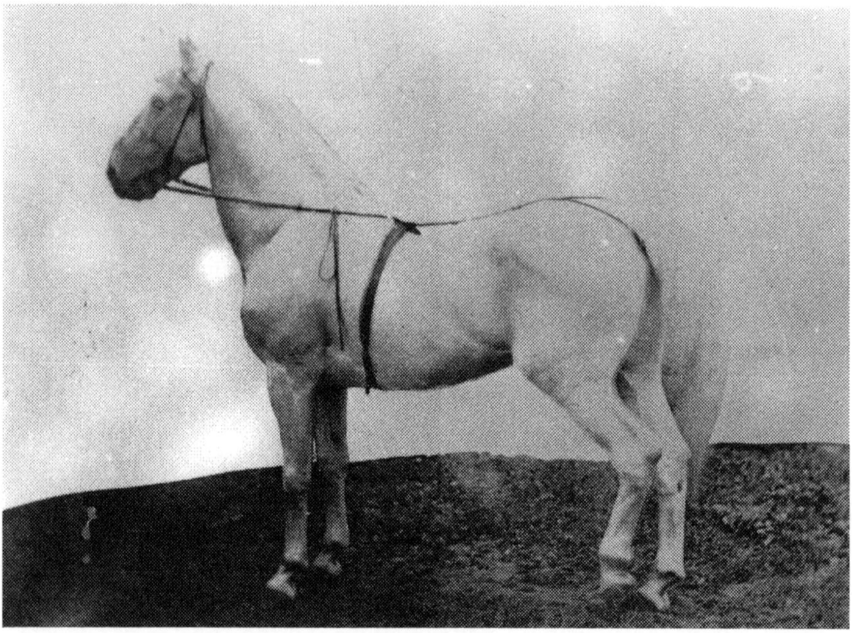

Excelsior's successor, dubbed Excelsior, Jr., was blind, yet did the same remarkable tricks.

clusions what is best for the future." He promised to send along a few dollars after his benefit that night—it raised $1,000—and also offered to sell one-third of the Great Show to Jacob for $5,000, either because he needed money or to help Jake and Libby. Still, for all the gloom, there was family. Dan's daughter, Libby, was with him, and she and Rebecca, "well and happy," sent their love. Joy in his marriage did buoy his spirits. He was not only "in love up to my eyes," he could now "See my way out which is a Remarkable thing with man when he gets in as far as Ive been."[11]

Gloom was growing nationally. Fort Sumter had been fired on. Lincoln called for volunteers and suspended habeas corpus. A Baltimore mob attacked Union soldiers. Southern ports were blockaded. Each new episode beat a tattoo on the drumhead of war. The *Clipper* had stopped calling for tolerance: "We want no more secession talk in our theatres; we have submitted to it long enough, and the sooner it is 'wiped out,' the better." As casualties grew, another battle had been joined on the home front that would prove equally important. Now that the country had its war, what did it mean? What was the purpose of the mounting deaths? What later ages saw as the abolitionist's moral high ground was countered by another ideal. The country stood as a beacon of liberty to the world because it had been founded in the rule of law, a triumph over the age-old rule of power. The keystone of that rule of law was the Constitution, a careful balance of regions and interests. Unfortunately, that rule of law countenanced slavery, and that balance of interests prevented reform. Beecher agreed with emancipation in theory, but preached that we "who boast of our Constitution must not violate it ourselves in putting down those who violate it." Because abolitionists were in such a minority that they seemed unlikely to win through constitutional means, many people believed they were waging a kind of guerrilla war—a new phrase from the Napoleonic era—while their wild ideas were cynically exploited by the North to further a lust for power. "Southern rights" was primarily a euphemism for slavery, but it also represented a fear that the North, with its manufacturing power, moral condescension, and "go," was growing tyrannical. The Republicans in turn suspected that Northern Democrats offered aid and support to the Slave Power.[12]

Leaping into the fray, Rice risked becoming a partisan favorite. The "secret of this celebrated humorist's success" was his "fearless habit of speaking aloud even unpalatable truths." The *Cincinnati Enquirer* swore that "no other man could have so braved the Southern tornado . . . at a time when New Orleans was running over with Secession. And upon the other hand there are none who can storm the strongholds of Abolitionism and beard the irrepressible negro worshiper to his teeth, with so little chance of being subjected to mob violence." Upon hearing his "talismanic name," Cincinnatans went not only to be amused but also instructed, "for there is more sound knowledge to be gleaned from Dan's philosophy, than out of any political stump orator we know of." His sarcasm cut like a two-edged sword, so "the ultras all round have to take it."[13]

Then came one of the most significant tales of Rice's life, expanded from the early, simple denial of disloyal words. The *Enquirer* laid out the revised story.

> There was an act of horsemanship in which the rider waved the "Star-Spangled Banner" to the same glorious air by the orchestra. The first ap-

> pearance of the flag, and the first few bars of the music, elicited a loud hiss by a stalwart individual . . . which was taken up until it swelled into a seeming universal chorus. Dan was in front, and as the storm increased, he dashed thro' the audience, cleared the orchestra, and waving to the "gentle musicians" to be silent, he faced the excited crowd.
>
> It was the night of the passage of the Ordinance of Secession, and the Union minority was crushed into silence by the fury and madness of the hour. There was one man, however, who did not flinch to defend the old flag and its thirty-four stars, one and inseparable. As he proceeded, a score of revolvers were leveled at him, but with the physical pluck which is part of his nature, and the moral courage derived from a good cause, he remained unflinching. . . .
>
> The American South, as well as North, admire pluck, and while the above manly conduct elicited a cheer "for Dan Rice," the act was continued, the flag waved, and the *Star Spangled Banner* played by the orchestra.[14]

Closing Cincinnati on New Year's Day, Rice continued his working honeymoon and took his bride to Washington. There, he played for two weeks with King's National Circus, around the corner from Ford's Theatre. Rice was the "Eloquent Expounder of the Realities of Life," who will "Sing the Song for the Union!" Whatever he said in the heart of the North's war effort drew standing-room crowds. Even though King had been running his show since November 4, he could raise ticket prices to 75¢ by presenting this "Logical Arguer, Facetious Joker and Philosophical Wag."[15]

Next at New York's Old Bowery Theatre, for four weeks with Stickney and another National Circus, Rice gave his opinions "on the war, . . . on Greeley, . . . on 'papers,' . . . on Dixie, . . . on 'things.'" Like Rice, Bennett at the *Herald* believed that the "*Tribune* itself is a proof that the abolitionists are disunionists." The *Herald* called the rival editor "that horrible monster, Greeley" a dozen times through a two-column attack, for urging that the American flag be torn down as a "polluted rag." Meanwhile, the paper praised Rice for his admiring crowds, "not a few of them from the fashionable quarter of the town." That echoed *Leslie's Illustrated,* which saw refined Rice rendering Stickney's "a place of fashionable resort."[16]

"Danl. Rice & Ly" went to Philadelphia, staying at the Continental Hotel.[17] He had an engagement for the first two weeks in March at the

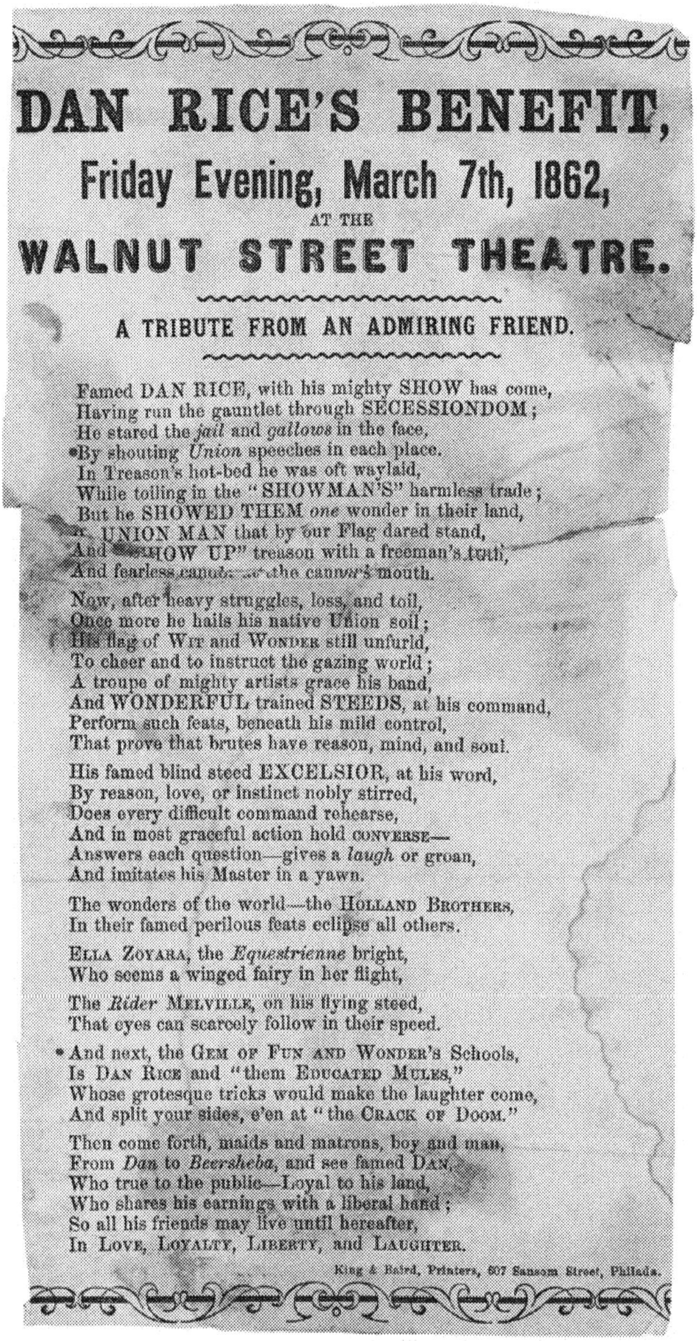

DAN RICE'S BENEFIT,

Friday Evening, March 7th, 1862,

AT THE

WALNUT STREET THEATRE.

A TRIBUTE FROM AN ADMIRING FRIEND.

Famed DAN RICE, with his mighty SHOW has come,
Having run the gauntlet through SECESSIONDOM;
He stared the *jail* and *gallows* in the face,
By shouting *Union* speeches in each place.
In Treason's hot-bed he was oft waylaid,
While toiling in the "SHOWMAN'S" harmless trade;
But he SHOWED THEM *one* wonder in their land,
A UNION MAN that by our Flag dared stand,
And "SHOW UP" treason with a freeman's truth,
And fearless [illegible] the cannon's mouth.

Now, after heavy struggles, loss, and toil,
Once more he hails his native Union soil;
His flag of WIT and WONDER still unfurld,
To cheer and to instruct the gazing world;
A troupe of mighty artists grace his band,
And WONDERFUL trained STEEDS, at his command,
Perform such feats, beneath his mild control,
That prove that brutes have reason, mind, and soul.

His famed blind steed EXCELSIOR, at his word,
By reason, love, or instinct nobly stirred,
Does every difficult command rehearse,
And in most graceful action hold CONVERSE—
Answers each question—gives a *laugh* or groan,
And imitates his Master in a yawn.

The wonders of the world—the HOLLAND BROTHERS,
In their famed perilous feats eclipse all others.

ELLA ZOYARA, the *Equestrienne* bright,
Who seems a winged fairy in her flight,

The *Rider* MELVILLE, on his flying steed,
That eyes can scarcely follow in their speed.

And next, the GEM OF FUN AND WONDER'S Schools,
Is DAN RICE and "them EDUCATED MULES,"
Whose grotesque tricks would make the laughter come,
And split your sides, e'en at "the CRACK OF DOOM."

Then come forth, maids and matrons, boy and man,
From *Dan* to *Beersheba*, and see famed DAN,
Who true to the public—Loyal to his land,
Who shares his earnings with a liberal hand;
So all his friends may live until hereafter,
In LOVE, LOYALTY, LIBERTY, and LAUGHTER.

King & Baird, Printers, 607 Sansom Street, Philada.

Rice increasingly focused on Union patriotism.

Walnut Street, a venerable theater and circus venue built in 1811 by Pepin and Breschard, and originally called the Olympic Theatre. Now, half a century later, a "fashionable" audience warmly welcomed "the comical genius." The bill advertising his benefit the first week was A Tribute From An Admiring Friend, beginning with an account of running "the gauntlet through SECESSIONDOM."

> He stared the *jail* and *gallows* in the face,
> By shouting *Union* speeches in each place.
> In Treason's hot-bed he was oft waylaid,
> While toiling in the "SHOWMAN'S" harmless trade;
> But he SHOWED THEM *one* wonder in their land,
> A UNION MAN that by our Flag dared stand,
> And "SHOW UP" treason with a freeman's truth,
> And fearless candor at the cannon's mouth.[18]

Here was Rice as glorious Union hero.

The *Sunday Dispatch* disagreed, setting off a squabble around the country. Greeting Rice with the old rumors, it challenged him to explain his politics. Rice met fire with his usual fire. Quoting Ben Franklin about those who hide behind their "battery of type," he stated his position. "I honor an honest press as the grand palladium of our liberties, but your noisy, puffy, gassy sensation newspaper no more represents the *true* press than a hog represents holiness." In New York, the *Clipper* dredged up the old accusations, and expressed surprised that patriotic Philadelphia allowed him to perform. The *Enquirer* in Cincinnati dismissed the whole thing as "balderdash," to which the *Clipper* shot back, "Why this sympathy for a secession showman? Is the *Enquirer* tinctured with like principles?"[19]

Exasperated by Rice's continued popularity, the *Philadelphia Dispatch* and the *Clipper* in New York worked each other into a lather, like overheated horses pushing each other in a race. The *Dispatch* reprinted the *Clipper* attack and added a longer one, "SECESSIONISM AT THE WALNUT STREET THEATRE.—ROTTEN EGGS AND TRAITOROUS SYMPATHIES." Despite Rice's "lately discovered Unionism," reinforced with a red, white, and blue costume covered with stars, he "concluded to brazen it out with an acknowledgment of his secession proclivities even now." According to the *Dispatch,* he repeated a speech he had made in the South claiming that region had been wronged. He added, "I believed so then, and I believe so now."

> Upon the utterance of this infamous and insulting sentiment a perfect storm of hisses broke forth, intermingled with applause from his dead head friends. The hissing rather seemed to disconcert him, for it was violent and prolonged, and the signs of disapprobation continued during the rest of the performance whenever Rice appeared.

In the *Dispatch* account, Rice plaintively cried to the crowd. "What have I done? what have I done?" The next night, "treated to a few more eggs," the clown said nothing about secession, and "appeared to be pretty well cowed down." On Saturday, with eighty police in attendance, Rice delivered "cheap buncumbe," trying to explain away his words in the South alternately as jokes and self-preservation. The *Dispatch* presumed sarcastically "that if Dan ever gets back to Dixie he will protest that his professions of loyalty in the North were to save his head from being knocked off, and that his admiration for the Union expressed when in the ring was all a joke!"[20]

The trouble with the account is that no other Philadelphia paper mentioned the alleged riot or any thrown eggs. The *Cincinnati Enquirer* dismissed it as the ranting of enemies. Most likely, there had been hisses covered by cheers from Rice's supporters and quelled by the police. The following week, the *Clipper* suggested as much. As it continued its assault on Rice, taking a swipe at his aspiration by calling him "McLaren, *alias* Rice," it asked why the police had squelched disapproval of Rice. Rather than the scene of a riot, the Walnut Street seems to have been the site of frustration for Rice's foes because they could not make their voices heard. (A week later, the *Clipper* reported that Mrs. Garrettson, the theater lessee, had attempted to close the engagement, but Rice insisted on continuing.)[21]

Yet even if every detail was a lie, there was truth in the account. The glory of antebellum amusements had been the creation of performance across the footlights. The embrace between the performer and the disparate people in the seats, forged into that mysterious body called an audience, was often uneasy, marred by violence and struggles for supremacy, but the resulting performance was the community's thinking out loud about what it wanted, feared, worried, hoped. "Community," after all, is not a numerical accumulation of the like-minded but people with human differences working through social accommodation for a modicum of civic harmony. Antebellum performance glory reached its pinnacle with Rice. Other performers did what he did but few so well, and none so famously. For "everybody has heard tell of Dan Rice; everybody has seen Dan Rice, at least no individual can be found, possessed in his or her senses, that would be silly enough to say that Dan Rice was not as well known as their best friend, for it would only reason an obtuseness only equaled by a person born in the wilderness and vegetated out of the reach of humanity."[22]

Increasingly though, comedy and talk, Rice's tools, were no longer sufficient. Of course, nothing was sufficient in this civil explosion of war, but his tools, and the audience bond they forged, had been the bedrock of his career. Now his ability to bond himself to audiences was faltering. He was still able to connect masterfully at particular performances. If nothing else, the Philadelphia attack shows itself a fiction by depicting a plaintive clown, pleading. But his pointed political talk no longer delighted widely. Where Rice once reached across classes and regions, the war fragmented audiences. If many believed that Rice was a brave and noble patriot, there was another side that saw him as an equivocator, or worse, a traitor. Critics such as Greeley who had long disliked him had new ammunition. Worst for Rice, he could no longer forge disparate clusters of people into any kind of a sustained whole over time. He continued to mock his opponents. He continued to draw crowds. The country had over 34 million people now, twice as many as when he began performing. But the broad communal audience of his glory days was disappearing. So the story of the Walnut Street Theatre carried metaphorical truth in the picture of a bewildered Rice before an audience he could not master. "What have I done?"

31

A MUTED VOICE

Rice's career shot fireworks of contrasting trajectories. His personal appeal blazed into the sky as if it would never come down. People flocked to his hits on the times, to his remarkable animals, and most of all, to the fellowship he created with them. Their concerns were given a thorough airing in the infinite circle of this fellow of infinite jest. A much different fate met the other symbolic rocket, his business path. While occasionally bouncing high, it often scudded along the ground, shooting off sparks on a haphazard course.

Rice was not ignorant in business. He could not have taken shows out year after year without some financial acumen. Yet he paid no steady attention to business details or to the long-range view required for success. He spent lavishly. Having known stark poverty, Rice was generous, with family, friends, strangers, and with himself. If all his donations had been concentrated in one place, he would have been warmly remembered in that place as a public benefactor. Mostly though, money flowed in and out, like the tide, and as abundantly. In the fond words of an agent, Rice "never allowed private obligations to check his ebullitions of public spirit."[1]

Rice got financing for the 1862 season from an unlikely source, Doc Spalding. For both, it was more than a business decision. Rice might have found money elsewhere, and Spalding could have invested in other shows. Yet they were back together, Dan blustering past possible chagrin. Amity did not mean equality. Dan needed money, but all Doc needed was another place to invest. For contributing $5,000 in capital, he received half the profits. Spalding himself, seeing that the war had eliminated the South for touring, looked to a South American tour. Transported on the brig *Hannah,* the Spalding & Rogers' Orion Circus was on the road to Rio. Spalding did not go, taking no part in the day-to-day vicissitudes of trouping.[2]

Meanwhile, Dan watched as Maggie continued in the business, going out as "directress" of "Goodwin & Wilder's North American Circus and Mrs. Dan Rice's Great Show." The *Clipper* enjoyed this turn of events. Maggie was a "true Union woman"—patriotism overlaying refinement—and free of "the 'late humorist,' whose political suicide leaves room" for her show. She took many of Dan's performers. They were described in a publicity pamphlet interspersed with almanac-like tips: cake recipes, a way to render children's clothes flame resistant, a "New Method of Compounding Interest." Their daughter Libby now had a featured act, a "Beautiful Pastoral Scene" on horseback. The other Libbie, Dan's sister and now Mrs. Showles, appeared as the American Female Horse Tamer. Her new husband, Jacob, continued his versatility. As the Antipodean Equestrian, he balanced a ball with his feet while riding on his back on a horse; when he was Le Monarque De Feu, he swung in the air and fire flew out of a headgear as he spun. He also presented Maggie's mules, named for prominent prizefighters, John C. Heenan and Tom Sayers. Comic mules had become a staple of circuses since their introduction by Rice. (Lent, his rift with Rice not healed, billed his mules, "P. T. Barnum" and "Dan Rice," as "the smallest and wickedest specimens of the mule race in existence.") Also on Maggie's show were two Charleys, Dan's former agent, Castle, and of course, her young husband, Warner. Warner's position as treasurer might have been expected to earn him a promotion to manager, but Maggie held the reins.[3]

She also borrowed Dan's title, the current Mrs. Warner leading Mrs. Dan Rice's Great Show. While she could legitimately claim the name after years of marriage, she did not use it for self-identity but to capitalize on the fame of her ex-husband and his circus. Dan was annoyed. In April, he wrote to *The Programme,* a show-business periodical, to alert the profession that his former wife was now Warner's wife or—getting snippy—"(so says the report)." No more Mrs. Rice, "therefore she is *Mrs. Charles Warner.*" Beyond personal feelings, Dan had a legitimate business complaint, especially when word about shows on the road still came mostly from the bills tacked and pasted on every vertical surface in town. Newspapers confused things by greeting Maggie in "Dan Rice's Great Show." Finally, Dan sued in New York, winning an injunction against Maggie's use of "Show" or "Great Show" in connection with the name Rice. Even so, her publicity continued to join them into the next year.[4]

The *Clipper* still had a grudge on, mocking Rice's new "circus-ism, dispensing with clowns, and soliciting the patronage of the clergy and Sabbath-schools! Bow-wow!" Nevertheless, he continued to draw. After a winter in Cincinnati, New York, Philadelphia, and Baltimore, Rice started a tour out of Girard again. He advertised it as his last stand before departing for Europe. With circuses competing over less territory during the war, a European tour would have made sense, but Rice stayed home. He continued to play the Zoyara card, now with Charley Reed as Zoyara, himself replaced as the show's child star by Estelle "Zoyara" Barclay's brother, Fred.[5]

Newspaper accusations of Southern sympathy became infrequent as Rice, taking every opportunity to cheer the Union, embodied what Lowell, Massachusetts deemed "patriotism, politics & piety." In Girard, when Rice heard that Federal troops had captured New Orleans, he fired salutes from his lawn to alert his neighbors to the news.[6]

But if Rice was now going it for the Union, he did not, in the era's lingo, go the whole hog. With Republicans in charge, he kept trailing hints of anti-Republican beliefs. In Chicago after touring Canada, Rice honored the man who had run against Lincoln, donating $500 to the Douglas Monument Association in June 1862. He also teased patriots so extreme that they wouldn't ride to the South Side, and professed that the red cheeks, white teeth, and blue eyes of a girl "are as good a flag as a young soldier in the battle of life need fight under." As the season continued, Rice's agent Dr. Jones also solicited donations as agent for the monument; his visits to a town were a way to test its "political as well as amusemental proclivities." Similarly swimming against the Republican tide, Rice named a new horse "Stephen Douglas." In 1863, he got up a new spectacle, "Rebel Raid on a Union Picket." Of course, it ended in Union victory, but to sustain dramatic interest, Rice certainly threw in plenty of Rebel triumphs along the way. His ads also began to show a dramatic image labeled "Dan Rice's Great Show, On The Mississippi River, Running the Blockade At Memphis, Tennessee, Summer of 1861." The stirring picture glossed over the fact that he had played that Southern town in April 1861, and had run no blockade. A new songster, *Dan Rice's Great American Humorist Song Book,* showed the same muted patriotism, adding Union sentiments to the contents of Rice's first two, but with equivocation. "Things That I Like To See" was pushed to the front of the songs, to proclaim that Rice "would like North and South to leave slav'ry alone." A new song, "Flag of Union Forever," which borrowed "land of the free and the home of the brave" from the "Star-Spangled Banner," was dedicated to retired Gen. Winfield Scott rather than to any officer actually fighting the war. And of the many patriotic speeches Rice had made, he chose an 1862 oration referring to a then-recent disaster of the Union army in Virginia.[7]

Closing the touring season in Spalding's Albany winter quarters, Rice returned to Chicago for two weeks with the Mabie Brothers Circus. John Wilkes Booth was also in town, playing *Richard II.* Booth had been in Cincinnati the previous winter when Rice had mused nostalgic there "for the good old days of Whig and Democrat, when neighbors differing in politics walked arm in arm to the polls, cast their votes as they pleased without fear or favor, took their glass of old Bourbon in a friendly and social manner . . . and left the Constitution to take care of the institutions of the North and South." Did Rice and Booth now take a glass of old Bourbon together? The accusations that Rice favored the South would have been a lure for Booth, while gregarious Rice would drink with anyone in the profession. Though theater and circus had been diverging, a still significant overlap was evident at the hotels frequented by performers, in the theaters they still shared in the winter, and in the common concerns of touring. Booth certainly knew the world of circus. The four photographs he carried with him in his last days included Fanny Brown, a beautiful circus acrobat whose father had worked with Rice. It is not difficult to envision the two showmen over bourbon—a Southern drink—discussing the aggrieved South, perhaps whispering that abolitionists ruled Washington. That was still a common thought: In November 1862, the *Enquirer* decided that a "party that will sing the song of the old murderer, traitor and cut-throat, John Brown, is nothing but an Abolition party of the most revolting character." History does record one meeting Rice had with Southerners. Just as politicians choose their venues for symbolic purposes, Rice took the unusual step of meeting with Confederate soldiers imprisoned in Chicago. When he closed this winter run in the Garden City, he was hailed as "the greatest living showman."[8]

Rice hurried home to Girard. It was the first time in a decade that he had made only a single winter engagement. He attended Libby's wedding in January 1863. After years of trouping side-by-side, Dan's daughter and his favorite apprentice, Reed, had decided to troupe together. Libby and Charley married at the Presbyterian church, now presumably Rice's home church.[9] Like Libbie Showles, her namesake aunt, Libby Rice Reed was making a career of the circus. (Kate was on a more retiring course. Like her own namesake aunt, Catherine Manahan, Kate Rice did not become a performer.)

A second event called Dan home.

Rice: "Where are you going, Master?"
Ring Master: "I'm going to get a little air."
Rice: "Going to get a little heir, eh? Well, sir, name him after me."
Ring Master: "You seem to be very happy. I can account for your happiness."
Rice: "How so?"

Ring Master: "You've got a charming, beautiful wife."
Rice: "Look here, we've always been friendly, haven't we?"
Ring Master: "Of course we have, Mr. Rice."
Rice: "Then don't you ever again remark that I've got a charming wife."
Ring Master: "Why, Rice? There's nothing in it."
Rice: "No, but there might be."[10]

Now Dan's charming wife was going to have a baby. On February 22, when patches of snow stretched along the ridges like bones, Rebecca gave birth to a girl. Mother and child survived, but that was no foregone conclusion at a time when one in seven newborns died. They named the little baby Charlotte McConnell Rice, Lottie for short. "Charlotte" came from Rebecca's first name, from her own mother, and from a cousin. The new baby would have exempted Rice from the draft had he been called. Just turned forty, he was still eligible. By "a strange hocus pocus," of the sixteen men required for the Girard quota in the fall of 1862, eight were connected with the show business, including Thayer, Glenroy, and Crum, Dan's cousin. Rice did not replay his absence at the birth of his first child; he was there when Rebecca had the baby, and he returned during the ensuing season.[11]

Spalding put up the capital for another tour. He would not have persisted if they had not made money during their first year; now, they were looking for more with another "Dan Rice's Show (of the Dr. Spalding stripe)." One report put Rice's salary at $25,000 for the season, $1,000 a week and "equal to that of the President." It is unlikely that Spalding paid that much. The source of the claim, an Erie article as Rice was leaving Pennsylvania, suggests he was trying to impress his neighbors. Regardless of Rice's salary, this circus was small, a dog & pony (& monkey & mule) show. That did include the impressive Excelsior, Jr., representing "the *one horseness*" of this "One-Horse Show." Junior was advertised like the original, carried on a platform. Sister Libbie and Jake returned for a season with Dan after touring with Maggie in 1862. Family remained close to Dan and Maggie despite the split and Dan's lawsuit against Maggie for using "Rice," which had been mostly business. Rice's brother, Manahan, was also along as doorkeeper. The show had to be small because it traveled by train. Unlike later railroad circuses, which were huge, riding in scores of cars and forging their own routes, shows on rail in 1863 still had to fit on a few cars and follow the train line's schedule. Nevertheless, Spalding's use of trains shows that that he continued to be innovative. The ads featured a speeding engine, the sleek lines of its cow-catcher, giant spoked wheels, and the inverted cone of the smoke stack together symbolizing modernity, as advanced as a speeding car in the 1930s or a rocket in the 1960s. Playing on the title of a favorite song, patrons were urged to "Wait for the Wagon! The Great Steam Wagon."[12]

For Maggie's second season, Brien's National Circus and Great Show National Circus was billed as the first managed by a woman. No records confirm the claim. The "Brien" was John "Pogey" O'Brien, a former stage driver who was an unlikely person to entrust his show to a woman. But Maggie had a strong enough personality to make the claim plausible. Dan may have had a secret pride in his ex-wife's strength with pique that she was still "Rice." For though she had had dropped the name from the title, she announced "Mrs. Charles Warner" in small type, "Formerly" in smaller type, and "Mrs. Dan Rice" in the largest type of the ad, larger than the title. Libby remained on the bills as Rice despite her marriage; that name carried weight on a circus bill. Similarly brewing confusion, another ad proclaimed the show's motto in large letters: EXCELSIOR. The phrase her husband had made famous, "Great Show," remained. Another ad promised "A GENUINE CIRCUS," implicitly countering Rice's claim that his was other than a circus. The publicity included a dig at Dan: Maggie had been "wife of the somewhat famous clown."[13]

On August 20, as Rice was playing Willimantic, Connecticut, Lottie died, taken by pneumonia at six months. Rebecca was still at home, so the husband and his young wife grieved each alone. Over the baby's grave they erected a monument, four granite pillars and a cupola sheltering a carving of a baby in her crib.[14]

Dan tried to ward off grief with anger. Five days after his baby died, he got into a fight in Massachusetts on a miserable and rainy day. A man named Walter Rosebrooks refused to sit where directed because the seat was wet. Rosebrooks was a black man, and it would have been under-

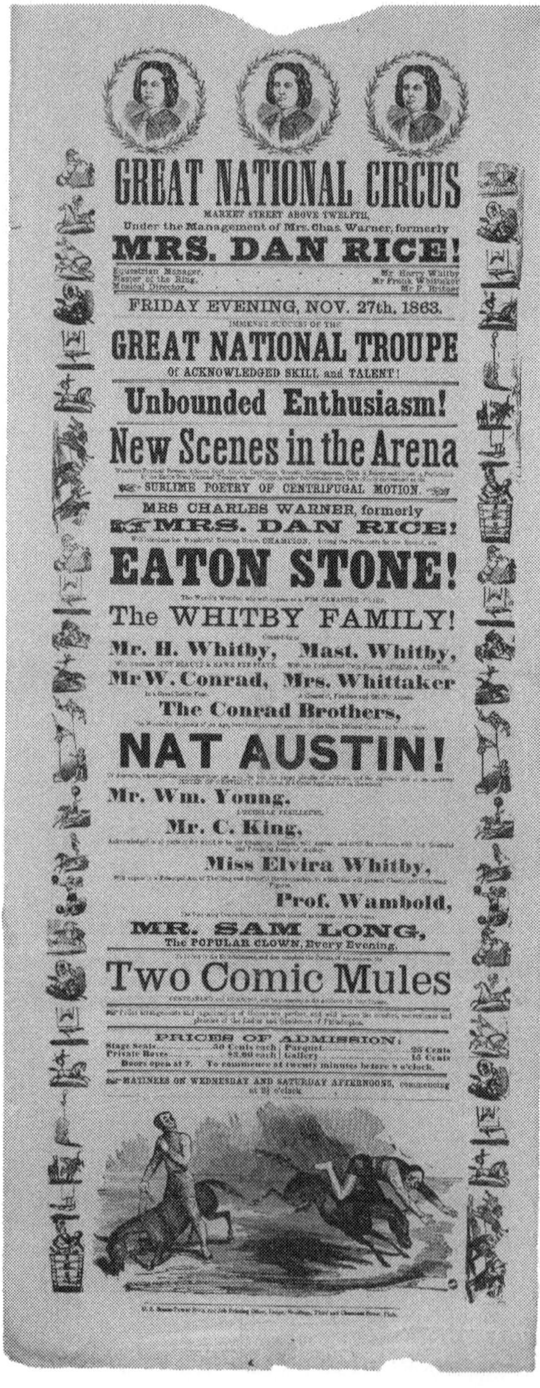

Maggie made sure that her bills reminded people of her former association with Dan Rice's Great Show.

standable if he believed the ushers were acting out of prejudice. They probably were. So, like Rosa Parks a hundred years later, Rosebrooks would not move. Rice then kicked him out of the tent so vigorously that Rosebrooks sued for assault and battery, and won $1,000. However, the state supreme court set aside the judgment on the principle that a showman may use as much force as the police to eject patrons. At a new trial, a jury awarded Rosebrooks $25 because Rice had used excessive force.[15]

His fortunes turning, his daughter dead, Dan kept on trouping.

32

"COLONEL" RICE

The Civil War began in improvisation. Despite all the fighting words, few people had prepared for a real fight. Both sides had to forge war machines in the midst of battle, the North's task difficult because it lost much of its officer corps, the South's because it was also creating a government. Stories of kinship across battle lines testified not only to conflicting loyalties but also to the war's improvised nature. Also improvised was the cause. At first, Lincoln said simply that the North fought to preserve the Union, but Democrats were suspicious. As Rice approached Ann Arbor in 1864, he would have agreed with the *Michigan Argus*: The Republicans wanted to "destroy slavery and let the Union take care of itself. George B. McClellan and the Democracy are pledged to restore and perpetuate the Union and let slavery take care of itself." Rice improvised, too. Through the first years of the war, he alternately defended and denied his Southern sympathies.[1]

As Rice took out an 1864 outfit on Spalding's money, a name, a photograph, and a connection figured prominently.

The name was an old one on a new performer. With her baby gone, Mrs. Dan Rice joined her husband on tour as a performer, presenting a mènage act, tutored by Dan. Rebecca was offered, like the original Mrs. Rice, as a role model for women, but more prominently, at the top of the ads. All was done "With the co-operation of Mrs. Dan Rice." Dan was trying to blend her into his world with a ready-made eminence.[2]

Dan persuaded Rebecca to perform.

The photograph was of Rice's tent, taken on July 9 in Jamestown, New York. Probably the earliest photograph of a tent on the lot, the black-and-white image is a far cry from pastoral nostalgia. The tent is shoehorned between sheds and "manufactories," separated from the sideshow tent by a foundry, and across the road from a furniture warehouse. The performers forming up for the parade seem dwarfed by the urban enterprise, and there is no crush of onlookers. Yet for all that, the photograph pictures a town transfigured, the daily routine suspended as if by magic. People stretch along the parade route, and the buildings themselves seem to watch, windows like eager eyes.[3]

The connection was with Lincoln. Abe and Dan were both known nationally for their humor—and criticized for their vulgarity. A letter writer to Lincoln assumed that the president knew of Rice: "For the sake of our

Country separate yourself from the Humbugs who surround you. Mr. Stanton reminds those who know him of a learned Pig, exhibited by Dan Rice, the noted Showman, many years ago." This year *Leslie's Illustrated* paired the president and the clown explicitly: "Busts of A. Lincoln and Dan Rice were placed together at the great fair in Chicago, and labeled 'The two American humorists.'" That was Chicago's Sanitary Fair, organized by the Sanitary Commission, a precursor of the Red Cross, to raise funds to improve conditions for wounded soldiers. People could support the war effort by buying handicrafts, observing military trophies and new inventions, or watching a tableau in the Children's Theatre. (Success spread this urban country fair to other cities; in Philadelphia, Rice donated receipts from his show, on the Academy of Music lot, to the local Fair.) The busts of the two famous funny men had been carved by the prominent sculptor Leonard W. Volk. Volk also designed the Douglas Monument, for which Rice had given a benefit. Soon after that, Rice had sat for Volk, then forged a joke from the experience.[4]

Jamestown, N. Y. on July 9, 1864. No. 1.—Albert Smith's Sash and Door Factory. No. 2.—Ford & Wood's Furniture Factory. No. 3.—Sprague, Steele & Co.'s Foundry Shop. No. 4.—Dan Rice's Circus. No. 5.—Gov. Fenton's Home.
Side Show
Bernard

Probably the earliest photograph of a circus on the lot, this shows Rice's tents wedged among buildings. (Arrows added.)

Rice: "I hit the drum too hard and made it bust."
Ringmaster: "'Burst' is the proper word. Always say burst, not bust."
Rice: "I'm glad you told me, for I want to tell the folks of Mr. Volk and the wonderful marble burst he is making of me."[5]

But folksy Abe and folksy Dan were not a matched set. Rice remained a resolute Democrat, arguing that Republicans violated constitutional ideals. In part, Rice kept at politics because he had built his career by speaking what was on people's minds, and he would not stop now. He also refused to retreat to "mere" amusement because he knew that controversy sells tickets. He was stubborn, too. Even as he saw that his jokes were not always landing well, he persisted, propelled by an abiding faith in his own ability.

There was another reason that kept him talking politics: principle.

As the war deepened, Rice saw himself as a necessary national voice spreading the Democratic gospel as he traveled the country, more widely than anyone else. Later, judgment would be made that Rice let politics go to his head, but he had been talking politics for years in the ring. And he had been persuasive, one reason for the ire he attracted. Politics went to Rice's head in the way it goes to most ambitious politicians' heads when they discover that they are reaching people. Increasingly, though, he needed what politicians need, a consistent image appealing to a core constituency. Gradually, like the war's improvisation, Rice's improvisation gave way to a concentrated effort. He started the season with an ad picturing a gentlemanly Rice flanked by American flags and bayonets. But, as attacks on his sincerity continued, he had to go further to prove his patriotism.[6]

So he resorted to fictions.

His career was rife with fictions, of course, but they had spoken to broader cultural truths. Now they supported a lie. Despite his genuine Union patriotism, his heart did lean toward Dixie and his head refused to support the policies of the Republicans, now identified with the Union. In "Rhymes on Philadelphia," he sang what few dared to admit in the bellicose North, that "I've loved the Southern shore." He stubbornly avoided a flag-waving title for his circus, even as Maggie called hers the Great National Circus, and Girard sent out Thayer & Noyes United States Circus. So he needed fictions to support the lie that he had always been a *Northern,* as opposed to a more generally *Union,* patriot. The claim that he faced down an armed a New Orleans mob was the first major fiction of his personal war campaign.[7]

Now he concocted another one: He was "Colonel" Rice, claiming the title from Zachary Taylor.

Circus men occasionally gave themselves military titles such as "Colonel" Cushing and "General" Welch, or "Capt. Van Orden" in advance of the *Floating Palace.* Rice was "Captain of all the Funny Fellows" in 1847, and his ads called him "Colonel" for two engagements early in the 1850s. Titles were more than a show business gimmick, though. In a country devoted to abolishing rank in society, little answered the urge to distinction better.

> He must have a handle to his name . . . so that if by accident he has not had the honor of being an officer in the militia, captain of a steamboat, proprietor of a hotel, nor been in any way attached to "soger clothes," steam, or roast beef lunches, he had better get a penny-a-liner to start him as—Major so-and-so, Colonel this, or General that.

Around the stables, many horse owners called themselves Colonel or Major, while, in Louisiana, Rice's would-be home, military titles were so "ridiculously common," that "every other man you meet is 'Colonel.'"[8]

In 1864, Rice adopted "Colonel" for good, with a supporting story that Taylor had awarded him the title in gratitude for his help in the 1848 presidential campaign. As a war measure, the value of this self-administered "Colonel" was subtle but strong. It rendered Rice military in a militaristic landscape, and invoked one of America's great war heroes. Postdating the honor to the 1840s also allowed him to suggest that when it came to patriotism, he was not, in the new phrase, a Johnny-come-lately.

Rice may have adopted the title in June, when he donated $200 to pay for Girard's draft substitutes. He donated more than any other person, and four times more than the bankers who were handling the money, Battles & Webster. Battles was a relative of Rebecca's, and Webster would go into business with her father, McConnell, who gave $25 himself. Rice's donation would not necessarily have impressed these community leaders;

in the time-honored tradition of snobbery, it could be dismissed as showy ostentation. Regardless of a $30,000 fantasy that Rice had single-handedly outfitted a regiment of Erie volunteers, the Pennsylvania 83rd, he did support the war effort. He donated a 120-foot round-top to the 83rd, commissioned a painting of their leader and local casualty, Col. John McLane, and gave money to the families of soldiers off at war. Later he noted that he had spent $9,000 toward the Union cause. (The *Clipper* was not impressed: In August, it hinted at Rice in a serialized story set in the circus of "Colonel Dick Hayes," a self-appointed colonel with a "habitual assumption of boisterous declamation.")[9]

Now politics became explicit. In September 1864, Erie Democrats nominated "Col. Dan Rice" for state senator. (It was not the first suggestion that he run for office: Three years before, Pennsylvania's *Clearfield Republican* had urged that he be sent to Congress. Nor was he the first performer with political thoughts. Edwin Forrest had toyed with the idea of leaving the stage for politics, and Rice's former rider, Levi North, had been elected a Chicago alderman in 1858.)[10]

Some suspected a publicity prank. The Erie *Gazette* sniffed that Rice was "perpetrating the biggest joke he ever got off." If frequency determined the quality of jokes, the politician-equals-clown witticism would be one of the best in the world. The comic actor Dan Marble had talked of being president, and the minstrel creation, the pretentious "Zip Coon," a burlesque of middle-class aspirations, was touted for that high office too. The *Spirit of the Times* had reversed the joke, making public figures into performers on the mock "Seward, Weed, Greeley & Co.'s Menagerie, Circus and Travelling Exhibition." More recently, Lincoln was depicted not only as a "villainous son of a b—h," but also as "a *circus tumbler* and a bastard!"[11]

Rice regularly encountered the joke. Cairo presumed in 1855 that "some country paper has nominated him for next President." In 1856 Rice's mules were "securing nominations." A year later the *Clipper* wondered whether Dan had entered the political arena. Two votes for him for Congress in Ohio prompted the *Erie Weekly Observer* in 1858 to observe that they had elected bigger clowns and worse men from that district. The jokes multiplied in 1859 to publicize his run at Niblo's. He jumped on the bandwagon himself in song: "Some people choose to name, for the coming President, / Your humble servant Rice, and on his election bent." In the fall the *Clipper* revived the gag: "The Rice ticket never was so much in demand. The people want to know Dan's platform on peaches and cream."[12]

Now it was no joke. Rice was in Cincinnati, his Great Show "a 'big thing' without ice," when he wrote to allow his name to be put in nomination. The *Erie Dispatch* declared that Rice would be supported by all the Democrats of the district, and many Republicans. It lauded him as a "hospitable, high-toned, and large-hearted gentleman," flowing with generosity. If elected—and "more surprising things have happened"—he would take his seat armed with not only practical experience of the world but also the comprehensive knowledge of what was needed in the crisis. In his letter of acceptance, Rice, while denying prior interest in party politics, declared that his "proclivities were formerly with the Whigs," and now were with the Democrats, who carried on their principles. He expressed the unusually modest thought that other men might be better suited but he agreed to let his name be brought forward. "When I see the great principles of personal liberty and the rights of property being cloven down by the men now running the machine of Government, 'the ancient landmarks' of the Constitution 'which our fathers set' removed, I feel like crying, in the language of the Holy Writ, 'cursed be he that removeth them.'"[13]

Rice's hymn to the Constitution was the Democrats's fundamental principle. It contrasted with the position articulated by Lincoln in his 1863 address at Gettysburg. That brief, powerful speech had crowned a long campaign of persuasion to define the meaning of both the war and the country. As explained by Gary Wills in *Lincoln at Gettysburg,* the address was a political argument from the famous first words to its stirring conclusion. "Four score and seven years ago" from 1863 was 1776, the year the Declaration of Independence was adopted, rather than the three score and fifteen to the ratification of the Constitution in 1788; this reflected the president's belief that the country's foundation lay in the ideal of equality embedded in the Declaration, an ideal compromised by the Constitution's acceptance of slavery. Similarly, at the end, to speak of a government "of the people, by the people, and for the people" was a carefully calculated thesis that the American people—and not their states, as secessionists claimed—had formed the national government.[14]

The Democrats chose Rice on September 13, when he was playing Lincoln's home, Springfield. The Chicago papers sparred over his patriotism; that is, his politics. The *Chicago Tribune* opened the dance with the headline, "Dan Rice and Disloyalty." It declared that Rice filled "his ring talk with disloyal utterances and flings at Lincoln and the war. A trimmer so cautious as this personage who once, it is said, actually gave a performance under the confederate flag, should understand that this style of thing will not pay in loyal communities." The *Tribune* found little to laugh at in his "quips and pasquinades persistently leveled at the President, the war, the government, and the anti-slavery sentiment of the north." Then, as he left town, it urged the press on his route to keep after him, to make sure his jokes did not "resemble a certain kind of soda—'drawn from *copper*.'" That last phrase refers to a chemical solution that uses copper, an allusion to the copperhead snake, which in turn was the sneer thrown at suspected traitors. According to Foster family stories, Rice, visiting at Mit's conservative Democratic home in Cleveland, met Clement Vallandigham, an Ohio politician regularly called a Copperhead, who was jailed for arguing against the war.[15]

Meanwhile, the *Chicago Post*, asking "Is Dan Rice Loyal?," thundered "Yes!" The *New York Tribune* and the local Republican papers "cannot comprehend how one can be loyal without being on the one hand an abolitionist and a devotee of Lincoln, or on the other in favor of 'peace at any price.' Mr. Rice is a Union man." In that he was "a representative man." The *Post* predicted that he would be elected, despite the Republican majority in his district, because his cause had been taken up by conservatives in both parties. Campaign protocol prohibited the nonstop campaigning of later years, so there would be few who could turn to the subject in as many places as Rice. He may have, as claimed, made more Union speeches than anyone else.[16]

Rice sent a letter accepting the nomination the day before his show moved to Jackson, Michigan, birthplace of the Republican Party. He declared himself a conservative citizen, grateful for the honor. Though no "worshipper at the shrine of any political dogma," Rice did acknowledge more political opinions than he usually admitted. Those who had nominated him were acquainted "with the views I have heretofore and throughout my life entertained." Paramount was the Constitution, which should be supported by "the people of the States and the people of all the States, and the States themselves." Less powerful than Lincoln's Gettysburg conclusion, this three-part phrase nevertheless stated the Democratic case: that the states had created the country. With Vallandigham's arrest recent, Rice again jabbed at Republican policies, declaring that the greatest danger to free institutions lay in partisanship. He invoked Jefferson: The majority should respect the rights of the minority, "to violate which would be oppression." Echoing Beecher, he urged that "we ourselves should be equally careful to respect and preserve the same standards to which we ask the support and allegiance of others." Rice vowed that he looked for the re-union of the people, "with all their interests combined."[17]

Rice ran an abbreviated campaign. He still had a show to troupe. Besides, he knew what those who chose him knew, that he was fighting an uphill battle. His was a Republican district—Lincoln had stopped there on his way to his inauguration, with Greeley along—and he faced an incumbent, Morrow Lowry. The *Erie Gazette*—where Greeley had once worked—gloated: "Our Democratic opponents seem to be hard up for a candidate this year. They have nominated a Vallandigham armistice-peace man for congress and a circus clown for state senate. They evidently anticipate defeat." There was some truth in the sneer, for the Democrats had passed over two candidates before settling on Rice. It was difficult to argue simultaneously for the Union and against the Republicans, who were running the war to save it. That was the problem facing the head of the ticket, Gen. George McClellan. A cartoon captured Little Mac's difficulty, depicting him as a circus performer standing on two horses, one wearing a blanket labeled "Peace," and the other, "War." In the background, Lincoln, wearing a jester's stripes, refers to one of the general's campaigns: "You tried to ride them two hosses on the Peninsula for two years, Mac, but it wouldn't work."[18]

After years of baiting editors, Rice became a newspaperman himself. Political newspapers were not unusual. Most newspapers of the time leaned one way or the other, and many were blazingly partisan. In this case, the *Girard Union* kept attacking Rice until he got fed up, bought it, and changed its name to the *Spectator.* The change showed another subtle equivocation of patriotism: The new title suggested that Rice was no Union enthusiast but a neutral observer.[19]

Rice's campaign revealed a significant change in his thought, as he relinquished implicit support for slavery. He had never advocated slavery itself. He had even sung that it would eventually disappear. Nevertheless, attacks on abolitionists shaded into a defense of the institution they were struggling to destroy. Certainly Rice's auditors in New Orleans believed that he was defending their "peculiar institution." Now he accepted the move toward emancipation. In a Fourth of July speech in Elmira, New York, Rice declared that "negroes are God's creatures, and shouldn't belong to Jeff. Davis, or any other man." He was recognizing the fundamental belief of abolitionism, even as he continued to renounce abolitionists. It was an important step for him. He included the speech, the only new one, in his 1865 songster.

Rice had changed; so had the United States. The crucible of war was burning away the belief that slavery was acceptable. The country almost literally had the "new birth of freedom" articulated by Lincoln at Gettysburg. Rice continued to oppose the president; but with the country, he decided that blacks "were not made for southern planters to vote on, nor northern fanatics to *dote* on." On the Fourth of July, he pronounced a folksy variation on Lincoln's theme: "Let every tub stand on its own bottom."[20]

For all the change wrought by Lincoln's leadership, much of it would have disappeared if he had lost the election. When he won, the *Cincinnati Enquirer* passed on what it deemed mournful news:

> Yesterday morning broke dark and lowering—the clouds were heavy—a drizzling and dismal rain was falling—and in every respect it was a cheerless and melancholy day; but a fit one for the re-election of Abraham Lincoln. The physical elements were in entire harmony with that state of the public morals and public intelligence that could repeat, after all the terrible lessons of the past, the horrid mistake of 1860.

Erie Democrats were dismal, too. Rice won the votes of nearly 7,000 neighbors, running ahead of the ticket, 40 percent to McClellan's 36 percent. But 40 percent still loses.[21]

The rocket of Rice's career was falling back to earth. Hard luck dogged him in 1864. Rochester brought bad weather, a remote circus lot, and other shows to buck against. In Washington, his tent at New York and 6th was distant from the entertainments between Grover's Theatre at 13th and Ford's new theater on 10th. (If amusement-loving Lincoln came to Rice's circus, as later claimed, no one recorded the visit.) The *Clipper,* deciding that the show did not present all it advertised, blamed Rice and absolved Spalding, the owner. July introduced national taxes to the circus, an annual federal license of $100, plus 2 percent of gross receipts. (Taxes meant revenue collectors, described as "bean spotters" because they used beans to count people entering the tent.) With Rebecca co-signing, Rice had to sell $5,000 worth of Girard property. Meanwhile, Charles Rogers, the partner Spalding had taken after Rice, retired a wealthy man. (Retirement may have been prodded by the shipwreck of their show as it returned from South America; by coincidence, it happened off Long Branch, home of Rice's people.)[22]

The new season did not improve matters. The *Philadelphia Sunday Dispatch* reported falsely but plausibly that Rice would be a "Lecturer on Horses" with Maggie's old circus. It was hard times all over for circuses. "Many a saw-dust performer will reach New York, at the close of the season, minus several week's 'sal.'" Rice took out a new show on the dime of Pogey O'Brien and Pogey's new partner, Adam Forbach, who had made a fortune peddling to the government during the war. It was a good war for business. When O'Brien could not pay $9,000 for horses Forbach had supplied in 1864, the horse dealer took a piece of the show and rechristened himself "Forepaugh," enabling him to use the pun 4-Paw as he developed into a major circus proprietor over the next decade. Now he and O'Brien backed the Mammoth Menagerie and Moral Exhibition of Rices.[23]

According to the publicity, Rice was paid $1,000 a week, guaranteed regardless of receipts. Did he really receive that astronomical salary, when young John Rockefeller was getting $5 a week as a clerk, and the *annual* urban wage was $500? In 1863, the claim had popped up only when Rice was near home, at the beginning and end of the tour. The Pittsburgh papers reported that, "but an humble boy" playing marbles, he had risen to be a star making $25,000 over the summer, "double the amount that President Lincoln gets" for six months work. That seems mere puffery for this "bred and born Pittsburgher."[24]

However, in 1865, Forepaugh wanted to make a splash in his new business so $1,000 is plausible. And reasonable. When Forepaugh became sole owner, the story circulated that O'Brien sold out because he had been frightened off by that huge expense. Later, in 1871, while expressing surprise that circus salaries reached $350 a week, the *New York Times* called Rice's $1,000 "hardly creditable but we have been assured of the fact." Old-timers, who knew the business, continued to pass on the amount as accurate. Perhaps clinching the matter, the *Clipper,* no fan of Rice's, declared his astronomical salary "a positive fact." As it had to acknowledge, "This is clowning it to some purpose."[25]

The grand salary and continuing acclaim obscured Rice's decline. Like a wave crashing on the shore, Rice still made a splash, but he no longer coursed through the cultural sea. A symbol of that diminishment lay in his failure to join Rebecca to his career. She did not go out again in 1865. Dan featured a horse named for his wife, but when the original Rebecca went home, he offered the horse to his sister. He sent regrets that he had not been able to teach the equine Rebecca's moves to Libbie, but he wrote a brief description: The horse waltzed, picked up a handkerchief, walked on its knees, fired a pistol, jumped over bars, and danced a polka—the waltz steps with different music. Rice's legendary clashes dwindled to a commotion with Lewis Lent, who was still sore about their squabble in Philadelphia. Their respective shows were both touring Ohio when Lent put out a rat sheet attacking Rice as no longer popular, and his show as no circus. Rice shot back his own scorn, and the *Clipper* joked about the "friendly interchange of professional courtesies." Diminishment continued. When Barnum was elected to Connecticut's legislature in April, a Rochester paper dredged Rice in, pretending to forget whether he had won or lost his own election. Troubled times threw "scum to the surface," so these two "mountebanks" made perfect associates for "the Drunkard" Johnson. The *Clipper* tried to make Rice a byword for fiction in a tale that folks had "Struck Ile" near Girard. "We might credit the report, were it not that the well supposed to have been struck is located on Dan Rice's farm; that spoils the story, in our opinion, Dan and his farm being more full of gags . . . than of oil." He was becoming less flesh-and-blood than a site of rumors. Some, like the tale of accidental poisoning in Michigan, killed him off.[26]

On the first day of November 1865, Rice scrambled to recoup, as fame, aspiration, and patriotism came together in a public ceremony making national news. To honor the Civil War dead of Girard, he arranged and financed a monument, said to be the country's first. Volk, who designed it, remembered Rice's commissioning it shortly after sitting for the bust, when he told Volk he had been accused of being a Copperhead, and so "proposed to get the 'Dead wood' on his enemies" with a monument.[27]

It is still there. The base, eight feet square at the bottom and stepped in as it goes up, with corners carved as upright cannons, supports a seventeen-foot-high Corinthian column draped in the American flag and topped by an eagle. A few locals, including an associate of Rebecca's father, objected when the borough council approved the site in June. They did not mind the national attention for the village, nor that Dan was paying the $5,000 cost—which he covered partly by selling a $1,500 parcel of land. The problem was the site on Main Street, in front of Rice's mansion. They railed that it memorialized Rice's arrogance more than the honored dead. When they lost in the council, they went to court to get an injunction, which ordered reconsideration. With the eyes of the country turning to their village, the council reconsidered, re-approved, and the work went ahead. (Not trusting his adopted home to keep his role alive in civic memory, the showman had "Erected by Dan Rice" chiseled on the base a week after the unveiling.)[28]

It was a perfect fall day, bright and crisp. *Harper's Weekly* reported the event to the country with a cover story. Cleveland and Cincinnati sent reporters, and the *Clipper*, in a now-rare positive notice for Rice, gave the dedication half a column. Special excursion trains brought as many as 10,000 people, "the largest and most enthusiastic assemblage of people ever held in this section." Not one to waste a crowd, Rice ended his season by giving two shows in Girard that day. After the morning performance, a noon salute of thirteen guns sounded over the village. Rice drew up his animals and wagons, with dignitaries as passengers, for a parade that began at 1:00 P.M. with the band chariot and its carved swans. (Carving, hallmark of the age's fine furniture, was making its way onto circus wagons.) Next came a carriage of veterans of the War of 1812, followed by marching soldiers from the recent conflict. Masons, Odd Fellows, and the fire department joined in full regalia. The most admired feature was an elephant-drawn wagon carrying the Daughters of Freedom, thirty-six young women, one for each of the re-united states.[29]

The ceremony, with Rice's mansion prominent in the background, began with a local general praising Rice's liberality and loyalty. Governor Andrew G. Curtin of Pennsylvania gave the principal address; letters from President Johnson, and Generals Grant, Meade, Sherman, and Hancock were read; and the former Ohio governor, David Tod, made a few remarks.[30] Still, for all the patriotism, Rice's political equivocation continued. As financial backer, he could have assigned his daughter Kate, one of the Daughters of Freedom, to represent Northern states, either Pennsylvania, her home; New York, where she went to school; or her birth state, New Jersey. Instead, Rice had her "personate" Louisiana. Similarly, one of the two young women presenting wreaths to Rice represented South Carolina, notorious as home of the most rabid Southern fire-eaters. Predictably, the Republican *Gazette* curled its lip at the man who paid for it all. "We give this much of a description, simply in justice to the heroes. . . . Whatever may have been the ruling motive of those who footed the bill, need not now be discussed."

Then the crowd called for Rice. Curtin had supplied the main address; Rice was comic relief. As normal as that division of duties now seems, it represented a monumental shift for Rice. He had risen to the peak of fame on his hits on the times. As war exploded, he had increased the politics in his performances. But people no longer wanted politics from Rice in the ring, the Republicans because they disagreed with him, the Democrats because they were reluctant to give more ammunition to the Republicans, who were already waving the bloody shirt. And neither side was sure what the showman believed. People had once relished Rice's talk because he seemed to be saying exactly what was on his mind, even when he placed it in a probable fiction. But through the course of the war he had shaded, explained, and justified so often that any comment he made now raised doubt. That is neither the best way to raise laughter nor to forge a bond with an audience. So, with his Rice stew of comedy, social issues, and politics no longer suiting public taste, he provided what people now expected of clowns: diversion.

The great talker joked that he had to be persuaded to talk. Curtin "insisted I should say something. (Laughter.) I can't say much, you know that. (Renewed laughter.)" He spoke briefly about the brave men they were honoring but capped it with another jest: Maybe he never stood ready to defend the country as they did, "but I always made a very good home guard. (Laughter.)" He teased that Curtin had come to see the girls, "but I give him credit for if he did, I am in the same boat. (Laughter.)" The governor had tried to kiss the girl presenting his wreath, but missed. "I made mine go nearer the mark. I struck the centre. (Laughter.) I have had better practice, I suppose. (Laughter.)" As the lowering sun cast a glow on the monument, Rice thanked his visitors and then returned to his comic theme, with a nod to the bleachers where the Daughters of Freedom stood. It was "a pyramid blooming with loveliness. (Laughter.) They are positively so inviting that I will run the Governor a race to that stand. I am well practiced and I can beat him, I think. I have kissed fully 7,000 ladies in this season alone."[31]

Lincoln, called to honor Civil War dead at Gettysburg, set forth a political proposition, that the country had been founded on the ideal of human equality. It was model leadership, as he led the country where it did not know it wanted to go but seemed inevitable when it got there. In his own realm, Rice had similarly led the country, persuading it that the best clowning was his heady mix of comedy and public issues. Now, honoring the Civil War dead himself, he diminished the expansive role he had pioneered. Instead of fervent words, Rice offered banter.

33

RICE FOR PRESIDENT

"Be careful, sir, Jefferson Davis is riding you."

The horse cantered.

"Now," said Rice, "General Grant is riding you."

Instantly the horse began to kick, and the Southern crowd roared. They would not care that the trick lay in the cues, "Be careful" and "Now," rather than in the respective names, which Rice switched in the North to make the former Confederacy's president the butt of the joke.[1]

Days after the monument dedication, Rice was in Georgia appearing with the Seth B. Howes' Great European Circus, run by Seth's nephew, Egbert. The show battled the United States Circus of Dan's old hands, Thayer and Noyes, on to New Orleans, but Rice faced a more specific problem. After five years of trying to establish his Union loyalty, he now faced Southern suspicion. One story told of a Mississippi drunk's bellowing that Rice had commanded a Negro regiment and shooting at him as he took tickets. When the bullet went through his coat, Rice coolly said, "Oh, put that up; we're used to that sort of thing here. Tickets! Tickets!"[2]

Rice turned north in February 1866 to lead Dan Rice's Circus & Menagerie out of Philadelphia. It was Forepaugh's headquarters, and Forepaugh's money again. When Rice wrote to his sister Libbie, sending his love to her, sister Kate, and the children, they were staying at the Philadelphia haunt of circus folks, Uncle Sam Miller's Hotel, as was his ex-wife. There was still some tension with Maggie. He explained to Libbie that he had not come to see her because "Maggie might have thought I done it with some object. She is so Suspicious besides it might have caused Some Remarks." Charley Warner had died in 1865, at Miller's, but Maggie continued as Mrs. Charles Warner. A manager remembered Rice's Washington stand as the first time he invited youngsters to his show for free. He had been doing that for years, so the memory signaled the circus's new role as a children's entertainment, though adults still constituted most of the audience. Similarly, circus was now often depicted as an amusement for black people, even though whites remained in the majority. In a society that saw blacks as inherently inferior, that was a perfect way to signal the lowbrow status of circus. So though Rice's 1866 show enjoyed greater attendance in the nation's capital than any circus had for years, the "colored population appear to be Dan's best patrons," according to the *Clipper.* (Despite attempts to make minstrelsy appear refined, its reputation as a common entertainment was solidified when "genuine darkey" performers—black men—began appearing.) In the ancient tradition of condescension, these diminishments were meant kindly. The middle class, now more comfortably secure in its position, did not need to mention those socially and economically below them, but could instead smile patronizingly at the amusements of the children, the masses, the "coloreds."[3]

The 1864 election had whetted Rice's appetite for political office. In March 1866, a Philadelphia paper passed on word that he had taken his name out of the running for governor because the Democratic platform did not stand strong enough for the Constitution, and he "would not be used by weak-kneed politicians to further their wild and wicked schemes for personal preferment." Then on August 1, Erie County soldiers "*Resolved,* That we believe Colonel Rice to be opposed to the policy of keeping the Southern States out of the Union, after spending so much treasure and so much blood to keep them in," therefore they urged him to run for Congress. There was some race-baiting in their support. They wanted someone who looked "more to the interests of the soldier and less to the negro race." But they were also remembering that when their pay had been months overdue, Rice had helped support their families. Other area citizens, including Noyes and Thayer, seconded the soldiers in a published letter, asking Rice if they could put his name forward as a candidate for the 19th Congressional District. Rice agreed. His friends had overcome the "natural objections I may have for political honors," especially as both Republicans and Democrats had signed, for "I belong to the people," rather than a party. Rice paid to have the correspondence printed for over a month in Erie's papers, under the headline "The People's Candidate for Congress." As he blanketed the district with handbills, his opponents were worried enough to circulate a rumor that he was withdrawing.[4]

His campaign enjoyed a boost when Johnson came to Erie. The president, accompanied by Secretary of State Seward, General Grant, Admiral Farragut, and General Custer, was trying to build political support. His "swing around the circle" would include a stop in Chicago to lay the cornerstone of the Douglas Monument to which Rice had contributed. Before Johnson's train arrived in Erie, the Democratic candidate for governor made a speech to the gathered crowd, and Rice made another. The *Erie Dispatch* had little use for what it called this "Copperjohnson club," but did report Rice's saying that he reluctantly spoke of politics. That may have gotten a laugh. Politicians, he said, "especially those of the radical party, were two hundred thousand per cent worse than a showman, and he disliked to fraternize with them." That got another laugh. Having handled comic mules, he would know how to handle the jackasses of Congress. The *Dispatch* called his speech "the most enjoyable portion of the 'show.'" When the president's party arrived, Grant declined to speak, saying he was sick. Rice rode along when the party continued to Girard, where he made another speech, to which Johnson replied. Then the presidential train continued west, and Rice returned to Erie. He had left Rebecca with the carriage, but she had driven it home. Perhaps they had misunderstood each other, or maybe she just got tired of waiting. Before making his way back to Girard, he dropped in on the editor of the *Dispatch.* A few days later, the paper called the nearby village of Girard Station "Dan Rice," and in a second item mentioned how "Gov." Rice lavished attention on Girard till it had all that "a people of taste and intelligence can desire for a home." If Rice "should leave Girard no one would be so greatly missed."[5]

Rice's campaign was going well. At the Democratic county convention on September 10, a rival who had organized Johnson's visit withdrew his name in favor of Rice's. At that point, the showman rose to speak to the meeting.

Then he did a curious thing. Rice declined the nomination. He told the assembled Democrats that they could not gain the support of their neighbors unless they rose above party feeling. He did allow his name to remain in play, but only if he could run on a "people's platform" rather than as a standard-bearer of the Democrats. Rice's maneuver effectively killed his candidacy. Delegates who had intended to support him took him at his word and turned to another man, William Scott. It is difficult to know what to make of Rice's move. Did he genuinely expect the Democrats to alter their platform, omitting the attacks on the Republicans that stirred the party faithful, attacks he had been making himself? The *Dispatch* professed itself mystified whether Rice had expected to be nominated or not. He may have decided that he could not win, and chose this way to avoid the prospect of losing. Some whispered that it was a gag for publicity, but the context shows otherwise. Perhaps the best interpretation takes him at his word: Rice believed that he could bridge the nation's acrimonious divisions. "I consider it my mission now to instruct and harmonize the people."[6]

Even with Rice's peculiar stand, he still had a chance. A list of candidates for Pennsylvania's congressional seats included three men for the 19th, the Republican Lowry and the Democrats Scott and Rice. Ultimately, Rice threw his support to Scott to avoid splitting the vote. Perhaps he had decided, as the *Dispatch* suggested, that "he is far better off as the director of a circus company at a salary of $1,000 per week than as a Congressman at $500 per term." But if Rice did not have the "peculiar tact" to be a politician, he had the analytical skill: Scott, running as a fervent partisan, lost to Lowry.[7]

Closing the season in November, with the *Clipper* still mocking his "sacred lecture tour," Rice took a vacation. Besides rest after a quarter century of working steadily, he may have decided he needed to devote more time to his young wife. Rebecca was twenty-three now, much more worldly than she had been as a bride. The fascination that the well-traveled Dan had once held for her diminished as she traveled herself. She now also had whatever wisdom or weight attended the loss of a child. She had tried her husband's trouping life but quit and come back to her quilts and the social world of Girard, among family and friends. Dan was frequently gone, for performances and now for politics. So on January 3, 1867, Dan and Rebecca left behind good sleighing in Girard to sail on the *Morro Castle* for Cuba. Their first vacation, it was also their first time off the continent, despite Dan's boasts of European triumphs. Havana was early in its career as a fashionable resort for the American well-to-do. They stayed two months, returning with souvenirs that included plants. White plum trees flowered every spring in Girard for years after, a memory of their one vacation.[8]

In 1867, Dan took out Dan Rice's Great Show and School of Educated Animals, some of the money coming from James Cooper, whose 1866 show had been led by Maggie. For all his trouble with money, Rice was financially sophisticated enough to weave a web of named, alleged, and actual interests in his shows so tangled that it will never be unraveled. On November 7, Rice wrote to Jacob to prepare him as a witness in a lawsuit. "What they want to prove by you is, that you sold Excelsior as well as the stock & fixtures to Spalding, and that you purchased Dan Rice's Great Show at Sheriff's sale in New Orleans in 1861, and sold it in 1862." The claim that Rice earned $1,000 a week was becoming habitual. In another farewell in Pittsburgh, when the city printers presented him with the works of Shakespeare, Rice declared that he had made more money than any six of the richest circus men in the world, and had given away a million and a half dollars of it, with documents to prove it.[9]

In May 1867, Rice had teased his own political aspirations, remarking that he might try for president next. He got the laugh, but as he toured the Great Lakes states, he looked around at the presidential prospects. Johnson would not get the support of his own party. Military service was considered poor preparation for executive office, despite Washington and

Jackson, so Grant and Farragut seemed unlikely possibilities. Others mentioned, like Vallandigham or the New York mayor Fernando Wood, had no widespread support because they were so closely associated with Democratic policies. Rice continued musing on the subject as he played Cleveland, making a pitch for the "working classes."[10]

Late in 1867, Rice decided to run for president. He started the ball rolling in September, when he put his name forward as a candidate in the *Girard Spectator.* The *Republican & Democrat* of Greensburgh, near Pittsburgh, copied the article, adding that Western papers and a soldiers' convention in Iowa supported Rice. Having "unadulterated patriotism, enlarged views, and a great practical mind, he controls the intelligent masses of mankind with that delightful ease which qualifies him for a great and popular leader." The politician made politics the opponent: He could pull the country from "the political quagmires in which our heated partizans and demagogues have placed them." Playing the new trump card of American politics, the newspaper called him "a second Abraham Lincoln." Not all comparisons to the martyred president were complimentary: One paper declared that Rice was a clown only by profession, "not, like Lincoln, *by nature!* No rude and vulgar jokes ever fell from his lips within sight of the mangled forms of his countrymen." Rice was "brave, honest and earnest," but Lincoln was the tool of knaves and demagogues; Rice has "done much *for* humanity! Lincoln did more against mankind!" More newspapers considered the political landscape and came to the same conclusion as Rice, that he was a legitimate candidate. The *New York Herald* classed him as a potential candidate with McClellan; the *World* named him with Peter Cooper and Greeley; a Buffalo paper yoked him with Grant and New York's Governor Horatio Seymour; and a Louisville journal with Seymour, Vallandigham, and ex-Presidents Pierce and Fillmore.[11]

Now the Greensburgh paper hoisted to its masthead the legend "For President in 1868: Col. Daniel Rice, of Pennsylvania." With him as standard bearer, "the blighting curse of Radicalism will be swept as with a hurricane from the country." Papers in Illinois, Tennessee, and Indiana concurred, including the *Elkhart Democratic Union,* which declared him an "offset to the ribboned aristocracy," and the *Nashville Banner,* which supported Rice for a workingman's ticket. His platform was standard Democratic fare, with sympathy for the defeated South and defense of the working man, both against the depredations of the "Moneyed or Political Aristocracies"—the Republicans. Rice declared that punitive measures against the South must be halted. States must retain their constitutional right to determine the qualifications of citizenship, a reproach to those who insisted that all blacks should be allowed to vote. Corruption should be ferreted out. Taxes should be equalized. Soldiers should receive preference for government office. Labor should be protected, and—a swipe at anti-Catholic prejudice—religious tolerance assured.

In the East, the *Philadelphia City Item* cheered the "shrewd, outspoken, hard-hitting" man. Formerly for Johnson, it now considered Rice the better man. The paper had only one hesitation: he had not embraced the Declaration's call for equality. Like most politicians on the rise, Rice attracted office seekers and moderated some views; he decided, on arriving in Philadelphia in February, that the Declaration was correct, that "all men are created equal."

Rice paid for the Girard, Pennsylvania monument, reputed to be the first dedicated to the Civil War dead.

Rice could not win over everyone. Where the *City Item* saw an admirable man and candidate, the *Philadelphia Bulletin* spied a venomous representative of the dastardly Democrats. It also hinted that Rice was drinking, a "spirit-ual man—ardently so." To remind editors of his patristic generosity, Rice sent out lithographs of his home with the monument prominently displayed. A Wisconsin paper thanked him for the lithograph, and suggested that he should be happy to stay home. The *New York Vindicator* mockingly mourned how low the nation had fallen, with prospects reduced to Frederick Douglass, Grant, and Rice. In Pennsylvania, the Lock Haven *Democrat* thought that Rice was "just as proper a person for the presidency as the 'late lamented,'" told fewer smutty jokes, and was smarter than Lincoln, but ultimately was better suited for the circus ring than the political one. The *New Castle Champion* averred that, unlike his opponents, Rice was no "bounty-breaking, hospital-swindling, sanitary-stealing, army-contracting, government-lobbying, orphan-making, humanity-crushing" villain.[12]

Predictably, Rice vigorously joined his own defense. When the *Ionia Sentinel* in Michigan attacked, he called the editors "mendacious blackguards and malicious liars." His religion came from the Bible, teaching him forgiveness; theirs came from Judas, teaching them betrayal. "Born of the flesh-pots of Egypt, the bastard offspring of shoddy and centralization," their principles were "the creed of the desperate and the damned; the prelude to destruction and the battle-cry of Hell." They charged him with unkind feelings toward colored people, but, he said, he had built the first church for slaves in the country. About the freed slaves, his critics were demagogues who acted only to "betray them as you have betrayed your country. You would make them an instrumentality for the revival of civil war," so that "with their blood you may patch up your broken power and establish another interregnum of rascality." His opponents were "serpents torn from the bodies of the Furies, by the hand of Discord, and fleeing, surcharged with venom. . . . One of your smiters, Dan Rice."[13]

Nineteenth-century candidates campaigned discreetly. Rice remained at home, working his contacts while enjoying local amusements. Pedestrianism was a favorite sport, and Rice shared a glass of wine at his home with a man who was making news walking from New York to Chicago. A new sport was catching on, so Girard boasted a Dan Rice Base Ball Club.

When Ralph Waldo Emerson came through Erie on a lecture tour in December, he spoke of the vitality of American language. "An eloquent man needs to know the whole language, that of the street as well as of the academy." Rice must have attended, for he wrote a campaign letter echoing the words America's grand old poet had spoken. "As I am of and from the people, it is but natural that I should express myself in plain, *democratic* language, rather than in the studied contrivances of speech which enable you to successfully play the editorial Bravo, and stab at one's good name in the sheltering obscurity of dastardly innuendo."[14]

Rice's candidacy for president of the United States suddenly ended in February, the letters and editorials ceasing. His refusal to run as a strongly partisan Democrat rendered his already difficult task impossible. The abrupt ending encouraged those who later believed that Rice's run had been a joke, but it would not be the first or the last time that a politician blazed briefly as a prospective president. Others carried less realistic fancies than Rice's. Whitman acted in 1856 as "though he were offering himself for the presidential nomination." Dan's old nemesis, Greeley, ran for president in 1872, and historians have deemed him one of the country's worst-qualified candidates. Peter Cooper, the businessman and philanthropist, for whom Rice said he had worked as a boy, ran for president in 1876 in a more quixotic effort than Rice's, garnering less than 1 percent of the vote. A century later, presidential primaries and television made that winnowing a common occurrence, flushing a flock of candidates every four years to be picked off one by one.[15]

P. T. Barnum was another politician. In 1865, the year after Rice ran for Pennsylvania's legislature, Barnum had won a seat in Connecticut. In 1866, Rice was a candidate for Congress and dropped out; in 1867, Barnum was a candidate for Congress and lost. Now the man who was famous for his museum exhibits and presentations such as Jenny Lind, but "always wanted to be known as a wit," was touring himself as a celebrity exhibit, lecturing on "The Art of Money Getting, or Success." On November 15, 1867, Erie flocked to his lecture, not for what one biographer called a "collection of platitudes," but because Barnum's fame glossed those platitudes with glitter. Rice attended and as resident celebrity acted the gracious host when they met after the lecture, "an illustration of Greek meeting Greek."[16] But Barnum was *the* nineteenth-century figure;

Rice's fame and skill were compared to Barnum's, not the other way around. And if the diminishment in Rice's career was not yet obvious to the world, he was too astute a judge of audiences, and Barnum too astute a judge of the business, not to notice.

As the two avatars of American amusement shook hands, the past faced the future of celebrity. Like Barnum, Rice was adept at self-promotion. An early twentieth-century retrospective of clowns declared that Rice was "the greatest talking and singing clown the world has ever produced," attributing greatness not only to his actions and words but to "publicity as well, which in America usually means fame." Nevertheless, Rice's strength lay in engaging the world, as the world engaged him. He had made his living, and forged his fame, by performing. As for Barnum, he was vitally active too, yet as he acknowledged, his success signally depended on "the liberal use of printers' ink."[17] Rice had been famous for what he *did,* Barnum for who he *was.* A bromide the next century held that a celebrity is famous for being famous. Barnum pioneered that territory.

PART 6

REVERSE OF SUCCESS

1868 – 1883

34

FOLLY TO FIGHT

Rice had a larger problem than Northern politics or Southern suspicion.

In 1868, the *Clipper* looked back on its fifteen years in operation: "American people have changed greatly since the Clipper was started; they are not so puritanic as they used to be . . . they display more taste; they spend more money; they brag less; they demand the best amusements; in short, they have *ripened.* This is well." A century later, a historian looked for reasons for the change and shrugged, concluding only that "something important happened to turn a portion of the old mixed theater audience away from rowdiness." Neither observer questioned what both saw as an improvement. "Something important happened," and, like God's separation of light from dark, it was deemed good.[1]

Even as later ages agreed with the 1868 *Clipper* that things had improved, they noticed a fall in enthusiasm, and wondered why. Yet it was no mystery. The *Clipper*'s "ripened" age resulted from a specific, identifiable historical process: The triumph of aspirational decorum. Audiences had learned to avoid interaction. Beyond performance, people withdrew from public engagement to a more private, inner-directed condition, what one historian called the fall of public man.[2]

Performers and audiences separated; audiences themselves, formerly mixed, became stratified, along with forms. "Art," which once meant craft, now became that rarified "something higher" the emerging middle class had been seeking as its esthetic ideal. Meanwhile, the violence of the Civil War seemed to confirm the risk of violence in unchecked masses and in amusements identified with those masses. Clinching the suspicion for many, Booth's assassination of Lincoln was not just an evil deed but the wicked manifestation of performance itself. Entertainment and art, more than opposite poles, became antagonists in the larger cultural drama of society. Through many attempts to define art in performance, one constant persisted: It was *not* entertainment. For theatre, ballet and opera to be art *required* some things to be less exalted; circus, with its violence and animal smells and bright colors and loud noises, fit this new lowbrow bill. Another constant was that formal art dwindled to the care of experts, who "accomplished tasks of expression which were difficult to accomplish in ordinary society." Later ages see this shift as inevitable, but it was more than coincidence that the post–Civil War years institutionalized "high" culture in the founding of New York's Metropolitan Museum and its Museum of Natural History, Boston's Museum of Fine Art, the Corcoran in Washington, and Cincinnati's Museum of Art.[3]

Rice, sensing the cultural shift, had been laboring to create a new performance genre—"sui generis"—like himself. Declaring that he was no clown but a humorist, and that his presentation was no circus, he might have dragged Dan Rice's Great Show up the performance hierarchy, leaving circus "entertainment" behind and forging a new form on his oratorical "art," some creative blend of refined lectures and boisterous amusement. Many people reacted to him as if he had done just that. Nor was this prospective elevation an impossible task. Ballet, which had once been more scorned than circus because it showed more leg, had risen. In part, that was because expert observers could project "artistic" meanings on the nonverbal form, for ballet was "the one form of theatre where nobody speaks a foolish word all evening."[4]

However, Rice's divided sympathies in the war had forced him to shackle the spontaneity that had been the foundation of his strength, pulling him back to the embrace of traditional circus. The old sneer that managers took him only to get his animals began to bear some truth. In 1865, Rice advertised his Mammoth Moral Menagerie as "Wholesome Pabulum," indicating intellectual nourishment, but that stimulating word soon boiled down to pablum, to mush. When the *Clipper* complained of his political harangues, it put "talking clown" in quotation marks, as if that were no venerable type but an aberrant strain. The paper contrasted Rice with other funnymen "most in favor with the masses, who prefer little jokes, or songs, or"—the venerable apology for bad clowning—"something of that sort." (Rice responded, writing to the editor that he called attention to the *Clipper* every day, "so that you may know I return Good for Evil—which is the way I do business.")[5]

The *Clipper* had been sniping at Rice since Fort Sumter, repeatedly decrying his "harangues." It had refused to apply "Colonel" to Rice, then finally did so, but ironically, in quotation marks. Ignoring the comic technique that paired ringmaster and clown in a mutual effort, it pronounced a need for the ringmaster to hold "the antics of the clowns in check," especially the antics of Rice. In 1868, after another clown retorted to a country editor, the *Clipper* made a pronouncement that would have prompted astonishment a decade earlier: "It is seldom that chin music can beat the pen. . . . One thing clowns should remember, that as a general rule, it's folly to fight against the press. Dan Rice attempted it in Morristown a couple of weeks ago and, although Dan was in the right, he came off second best." The *Clipper* had cheered Rice in his antebellum battles against Greeley, declaring the clown the winner. Now it warned him to hush. "A newspaper can go where the voice of Mr. [Merryman] can never reach."[6]

Some have decided that Rice's career faded because the growing size of American circuses made it physically impossible to be heard, but they had not grown yet. Two-ring circuses did not appear until 1873, and the first three-ring affair in 1881. Though larger tents would make Rice's intimate relationship with audiences more difficult, he had spoken to thousands at a time, in large tents and in city theaters. Even in the later, larger tents, ringmasters continued to talk. More significantly, the commonplace explanation that Rice's appeal succumbed to circus size ignores the diminished taste for interaction in audiences large and small. Rice's perfect rush didn't falter because tents got bigger; it faltered because the scope of performance got smaller.

Celebrated or scorned, "artistic" or not, Rice kept on.

After a December 1867 meeting of circus men in Philadelphia, at Uncle Sam Miller's, Rice prepared another Farewell Tour with the Dan Rice Circus and Menagerie, Adam Forepaugh again as proprietor. Rice's closing speech dripped dolefully. "Farewell, if we meet no more here below, may we all be gathered into the Kingdom of our Father, where there is no sorrow, neither weeping, but happiness." That matched the growing taste for sentimentality, but Rice could also have had the wretched season in mind. Neither the "swimmist," who ate and smoked underwater in an iron tank with windows, nor a learned pig in the sideshow could stimulate business. Rice and the Forepaughs blamed each other. Forepaugh's son, John, manager on the road, complained that Dan's speeches savored too much of politics, and Rice accused them of running things on the cheap. June brought a confrontation that put John in jail. The following month, Rice gave him "particular Jessie" from the ring in Troy, New York, blaming Forepaugh for stabling the horses two miles away and providing workingmen such bad accommodations that they had to make their own arrangements and pay themselves. Rice vowed that he had sold his name for a salary for the last time. No one said anything about $1,000 a week now. When Rice played Brooklyn in September, the ring carpet looked as if it had been "picked out of some junk shop." Finally, in November, as the show was "worrying out the . . . week" in Philadelphia, Rice quit, though they continued to use his name. Even the *Clipper* sympathized. "We do not think Dan has been treated right this season, and we are glad to find that he has had the nerve on more than one occasion to place the shortcomings of the show to the discredit of the proprietors."[7]

Dan did get some good news. On June 6, 1868, Rebecca gave birth to a boy, and they named him Dan Rice, Jr. As Rice's confrontation with Forepaugh came just after the birth, perhaps Dan's anxiety manifested itself in bluster, as it had when they lost Lottie. This child, though, was thriving. A photograph—"probably Dan Rice, Jr.," it says on the back—shows a chubby, healthy baby leaned back in a chair, its white baby clothes draped to the floor. Dan would say that he had divorced Maggie for the royal reason that she had not borne him a son. True or not, he now had that son. Maggie went by Warner, and his daughter performed as Libby Reed, but he saw someone to carry on his name.[8]

Kate had not performed for over a decade. More influenced by convent education than her sister, she had become a Catholic, taking her First Communion in 1864. A month after getting a baby brother, thanks to a stepmother her own age, she was singing and playing four-hand piano in a "Musical Soiree" at the Ursuline convent in Cleveland. While Libby continued in their father's circus footsteps, Kate briefly followed his political path, speaking at a Girard rally for Horatio Seymour, trustee of her old school in Utica and the Democratic presidential candidate. Not completely distancing herself from her father's show, she married his treasurer, Albert C. Wurzbach. He had been a Memphis watchmaker, and called himself "Captain" on an unsubstantiated claim of Confederate service. He was involved in a mystery before their marriage. In July 1868, a recent arrival in Girard, Margaret Riggs, died suddenly, and her daughter, Julia, took ill, prompting the Erie County district attorney to investigate for poision, though none was found. Rice was involved, having sold a lot on Rice Avenue to Riggs; then her manager, described as Rice's intimate acquaintance, took her body to Rice's house, where it was readied for transportation to Philadelphia for burial. The suspicion of foul play erupted again in September, in Riggs's will. It turned out that she was Wurzbach's divorced wife, and that Julia, who had left town, was their daughter. Wurzbach inherited the house that Riggs had been building, and late in that year it became the home of his bride, Kate Rice. She was twenty-two and he was forty-eight, the same age span as Dan and Rebecca.[9]

Girard remained one focus of Rice's restless energy. In 1867, he merged the town's *Spectator* and the *Crisis* of nearby Conneautville, which he had bought a decade before, naming the combined venture *Cosmopolite*—"citizen of the world." Stow remained editor. The pace of Rice's land deals picked up in 1868. He probably needed money so, with Rebecca co-signing, he sold many parcels, though he kept buying, too. Scrambling to stay ahead, he still envisioned the personal empire of property that his publicity had long boasted. In February 1869, he bought a local hotel, the Girard House, with a $2,000 mortgage. He also built a barn and a conservatory, which, Rice told a newspaper, had cost $20,000. Rice owned a farm five miles away and another one in town. In April 1868, the *Reading Times* declared it would "play the woman," peeping behind the curtain to describe the centerpiece of his holdings, his residential estate, surrounded by landscaped acres, "made leafy labyrinths by the sinuous hedges." The house itself was free of any "suspicion of the sawdust," any reminder of "the show 'shop.'" Instead, rare curiosities and costly souvenirs were set off tastefully by "dainty bits" of sculpture. The bust by Volk was surrounded by "one of the largest and best selected libraries in the country."[10]

The 1869 show, "Dan Rice's Own Circus!" proclaimed another Farewell Tour, his fifth or sixth. He brought out a new edition of his 1863 songster, as he had in 1866. The big draw remained blind Excelsior, Jr. Libby and Charley Reed were Queen of the Menage and American Centaur respectively, and the bills showed off a Rice cousin, Dick Clark, with a new Rice apprentice, Lizzie Marcellus, the "beautiful girl prodigy." Rice told of spotting the pretty little girl taking cows to pasture as he drove his buggy near Albany. He stopped to chat, then drove her home, asking on-the way if she had seen the circus. She had, and thought the clown an ugly old man. Rice teasingly identified himself, then gave her mother passes to his show. At the performance, Lizzie skipped into the ring, hugged him, and wouldn't go away. Bowing to her eagerness, he told her parents that he would take her on as an apprentice, knowing that she would get homesick and return in a few days. But she stayed, becoming virtually a member of his family. Rice said that he gave her every advantage his daughters had enjoyed; a bill he owed at New York's Academy of the Sacred Heart was probably Lizzie's overdue tuition.[11]

The 1869 bills sought to quell rumors that Rice was gone: "N. B.—Special attention is called to the $100 Reward, offered by Dan Rice, with reference to his non-appearance as Clown, &c." The vague wording ensured that no one could claim the reward. Showing in Iowa in July, he added old Civil War cuts of himself standing amid a bouquet of American flags, and of his steamboat running the blockade. In Evansville, Rice's agent proclaimed that "The River God is Coming!!"[12]

On June 21, 1869, circus history was made along the Mississippi—though no one knew it at the time. On that day, Rice played McGregor, Iowa, opposite the mouth of the Wisconsin River. The proprietor of the town's "One-Horse Harness Shop," a German immigrant, had anglicized his name from August Rüngeling. That summer day, Rice transfixed August's sons, the Ringling brothers. Though they saw other shows in their youth, they would later recall Rice as their inspiration for creating their own circus.[13]

This inconspicuously momentous event occurred during a terrible season. The *Clipper* had called the 1868 season the most disastrous circus had known; this one was worse. Rice did well in Cincinnati, making over $10,000 and giving himself $1,000 of it. But, like spring flooding, that was the high mark of the season. After that, he took in $300 a week, then dipped to $125. The *Clipper* yapped at him all summer. In mid-June, people were leaving his show "severely alone . . . preferring to visit a tent exhibition where they can be amused by a man in the garb of motley, and not be compelled to listen to a political harangue or a rodomontade by a person calling himself a jester." The following month, it quoted a Hannibal paper that the absence of face paint detracted from his jokes, themselves suggesting that "he had been a disappointed office-seeker." Even as the *Clipper* reported on rough times for all circuses, it kept blaming Rice for his troubles. "It requires a first class exhibition to attract the people now-a-days. They understand the difference between political harangues and true wit, and they absent themselves from concerns where the former is the principal stock in trade."[14]

As Rice toured Iowa, his critics forged new ammunition. It was the old tale of Robert Stickney's fall from his horse in 1858, brought up to date, which meant increased sentimentality. The agent for one of Rice's competitors, James Bailey, published a revised version of the story, adding Rice to the scene and transforming the silent teenage boy of the original account into "one of the prettiest angel-faced little girls we ever beheld." After the fictional angel-face fell, horror multiplied.

> Evidently much against her inclination, and in spite of her trembling and her tears, nature's protest against such inhuman barbarity, she was tossed again to her place. . . . Trembling and bruised, her cheeks pale with fear

> and pain, sobbing as if her little heart would break, she was again made to attempt the leap. Again she fell to the ground, this time striking heavily upon her head. She rolled directly under the horse's feet, and only by a sheer chance escaped a terrible death.

The concern of the people—clearly of a better class than the original version's "noisy spectators"—roused itself. "Cries and shouts were heard from all quarters. 'Shame,' 'That'll do,' 'Take her out,' came up from every side." Rice, blended into the ringmaster in this telling, complied, with ill-concealed insolence. "It would not answer to disregard such commands, and with a half leer and an assumed smile," he carried the sobbing little girl out. Rice was the perfect picture of melodramatic villainy here because the story came from a "rat sheet," circus publicity designed to make the opposition look bad. Accuracy did not matter as long as some papers repeated it, and some people believed it. Other papers picked this one up and added the detail that Rice joked about the fall with "a dirty pun of vulgarity, too indecent for publication." The show-business *Clipper* knew how unreliable rat sheets were. It also knew, in its institutional memory, that it had printed a Rice-less version of the story in 1858. But disingenuously, it reprinted it as a report of an actual incident.[15]

This would mostly be an intramural struggle, of little importance, except that those who seek to read about Rice more deeply than the publicity-fueled fictions inevitably turn to the *Clipper*, little aware of its bias. When the agent John A. Dingess quit Rice this season, the *Clipper* blamed it on his disgust at the "would-be President's harangues," but Dingess left due to a more traditional show business reason: Rice had stopped paying him. In a memoir, Dingess showed that the paper's estimation of the clown was not his. He wrote of Rice's strength, courage, and generosity. He also described Rice as "one of the finest extemporaneous speakers of the land." It "is impossible for the boys of today to understand the popular enthusiasm that Dan Rice's appearance aroused. It is no exaggeration to say that he was one of the biggest men in the country."[16]

Another benefit to understanding the bias in the *Clipper* attacks is that they revealed the shift in aspiration. The ideal of "higher things," once a defense against anxiety, had become barely disguised snobbery. As far as the "better sort" were concerned, circus—and especially Rice, in his lingering prominence—deserved disdain. That can be seen in one more incarnation of the fallen apprentice story, plagiarized by an actress who wrote a book proclaiming the "high aspirations . . . of dramatism." To reinforce her disdain for the "common run," the author also championed the new taste for silence, in theater and circus. "Personal communication" between the audience and the performers was "equally indelicate and unwise." She especially liked her clowns quiet.

> The circus clown and the stage clown of pantomime are two very different creatures. The one talks—and usually his wit is coarse, his humor vulgar, his jokes old and stupid. . . . The pantomime clown . . . has a wealth of laughter-provoking power in his whitened face. Pantomime, as a means of expressing ideas, may be one of the most beautiful of arts, in the hands of a man or woman of genuine artistic ability.

This growing bias against spoken eloquence explains why, half a century later, an old clown looking back did not mention Rice for his politics, his popularity, or his Shakespeare, but because he "taught the author the fundamentals of pantomime."[17]

Rice's steamboat the Will S. Hays

Still, Rice kept on. In fall 1869, he turned to Kansas, traveling on the stern-wheeler *Will S. Hays,* which he bought for $10,000. The boat was named for Rice's friend, a songwriter named William Shakespeare Hays, who had taken Stephen Foster's place as the foremost American songwriter. In Topeka, the local paper complained that Rice had become a grim joker who advocated Christian principles, morality, temperance, Sunday Schools, and female suffrage. The next day, Rice was arrested for flogging a man, who, he said, had insulted his daughter. When the judge fined him $25, the paper approved: Rice too often relied "wholly upon his muscle in maintaining his principles and positions." Patience was never one of Rice's virtues. His fights were increasingly hazardous: An apprentice recalled that Rice endured the "severest licking . . . I ever saw a man get," as the veteran showman swallowed his chew and couldn't work for days.[18]

For all its nagging, the *Clipper* did give an accurate impression of Rice's tour. He had "invested in a small concern, chartered a steamboat and paddled up small streams, stopping at little out of the way places, pitched a small tent and opened shop." On November 11, Rice's "curiosity sideshow" was at Friar's Point, Arkansas, downriver from Memphis. It was too windy to raise the tent, so Rice kept his outfit on the boat. As he looked for a change in the weather, the crowd grew on shore and kept drinking. The workers unloaded once the wind had settled; but it whipped up again, so everything went back on the boat, which pulled offshore. The crowd didn't care that the show was losing a day's receipts. They had lost a day's work themselves, and would see the show or "bust a biler." About 2:00 A.M., a gang, "led by an old Negro named 'Ginril,'" waved shotguns and demanded that Rice pull the boat in. The Colonel defied Ginril, so the gang fired, getting off fifty shots before the boat could move out of range.[19]

In 1870, Rice switched to a train, touring a "Trick Horse Ampliation and Asiatic Animal Spectacle." The showman who had once featured an elephant on a tightrope was reduced to boasting of the birth of twin calves. The small roster featured "Old" Dan and Lizzie, his Great Juvenile Premiere Equestrienne. In the spring, an Indiana paper complained that Dan "dressed magnificently, sang shockingly bad, attempted to preach and failed, and was only successful in raising a laugh when he spoke scoffingly of the President."[20]

A surviving ledger gives a sketch of the season. Rebecca was performing again, briefly. Most of the items for "Mrs. R" covered expenses, but in July she received $50 in salary. Libby and Charley Reed trouped with the show in the spring before they left with a $1,000 loan, Libby being pregnant. Dan gave Lizzie money and paid for her wardrobe. His sartorial influence showed when Marcellus was later described as "one of the best dressers that ever graced the arena." The ledger also recorded $1,100 on court judgments, and Rice's liquor bill. The circus had a bar on the steamboat, with running tabs for the workers. One groom was hired, ran up a bill of $7.50 at the bar during his first few days—on a groom's salary of $3 a week—and was fired. Dan's bill reached $15 a week. He generously picked up many tabs, but much of that liquor went down his own throat. It was a drinking age, and he joined in heartily. Rice also paid a fine, recorded as: "Luxury of choking a blackguard, $5."[21]

On September 22, 1870, as Rice was leading his show to close in Rochester, Daniel McLaren died in Girard. Rebecca left the tour to arrange for the funeral. A year later, on September 13, 1871, Hugh Manahan died, too. Between the deaths of Dan's two fathers, his granddaughter, Libby and Charley's Charlotte, died. Like his and Rebecca's Charlotte, also called Lottie, she, too, died at six months. After these losses, Dan would not have grieved much when Henry McConnell, Rebecca's father, died. He had never warmed to his son-in-law. In his will McConnell stipulated that none of the property given to Rebecca could be used to pay the debts of her husband. It was one last slap at the upstart clown, delivered from the grave.[22]

Old showmen would say that with his divorce from Maggie, Dan had lost his luck.[23] He must have begun to wonder whether that were true.

35

PARIS PAVILION

Rice believed he had found a way to beat the devil and carry a rail—to triumph despite handicaps. Reaching New Orleans in January 1871 with his nondescript Italian & American Circus, he saw a vision of the future.[1] It came in a glimpse of the past, the Paris Pavilion moldering in a warehouse. Four years earlier, Spalding and his partners had paid $125,000 to build the imposing structure for the world exposition in Paris. Wooden panels, eight feet by sixteen feet, interlocked to form the walls, topped by a blue-and-white painted canvas ninety feet in the air. The project had failed when Parisian authorities, spurred by local managers, enforced a law forbidding portable wooden buildings. Spalding's group shipped the majestic structure back across the Atlantic, to be stored in New Orleans. It was re-erected briefly in 1870, then dismantled again. Now Rice visited the warehouse. In the rows of wood panels and stacks of chairs, he saw the elegant arena it could be, his old aspirations in physical form. He saw recaptured glory and a rebuilt fortune. To cap the climax, he saw himself making a success of Doc's failure.

In March, putting some money down and giving notes to Spalding for the rest, Rice bought the Paris Pavilion with a St. Louis man, D. K. Prescott. To open in St. Louis in mid-April, they transported the Pavilion upriver and gathered a troupe featuring Lizzie Marcellus. Because people now expected contingents of clowns, Rice hired a bumbling "Felt-Crowned Fool"; a "French Grimaldi" who had allegedly escaped in a balloon from beleaguered Paris; "the Equestrian Joseph Jefferson," which meant a scenic act of Rip Van Winkle, a role being made famous by the comic actor Joseph Jefferson; and a German dialect clown, later called a Dutch comic. Of course, he also presented the "$100,000 Excelsior, Jr."[2]

The Pavilion repeated the attention to accuracy that Rice had devoted to his historical spectacles, only now instead he presented his own era's elite culture, an elegant parlor rather than knights in armor. Red velvet carpeting covered the floor, drapery beautified and soundproofed the walls, and lace festooned the openings. For lighting beyond the gas chandelier ringing the center pole, sconces rode the wall and glass globes

DAN RICE, PROPRIETOR AND MANAGER

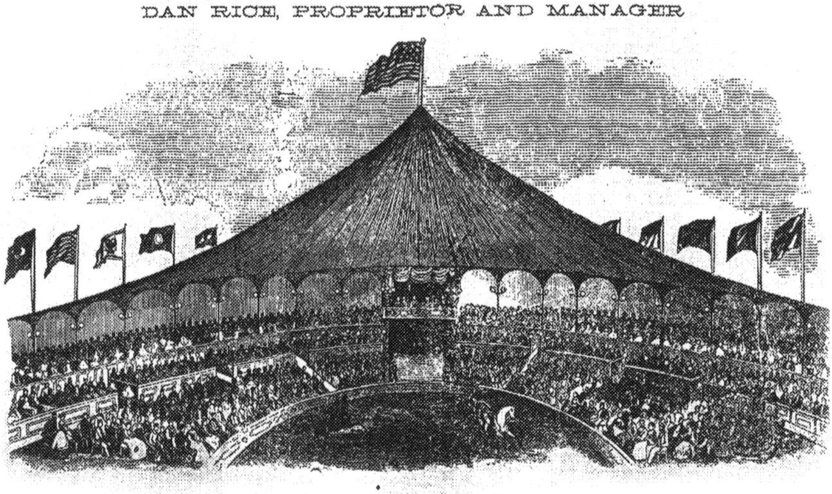

THE PARIS PAVILION

Rice tried to make a success of one of Spalding's few failures, the wooden-sided, canvas-topped Paris Pavilion.

stood at each box. At the ceiling, national flags of silk hung from velvet ropes. Rice kept the French names of the sections, the "Premieres" of cane-bottomed chairs, the "Loges," a second ring of boxes with cushioned benches, and the "Secondes," or Family Circle, 1,700 customers altogether. Rice put his band in a box above the performers' entrance. Across the ring, over the audience entrance, Rice flattered newspapermen by converting what had been intended as seating for the French emperor into an "Editorial Box." Elegance extended into "withdrawing rooms," where combs hung from chains and decorative fish sprayed perfume with each use of the towel rolls. That new middle-class luxury, toilets, flushed into city sewers.[3]

The structure took days to erect and dismantle, a major drawback for a touring show, but Dan had a plan. He sent the structure on to larger cities while using the title for tent performances in towns between. Some dates remained open though, which meant reduced income. That summer, a credit rating showed Rice verging on bankruptcy; his debts amounted to $40,000, but his real estate and personal property would fetch less than $30,000. With all his resources in the Pavilion, Rice had no sideshow, menagerie, or parade. Naturally, he made that a virtue. "No humbug sideshows are permitted on the grounds, and the audience will be nourished with plentiful supply of ice water."[4]

Before the season, Rice had paid a call on his mother's people in Long Branch, where they must have chatted about cousin W. C. Crum's new job. He was now treasurer of P. T. Barnum's Great Traveling Museum, Menagerie, Caravan and Hippodrome.[5]

Barnum is a strange duck in the circus world. His name descends through history as the quintessential circus man, but he had little involvement in circus for much of his career. He had sold circus tickets in 1836; after that he produced traveling museums and menageries, Jenny Lind and Tom Thumb, but no circuses.[6] Then Coup and Castello came calling.

In 1870, William C. Coup and Dan Castello had taken out a small Wisconsin show. Concluding with a profit and seeking to expand, they contacted Barnum about using his name. He declined. He had retired, and his friends and family advised against the proposal. But Coup persisted until, on October 8, Barnum relented. He agreed to the use of his name, and loaned his expertise to create the show's museum department. (He placed his son-in-law on the show as assistant to Crum.) As Barnum wrote to his Boston Museum compatriot, Moses Kimball, "I *thought* I had finished the show business (and all other), but just for a flyer I go it once more."[7] Success has many fathers: Coup and Barnum eventually disagreed about which one had been the major force in the enterprise, a dispute that continues. Barnum's biographers see his energy sailing the circus on new tides of grandeur; others give the credit to Coup, a circus man who had to persuade a hesitant Barnum and who managed the show on the road. In either case, Barnum might be little known now but for Coup's invitation. Jenny Lind and Tom Thumb were sensations, and Barnum was the nineteenth-century master of self-promotion, yet his name might have dwindled but for its survival in Barnum & Bailey, successor to the Coup-Barnum circus.

Rice had politely endured Barnum's ascendant celebrity after the 1867 lecture in Erie. He knew well the fame of his fellow showman, and capitalized on it. After offering $5 to anyone who named a baby for him, he delivered the punchline: "I've shaken hands with forty-three men this morning who had named babies after me and my last five-dollar bill has been paid out. You'd better strike Barnum when he comes."[8]

Now as Phineas joined the world of circus, with what the *Clipper* called the "great show," Dan had the chance to establish his name and show as greater. The outfits day-and-dated in Albany, that is, they showed at the same place at the same time, August 22–23, 1871. The promise on Rice's bills that he had no "humbug sideshow" was a swipe at the Great Humbug, though Barnum now shied from that old nickname. As both shows drew good crowds, it would seem to have been a victory for Rice. He had gone toe-to-toe with Barnum's larger and more publicized circus, and beaten him to a draw. But triumph was fleeting. A high mark of the season for Rice, Albany was simply another stand for the Barnum show. Even the advantage Rice had, that he directly engaged each audience in person, had become less crucial. As America grew, its business and pleasure became less direct. The new business vehicle, the corporation, after all, is a theory—an abstract "corpus," or body—endowed with limited liability to take the financial risk of business from the shoulders of real, unabstract people. (Some believed that corporations were immoral for eliminating personal responsibility.) The site of work was a similar abstraction.

Where workers had formerly engaged in a task together, functions were increasingly scattered among far-flung venues, places and times. Suppliers, buyers, laborers, managers, and financiers might operate in different places, unknown to each other personally. The same shift was taking place in performance. Its work had once been done over the footlights, the antebellum performance created jointly by the performer and the audience, that paradoxically intimate community of strangers. No one mastered that connection better than Rice. But the site was changing. With audiences less engaged, a new creature, the director, rehearsed and announced the meanings of plays before performance, while critics judged afterwards whether it worked—and benefactors gave a final, financial benediction. Quieter, less engaged audiences were also less secure in their tastes, so they deferred to those experts. Reputations that had flourished in the daily interplay with audiences increasingly depended on what would be called marketing (which employed techniques borrowed from circus). The fact that Rice placed himself daily before the people for their judgment mattered less now than Barnum's publicity machine. Seeing Barnum became an experience competing with the anticipation beforehand and the privilege of boasting about it.[9]

This season made the difference manifest. Coup and Castello, buoyed by Barnum's name, made $400,000; Rice's big gamble failed and he lost $60,000. As Spalding had known, the Paris Pavilion was too expensive to use for a traveling show. There were stops in the East to eke out the season—Rice played New York City for the first time in a decade—but the money was gone. He had been selling off land in Girard; it was not enough. He closed on Thanksgiving Day in Baltimore and put his wooden arena into storage. Three years later, junk dealers and curiosity seekers poked through the moldy remnants of Rice's dream before paying 35¢ for each of few usable chairs and $34 for three hundred yards of Brussels carpet.[10]

Rice tramped south from Baltimore in the fall of 1871, using the Pavilion title and Spalding's money. Rebecca was back on the road. It seems likely that Dan, Jr., four, was left behind with his mother's family. Rebecca might brave their disapproval to rejoin her husband; she probably could not defy them about the child. Harry Spalding was manager, keeping an eye on his father's interest. The treasurer was James Henry Howland, who would marry Dan's sister, Catherine. Maggie and daughter Kate had married his treasurers too. After years with Dan, the Rice women apparently appreciated a man who kept his eye on the balance sheet.[11]

Small incidents peppered Rice's show in 1867. In New Orleans, Rice played for Grand Duke Alexis Romanoff Alexandrovitch of Russia; Lizzie Marcellus dressed in white velvet and used golden silk ribbons as reins for the occasion. In Kansas, the *Olathe Mirror* appreciated the absence of fights, "unusual for show days," but Dodge City drama came to Baxter. When a drunken marshal, waving a pistol, tried to collect a second license fee from a candy peddler, Henry Spalding rushed to object, and the marshal shot him three times. Spalding drew a revolver himself, wounding the lawman. Doc's son went to St. Louis to mend, and returned to the show in mid-July. Meanwhile, Maggie popped back into the picture. Rice had his circus in McGregor, Iowa, again, while she was with a show across the Mississippi in Wisconsin, when a fight broke out between members of the two shows. An account denying a larger battle added that "relations between the Mrs. Charles Warner and her former husband, Dan Rice, are amicable and governed by respect. Divorced for years, when they do meet—which is seldom—it is upon a friendly basis." A year later, Rice's band led the company to the cemetery at Great Barrington, Massachusetts, where Charley Warner had been buried in 1865. Dan's rapprochement with Maggie continued.[12]

Rice was no longer a newspaperman, having lost his *Cosmopolite* to sheriff's auction. His credit ratings trailed him like ghosts. In July 1872, he was "genly consid at present as insolvent"; in December, "working hard to get out of debt." Now water slapped against another steamboat hull and cascaded off its wheel on another ride around America's rivers. In New Orleans, he had to pay a $500 fine for failing to get an inspection. It would be a lethal year, with five deaths on the show, including that of his cousin, Clark.[13]

Even as his career slid, Rice retained his skill at reading audiences. He knew that people wanted sentimentality. In its 1873 season preview, the *Clipper* reflected that new taste. While circus performers are "lighthearted and gay" as a class, clowns "always seem, out of the ring, the gravest and most taciturn of the race." (The frequently sentimental tramp clown had not appeared yet because "tramp" did not become a synonym for hobo until the increased industrialization of the 1870s.) Dan could deliver the sentimentality of nostalgia. Since 1869, he had been advertising his "'Old Time' character of Clown," and himself as aged. Not yet fifty, he presented himself as "one of the oldest showmen in the country." One paper declared that he was sixty-five. Treating his audiences to a fond look back, he would be "Old Dan Rice." Out again with Spalding's backing, he plastered his grandiloquent title on cards and stationery, Dan Rice's Museum, Circus, Coliseum, Menagerie, and School of Trained Animals, with the letterhead adding a parade of animals in front of seven huge tents. As Rice took his show into Canada, there was also a "Dan Rice's Paris Pavilion Circus" playing Kansas without him, despite the ads' use of his face. Papers could still legitimately say that Rice "is as well known from one end of the continent to the other as President Grant or P. T. Barnum," but he was increasingly a figurehead, a fading name to conjure rather than the real thing.[14]

While Rice's title echoed Barnum's bombast, Barnum was taking a leaf from Rice. Coup, Barnum, and Castello had built from strength to strength. Others had tried the rails, including Spalding, but the triumvirate's huge show on sixty-five cars in 1872 made the rolling experiment famously successful, a turning point in circus transportation. In 1873, they

Rice still promised multitudes of wonder, even on his stationery.

made another important mark in circus history when they adopted the slogan "The Greatest Show on Earth." It is one of the few things Barnum does not take credit for, and no one knows who thought it up. However, their publicity man, the "Director of Publications" was Rice's cousin, Crum.[15] Proclaiming the Greatest Show on Earth, Coup and Barnum echoed a resonance stirringly sounded by Rice's Great Show.

Four decades after Rice started his working life in the Panic of 1837, his show stumbled to a close in a bigger depression. Jay Cooke and Company collapsed on September 18, precipitating the Panic of 1873. The New York Stock Exchange closed for ten days, and in an early display of globalization, markets tumbled around the world. Among the 10,000 businesses that failed were Howes's circus dynasty and Rice's Midwest outfit. (Rice later called his losses a personal betrayal by his alleged friend, Cooke.)[16]

February 1874 brought two more deaths. That month Rice's old ringmaster and partner, Frank Rosston, passed on. In a business rife with shifting combinations, Rice and Rosston had worked together for fifteen years, and Frank had named his oldest son Daniel. This same February, Doc Spalding buried his own son. Henry had seemed to be progressing well from the gunshot wounds, but he died at his father's home in Saugerties, New York, on February 4. On the same day, Doc seized Dan's Girard property on a claim of $72,000. Was the date a coincidence, or did Spalding blame Rice for Henry's death? Included in Rice's losses was a farm that had been in Rebecca's family for years. On April 7, Spalding foreclosed in Cook County, Illinois, on Rice's Hyde Park property, and on May 4, asserted a claim to more of Rice's Girard property.[17] Earlier, midway through the nineteenth century, the potential for an amazing partnership between the great circus manager and the greatest American circus clown had vibrated like a banjo string. Even during their titanic feud, creative tension had quivered between Doc and Dan. Now, the string broke.

The clown struggled through 1874. His perfect rush had slowed to a crawl. Or a stagger.

"Have you hurt yourself lifting the lady on her horse?"

"Yes. You see, Master, I'm getting old. It is hard to raise a girl now."

"Yes, I see you are getting very old."

"Yes, Mr. Master, but I am strong and lusty, for in my youth I did not apply the hot, rebellious liquors to my blood."

"No, but you have made up for it in your advanced years."

Rice had always been a gregarious drinker in a gregarious, well-liquored age. That social practice wobbled into a habit he couldn't control. One night, foiled in his search for a drink in a temperance town, he gathered the band to serenade the local banker, who invited them in to share his private stock.[18]

He also could not control money. It flowed through his life like water rolling off a paddlewheel. Starting in the show business on his own, he had built a career on his native wit, and he had done it all over again with the One-Horse Show. His tremendous appeal kept finding him backers for decades. But he was no longer young, the country was in a depression, and his name did not carry its old clout.

On February 9, 1875, he filed for bankruptcy in U.S. District Court. He owed almost $85,000 to nearly two hundred people from New Orleans to Canada, plus a $500 jewelry bill in Dresden, Germany. There were obligations for back pay, loans across the show world, and debts to doctors, lawyers, lithographers, and carpenters. Rice's Paris Pavilion partner, Prescott, claimed $3,500. A New York sail maker had $1,200 coming for canvas. Rice owed hundreds for shipping, thousands for printing and advertising, and more thousands on steamboats. The largest creditor was Spalding, for one-third of the total debt. Dan owed his old Pittsburgh pals, George Evans and Mit Foster. His indebtedness included nearly $3,500 to Mr. and Mrs. A. C. Wurzbach—daughter Kate and her husband. Money was due to Charles Stow, his former editor, now with Barnum; to Lizzie Marcellus, living in Girard; and—particularly rankling—to his mother-in-law. One other name in the list hinted at a combination of reconciliation and embarrassment: Mrs. Charles Warner, New York City. Dan owed Maggie $337.[19]

36

IS LIFE WORTH LIVING?

As Rice floundered, the sentimentalized picture of the circus was being perfected. In *The Adventures of Huckleberry Finn*, published in 1884, Mark Twain depicted the "real bully circus" that the American imagination was coming to treasure. Huck gazes in wide-eyed wonder at men riding easy, the women beautiful, and the whole "a powerful fine sight," making the audience wild with excitement. The "quick as a wink" clown said such funny things "it most killed the people."

Some have decided that Twain was describing Rice's circus, which he saw when he was young Sam Clemens. But the description, even if an accurate depiction of Rice's show, is false in a way, what Huck would call a stretcher. For one thing, the glowing image of circus is thematically inconsistent in the book, in which Twain otherwise contrasts nature against human institutions and practices, all narrow, tawdry or corrupt. Pursuing his satirical cynicism about life on shore, he could have used these three pages in the book to depict shabby costumes, inept riders, and clowns who raised laughs only with obscenity. Instead, relying on the sentimentality he otherwise mocked, Twain penned a valentine to the American circus. He similarly altered his central character. Though unsophisticated, Huck is not childlike, and much of the power of the novel lies in the ironic gap between what the reader knows and what Huck ingenuously describes. Yet at Twain's glorified circus, Huck—as hackneyed publicity would put it—becomes a child again. Discernment is replaced by open-mouthed wonder at the "splendidest sight that ever was." No Hollywood happy ending could do better. This glorified image, framed by its temporarily childlike observer, was important to Twain, as he made it literally central. Critics have complained about the lack of structure in *Huckleberry Finn* but there is at least this: He placed the circus scene exactly in the middle of the book, in the twenty-second of forty-three chapters. Twain's sentimentalized circus is a pivot of the action.[1]

Twain's masterful depiction burrowed deep into cultural consciousness because it precisely fit America's new view of the circus as the epitome of nostalgia and childlike innocence. That sweetly sentimental image had already grown so bloated that it made an easy target for ridicule. Slang flipped that image on its head, turning "circus" into a colloquialism meaning an obscene exhibition by prostitutes. Meanwhile, veterans grumbled about the sentimental bloat. The author of the *Clipper*'s 1875 season preview confessed that he had lost his enthusiasm for the circus with the downfall of Rice in the 1860s.[2]

Rumors had put him on a California tour, but in the spring of 1875, Rice signed on with George W. DeHaven's America's Racing Association, International Hippodrome, Menagerie and Congress of Nations. Matching its bombastic title to the largest spread of canvas of the day, the show suffered blowdowns and dodged creditors until it died in New York's North Country, where the state faces Canada across the St. Lawrence River. In September Rice made his way back to Cincinnati to try Dan Rice's New Show of Educated Bronchos. Two weeks later Coup brought Barnum's Hippodrome to town.[3]

Of all the era's prominent figures, the fleetingly or lastingly popular, the infamous and the famous, two stood out, P. T. Barnum and Dan Rice. People mid-century knew that something "Ricean" or "Barnumesque"

A prostitute "playing circus" with customers.

would be exciting. It made sense then that their names had been connected. In 1875, the connection became official. Coup hired Rice for the three-day run. But this was no joining of equals. Rice's dimmed star simply fell briefly into Barnum's gravitational pull. Barnum, off in Bridgeport, may not have even known about the hire, while Rice nestled briefly in the ads among a balloon ascension and the Dazzling Amazonian March of two hundred girls in silver armor.[4]

Fighting on alone, Rice continued to bluster. He added a decade to his experience with "1836 Dan Rice's 1876 / New Show and / Centennial Exposition." Advertising for agents, he crowed, "Have enlarged canvas three times . . . standing room at a premium." He had little to back up the big words, though. A story tells that Rice brought his circus to a town in which another show had put up its handbills and heralds. After Rice pretended that the ads were for him, his competitor objected. "I don't think it's the fair thing, Dan, to play on my printing."

"I hadn't any printing of my own. I had to play on somebody's."

By June, Rice left his bandwagon behind, and then the performers confiscated his show and sold it for back wages due. As a credit report put it, he was "Gd for 00."[5]

When Rice joined Cook's English & American Circus in eastern Kentucky, his former protégée, Lizzie Marcellus, was on the show with her new husband, Harry Codona. Rice had tried to have the marriage stopped. He was fond of her and did not approve of Codona, who in turn thought Rice was too fond. Rice, in Canada as the wedding approached, tried to wire a Kansas sheriff to stop it but the wire had come too late. Now together on a roster, Dan, Harry and Lizzie made a volatile mix, which erupted late one night on a boat in the upper Mississippi. Harry brandished a razor at Lizzie, she screamed, and Dan flew to her rescue. The story may have been embellished, but reports did have Rice and an equestrienne leaving the show together, and soon after, Marcellus divorced Codona.[6]

After an ill-fated attempt at a Louisiana circus, Rice took out a summer tour in 1877, reviving the title of his ascendancy, "Dan Rice's Great Show." Once, that had said everything; now he had to make it sound grander, advertising it as "Positively the Greatest Show on Earth or Water!" Sister Libbie and brother Jake brought along their newly adopted son, Willie. Having spotted the boy turning flips as he played with his friends, they received his parents' permission to adopt him. Willie Showles would become one of circus's best riders.[7]

In 1878, skipping Memphis because creditors had the sheriff waiting, Rice tried Kansas again, teetering between good days and bad. He took more family along, Anna and Nina Howland, the equestrienne daughters of his sister Catherine. In Topeka, Rice's horse and buggy were held for what he owed, and a hotel proprietor kept the showman's trunks till the bill was paid. Rice swung a loan to pay but, according to a jaundiced account, he made a spectacle of himself on the street, cursing and sobbing at the indignity.[8]

Rice thought he would have better luck among the gold-seekers in the Black Hills of South Dakota, so he turned his boat, the *Damsel,* north on the Missouri River in July, riding the border of Nebraska. North of Omaha, the performers stayed the night at a hotel while the boat, steaming ahead, ran into "one of the most terrific tempests . . . ever witnessed in Nebraska." The boat sank near Decatur. Excelsior and the ship's bell were saved but everything else, $20,000 worth, was lost. Rice had no insurance. What could be salvaged was sold at auction, and Rice presented the bell to Decatur in gratitude for the town's help. Leaving Excelsior behind to recover, Rice soldiered on in killing heat, letting the river return him south to Kansas, where a Topeka paper awaited his "phunnyisms." An ad in the *Belleville Telescope* meant to signal eagerness when it inadvertently underscored stark reality: "Old Dan in the Ring Yet / Can't Quit." He could be shut down, though. The Sedalia, Missouri sheriff attached part of the show, and the Kansas City sheriff got the rest as Rice tried to sneak out of town. He was out of business again. The *Clipper,* thawed by his troubles, commended his pluck enduring "reverses and accidents enough to discourage any ordinary mortal."[9]

Reverses now included the death of Excelsior, Jr. Held in St. Louis for freight charges of $52, the incomparable white horse, more remarkable than the original Excelsior, died on November 17, twenty-eight years old. Rice honored his last great animal attraction with stories about a mile-long funeral procession and that Henry Wadsworth Longfellow confided that Excelsior made him believe in a heaven for horses.[10]

Drink began to submerge Dan. He reportedly refused an offer to name his own salary if he would agree to avoid alcohol until the end of the season, as a guarantee of sobriety. Back in St. Louis at the end of 1879, Rice reportedly got religion, converted by the famed temperance man, Rev. Dwight Moody. That news made the front page of the *New York Tribune,* the paper of his old nemesis, the teetotaling Greeley. Rice said the conversion happened as he listened to a song his mother had sung, hitting him "right square in the soft spot, you know." Weeping like a child, "I had to go; I was forced to it. I just caved right in." It has never been clear how sincere Rice's temperance was. He would later joke that it had all been a sham, that he had gin in his water pitcher as he lectured on temperance, but it is not unusual for someone embarrassed by early ardor to pass it off as a joke. (Whitman said that he had tossed off a temperance novel while drunk.) Like most people, Rice had mixed motives. A drunk, he looked for a way out; a showman, he cocked an expert's eye at the temperance crowd, and decided he could do as well as Moody.

On Sunday, December 21, Rice took his maiden voyage on the dry seas of temperance lecturing. Before a small St. Louis crowd, he imitated how he used to stagger about the streets, and told jokes. "'Gen. Grant's a great man, Gen. Grant gets drunk, I and Gen. Grant have been drunk together. I am a great man, too. He's a great man, so'm I, hic.' [Laughter.]" Of course, the raw meat for a temperance audience is tales of degradation. Confessing that he had not gone to bed with a sober brain in five years, Rice mourned the loss of three fortunes to drink.[11]

Sincere or not, his conversion did not suddenly transform his life. In the longest article it ever devoted to Rice, the *New York Times* reported that his lecturing met "the reverse of success," including a sad little audience totaling one janitor and the local editor. As Rice continued living "by his wits and off of casual acquaintances," he apparently was still sincere in his drinking. During an interview over a glass of wine, Rice explained to the reporter that he favored moderation over abstinence, but his moderation made his exhilaration "staggeringly conspicuous." The *Times* saw little difference between the circus and alcohol—"Tan-bark and toddy"; so the "notorious showman" could choose his poison.[12]

Rice had reached bottom. No more was heard of him for eight months, as he shambled somewhere with sunken eyes and a shabby suit in degraded obscurity.

Lost in a bottle, he may have missed the passing of Gilbert Spalding. A few years earlier, Wessel T. B. Van Orden had died. After taking the blame as advance man for the Paris Exposition fiasco, Rice's old nemesis had drifted away from circus, and then had a breakdown. Despite the ancient bitterness and Rice's own fall, did he empathize with a man who also owed Spalding money, nearly $10,000? Unlike Dan, Doc always kept an eye cocked on the balance sheet, even with family. Now Spalding himself

Rice's "palatial" Girard holdings dwindled to a few, overgrown remnants like this gazebo.

was gone. South for his health, he died in New Orleans on April 6, 1880. Rice now warranted no mention in the obituaries but their feud had united them more deeply than any partnership. The two men had enacted a kind of parody marriage, as they fought for better and for worse, in sickness and in health, till death did them part.[13]

Rice roused himself, venturing out in 1880 and 1881 with small shows, including one on a side-wheeler called the *Floating Palace*, Spalding's old name. Limping into Wheeling at the end of 1881, Rice occasionally gave lectures on reform in nearby towns, scratching through the winter to find money for food and a place to stay. Driving another stake into his reputation, a sketch of Thayer's life erased Rice from his triumphant 1858 season, in the claim that Thayer, not Rice, had been "Dan Rice" in the ring.[14]

The old showman did not go home, because he no longer had one. After twenty years of long-distance marriage, Rebecca sued for divorce in 1881. Dan had devoted more attention to the circus than to their son, and had spent more time with Lizzie than with her. He did not oppose the divorce, which officially ended a relationship long dead. It is striking that in his interviews and reminiscences, Dan rarely mentioned Rebecca or Dan Jr. Estrangement would not have been all his fault, though. Rebecca's people had never considered him family. His fall confirmed what their small-town gentility had craved to believe, that he was not solid. Years later, the McConnells were still angry. "Why did Dan Rice come to Girard and with the breath of a Demon blast a beautiful life?" He had put Girard on the map but now it didn't want to know him. A friend said later that "Rice could not borrow five dollars in Girard if he needed it."[15]

The *Chicago Tribune* sent a reporter to Wheeling to interview Rice. The resulting report spawned new Rice stories, such as the one about his being invited to dine by Garfield. A whiff of the old politics lingered: Rice said that Garfield's death unnerved him, while Lincoln had "died at the right time." Beyond the usual bluster, that he had been worth a million, for instance, Rice was in melancholic retreat from the powerful public figure he had been. Dan said, "A circus-clown is not a very elevated character in the eyes of the world, but with all his failings a circus-clown has a heart, and doesn't the Bible say, 'Judge not that ye be not judged.'" According to the reporter, Rice had no friends, scarce food, and few clothes. "Whisky and time are fast doing their work for old Dan. The light of his life is fast going out, the silver cord is being loosed, the golden bowl is being broken." Now he sunk in "pools of doubt and despair." After all Rice had been through, the reporter suggested that he ask, "Is life worth the living?"[16]

Rice stirred himself again, signing in March 1882 for a cross-country jaunt on John Robinson's 10 Big Shows. Rice was variously called lecturer, ringmaster, and master of ceremonies, but he would do little more than appear in the ring. His salary, advertised as equal to the president's, was $30 a week, as much as a bearded lady made. The show put out *Dan Rice's Old Time Circus Songster,* but like an 1873 Rice songster, it had no songs he wrote, old or new. As preparations proceeded in Cincinnati, bad news floated upriver. Rice's protégée, Lizzie Marcellus, died with her children and husband, Rice's former partner, William Stowe, in a horrific steamboat fire near Memphis. Dan felt the loss of Lizzie particularly deeply, expressing concern that both deflected and reflected his pain.

"Oh, my God! what will be the feelings of that poor mother when she hears of her daughter's death?"[17]

Go west, old man. Rice now rode with Robinson's show to San Francisco on the Union Pacific and Central Pacific railroads. The golden age of American railroad met the golden age of the large circus in complaints that Robinson had three rings—two side-by-side and a track around them—rather than the old single ring where attention could be paid to one act. There was another complaint that became proverbial. To "give 'em a John Robinson" meant to speed through the show, as he regularly did. The circus train outraced a prairie fire in Nebraska, and the show performed for prisoners in the Wyoming Territory. Rice would say that he dined with Brigham Young in Salt Lake City and spoke in the Tabernacle, but the local press reported nothing like that and treated him with indifference. A grander tale told of San Francisco's tumultuous welcome and a romantic reunion with the widow of the wealthy Californian, Mark Hopkins, but again there was nothing to it. The *San Francisco Chronicle* failed to mention him and the *Daily Alta Californian* offered faint praise: "The old circus man and veteran amusement caterer, Dan Rice, also appeared and made a short address to the audience, which was well received." He could have been the after-dinner speaker at a church social.[18]

The show returned to Cincinnati on the Atchison, Topeka, and Santa Fe, and Rice cast about for paying work again. He could ponder the declaration in the *Cincinnati Commercial Gazette* that the talking clown's time was past, "the silent clown now usurping his place." It was no accident of chronology that Rice's decline was simultaneous with the rise of another "funniest man" in America, George L. Fox, a stage pantomime clown who used the circus clown's traditional white face and skull cap. Though Rice certainly enjoyed the assessment that he was, as a talking clown, "undoubtedly the greatest that ever lived," the article then pictured him as an instinctive but ignorant buffoon, paraded through the streets in a coach "with a handsomely bound copy of the great William's works open before him, when, had his life depended upon it, he could not have spelled out a single word of the text." The clown who had delighted Cincinnati with clever word play had retrospectively become a foolish illiterate.[19]

Making his way to New York, Rice gave a temperance lecture, recommending the "jimjams"—delirium tremens—as a way to persuade men not to drink. The *New York Times* teased that Rice's stories all used hackneyed formulas, concluding with virtue rewarded and vice punished. Rice next signed up with A. M. Nathans's circus, billed as the Great One-Ring Show to distinguish it from larger affairs. Nathans put Rice's face in profile on the cover of the show's courier, his nose prominent. The gray flecking the old showman's hair and streaking his long goatee helped Nathans's nostalgia pitch. "Those who saw him in their youth can now see him again in their declining days." The *Clipper,* which had been running front-page pictures of members of the profession for years, finally got around to Rice. A few issues later, picturing "The Clown's Dream," the paper did not name Rice but suggested him by referring to "the almost forgotten trick mules, Pete and Barney," and to the smile of the sleeping clown dreaming of the "greatest show on earth."[20]

Rice's daughter, Catherine, joined him on tour. (Libby was off in Russia with Charley Reed and their brood, which grew to sixteen children.) Catherine's husband, Wurzbach, had died recently, and an old awkwardness revived. Julia, the daughter of his first wife suddenly appeared in Girard and claimed his body. Catherine may have joined her father because she had lost her home: The "Wurzbach Place" was later sold in the name of the children of Julia Wurzbach Caulkin.[21]

On June 8, Rice left Nathans's and returned to Erie. The immediate suspicion was that he had been drinking again. Another reason may have been his anger after A. M. Nathans's brother, J. J., along with Spalding's estate, foreclosed on Rice's home. His return to the show in September, however, suggested a more traditional answer: He had not been getting paid. He may have returned to improve his standing to sue. Immediately after his arrival in Garnett, Kansas, the show folded. He wrote to Foster that he had "opened the Dance," suing to attach horses for $1,600 in back pay. While other performers waiting on their claims got up an *Uncle Tom's Cabin* or went to work on farms or as domestics, Rice tried to lecture. After exchanging letters with Mit, "My Dear warm hearted friend," and following a poorly attended lecture, Rice left Kansas, his claims undecided.[22]

PART 7

OLD UNCLE DAN

1884 ☛ 1900

37

MORE FUN THAN YOU CAN COUNT

Well, I guess I am about the livest dead man you ever saw; although I was once asked to accept a coffin. I had partially broken down from exhaustive labors in the ring and taken a short season of rest, after which I rejoined the show. I was approached by a long, lank funeral-visaged individual, who tried very hard to look pleasant, and warmly shook my hand. "You don't know me," said he, "but I'll never forget you, Dan. You gave me a pony when I was a boy. I'm in the undertaking business and rich now, Dan, and I want to do something for you. You are always traveling, and like as not, you'll get away down in Arkansas, Texas, or some other benighted place and die. Here's my card, and if you will hand it to a friend at your bedside and have him telegraph me, I'll send you a first class coffin to remember me by."[1]

In 1884, Rice embarked on a lecture tour, sporadic at first, booking talks for $50 when he could get them. Starting in Florida, Georgia, and Alabama, he hit his stride in Texas in 1885 and 1886. It is not difficult to envision Rice's goatee waggling its usual punctuation as he presented his talks in halls, theaters, and opera houses, nor to see him more casually, a sombrero perched over his rosy face as he chatted with a reporter from the stuffed chair of another Lone Star hotel lobby.[2]

"After a century's reign, the circus is dethroned."[3]

First, not giving up on his old business entirely, Rice ventured a ten-cent circus in New Orleans' French Quarter. There, he picked up a few dollars endorsing Buffalo Bill Cody's Wild West. Like "spectacle," the word "show" had fallen to a synonym for tawdry ostentation, so Cody spurned it, insisting that his was no Wild West *Show,* but simply a "Wild West." Rice capitalized on that prejudice in his lectures, vowing that he would never again lend his name to shows. "The association is so disreputable, with here and there an exception, that no man with self respect or who places any value upon public opinion, can identify himself with such infamously conducted conglomerations." That was a jab at the major showmen of the day, like Forepaugh, Barnum, and Bailey. It did not refer to the Ringling boys, who were just starting their career, having sought out the retired showman, Fayette Lodawick "Yankee" Robinson, for the prestige of his name, the way Coup and Castello had turned to Barnum. The way someone might have approached Rice. "Yankee Robinson's Great Show and Ringling Brothers Carnival of Comedy" in 1884 echoed Rice's Great Show. [4]

In between, Rice rested in Florida with his cousin, W. C. Crum. Circus folks had discovered the state as a place to winter, and Crum lived in Tampa now. As obstreperous as Dan, W. C. had moved there after an arrest for assault at his newspaper in Rochester. While visiting, Dan wrote to Mit again, employing the florid style then in fashion.[5]

> My Highly Esteemed friend,
>
> It is with infinite pleasure I Sit down this beautifull morning under the Shade of orange trees, to write a few lines to one of my Boyhood friends. The balmy breeze of South Florida and the magestic pines, and tropical Yew together with the influences of a Christian home wherein dwell those I love, Make all So Lovable in nature, that I can not for a Moment permit any one to creep into my pleasure freighted Mind, only those that are fit, both by instinct and Education to be companions of my thoughts. . . . Well, Old Boy, I must close. Let me have a few lines.[6]

Rice's usage—though not his handwriting—had vastly improved since he "rotre" to Mit in 1843. It is said about some performers that they read their own publicity, meaning they believe what their press agents write about them; Rice had read his agent's ornate words, and learned.

> I vary my labors with occasional strolls beneath the umbrageous shade of the park, where I spend much time in silent meditation over the grassy hillocks of the distinguished dead. Strange employment for a professional jester? True. 'Tis strange, 'tis passing strange; yet stranger things may overcome us like a summer cloud without our special wonder.

Rice started his lecture tour in a pious vein, speaking in churches, and giving benefits to erect new ones. Discussing recent revisions of the Bible, Rice defended the King James version, saying, as he had of the alleged song he heard during his alleged conversion, that "it was good enough for his mother." People testified to the accuracy of the details of his (fictive) trip to the Holy Land, and he told of ministers sobbing at the "Clown's Prayer Over a Dying Man." Since many considered him fit for the pulpit, it was not odd that he was invited to address Waco University students in chapel, or that Sam Houston's former pastor and now that university's president, Dr. Rufus Burleson led a contingent the next day to Rice's lecture at the Garland Opera House.[7]

> Among the many beautiful thoughts suggested by the surroundings, reflecting the struggles and triumph of life and the inevitable end of all, I am consoled by this gem of Tom Moore's, who wrote "Lalla Rookh":
>
> "Let fate do her worst, there are moments of joy,
> Bright dreams of the past that she cannot destroy—
> You may break, you may shatter the rose if you will,
> But the scent of the roses will hang 'round still."[8]

Rice retained the old spontaneity, founded on his phenomenal memory of items he had read, things he had seen, people he had known. The culture that had prized oral expression was fading but his words kept spinning, his beard wagging. Observers' attempts to capture his kaleidoscopic range themselves became a kaleidoscope of word pictures. He dropped "from the sublime to the ridiculous, and [flew] from the senti-

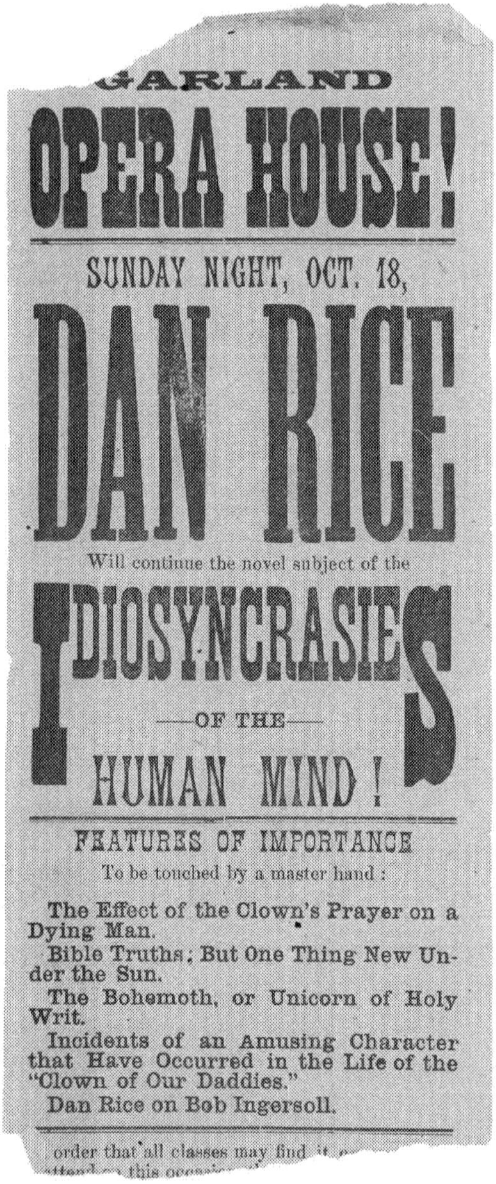
GARLAND

OPERA HOUSE!

SUNDAY NIGHT, OCT. 18,

DAN RICE

Will continue the novel subject of the

IDIOSYNCRASIES

—OF THE—

HUMAN MIND!

FEATURES OF IMPORTANCE

To be touched by a master hand:

The Effect of the Clown's Prayer on a Dying Man.

Bible Truths; But One Thing New Under the Sun.

The Behemoth, or Unicorn of Holy Writ.

Incidents of an Amusing Character that Have Occurred in the Life of the "Clown of Our Daddies."

Dan Rice on Bob Ingersoll.

order that all classes may find it

Rice pulled himself out of the bottle and began anew as a lecturer.

mental and pathetic to the humorous with a grace and ease of method that were absolutely remarkable." With spell-binding eloquence, "he would improvise beautiful rhythms and interpolate the rarest gems from English literature, showing a wonderful familiarity with contemporary writings." Sometimes topics spun too fast: "His changes from the sublime to the ridiculous are so quick that it is difficult to follow the thought of the speaker." Nevertheless, Rice "seems to be a walking, living encyclopedia" keeping the audience "in a brown study, then in a giggle, and then in a roar of laughter." He gave off the "sparkle of mental champagne."[9]

> I did get very religious thoughts in the Holy Land, but lost my religion while riding in a gondola with a beautiful dulcina on the Bay of Naples. Temperance lecturing? No, I've quit drinking altogether.[10]

True believers like their preaching straight, with no comic chaser, but the old trouper gradually returned to his old irreverence. The laughter of crowds again washing over him helped revive his spirits but there may have been more to it. Newspapers dropped hints that his periodic illnesses may have been caused by drink. He told a reporter that he did not suffer from the dengue fever of southern climes, "but he only winks when you ask him to tell you just what it is." Reference to Rice "in Stude's coffee parlor, or some place near there" suggest a bar, and a Texarkana paper applied to Rice what the whole country knew as the catchphrase of that lovable fictional drunk, Rip Van Winkle: "May he live long and prosper." Retaining his skill at ingratiating himself with his listeners, Rice even extolled the virtues of Lone Star Beer.[11]

> Texas? Grand, sir, grand. Finest country I ever saw. Why, if some of these old croakers who think Texas a wild, uncivilized country could take at peep at it to-day they would be actually paralyzed with astonishment. I have always enjoyed myself everywhere, but I think the most fun I ever had in a short time was in Texas. Several years ago a friend of mine got into trouble with his circus in southern Texas and telegraphed me to come on and help him out. I ran the show for six weeks and got him clear. I stood in with the cowboys and had more fun than you can count on your fingers.[12]

As in the old days, Rice's local "hits" formed a key part of his appeal. He told of friendship with prominent citizens, lavished praise on each town, and said that he might become a citizen of Texas.

> I tell you, young man, Galveston has a beach and surf that are unexcelled anywhere. I have seen Long Branch, Brighton, Saratoga, Newport

and all the famous watering-places—in natural advantages none compare with Galveston. I tell you I am proud to own the place.[13]

Claiming affinity with the locals is one thing; Rice claimed Galveston. The old report that he owned thousands of acres in Texas gave way to a specific claim to the island of Galveston and to land along the Rio Grande. Rice said his rights derived from old Spanish land grants, by way of Daniel McLaren of New York City, without mentioning that McLaren was his father. It is difficult to assess the validity of Rice's claims. Neither the state's General Land Office nor individual counties have records of Rice. On the other hand, the specificity of his claims and his use of former governor Oran Milo Robert as his lawyer suggest that it was not totally fiction. Rice may have retained Roberts in a bow to politics, a subject that still grabbed the showman's interest.[14]

I was nominated myself in 1865 by the soldiers and people to represent in Congress the Nineteenth District of Pennsylvania. In my letter of withdrawal to my numerous friends, after thanking them for the honor conferred upon me, I stated my reasons, as follows. First, I felt myself totally inadequate to discharge the duties of so important a trust; and secondly, I had labored for years to establish a good reputation and did not want to lose it by going to Congress.

Even as he joked, Rice could not relinquish his opinions. When he told of declining the Democratic nomination for the presidency in 1868 after learning he would have to pay $100,000 for the prize, his audiences knowingly nodded about the corruption in the 1880s. His tales of prominent politicians similarly carried a taste of his old partisanship. Grover Cleveland, the first Democratic president since Buchanan, was a man of the people, for he "had blacked my boots, done it well and was not ashamed to acknowledge it." In contrast, while saying he knew Grant better than anyone else knew him, Rice reminded people of the corruption that flourished during that Republican presidency by calling the Union hero "one of the most unsuspecting men in the world." Rice's politics could move beyond veiled implications.[15]

On the occasion of Zachary Taylor's inspection, the roll was called, and all answered but Timothy Donahue. An orderly was dispatched to the

> camp, when Timothy was seen coming, staggering, with musket on shoulder, fell in and the Captain addressed him in very stern tones: "Timothy, you are drunk on duty. I had hoped on this occasion to have General Taylor make some recognition of your many gallant deeds, by shaking hands with you, but here you are drunk on duty." He answered "Hist, Captain, not another word. I have only to ask how do you expect all the virtues in a man for $13 a month."

Rice transformed the ethnic joke of a drunken Irishman into a political barb, with a moral: "You capitalists in every line, think of the remark of the Irishman when you are cutting laborers' wages and pinching the monarchs of muscle down to a pittance, scarcely half enough to support their wife and children." Rice's sentiments might be read as self-interest, a performer pandering to his audience, except that his genteel talks did not draw workingmen crowds. As hard times led to labor tension and strikes, he ignored the safety of silence to reproach those who reduced wages. He warned that armed conflict was probable if business did not stop its oppression, and Chicago's Haymarket Riot in May 1886 starkly confirmed his point. When Rice defended workers struggling "against the crushing and encroaching policy of the financial cormorants of Wall Street," he could have been a Socialist agitator on New York's Lower East Side.[16]

> Remember, don't get old, if years have crept up on you. I propose to remain in the harness until the last. I am organizing now in Cincinnati and preparing to start out upon the road again next season. These lectures that I deliver are a little sideplay. I can't abide idleness, and must be doing something. I would die if I could not find work. For over fifty years I have been in the ring and nobody has knocked me out yet. Yes, sir, I have traveled more miles than any other man living and endured vicissitudes that volumes alone could express. Shipwrecked twice, cast away on the coast of Morocco, both limbs fractured below the knees, ankle bones crushed, collar bone dislocated and with three ribs broken. You might say that I am slightly disfigured and then add truthfully that I am still in the ring.[17]

On January 23, 1886, Rebecca arrived in San Antonio to tend her ailing son, Dan Jr., at the Southern Hotel. Two weeks later, Dan, in town for lectures, took a room at the same hotel.[18]

> There is no justification for divorce, and every divorced man must ever afterwards, no matter what his condition, feel a gnawing at his heart strings; the breach in the domestic unity, once accomplished, cannot be restored, and I therefore urge vigorously that nothing should be permitted to estrange, even temporarily, the affections of husband and wife.[19]

Nothing records that Rice enjoyed the traditional conclusion of the temperance story, the reformed drunk's return to the loving embrace of family. He and Rebecca may have met, for he did begin to refer to his son in his talks, and to speak reverently about marriage on occasion. Yet even as he ladled out tributes to Woman as the "most perfect handiwork of God"—sentiments an Austin woman called "taffy"—Rice continued to

Though Dan finally had someone to carry on his name, Dan Rice, Jr. did not join circus but became an engineer.

make jokes. There was that gondola-borne "dulcina" tempting him from religion, and the "somewhat racy" story of finding himself shipwrecked on the Mississippi, being taken in by a woman, and trying to decide where it would be safe to sleep in case her husband returned that night. The hint of sexual tension was repeated when Rice confided to audiences that "his young second wife pronounced him after a few months of married life, the gayest old duck" around.[20]

> Woman, ah, woman. If she wants money, give it to her. If you haven't it, raise it anyway. Pursue this course and if it is not productive of good in one way, it will be in another, for she'll fret herself to death.Twice married and I still live.[21]

38

SNAKE OIL

Thrice married.

In 1887, Rice took another bride, Marcella C. Robinson, the lively "Cattle Queen of Lavaca County." Born in Tennessee in 1841, she grew up in Schulenburg, Texas, between San Antonio and Houston. At nineteen, she had married Robert Greathouse, a pioneer of Western cattle drives that would become part of Western lore. Starting a herd to Kansas in May 1867, he died on the trail, leaving Marcella and four children. Rich in cattle, she didn't have the cash to get his body home, so she had to petition the court to sell 150 head. A second husband, Dr. Camille DeGoffredo, pawned her jewelry with the promise to move them to New Orleans, but grabbed the money and went by himself, so Marcella got a divorce and her jewels back, too. In 1875, she took her next husband, James Robinson, but the bloom soon wore off the yellow rose. Robinson's family remembered Marcella as mean, but she looked at it differently. In 1885, soon before Robinson died, she was talking about "horrid men" and telling friends that she was on a mission to persuade women that they only needed confidence in themselves to live lives independent of men. She did her best to prove it, trying to elbow her way into the all-male Southern Live Stock Association.[1]

Once again, Rice had found a woman with spirit. She drove her carriage in a dash through San Antonio's streets, and, told that she had left a diamond at a dress fitting, she replied, "Dear me, I believe I did leave one of my rings. Never mind; I'll call for it." She was reputed to be wealthy,

In Texas, Rice found his third wife, Marcella Jones Greathouse DeGoffredo Robinson, the "Cattle Queen of Lavaca County."

though most of it was in cattle and land, including a reported 100 million acres in Mexico. She had a square face, like Maggie's, and wore her hair unfashionably but practically short, in tight curls close to her head. On his side, Dan had filled out from the wreck of a man he had been to a prosperous 190 pounds, ten pounds more than Marcella. His trademark goatee now flowed a white waterfall of hair off his chin. Sometime in 1886, the couple got engaged, perhaps in Schulenburg, her hometown, when he was there for a March lecture. It may have been in San Antonio. Between lectures in surrounding towns, he put up at the Southern Hotel, where Marcella also stayed. Charming his way around Marcella's suspicion of men, he was less successful with her family. Rumors floated for a year that "powerful influences" would prevent the marriage. Reports of a drunken Rice in a Cincinnati jail did not help his cause. More pertinent was the family's Catholicism. He converted for the wedding and her local status helped get the couple's earlier marriages annulled, but that would not have pleased her four grown children. Nevertheless, at her daughter's home in Hallettsville, as a future bishop of San Antonio presided, Marcella Jones Greathouse DeGoffredo Robinson and Daniel Rice McLaren celebrated Mass and were married on June 7, 1887.[2]

The *New York Times* account of the wedding called Rice a "veteran Cincinnati showman," and by July they were in the Queen City, before making their way to Erie, to stay with his daughter, Catherine. Dan and Marcella were on a tight budget. Either the Cattle Queen had little cash or she was suspicious; or perhaps Rice's pride kept him from asking for money. Though Marcella returned to Texas over the winter because of her arthritis, they remained a happy couple. Rice told a reporter that she was devoted to him, "a devotion he repays with unstinted liberality." She wrote to a friend the same a year later: "My husband is all the world to me and I to him." When Marcella returned, they went to New Jersey to stay with Libbie and Jake, who had opened a livery stable in the old Manahan family seat in 1885. In the generous tradition of Rice's family, the Showles kept open house for circuses that came through. A newspaper picture captured Dan as the image of retired gentry, walking along the Atlantic shore, toting a fashionable cane, and sporting a straw boater shaped like the porkpie hat Buster Keaton would wear.[3]

In mid-August, Dan, Marcella, and the Showles paid a visit to the Frank Robbins circus showing in Long Branch. A flurry of reports in 1886 had asserted that Rice would go out with Robbins or others, but nothing came of them. The closest it got was the day after Rice's visit, when he appeared in Robbins's ring and kept 5,000 spectators laughing for half an hour. It was his standard talk: He had been in every county on the globe; reports of his conversion were wrong because his was the religion of humanity; he had made $1,000 a week for nine years, and had to borrow money to get home. As for what he did with all that money, in Texas he had boasted of giving $400,000 to charity, but now he simply said, "I had lots of fun." He bragged of his bright, handsome wife, who was helping him prepare a book, *The Clown's Wisdom.* Rice also gave his opinion on the state of clowning: Once philosophers, clowns had fallen to be only a vulgar punsters, catering to "the vitiated appetites of the uncultured minds of the masses."[4]

Not surprisingly for a talker like Rice, he made a few contributions to the language. Of course, he spread, if he did not coin, "one-horse," now in general circulation. When Longfellow saw Whitman in New Jersey, he called it "a sort of one-horse visit." A Chicago paper told of a circus manager who paid a college professor to create a classical name, only to discover that "monohippicaggregation" meant a one-horse show. Slang is rarely attributable to one person, but Rice was one exception. To squelch those who dismissed him as a has-been, Rice reminded people that he was no "never-was." As he kept hustling for work, he played the same verb another way, telling of when he was looking for a double-somersault performer:

> One man said he "used to" do the act, but was out of practice. Another said he believed would soon "get there." And so on. When they all made their excuses, claims and promises, old Dan, with deep disgust, said, "Twenty-five 'used to be's' and twenty-five 'going to be,' and not a thunderin' 'is-er' in the lot. I want an 'is-er.'"[5]

Dan would be an is-er. First he tried his hand at selling snake oil. "Merry-Andrew," an early synonym for clown, may have derived from a medieval quack who sold his nostrums by haranguing the population; now it was Rice's turn. In lectures at the Long Branch Opera House and at Robbins's show, he pitched Jo He, the Texas Panacea. He was the product's agent for "suffering humanity" in New York and New Jersey. ("Jo He" probably came from a name invoked in the publicity, "Johephus of the Hebrews"—Josephus, famous Jewish general and historian.) Rice published letters of endorsement that, taken orally or applied to the skin, Jo-He cured dropsy, neuralgia, heart trouble, kidney trouble, and blindness. In another venture, he set up as a dealer in southwestern lands. There was a rumor that he planned to trade Lone Star land for a hotel in Long Branch, but no record has been found of a sale or swap. Rice considered returning to gambling, certain that Marcella had changed his luck, but she would not allow it. That was what the *Troy Budget* reported in an account of bravado in the old days, that he bet half his circus against a Mississippi steamboat, lost, then bet the other half, and lost all. Now he bragged that Marcella was one of the finest women who ever lived, and the first who could control him. "She told me I must not drink or play cards and I have not done so."[6]

Rice also turned his hand to writing. Another old circus man would speak glowingly of newspaper critics, "whose voice proclaims success or defeat in tones of thunder. The makers of history. The moulders of public opinion and the architects of reputation." That voice had been Rice's, complete with tones of thunder, but as eagerness for oral expression would continue to wane, public discussion increasingly shifted to print. Rice complained that the clown's "gradual decadence" had been caused by the "encroachments on the field of fun by the newspaper paragrapher." Nor was he alone in that judgment. The *Nation* in 1882 speculated that much of the talent once found in circus clowns now went into journalism.[7]

One "encroaching" writer Rice mentioned in particular was Mark Twain. More than any circus performer, Twain was Rice's successor. Twain was reported to have said that his ambition had been to be a circus clown, and the goateed clown complained that the mustached writer stole his jokes. Of course Twain was a comic performer, too. In 1866 the *Clipper,* after mocking Rice's "sacred lecturing tour," applauded Twain's lectures in California. Three years later, Twain toured with Josh Billings (Henry W. Shaw) and Petroleum V. Nasby (D. R. Locke) under the collective title,

"The American Humorists," an echo of Rice's Great American Humorist. But these latter-day American Humorists were primarily writers, their talks a way to grab extra dollars from their literary fame. When Billings lectured in Erie, the *Dispatch* judged that he wrote better than he spoke. Nevertheless, an increasingly literate culture decided that Twain, refining his approach to suit the privacy of individual readers, was funnier than Rice, or in a variation on the theme, that earlier audiences had been unsophisticated. But Rice's humor was meant for a large, rowdy crowd. As Rice pointed out, a newspaper audience could not catch the subtle wit conveyed by "an inflection or modulation of the voice." To read Rice's words, without his inflections or facial expressions, and absent the embrace of a turbulent crowd, is like trying to understand the power of a great singer's voice by reading lyrics.[8]

Rice bent to the times and became a writer himself. He got some of his pieces in *Texas Siftings,* one of the nation's most popular weeklies. The *Siftings* articles were unsigned, but it seems likely that Rice wrote those he saved in his scrapbook, "The Clown Who Tried to Play Richard," "What Prevented Dan Rice From Being Carried Off By Yellow Fever," and the (auto) biography in "Siftings' Portrait Gallery." There was also a piece about New York's Everett Hotel, a haunt of newspapermen, where Rice was staying; he may have written it in exchange for a room. Rice also contributed a romance in serial form and a weekly potpourri of the "Clown's Wisdom" to the *Long Branch News,* and an animal story to the *Los Angeles Times.* He joined the Arctic explorer, Robert E. Peary, and others, in relating *Fifty-two Stories of Animal Life and Adventure.* Rice's contribution, "Fifty Years With A Menagerie," profiled "Patsy, the Peerless Pig," and revealed Dan's exploits training a cat orchestra, caging an escaped tiger, and surviving an elephant stampede. When monkeys were dying on his show, he related that rivals said the animals killed themselves because they were disgusted by Darwin's theory that man had descended from them. For his "scintillating apothegms," Rice collected odds and ends of clippings. In addition to a satirical poem on blue blood from the *Harvard Lampoon,* his scrapbooks included tidbits about roses, the origin of trump in cards, woman's suffrage, Bismarck as a swordsman, goat-based taxes in Kurdistan, and a woman steamboat captain.[9]

As the 1880s closed, Rice carryied his years "stanchly" as one of the picturesque features of Long Branch. It was at the height of its fashion as a resort, a summer home of presidents since Grant. Unfortunately, Marcella could barely get out of their room. She wrote to her friends in Texas that the "plaguey demon" of rheumatism had kept her confined for eight months. She also confided that "it is *'change of life'* affecting me." She wrote that Dan, "one of the best men living," soothed her with his love and devotion. They planned a visit to Texas, waiting only for Dan to clear up his current business; Marcella did not realize how often he had waited for business to clear up. Inviting her friends to visit, she was still concerned about their opinions. "You must get acquainted with my husband. I am anxious that you should know each other. You will be bound to love him." In October, when the Rices failed to pay their board bill, the landlord seized their trunks. Again, her reluctance, his pride, or her poverty behind the million-dollar stories prevented her from paying.[10]

Marcella then mostly disappeared from Rice's life. One story sent her to Europe by herself. Another depicted her sons paying Dan $6,000 a year to clear out, warning they would shoot him on sight if he returned. (Rice would have been thrilled with $60 a year.) To her last days in San Antonio in 1908, however, Marcella called herself Mrs. Dan Rice.[11]

Back in New York, Rice worked to keep his hand in. He appeared at a testimonial at the Union Square Theatre, and got a benefit there in return on May 11, 1890. That fall, he traveled to Yonkers to give a talk for the Young Men's Catholic Association, the program ending with the century's song, "Home, Sweet Home." In between those performances, April brought sad news from Europe. Libby, Dan and Maggie's first-born, died of consumption on the road from Warsaw. His reaction is not recorded.[12]

Rice continued political. As 1891 began, the Democratic Party of New York City invited him to attend the opening of its new clubhouse on Fifth Avenue. He saved clippings such as "Why I am not a Republican" (denouncing "consolidating" Federalism) and he declared that he had bet $250,000, the value of Tennessee property he said he owned, on the 1884 election of the Democrat Cleveland. There was even a political message in Rice's yarn of being held up on an Iowa train by the Jesse James gang in 1873: The outlaw chief recognized Rice and let him go, for "We never Robed a Southern Man in our lives if we new it."[13]

Dan's elder daughter married a Rice apprentice and became a star as Libbie Rice Reed, while his younger daughter Kate left circus.

In 1890, the *Clipper* teased Rice about his periodic announcements of his returning to the ring. "We all know that you 'can't quit,' that you never grow old, that you rocked the cradle of the show business, and that you will always be 'Old Dan Rice.'" In 1891, however, the rumors came true.[14]

It was "Dan Rice's Big One-Ring Show!" The roster was undistinguished and small. Barnum & Bailey, the "Greatest Show on Earth," capitalized at $3,500,000, had as many clowns as Rice had performers, twenty. But stroking his white goatee and puffing on a wooden pipe at Everett's, smoke rising above his balding head, Rice knew just what to say. Like every proprietor of a one-ring circus since the rise of three-ring shows, he made a virtue of smallness. "I think the public is getting tired of variety shows under a tent, gilded gee gaws and spangles, and a lot of ballet dancers." A four-page courier featured endorsements, Rice's profile, goatee and large nose prominent, and a flurry of publicity. The *Times* carried a major piece, the *Herald* and *Sun* noticed the show, the *National Police Gazette* ran an illustrated story, and the *Clipper* printed items about it. Rice promised the "Circus of the Future," unlike the contemporary one, where "mediocrity reigns." Like an actor of the future plugging a new movie, Rice gave a talk at Knickerbocker Hall and appeared at benefits. He must have relished clipping the quotation from his old nemesis, the *Tribune:* "As there never was but one Shakespeare, so there never will be but one Dan Rice."[15]

The show opened mid-May in Jersey City amid plans to take it into New England, where the "people are really well educated," said Rice, and then to California and Australia. But Rice caught a severe cold and collapsed in the ring. He returned. Then a storm knocked over the tent. Rice's comeback was over. He accurately predicted that "a base imitation" would someday be foisted on the public.[16] But after half a century, Dan Rice would be part of no more Dan Rice shows.

39

HONEST ABE'S UNCLE SAM

The American circus was a hundred years old and Dan Rice, who had lived through most of it, was seventy when he returned to Long Branch. Throughout his life the once homeless, virtually orphaned boy had pulled wives, children, siblings, cousins, apprentices and associates around him, and the extended family he created had sustained him. Now family took him in, cousin Delia Crum Brown and her husband John opening their Norwood Avenue home to him around 1893. He had been hanging around New York, living on 21st Street and giving the occasional speech, which "he seemed ever willing to do." But the collective memory of his glory, especially in showmen who knew best what he had been, was passing. Noyes and North died in 1885, Robinson in 1888, Forepaugh in 1890, Barnum and Nathans in 1891, Thayer and Wallett in 1892. In 1894, Rice reunited with fellow old-timers—including Barnum's old partner, Dan Castello—for a one-day stand at Newark's Grand Opera House. Mostly though, he stayed in Long Branch, where family occupied his thoughts. He wrote to his sister Libbie in 1894, greeting her with the thought that "all in this life are liable to meet death," and urging her, in case "sad fate befallen me," to use half the proceeds from his yet-unwritten biography to care for their "Beloved" Kate. If Libbie died, he continued in his morose mood, the duty fell on Jacob, "whom I love and honor." A few years later, Dan asked about the other Kate, his daughter, in a letter to her son, Bert Wurzbach, an Erie newspaperman. He cared about his grandson too, who was flirting with the notion of joining the Klondike gold rush; "your old G. Poh" advised him to avoid gold fever, that "'swindling Jade' 'Giddy fortune.'" Rice also asked Bert if he could recommend an Erie lawyer, for a matter to be kept "Sub Rosa until the time comes to move on the Chess board of Events." Rice still thought of himself as a player, though he had few pieces left for the game.[1]

Once a buster, a man of strength and presence, he had become an old man, his robust goatee now a scraggle of hair. One photograph shows him huddled in a coat that once fit, sitting in a one-horse buggy. The picture meant to convey that he still held the reins, but it's a bleak image, the horse, buggy and old man starkly alone in an empty Long Branch field on an overcast day. Rice now fit the slang of his youth, a man so thin he had to lean against a sapling to cuss. Still, he had his voice. The family remembered it booming through the neighborhood when he went out to feed the chickens, his frail body incongruously spouting songs, curses, demands. "Anyone in the sound of my voice, get me a drink!"[2]

On November 1, 1895, Rebecca died in Girard after a run of poor health. Dan did not attend the funeral. Whatever he felt, he had been less successful family-building there. The statues on his estate were scattered, a handful eventually placed around the borough hall. The monument that he had bought and neighbors fought was mostly ignored. The town he had put on the map wanted nothing to do with him.[3]

Dan did follow the career of one son of Girard, Dan Jr. The father clipped notices about his son at RPI, Rensselaer Polytechnic Institute, in Troy, New York, where Rebecca lived while the boy was in school, and about Dan Jr.'s career as a civil engineer, appointed Girard's county surveyor. Nor did Dan Sr. keep his distance. In that 1894 letter to sister Kate, he mentioned that he was heading into New York to see Dan Jr. Still, in his will, father ignored the son and referred to daughter Kate as "my sole and only legitimate heir." (Dan Jr. later took his wife and children to North Dakota, then drifted west, working in Spokane through the 1920s and falling victim to drink or the Depression in San Francisco. Ultimately Girard had no more use for the son than the father. Informed of Dan Jr.'s death in 1936, relatives wired the coroner that "it is immaterial to us what disposition is made of the body," and he was buried in a potter's field thousands of miles from home.)[4]

A poignant attempt to show the great performer figuratively still holding the reins.

Some later tried to boost themselves into family. In 1901 Nancy Rice McLaren of Indianapolis fantasized that she had been married to Dan, and Cincinnati history records bargeman Bill Rice, an alleged brother. Alexander Graham Bell got in on the act when he wrote to Professor Samuel Langley of the Smithsonian about Almenia Rice, supposedly Dan's wife. In 1911, an Ella Rice decided that she was Dan's daughter, born on his circus in England and with him when he died in 1888 in Horseheads, New York, while building an airship to fly the Atlantic.[5]

Just as Rice forged family out of disparate people, binding them together in abiding love and respect, he similarly forged a career. One of the mysteries of performance is that, in a sense, it does not exist. A singer can warble standards, a juggler can manipulate seven objects, a comedian can prattle but none of those quantifiable things are exactly *performance,* or every soprano who hits high notes would be a diva. Performance creates a reality that transcends its elements, just as the magician defies the reality that there is no such thing as magic, by creating the illusion, beyond particular tricks, that magic is being done. Dan accomplished that alchemy with his career, building on a scattered variety of attributes and talents—his strength and his mighty voice, his singing, humor and oratory, his facility with animals and his ability to sense an audience's inclinations—to *create* a persona and performance that had never before been seen, billowing on the wind of his stories.

It is ironic that many stories continuing to define Dan Rice emerged from the conflict that began his downfall, the Civil War. That defining could be dictionary literal: "U.S. circus clown, circus owner, and Union patriot." Though he did support Union, that third element of the definition perpetuates the larger fiction Rice peddled, that he was a Northern partisan, even an abolitionist who could never bring his "muse to sing of the sweet and sunny side of secession."[6]

Rice had long spun three patriotic fictions in particular: that he defied secessionist hotheads in New Orleans; that Taylor had named him "Colonel"; and, one of "the most important incidents in his career," that he had reprimanded Southern medical students. A decade and a half after the war ended, as clear memories of it faded into a national romance, he added a fourth: Rice began to proclaim that he had been great friends with Abraham Lincoln. The fable grew to become the most important of all the stories, more prominent than any facts of Rice's life. (For greater plausibility, Rice postdated the connection, adding Lincoln to a half-century old story from *Sketches*, of a backwoods horse race in Illinois, where charlatans tried to get him drunk so they could cheat him. Now Abe entered the story as the race's honest judge.)[7]

This new fiction joined the two humorists as comrades during the war, Dan buoying Abe's spirits with his humor, usually with some stuffy character as contrast to the homespun pair. In one variation, set in Rice's dressing tent, Lincoln perches on a trunk, his long legs stretched out in the small space, while Mary Lincoln tries to maintain her dignity in the background. In another, Abe has sent a carriage to bring Dan to the White House, to get his friend's sense of the country's mood. They were trading jokes when Judge Throckmorton came calling. "Well, Dan," Rice said Lincoln said, "he's a big bug from Massachusetts, and it won't do to deny him now that he's sent in his name. But you stay, and I'll soon get rid of him." After enduring the judge's complaints about the conduct of the war—conduct supported by Rice, the story implied—the president interrupted and introduced the clown, which propelled Throckmorton to a sputtering, indignant retreat. The *St. Louis Republican* made the 1879 purpose of the story clear. "This anecdote—the authenticity of which is unimpeachable—ought to put Dan Rice's loyalty far beyond all suspicion, and he can afford to defy Republican malice now and forthwith." Of course, the authenticity *was* impeachable. No stories appeared until fourteen years after the assassination, and it took Rice two more decades to add Lincoln to the horse race tale. Ignored in all were Rice's repeated attacks on Lincoln and his "Black Republican" policies.[8]

However, the fact that Abe and Dan were not friends does not dispose of the case. Rice's 1901 biographer reprinted a letter allegedly written by Simon Cameron, Lincoln's first secretary of war, in response to Rice's invitation to the monument ceremony.

> Well I do remember accompanying you to see Mr. Lincoln when you took him the draft on the United States Treasury over from General Fremont for $32,000 in payment of steamboat "James Raymond" which he forced into service at St. Louis, and how grateful he and Mr. Seward and Mr. Stanton were when you asked them to distribute it to the widows and orphans of the soldiers. Again regretting that I will not be able to be present on the first of November, I am, my dear sir, very truly yours, Simon Cameron

Again, authenticity is impeachable. No original has been found, the size of the donation was remarkable for anyone, much less cash-strapped Rice, and he does not appear in the day-by-day record of Lincoln's life. Yet much argues for the letter's reliability. The military had in fact taken over Rice's steamboat during the war, and the generous showman was not only fond of the grand gesture, he badly needed to prove himself a Union patriot. Cameron, the major figure in Pennsylvania politics, would have been invited to the ceremony and written his regrets. And despite an impulse to glorify Rice, the 1901 biographer was scrupulous in her use of documents. Since it would have been no surprise that the two political funnymen met, the Lincoln fictions, like many another Rice story, may be built on an actual event.[9]

Nevertheless, the Lincoln stories remain predominantly false. Why were they so readily accepted?

Beyond plausibility, the Rice-Lincoln fiction took hold because it fit other fictions the country was embracing in the aftermath of the Civil War. Obscured were the war's fierce anger and the harsh policy differences, the summer patriots who had avoided service by paying a bounty and the profiteers who had gotten rich off their fellow citizens' misery. In the new idyllic view, both sides had been equally gallant in fighting for equally noble causes, the North to free the slaves, the South to protect values. Few now remembered that they had shouted for Lincoln's death or Lee's as a traitor. Slavery was now generally conceded to be a wrong but most whites, relieved that there had been no revolution of equality, comfortably accepted a system of second-class citizenship for blacks—"Jump Jim Crow" dancing and singing transformed into Jim Crow laws. In this communal amnesia, Lincoln, the most reviled president in American history, became retrospectively beloved in the North and respected in the South. Compared to that whopper, Rice's fictions were small potatoes and few on the hill. So the *St. Louis Republican* could sneer that a rural editor was making up stories of Rice as a Democrat, for the clown's politics were "of very little consequence to himself or anybody else." (A twentieth-century source went further, telling of Rice's campaign for the *Republican* nomination for president.)[10]

The culminating element in Rice's patriotic elevation, albeit a claim he did not make himself, was that he had been the model for Uncle Sam.

Uncle Sam had been decades in the making. First came Brother Jonathan, a rural, populist figure. Reinforcing that countrified image was the stage Yankee, originally seen in the first American comedy, *The Contrast,* in 1787. A quarter century later, "Uncle Sam" appeared, described in the *Troy Post* of September 7, 1813 as a "cant name" for the government. Jonathan and Sam coexisted for a while as representatives of the people and government respectively. In fact, the first image of Uncle Sam was joined in an 1836 picture with his rustic cousin, Brother Jonathan, and *Bartlett's Dictionary of Americanisms* in 1849 included Brother Jonathan in the definition of Uncle Sam. A Currier & Ives print in 1856, on the split in the Democratic Party over slavery, could have been showing either Sam or Jonathan in top hat and striped pants. So it continued until Uncle Sam grew his chin whiskers, like Rice's distinctive goatee, with no mustache. Thomas Nast created the culminating image in 1869, notably in "Uncle Sam's Thanksgiving Dinner" in *Harper's Weekly*.[11] Nast, probably the foremost promulgator of the image as it is now known, was an ardent Republican who would emphatically not have chosen the ardent Democrat Rice as his model. Nor, again, did Rice himself claim to be Uncle Sam.

And yet, Dan Rice is the closest thing America has had to an embodiment of Uncle Sam. He traveled nearly all the country, and the country knew him as well as it knew anyone else. His signature goatee and top hat made him an instantly recognizable symbol. If brand-name recognition had been a common concept at the time, Rice would have been Coca-Cola. He combined the current events and comic flair of a political cartoon. He also combined in himself the country's conflicted sense of itself as simultaneously populist and elevated, a conflict symbolized by Uncle Sam, a democratic icon in formal clothes. Mythic truth aside, Rice looked the part, or rather the part looked like him. Top-hatted, goateed Uncle Sam could be a caricature of Rice, including those formal clothes. Rice himself had adopted a visually patriotic image. His *Pictorial* of 1858 pictured him in striped pants and a starred top, and his 1860 songster put him in another flag suit. (That songster also included the lyrics to Rice's song, "Uncle Sam," to the tune of "Brother Jonathan.")[12] If America had an actual Uncle Sam, it was Dan Rice.

Rice's stories multiplied into the 1890s as he tried pulling together his memoirs into a biography, dragging trunks of heralds, handbills, and scrapbooks from place to place.

> Lord, child, there never was a man had such a life as I. I have worked in a glue factory, been a clown, a preacher, a temperance lecturer, a hard

> drinker, had the jimjams, been left for dead time and again, fought man and beast, beat 'em both, been rich and poor, up and down, married and single, and I'm good for it all over again.

He saved obituaries and solicited accounts from former colleagues. (One bragged in an interview that he sent sixty pages to Rice and had a more interesting life; Dan kept the interview but dumped the pages.) Never shy about controversy, Rice even clipped press attacks. He pasted in his own published compositions, including a poem which he said expressed his life's philosophy:

> For heaven's sake, a quiet life,
> A constant friend, a loving wife;
> A good repute, a fund in store,
> O what can man desire more?

Friends were dead, he had lost three wives, and he had no fund in store, but the poem put Rice once more in step with his times, awash in honeyed sentimentality. That sentimentality was especially true about circus. Clowns were being called "joeys," ostensibly a traditional name for clowns based on one of the early great ones, Joseph Grimaldi, but the sweet diminutive appeared generations after Grimaldi's death, probably as some writer's mawkish invention. Similarly, circus completed its alteration from the boisterous affair it had been in Rice's day to a field of nostalgia, like Christmas, which itself had been transformed from a day of public rowdiness into a nostalgic event focused on children—and consumers. Meanwhile, like the newly benevolent figure of Santa, Rice became Old Uncle Dan, the children's favorite. That historical process was applied to other public men, like Barnum and Rockefeller. It was no coincidence that years later, a writer concocted a yarn that Rice played Santa Claus when he was stranded in Kansas. (Like Uncle Sam, the roly-poly Santa Claus image came significantly from the pen of Nast.) Rice's poem of the quiet life concluded with a word picture of modern technology combined with sentiment, a child at night calling an operator on the phone: "And softly as we listened, came stealing down the stairs; / H'lo, Central! Give me heaven; I want to say my prayers." Rice's rowdy audiences in 1850 would have howled in derision; his readers half a century later sighed. Adopting sentimentality, Rice propelled his own diminishment, reinforcing the new idea that one clown was any clown, and all clowns were necessarily for kiddies.[13]

Rice floundered in his attempt to write the story of his life. As an interviewer pointed out, the showman did "not hold onto a subject with a bull-dog tenacity." In 1891, the *New York Herald* announced the imminent publication of Rice's recollections, "and if he writes as well as he talks his book will be a veritable library of wit and humor," but nothing appeared. Two years later, Rice asked a Dr. Frederick Valentine of New York to undertake the book, joking that Valentine should buy insurance because of the fates of the six others who had tried to write his life story: "Yes, the first died, the second broke his leg, the third lost his mother-in-law and went crazy with joy, the fourth caught consumption, the fifth gave it up as a hopeless job, and the sixth merely copied some of my incoherent manuscript and got a hundred dollars out of me—which I blush to confess." Valentine failed too, writing only a sketch of "Rice's Personality." Within a month, Rice was back at the task himself, "three times and over busy, working on my troublesome history." One account cautioned that his autobiography would be entertaining, "if it is ever published. . . ." Reports of Rice's memoirs became nearly as constant as word of his farewell tours in the 1860s, or his circus plans in the 1880s.[14]

Finally Rice found his biographer, as he charmed one more woman. It was Delia's sister-in-law, Maria Ward Brown, a school teacher and unmarried, what they called a spinster. As Dan and Maria (pronounced Mariah) became chums, he realized that she had a way with words suited to his seventy-year old ears. She also knew how to use that new invention, the "type-writer." He once again enlarged his family circle as they became a kind of couple. He told a nephew that he hoped Maria would find a man worthy of her hand, heart and "Intellectial Head," and she returned his affection, sending her "Beloved Cousin" a shamrock from a trip to Ireland in 1895, with wishes for him "to reach at least the *Hundred Mile Stone.*" She wrote the stories he told while he stood at her shoulder, making corrections and cracking jokes. She did eventually complete the book, publishing it herself in New York, but lost money on it. (Some in the family blamed Dan. Maria's niece was so exasperated that during the Depression, she took his papers to the backyard and burned them.)[15]

On the reverse side: "Maggie, Dan Rice's first wife, when, on hearing he was ill, came to Long Branch, 1898"

As Dan struggled with Bright's disease, a urinary illness involving high blood pressure, Maggie returned to care for him. She held no grudge about the divorce, though others carried one on her behalf. Rice saved a sardonic poem a Pittsburgh man sent him that blamed his selfishness for the divorce. Family stories bring Kate to Long Branch too, tending her father and then her mother, who passed on exactly four months after Dan.[16]

On February 22, 1900, Dan Rice McLaren died in Long Branch. All the pallbearers were relatives, which meant that he had family to the last but also that his professional obscurity was complete. In a token nod to Rice's old glory, there were obituaries in the *New York Times, Herald, Tribune, Sun;* in the show business papers, the *Clipper* and the *Dramatic Mirror;* and in a few papers across the country. Rice's will, in which he called himself a "commedian," showed him inept with money to the end: He bequeathed land he didn't own and book proceeds that never came in.[17]

Nine months after he died, another story had him jailed as a drunk in Cincinnati.[18]

"The history of his own circus life reads more like a romance than a well-established fact," but fact it was. For all the fictions that floated his career, Rice's greatness transcended self-aggrandizement. At the height of his powers, he helped change the way Americans perceive performance. When citizens fret about a politician's sincerity, they follow forces brewing with Rice. When people accord high status to opera or ballet or Shakespeare, and decide that comedy movies are inherently lesser than "serious" films, they are buoyed by the idea of judging by categories, an idea established as Rice was trying to "raise" the circus. When theater theoreticians began touting "realism" and "sincerity" late in the nineteenth century, they were codifying ideas that had been rumbling through the landscape Rice had reigned.[19]

For years upon years, in thousands of performances before a million people and more, Dan Rice forged human connection through emotion, thought and enjoyment, by the sheer power of his talent. The great clowns

Rice, as he hoped to be remembered: Strong, commanding, and fierce.

of earlier history had limited audiences; the great clowns of the twentieth century enjoyed larger audiences than Rice's, but they are mostly known through electronic media such as movies, fixed after many takes, unalterable. Rice made it up on the spot, adjusting to each crowd and to his country so well that he forged a powerful career no circus performer has known, no clown has known, few others have known. It was no puff when a showman wrote, "Dan Rice was the greatest and most original clown this or any other country ever produced, and his record will yet be written in history as that of one of the great men of the 19th century."[20]

The crowd drifts away, into the dark on a hum of conversation.[21] The quiet feels deep after the noise of the circus, after the laughter, the storm of applause, the brassy crash of the band. Anyone turning to look back sees sidewalls coming down, and the mound of the circus ring. In the emptying space, men line up the wagons and cages and animals, and move them off. It had seemed so big, a thousand people and a thousand sights, lit by hundreds of candles. Now it is barely there, nearly a "never was." It is trampled grasses under a top, ringed by side poles. Beyond the torches, a child yelps for ma, a few good-byes pop the night, a last flirt is flung, and the quiet grows. The canvasbacks talk little as they ready the show to move. Getting the heavy canvas down is hard; then it will have to be divided into its sections, folded and rolled and wrestled onto wagons. Already feeling the labor coming long into the night ahead of them, men plod and voices trail. The last wagon clears the tent.

"Lower away!"

The canvas top starts to sink, slowly. The weight the center pole had shared with the side poles now pushes on them alone, straining. The rest of the poles are pulled out of their sockets.

"Let her go!"

The majestic circus tent floats on the air, settles, rides down in surges and sighs. Air escapes, it settles lower. It huffs. Air rolls to one side, rippling the canvas like a wave. Lower, another huff. The canvas that had held great humanity settles, settles, settles, lies flat and still.

NOTES

Abbreviations

Blue: Scrapbook compiled by Rice. [Dark blue cover.] Author's collection.
CWM: Circus World Museum, Baraboo, Wis.
Great Show: Ledger for Rice's circus, 1857–1858, and scrapbook covering 1890s. Author's collection.
HTC: Harvard Theatre Collection, Cambridge, Mass.
Hertzberg: Hertzberg Circus Collection, San Antonio Public Library.
Kunzog-Adams: Photocopies of John Kunzog's papers from Earl Adams, Jamestown, N.Y. Author's collection.
Mercyhurst: Dan Rice Family Collection, Mercyhurst College, Erie, Pa.
MCNY: Museum of the City of New York.
New Orleans: Ledger for Rice's circus, 1852 and 1856, and scrapbook. [No cover, first entry for New Orleans.] Author's collection.
NYPL-LC: New York Public Library for the Performing Arts, Lincoln Center.
Onondaga: Onondaga [N.Y.] Historical Association.
Pfening: Private collection, Fred D. Pfening Jr. and Fred D. Pfening III, Columbus, Ohio.
Polacsek: John F. Polacsek, Director, Dossin Great Lakes Museum, Detroit, Mich.
Rice!: Scrapbook compiled by Dan Rice, primarily 1884–1886. (Title pasted on cover, "Dan Rice!") Author's collection.
Thayer: Stuart Thayer, circus historian, Seattle, Wash.
Tibbals: Private collection, Howard Tibbals, Oneida, Tenn.
Note: William L. Slout's biographical dictionary, *Olympians of the Sawdust Circle,* was an invaluable source of information.

Prologue

1. Charles Stow, "The Pioneers of the American Circus," *Theatre Magazine* 5 (Aug. 1905): 192–194; Stuart Thayer, *Annals of the American Circus: Volume 3, 1848–1860,* Seattle, Wash: Dauven & Thayer, 1992, 90; John J. McCusker,

How Much Is That in Real Money?: A Historical Price Index for Use as a Deflator of Money Values in the Economy of the United States, Worcester, Mass.: American Antiquarian Society, 1992, 328–332.

2. Mark Twain, *Adventures of Huckleberry Finn,* 1884, Boston: Houghton-Riverside, 1958, 124–126.
3. Jeffrey McQuain, *Never Enough Words,* New York: Random House, 1999, xvii; *Cincinnati Daily Enquirer,* 17 May 1857.
4. Series Y, "Voter Participation in Presidential Elections, 1824 to 1868," *Historical Statistics of the United States,* Part 2, Washington, D.C.: Bureau of the Census, 1975.

Chapter 1: Home, Sweet Home

1. Maria Ward Brown, *The Life of Dan Rice,* Long Branch, New Jersey: Author, 1901, 1–3 (hereafter cited as Brown). Rice told his stories to Brown, a relative, who patched together a memoir-biography and a random collection of clippings, letters, and speeches in one volume.
2. Jessie Manahan Reed, "The Crum Family," 5, 7–8, Collections of Barbara Carver Smith, Monmouth County Historical Society; William S. Stryker, comp., *Official Register of the Officers and Men in the Revolutionary War,* Baltimore: Genealogical Publ., 1967, 171; Brown 2–11; on Methodists, Nathan O. Hatch, "The Democratization of Christianity and the Character of American Politics," 92–120 in *Religion in American Politics: From the Colonial Period to the 1980s,* Mark A. Noll, ed., New York: Oxford Univ. Press, 1990, 97; also, Sean Wilentz, *Chants Democratic: New York City and the Rise of the American Working Class, 1788–1850*, New York: Oxford Univ. Press, 1984, 81; e-mail to author, 13 Oct. 1999, Dr. Kenneth E. Rowe, Drew Univ.; Sydney E. Ahlstrom, *A Religious History of the American People,* New Haven & London: Yale Univ. Press, 1977, 437; e-mail to author, 19 Feb. 1999, L. Dale Patterson, archivist, United Methodist Church Archives.
3. *Lowell (Mass.) Daily Courier,* 24 Sept. 1863.
4. Brown 238; Douglas Southall Freeman, *George Washington: A Biography, vol. 6: Patriot and President,* New York: Charles Scribner's Sons, 1954, 253; *Index of Marriages and Deaths in New York Weekly Museum, 1788–1817,* vol. 2 H–Z, Worcester, Mass.: American Antiquarian Society [1952]; City directories; on Moving Day, *Pittsburgh Gazette,* 5 May 1849; Edwin G. Burroughs and Mike Wallace, *Gotham: A History of New York City to 1898,* New York: Oxford Univ. Press, 1998, 476–479, 500; Alvin F. Harlow, *Old Bowery Days,* New York: Appleton, 1931, 179.
5. *Evening Post,* 24 Jan. 1823; New York State Census, 1850, Saratoga Springs; Daniel Scott Smith and Michael S. Hindus, "Premarital Pregnancy in America 1640–1971: An Overview and Interpretation," *Journal of Interdisciplinary History* 4 (Spring 1975): 537–570; Hendrik Hartog, *Man & Wife in America,* Cambridge: Harvard Univ. Press, 2000. Rates may have been higher: English records suggest that from 40 to 50 percent of English brides in 1800 were pregnant,

Lawrence Stone, *Family, Sex and Marriage: England 1500–1800,* New York: Harper & Row, 1977.

6. *Journal of the Proceedings of the Legislative Council of the State of New Jersey,* New Brunswick, 1825, 102–111; *Votes and Proceedings of the Fifty Second General Assembly of the State of New Jersey,* 1828, 62–64; *Financial Cyclopedia of the State of New Jersey,* Newark: Expositor Company, 1908, 58–62.
7. *New York City Methodist Marriages, 1785–1893, vol. 1: Index of Brides,* comp. William Scott Fisher, Camden, Maine: Pictor Press, 1994; New Jersey 1850 Census; 1823 and 1831 city directory; Brown 11–13, 27, records Manahan as partner with David S. Mills, also in city directories; obituary, Elizabeth Showles, 19 March 1924, Author's Collection; Brown 13; John Anderson, conversation with author, 15 Dec. 1998.
8. Brown 3–5, 13–22; Burroughs and Wallace 384–384, 534–535, 805; David S. Reynolds, *Walt Whitman's America: A Cultural Biography,* New York: Random House-Vintage, 1996, 227–228.

   In his tales of Burr, Rice deviated from his usual practice in yoking his family to someone popular. After his 1808 expedition to form a Western empire and his subsequent trial, Burr was universally regarded as a traitor, and a trifler with women's hearts as well, in all "a festering mass of moral putrefaction," qtd. in Merrill D. Peterson, *The Jefferson Image in the American Mind,* New York: Oxford Univ. Press, 1960, 144. Yet, devoting more of his memoirs to Burr than to his mother or Manahan, Rice followed his father's opinion and portrayed Burr as a misunderstood hero, always "misinterpreted, because of a universal failure to approach his nature correctly," Brown 3–11.
9. Brown v and 16; "The Crum Family," 6; herald, "Dan Rice & Co.'s Metropolitan . . . Circus!" 4 July 1848, Harvard Theatre Collection (hereafter HTC).
10. Harlow 148, 179; D. S. Reynolds 408; *Topeka (Kan.) Daily Capital,* 5 Jan. 1880.
11. Philip Hone, *The Diary of Philip Hone, 1828–1851,* rev. ed., Allan Nevins, ed., New York: Dodd, Mead, 1936, 145; Brown 14; Harlow 199; Burroughs and Wallace 477, 486.
12. McCabe 127; Jerry E. Patterson, *The City of New York: A History Illustrated from the Collections of the Museum of the City of New York,* New York: Abrams, 1978, 107; Brown 198; Burroughs and Wallace 439.
13. Burroughs and Wallace 437, 491, and 605; Wilentz 248, 256–262; Hone 94, 211–212; Patterson 112.
14. Harlow 209 and 188; Burroughs and Wallace 633–634; Hone 40, 134–135, 195; D. S. Reynolds 100; Dale Cockrell, *Demons of Disorder: Early Blackface Minstrels and Their World*, Cambridge: Cambridge Univ. Press, 1997, 115, 193.
15. *New York Mirror,* 29 Dec. 1832, qtd. in Stephen M. Archer, *Junius Brutus Booth: Theatrical Prometheus,* Carbondale: Southern Illinois Univ. Press, 1992, 121; Harlow 247–248.
16. Brown 20–21; Charles Hamm, *Yesterdays: Popular Song in America,* New York: W. W. Norton & Co., 1979, 76.
17. Brown 12–16; Burroughs and Wallace 589–594; "Cholera Health Reporter," MCNY, MS. Coll., Cab. 3, Box 180.

18. Burroughs and Wallace 586–598; Hone 185–186, 193, 198.
19. Letter, 14 July 1998, and telephone conversation, 18 Dec. 1998, Jessica Silver, Parish Historian, Trinity Church, New York City; and 30 Apr. 1999, letter, Bob Heman, Archives Assistant; Brown 27.
20. Reed, "Crum Family," 7.
21. Hamm 165, 270. John Howard Payne wrote the song lyrics, to music by Henry Bishop, and adapted the libretto from his play *Clari.*

Chapter 2: Go West, Young Man

1. Burrows and Wallace 609–618.
2. Brown 40–48. On Dusty Foot, *Spirit of the Times* (hereafter *Spirit*), 11 June 1836, 132; on Clay, *Chicago Tribune,* 25 Nov. 1881, 7; on Harrison, clipping, "What Dan Rice Recalls," c. 1891, Circus World Museum (hereafter CWM); "Dan Rice's Old-Time Show," *New York Sun,* 14 June 1891; on *Moselle, Lloyd's Steamboat Directory and Disasters on the Western Waters,* Cincinnati, 1856, 89–93.
3. George E. Condon, *Stars in the Water: The Story of the Erie Canal,* Garden City, N.Y.: Doubleday, 1974, 130.
4. Charles Dickens, *American Notes for General Circulation,* 1842, John S. Whitley and Arnold Goldman, eds., London: Penguin Classics, 1985, 140.
5. Brown 31, 54–55; *San Antonio Daily Express,* 23 June 1886, "Dan Rice!" scrapbook 56 (hereafter Rice!), author's collection.
6. "Dan Rice," *Dramatic Mirror,* 3 March 1900; Wilentz, 403; Lewis E. Atherton, "Daniel Howell Hise, Abolitionist and Reformer," *Mississippi Valley Historical Review* 26, no. 3 (Dec. 1939): 345; *New Orleans Delta,* 18 Jan. 1854; "What Dan Rice Recalls," c. June 1891, CWM. Also Brown 49–52.
7. City directory, 1837, 183–184; George Templeton Strong, 8 Jan. 1856, qtd. in *The Hone and Strong Diaries of Old Manhattan,* ed. Louis Auchincloss, New York: Abbeville Press, 1989, 100; Brown 35; letter, Seth C. Rhodes to "Librarian, Pittsburgh, Pennsylvania," 8 Feb. 1953; city directory, 1837.
8. Dickens, *American Notes,* on "counting-house," 77; on Boston, 76 and 106; Mississippi, 230; Ohio, 235; low public life, 287; Pittsburgh, 200. On Dickens's visit to Pittsburgh, Evelyn Foster Morneweck, *Chronicles of Stephen Foster's Family,* 2 vols., Pittsburgh: Foster Hall Collection, Univ. of Pittsburgh Press, 1944, 232–233; Rice on Dickens, *San Antonio Daily Light,* 23 Sept. 1886.
9. City directory, 1837, 278–279; on Rice's claimed friends, Brown 29–31, 54, 152, and Rice memo, c. 1895, Museum of the City of New York (hereafter MCNY); on Repperts, Brown 37–40, 51–52; *Marietta Intelligencer,* 11 Oct. 1839; *Gazette,* 12 Oct. 1839; 1840 Ohio census.
10. Brown 13, 17; [Evan Orden, Wessel T. B.], *Sketches from the Life of Dan Rice, the Shakspearian* [*sic*] *Jester and Original Clown*, Albany, N.Y., 1849, 83–84; *Dan Rice's Amphitheatre,* New Orleans, c. 1854, New York Public Library; Henry Marie Brackenridge, *Recollections of Persons and Places in the West,* Philadelphia: Lippincott, 1868, 62, qtd. in Ken Emerson, *Doo-dah! Stephen Fos-*

ter and the Rise of Popular Culture, New York: Simon & Schuster, 1997, 129, 157, 160–161.

11. Morrison Foster, *Biography, Songs and Musical Compositions of Stephen C. Foster,* 1896, New York: AMS Press, 1977, 15; Morneweck on Rice, 262–264, 474–475; on Mit's jobs, 164–169, 182, including 7 Aug. 1840 letter, Mrs. Foster to William B. Foster, Jr.
12. Morneweck 229, 221, 257–260; ad, "Briare's Ice Cream Saloon," *Daily Albany Argus,* 4 July 1842; 12 Jan. 1840 letter, qtd. Morneweck 171; 7 Oct. 1840 letter, qtd. in Morneweck 184.
13. *Sketches* 83; *San Antonio Daily Express,* 23 June 1886, Rice! 56.
14. *Keokuk, Iowa Gate City,* 7 Oct. 1881, CWM; *Girard, Pa. Cosmopolite* 19 Jan. 1922, 1, qtg. *North East Sun,* 13 Aug. 1881.

Chapter 3: Learned Pig, Learning Dan

1. R. W. G. Vail, *Random Notes on the History of the Early American Circus.* Barre, Mass: Barre Gazette, 1956, 26; Ricky Jay, *Learned Pigs and Fireproof Women,* New York: Farrar, Straus and Giroux, 1986, 8–23.
2. Sketches 5–12; Brown 55–60. Barnum bought Heth from others, Neil Harris, *Humbug: The Art of P. T. Barnum,* Chicago: Univ. of Chicago Press, 1973, 21. Rice also claimed around 1890 that he and Kise modernized the banjo, New Orleans 40 (Rice ledger/scrapbook).
3. *Reading Standard,* 24 Sept. 1855, CWM.
4. Phone conversations with animal trainer Dawnita Bale, of the famous Bale circus family, 19 and 22 March 1999; Dean Chambers, the clown "Elmo Gibb," e-mail, 20 Nov. 1998; Bill Ballantine, *Wild Tigers and Tame Fleas,* New York: Rinehart, 1958, 36; Rice, "Fifty Years with a Menagerie," *52 Stories of Animal Life and Adventure,* London: Hutchinson, 1903, 12–13.
5. The same method appeared in the first novel written and published west of the Alleghenies, Hugh Henry Brackenridge, *Modern Chivalry,* 1792, ed. Lewis Leary, New Haven: College & Univ. Press, 1965, 40; Brown 173.
6. Jay 105.

Chapter 4: "Circus"

1. On Rice's size, John Glenroy, *Ins and Outs of Circus Life,* Boston, 1885, 77; *New York Daily Graphic* 12 Jan. 1888: 517; W. C. Coup, *Sawdust & Spangles: Stories & Secrets of the Circus,* Chicago: Stone, 1901, 217; Edgar White, interview, "The Oldest Living Clown," *Circus Scrap Book* 1, no. 4 (Oct. 1929): 32; *Pittsburgh Post,* 9 Mar. 1843; on riding school, Stuart Thayer, *Annals of the American Circus. vol. 1: 1848–1860,* Manchester, Mich.: Peanut Butter Press, 1976, 3.
2. Nicholas Kanellos, "A Brief Overview of the Mexican-American Circus in the Southwest," *Journal of Popular Culture* 18, no. 2 (Fall 1984): 74–84, also discusses a clown, "el loco de los toros," at a Mexico City bullfight in 1769; George Speaight, *A History of the Circus,* London: Tantivy Press, 1980, 24–25; Thayer,

Annals 1: 120, rprt. Ricketts handbill; James S. Moy, "Entertainments at John B. Ricketts' Circus, 1793–1800," *Educational Theatre Journal* 30 (May 1978): 186–120.

Circus lore says that the ring is 42' because it creates the centrifugal force to keep the standing rider on the circling horse but that force varies with the horse's speed. Astley's ring was 60 feet. The now traditional 42' is probably a compromise. Smaller rings make a tighter circuit for the horse, and tricks more difficult; larger rings reduce the number of seats, and thus the income. Because circus was international early, size was standardized, Speaight, *History* 44.

3. Thayer, *Annals* 1: 8, qtg. 3 Nov. 1794 *Philadelphia General Advertiser;* on French troupe, 38; on Harvard, 41; on prediction, 148.
4. Thayer, *Annals* 1: 112; Speaight, *History* 49; A. H. Saxon, *Enter Foot and Horse: A History of the Hippodrama in England and France,* New Haven: Yale Univ. Press, 1968.
5. Thayer, *Annals* 1: 56, 134, 144; Speaight, *History* 34.
6. Thayer, *Annals* 1: 154–155.
7. Thayer on arrest, 1: 222; on the original 400, 239; on menagerie, 103, 171, and 210; on rope-walkers, 48; on strongwoman, 88; on slack rope, 60; William B. Wood, *Personal Recollections of the Stage,* Philadelphia, 1855, 79, on "Whirligig." On the self-asphyxiation, Joseph Cowell, *Thirty Years Passed Among the Players in England and America,* 1844, Hamden, Conn.: Archon, 1970, 79, recounted that the "boxes were always filled with the fair sex whenever the feat was advertised," perhaps because cutting off the flow of oxygen to the brain can cause an erection.
8. *Mercury and Democrat,* 25. Aug. 1841; *Pittsburgh Post,* 26 May 1843; "Old Amphitheatre," Hertzberg Circus Museum (hereafter Hertzberg). Before Nichols left his headquarters in Albany, a letter was held there for a "Daniel Rice," *Albany Argus,* 2 Dec. 1842. On Nichols, Thayer, *Annals* 2: 94.
9. *Pittsburgh Post,* 20 Jan.–11 Mar. 1843.
10. Brown 52–53.
11. *Sketches* 15, 32–39; Brown 57, 70–78. An obituary places Billy Whitlock "at Barnum's Museum when Dan Rice was a 'strongman' there" (*Clipper,* 13 Apr. 1878, 21), but Whitlock probably got the story when he toured with Rice in 1855.
12. On Philadelphia, Brown 68–69, and *West Chester* (Pa.) *American Republican,* 2 Oct. 1855; on strongman tour, Earle Forrest, *History of Washington County,* vol. 1, Chicago: Clarke, 1926, 924; on "negro dancing," J. M. Fuller, "Oh, That I Were an Actor," blue-covered Rice scrapbook (hereafter "Blue"): loose clipping; Cockrell 69; on "histriones," Speaight, *History* 12, 102.
13. Rice letter to Morrison Foster, 17 June 1843, Foster Hall Collection, Stephen Foster Memorial, Pittsburgh; Morneweck 258, 266.
14. On puppets, "Dan Rice's Start," 11 Dec. 1889, CWM, and Isaac J. Greenwood, *The Circus,* New York: 1898, 116; on blackface, S. S. Sanford letter, *Clipper,* 27 May 1871, 57; Lindsay did not name Rice in his memoirs, *History of the Life, Travels and Incidents of Col. Hugh Lindsay,* 1859, 1883, 83, nor did Rice make

the list of Lindsay protégés in T. Allston Brown, "A Complete History of the Amphitheatre and Circus," *Clipper* 19 Jan. 1861, 320 (hereafter cited as T. Allston Brown, *History*); on PZG, *Harrisburg Democratic Union*, 21 June 1843, and Thayer, *Annals* 2: 112, 286–287; on Turner, Thayer, *Annals* 2: 291, and *Pittsburgh Post,* 14 and 20 June, 1843; on other shows, Thayer, "The Out-Side Shows," *Bandwagon* 36, no. 2 (1992): 24–26.

15. Rice letter to Morrison Foster, 24 July 1843, Foster Memorial. A large Boston circus, Welch & Mann, paid their stars less this year, Thayer, *Annals* 2: 119.
16. On "Dusty Foot," John Paisley letter to Maria Ward Brown 15 Mar. 1900, Blue, end piece; on "Rice" explanations, Rice obituaries; Speaight, noted British circus historian, letter to author, 27 Dec. 1991; Brown 2; "Excerpts from Family Scrap Books In Possession of Mrs. Harry P. Heldt," *Genealogical Records, Shrewsbury, New Jersey, 1939,* Monmouth County Historical Assoc.; on pudding, John C. Kunzog, *The One-Horse Show: The Life and Times of Dan Rice, Circus Jester and Philanthropist,* Jamestown, N.Y.: Author, 1962, 3.
17. Carl Wittke, *Tambo and Bones: A History of the American Minstrel Stage,* 1930, Westport, Conn.: Greenwood Press, 1968, 34.
18. T. Allston Brown, "The Origins of Negro Minstrelsy," in Charles H. Day, *Fun in Black,* New York, 1874, 5–7, qtd. in Robert C. Toll, *Blacking Up: The Minstrel Show in Nineteenth-Century America,* London: Oxford Univ. Press, 1974, 27, 44–45. Also, Carl Wittke; Dale Cockrell; and Eric Lott, *Love and Theft: Blackface Minstrelsy and the American Working Class,* New York: Oxford Univ. Press, 1993; on T. D. in circus, *New York Clipper,* 14 Dec. 1867, 281; on Nichols, Thayer, *Annals* 2: 10; on common circus blackface, Wittke 12.
19. *New York Herald,* 6 and 9 Feb. 1843; *Clipper,* 27 May 1871, 57; 20 June 1874, 95; 19 May 1877; "William M. Whitlock," 13 Apr. 1878, 21; and "Pioneers of Minstrelsy," 13 Mar. 1880, 401; on Rice's name, *Baltimore Sun,* 11 Apr. 1846; Brown 56. *Sketches*, 3, said that estrangement from rich parents prevented Dan from using his "patronymic."
20. Twentieth-century authors who have confused the two men include Lawrence Levine, *Highbrow / Lowbrow: The Emergence of a Cultural Hierarchy,* Cambridge: Harvard Univ. Press, 1988, 90; Carl Sandburg, *Abraham Lincoln: The War Years,* New York: Harcourt, 1939, vol. 3, 300; Bernard DeVoto, *Mark Twain's America,* 1932, Westport, Conn.: Greenwood Press, 1978, 33–34; Philip C. Lewis, *Trouping: How the Show Came to Town,* New York: Harper, 1973, 167; Sam Dennison, *Scandalize My Name: Black Imagery in American Popular Music,* New York: Garland, 1982, 185–186; and Russell Sanjek, *American Popular Music and Its Business: The First Four Hundred Years,* vol. 2: *1790–1901,* New York: Oxford Univ. Press, 1988, 166, 168. *Variety* reported a proposed movie on the "nineteenth-century minstrel Dan Rice" (10 Sept. 1964).
21. William G. B. Carson, *Managers in Distress: The St. Louis Stage, 1840–1844,* St. Louis: St. Louis Historical Documents Foundation, 1949, 14–18; George C. D. Odell, *Annals of the New York Stage,* 15 vols., New York: Columbia Univ. Press, 1927–1949, vol. 4, 440, 603; Thayer, *Annals* 2: 109–110; on Foster, Brown 61–64 and 429–432. Rice's "Hard Times" mostly repeats English broadsides, John

Harrington Cox, *Folk-Songs of the South,* New York: Dover, 1925, 511–513; Peter Kennedy, ed., *Folksongs of Britain and Ireland,* London: Cassell, 1975, 505, 536–537.

22. For clarity, Dan's sister will be referred to as "Libbie" and his daughter as "Libby," though both spellings were used for both of them.
23. *Davenport Gazette,* 28 Mar. 1844; City Council Minutes, City of Davenport, Iowa, 30 March 1844, 112; *Sketches* 65–71; Joseph S. Schick, *Early Theater in Eastern Iowa,* Chicago: Univ. of Chicago Press, 1939, 179, 185, 207; on Palmer, Bruce E. Mahan, "Three Early Taverns, *Palimpsest* 3, no. 8 (Aug. 1922): 259–260.
24. *Sketches* 65–71; Brown 66.
25. On St. Louis connections, *Chicago Tribune,* 15 June 1858, 12; *Dan Rice's Budget,* 1 Jan. 1860; Brown 43–47; Noah Ludlow, *Dramatic Life As I Found It,* St. Louis, 1880, 607; *Sketches* 26–29; Brown 87–89; Carson 162; on Joseph Smith, Brown 46–47; Fawn M. Brodie, *No Man Knows My History: The Life of Joseph Smith, the Mormon Prophet,* New York: Knopf, 1946, 84, qtg. *Kirtland, Ohio Evening and Morning Star,* Apr. 1834 and *Latter-Day Saints Messenger and Advocate,* Dec. 1835 (Carson, 197, discussed a now-lost play in St. Louis on "the schemes of the Mormons at Nauvoo"); *Sketches* 13–25. Neither Dan Rice, Manahan, nor McLaren appears in the records for these years. Roger D. Launius and F. Mark McKiernan, *Joseph Smith, Jr.'s Red Brick Store,* Macomb: Western Illinois Monograph Ser., No. 5, 1985; letter to author, James L. Kimball, Research Library, History Dept., Church of Jesus Christ of Latter-Day Saints, Salt Lake City, Utah, 25 Sept. 1990; letter to author, Ronald E. Romig, Church Archivist, History Comm., Reorganized Church of Jesus Christ of Latter-Day Saints, Independence, Mo., 17 Dec. 1990.
26. Walt Whitman, tarred-and-feathered, was laid up for a month, D. S. Reynolds 71.
27. Thayer, *Annals* 2: 127, 319; Thayer e-mail to author, 2 June 1999. On unspecified evidence, William Lambert, *Showlife in America,* East Point, Ga.: Will Delavoye, 1925, 209, ties together aspects of Rice's early career: "He was playing with Spaulding [*sic*] and Rogers in the side show for Kries [Kise] who had his educated pig there, that and the Jim Crow song and dance being the features. One day George Knapp, the big show clown, was taken sick and Dan Rice was asked to clown the show till he was better."
28. "Dan Rice's Old-Time Show," *New York Sun,* 14 June 1891; Brown vi, 98–100. Elsewhere, Rice claimed he started in circus with Nathan Howes in 1841, Brown 68–69.

Chapter 5: Clown to the Ring

1. Thayer, *Annals* 2: 21–22, 129, 173–174, 324–325; handbill, "Ethiopean Serenaders!" (1845), author's collection; *Herald,* 28 Oct.–3 Nov. 1845; Odell 5: 229–230.
2. *Herald,* 28 Oct. 1845.

3. *Baltimore Sun,* 17 Dec. 1845 (hereafter, *Sun*); Brown 293.
4. *Herald,* 24 Jan.–26 Feb. 1846; Odell 5: 225; lithograph, HTC. The sword pose was used by Nichols for his strongman (Thayer letter to author, 9 Mar. 1992); by Spalding for a later clown (*Spalding and Rogers' New Railroad Circus,* 1856); and by Rice (*Sketches* cover; *Marietta Intelligencer,* 9 June 1852).
5. *Sun,* 11 Apr. 1846. Also *Philadelphia Public Ledger,* 9 Nov. 1846 (hereafter *Public Ledger*).
6. D. S. Reynolds 68; *Spirit,* 5 Nov. 1842, 432; Speaight, *History* 89, 96.
7. *Sun,* 20 Jan., and 3, 11 Apr. 1846; Thayer, *Annals* 1: 120, 112–116.
8. George Speaight, the dean of English circus historians, suggests that the contrast of discipline and disorder is so important that it doesn't matter whether a clown is funny. Speaight, *History* 96–97.
9. Brown 298, 283.
10. Speaight, "A Note on Shakespearean Clowns," *Nineteenth Century Theatre Research* 7, no. 2 (Autumn 1979): 93–98; *Sun,* 11 Apr. 1846; Ray B. Browne, "Shakespeare in America: Vaudeville and Negro Minstrelsy," *American Quarterly* 12 (1960): 376–382; James Ellis, "The Counterfeit Presentment: Nineteenth-Century Burlesques of *Hamlet,*" *Nineteenth Century Theatre Research* 11, no. 1 (Summer 1983): 29–50; Claudia D. Johnson, "Burlesques of Shakespeare: The Democratic American's 'Light Artillery,'" *Theatre Survey* 21 (May 1980): 49–62; A. H. Saxon, "Shakespeare and Circus," *Theatre Survey* 7, no. 2 (Nov. 1966): 59–79.
11. *Dan Rice's Original Comic and Sentimental Poetic Effusions,* 1859, 1, 14 (hereafter, *Effusions*); *Spirit,* 8 May 1841, 120, qtg. *Dublin University Magazine,* April 1841; *St. Louis Daily Reveille,* 16 May 1848.
12. Odell 4: 664.
13. Brown 23; Jessie Manahan Reed, "The Crum Family," Collections of Barbara Carver Smith, Monmouth County (N.J.) Historical Soc., 7; *Entertaining a Nation: The Career of Long Branch,* Writer's Project, Works Projects Administration, State of New Jersey, American Guide Series, Long Branch: 1940, 31–32; 1850 Census.
14. *Rochester Daily Democrat,* 8 Sep. 1846; Brown 292.
15. *Buffalo Morning Express,* 28 Aug.–2 Sept. 1846.
16. *Sketches* 57–63.
17. Thayer, *Annals* 2: 20; *United States Gazette,* 3 Oct. 1846 (hereafter *U.S. Gazette*).
18. Thayer, *Annals* 2: 19, 52, 82, 99, and 139, 1: 210, and 3: 77; "The Circus," American Sunday-School Union [1846], author's collection.
19. *U.S. Gazette,* 3 and 30 Oct. and 30 Nov. 1846; *Public Ledger*, 8 Mar. 1847; on Blackburn, Brown 171, 180.
20. *Public Ledger*, 6 and 8 Mar. 1847; John J. Jennings, *Theatrical and Circus Life,* St. Louis, 1882, 597; Brown 337–339.
21. *U.S. Gazette,* 17 Nov. 1846; *Public Ledger,* 3 Mar. 1847. In a later story of the learned pig, Rice said that he used the alias "Seth" himself.
22. *U.S. Gazette,* 12 and 18 Jan. and 7 May 1847; *Public Ledger,* 7 May 1847.

23. Emerson, *Doo-dah!* 127; *Effusions* 6, 7, 9, 11, 13, 26.
24. *Post,* 17–18 Sept. 1847.
25. *Herald,* 28 Oct. 1847; also see *Spirit,* 30 Oct. 1847, 428; Park Benjamin, "Dan Rice, The Celebrated Shaksperian Clown," *New World,* 30 Oct. 1847, Brown transcript, Tibbals Collection. Like Rice, Benjamin had his own "Hard Times," which he delivered in lecture tours, *Enquirer,* 22 Nov. 1857; *New York Evening Post,* 15 Feb. 1858.
26. *Herald,* 31 Oct.–1 Nov. 1847.

Chapter 6: Spalding and Spicy Rice

1. Thayer, *Annals* 2: 127.
2. *Clipper,* 17 Apr. 1880, 25; *St. Louis Missouri Republican,* 1 Feb. 1880, 5; Lewis B. Lent interview, *New York Sunday News,* 3 Feb. 1884. On Kendall, *Picayune,* 20 Nov. 1848; Thayer, *Annals* 1: 139, and 2: 23. Kendall soon engaged in a famous contest with the valve cornetist, Patrick Gilmore, Robert E. Eliason, *Keyed Bugles in the United States,* Washington, D.C.: Smithsonian Institution Press, 1972, 23–26.
3. *Mobile Daily Advertiser,* 5 Jan. 1848, qtd. in James H. Dormon, Jr., *Theatre in the Antebellum South: 1815–1861,* Chapel Hill: Univ. of North Carolina Press, 1967, 196. Also John A. Dingess, *Memoirs* 312, CWM (original ms., Hertzberg).
4. Clipping, Mobile, 17 Jan. 1848, Kunzog-Adams; *Effusions* 14; Falconbridge [Jonathan Kelly], *Dan Marble,* New York, 1851, 75; Brown 172.
5. "Scraps from Dan Rice's Diary," *Spirit,* 17 Mar. 1849, 37–38. On McKinstry, *Dictionary of Alabama Biography;* on Childress, 1814–1938 list, Frances Beverly Collection, Mobile Public Library; on Cass and Van Buren, Seba Smith, *The Life and Writings of Major Jack Downing,* Boston, 1833, 216–217.
6. John Chase, *Frenchmen, Desire, Goodchildren,* New Orleans: Crager, 1949, 82–83; Thayer, *Annals* 1: 85–86.
7. *Picayune,* 22 Dec. 1848; *Mobile Register,* 6 Jan. 1848; *Delta,* 5 Feb. 1848.
8. Brown 111–112; *New Orleans Mercury,* 5 Mar. 1848, qtd. in Kunzog 52.
9. Dickens, *American Notes* 207.
10. *Enquirer,* 11–17 Apr. 1848; Thayer, *Traveling Showmen: The American Circus Before the Civil War,* Detroit: Astley & Ricketts, 1997, 64; *Reveille,* 10–30 Apr. and 6 May 1848.
11. *Enquirer,* 13 Sept. 1848; Thayer, *Annals* 3: 14, qtg. Hall Letters, Henry Ford Museum, Dearborn, Mich.; Thayer e-mail, 29 Nov. 1999. *Sketches,* 16, had joked about Rice and the Mormon Smith as "projectors." Beyond cultural chest-thumping, projectors eased the way for reforms such as abolition. Thomas Haskell, "Capitalism and the Origins of the Humanitarian Sensibility," *American Historical Review* 90 (Apr. 1985): 339–361; 90 (June 1985): 547–566.
12. Thayer, *Traveling Showmen* 11–21, 30, 60–61; *Pittsburgh Post,* 17 July 1848; (*Enquirer,* 7 Apr. 1848, qtg. Nashville *Orthopolitan,* put the tent's capacity at 4,000 people); *Reveille,* 21 June 1848; and 30 June, qtg. *Quincy (Ill.) Whig.*

13. Vital Statistics file and Van Orden Vertical file, Greene County Historical Soc.; *Albany Argus*, 16 Nov. 1844; e-mail, 9 July 1999, Marti Spalding, Spalding Memorial.
14. "Circus!" herald, Grand Gulf, Miss. [21 Oct. 1848], HTC; *Reveille,* 21–25 May, 21 June and 30 June 1848.
15. *Reveille,* 23 May 1848; S. S. Sanford letter, *Clipper,* 28 May 1871, 57. Also *Marietta Intelligencer,* 3 Aug. 1848; *Picayune,* 9 Nov. 1848.
16. Dan Rice & Co.'s herald, Evansville, 4 July 1848, HTC; also *Quincy* (Ill.) *Whig,* 20 June 1848; *Pittsburgh Gazette,* 15 July 1848; Schick 188. If Smith's widow was offended by the depiction of her husband in *Sketches,* she did not blame Rice, for she dined with him again in 1852, Glenroy, 71, 97. The English clown Wallett remembered boarding with Mrs. Smith, *The Public Life of W. F. Wallett,* John Luntle, ed., London, 1870, 111.
17. *Hannibal Journal,* 29 June 1848; *Reveille,* 16 May 1848.
18. *Reveille,* 30 Apr. 1848.
19. *Mobile Register,* 6 Jan. 1848; *Pittsburgh Post,* 18 and 27 July 1848.
20. *Enquirer,* 15–18 Aug. 1848; *Delta,* 9 Apr. 1853. Van Orden managed the North American in 1844 and Rice's show, Thayer, *Annals* 2: 15. On Spalding's colors, *Clipper,* 17 Apr. 1875: supplement.
21. *Crescent,* 10 Nov. 1852.
22. Glenroy 72; *Random House Historical Dictionary of American Slang,* vol. 1, J. E. Lighter, ed. New York: Random House, 1994 and 1997; Hans Nathan, *Dan Emmett and the Rise of Early Negro Minstrelsy,* Norman: Univ. of Oklahoma Press, 1962, 260–266.
23. *U.S. Gazette,* 5 Feb. 1847; *Delta,* 5 Feb. 1848; Dingess 311–312; Capt. James Hobbs, *Wild Life in the Far West,* Hartford, Conn., 1874; on Baton Rouge, Glenroy 72–73; Brown 108–111; Richard C. Bain and Judith H. Parris, *Convention Decisions and Voting Records,* Washington, D. C.: Brookings, 1973, 36–43; William Safire, *Safire's New Political Dictionary,* New York: Random House, 1993, 42–43; Brown 149.
24. *Delta,* 14 Nov. 1848; "Dan Rice and Van Orden! The Other Side of the Question!" herald, 17 Jan. 1851; "Dan Rice's Bulletin! Number One!" herald, 24 Jan. 1851; and "Crucible," herald, 27 Jan. 1851, HTC and Hertzberg.
25. *Picayune,* 9 Nov. 1848; on fire company, *Delta,* 25 Nov. and 5 Dec. 1848; on races, *Delta* and *Picayune,* 28 Nov., 1, 8 and 9 Dec. 1848; on rider, *Picayune* and *Delta,* 7 and 12–13 Dec. 1848; on riding school, *Picayune,* 15–16 Dec. 1848; on cane, Brown 494–495; *Picayune,* 22 Dec. 1848. Rice would claim that Aroostook was one of his mounts when he was a jockey, Brown 36.
26. *Delta,* 15 Nov.–5 Dec.; *Picayune,* 1 and 12 Dec. 1848. The theater's darkness was ironic. In the 1830s, James H. Caldwell aimed to build the best theater in the country, which meant using the innovation of gas lighting. Since New Orleans had no company for gas lighting, Caldwell took two years off to create one. In 1835, he returned to the stage, opening his gorgeous, gas-lit St. Charles Theatre. Warren Kliewer, "A Family of Actors," ms., 56–58, author's collection.
27. *Delta,* 23 Nov., and 6–14 Dec. 1848.

28. *Delta,* 16 Dec. 1848.
29. *Delta* and *Picayune,* 7 Dec.; on the rumored collusion, 14 Dec. 1848.

Chapter 7: Reading, Not Acting Clown

1. *Spirit,* 16 Dec. 1843, 494; *Clipper,* 26 July 1856, 110; Robert E. Wiebe, *The Opening of American Society: From the Adoption of the Constitution to the Eve of Disunion,* New York: Knopf, 1984, 295; Charles H. Haswell, *Reminiscences of an Octogenarian of the City of New York (1816 to 1860),* New York: 1896, 439. See Victor Emeljanow, "Erasing the Spectator: Observations on Nineteenth Century Lighting," *Theatre History Studies* 18 (1998): 107–116.
2. Richard Butsch, *The Making of American Audiences: From Stage to Television, 1750–1990*, Cambridge: Cambridge Univ. Press, 2000, esp. introduction and 44–95; William Oxberry, *The Actor's Budget of Wit and Merriment,* London, 1820, 185; *Spirit,* 4 Sept. 1841, 324, and 17 Sept. 1853, 368.
3. *Spirit,* 25 Sept. 1846, 109; on Forrest as purported acrobat, 14 Oct. 1843, 396; Forrest's version, *Public Ledger,* 22 Nov. 1848; *Clipper,* 1 Nov. 1862, 230; on Macready, *Spirit,* 30 Nov. 1844, 430; 29 Apr. 1848, 120; 6 May 1848, 132; 20 May 1848, 156; 10 June 1848, 181 ("sad failure"); 24 June 1848, 205; 5 Aug. 1848, 281; Ludlow 593–598. Richard Moody, *The Astor Place Riot,* Bloomington: Indiana Univ. Press, 1958, 76.
4. *Picayune,* 22–28 Dec., and *Delta* 17 and 23 Dec 1848, including civic-minded attempts to ignore cholera or blame it on low morals; Glenroy 73–74; *Reveille,* 31 Dec. 1848; *Enquirer,* 10–11 Jan. 1849; *Public Ledger*, 22–27 Jan. 1849. *Herald,* 4–5 and 10 Feb.; *Morning Sun,* 6 Feb. 1849.
5. *Spirit,* 10 Feb. 1849, 612.
6. *Spirit,* 14 Oct. 1848, 408. The same issue mentioned burlesques, *Mr. McGreedy* at the Chatham Theatre and *Who Got Macready?* at the Olympic.
7. Thayer, *Annals* 2: 11; 3: 15–16, 84–87; *Enquirer,* 7 Oct. 1848.
8. *Spirit,* 17 Mar. 1849, 37–38; "A Book As Is A Book," *Enquirer,* 29 Apr. 1849; *Sketches* 3, 81, 84, 76, 65, 82; Paul E. Johnson, *A Shopkeeper's Millennium: Society and Revivals in Rochester, New York, 1815–1837,* New York: Hill, 1978, 8, 136; *Harper's,* Jan. 1857, 270.
9. *Sketches,* appendix, 3, and 86.
10. "Traveling Season of 1849," hw ms. [9 May 1849], Tibbals Collection; on Johnson, *Picayune* and *Delta,* 22 Nov. 1848; *Sketches,* appendix; on Spalding's share, *Enquirer,* 4 May 1849; Brown 112; Van Orden-Rice heralds, Jan. 1851, HTC; *Enquirer,* 2–8 May 1849; on Apollonicon, Thayer, *Annals* 3: 14–15; on Rice's wagons, Lewis E. Atherton, "Daniel Howell Hise, Abolitionist and Reformer," *Mississippi Valley Historical Review* 26, no. 3 (December 1939): 346; on Louis Phillippe, Brown 298, 28.
11. *Sketches* appendix; *Cincinnati Enquirer,* 1 and 8 May 1849; *Pittsburgh Gazette,* 15 May 1849, 3; *Rochester Advertiser,* 22 June 1849; *Syracuse Reveille,* 14 July 1849; on Poneyantum, *Picayune,* 28 Nov. 1848.

12. W. C. Crum, "Romance in Real Life," *Florida State Republican,* c. 1890s, qtd. Brown 237–239. W. C. and the family Bible called Gardner a minister, but the census listed him as a farmer. The Methodist Episcopal clergyman noted in the census lived between Gardner and his brother, Richard.
13. "Things in New York," *Public Ledger,* 29 Nov. 1847; *Spirit,* 6 May 1848, 132. Antithesis also ignores a third *Macbeth* that night, Thomas Hamblin's at the Bowery Theatre, *Spirit,* 12 May 1849, 144.
14. *Pittsburgh Gazette,* 12 May 1849, and 16 May, qtg. *New York Herald,* 11 May 1849; H. M. Ramney, "Account of the Terrific and Fatal Riot at the New York Astor Place Opera House," New York, 1849; Burrows and Wallace, 760–766; Moody 136–175.
15. D. S. Reynolds 165–166.
16. On *Millingar, Enquirer,* 10 and 11 May 1849, and Frederick Way, Jr., *Way's Packet Directory, 1848–1983*, Athens: Ohio Univ. Press, 1983, 241 (A few months later, Dunning Foster bought the boat, and in 1852, his brother, Stephen Foster, rode it on his only trip south of Kentucky. Emerson, *Doo-dah!* 148, 187–188); on Rice, *Gazette,* 17 May 1849; on fights, Thayer, *Annals* 2: 130–131, and *Pittsburgh Post,* 22 May 1849; *Gazette*, 18–19 May 1849; *Pittsburgh Post,* 17–24 May 1849. A year later, the council's police arrested the mayor, while his police arrested council members, *Post,* 7–12 Oct. 1850.
17. Evelyn Barrett Britten, *Chronicles of Saratoga,* Saratoga Springs: Author, 1959, 381; Cornelius E. Durkee, *Reminiscences of Saratoga, Reprinted from the* Saratogian*, 1927–1928*, 10, 121; Hugh Bradley, *Such Was Saratoga,* Doubleday: Doran & Co., 1940, 77, 96; Nathaniel Bartlett Sylvester, *History of Saratoga County, New York: 1609–1878,* Philadelphia, 1878, 167; George Waller, *Saratoga: Saga of an Impious Era,* Englewood Cliffs, N.J.: Prentice, 1966, 79; Daniel McLaren, *The Pavilion Fountain at Saratoga,* 2d ed., New York, 1842; New York City directories, 1832 and 1839.

    McLaren's scheming did not make him immune to schemes. Harman Blennerhassett had been a co-defendant with Aaron Burr in the failed Western empire. Later, swindlers impersonated the Blennerhassetts at spas, and McLaren was taken in by one, paying the board of a woman posing as Harman's widow. Brown 6–8; clipping, 28 Nov. 1890, New Orleans–61. Milton Lomask, *Aaron Burr: The Conspiracy and Years of Exile, 1805–1836,* New York: Farrar, Straus, Giroux, 1992; letter to author, Ray Swick, Historian, Blennerhassett Island Historical State Park, 21 March 1999.

Chapter 8: Foreclosure

1. "The Finest Beaver," Account book, p. 76, Dan Rice Collection, Mercyhurst College Archives.
2. *Sun,* 22, 27, and 29 Oct. 1849; on Leonard's hospital work, *Sun,* 18 Dec. 1845; *Spirit,* 8 Dec. 1849, 504.
3. Glenroy 75; Thayer, *Annals* 3: 31.

4. Glenroy 76.
5. New Orleans Ledger, 20 June 1856 entry: "1849–50 feed bill, per Van Orden $34"; *Delta,* 13 Dec. 1860.
6. *Morning Star,* 5 and 7 Dec. 1849.
7. *Evening Bulletin,* 1 Jan. 1850; Rice-Van Orden heralds, Jan. 1851, HTC.
8. 1850 New Jersey Census, Ocean Township, Monmouth County (Hugh was recorded as "U. Manahan"); *Entertaining A Nation* 31–32.
9. Thayer, *Annals* 3: 20–21; *Nashville Republican Banner,* 26 May 1848, qtd. in Thayer, *Annals* 3: 21; *Wilmington (N.C.) Commercial,* 5 February 1850; *Spirit,* 16 March–20 Apr. 1850; Brown 351–53, qtg. *Charleston Literary Gazette.*
10. *Sun,* 7–16 and 21 Jan., 4 Feb., 12 and 19 Mar. 1850.
11. "Dan Rice's Circus," herald, c. Sept. 1850, HTC.
12. *Effusions* 13–14, 19–20, "Song of Baltimore" to Emmett's tune, "Boatman Dance."
13. *Effusions* 9–10; Brown 485–488; *New York Herald,* 7 Feb. 1849.
14. Brown 270–271; Stephen B. Oates, *Approaching Fury: Voices of the Storm, 1820–1861,* New York: HarperCollins, HarperPerennial, 1997, xv, 13–14, 88, 143–144, 150.
15. *Camden West Jerseyman,* 24 July 1850; *Jersey City Daily Telegraph,* 29 July 1850; Brown 429–432; (*Effusions* 24–25, and Brown, 61–64, print the versions without Van Orden); on "Devil," *Effusions* 7–9, Brown 478–481, and single sheet, HTC; *Syracuse Standard,* 9 Sept. 1850.
16. *Rochester Daily Advertiser,* 21–27 Sept. 1850; *Buffalo Morning Express,* 30 Sept. 1850.
17. *Enquirer,* 8–13 Nov. 1850.
18. Kunzog 7, 78–81; Brown 128; Rice to Morrison Foster, 15 Nov. 1850, Foster Hall Collection; Emerson, *Doo-dah!* 174.
19. Brown 128, 209; *Clipper,* 1 July 1876, 108, on 10 June 1856 stand.
20. Hyatt Frost, "News of the Circus Ring," *Dramatic News,* 29 Dec. 1894, Hertzberg.
21. Timothy Flint, *Recollections of . . . the Mississippi,* 1826, qtd. in Jonathan Raban, *Old Glory: An American Voyage,* New York: Simon and Schuster, 1981, 293.
22. John Hanners, "'It was Play or Starve': John Banvard's Account of Early Showboats," *Theatre Research International* 8, no. 1 (Spring 1983): 54–61; *Spirit,* 5 Sept. 1857, 358.
23. Brown 201–210; Thayer, *Annals* 3: 53; *Pittsburgh Gazette,* 4 July 1853, called Johnson Spanish; Albert Parry, *Tattoo: Secrets of A Strange Art as Practiced Among the Natives of the United States,* New York: Simon and Schuster, 1933, 58–59; Glenroy 32; *Picayune,* 1 Feb. 1852; Thayer, *Annals* 2: 60; Arthur Loesser, *Humor in American Song,* New York: Howell, 1942, 92–94.
24. Thomas L. Nichols, "Yankee Speech," *Forty Years of American Life,* 1864, New York: Stackpole Sons, 1937, 68.

Chapter 9: One-Horse Story

1. Kunzog 85. Rice originally put the sneer in Van Orden's mouth, *Effusions* 17.
2. *Effusions* 30, Brown 459–461, and "Rochester Song No. 3," New Orleans, 1852, Louisiana Collection, Tulane Univ.; *New York Herald,* 8 July 1849, qtd. in Johannes Dietrich Bergmann, "The Original Confidence Man," *American Quarterly* 21 (Fall 1969): 560–577. In 1855 the "original Confidence Man" was in the Albany jail, *Argus,* 1 May 1855; *Effusions* 3; Brown 289.
3. *Picayune,* 22 Dec. 1850.
4. *Delta,* 20 Dec. 1850; *Crescent,* 2–3 Jan. 1851; *Picayune,* 2, 10 and 20 Jan. 1851.
5. "Lost Chickens," *Effusions* 17, and Brown 455–456; "Polka," *Effusions* 28–29, and Brown 469–471; "Pills and Quills; or, The Beginning and End of Dan Rice's Circus," [c. 1851], New-York Historical Society (hereafter N-YHS); Thayer, *Annals* 3: 85–87; Thayer e-mail, 30 July 2000.
6. *Crescent,* 17 Jan. 1851; *Picayune,* 18 Jan. 1851; *Delta, Crescent,* and *Picayune,* 22 Feb. 1851; Brown 126–129.
7. "DAN RICE AND VAN ORDEN! / THE OTHER SIDE OF THE QUESTION!" herald, 17 Jan. 1851, Hertzberg.
8. Richard L. Berke, "What a Mind!" *New York Times,* 25 June 2000, sec. 4, pp. 1, 3.
9. *Crescent,* 15 Jan.; *Picayune,* 18 Jan.; *Delta,* 17 Jan. 1851.
10. "Bulletin" and "Crucible," Hertzberg.
11. "Rochester Song No. 3."
12. Thayer, *Traveling Showmen* 65, on the Drummond light. "Spaulding," *Effusions* 26–27; *Dan Rice's American Humorist & Shaksperian Jester*, Philadelphia, 1860 (hereafter *American Humorist*) 28–29; Brown 437–438; (Herman Melville compared the title character in his 1856 novel, *The Confidence-Man,* to the Drummond Light, to depict him as an original); on Rice's electric light, *Crescent,* 11 and 14 Jan. 1851; on *Richard III, Picayune,* 26 Jan. 1851; on Smith, *Delta,* 26 Feb.; *Crescent,* 26 Feb. 1851; on Jackson Monument, *Delta,* 5 Jan., 6 and 9 Feb. 1851; *Picayune,* 25 Feb. 1851; "Song—1852 [sic]," *Effusions,* 31–32.
13. William R. Denslow, *10,000 Famous Freemasons,* vol. 4, Missouri: Transactions of the Missouri Lodge of Research, 30–31, c. 1961; Speaight, *History* 150–151.
14. *Delta,* 11 Feb. 1851.
15. *Effusions* 16–17. "Lost Chickens" was juxtaposed to the Lind "Ode."
16. *Delta* and *Crescent,* 11 Feb. 1851; *Effusions* 16–17, 29–30; Brown 457–459, 467–469.
17. *Crescent,* 11 Feb.; *Picayune,* 12 Feb. 1851; Brown 226; *Crescent,* 19 Feb.; *Delta,* 1 Mar. 1851.
18. *Picayune,* 12 Feb.; *Crescent,* 11 Feb.; *Delta* and *Picayune,* 22 Feb.; *Crescent,* 6 Mar. 1851; *New Orleans News-Letter,* qtd. in *Pittsburgh Post,* 14 June 1851.
19. *Crescent,* 11 Feb. 1851.

Chapter 10: Like a Phoenix

1. *Enquirer,* 24 May; *Pittsburgh Post,* 26 June; *Utica Daily Gazette,* 29 July; *Syracuse Standard,* 20 Aug. 1851.
2. *Hawesville (Ky.) Clarion,* ca. 1900, Account Book, 76, Mercyhurst. In 1917, another doctor's son told of trading a white stallion to Rice for a pony, in Potosi, Missouri. Guy Bryan, Folder 16, Bryan Obear Collection, Western Historical Manuscript Collection, University of Missouri (Columbia); *Pittsburgh Gazette* and *Post,* 26 June 1851.
3. *Enquirer,* 5 June 1851.
4. *Pittsburgh Post,* 26 June 1851; Morneweck, 389.
5. *Bloomington (Ill.) Daily Pantagraph,* 16 July 1858; on Castle, Charles H. Day, *Ink from a Circus Press Agent,* William L. Slout, ed., San Bernardino, Ca.: 1995, 27, 157, 177; *Clipper,* 4 Mar. 1882, 817 and 830; and Glenroy 68–69; on orphans, *Post,* 4 June 1851, qtg. *Natchez Free Trader; Post,* 26 June 1851.
6. *Post,* 4 July 1851; Ralph Waldo Emerson, "Self-Reliance" and other essays, *The Selected Writings of Ralph Waldo Emerson,* Brooks Atkinson, ed., New York: Modern Library, 1940, 146.
7. *Picayune,* 26 Dec. 1850.
8. *Enquirer,* 5 June 1851; *Rochester Democrat,* 21 and 25 July, 8 Sept. 1851.
9. *Buffalo Express,* 17 July; *Rochester Democrat,* 21 and 25 July; *Spirit,* 2 Aug., 279; *Syracuse Standard,* 1 Sept. 1851.
10. "The Circus," American Sunday-School Union [1846], author's collection; Beecher, *Lectures to Young Men,* 1845, Boston, 1846, "Popular Amusements," 231–251; *Sketches* 42–47; Brown 345–349; *Indianapolis Journal,* 1 Mar. [1890s], HTC. The men named, the Methodist Charles Dunning and the Presbyterian Graves, both served around Weedsport. *Minutes of the Northern New York Conference–Methodist Episcopal Church,* Westown, N.Y., 1877, 56–57; e-mail, Susan J. Flacks to author, Presbyterian Historical Society, 9 June 2000.
11. Glenroy 87–89.

Chapter 11: Alternating Ringmasters

1. *Delta* and *Picayune,* 13–14 Jan. 1852; *Crescent,* 15 Jan. 1852.
2. Ludlow 719–720; *Crescent,* 13 Jan. 1852; *Delta* and *Picayune,* 18 Feb. 1852.
3. *Enquirer,* 10 Oct. 1851, on steamboat; *Picayune,* 9 Feb. 1851 on Barnum; *Delta,* 1 and 18 Feb. and 14 Nov. 1852; *Crescent,* 4 and 18 Jan. 1854; *Dan Rice's Interlude,* 30 Nov. 1854; *Crescent,* 9 Dec. 1853.
4. *Picayune,* 29 and 31 Dec. 1851; on the bout, *New York Morning Star,* 8 Feb. 1849; *Sun,* 1 Mar. 1849; and *Effusions* 20–21; on Rice's offerings, *Picayune,* 12 Dec. 1851; 12 Jan., 28 Jan., 14 Feb., 16 Mar. and 27–28 Mar. 1852.
5. *Picayune,* 25 Feb. 1852; Wittke 139, 168; Coup 215; Nathan 133.
6. *Crescent,* 6–10 Mar. 1851 and 15 Jan. 1852; *Delta,* 15 Jan. 1852; Picayune, 22 Dec. 1851, 15 Jan. and 4 March, 1852; e-mail, 14 Dec. 1999, Dr. Charles Nolan,

Archivist, Archdiocese of New Orleans. Brown 358–359; on another church benefit, *Picayune,* 27 Jan. 1854.

7. *Picayune,* 9 Mar. 1851; 20 Jan., 28 Feb. and 12 Mar. 1852; also *Crescent* and *Delta,* 12 Mar. 1852.
8. *Galveston Weekly News,* 17 Nov. 1848, qtd. in Thayer e-mail, 2 June 1999; *Crescent,* 12 Mar. 1852; Thayer, *Annals* 3: 206; *Picayune,* 23 Dec. 1851.
9. *Enquirer,* 8 and 10 Oct. 1851; *Delta,* 5 Feb. 1851; Wallett 68, 153–154, viii-ix; ("Rees' Encyclopedia," qtd. in Brown 167–170, copied from or was copied by Wallett). In his otherwise admirable survey of clowns, John Towsen posited the existence of a "daring political jester" on the evidence of apocrypha, anecdotes in which jesters mocked outsiders, and the fiction of Shakespeare's *Twelfth Night.* Towsen, *Clowns,* New York, Hawthorn Books, 1976, 21–30.
10. *Picayune,* 23 Nov. 1851.
11. Wallett 107–108; Glenroy 89–90; Brown 124–125; *Effusions* 7; *Picayune,* 15 Mar. 1852.
12. *Picayune,* 3 Feb.–5 Mar. 1852; Wallett 187–188; *Delta,* 19 Feb. 1852; Brown 172.
13. *Picayune,* 4–8 Apr. 1852; *Crescent*, 23 Mar. 1852; Slout entries, and Thayer e-mail, 5 Jan. 2000; on "Dan Rice" horses, *Crescent*, 6 Feb., 16 Nov., 7, 8 and 24 Dec. 1852, 5 and 16–17 Mar. 1853; *Picayune,* 16 Nov. 1852 and 21 Jan. 1855; *Delta,* 24 Dec. 1852, 21 Jan. and 21 Dec. 1855; and *Spirit,* 9 Apr. 1853, 19, and 24 Feb. 1855, 18; *Michigan Argus,* 27 June 1862; *Picayune,* 17 Mar. 1852.

Chapter 12: Curses, Foiled Again!

1. Glenroy 92–93; Brown, 116. The showman, W. C. Coup, told of even greater bravery, when Rice faced down a man with a pistol in Mississippi, Coup 217–219.
2. Thayer, *Annals* 3: 53; Slout, "The Great Roman Hippodrome of 1874: P. T. Barnum's 'Crowning Effort,'" *Bandwagon* 42, no. 1 (1998): 34; Thayer, *Traveling Showmen,* 61–62; e-mail to author, 24 Sept. 2000; *Delta, Picayune,* and *Crescent,* 21–25 Mar. 1852. Rice's tournament spectacle seems to have influenced Mobile's New Year Carnival pageantry, *Picayune,* 6 Jan. 1855.
3. *Clipper,* 13 Jan. 1883, 702, on Crum; "Dan Rice's Big Poker Game," c. 1890s *[New York Sun],* CWM; (Canada Bill later had a national reputation as a gambler, *Enquirer,* 11 Sept. 1875); Rice letter, *New York Sun,* n.d., CWM.
4. *Enquirer,* 23 Apr. 1852; *Mobile Register*, 8 Nov. and 8 Dec. 1852; Thayer, *Annals* 3: 48–51; Penelope M. Leavitt, *Spalding and Rogers' Floating Palace, 1852–1860,* diss. Washington State Univ., 1979; *Enquirer,* 22 Apr. 1852; clipping, Blue 115.
5. *Effusions* 7; *Delta*, 9 Apr. 1852, qtg. *New York Mirror.*
6. Glenroy 93–96; Brown 116–118; Frost, "Circus Ring," *Dramatic News,* 28 Dec. 1894; Rice set the same story in Paducah, "Dan Rice. A Characteristic Private Letter," c. 19 July 1890, CWM; *Pittsburgh Post,* 18 June 1852.
7. Brown 471–473; *Crescent,* 10 Nov. 1852.

8. Brown 471–473.
9. *Hannibal Journal,* 29 June 1848; *Tri-Weekly Messenger,* 24 Aug. 1852; on Congo Square, Chase 84; *Mobile Register,* 12 Jan. 1853; *Effusions* 28–29.
10. Glenroy 98.

Chapter 13: The Barnum of New Orleans

1. *Crescent,* 8 Nov. 1852.
2. *Crescent,* 10 Nov. 1852.
3. *Delta,* 29 Dec. 1854; *Crescent,* 13 Jan. 1852.
4. *Crescent,* 10–13 Nov. 1852; *Mobile Register,* 18 Nov. 1852.
5. *Register,* 9–19 Nov. and 10–17 Dec. 1852.
6. Glenroy 76; *Enquirer*, 17 Nov. 1861.
7. *Register,* 15–17 Dec. 1852; 12 Jan. 1853; "Letter from the First Private, Mobile," *Delta,* 23 Dec. 1852; on hospital tax, *Delta,* 31 Dec. 1853; on Spalding license, *Register,* 6 Dec. 1852; *Delta,* 14 Dec. 1852; *Crescent,* 17 Dec. 1852.
8. *Register,* 8 Dec. 1852–18 Jan. 1853.
9. *Crescent,* 4 Sept. 1852, 31 Dec. 1852–6 Jan. 1853; Glenroy 98–99; *Register,* 12 Jan.–7 Feb. 1853.
10. *Picayune,* 23 Jan. 1855, on Museum cost; *Crescent,* 26 Feb. 1853; New Orleans ledger, author's collection; Ralph Hyde, *Panoramania: The Art and Entertainment of the 'All-Embracing' View,* London: Trefoil, 1988, 125–130.

    Barnum had presented his Wooly Horse, captured by John Fremont in his Western expeditions. Neil Harris, *Humbug: The Art of P. T. Barnum,* Chicago: Univ. of Chicago Press, 1973, 104. The footnote to this item repeats Rice's fiction that he had been a strongman for Barnum, although Harris modified the punch line to make Rice, not Barnum, the humbug of the empty barrel.
11. *Public Ledger,* 5 June 1848; *Delta,* 8 Sept. 1852; *Crescent,* 8, 11, and 16 Feb. 1853.
12. Harris 310, also 50.
13. *Crescent,* 3 Jan. 1853; *Picayune,* 11 Oct. 1852; 4 Jan. and 2 Apr. 1853.
14. *Crescent,* 18, 24–27 Jan. and 4–11 Feb. 1853; *Picayune* and *Delta,* 23 Jan. 1853; Barnum letter to James L. Hutchinson, 29 June 1885, in A. H. Saxon, ed., *Selected Letters of P. T. Barnum,* New York: Columbia Univ. Press, 1983, 263; *Picayune,* 28 Jan. and 19 Feb. 1853; *Delta,* 24 Feb. 1853; *Amphitheatre* 7.
15. *Picayune,* 28 Jan. 1853, qtg. *Register,* 3 Dec. 1852; *Crescent,* 16 Dec. 1852, qtg. *Register*; *Crescent,* 15 Jan.–16 Mar. 1853; on made-up words, *Crescent,* 8 Dec. 1852; *Register,* 20 Nov. 1852.
16. *Register,* 7 Feb. 1853; *Crescent,* 10 and 25 Feb., 21 Mar. 1853.
17. *Delta,* 9 Dec. 1852; *Crescent,* 28 and 7 Feb. 1853.
18. *Register,* 8 Dec. 1852; *Crescent,* 26 and 28 Jan. 1853; "Dan Rice's Valedictory," *Effusions* 2–3.
19. *Delta,* 10 Mar. 1853; *Crescent,* 21 Mar. 1853.
20. *Crescent,* 2, 5, 7, and 23 Mar.; *Delta,* 24 Feb., 1 Mar., 28 Apr., and 3 May; *Picayune,* 5 and 9 Mar., and 17 Apr. 1853.

21. *Picayune,* 27 Mar.; *Delta,* 25 and 29 Mar; *Crescent,* 26 and 28 Mar. 1853.
22. *Picayune,* 1 Apr. 1853; *Delta,* 2 Apr. 1853. Seventy years later, the Ringling brothers' lawyer argued the value of circus goodwill in a federal case. John M. Kelly and Fred D. Pfening III, eds., "Taxable Value of Circus Goodwill," *Bandwagon* 12, no. 1 (1968): 3–14.
23. *Delta,* 1 May; *Picayune,* 1 and 10–12 May; *Crescent,* 4 Apr. 1853.

Chapter 14: See the Elephant

1. *Delta,* 30 Mar. 1853; *Erie, Penn. Chronicle,* 19 July 1853; lithograph, Hertzberg; "Circus," *Knickerbocker* 13, no. 1 (1839): 72.
2. *Enquirer,* 1 June 1853; *Louisville Courier,* 1 Oct. 1853; *Crescent,* 30 Mar. 1852; *Pittsburgh Post,* 6 July 1853 (The Boy's handler sued for back pay, "New Orleans" ledger, 12 Aug. 1856); *Spirit,* 29 Jan. 1853, 600; *Newport Daily News,* 8 June 1956.
3. *Marietta Intelligencer,* 18 June 1853; *Erie Chronicle* 19 July 1853; *Covington Journal,* 20 Aug. 1853; S. D. Dickinson, "Showboats and Circuses," *Arkansas Gazette,* 28 Nov. 1948, B1, 7. On the mules, *Picayune,* 8 Jan. 1852; Thayer e-mail to author, 11 May 1998; *Effusions* 3–6; Brown 442–447.
4. *Spirit,* 12 Feb., 613; 19 Mar., 60; 26 Mar., 72; 2 Apr., 84; 30 Apr., 132; 7 May 1853, 144; *Clipper,* 28 May, 4 June, and 8 Oct. 1853; Thayer, *Annals* 3: 71–72.
5. *Register,* 18 Nov.; *Crescent,* 20 Nov. and 1 Dec. 1852; *Enquirer,* 27 Sept. 1853.
6. *Spirit,* 20 Aug. 1853, 324; *Picayune,* 1 Dec. 1848; *Crescent,* 24 Jan. 1851; Glenroy 75, 96.
7. Thayer, *Annals* 3: 175, 178, 180, 182, 185, 193, 194, 196, 198, 202.
8. Thayer, *Annals* 3: 29–30, 155, 187–188; *Cincinnati Gazette,* 27 July 1852.
9. *Enquirer,* 1–15 June 1853; *Pittsburgh Post,* 6 July 1853.
10. *Enquirer,* 24–28 Aug. 1853.
11. *Delta,* 9 Dec. 1860; Brown 274. The *Historical Dictionary of American Slang,* vol. 2, J. E. Lighter, ed., New York: Random House, 1997, cites 1853 as the first use of "one-horse," though it missed Rice's ironic meaning.
12. *History of Erie County, Pennsylvania*; Chicago, 1884, 835–850; on the railroad, *Crescent,* 16 and 29 Nov. 1852.
13. James Barker, interviewed in John Kelley, "Dan Rice Celebration is Suggested by Girard Men," *Chicago Daily Tribune,* 13 Apr. 1937, Hertzberg.
14. *Pittsburgh Post,* 6 July 1853; sale and property described in 12 Dec. 1859 mortgage to McClure, Erie Recorder of Deeds; also John Miller, *A Twentieth Century History of Erie County, Pennsylvania,* vol. 1, Chicago: Lewis Publ., 1909, 470; (Kunzog, 94, writes that Rice first bought land in Girard midsummer 1852, and S. S. Freeman, 12, refers to the same year); on steamboat, *Billboard,* 16 Oct. 1920, 57–59; Denslow 30–31; letter to author, 20 Aug. 1998, Frederick A. Parker, Jr. Secretary, Holland Lodge No. 8, New York City; Rice letter, 20 Aug. 1888, qtd. in "Dan Rice's Gratitude," Greenville, Pa. newspaper, 7 Oct. 1889, Rice! 74.
15. *Picayune,* 12 Dec. 1851.

16. Thomas Moore, *Lalla Rookh: An Oriental Romance,* London, 1817; Emerson, *Doo-dah!* 42–43; *Picayune,* 22 Mar. 1852; *Spirit,* 13 Aug. 1859, 316. Moore's ultimate reputation was set more by the fact that, entrusted with the memoirs of his friend, Lord Byron, he burned them.
17. Thayer, "The Elephant in America 1840–1860," *Bandwagon* 35, no. 3 (1991): 35–36; Thayer, *Annals* 3: 53–54. *Covington Journal,* 20 Aug. 1853; "imported" in *Enquirer,* 21 Aug. 1853. On Noyes, "Lives of Famous Showmen," 4 Mar. 1911, Hertzberg. Kunzog, 100, writes that Rice bought Lalla Rookh from Seth Howes for $5,000 in New York.
18. *Enquirer*, 12 and 18 Aug.; *Covington Journal,* 20 Aug. 1853; Lewis E. Atherton, "Daniel Howell Hise, Abolitionist and Reformer," *Mississippi Valley Historical Review* 26, no. 3 (Dec. 1939): 346; "Lalla Rookh's Walk," *Crescent,* 8 Mar. 1854.
19. *St. Louis News,* 15 Oct. 1853, qtd. *Picayune,* 26 Oct. 1853; *Erie Chronicle* 19 July 1853; *Helena (Ark.) Southern Shield,* 12 Nov. 1853, qtd. in S. D. Dickinson, "Showboats and Circuses," *Arkansas Gazette,* 28 Nov. 1948, B1.

Chapter 15: People's Choice

1. D. S. Reynolds 119; *Register,* 14 Jan. 1853, based on the 1850 census.
2. *Crescent,* 19 Feb. 1851; *Delta,* 19 May 1854, qtg. *Westminster Review*; *Register,* 15 Dec. 1852.
3. *Clipper,* 29 Oct. 1853; *Crescent,* 9 Feb., *Picayune,* 15 Feb. and *Delta,* 16 Feb. 1854.
4. *Crescent,* 16–17 Feb.; *Picayune,* 17 Feb.; *Delta,* 17 Feb. 1854; *Spirit,* 25 Feb. 1854, 17.
5. *Amphitheatre* 5–6; *Crescent,* 30 Nov.; *Delta,* 4 Dec.; *Picayune,* 6 Dec. 1853; Edwin L. Jewell, "Academy of Music," *Jewell's Crescent City Illustrated,* New Orleans, 1873, 164, picture on 269; John S. Kendall, *The Golden Age of the New Orleans Theater,* Baton Rouge: Louisiana State Univ. Press, 1952, 467.
6. *Crescent,* 12 Dec. 1853; *Delta,* 4 and 12 Feb. 1854; 12 Dec. 1853, 3 Dec. 1848; Spartacus.schoolnet.co.uk/Chrepublican, 12 Aug. 1999.
7. *Delta,* 1, 4, and 27 Dec.; *Picayune,* 4 and 22 Dec. 1853, 5 and 17 Jan. 1854.
8. *Amphitheatre* 7; *Picayune,* 23 Dec. 1853, and 1 and 5 Jan. 1854; *Crescent,* 27–30 Dec. 1853, and 20–26 Jan. 1854; *Delta,* 9 Jan. 1854.
9. *Crescent,* 1–2 and 8–9 Feb. 1854; *Delta,* 3 Dec. 1853; *Picayune,* 1 Feb. 1854.
10. *Delta,* 30–31 Jan. 1854; Brown 276; *Picayune,* 3 Feb. 1854.
11. *Delta* and *Picayune,* 7 and 18 Mar. 1854.
12. "Uncle Tom's Cabin," *Effusions* 25–26; Brown 438.
13. *Crescent,* 7, 9, 13, 18, and 22 Mar., and 1 Apr. 1854; *Picayune,* 7 Mar. and 2 Apr. 1854.
14. Maggie, *Crescent* and *Picayune,* 6 Apr.; Dan, *Picayune,* 9 and 13 Apr. 1854.
15. *Picayune,* 13 Apr. 1854; *Delta,* 22 Nov. 1853 and 9 Apr. 1854.
16. *Picayune,* 9 Apr. 1854; *Delta,* April 6, 14 May, and 2 July 1854.
17. *Crescent* and *Delta,* 15 April 1854; "brain," *Crescent,* 10 Nov. 1852.

Chapter 16: $100,000

1. Thayer, "Lexicon," July 2000, transcripts to author.
2. Thayer, *Annals* 1: 83, *Showmen* 61, and e-mail to author, 24 Sept. 2000; city council minutes, Lyons City (North Clinton), Iowa, 2 Aug. 1861; Ron Ryder, *Combined Editions, Ryder Pictorial 1959–1962–1964,* Boonville, N.Y.: Ryder's Hardware.
3. Coup 76–80; John Tryon, *The Old Clown's History,* New York, 1872, 86–88.
4. Robert E. Wiebe, *The Opening of American Society*, New York: Knopf, 1984, 285; D. S. Reynolds 308 on overlap, 173 on Beecher in crowd; Nichols 1: 374. Jokes on Beecher as a performer, *Clipper,* 9 Mar. 1861, 375; *Enquirer,* 20 July 1863.
5. D. S. Reynolds 154–194; "Bloomer Song," sheet music, 1854, Louisiana Collection, Tulane Univ.; *Crescent,* 7 Jan. 1853; on other arrests of pants-wearing women, *Pittsburgh Post,* 25–27 June and 2 July 1851; *Crescent,* 13 Jan. 1854; Brown 292; *Effusions* 18–19.
6. *Kentucky Statesman,* 25 July 1854; *Rochester Daily Union,* 18 Sept. 1854, qtg. *Buffalo Evening Post; Enquirer,* 1 Nov. 1854, qtd. in Kunzog-Adams Papers.
7. *Amphitheatre* 1–4.
8. "Contemporary Newspaper Opinion of Dan Rice," *Billboard,* 12 Jan. 1907, 26; *Rochester Daily Union,* 20 Sept. 1854.
9. Brown 138, 6, 117, 184; conversation with John Anderson, 15 Dec. 1998.

Chapter 17: Bearded in His Den

1. *Delta,* 24 Feb. 1854; Morneweck, 405, 565.
2. *Enquirer,* 11–12 Nov. 1854; New Orleans ledger.
3. *Picayune,* 9 Nov. 1854; *Dan Rice's Interlude,* 30 Nov. 1854, MCNY; *Delta,* 16 Dec. 1854.
4. *Delta,* 24 Dec. 1854, also *Picayune.*
5. Kunzog 113–114; *Delta,* 12 Nov. 1852; also, 4 Jan. 1854. *Random House Dictionary,* 2d ed., 1987, dates "peanut gallery" thirty years later.
6. *Picayune,* 24 Dec., and *Delta,* 26 and 28 Dec. 1854; *Picayune,* 6 Jan. 1855; *Delta,* 6 and 8 Jan. 1855; Kendall, 475–476; Jewell 151; *Crescent,* 27 Dec. 1852.
7. *Picayune,* 23 Jan. 1855. Robertson's husband, Dionysus Bourcicault, gave a few lectures then, but he would find greater success as Dion Boucicault, playwright, theater manager, and American show business leader.
8. Shreveport *South-Western,* 7 Mar. 1855; Thayer, *Annals* 3 106–107, 206.
9. Kunzog 115, 108; Brown 138.
10. *Picayune,* 18 Mar. 1852.
11. *Bulletin,* 2–14 Apr. 1855; *Philadelphia Sunday Dispatch* (hereafter *Sunday Dispatch*), 1 Apr. 1855.

Chapter 18: Dan Rice's Great Show

1. *Picayune,* 2 Mar. 1852; Thayer, *Annals* 3: 80–81; *Baltimore American,* 17 Mar. 1859.
2. Brown 139; on Showles, *Picayune,* 2 Feb. 1854; on Reed, *Pittsburgh Daily Union,* 19 Oct. 1854, and interview, "Oldest Living Bareback Rider," *Billboard,* 23 Mar. 1929, 65; on Thayer, "Lives of Famous Showmen," 4 Mar. 1911, Hertzberg; on Dan's sister, "The Late Mrs. Showles," *York Dispatch,* 15 Mar. [c. 1923], Hertzberg.
3. "Noted Kentucky-Born Author Recalls Thrill of First Circus," *White Tops,* May-June 1947, 23, rprnt. 1935 article; *Lansing (Mich.) State Journal,* 28 Apr. 1955, qtg. *Lansing Semi-Weekly Republican,* 9 May 1876; *Trenton State Gazette,* 5 Sept. 1855; on Spalding's horse on a platform, *Crescent,* 11 Jan. 1851.
4. *West Chester (Pa.) American Republican,* 2 Oct. 1855; Rice later gave a different version, that the bills of the headstand were accidentally posted upside down, "What Dan Rice Recalls," c. June 1891, CWM; Brown 262; "Circus Managers of the Past," *Clipper,* 13 Dec. 1879, 300.
5. Thomas Frost, *Circus Life and Circus Celebrities*, London, 1875, 117; e-mail, Fred Dahlinger, Director, CWM, 8 Mar. 2000; e-mail, Dean Chambers, elephant presenter, 6 Apr. 2000; phone, Barbara Woodcock, 7 Apr. 2000; letter, Bill Woodcock, 26 Apr. 2000 (the Woodcock family has been training animals since the 1850s); *Philadelphia Sunday Mirror,* 21 Feb. 1858; Scrapbook 7, Mercyhurst. Two preeminent circus historians have scoured the archives and concluded, despite their skepticism, that it had been done. Speaight, *Circus* 11, 86, and letter to author, 15 May 2000; Thayer, *Annals* 3: 54. Also Frost, *Circus Life*, 111–117.
6. *Trenton State Gazette,* 5 Sept. 1855. Rice did hedge his bet this year, occasionally calling it "Rice's Great Circus Show."
7. *West Chester (Penn.) American Republican,* 2 Oct. 1855, qtg. *Reading Gazette.* "Dan Rice's Gratitude," Greenville, Pa. newspaper, 7 Oct. 1889, Rice! 74.
8. Syracuse clipping, 8–9 June 1855 engagement, Onondaga Historical Assoc. (hereafter Onondaga).

Chapter 19: Servis Renderd

1. Rice's finances and personal comments this chapter, New Orleans ledger.
2. Glenroy 89; *Enquirer,* 11–14 Oct. 1851; Day, *Ink,* 128–29; Rice letters to E. Brinton, 5 Oct. and 4 Nov. 1855, CWM. Strobridge apparently began printing circus posters, for which it would become renowned, with one for Rice, "whiskers and all," John W. Merten, "Stone by Stone Along a Hundred Years With the House of Strobridge," *Bulletin of the Historical and Philosophical Society of Ohio* 8, no. 1 (Jan. 1850): 15.
3. *Spirit,* 29 Dec. 1855, 542; *Sun,* 17, 24–29 Dec. 1855; 2 Jan. 1856.
4. Saxon, *Enter Horse and Foot* 173–204. Rice sang about Menken in "Dan Rice's Original Budget of Photographs," *Dan Rice's Songs, Sentiments, Jests, and Stories,* New York, 1865 (hereafter *Songs, Sentiments*), 14. (Calling his descriptions

"photographs," Rice was again capitalizing on new technology.) On the "half nude," Speaight, *Circus* 74–76.

5. "Old Time Clown," *Boston Globe,* 19 Mar. 1907, New York Public Library for the Performing Arts, at Lincoln Center (hereafter NYPL-LC); *Joe Miller's Jests, or the Wit's Vade-mecum. A facsimile of the original "Joe Miller" (1739),* New York: Dover, 1963, 164, 85, 176, 153.
6. *Enquirer,* 12 Jan. 1856.
7. *Opelousas (La.) Courier,* 13 Jan. 1856, qtd. *Delta,* 23 Jan.; *Vermillionville Echo,* 19 Jan. 1856, qtd. *Crescent,* 24 Jan.; Rice letter to Brinton, 9 Feb. 1856, CWM.
8. Brown, 298; *Cairo Weekly Times and Delta,* 5 Dec. 1855.
9. *Spirit,* 19 Jan. 1856, 577; Cushing heralds, 1 Feb. 1856, Ringling Museum, Sarasota; 8 Feb., American Antiquarian Society.
10. Mortgages, 17 Dec. 1859 and 7 Nov. 1865; Erie Co. records.
11. *Enquirer,* 15 June 1856; Thayer *Annals* 3: 101, 107, 122, on proprietors; Slout, *Clowns and Cannons: The American Circus During the Civil War,* San Bernardino, Cal.: Borgo Press, 1997, 107.
12. In his memoirs, Rice transformed that loss into a loan to a Cincinnati butcher who had helped him during his Spalding feud, Brown, 199–200; Thayer *Annals* 3: 260.
13. Thayer, *Traveling Showmen* 6.

Chapter 20: Hey, Rube!

1. Walt Whitman, "The Circus," *Life Illustrated,* 30 Aug. 1856, in *New York Dissected,* Emory Holloway and Ralph Adimari, eds., New York: Rufus Rockwell Wilson, 1936, 193–196; *Enquirer,* 1 Jan. 1860.
2. D. S. Reynolds 174, 154–194 generally.
3. Ibid., 49–50, 71, 174; Rice's observations in this chapter fare from his "Great Show" Ledger, author's collection. In London, officers stood guard at Madame Vestris's theater, and "at the entrance of *every other* place of public amusement," Anna Cora Mowatt, *Autobiography of an Actress,* Boston, 1854, 80.
4. Thayer, *Annals* 1: 23; *Public Ledger,* 5 June 1848; *Sun,* 25 Oct. 1849; *New York Tribune,* 27 Sept. 1850, qtg. *Utica Gazette,* clipping, Onondaga; *Delta,* 16 Nov. 1848; *Enquirer,* 9 May 1852; Thayer, *Traveling Showmen,* 91; *Enquirer,* 1 June 1856.
5. Coup 7, also 192–200, 212–213. Also Ralph Keeler, *Vagabond Adventures,* Boston, 1870, 179, 190–191; and Tryon 222–228.
6. Harvey W. Root, *The Ways of the Circus, Being the Memories and Adventures of George Conklin, Tamer of Lions,* New York: Harper, 1921, 233; Brown, 104, 177; Frost, *Circus Life,* 208 (the volume consulted included a reader's penciled notation, "Ann Arbor," next to discussion of rough show towns); *Bloomington (Ill.) Pantagraph,* 21 July 1858.
7. *Rochester Daily Union,* 27 May 1856; Dingess 350; H. G. Wilson, *Official Route Book of the Pawnee Bill Wild West Show,* Piqua, Ohio, 1898, 69; Thayer, "The History of the Concert or After-Show," *Bandwagon* 41, no. 5 (Sept.–Oct. 1997):

10–12; *Enquirer,* 6 July 1856; James A. Inciardi and David M. Peterson, "Gaff Joints and Shell Games," *Journal of Popular Culture* 6, no. 3 (Spring 1973): 591–606; *Baltimore American,* 15 Dec. 1857; *Public Ledger,* 19 Jan. 1847.

8. Brown 176–179; Keeler 179; Glenroy 73. Don B. Wilmeth, *The Language of Popular Entertainment,* Westport, Conn.: Greenwood Press, 1981, 129, passes on a tale that "Hey, Rube!" summoned a local lawyer, though it is implausible that circus men under siege would passively wait the intervention of a towner. Circus folks later also called a fight a "clem."
9. Charles Stow, "The Pioneers of the American Circus," *Theatre Magazine* 5 (Aug. 1905): 194; Coup 214–221; *Lawrence (Mass.) Sentinel,* 26 July, 1856, Mercyhurst, Box 2; "Recollections of Dan Rice," [1880s], CWM.
10. "Prince of the Circus Ring," c. Feb. 1900, CWM; *Norristown Register & Democrat,* 26 Aug. 1856; Geneva, N.Y. advertisement, 29 May 1856, rpt. 4 Sept. 1875 *Clipper,* 180.
11. *Rochester Advertiser*, 12 June 1849, qtd. in Ruth Rosenberg-Naparsteck, "A History of the Circus in Rochester," *Rochester History* 49, no. 3 (July 1987): 5; *Oswego (N.Y.) Times and Journal,* 3 June, and *Daily Palladium,* 4 June 1856, Scrapbook 4 and 6, Mercyhurst; *Syracuse Standard,* 4 June 1856, Onondaga.
12. *Hudson Daily Star,* 14 Aug. 1856, Blue 108; *Syracuse Standard,* 18 Aug. 1856; *Clipper,* 23 Aug. 1856, 143; New Orleans ledger.
13. Thayer, *Annals* 3: 107; *Sun,* 22 Sept. 1856.
14. Twain 125–126.
15. New Orleans ledger 8.

Chapter 21: Cabinet of Curiosities

1. *Mackenzie's,* Mercyhurst; Kunzog 372–373.
2. *Girard (Pa.) Cosmopolite,* 19, Jan. 1922, 1, quoting *North East (Pa.) Sun,* 13 Aug. 1881, Dan Rice Collection, Mercyhurst.
3. "New Orleans" Ledger, 21 Nov. 1856; Rice to Brinton, 18 Dec. 1856, qtd. *Richmond Times-Dispatch,* 18 Oct. 1931 (from Thayer); *Washington (D.C.) Daily National Intelligencer,* 13 and 28 Feb. 1857.
4. *Union,* 27 Feb. 1857.
5. *Evening Star,* 2–7 Mar. 1857.
6. "Captain Dan Rice," 4 Mar. 1857, Brown University Library.
7. Emerson, *Doo-dah!* 10, 52, 74, 234.
8. *Sunday Dispatch,* 15 Mar.; *Public Ledger,* 10–13 and 21 Mar.; and *Bulletin,* 2 Apr.; *Baltimore American,* 2 Mar.; *Sun,* 3 Apr. 1857.
9. *Sun,* 26 Mar. 1857.

Chapter 22: A Genius for Fun

1. *Enquirer,* 24 May 1857; Brown 278.
2. *Sketches* 40; Great Show ledger; *Pictorial,* June 1857, Tibbals Collection.

3. Jonas Barish, *The Antitheatrical Prejudice,* Berkeley and Los Angeles; Univ. of California Press, 1981; *Picayune,* 10 Dec. 1851; Richard Sennett, *The Fall of Public Man,* 1977, New York: Random-Vintage, 1978; Bettyann Holtzmann Kevles, *Naked to the Bone: Medical Imaging in the 20th Century,* New Brunswick, N.J.: Rutgers Univ. Press, 1997.
4. 1857 *Pictorial*; S. S. Freeman, "It All Began with a Clown," 1A, on Rice's purchase of the newspaper in the 1850s; Dickens, *Hard Times,* 1854, New York: Penguin, 1969, 82; clipping, Cincinnati, c. Nov. 1861, Blue 47; Walter Kerr, *How Not to Write A Play,* New York: Simon & Schuster, 1955, 27–29, 36; *Philadelphia Evening Bulletin,* 19 Feb. 1858, Scrapbook 21, Mercyhurst.
5. *Pictorial,* qtd. in *Enquirer,* 15 May 1857.
6. *Rochester Union & Advertiser,* 6 May 1857.
7. Howes & Cushing also took Rice performers Rosston, Murray, and Holland to England, Speaight, *History* 106; *Sunday Dispatch,* 8 Mar. 1857; Brown 183–184. Egbert Howes, Seth's nephew, paid Rice $800, perhaps as compensation, Great Show ledger, May 1858. Also Jeanne Chretien Howes, *The Howes Circus Story,* Weston, Conn.: Author, 1990, 26, 43–44; on rhinoceros, *Clipper,* 23 July, 1859, 110.
8. "The Docile Rhinoceros," [hw: *The Mercury,* 21 Mar. 1858], HTC; Richard J. Reynolds III, "Circus Rhinos," *Bandwagon* 12, no. 6 (1968): 12; Reynolds e-mail to author, 27 Mar. 2000; 1858 *Pictorial.*
9. *Union & Advertiser,* 26 May; *Syracuse Standard,* 9 June; *Oswego Palladium,* qtd. in *Syracuse Standard,* 10 June; *Girard Dispatch* [c. 10 Aug. 1857], Blue 114.
10. *Toronto Daily Globe,* 16 July; *Brooklyn Daily Eagle,* 19 and 26 Sept. 1857; *Pittsburgh Post,* 1 Nov. and 12, 17 and 26–31 Oct. 1857; on Spalding, *Enquirer,* 11 Oct. 1857.
11. "Dan Rice's Song at Niblo's Garden," *Effusions* 23.
12. John Driscoll, *All That Is Glorious Around Us: Paintings from the Hudson River School,* Ithaca: Cornell Univ. Press, 1997, 18–19.

Chapter 23: Excelsior!

1. *Tribune,* 15 Jan.; *Times*, 12 Feb. 1858; Great Show ledger.
2. *Programme,* New York, 21 Jan. and 3 Feb. 1858, MCNY.
3. Great Show ledger, 7 and 8 Dec. 1857.
4. Speaight, *History* 73–74.
5. Richard Jackson, ed., *Popular Songs of Nineteenth-Century America,* New York: Dover, 1976, 269.
6. "The Late Mrs. Showles," Hertzberg; Bible, Dan Rice Collection, First Methodist Church, Long Branch, N.J.; Great Show ledger, 8 Dec. 1857; 1858 *Pictorial; Tribune,* 27 Jan. 1858.
7. Great Show ledger, Dec. 1857, and 5 Feb. 1858.
8. *Delta,* 13 Dec. 1860.
9. *Sun*, 4 Jan. 1858; John Adams to Benjamin Rush, Quincy, Mass., 21 June 1811,

Heineman Ms. 1c, Heineman Collection, Morgan Library; *Baltimore American,* 4 Jan. 1859; D. S. Reynolds 107.

10. Henry Wadsworth Longfellow, *Complete Poetical Works,* 1866, Boston: Houghton: 1922, 19; Burton J. Bledstein, *The Culture of Professionalism: The Middle Class and the Development of Higher Education in America,* New York: Norton, 1976.
11. Robertson Davies, *What's Bred in the Bone,* New York: Penguin, 1985, 151; *Brooklyn Daily Eagle,* 23 Sept. 1857; *Clipper,* 31 March 1860, 398.
12. *Herald,* 7–8 Feb. 1858; Brown 325.
13. *Enquirer,* 17 Apr. 1848; *Amphitheatre* 1–3; *Harper's,* Nov. 1855, 858; 1858 *Pictorial.*
14. On "Excelsior," *Public Ledger,* 19 Dec. 1846; *Pittsburgh Post,* 28 June and 4 Dec. 1853; *Enquirer,* 2 May 1858; *Clipper,* 17 May 1860, 34, and 14 Aug. 1858, 135. Above the bed in which Lincoln died was an engraving of Bonheur's celebrated 1857 "Horse Fair," Asia Booth Clark, *The Unlocked Book: A Memoir of John Wilkes Booth,* New York: Putnam, 1938, 175.
15. *Philadelphia Mercury,* c. Mar. 1858, Scrapbook 11, Mercyhurst; Great Show Ledger, 5 Apr. 1858; *American & Gazette,* 13 Mar. 1858, Scrapbook 3, Mercyhurst.
16. Haswell 542; Hone 754.
17. *Sketches* 81; *Amphitheatre* 4.
18. Mowatt 152–155.
19. Harris 138, qtg. *Journals of Ralph Waldo Emerson,* 1900–1914, vol. 7, 247; *Halifax, Nova Scotia Evening Express,* 16 July 1862.
20. *Jamestown (N.Y.) Journal,* 9 May 1856; "Niblo's Garden," 18 Jan. 1858, facsimile, NYPL-LC; 1858 *Pictorial.*
21. D. S. Reynolds 214–217. Also, Barbara Welter, "The Cult of True Womanhood: 1820–1860," *American Quarterly* 18, no. 2 (summer 1966): 151–174; Stuart M. Blumin, "The Hypothesis of Middle-Class Formation in Nineteenth-Century America: A Critique and Some Proposals," *American Historical Review* 90 (1985): 299–338; Ann Douglas, *The Feminization of American Culture,* New York: Knopf, 1977; Karen Halttunen, *Confidence Men and Painted Women,* New Haven: Yale Univ. Press, 1982; Mary P. Ryan, *Cradle of the Middle Class: The Family in Oneida County, New York, 1790–1865,* Cambridge: Cambridge Univ. Press, 1981; and Christine Stansell, *City of Women: Sex and Class in New York, 1789–1860,* New York: Knopf, 1986.
22. 1858 *Pictorial*; *Harper's,* Sept. 1851, 709; also *Pittsburgh Post,* 20 July 1848; clipping, c. 5 Mar. 1858, Scrapbook 23, Mercyhurst; "Curiosities of Dan Rice's Great Show," Philadelphia, c. March 1860, HTC; *Bulletin,* 2 Apr. 1858, Scrapbook 26, Mercyhurst.
23. Letter, Fred Greene to Mrs. Dan Rice, Philadelphia, 1 May 1858, Box 1, Mercyhurst.
24. *New York Evening Post,* 19 Jan. 1858.
25. 1857 *Pictorial.*
26. Glenroy 70, 10; *Clipper,* 12 Feb. 1859, 242.

27. Sherwood 27; Reed, "Oldest Living Bareback Rider," *Billboard,* 23 Mar. 1929, 65.
28. *Clipper,* 10 Apr. 1858, 407, qtg. *Evening Journal.*
29. *Evening Journal,* c. Feb.–Mar. 1858, Scrapbook 15 and 19, Mercyhurst; *Herald,* 13 Feb. 1858.

Chapter 24: Daniel McLaren

1. *Spirit,* 20 Feb. 1858, 24; *Evening Journal,* c. Mar. 1858, Scrapbook 27, Mercyhurst; *Clipper,* 6 Mar. 1858, 367; route information, Hertzberg.
2. *Pittsburgh Post, Gazette,* and *Dispatch,* 15–21 Nov. 1859; *Clipper,* 29 May 1858, 42.
3. Emerson, *Doo-dah!* 243–244; Morneweck, 2: 548, dates the complimentary pass 1863, but Dan and Mit were both in Philadelphia in 1858, and not in 1863; *Pittsburgh Post,* 24 Apr. 1858; Great Show Ledger, 18 Apr. 1858.
4. *New York Times,* 19 Jan. and 9 Feb. 1858.
5. Halttunen 107, 184; *Harper's,* Nov. 1855, 843; *Chicago Tribune,* 8, 15–18 June 1858.
6. *Kenosha Times,* 17 and 24 June, 1 July 1858.
7. *Spirit,* 11 Nov. 1848, 456; also 26 Oct. 1844, 420; *Clipper,* 18 Oct. 1856, 206. Also *Clipper,* 6 Nov. 1858, 230: "During election week there is always a 'let up' in the attendance at theatrical exhibitions."
8. *Boston Herald,* 13 Dec. 1858.
9. D. S. Reynolds 169–170.
10. Thayer, "Mr. Lincoln, Senator Douglas and the Circus," *Bandwagon* 93, no. 3 (1999): 30–31. Levi North's circus seating was rented for the sixth Lincoln-Douglas debate, in Quincy on October 13, but they collapsed. Van Amburgh's tent may have been used on May 9, 1860, for the Decatur convention that made Lincoln the choice of Illinois Republicans for President. Thayer, *Traveling Showmen* 92. Lincoln did speak in a circus tent, on September 9, William E. Baringer, ed., *Lincoln Day by Day: A Chronology,* Earl Schenk Miers, ed.-in-chief, vol. 2: 1849–1860, 228.
11. *Cincinnati Daily Commercial,* 2 Sept. 1858; *Clipper,* 14 Aug. 1858, 135; clipping, Blue 105.
12. *Bloomingtom (Ill.) Daily Pantagraph,* 16 July; *Clipper,* 25 Sept., 182; *Clipper,* 17 July, 103 and 24 July, 111; *Enquirer,* 25 July 1858.
13. *Enquirer,* 4 July; *Clipper,* 17 July, 103; 14 Aug. 1858, 135.
14. *Marietta Intelligencer,* 8 Sept. 1858.
15. Robert Browning, "Andrea del Sarto," 1855, in *The Poems and Plays of Robert Browning,* New York: Modern Library–Random House, 1939, 219; Stansell 93; McCabe 64–65; Roy Rosensweig, *Eight Hours for What We Will: Workers and Leisure in an Industrial City, 1870–1920,* Cambridge: Cambridge Univ. Press, 1983, 142; *Lord Chesterfield's Letters to his Son,* London, 1774, vol. 1, 329; *Crescent,* 5 Dec. 1851.
16. Mowatt 241–244.

17. *Bulletin,* 3 Mar. 1858; Scrapbook, 15, Mercyhurst; Mowatt 313; *Clipper,* 29 Dec. 1860, 296.
18. *Clipper,* 9 Oct. 1858, 198, two items; *Spirit,* 16 Oct. 1858, 432; *Clipper,* 30 Oct. 1858, 218. Later, the Louisville *Courier* declared that Rice had sold out to McLaren & Farwell because of ill health, 28 Aug. 1860, Blue 22.

Chapter 25: Grammatical Assassin?

1. *Tribune,* 22 Jan. 1858; Odell 7: 55. Historians have treated this passage as emblematic of Rice's performance, like Odell in a typical twentieth-century bias against nontheatre performance: "How often have we cried out in utter weariness for the segregation of . . . Circus [which] no longer stuck like a leech to the regular plays," 4: 664. Clipping, Blue 2; *Clipper,* 8 Jan. 1859, 303; *Tribune,* 28 Jan. and 27 Feb. 1859.
2. *Delta,* 25 Dec. 1854; also the *Enquirer,* 10 Oct 1852; *Clipper,* 12 Feb. 1859, 342.
3. *New York Times,* 26 Jan., 2, 12 and 26 Feb. 1859; *Clipper,* 18 Dec. 1858, 278; Erie County Records, Jan. 1857, Apr. and May 1858; *History of Erie County*, 1884, 846; Miller 470.
4. "A Speech Delivered at the Metropolitan Hotel," *American Humorist* 21–22. This second Rice songster dates the speech as 1858, but it seems most likely that it is the one mentioned in the 8 Jan. 1859 *Clipper*; also Brown 363–364.
5. *Herald,* 31 Jan. 1859; *Clipper,* 8 Jan. 1859, 303, and 12 Feb. 1859, 242; *New York Atlas,* 6 Feb. 1859, Blue 110; *Tribune,* 17 Feb. 1859.
6. *Clipper,* 5 Mar. 1859, 366.
7. *Tribune,* 7 Feb. 1859.
8. *Porter's Spirit,* 21 Jan. 1860, 327; 1856 *Pictorial*; *Picayune,* 29 Nov. 1854; *Enquirer,* 13 Feb. 1859; *Picayune,* 12 Nov. 1854; *Philadelphia Evening Argus,* 17 Feb. 1858, Scrapbook, 19, Mercyhurst.
9. 1858 *Pictorial*; "Special to the Indianapolis Journal," 1 Mar. [c. 1895], HTC; Kunzog 143.
10. *Washington Morning Chronicle,* 9 June 1864; Thomas Ford, *A Peep Behind the Curtain,* Boston, 1850, 66–68; Burroughs and Wallace 634.
11. Benjamin, "Dan Rice," Tibbals Collection.
12. *Porter's Spirit,* 4 Oct. 1856, 69; "Contemporary Newspaper Opinion of Dan Rice," *Billboard,* 12 Jan. 1907, 26.
13. *Clipper,* 26 July 1856, 110; *Delta,* 3 Mar. 1853; also "The Right of Hissing," *Spirit,* 16 Dec. 1843, 494; and "Hissing at the Theatre," *Picayune,* 29 Jan. 1854; *Delta,* 5 and 22 Jan. 1854; D. S. Reynolds 172, qtg. Walt Whitman, vol. 6, *Notebooks and Unpublished Prose Manuscripts,* Edward F. Frier, ed., New York: New York Univ. Press, 1984, 2, 234.
14. D. S. Reynolds 174, 191, and 286, qtg. 10 Nov. 1858 *Daily Times.*
15. *Porter's Spirit,* 19 Feb. 1859, 400; Richard Butsch, *The Making of American Audiences: From Stage to Television, 1750–1990,* Cambridge: Cambridge Univ. Press, 2000; *Harper's,* Nov. 1855, 843; *Ann Arbor Peninsula Courier,* 13 June 1862.

16. *Clipper,* 19 Feb. 1859, 350; *Spirit,* 16 Apr. 1859, 414.
17. *Boston Herald,* 13 Dec. 1858; *Philadelphia City Item,* 12 Mar. 1859, Blue 106; *Sun,* 24 and 29 Mar. 1859; *American,* 19 and 24 Mar. 1859, and 14 Dec. 1857; *Enquirer,* 26 Aug. 1858.
18. Adv., 7 Apr. 1859, Blue 5.
19. *Porter's Spirit,* 2 Apr., 70, and 19 Mar. 1859, 48; "Card from the Management" and "National Circus," Philadelphia, c. Mar. 1859, Scrapbook 49, Mercyhurst.
20. *Tribune,* 11 Apr. 1859.

Chapter 26: The End?

1. *Baltimore American,* 7 Oct. 1859; *Sun,* 8 Oct. 1859.
2. *Hannibal Tri-Weekly Messenger,* 31 Aug. 1852; *Pittsburgh Post,* 6 July 1853; *Clipper,* 7 May 1859, 23.
3. *Amphitheatre* 4; Mowatt 425; *Clipper,* 18 December 1858, 278.
4. Rice letter to W. C. Crum, 21 June 1859, Pfening Collection; *Enquirer,* 29 May 1859; *Clipper,* 7 May 1859, 22, and 18 Dec. 1858, 278; bill of sale, Earl Chapin May Papers, CWM, Dahlinger e-mail, 3 June 2000. Letter, Maggie Rice to "My Dear Children," 12 Mar. "1589" [1859], Box 1, Mercyhurst.
5. *Clipper,* 11 Sept., 166, and 7 May 1859, 22; handwritten contract, pictured in Kunzog 146, and photocopy Kunzog-Adams; *Effusions* 21–22.
6. *Enquirer,* 29 May 1859; *Clipper,* 11 June 1859, 62; herald, "Dan Rice's Great Show," Portsmouth, N.H., 29 June 1859, Hertzberg; *Lowell Daily Journal and Courier,* 2 and 5 July 1859; clipping, Blue 41; *Clipper,* 16 July 1859, 103. On Connecticut, *Clipper,* 6 Aug., 126–127, and 27 Aug. 1859, 150; *Enquirer,* 21 Aug. 1859.
7. Kunzog 158; *Clipper,* 3 Sept., 159; 10 Sept., 166; 3 Dec. 1859, 263; *Enquirer,* 16 Oct. 1859; *Clipper,* 1 Oct. 1859, 191.
8. *Clipper,* 11 June 1859, 20; Great Show Ledger, after 23 Apr. 1858; *Circular and Catalogue of the Utica Female Seminary for 1859–1860,* Utica, 1859; T. Wood Clarke, *Utica for a Century and a Half,* Utica: Widtman Press, 1952, 175; John J. Walsh, *Vignettes of Old Utica,* Utica: Dodge Graphic Press, 1982, 139; Kate Rice letter to Maggie Rice, 22 Mar. 1861, Box 1, Mercyhurst; *Songs, Sentiments* 62.
9. *Clipper,* 30 Apr., 14; *Enquirer,* 8 May; *Clipper,* 21 May, 38; clipping, qtg. *Utica Daily Observer*, 30 May, Blue 29; *Enquirer*, 5 June; *Clipper*, 9 July 1859, 94; *Fort Plain, N.Y. Register,* 19 June 1856, Scrapbook 12, Mercyhurst; "Curiosities of Dan Rice's Great Show," Philadelphia, c. Mar. 1860, HTC.
10. *Syracuse Standard,* 16 June and 20 Aug. 1859, Onondaga; *Enquirer,* 19 June and 28 Aug. 1859; *Clipper,* 10 Mar. 1860, 375; 31 Mar. 1860, 398; clipping, "Special to the Indianapolis Journal," c. 1890, HTC.
11. Letter, Margaret Rice to her daughters, 15 Sept. 1859, Box 1, Mercyhurst; *Rochester Union and Advertiser,* 20 Sept. 1859; *Syracuse Tribune,* 21 Sept. 1859, Onondaga; *Enquirer,* 25 Sept. 1859.
12. *Sun,* 15 Oct. 1859; D. S. Reynolds 119, also 49, 117–124, 415, 472–473.

Chapter 27: Ring Cycle

1. "Curiosities of Dan Rice's Great Show," Philadelphia c. Mar. 1860, HTC.
2. *Enquirer,* 23 Oct. 1859. A year later, McLaren presented Blondin walking the tightrope while carrying his agent in a sack; few agents show such dedication. Bill, "D. McLaren, Sole Lessee," 10 Nov. 1860, Hertzberg. Isaac J. Greenwood, *The Circus,* New York, 1898, 116, wrote that Rice owned the Walnut Street Theatre.
3. *Budget,* 6 Feb. 1860.
4. *Enquirer,* 25 Mar. 1860; *Sunday Dispatch,* 6 Nov. 1859 and 19 Feb. 1860; heralds, "Dan Rice's Great Show," 23 Feb. 1860, and "The Elephant of Siam," c. Feb. 1860, American Antiquarian Society; Jack Beeching, *The Chinese Opium Wars,* New York: Harcourt Brace Jovanovich, 1975, 267–277; handbill, "Dan Rice's Great Show," Philadelphia, 10 Mar. 1860, Somers (N.Y.) Historical Society; *Sunday Dispatch,* 25 Mar. 1860; *Songs, Sentiments* 62.
5. *Clipper,* 12 Nov. 1859, 239, 14 Jan. 1860, 311, and 21 Jan. 1860, 319; *Sunday Dispatch,* 11 Mar. 1860; *Baltimore American,* 3 Apr. 1860; *Clipper,* 24 Dec. 1859, 287; *Budget,* 1 Jan. 1860; Erie County records.
6. Rice later said that the sheriff involved, Roddy Patterson, had steered him to the job at the Arsenal, Brown 49; Thayer, *Annals* 2: 93; *Post, Gazette,* and *Dispatch,* 15–21 Nov. 1859. The *Dispatch* reported damages at $4,350, but the lower figure is more likely; also *Louisville Courier,* 28 Aug. 1860.
7. *Budget,* 1 Jan. 1860; *American Humorist* 27, 38–39.
8. M. Willson Disher, ed., *The Cowells in America,* London: Oxford Univ. Press, 1934, 25.
9. *Clipper,* 13 Dec. 1879, 300; Charles Bernard, "Old-Time Showmen," *Billboard,* 14 July 1934, 37; *Porter's Spirit,* 4 Feb. 1860, 368; *Spirit,* 11 Feb. 1860, 12; *Clipper,* 25 Feb. 1860, 359; and 3 Mar. 1860, 367. The last name may have come from an "African giant, Mr. Zoyara," presented by the Christy Minstrels, *Clipper,* 25 Feb. 1860, 359.
10. Raymond Toole-Stott, *Circus and Allied Arts: A World Bibliography, 1500–1957,* Derby, Eng.: Harpur, 1958–1971, 303; *St Louis Bulletin,* 22 Oct. 1860, Blue 28; also *Enquirer,* 4 Nov. 1860; *Clipper,* 17 Nov. 1860, 247.
11. *Clipper,* 17 Mar. 1860, 383; *American,* 27 Mar. 1860; *Baltimore Republican,* 21 Apr.; *Baltimore Patriot,* 21 Apr.; *Baltimore Clipper,* 23 Apr.; and *Washington States & Union,* 25 Apr. 1860, all Blue 6; *Clipper,* 10 Mar. 1860, 375.
12. *Budget,* 6 Feb. 1860; *Enquirer,* 1 Jan. 1860.
13. *Porter's Spirit,* 31 Dec. 1859, 280; *Sunday Dispatch,* 25 Dec. 1859 and 1 Jan. 1860. See the *Public Ledger,* 18 Mar. 1858, on the schools' national eminence. The Women's Medical College, now part of Drexel University, was founded in 1850. *Clipper,* 19 Jan. 1861, 320.
14. "Great Union Speech," lithograph, Hertzberg; *Budget,* 1 Jan. 1860; "Dan Rice's Great Show," 16 Jan. 1860, Tibbals; *Clipper,* 31 Dec. 1859, 295; *Enquirer,* 1 Jan. 1860.

15. D. S. Reynolds 472–473, also 119, 124 and 372–373, 389.
16. *American Humorist* 30–32, 23–25, 11–12, 29, 32–35, 72.

Chapter 28: House Divided

1. On "Dixie," "Bryant's Programme & Songs," New York, 1859, author's collection; and *Clipper,* 16 Feb. 1861, 348; Calhoun cited in Eric Foner, *Free Soil, Free Labor, Free Men,* London: Oxford Univ. Press, 1970, 308.
2. Blue 8–10: *Washington Intelligencer, Star,* and *States & Union,* 27 Apr. 1860; *Richmond Dispatch,* 12 May; and *Whig,* 14 May 1860; *Petersburg Express,* 15 May; and *Intelligencer,* 15 May 1860. On Maggie, *Clipper,* 2 June 1860, 55.
3. "Things That I Like To See," *American Humorist* 23–25.
4. Blue 13–14: *Raleigh Register,* 30 May 1860; *Daily Democratic Press,* 29 May 1860; *Raleigh Standard,* 30 May 1860.
5. *Clipper,* 22 Dec. 1860–9 Feb. 1861, on Rice, final installment, 344.
6. On Buffalo, *Clipper,* 10 Apr. 1858, 407; on "Shovelry," *New York Times,* 8 Feb. 1858; *Clipper,* 20 Feb. –7 July 1858; on Philadelphia "Dream of Shovelry," *Clipper,* 27 Mar. 1858, 391; 17 Apr. 1858, 415; on *Mazeppa, Clipper,* 4 Sept. 1858, 158; on T. D. and Dan, *Clipper,* 26 Mar. 1859, 386; 31 Dec. 1859, 296.
7. On Chanfrau, *American,* 7 Apr. 1860, and Alvin F. Harlow, *Old Bowery Days,* New York: Appleton, 1931, 213; on Germany, bill in photocopy, Thayer, from Peter Brauning of Germany (Howes & Cushing took a circus to Germany in partnership with a London banker named Fillingham; later, Rice's fiction of touring Europe as a strongman included Fillingham as the agent, Brown 740); on Wilson, *Daily Alta California,* 29–30 May 1860, qtd. Thayer, *Annals* 3: 127; *Clipper,* 2 June 1860, 55, 5 Jan. 1861, 303; on Rice's warning, "Dan Rice's Great Show," 29 June 1859, Hertzberg.
8. Erie County records, 27 June 1860; contract, 1 Aug. 1860, Box 1, Mercyhurst; *Clipper,* 18 Dec. 1858, 278; 29 Jan. 1859, 326.
9. Ira Mark Ellman, Paul M. Kurtz, Katharine T. Bartlett, *Family Law,* Charlottesville, Va.: Michie Co., 1986, 162–165; Laws of Pennsylvania, 1815 (chap. 4104), supplements 1817 (chap. 4325) and 1854 (no. 629); *Young v. Young,* 82 Pa. Super. 492, 1924, Lexis 4; contract and bill of sale, 9 Aug. 1860, typescript, Kunzog-Adams; Kunzog 179; *North East (Pa.) Sun,* 13 Aug. 1881, qtd. *Erie Cosmopolite,* 19 Jan. 1922, 1; *Clipper*, 20 Oct. 1860, 24; clippings, c. 1863, Scrapbook 18 and 25, Mercyhurst; "Great National Circus," c. July 1863, Scrapbook 48, Mercyhurst.
10. D. S. Reynolds 476–477.
11. *Cincinnati Commercial, Enquirer, Gazette, Post* and *Times,* 9–10 Aug. 1860, Blue 14–20; *Clipper,* 25 Aug. 1860, 150–151; *Spirit,* 1 Sept. 1860, 364.
12. *Clipper,* 29 Sept. 1860, 191; Vincennes, Ind., c. 15 Sept. 1860; *Clipper,* 11 Aug. 1860, 135.

13. *Madison (Ind.) Courier,* 23 Aug. 1860, Blue 28; *Louisville Courier, Democrat,* and *Journal,* 27 Aug.–1 Sept. 1860, Blue 22, 24, 26 and 28; *Enquirer,* 3 Sept. 1860; *Springfield Daily Illinois Journal,* 3 Oct. 1860, Thayer.
14. *Picayune,* 22 Mar. and *Delta,* 3 Apr. 1854; Kunzog 170, and Way, *Packet Director* 242; *St. Louis Bulletin* and *Express,* 20–22 Oct. 1860, Blue 28; *Memphis Avalanche,* 8 Nov. 1860; *Memphis Appeal, Argus, Avalanche, Bulletin,* and *Enquirer,* 8–13 Nov. 1860, Blue 30–32.

Chapter 29: Southern Sympathy

1. *Crescent,* 28 Jan. 1861.
2. *Clipper,* 23 Mar. 1861, 391; *Delta,* 11 and 13 Dec. 1860
3. *Clipper,* 2 Feb. 1861, 335; Irwin Silber, *Songs of the Civil War,* New York: Columbia Univ. Press, 1960, 49; Richard Barksdale Harwell, *Songs of the Confederacy,* New York: Broadcast, 1951, 28–31.
4. *Delta,* 18 Jan. 1861, Blue 36; *Algiers (La.) Newsboy,* 11 Dec. 1860, qtd. in Brown 362–363; *Delta,* c. Jan. 1861, Blue 42.
5. *Delta,* 16 and 22 Dec. 1860; 22 Jan. 1861.
6. *Delta,* 11 Dec. 1860; 27 Jan. 1861; D. S. Reynolds 119; *Clipper,* 8 Dec. 1860.
7. *Delta* and *Picayune,* 2 Feb. 1861; clipping, Alexandria, La., 23 Feb. 1861, Blue 32; *Natchez Daily Free Trader,* 15 Mar. 1861, Blue 36.
8. *New York Times,* 16 Jan. 1858; Haswell 526; *Clipper,* 9 Feb. 1861, 343, and 18 May 1861, 38.
9. *Delta,* 9 Feb. 1861; "Local Intelligence," c. Dec. 1860, Blue 35; clipping, *Algiers (La.) Newsboy,* 8 Dec. 1860, Blue 34; *Delta,* 3 Feb. 1861. Kunzog, 169, wrote that father and son had a falling out in 1859.
10. Contract and bill of sale, 9 Aug. 1860, typescript, Kunzog-Adams (Kunzog 179); Kate Rice letter to "My Dear Ma," 23 Mar. 1861, Box 1, Mercyhurst; "Charles Warner," *Clipper,* 9 Sept. 1865, 175; *Great Barrington (Mass.) Berkshire Courier,* 19 Apr. 1861, qtd. in S. S. Freeman, "Girard's Dan Rice," *Girard Cosmopolite Herald,* 30 July 2000, 10A.
11. *New York Tribune,* 13 May 1861; A. M. Judson, *History of the Eighty-Third Regiment Pennsylvania Volunteers*, Erie, Pa., 1865, 21; Miller 471; Speaight, *History*, 65–66; *Norristown (Pa.) Register & Democrat,* 26 Aug. 1856, CWM; *Enquirer*, 3 Feb. and 17 May 1861; *Clipper,* 29 Dec. 1860, 295; *Frank Leslie's Illustrated Newspaper,* 11 May 1861, 406; *Clipper*, 9 Feb., 342; 2 Mar., 363; 13 Apr., 415; and 4 May 1861, 23; *New Orleans Commercial Advertiser,* 26 Jan. 1861, Blue 40.
12. *Clipper,* 2 Mar. 1861, 363.
13. *Enquirer* and *Commercial*, 15–18 May 1861.
14. *Enquirer,* 19 May 1861.
15. Clippings, "Excitement in Wheeling," c. 27 May 1861, Blue 41; and *St. Louis Democrat,* 20 June 1861, Blue 45; clipping, "Dan Rice in Western Virginia," c. 27 May 1861, Blue 43. Nearby George McClellan defeated Confederate forces in one of the first battles of the war.

16. *Clipper,* 25 May 1861, 47; 1 June, 54–55; 15 June, 71; 22 June, 78; 29 June, 87; 6 July, 95; 17 Aug., 142–143.
17. *Republican,* c. June 1861, Blue 122; *Democrat,* 25 June, Blue 121; St. Louis clipping, c. June 1861, Blue 45; Brown 144, 219; *Way's Packet Directory,* 242; "List of Vessels . . . Employed by the Quartermasters' Department," National Archives, Record Group 92, Entry 1418; *Lyons City Advocate,* 27 July 1861. Rice associated himself with Jefferson Davis, saying that he met the young lieutenant at Wisconsin's Fort Winnebago—Rice never got there—and that they reunited at Davis's Mississippi plantation in the fall of 1854—the senator was in Washington then. M. W. Brown 98, 138; Andrew Jackson Turner, "The History of Fort Winnebago," *Army Life in Wisconsin Territory,* Madison: 1898; William C. Davis, *Jefferson Davis: The Man and His Hour,* New York: HarperCollins, 1991, 240–242.
18. *Enquirer,* 1 and 15 Sept. 1861; *Lyons City Advocate,* 27 July 1861; clipping, Blue 116; "'Old Put' Drowns," Iowa Clipping File 2: 240, State Historical Society of Iowa; *La Crosse (Wis.) Tri-Weekly Democrat,* 20, 28 and 30 Aug. 1861; *Clipper,* 31 Aug., 158–159; 14 Sept., 174, and 21 Sept. 1861, 182.
19. *Cleveland Daily Herald,* 10 Aug. 1861, Blue 121; *Plain Dealer* reported in *Erie Gazette*, 15 Aug. 1861, qtd. in S. S. Freeman, "A Spy Among Us?" *Girard Cosmopolite Herald,* 6 Aug. 2000, 2A ; Brown 378–380; *Erie Weekly Gazette,* 29 Aug. 1861, qtg. *Girard Union*; *History of Erie County*, 1884, 466; *Chicago Post,* 12 Sept. 1861; *Chicago Tribune,* 11–14 Sept. 1861. Brown 220, printed a letter allegedly from Douglas to Rice, attesting to Rice's wisdom and his sincerity in warning Secretary of War Edwin Stanton of threats on his life.
20. *Enquirer,* 20 Oct. 1861; *Utica Evening Telegraph,* 31 Oct. 1861; *Clipper,* 23 Nov. 1861, 255.
21. *Erie Dispatch,* 5 Oct. 1861, qtd. in Brown 367–369; *Erie Weekly Observer,* 5 Oct. 1861, Blue 46, 119 (qtd. in Brown 424); *Erie Weekly Gazette,* 26 Sept. 1861; *Enquirer,* 28 Oct. 1861.
22. *Girard Union,* 30 Sept. 1861, Blue 46.

Chapter 30: Union, Alias Peace

1. "A Ticklish Subject," *Songs, Sentiments* 36.
2. Laura G. Sanford, *History of Erie County, Pennsylvania,* Philadelphia, 1862, 201; *History of Erie County*, 1884, 61; clipping, *Syracuse Journal,* 14 July 1860, Onondaga.
3. S. S. Freeman, *The Battles Story,* Fairview, Pa.: Author, 1992, 23–24.
4. Brown 321.
5. Clipping, Girard, c. Mar. 1858, Scrapbook 5, Mercyhurst; Miller 470.
6. "A Professor in Girard," c. Nov. 1861, Blue 4; "Teacher's Institute Near Fizzle by Dan Rice's Marriage," *Girard Cosmopolite,* 11 Mar. 1955 (both sources citing the Pennsylvania *School Journal*); *Enquirer,* 8 Sept. 1861, quoting and correcting *New York World,* 6 Sept. 1861.

7. Letter, Rice to Jacob Showles, 14 Feb. 1862, MCNY; Mary Kupiec Cayton, Elliott J. Gorn, and Peter W. Williams, eds., *Encyclopedia of American Social History,* vol. 1, New York: Charles Scribner's Sons, 1993, 94; Phillip A. Gibbs, "Self Control and Male Sexuality in the Advice Literature of Nineteenth-Century American, 1830–1860," *Journal of American Culture* 9, no. 2 (Summer 1986): 41; Reed, "Oldest Living Bareback Rider," *Billboard,* 23 Mar. 1929, 65.
8. *Cleveland Plain Dealer,* 5 Nov. 1861, Blue 3.
9. *Clipper,* 23 Nov. 1861, 255; *Enquirer,* 27 Nov. 23 1861.
10. *Enquirer,* 12 Nov.–2 Dec. 1861, and 5 Jan. 1862; *Daily Dramatic Review,* 21 Nov. 1861, Blue 122; Kingsley-Zoyara had married Stickney, Charles Bernard, "Old-Time Showmen," *Billboard,* 14 July 1934, 37.
11. Rice to Jacob Showles, 14 Feb. 1862, MCNY.
12. *Clipper,* 20 Apr. 1861, 6; *Enquirer,* 3 Dec. 1861. The pro-Southern, New York-based *Spirit of the Times* ceased publication on June 22, 1861, *Porter's Spirit of the Times* carried on until 14 Dec. 1861, and *Wilkes' Spirit of the Times* continued after that.
13. *Enquirer,* 7–10 Nov., and 1–8 Dec. 1861.
14. *Enquirer,* 8 Dec. 1861.
15. *Clipper,* 25 Jan. 1862, 327; *Washington (D.C.) Evening Star,* 6, 14, and 17 Jan. 1862.
16. *Herald,* 25–27 Jan. 1862; *Frank Leslie's Illustrated,* 22 Feb. 1862, 215.
17. *Inquirer,* 1 Mar. 1862.
18. *Inquirer,* 1–6 Mar.; *Bulletin,* 1–6 Mar. 1862; "Dan Rice's Benefit," handbill, 7 Mar. 1862, author's collection.
19. *Dispatch,* 2 Mar. 1862; *Songs, Sentiments* 63; *Clipper,* 15 Mar. 1862, 383; *Enquirer,* 16 Mar. 1862; *Clipper,* 29 Mar. 1861, 395.
20. *Dispatch,* 16 Mar. 1862.
21. *Enquirer,* 23 Mar. and 13 Apr. 1862; *Clipper,* 22 Mar. 1862, 391; 29 Mar. 1862, 399.
22. *Enquirer,* 9 Nov. 1861.

Chapter 31: A Muted Voice

1. Dingess 339.
2. Brown 145; *Enquirer,* 23 Feb. and 6 Apr. 1862.
3. *Clipper,* 5 Apr. 1862, 407; *Handbook of the Arena,*1862, Tibbals; *Enquirer*, 6 Apr. 1862; *Clipper,* 2 Feb. 1861, 335, and 12 May 1860, 30. Heenan had joined Howes and Cushing's circus in England after his boxing career had ended. Though Mark Twain named his character Tom Sawyer after "sawyers," river snags that could saw through the hull of steamboat, his pen caught an echo of the era's popular Tom Sayers.
4. *Programme,* 7 Apr. 1862, Scrapbook 33, Mercyhurst; *Charleston Advertiser,* Rhode Island or New Hampshire, c. 1862, Scrapbook 45, Mercyhurst; *Clipper,* 22 Aug. 1863, 150.

5. *Clipper,* 18 Oct. 1862, 211; *Erie Weekly Gazette,* 1 and 9 May 1862; *Ann Arbor Peninsular Courier,* 13 June 1862; *London (Ontario) Advertiser*, 23 Aug. 1862. Slout, *Olympians,* passes on a report that Rice adopted Fred Barclay, reflecting Rice's close involvement with his apprentices more than a legal fact.
6. *Lowell (Mass.) Daily Courier,* 23 Sept. 1863; *Dan Rice's Great American Humorist Song Book,* New York, 1863, 4–5; *Enquirer,* 1 June 1862.
7. *Chicago Tribune,* 28 June 1862; Brown 145, 91, and 315; *Clipper,* 26 July 1862, 119; *Essex (Mass.) Statesman,* 19 Sept. 1863; *Harrisburg (Pa.) Patriot and Union,* 8 Oct. 1863; *Great American Humorist,* 11–14, 18, 5–6.
8. *Enquirer,* 4 Dec. 1861; on Booth, Thayer, e-mail, 15 July 2000; Gene Smith, *American Gothic: The Story of America's Legendary Theatrical Family—Junius, Edwin, and John Wilkes Booth,* New York: Simon & Schuster, 1992, 213; *Clipper,* 10 Sept. 1864, 169 (Perhaps the actor trumped the clown's tales of bravery by boasting that he had taken a bullet in the leg at a shooting gallery in Georgia; Booth could depict himself as no stranger to wounds, and not fearful of them, *Clipper,* 27 Oct. 1860, 223); *Enquirer,* 9 Nov. 1862; *Erie Weekly Gazette,* 18 Apr. 1863; *Chicago Post,* 23 Dec. 1862; also *Chicago Tribune,* 5 Jan. 1863.
9. S. S. Freeman, "The Wurzbachs and the Legend of Their House," Part 1, *Girard Cosmopolite Herald,* 10 Jan. 1993.
10. Brown 295–296.
11. "Infant Mortality Rates for Massachusetts, 1860–1864," *Historical Statistics of the United States,* U.S. Department of Commerce, 1975, 57; S. S. Freeman, *Battles* 25; *Clipper,* 8 Nov. 1862, 235; Rice autograph, 20 May 1863, MCNY.
12. *Clipper,* 27 Sept. 1862, 191; 4 Oct. 1862, 199; *Erie Weekly Gazette,* 30 Apr.; *Erie Observer,* 2 May 1863, qtd. in Kunzog 214; on Excelsior, Jr., Batavia, N.Y., 13 June 1863, Blue 117; "Dan Rice's Great Show," herald, Aug. 1863, MCNY; "Dan Rice's Great Show," Salem, Mass., 19 Sept. 1863, CWM; *Reading Times,* 14 Oct. 1863.
13. *Pittsburgh Post,* 30 June 1863; e-mail, Slout to author, 15 Dec. 2000; Thayer to author, 16 Dec. 2000; *Clipper,* 18 Apr. 1863, 6; *Syracuse Journal,* 31 July 1863; clipping, Jamestown N.Y., 20 June 1863, Adams-Kunzog; *Newton (N.J.) Sussex Register,* 2 Oct. 1863, Scrapbook 24, Mercyhurst.
14. "Dan Rice's Great Show," herald, 20 Aug. 1863, MCNY; letter to author, 12 Feb. 1992, Betty Gardner (Rice's great-granddaughter).
15. *Worcester (Mass.) Aegis and Transcript,* 31 Dec. 1864 and 1 Apr. 1865; *Clipper,* 7 Jan., 311, and 8 Apr. 1865, 414.

Chapter 32: "Colonel" Rice

1. *Ann Arbor Michigan Argus,* 23 Sept. 1864.
2. *Syracuse Journal,* 7 May 1864. Rice's performers this season included Kate Ormand, who was the adopted daughter of Margaret Ormand, the Miss Delsmore implicated in the affair with Spalding.

3. Robert D. Good Collection, CWM; e-mail to author, Fred Dahlinger, Jr., CWM, 23 July, 2001; John and Alice Durant, *Pictorial History of the American Circus,* New York: A. S. Barnes, 1957, 44; letter to author, 21 Aug. 2000, Norman P. Carlson, Fenton History Center, Jamestown.
4. John P. Sanderson letter to Abraham Lincoln, 4 July 1862, Chicago, Papers of Abraham Lincoln, Robert Todd Lincoln Collection, Library of Congress; *Leslie's Illustrated,* 19 Mar. 1864, 403; *Chicago Post,* 28 Oct.–8 Nov. 1863, and 17 Mar. 1864; *Report of the Northwestern Sanitary Commission, Branch of the U.S. Sanitary Commission, for the Months of May and June, 1864,* Chicago, 1864, 24; *Sunday Dispatch,* 5 June 1864; *Catalogue of Paintings, Statuary, Etc., in the Art Department of the Great North-Western Fair*, Chicago, 1865, 11; *Chicago Tribune,* 28 June 1862. Volk organized the Fair's Fine Arts gallery, *Catalogue,* 2; *Chicago Post,* 29 Oct. 1863. The Little Giant had supported Volk, a relative, through his artistic education. Volk, *History of the Douglas Monument at Chicago,* Chicago, 1880; Robert W. Johannsen, *Stephen A. Douglas,* New York: Oxford Univ. Press, 1973, 466, 619.
5. Kunzog 233.
6. *Syracuse Journal,* 7 May 1864.
7. *Songs, Sentiments,* 56–58 (Compare Whitman's enduring affection for "O magnet South! O glistening perfumed South! My South!" D. S. Reynolds 121); *Clipper,* 26 Mar. 1864, 398.
8. *Enquirer,* 13 Sept. 1848; *Mobile Register,* 12 Jan. 1853; *Picayune,* 19 Jan. 1855; "Captain Dan Rice on Buchanan's Cabinet," Mar. 1857; *Delta,* 9 Dec. 1860; on "Colonel," *Washington Daily Union,* 8 June 1850; *Picayune,* 30 Dec. 1852; on titles, Ford 67; *Harper's,* Aug. 1859, 579.
9. "Girard's Quota Nearly Full," [*Girard Union,* June 1864], Blue 124; Judson, *History of the Eighty-Third,* does not mention Rice; *Erie Daily Dispatch,* 7 Feb. 1866; Brown 421–423; S. S. Freeman, "Spy?" *Girard Cosmopolite Herald,* 6 Aug. 2000, 10A; Rice memo, "83d Regiment," c. 1895, MCNY; "The Pride of the Arena," *Clipper*, 27 Aug.–12 Nov. 1864; *Jamestown (N.Y.) Journal,* 8 July 1864.
10. *Clearfield (Pa.) Republican,* 18 Dec. 1861, Blue 119; Moody, 42; Thayer 3: 101.
11. *Erie Gazette,* 22 Sept. 1864, qtd. in S. S. Freeman, "Clown," 8A ; Kelly 204; Cockrell 93; *Clipper,* 2 Feb. 1861, 335, and 1 Sept. 1866, 167, qtg. a Kentucky politician.
12. *Cairo Weekly Times and Delta,* 5 Dec. 1855; *Clipper,* 5 July 1856, 87; and 12 Sept. 1857, 167; *Erie Weekly Observer,* 23 Oct. 1858; *New York Herald,* 31 Jan. 1859; *Girard Republican,* 18 Feb. 1859, Blue 2; *Clipper,* 8 Jan., 303, and 12 Feb. 1859, 342; *Effusions* 23; *Clipper,* 10 Sept. 1859, 166.
13. *Enquirer,* 2 Aug. 1864; *Erie Dispatch,* 15 Sept. 1864.
14. Gary Wills, *Lincoln at Gettysburg: The Words That Remade America,* New York: Simon & Schuster, 1992. Edwin Forrest had earlier articulated similar thoughts in a Fourth of July speech saying they met not to celebrate military triumph but a grand "experiment"—Lincoln's "proposition"—in the birth of the nation,

then "Threescore years and two" ago, *Pittsburgh Mercury,* 15 Aug. 1838. On other precursors of Lincoln's address, Don E. Fehrenbacher, *Lincoln in Text and Context,* Stanford, Calif.: Stanford Univ. Press, 1978, 285.

15. *Chicago Tribune,* 23–24 Sept. 1864; Morneweck 2: 529.
16. *Chicago Post,* 24 Sept. 1864.
17. S. S. Freeman, "Spy?" *Girard Cosmopolite Herald,* 6 Aug. 2000, 1–2A; photographic facsimile, "Dan. Rice's Letter of Acceptance," 1 Oct. 1864, author's collection; Brown 418–421.
18. *Nelson's Biographical Dictionary and Historical Reference Book of Erie County, Penn.,* Erie, Pa., 1896, 143; Sandburg 3: 235.
19. S. S. Freeman, "Clown," 1A. Though the notice named another man as the new owner, it "was generally known" that the paper was Rice's.
20. "Dan Rice's Fourth of July Oration," *Songs, Sentiments,* 64–66.
21. *Enquirer,* 9 Nov. 1864; *History of Erie County*, 1884, 384. S. S. Freeman's "Clown," and "Dan Rice's Monument," *Pennsylvania Heritage* 12, no. 4 (Fall 1986): 10–15.
22. *Clipper,* 14 May 1864, 38; *Washington Morning Chronicle,* 8–13 June 1864; *Clipper,* 11 June 1864, 71; 16 July 1864, 110, and 4 July 1868, 102; *Enquirer,* 18 Apr. 1864.
23. *Sunday Dispatch,* 22 and 29 Jan. 1865; *Clipper,* 17 June 1865, 78.
24. *Historical Statistics of the United States,* Bureau of the Census, 1975, Part I, 165; Ron Chernow, *Titan: The Life of John D. Rockefeller, Sr.,* New York: Random House, 45–47; *Pittsburgh Gazette,* 17 and 27 Oct.; and *Post,* 24–30 Oct. 1863.
25. "Dan Rice.—A Sketch," *Billboard,* 12 Jan. 1907, 26; *New York Times,* 15 Jan. 1871, 8; *Clipper,* 25 Mar. 1864, 398.
26. Rice letter to "My Dear Sister," 22 Apr. 1866, MCNY; *Clipper,* 14 Oct. 1865, 214–215; *Rochester Union and Advertiser,* 6 Apr. 1865; *Clipper,* 5 Aug. 1865, 135; 10 June, 70.
27. Volk's reminiscences, vol. 8: 17–18, 61–62, Item #5137, *A Catalog of the Alfred Withal Stern Collection of Lincolniana in the Library of Congress* (1960), 467.
28. *Clipper,* 18 Feb. 1865, 359; S. S. Freeman, "Dan Rice's Monument."
29. *Harper's Weekly,* 25 Nov. 1865, 737–738; *Clipper,* 11 Nov. 1865, 247; *Erie Weekly Gazette,* 9 Nov. 1865.
30. A former foe, the Republican publisher from Philadelphia, J. W. Forney, also wrote, attesting that Rice's noble war actions "deserve to be remembered and honored by the country," *Pittsburgh Post,* 6 July 1866.
31. *Erie Daily Dispatch,* 2 Nov. 1865; *Erie Weekly Gazette,* 9 Nov. 1865; *Erie Observer,* qtd. in Kunzog 236–237; *Girard Union,* 2 Nov. 1865, Lincoln Museum, Fort Wayne, Ind.

Chapter 33: Rice for President

1. Robert Edmund Sherwood, *Here We Are Again: Recollections of an Old Circus Clown,* Indianapolis: Bobbs-Merrill, 1926, 60–61.

2. *Clipper,* 25 Nov. 1865–13 Jan. 1866; Charles Stow, "The Pioneers of the American Circus," *Theatre Magazine* 5 (Aug. 1905): 192–194 (In addition to his circus agentry, Stow had been editor of Rice's *Cosmopolite*).
3. Rice to "My Dear Sister," 22 Apr. 1866, MCNY; *Clipper,* 9 Sept. 1865, 175, and 8 Sept. 1866, 175; John B. Doris, "Dan Rice—A Sketch," *Billboard,* 12 Jan. 1907, 6; *Boston Herald,* 5–9 Aug. 1856; *Clipper,* 14 Apr. 1866, 7; *Enquirer,* 29 May 1865.
4. *The Age,* 9 Mar. 1866, Blue 1; Brown 421–423; *Dispatch,* 6 Aug.–28 Sept. 1866; clipping of Rice letter, "Won't Give It Up," 28 Aug. 1866, author's collection.
5. *Dispatch,* 3–7 and 15 Sept. 1866. Kunzog, 247, places Rice at the unveiling of the Douglas Monument in Chicago three days later.
6. *Dispatch,* 11 and 15 Sept. 1866; *Picayune,* 1 Dec. 1865, 9, qtg. *Mobile Times,* 28 Nov.
7. *Dispatch,* 26 and 29 Sept. 1866.
8. *Clipper,* 3 Nov. 1866, 239; *Dispatch,* 21 Nov. 1866; Jeanne Celli, Rebecca's great-great-granddaughter, phone conversation with author, 7 Sept. 2000; *Dispatch,* 12 and 15 Jan. 1867; Kunzog 433.
9. Rice letter to Jacob Showles, 7 Nov. 1866, MCNY; Brown 243; transcript, *Erie Dispatch,* 16 Mar. 1867, Adams-Kunzog; *Pittsburgh Post* and *Gazette,* 28 Oct.–4 Nov. 1867; *Commercial,* 4 Nov. 1867, qtd. in Kunzog 250–251; *Erie Weekly Dispatch,* 16 Nov. 1867; *Clipper,* 16 Nov. 1867, 255.
10. *Marietta (Ohio) Times,* 30 May 1867; *Clipper,* 6 July 1867, 102.
11. *Spectator,* qtd. in Brown 400–401; *Greensburg (Pa.) Republican and Democrat,* 11 Sept. 1867; Rice for president, Tibbals 1867–1868 clippings; most rpt. in Brown 392–424.
12. "Home of Dan Rice," photograph of lithograph, author's collection.
13. Tibbals 1867; Brown 223–225.
14. *Dispatch,* 18–25 Nov., 26 Oct., and 6 Dec. 1867.
15. D. S. Reynolds 351; Leslie H. Southwick, *Presidential Also-Rans and Running Mates, 1788–1996,* 2d ed., Jefferson, N.C.: McFarland, 1998, 337–345. Rice piggy-backed himself onto Cooper's run, claiming that he had distributed 300,000 circulars for him. Brown 17, 19; Miriam Gurko, *The Lives and Times of Peter Cooper,* New York: Thomas V. Crowell, 1959, 224.
16. Dingess 368; Harris 156; *Dispatch,* 13 and 16 Nov. 1867.
17. J. Milton Traber, "The Lives of Famous Clowns," *Billboard,* 23 Dec. 1911, 5; *Erie Dispatch,* 31 Oct. 1866.

Chapter 34: Folly to Fight

1. *Clipper,* 11 Apr. 1868, 2; Patricia C. Click, *The Spirit of the Times: Amusements in Nineteenth-Century Baltimore, Norfolk, and Richmond,* Charlottesville: Univ. Press of Virginia, 1989, 52.
2. Richard Sennett, *The Fall of Public Man,* New York: Random House, 1977, 313–323.

3. Raymond Williams, *Culture and Society: 1780–1950,* New York: Harper, 1966, xv–xvi; also Levine, *Highbrow/Lowbrow*; Bruce A. McConachie, *Melodramatic Formations: American Theatre & Society, 1820–1870,* Iowa City: Univ. of Iowa Press, 1992; James H. Johnson, *Listening in Paris: A Cultural History,* Berkeley and Los Angeles: Univ. of California Press, 1995.
4. Edward Denby, qtd. in Terry Teachout, "Beyond the Sugar Plum Fairy," *New York Times Book Review,* 3 May 1998, 13.
5. *Daily Dayton Empire,* 8 Aug. 1865; *Clipper,* 6 Jan. 1866, 65; 10 Mar., 383; Rice letter to *Clipper,* 12 May 1867, HTC.
6. *Clipper,* 6 June 1870, 70; 27 Nov. 1869, 265; on "harangues," 10 Mar. 1866, 383; 11 July 1868, 118; 12 June 1869, 79; 28 Aug. 1869, 167 (twice); 30 Oct. 1869, 239; 26 Oct. 1878, 244; on newspaper reach, 16 May 1868, 46.
7. *Clipper,* 21 Dec. 1867, 295; 4 Apr 1868, 414; "Dan Rice Farewell," *White Tops* (Dec. 1937): 20, qtg. *Hartford (Conn.) Times,* 30 July, 1868; *Clipper,* 28 Mar. 1868, 407; 11–18 Apr. 1868, 6, 14; 18 July, 118; *Clipper,* 12 Sept. 1868, 182; 7 Nov. 1868, 247.
8. Photograph, MCNY.
9. "Musical Source," Ursuline Chapel, Cleveland, 9 July 1868, Account book 2, Mercyhurst; "The Great River Show," 1864, Pfening Collection; Erie County records; S. S. Freeman, "The Wurzbachs," parts 1 & 2, *Girard Cosmopolite Herald,* 10 and 17 Jan. 1993.
10. S. S. Freeman, "Clown," 1A; *Clipper,* 27 Mar. 1869, 407; *Leavenworth (Kans.) Times & Conservative,* 8 Aug. 1868; *Reading Times,* 22 Apr. 1868, qtg. *New York Commercial Advertiser.*
11. "Dan Rice's Ultimatum," 17 Apr. 1869, CWM; Brown 425; *Quincy (Ill.) Daily Herald,* 19 May 1869; *Clipper,* 25 Jan. 1873, 348; *Memphis Daily Appeal,* 2 Apr. 1882; "In Bankruptcy," 20 Mar. 1875, Kunzog-Adams.
12. *Clinton (Iowa) Daily Herald*, 19 May 1869; *Evansville Ind. Daily Journal*, 9 Sep. 1869.
13. *Baraboo (Wis.) Republican,* 23 June 1855; 30 Aug. 1857. Thayer, "The Circus That Inspired the Ringlings," *Bandwagon* 40, no. 3 (1996): 23–25. [Albert Ringling], *Life Story of the Ringling Brothers,* Chicago: Donnelley, 1900, 21–25; "Romance and the American Circus," *Chicago Sunday Record-Herald,* 16 Apr. 1911; Charles Ringling interview, *Public Ledger,* 26 Mar. 1921; Henry Ringling North and Alden Hatch, *The Circus Kings,* Garden City, N.Y.: Doubleday, 1960, 47–54.
14. *Clipper,* 18 July 1868, 118; 30 Oct. 1869, 239; Frost, *Circus Life* 205; Dingess, memoirs, 347; *Clipper,* 12 June 1869, 79; 31 July 1869, 135, qtg. 19 July *Hannibal (Mo.) Courier;* 28 Aug. 1869, 167.
15. *Clipper,* 24 July 1869, 127; *Davenport Democrat,* 4 May 1869.
16. *Clipper,* 28 Aug., 167; 11 Sept., 183; 16 Oct. 1869, 223; Dingess 338, 345–348.
17. Olive Logan, *Before the Footlights and Behind the Scenes,* Philadelphia, 1870, 360–366, 307, 111, 372 (Jennings 538, repeated the tale and made Logan a first-hand witness); Sherwood 148.

18. Rice! 74; Brown 154, 262; Morneweck 389–390, 403; *Topeka (Kans.) Daily Commonwealth,* 17–18 Aug. 1869; "Col. Dan Rice," 1869 Ledger, author's collection; Sherwood 61.
19. *Clipper,* 11 Dec., 28; 30 Oct., 239, and 13 Nov. 1869, 255; S. D. Dickinson, "Showboats and Circuses," *Arkansas Gazette,* 28 Nov. 1948, B1.
20. "Dan Rice's Rail and Steamer Circus," 24 Aug. 1870, CWM; *Evansville Daily Journal,* 16 May 1870, CWM.
21. "Dan Rice's Own Circus," 1870 Ledger, pp. 58, 60, 134–140, Mercyhurst; on Mrs. Rice 184–185, on Marcellus, 186, $600 fine, 112; firing, 4.
22. Letter to author, 29 Feb. 1992, David Wiley, Clerk of Records, Erie County, Penn.; *Saratoga Springs (N.Y.) Saratogian,* 6 Oct. 1870; 1870 Ledger, 140, 184, Mercyhurst; Inventory of Hugh Manahan, 17 Oct. 1871, New Jersey State Archives; S. S. Freeman, *Battles* 32.
23. *New York Sun,* 23 Feb. 1900; Brown 251.

Chapter 35: Paris Pavilion

1. *Clipper,* 21 Jan. 1871, 335; *New Orleans Republican,* 19 Jan. 1871, Historic New Orleans Collection.
2. *Ann Arbor Michigan Argus,* 26 May 1871; and *Ann Arbor Peninsular Courier,* 26 May and 2 June 1871.
3. *Clipper,* 25 Mar. 1871, 407; *Baltimore American and Commercial Advertiser,* 16 Nov. 1871, qtd. in Slout, "The Recycling of the Dan Rice Paris Pavilion Circus," *Bandwagon* 42, no. 4 (1998): 13–21; *Syracuse Journal,* 26 July 1867, Onondaga; *Clipper,* 7 Oct. 1871, 214; *Baltimore Sun,* 14 Nov. 1871; seating chart, MCNY. Various accounts boosted capacity to 2,000—Baltimore *Sun,* 11 Nov. 1871; 3,500—*Syracuse Journal,* 30 Mar. 1867, Onondaga; 4,400—*Clipper,* 17 Apr. 1880, 25; 5,000—Kunzog 271; 8,000—*New York Times,* 27 Aug. 1874, 2.
4. *Buffalo Daily Courier,* 1 July 1871, qtd. in Slout, "Recycling" 12–14 and 20; "Dan. Rice," 22 June 1871, PA vol. 61, R. G. Dun & Co. Collection, Baker Library, Harvard Business School.
5. Visit of 8 Feb. 1871 recorded, Crum Family Bible, Monmouth County Historical Society.
6. Thayer, *Annals* 3: 65–67, 220; Slout, *A Royal Coupling,* San Bernardino, Cal.: Emeritus Enterprises Publ., 2000, 1–4; *Clipper,* 16 Mar. 1867, 391.
7. Thayer, "P. T. Barnum's Great Travelling Museum, Menagerie, Caravan and Hippodrome," *Bandwagon* 20, no. 4 (1976): 4–9; Slout, *A Royal Coupling* 1–5; Saxon, *Selected Letters of P. T. Barnum,* New York: Columbia Univ. Press, 1983; clipping, "When William C. Coup and Daniel Castello Came Out of the West," Hertzberg.
8. *Detroit Free Press,* 31 May 1873.
9. *Clipper,* 19 Aug., 159; and 2 Sept. 1871, 175; Slout, "Recycling" 15; Alan Trachtenberg, *The Incorporation of America: Culture and Society in the Gilded Age,* New York: Hill, 1982.

10. *Baltimore American and Commercial Advertiser,* 13 Nov. 1871; *Sun,* 14 Nov. 1871; Erie County records; *New York Times,* 27 Aug. 1874, 2.
11. *Clipper,* 30 Dec. 1871, 311.
12. *Picayune,* 15–17 Feb. 1872; *Olathe (Kans.) Mirror,* 18 May 1872; *Ft. Scott (Kans.) Daily Monitor,* 24 May 1872; *Clipper,* 22 June, 95; 13 July 1872, 119; 3 Aug. 1872, 143; 11 Oct. 1873, 223.
13. "Dan. Rice," 2 July and 30 Dec. 1872, PA vol. 61, R. G. Dun & Co. Collection; *Clipper,* 18 Jan. 1873, 335; Way 28; *Atchison (Kans.) Daily Champion,* 27–28 May. 1873, *Clipper,* 21 and 18 Sept. 1872, 199, 207, 25 Jan., 348; 22 Feb., 375; 25 Oct., 239; 8 Nov., 255; 20 Dec. 1873, 303. The *Cosmopolite* continues, the grand title Rice gave it jokingly transformed locally into the "Cow's Appetite," phone conversation, editor Valerie Myers, 21 Mar. 2001.
14. *Clipper,* 19 Apr. 1873; Frost, *Circus Life*, 286–287; Roy Rosenzweig and Steve Brier, *Who Built America?* CD, American Social History Project, 261; *Evansville (Ind.) Daily Journal,* 9 Sept. 1869; *Atchison (Kans.) Daily Champion,* 11 Aug. 1869; "Dan Rice's Tripartite . . . Circus," 24 Aug. 1870, CWM; *Mobile Daily Register,* 23 Jan. 1872; *Osage Mission (Kans.) Neosho County Journal,* 18 May 1872; Rock Island ad, 14 July 1869, qtd. in Dingess 347; *Leavenworth (Kans.) Daily Commercial,* 7 Aug. 1869; *Clipper,* 8 Feb. 1873, 359, referring to it as the Spalding, Henderson & Ryan show. Also *Clipper,* 15 Mar., 399; 29 Mar. 1873, 415; stationery, author's collection. *Leavenworth (Kans.) Daily Commercial,* 22 May 1873; John Trewolla, a performer, had a one-third stake in this one, and S. E. Crane, the manager, may have had another third, *Clipper,* 29 Mar. 1873, 415.
15. Fred Dahlinger, "The Development of the Railroad Circus," *Bandwagon* 27, no. 6 (1983): 6–11; 28, no. 1 (1984): 16–27; Thayer, "P. T. Barnum's Great Museum, Menagerie, Hippodrome and Traveling World's Fair: Season of 1873," *Bandwagon* 41, no. 4 (1997): 26–30; *Clipper,* 25 Jan. 1873, 348.
16. Brown 163–164; *New York Times,* 27 Aug. 1874, 2; *Clipper,* 29 Nov., 271; 6 Dec. 1873, 287.
17. *Clipper,* 7 Mar. 1874, 391; *Clipper,* 26 July 1873, 135; 14 Feb. 1874, 368; Erie County records; *Clipper,* 18 Apr. 1874, 23; S. S. Freeman, *Battles* 44.
18. *Clipper,* 20 June 1874, 95; 8 Aug. 1874, 151; Brown 285; *Topeka (Kans.) Daily Capital,* 5 Jan. 1880; Pete Conklin, qtd. in David W. Watt, "Side Lights on the Circus Business," *Bandwagon* 44, no. 5 (2000): 47. The reference to "rebellious liquors" is to Adam in Shakespeare's *As You Like It,* the character representing extreme old age.
19. "In Bankruptcy," 20 Mar. 1875, Adams-Kunzog; *Clipper,* 27 Feb. 1875, 38; e-mail, L. Dale Patterson, Archivist, United Methodist Church Archives, 21 May 2001.

Chapter 36: Is Life Worth Living?

1. Dixon Wecter, *Sam Clemens of Hannibal,* Boston: Houghton-Mifflin, 1952, 187–192; Walter Blair and Victor Fisher, eds., *The Works of Mark Twain,* vol. 8,

Adventures of Huckleberry Finn, Berkeley and Los Angeles: Univ. of California Press, 1988, 411 and 414.

Twain may have been borrowing from Rice Shakspeareianism a few pages earlier in the pastiche spouted by the fake Duke: "To be, or not to be; that is the bare bodkin / That makes calamity of so long life; / For who would fardels bear, Till Birnum wood do come to Dunsinane, / . . . / But soft you, the fair Ophelia: / Ope not thy ponderous and marble jaws, / But get thee to a nunnery—go!" *Huckleberry Finn*, 1958, 115.

2. *Historical Dictionary of American Slang*, first citation, 1878. ("Hippodrome" had come to mean a rigged horse race, and then fraud generally.) Chess L. Briarmead, "The American Circus," *Clipper,* 17 Apr. 1875, supplement 2.
3. *Clipper,* 13 Feb., 367; 27 Feb, 383; 17 Apr.–24 July 1875; "Herkimer, June 1, 1875," DeHaven handbill, CWM. DeHaven tried to recoup by suing Barnum for $50,000 for libel, but P. T. shrugged—"it doesn't amount to shucks"—and nothing came of it, *Enquirer,* 1 and 7 Oct. 1875.
4. *Enquirer,* 13 Sep.–9 Oct. 1875; *Clipper,* 11 Sep.–2 Oct 1875; W. Quinett Hendricks, *Stranger Than Fiction* [Wooster, Ohio:] Author, 1928, 24. A circus memoir added another alleged connection, with Rice as witness to the memoirist's contract with Barnum in April 1887, Sherwood 80–81.
5. *Dallas Weekly Herald,* 1 Feb. 1876; *Clipper,* 29 Jan., 351, and 19 Feb. 1876, 375; "When William C. Coup and Daniel Castello Came Out of the West," Hertzberg; *Portsmouth (Ohio) Times,* 17 June 1876; *Gallipolis (Ohio) Bulletin,* 7 June 1876; Way 166; "Dan. Rice," 12 July 1876, 20 Jan. and 4 June 1877, PA vol. 61, R. G. Dun & Co. Collection.
6. *Clipper*, 23 Aug. 1873, 167; *Memphis Daily Appeal,* 2 Apr. 1882; John F. Polacsek, "The Stowe Bros. Circus—A Real Family Tradition: Part One," *Bandwagon* 29, no. 1 (1985): 49–56; *New York Mercury,* 21 Apr. 1876; *Clipper,* 22 July 1876, 134; *Memphis Daily Appeal,* 2 Apr. 1882.
7. *Clipper,* 28 Oct. 1876, 244; and 6 Jan. 1877, 327; *Metropolis (Ill.) Promulgator,* 15 Sept. 1877, Polacsek; *Clipper,* 31 Mar., 7; and 28 Apr. 1877, 39. Also John Daniel Draper, "A Celebrated Rider: William Showles," *Bandwagon* 45, no. 1 (2001): 19–23; "The Late Mrs. Showles," 15 Mar. 1924, Hertzberg.
8. *Clipper,* 9 Mar. 1878, 399; *Wyandotte (Kans.) Herald,* 6 June 1878. On Howland and Jennier, Box 1, Mercyhurst; *Topeka Daily Capital,* 9 Jan. 1880; *Daily Commonwealth,* 9 Jan. 1880.
9. *Omaha Republican,* 11, 17–18 July 1878; *Decatur (Neb.) Burtonian,* 18 July 1878, contributed by Ronald W. Hunter, Omaha. (Bell and boat are still there, the former in a church belfry, and the Damsel silted over, Letter to author, 26 Oct. 1991, Decatur Village Clerk Peggy A. Davis.) *Blue Rapids (Kans.) Blue Valley Telegraph,* 6 Sep. 1878; *Topeka Daily Commonwealth,* 5 Sept. and *Daily Blade,* 6 Sep. 1878; *Belleville (Kans.) Telescope,* 29 Aug. 1878; *Clipper,* 26 Oct. 1878, 244.
10. *Clipper,* 30 Nov. 1878, 287; Brown 498–500.
11. D. S. Reynolds 96; *New York Tribune,* 21 Dec. 1879; *St. Louis Republican,* qtd.

Columbus Dispatch, 21 Dec. 1879; *New York Times,* 27 Dec. 1879, 4; *Topeka (Kans.) Daily Capital,* 24 Dec. 1879; and *Clipper,* 3 Jan. 1880, 323.

12. *New York Times,* 3 Feb. 1880, 4.
13. Estate of Wessel T. B. Van Orden, statement of Edmund H. Van Orden, 3 Sep. 1877, Greene County Historical Society; *Clipper,* 10 Nov. 1877, 259; 10 Apr., 19; and 17 Apr. 1880, 27; *Picayune,* 7 Apr. 1880; *Albany Evening Times,* 12 Apr. 1880 and *Albany Argus,* 12 and 14 Apr. 1880. (On no discernible evidence, Kunzog, 329, puts Rice at Spalding's funeral.)
14. *Clipper,* 16 Oct., 239; 18 Dec. 1880, 307; 5 Feb.–9 Apr., 13 Aug., 731; 1 Oct., 451, and 5 Nov. 1881, 537; 28 Jan. 1882, 733; Way 77; *Memphis Appeal,* 26 Oct. 1880; *New Orleans Time Picayune,* 19 Feb. 1881; Polacsek, "The Stowe Bros. Circus—A Real Family Tradition: Part Two," *Bandwagon* 30, no. 3 (1985): 14–21.
15. *Keokuk (Iowa) Gate City,* 7 Oct. 1881, CWM; "Aunt Townsend" to Charlotte Webster Battles, 1887, qtd. in S. S. Freeman, "Spy," *Girard Cosmopolite Herald,* 6 Aug. 2000, 10A; C. C. G. Sturtevant, "Little Biographies of Famous American Circus Men," *White Tops* (Oct. 1928): 7. Girard disdain continued into the twentieth century, remembered by Rice's New Jersey relatives into the twenty-first.
16. *Chicago Tribune,* 25 Nov. 1881, 7; *Topeka (Kans.) Daily Capital,* 29 Nov. 1881.
17. *Clipper,* 25 Feb.–9 Sep. 1882; Hendricks 37–38; "John Robinson's 10 Big Shows Combined," John Robinson Papers, Cincinnati Historical Society; clipping, *Show World,* c. 1882, rpt. of Rice's contract, 18 Mar. 1882, NYPL–LC; *Eldorado (Kans.) Butler County Democrat,* 5 Oct. 1882. On salaries, *Columbus (Ohio) Dispatch,* 2 Apr. 1883, Polacsek. *Dan Rice's Song Book*, n.p. [1873], Tibbals; *Dan Rice's Old-Time Circus Songster,* New York, 1882, Newberry Library, Chicago; on Marcellus, *Clipper,* 8 Apr., 42, and 22 Apr. 1882, 76; *Memphis Appeal,* 2 Apr. 1882.
18. *Clipper,* 22 Apr. 1882, 76; *Salt Lake Daily Herald,* 15 July 1882, 8; *New York Times,* 13 Apr 1891, 3; Brown 161–163; *Kearney (Neb.) New Era,* 7 June 1882; *Daily Alta Californian,* 29 Aug. 1882.
19. *Cincinnati Commercial Gazette,* 3 June 1883; Lawrence Senelick, *The Age and Stage of George L. Fox: 1825–1877,* Hanover, N.H.: Tufts Univ.–Univ. Press of New England, 1988.
20. Brown 19; *New York Times,* 9 Apr. 1883, 5; *New York Herald,* 9 Apr. 1883, 3; courier, Nathans & Co.'s New Consolidated Shows [Syracuse, 25 May 1883], CWM; *Clipper,* 21 Apr. 1883, 65; *Oswego (N.Y.) Gazette,* 17 Apr. 1883, Somers (N.Y.) Historical Society; *Police Gazette,* 1 Apr. 1883; *Clipper,* 5 May 1883, 97.
21. *Clipper,* 8 Oct. 1881, 467; 25 Mar. 1882, 8; *Fond du Lac (Wis.) Daily Reporter,* 31 Mar. 1883, Polacsek; Erie County records; S. S. Freeman, "The Wurzbachs," parts 1 & 2, *Girard Cosmopolite Herald,* 10 and 17 Jan. 1993.
22. *Clipper,* 16 June 1883, 206; *Philadelphia Times* qtd. in clipping, *Columbus (Ohio) Dispatch,* 4 July 1883, Polacsek; Freeman, "The Wurzbachs;" *History of Erie County*, 1884, 846; *Clipper,* 29 Sep. 1883, 456; Orin C. King, "Only Big

Show Coming, Chapter Five, Part Two," *Bandwagon* 33, no. 1 (1989): 43–47; Rice letters to Morrison Foster, 20 and 28 Sept. 1883, and circular, "Lecture: Dan Rice," 27 Sep. 1873, Foster Hall Collection.

Chapter 37: More Fun Than You Can Count

1. *Dallas Daily Herald,* 7 June 1885, Rice! 22.
2. Rice letter to Thomas Risk, 10 Dec. 1884, Hertzberg; *Waco Examiner,* 30 Jan. 1886, Rice! 40; sombrero pictured in *Houston Herald,* c. Sept. 1885, Rice! 35.
3. *Picayune,* 22 Dec. 1884.
4. *Chicago Tribune,* 24 Mar. 1885; *Louisville Commercial,* c. Oct. 1884, Rice! 5; Henry Ringling North and Alden Hatch, *The Circus Kings: Our Ringling Family Story,* Garden City, N.Y.: Doubleday, 1960, 77.
5. *Clipper*, 2 Feb. 1884, 782; Brown 237–239; on Crum, *Rochester Union & Advertiser,* 25 Apr. 1876; *Clipper,* 31 Jan. 1874, 351; 23 Dec. 1882, 646; as local postmaster, Crum was killed by a mob in 1901 for appointing a black assistant, *Clipper*, 9 Mar. 1901, 29. On Rosston in Florida, *Clipper,* 7 Mar. 1874, 391; on Robinson, "Famed Circus King," 4 Aug. 1888, Hertzberg.
6. Rice letter to Morrison Foster, 26 Jan. 1884, Foster Hall Collection.
7. *Jackson (Tex.) County Progress,* 19 Mar. 1886, Rice! 1; clipping, Waco, 18 Oct. 1885, Rice! 61; *Houston Post,* 25 June 1885, Rice! 32; *Waco Daily Examiner,* 15 Oct. 1885. The following year, Baylor and Waco Universities combined, with Burleson as president.
8. *Houston Herald,* c. 12 Sept. 1885, Rice! 35.
9. *Galveston Daily News,* 22 Aug. 1885, Rice! 33b; *Weimar Gimlet,* 25 Feb. 1886, Rice! 44; *Chattanooga (Tenn.) Daily Times,* 1 July 1884, Rice! 59; *Brackett News,* 18 Sept. 1886, Rice! 58; *Dallas Daily Times,* 11 June 1885, Rice! 24.
10. Clipping, Wharton, Tex., spring 1886, Rice! 48; clipping, Pine Bluff, Ark., c. Apr. 1885, Rice! 10.
11. Clipping, Oct. 1885, Rice! 36; *Houston Post,* 12 Sept. 1885, Rice! 34; *Texarkana Daily Public Opinion,* 30 May 1885, Rice! 18; *Eagle Pass Journal*, 18 Sept. 1886, Rice! 58.
12. *Dallas Daily Herald,* 7 June 1885, Rice! 22.
13. *Galveston Daily News,* 22 Aug. 1885, Rice! 33b.
14. *Clipper,* 18 Dec. 1858, 278; clipping, Houston, 9 Sept. 1885, Rice! 2.
15. *Dallas Daily Herald,* 7 June 1885, Rice! 22; "Dan Rice's Lecture," Rice! 47; *Waco Examiner,* c. 27 Oct. 1885, Rice! 37.
16. *Houston Post,* 12 Sept. 1885, Rice! 34; clipping, Victoria, 13 Mar. 1866, Rice! 51; *San Antonio Daily Light,* 5 May 1886.
17. *Williamson County Sun,* c. Feb. 1886, Rice! 21; *Louisville Commercial,* 1884, Rice! 5.
18. *San Antonio Light,* 23 Jan. and 11 Feb. 1886; *Weimar Gimlet,* 1 Apr. 1886, Rice! 44.
19. Clipping, Victoria, Tex., 13 Mar. 1886, Rice! 51.

20. "Dan Rice's Lecture," Rice! 47; *Austin Statesman,* 20 June 1885, Rice! 30; clipping, spring 1886, Rice! 47.
21. Clipping, fall 1885, Rice! 29; *Eagle Pass Journal,* 18 Sept. 1886, Rice! 58.

Chapter 38: Snake Oil

1. Marriage Records, Lavaca County, Vol. B, 45; Vol. C, 151; Vol. D, 177; Vol. E, 337. On Greathouse, Paul C. Boethel, *On the Headwaters of the Lavaca and the Navidad,* Austin, Texas: Von Boeckmann-Jones, 1967, 173. On DeGoffredo, Minutes of the District Court of Lavaca County, Vol. F, 135, 26 July 1875, qtd. in Boethel letter to Leopold Morris, 3 June 1950, Boethel Archives, Friench Simpson Memorial Library, Hallettsville, Texas. On Robinson, "Sarah Ann Robinson," *Fayette County Texas Heritage,* vol. 2, Fayette Co. History Book Committee, 1996, 398. *San Antonio Light,* 10 June 1885, 4.
2. Clipping, Schulenburg, c. Mar. 1886, Rice! 44; *Clipper,* 5 Jan., 695; and 5 Feb. 1887, 738 (Cincinnati police denied the rumors, *Clipper,* 3 Apr. 1887, 84); *Hallettsville Enterprise,* 8 June, qtd. in *Girard Cosmopolite Herald,* 16 June 1887; *New York Times,* 9 June 1887, 1; *New York Herald,* 9 June 1887; *Louisville Courier-Journal,* 13 June 1887. Though the remarriage of a divorced Catholic was complicated, it was not impossible, e-mail to author, 19 Dec. 2000, Alan Krieger, Theology Librarian, University of Notre Dame.
3. *Clipper,* 23 July 1887, 290; Blue 104; New Orleans 57, 13; *Appleton's Cyclopædia of American Biography,* 1888. *Erie Sunday Morning Gazette,* 7 Aug. 1887; *New York Daily Graphic,* 12 Jan. 1888, 517 and 519.
4. *Clipper,* 13 Feb., 756; 13 Mar., 820; and 3 Apr. 1886, 37; "Tumblers and Breakers," 18 Aug. 1888, CWM; "Route Book, Frank A. Robbins' New Shows," 1888, 24, Robert F. Sabia; *Galveston Daily News,* 22 Aug. 1885, Rice! 336; "What Dan Rice Recalls," c. June 1891, CWM.
5. *Clipper,* 6 Jan., 678; 10 Feb. 1883, 759; *Historical Dictionary of American Slang,* vol. 2, 648, and vol. 1, xxxv; on "is-er," *Clipper,* 3 Sept. 1887, 391.
6. Robley Dunglison, *Dictionary of Medical Science,* 1844 (The story is debunked in Charles Earl Funk, *Horse Feathers and Other Curious Words,* New York: Harpers, 1958); *San Antonio Light,* 10 Feb. 1886; clippings, New Orleans 11, 62, and 86; Blue 114; on land sales, stationery, author's collection; *Long Branch News,* c. Oct. 1888, Kunzog 421; New Orleans 13, 58.
7. *Clipper,* 16 May 1868, 46; Louis E. Cooke, "Reminiscences of a Showman," *Newark Evening Star,* 1 Nov. 1915; also *Fond du Lac (Wis.) Daily Reporter,* 9 June 1885, Polacsek; clipping, "What Dan Rice Recalls," c. June 1891, CWM; *Nation,* 3 Aug. 1882, 83.
8. *Clipper,* 3 Nov., 239, and 17 Nov. 1866, 255; Justin Kaplan, *Mr. Clemens and Mark Twain,* New York: Simon & Schuster, 1983, 57, 94, and 111; *Enquirer,* 1 Jan. 1885, 5; on Twain's ambition to be a clown, Sherwood 219–220; on Rice's claim of joke theft, *New York Daily Graphic,* 12 Jan. 1888; *Erie Daily Dispatch,* 19 Feb. and 15–22 Nov. 1867; "What Dan Rice Recalls," c. June 1891, CWM.

9. "Texas Siftings," *The New Handbook of Texas,* vol. 6, Austin: Texas State Historical Association, 1996, 405–406; *Siftings,* pieces, Blue 49 and New Orleans 5–6; Blue 102; *Long Branch News,* c. 1894, Blue 47; *New York Tribune,* 7 Nov. 1897, illustrated supplement, 6; clipping, c. Dec. 1895, New Orleans 17; Rice, "Fifty Years," *Fifty-Two Stories of Animal Life and Adventure,* ed. Alfred H. Miles, London: Hutchinson, 1903, 11–28.
10. *Clipper,* 27 July 1889, 321; letter, "DeWitt Cottage," Rice to Ben W. Austin, 16 Apr. 1889, Circus Collections, Illinois State University, Milner Library—Special Collections; Marcella Rice letters to M. B. West, 26 July and 19 August 1889. On Long Branch, *Cincinnati Daily Gazette,* 5 Aug. 1875; Rice recalled visits with Vice President Hobart in 1899, Brown 195–197; *Freehold (N.J.) Transcript,* 18 Oct. 1889, New Orleans 14; *Clipper,* 19 Oct. 1889, 550.
11. "Old Dan Rice," *Chicago Times-Herald,* c. Apr. 1895, MCNY; letter, T. S. Woodruff to J. E. Reed, Erie County Historical Society, 27 Dec. 1923, York Historical Society; *Hallettsville (Tex.) Herald,* 23 Apr. 1908.
12. New Orleans 13, 58; *New York Herald,* 24 Mar. 1890, 4; *Clipper,* 10 May, 139, and 17 May 1890, 150; handbill, "Young Men's Catholic Association," 12 Nov. 1890, New Orleans 75; *Clipper,* 17 Apr. 1886, 68; 29 Sept. 1888, 458; 3 May 1890, 126.
13. Invitation, 10 Jan. 1891, New Orleans 71; clipping, *Long Branch News,* 17 Nov. 1888, New Orleans 9; on Cleveland, New Orleans 19 and 35, and Black 104; Brown 263–264; *Memphis Daily Appeal,* 8 Apr. 1882.
14. *Clipper,* 2 Aug. 1890, 323.
15. *New York Times,* 13 Apr. 1891, 3; "Dan Rice's Big One Ring Show!" herald, 17 June 1891, Tibbals; *Herald,* 14 Apr., 10 and 18 June 1891, 3; *Sun,* 14 June 1891; *National Police Gazette,* 9 May 1891; *Clipper,* 18 Apr.–20 June 1891; Brown 172, 179–180; on Rice's talk, Odell 14: 770, and *New York Herald,* 5 Apr. 1891, 8; loose Blue clipping.
16. *Clipper,* 6 June, 214, and 13 June 1891, 220; Blue 105; *Billboard,* 1 Jan. 1923, 75; *Herald,* 18 June 1891, 3, 5; New Orleans 22, c. 1894. In 1892, an "Old Dan Rice Circus" toured Kansas, Orin C. King, "Backed by Unlimited Millions," *Bandwagon* 37, no. 3 (1993): 32–38. The twentieth century saw a fake Dan Rice, Jr., on a 1905 circus, and Dan Rice Circuses in 1911, 1936, 1937, and 1954, CWM.

Chapter 39: Honest Abe's Uncle Sam

1. *National Cyclopædia of American Biography,* 1893; *Detroit Free Press,* 23 Feb. 1893; Odell 26: 433; Charles H. Day, "History of American Circus and Tented Exhibitions", 9 Nov. 1906, Hertzberg; clippings, New Orleans 19, 22, 63; Rice letter to Libbie Showles, 2 Mar. 1894, MCNY; Rice letter to Bert Wurzbach, 29 July 1897, Mercyhurst, Box 1.
2. John Anderson conversation with author, 19 Jan. 1998.
3. By the mid-twentieth century, Girard began to rediscover and reclaim Rice.
4. Blue 1, 105, loose clipping; New Orleans 22; letter to author, 1 Oct. 1998, John Dojka, Institute Archivist, Folsom Library, Rensselaer Polytechnic Institute;

Last Will and Testament, Dan Rice McLaren, 28 Apr. 1899, probated, 24 Apr. 1900, New Jersey State Archives; Jeanne Celli (Rice Jr.'s great-granddaughter) phone conversation with author, 7 Sept. 2000; Betty Gardner (Rice's great-granddaughter) letter to John Kunzog, 2 Apr. 1977, Kunzog-Adams; letter to author, Glenn Mason, Director, Eastern Washington State Hist. Society, 2 Oct. 1991; *San Francisco Examiner,* 9 Apr. 1936.

5. On Nancy "Rice," 10 Mar. 1901, Account book, 1, Mercyhurst; on Bill Rice, "First Showboat," Public Library of Cincinnati and Hamilton County; on Almenia Rice, letter from Bell to Langley, 15 Feb. 1902, Library of Congress, Alexander Graham Bell Papers, Series: General Correspondence, Folder: Samuel P. Langley, 1888–1904; on Ella "Rice," Jeanne Judson, "Tales of an Old Circus," *Billboard* (3 June 1911): 24, 52.
6. *Random House Dictionary*, 1993; "Old Dan Rice," *Chicago Times-Herald,* c. April 1895, MCNY; "What Dan Rice Recalls," c. June 1891, CWM.
7. *Sketches* 72–80; Brown 43–53. Don Carle Gillette turned Rice's Lincoln fiction into an inaccurate biography with a great title, *He Made Lincoln Laugh,* New York: Exposition Press, 1967.
8. *Clinton (Iowa) Daily Herald,* 2 Sept. 1879, CWM; *St. Louis Republican,* qtd. in *Parsons (Kans.) Sun,* 27 Sept. 1879, 7.
9. Brown 219, 145; *List of Vessels Chartered, Hired . . . During the Late Rebellion,* 192, National Archives. John B. Doris, a showman, mentioned that "Mr. Rice never tired of recalling" Lincoln's visit to the tent in 1863, though the Great Show did not play Washington that year, Brown 239–240.
10. *San Francisco Examiner*, 9 Apr. 1936.
11. "Uncle Sam: A Face of the Nation," exhibit, New-York Historical Society, Ann Weisman, curator, Aug. 1999.
12. *American Humorist* cover, 30 and 78.
13. *New York Daily Graphic,* 12 Jan. 1888, 517; New Orleans 85; *Dictionary of Historical Slang,* first "joey" citation, 1889; *Clipper,* 30 Mar. 1889, 39; Roland Butler, "When Dan Rice Played Santa Claus," *Billboard* (8 Dec. 1928): 108. An early picture of Santa showed a Rice-like goatee, *Daily Albany Argus,* 27 Dec. 1842.
14. New Orleans 57; "Du Chaillu [explorer] and Dan Rice in Literature," *New York Herald,* 25 Oct. 1891, 28; Brown 245–47; Rice letter, 14 Nov. 1893, rpt. in clipping, Blue 114; *Picayune,* 25 Dec. 1892; clipping, 8 Dec. 1896, New Orleans 22. This Dr. Valentine may have been the performer of that name in 1843 at Barnum's American Museum (Harris 41), in New Orleans (*Crescent,* 9 Jan. 1852), and with Tom Thumb in Cincinnati (*Enquirer,* 18 May 1856).
15. Rice to "My dear young friend," 14 Dec. 1897, author's collection; envelope, Maria Ward Brown to Rice, 1 Apr. 1895, MCNY; poems, 1897 and 1898, author's collection; John Anderson phone conversation with author, 14 July 1998. Brown got notices for her book in Philadelphia and New York, where the *Herald* announced itself satisfied by Brown's "quaint naivete of language," *Philadelphia North American,* 28 Dec. 1900; *New York Herald,* 24 Aug. 1901, 13.
16. Sister Kate lost her husband, James Howland, to the disease, 27 Feb. 1900. "James Howland," 2 Mar. 1900, Account book 45, Mercyhurst; Maggie photo,

MCNY; on Whittaker, Brown 483–484, and Tom Whittaker to Rice [c. 1890s], author's collection; on Kate, *Girard Cosmopolite Herald,* 22 June 1900, qtd. in S. S. Freeman, "The Wurzbachs," part 2, 17 Jan. 1993

17. *Clipper,* 3 Mar., 7, and 7 Apr. 1900, 134; clippings, author's collection; Last Will and Testament, Rice McLaren, 28 Apr. 1899, New Jersey State Archives.
18. *Madison (Wis.) Democrat,* 22 Nov. 1900, CWM.
19. *Chicago Tribune,* 25 Nov. 1881, 7.
20. Joseph Warner, "Dan Rice, Showman," *Lansing (Mich.) Journal,* 22 Feb. 1893.
21. Inspired by Cooke, "Reminiscences," 6 Jan. 1916.

BIBLIOGRAPHY

Books and Journals

Ahlstrom, Sydney E. *A Religious History of the American People.* New Haven: Yale Univ. Press, 1977.

Appleton's Cyclopædia of American Biography. New York, 1888.

Archer, Stephen M. *Junius Brutus Booth: Theatrical Prometheus.* Carbondale: Southern Illinois Univ. Press, 1992.

Atherton, Lewis E. "Daniel Howell Hise, Abolitionist and Reformer." *Mississippi Valley Historical Review* 26, no. 3 (Dec. 1939): 342–358.

Auchincloss, Louis, ed. *The Hone and Strong Diaries of Old Manhattan.* New York: Abbeville Press, 1989.

Bain, Richard C., and Judith H. Parris. *Convention Decisions and Voting Records.* Washington, D.C.: Brookings, 1973.

Ballantine, Bill. *Wild Tigers and Tame Fleas.* New York: Rinehart, 1958.

Baringer, William E., ed. *Lincoln Day by Day: A Chronology.* Vol. 2: 1849–1860. Earl Schenk Miers, ed.-in-chief. Washington, D.C.: Lincoln Sesquicentennial Commission, 1960.

Barish, Jonas. *The Antitheatrical Prejudice.* Berkeley and Los Angeles: Univ. of California Press, 1981.

Bartlett, John. *Dictionary of Americanisms.* 1849. New York: Crescent Books, 1989.

Beecher, Henry Ward. *Lectures to Young Men.* 1845. Boston, 1866.

Beeching, Jack. *The Chinese Opium Wars.* New York: Harcourt Brace Jovanovich, 1975.

Bergmann, Johannes Dietrich. "The Original Confidence Man," *American Quarterly* 21 (Fall 1969): 560–577.

Berke, Richard L. "What a Mind!" *New York Times,* 25 June 2000, sec. 4, pp. 1, 3.

Bernard, Charles. "Old-Time Showmen." *Billboard* (14 July 1934): 37.

Bledstein, Burton J. *The Culture of Professionalism: The Middle Class and the Development of Higher Education in America.* New York: Norton, 1976.

Blumin, Stuart M. "The Hypothesis of Middle-Class Formation in Nineteenth-Century America: A Critique and Some Proposals." *American Historical Review* 90 (1985): 299–338.

Bode, Carl. *The American Lyceum: Town Meeting of the Mind.* 1956. Carbondale: Southern Illinois Univ. Press, 1968.

———. *The Anatomy of Popular Culture, 1840–1861.* Berkeley and Los Angeles: Univ. of California Press, 1959.

Boethel, Paul C. *On the Headwaters of the Lavaca and the Navidad.* Austin, Texas: Von Boeckmann-Jones, 1967.

Brackenridge, Hugh Henry. *Modern Chivalry.* 1792. Lewis Leary, ed. New Haven: College & Univ. Press, 1965.

Bradley, Hugh. *Such Was Saratoga.* New York: Doubleday, Doran & Co., 1940.

Briarmead, Chess L. "The American Circus," *Clipper,* 17 Apr. 1875, supplement, p. 2.

Britten, Evelyn Barrett. *Chronicles of Saratoga.* Saratoga Springs: Author, 1959.

Brodie, Fawn M. *No Man Knows My History: The Life of Joseph Smith, the Mormon Prophet.* New York: Knopf, 1946.

Brown, Maria Ward. Cited as "Brown." *The Life of Dan Rice.* Long Branch, N.J.: Author, 1901.

Brown, T. Allston. Cited as "T. Allston Brown." "The Origins of Negro Minstrelsy," in Charles H. Day, *Fun in Black.* New York, 1874.

———. "A Complete History of the Amphitheatre and Circus." *Clipper,* 22 Dec. 1860–9 Feb. 1861.

Browne, Ray B. "Shakespeare in America: Vaudeville and Negro Minstrelsy." *American Quarterly* 12 (1960): 376–382.

Browning, Robert. "Andrea del Sarto." 1855. *The Poems and Plays of Robert Browning.* New York: Modern Library–Random House, 1934.

Burroughs, Edwin G., and Mike Wallace. *Gotham: A History of New York City to 1898.* New York: Oxford Univ. Press, 1998.

Butler, Roland. "When Dan Rice Played Santa Claus." *Billboard* (8 Dec. 1928): 108.

Butsch, Richard. *The Making of American Audiences: From Stage to Television, 1750–1990.* Cambridge: Cambridge Univ. Press, 2000.

Carson, William G. B. *Managers in Distress: The St. Louis Stage, 1840–1844.* St. Louis: St. Louis Historical Documents Foundation, 1949.

Catalogue of Paintings, Statuary, Etc., in the Art Department of the Great North-Western Fair. 2d ed. Chicago, 1865.

Cayton, Mary Kupiec, Elliott J. Gorn, and Peter W. Williams, eds. *Encyclopedia of American Social History.* Vol. 1. New York: Charles Scribner's Sons, 1993.

Chase, John. *Frenchmen, Desire, Good Children.* New Orleans: Crager, 1949.

Chernow, Ron. *Titan: The Life of John D. Rockefeller, Sr.* New York: Random House, 1998.

Circular and Catalogue of the Utica Female Seminary for 1859–1860. Utica, N.Y., 1859. Utica Public Library.

"Circus." *Knickerbocker*, 13, no. 1 (1839): 72.

Clark, Asia Booth. *The Unlocked Book: A Memoir of John Wilkes Booth.* New York: Putnam, 1938.

Clarke, T. Wood. *Utica for a Century and a Half.* Utica: Widtman Press, 1952.

Click, Patricia C. *The Spirit of the Times: Amusements in Nineteenth-Century Baltimore, Norfolk, and Richmond.* Charlottesville: Univ. Press of Virginia, 1989.

Cockrell, Dale. *Demons of Disorder: Early Blackface Minstrels and Their World.* Cambridge: Cambridge Univ. Press, 1997.
Condon, George E. *Stars in the Water: The Story of the Erie Canal.* Garden City, N.Y.: Doubleday, 1974.
"Contemporary Newspaper Opinion of Dan Rice." *Billboard* (12 Jan. 1907): 26.
Cooke, Louis E. "Reminiscences of a Showman." *Newark Evening Star,* 27 May 1915–6 Jan. 1916.
Coup, W. C. *Sawdust and Spangles: Stories and Secrets of the Circus.* Chicago: Stone, 1901. [Coup died in 1895, no other author/editor named.]
Cowell, Joseph. *Thirty Years Passed Among the Players in England and America.* 1844. Hamden, Conn.: Archon, 1970.
Cox, John Harrington. *Folk-Songs of the South.* New York: Dover, 1925.
Dahlinger, Fred, Jr. "The Development of the Railroad Circus." *Bandwagon* 27, no. 6 (1983): 6–11; 28, no. 1 (1984): 16–27; 28, no. 2 (1984): 28–36; 28, no. 3 (1984): 29–36.
Davies, Robertson. *What's Bred in the Bone.* New York: Penguin, 1985.
Davis, William C. *Jefferson Davis: The Man and His Hour.* New York: HarperCollins, 1991.
Day, Charles H. "History of American Circus and Tented Exhibitions," 9 Nov. 1906. Hertzberg.
———. *Ink From a Circus Press Agent.* William L. Slout, ed. San Bernardino, Ca.: Borgo Press, 1995.
Dennison, Sam. *Scandalize My Name: Black Imagery in American Popular Music.* New York: Garland, 1982.
Denslow, William R. *10,000 Famous Freemasons.* Vol. 4. Missouri: Transactions of the Missouri Lodge of Research, c. 1961.
DeVoto, Bernard. *Mark Twain's America.* 1932. Westport, Conn.: Greenwood Press, 1978.
Dickens, Charles. *American Notes for General Circulation.* 1842. John S. Whitley and Arnold Goldman, eds. London: Penguin Classics, 1985.
———. *Hard Times.* 1854. New York: Penguin, 1969.
Dickinson, S. D. "Showboats and Circuses." *Arkansas Gazette,* 28 Nov. 1948.
Dingess, John A. Memoirs. c. 1890. Transcript, Dan Draper, CWM. Original ms., Hertzberg.
Disher, M. Willson, ed. *The Cowells in America.* London: Oxford Univ. Press, 1934.
Doris, John B. "Dan Rice.—A Sketch." *Billboard* (12 Jan. 1907): 6.
Dormon, James H., Jr. *Theatre in the Antebellum South: 1815–1861.* Chapel Hill: Univ. of North Carolina Press, 1967.
Douglas, Ann. *The Feminization of American Culture.* New York: Knopf, 1977.
Draper, John Daniel. "A Celebrated Rider: William Showles." *Bandwagon* 45, no. 1 (2001): 19–23.
Driscoll, John. *All That Is Glorious Around Us: Paintings from the Hudson River School.* Ithaca: Cornell Univ. Press, 1997.
Dunglison, Robley. *Dictionary of Medical Science,* 1844.
Durant, John and Alice. *Pictorial History of the American Circus.* New York: A. S. Barnes, 1957.

Durkee, Cornelius E. *Reminiscences of Saratoga, Reprinted from the* Saratogian, *1927–1928*. [Saratoga Springs] 1928.

Eliason, Robert E. *Keyed Bugles in the United States.* Washington, D.C.: Smithsonian Institution Press, 1972.

Ellis, James. "The Counterfeit Presentment: Nineteenth-Century Burlesques of *Hamlet.*" *Nineteenth Century Theatre Research* 11, no. 1 (Summer 1983): 29–50.

Ellman, Ira Mark, Paul M. Kurtz, and Katharine T. Bartlett. *Family Law.* Charlottesville, Va.: Michie Co., 1986.

Emeljanow, Victor. "Erasing the Spectator: Observations on Nineteenth Century Lighting." *Theatre History Studies* 18 (1998): 107–116.

Emerson, Ken. *Doo-dah!: Stephen Foster and the Rise of Popular Culture.* New York: Simon & Schuster, 1997.

Emerson, Ralph Waldo. "Self-Reliance" and other essays, *The Selected Writings of Ralph Waldo Emerson.* Brooks Atkinson, ed. New York: Modern Library, 1940.

Entertaining a Nation: The Career of Long Branch. Writer's Project, Works Projects Administration, State of New Jersey, American Guide Series, Long Branch: 1940.

Falconbridge [John Kelly]. *Dan Marble, A Biographical Sketch of the Famous and Diverting Humorist.* New York, 1851.

Fehrenbacher, Don E. *Lincoln in Text and Context.* Stanford, Cal.: Stanford Univ. Press, 1978.

Financial Cyclopedia of the State of New Jersey. Newark: Expositor Company, 1908.

Flint, Richard W. "The Circus in America." *Quarterly Journal of the Library of Congress* 40, no. 3 (Summer 1983): 202–233.

Foner, Eric. *Free Soil, Free Labor, Free Men.* London: Oxford Univ. Press, 1970.

Ford, Thomas. *A Peep Behind the Curtain.* Boston, 1850.

Forrest, Earle. *History of Washington County* [Pa.]. Vol. 1. Chicago: Clarke, 1926.

Foster, Morrison. *Biography, Songs and Musical Compositions of Stephen C. Foster.* 1896. New York: AMS Press, 1977.

Fox, Charles Philip. *Circus in America.* Waukesha, Wis.: Country Beautiful, 1969.

Freeman, Douglas Southall. *George Washington: A Biography, Vol. 6: Patriot and President.* New York: Scribners, 1954.

Freeman, Sabina Shields. "A Spy Among Us?" *Girard Cosmopolite Herald,* 6 Aug. 2000.

———. "Girard's Dan Rice." *Girard Cosmopolite Herald,* 30 July 2000.

———. "The Wurzbachs and the Legend of Their House," parts I & II. *Girard Cosmopolite Herald,* 10 and 17 Jan. 1993.

———. "Dan Rice's Monument: Patriotism or Circus Promotion." *Pennsylvania Heritage Magazine* 12, no. 4 (Fall 1986): 10–15.

———. "It All Began with a Clown." *Girard Cosmopolite Herald,* 30 July 1991.

———. *The Battles Story: The Life and Times of the Battles Family of Girard, Pennsylvania.* Fairview, Pa.: Author, 1992.

Frost, Hyatt. "News of the Circus Ring." *Dramatic News,* 29 Dec. 1894. Hertzberg.

Frost, Thomas. *Circus Life and Circus Celebrities.* London, 1875.

Funk, Charles Earl. *Horse Feathers and Other Curious Words.* New York: Harpers, 1958.

Gibbs, Phillip A. "Self Control and Male Sexuality in the Advice Literature of Nineteenth-Century American, 1830–1860." *Journal of American Culture* 9, no. 2 (Summer 1986): 37–42.

Gillette, Don Carle. *He Made Lincoln Laugh: The Story of Dan Rice.* New York: Exposition Press, 1967.

Glenroy, John. *Ins and Outs of Circus Life.* Boston, 1885.

Greenwood, Isaac J. *The Circus: Its Origins and Growth Prior to 1835.* New York, 1898.

Gurko, Miria. *The Lives and Times of Peter Cooper.* New York: Thomas V. Crowell, 1959.

Halttunen, Karen. *Confidence Men and Painted Women: A Study of Middle-Class Culture in America, 1830–1870.* New Haven: Yale Univ. Press, 1982.

Hamm, Charles. *Yesterdays: Popular Song in America.* New York: W. W. Norton & Co., 1979.

Hanners, John. "'It was Play or Starve': John Banvard's Account of Early Showboats." *Theatre Research International* 8, no. 1 (Spring 1983): 53–64.

Harlow, Alvin F. *Old Bowery Days.* New York: Appleton, 1931.

Harris, Neil. *Humbug: The Art of P. T. Barnum.* Chicago: Univ. of Chicago Press, 1973.

Hartog, Hendrik. *Man & Wife in America.* Cambridge: Harvard Univ. Press, 2000.

Harwell, Richard Barksdale. *Songs of the Confederacy.* New York: Broadcast, 1951.

Haskell, Thomas. "Capitalism and the Origins of the Humanitarian Sensibility." *American Historical Review* 90 (Apr. 1985): 339–361; 90 (June 1985): 547–566.

Haswell, Charles. H. *Reminiscences of an Octogenarian of the City of New York (1816 to 1860).* New York, 1896.

Hatch, Nathan O. "The Democratization of Christianity and the Character of American Politics." In *Religion in American Politics: From the Colonial Period to the 1980s.* Mark A. Noll, ed. New York: Oxford Univ. Press, 1990.

Hendricks, W. Quinett. *Stranger Than Fiction.* Wooster, Ohio: Author, 1928.

History of Erie County, Pennsylvania. Chicago, 1884.

Hoffman, Andrew. *Inventing Mark Twain: The Lives of Samuel Langhorne Clemens.* New York: William Morrow and Co., 1997.

Hone, Philip. *The Diary of Philip Hone, 1828–1851*, rev. ed. Allan Nevins, ed. New York: Dodd, Mead, 1936.

Howes, Jeanne Chretien. *The Howes Circus Story.* Weston, Conn.: Author, 1990.

Hutchinson, Robert, ed. *Joe Miller's Jests, or the Wit's Vade-mecum. 1739.* New York: Dover, 1963.

Hyde, Ralph. *Panoramania: The Art and Entertainment of the 'All-Embracing' View.* London: Trefoil, 1988.

Inciardi, James A. and David M. Petersen. "Gaff Joints and Shell Games: A Century of Circus Grift." *Journal of Popular Culture* 6, no. 3 (Spring 1973): 591–606.

Jackson, Richard, ed. *Popular Songs of Nineteenth-Century America.* New York: Dover, 1976.

Jay, Ricky. *Learned Pigs and Fireproof Women.* New York: Farrar, Straus and Giroux, 1986.

Jennings, John J. *Theatrical and Circus Life; or Secrets of the Stage, Greenroom and Sawdust Arenas.* St. Louis, 1882.

Jewell, Edwin L. "Academy of Music," *Jewell's Crescent City Illustrated.* New Orleans, 1873.

Johannsen, Robert W. *Stephen A. Douglas.* New York: Oxford Univ. Press, 1973.

Johnson, Claudia D. "Burlesques of Shakespeare: The Democratic American's 'Light Artillery.'" *Theatre Survey* 21 (May 1980): 49–62.

Johnson, James H. *Listening in Paris: A Cultural History.* Berkeley and Los Angeles: Univ. of California Press, 1995.

Johnson, Paul E. *A Shopkeeper's Millennium: Society and Revivals in Rochester, New York, 1815–1837.* New York: Hill, 1978.

Judson, A. M. *History of the Eighty-Third Regiment Pennsylvania Volunteers.* Erie, Pa., 1865.

Judson, Jeanne. "Tales of an Old Circus." *Billboard* (3 June 1911): 24–25.

Kanellos, Nicholas. "A Brief Overview of the Mexican-American Circus in the Southwest." *Journal of Popular Culture* 18, no. 2 (Fall 1984): 74–84.

Kaplan, Justin. *Mr. Clemens and Mark Twain.* New York: Simon, 1966.

Keeler, Ralph. *Vagabond Adventures.* Boston, 1870.

Kelly, John M. and Fred D. Pfening III, eds. "Taxable Value of Circus Goodwill." *Bandwagon* 12, no. 1 (1968): 3–14.

Kendall, John S. *The Golden Age of the New Orleans Theater.* Baton Rouge: Louisiana State Univ. Press, 1952.

Kennedy, Peter, ed. *Folksongs of Britain and Ireland.* London: Cassell, 1975.

Kerr, Walter. *How Not to Write A Play.* New York: Simon & Schuster, 1955.

Kevles, Bettyann Holtzmann. *Naked to the Bone: Medical Imaging in the 20th Century.* New Brunswick, N.J.: Rutgers Univ. Press, 1997.

King, Orin C. "Backed By Unlimited Millions." *Bandwagon* 37, no. 3 (1993): 32–38.

———. "Only Big Show Coming, Chapter Five, Part Two." *Bandwagon* 33, no. 1 (1989): 43–47.

Kliewer, Warren. "A Family of Actors." Typescript, 1999. Author's collection.

Kunzog, John C. *The One-Horse Show: The Life and Times of Dan Rice, Circus Jester and Philanthropist.* Jamestown, N.Y.: Author, 1962.

Lambert, William. *Showlife in America.* East Point, Ga.: Will Delavoye, 1925.

Launius, Roger D., and F. Mark McKiernan. *Joseph Smith, Jr.'s Red Brick Store.* Macomb: Western IL Monograph Ser., No. 5, 1985.

Leavitt, Penelope and James S. Moy. "Spalding and Rogers' Floating Palace, 1852–1859." *Theatre Survey* 25, no. 1 (May 1984): 15–28.

Levine, Lawrence. *Highbrow / Lowbrow: The Emergence of a Cultural Hierarchy.* Cambridge: Harvard Univ. Press, 1988.

Lewis, Philip C. *Trouping: How the Show Came to Town.* New York: Harper, 1973.

Lindsay, Hugh. *History of the Life, Travels and Incidents of Col. Hugh Lindsay.* Philadelphia, 1859.

Lloyd, James T. *Lloyd's Steamboat Directory and Disasters on the Western Waters.* Cincinnati, 1856.

Loesser, Arthur. *Humor in American Song.* New York: Howell, 1942.

Logan, Olive. *Before the Footlights and Behind the Scenes.* Philadelphia, 1870.
Lomask, Milton. *Aaron Burr: The Conspiracy and Years of Exile, 1805–1836.* New York: Farrar, Straus, Giroux, 1992.
Longfellow, Henry Wadsworth. *Complete Poetical Works.* 1866. Boston: Houghton, 1922.
Lord Chesterfield's Letters to His Son. Vol. 1. London, 1774.
Lott, Eric. *Love and Theft: Blackface Minstrelsy and the American Working Class.* New York: Oxford Univ. Press, 1993.
Ludlow, Noah M. *Dramatic Life As I Found It.* St. Louis, 1880.
Mackenzie's Five Thousand Receipts in All the Useful and Domestic Arts. Philadelphia, 1856. Mercyhurst.
Mahan, Bruce E. "Three Early Taverns." *Palimpsest* 3, no. 8 (Aug. 1922): 250–260.
McCabe, James D., Jr. *Lights and Shadows of New York Life.* 1872. New York: Farrar, Straus and Giroux, 1970.
McConachie, Bruce A. *Melodramatic Formations: American Theatre & Society, 1820–1870.* Iowa City: Univ. of Iowa Press, 1992.
McCusker, John J. *How Much Is That in Real Money?: A Historical Price Index for Use as a Deflator of Money Values in the Economy of the United States.* Worcester, Mass.: American Antiquarian Society, 1992.
McLaren, Daniel. *The Pavilion Fountain at Saratoga,* 2d ed. New York, 1842. American Antiquarian Society.
Merten, John W. "Stone by Stone Along a Hundred Years with the House of Strobridge." *Bulletin of the Historical and Philosophical Society of Ohio* 8, no. 1 (Jan. 1850): 15.
Miller, John. *A Twentieth Century History of Erie County, Pennsylvania.* Vol. 1., Chicago: Lewis Publ., 1909.
Moody, Richard. *The Astor Place Riot.* Bloomington: Indiana Univ. Press, 1958.
Moore, Thomas. *Lalla Rookh: An Oriental Romance.* London, 1817.
Morneweck, Evelyn Foster. *Chronicles of Stephen Foster's Family.* 2 vols. Pittsburgh: Foster Hall Collection, Univ. of Pittsburgh Press, 1944.
Mowatt, Anna Cora. *Autobiography of an Actress.* Boston, 1854.
Moy, James S. "Entertainments at John B. Ricketts' Circus, 1793–1800." *Educational Theatre Journal* 30 (May 1978): 186–220.
Nathan, Hans. *Dan Emmett and the Rise of Early Negro Minstrelsy.* Norman: Univ. of Oklahoma Press, 1962.
National Cyclopædia of American Biography. 1893.
Nelson's Biographical Dictionary and Historical Reference Book of Erie County, Pennsylvania. Erie, Pa., 1896.
New York City Methodist Marriages, 1785–1893. Vol. 1: *Index of Brides.* Compiled by William Scott Fisher. Camden, Maine: Pictor Press, 1994.
Nichols, Thomas L. *Forty Years of American Life.* 1864. New York: Stackpole Sons, 1937.
North, Henry Ringling and Alden Hatch. *The Circus Kings: Our Ringling Family Story.* Garden City, N.Y.: Doubleday, 1960.
Oates, Stephen B. *Approaching Fury: Voices of the Storm, 1820–1861.* New York:

HarperCollins, HarperPerennial, 1997.
Odell, George C. D. *Annals of the New York Stage.* 15 vols. New York: Columbia Univ. Press, 1927–1949.
Oxberry, William. *The Actor's Budget of Wit and Merriment.* London, 1820.
Parry, Albert. *Tattoo: Secrets of A Strange Art as Practiced Among the Natives of the United States.* New York: Simon and Schuster, 1933.
Patterson, Jerry E. *The City of New York: A History Illustrated from the Collections of the Museum of the City of New York.* New York: Abrams, 1978.
Peterson, Merrill D. *The Jefferson Image in the American Mind.* New York: Oxford Univ. Press, 1960.
Polacsek, John F. "The Stowe Bros. Circus—A Real Family Tradition," parts 1 and 2. *Bandwagon* 29, no. 1 (1985): 49–56; 30, no. 3 (1985): 14–21.
Raban, Jonathan. *Old Glory: An American Voyage.* New York: Simon and Schuster, 1981.
Ramney, H. M. *Account of the Terrific and Fatal Riot at the New York Astor Place Opera House.* New York, 1849. Author's collection.
Random House Historical Dictionary of American Slang. Vols. 1–2. J. E. Lighter, ed. New York: Random House, 1994 and 1997.
"Red Republican." [database online]. 12 Aug. 1999. www.spartacus.schoolnet.co.uk.
Reed, Charles. Interview. "Oldest Living Bareback Rider." *Billboard* (23 Mar. 1929): 65.
Reynolds, David S. *Walt Whitman's America: A Cultural Biography.* New York: Random House–Vintage, 1996.
Reynolds, J. Richard III. "Circus Rhinos." *Bandwagon* 12, no. 5 (1968): 4–13.
Rice, Dan. "Fifty Years with a Menagerie." *52 Stories of Animal Life and Adventure.* London: Hutchinson, 1903.
Ringling, Albert. *Life Story of the Ringling Brothers.* Chicago: Donnelley, 1900.
Ringling, Charles. Interview. Philadelphia *Public Ledger,* 26 Mar. 1921.
Root, Harvey W. *The Ways of the Circus, Being the Memories and Adventures of George Conklin, Tamer of Lions.* New York: Harper, 1921.
Rosenberg-Naparsteck, Ruth. "A History of the Circus in Rochester." *Rochester History* 49, no. 3 (July 1987): 5.
Rosensweig, Roy. *Eight Hours for What We Will: Workers and Leisure in an Industrial City, 1870–1920.* Cambridge: Cambridge Univ. Press, 1983.
Ryan, Mary P. *Cradle of the Middle Class: The Family in Oneida County, New York, 1790–1865.* Cambridge: Cambridge Univ. Press, 1981.
Ryder, Ron. *Combined Editions, Ryder Pictorial 1959–1962–1964.* Boonville, N.Y.: Ryder's Hardware, 1964.
Sandburg, Carl. *Abraham Lincoln: The War Years.* Vol. 3. New York: Harcourt Brace Jovanovich, 1926.
Sanford, Laura G. *History of Erie County, Pennsylvania.* Philadelphia, 1862.
Sanjek, Russell. *American Popular Music and Its Business: The First Four Hundred Years. Vol. 2: 1790–1901.* New York: Oxford Univ. Press, 1988.
"Sarah Ann Robinson." *Fayette County Texas Heritage.* Vol. 2. Fayette Co. History Book Committee, 1996.

Saxon, A. H. "Shakespeare and Circuses." *Theatre Survey* 7, no. 2 (Nov. 1966): 59–79.
———. *Enter Foot and Horse: A History of the Hippodrama in England and France.* New Haven: Yale Univ. Press, 1968.
———. *Selected Letters of P. T. Barnum.* New York: Columbia Univ. Press, 1983.
Schick, Joseph S. *Early Theater in Eastern Iowa.* Chicago: Univ. of Chicago Press, 1939.
Senelick, Laurence. *The Age and Stage of George L. Fox, 1825–1877.* Hanover, N.H.: Tufts Univ.–Univ. Press of New England, 1988.
Sennett, Richard. *The Fall of Public Man.* 1977. New York: Random House–Vintage, 1978.
Sherwood, Robert Edmund. *Here We Are Again: Recollections of an Old Circus Clown.* Indianapolis: Bobbs, 1926.
Silber, Irwin. *Songs of the Civil War.* New York: Columbia Univ. Press, 1960.
Slout, William L. "The Great Roman Hippodrome of 1874: P. T. Barnum's 'Crowning Effort.'" *Bandwagon* 42, no. 1 (1998): 29–34.
———. "The Recycling of the Dan Rice Paris Pavilion Circus." *Bandwagon* 42, no. 4 (1998): 13–21.
———. *A Royal Coupling: The Historic Marriage of Barnum and Bailey.* San Bernardino, Cal.: Emeritus Enterprises Publ., 2000.
———. *Olympians of the Sawdust: A Biographical Dictionary of the Nineteenth Century American Circus.* San Bernardino, Cal.: Borgo Press, 1998.
———. *Clowns and Cannons: The American Circus During the Civil War.* San Bernardino, Cal.: Borgo Press, 1997.
Smith, Daniel Scott, and Michael S. Hindus. "Premarital Pregnancy in America 1640–1971: An Overview and Interpretation." *Journal of Interdisciplinary History* 4 (Spring 1975): 537–570.
Smith, Gen. *American Gothic: The Story of America's Legendary Theatrical Family—Junius, Edwin, and John Wilkes Booth.* New York: Simon & Schuster, 1992.
Smith, Seba. *The Life and Writings of Major Jack Downing.* Boston, 1833
Southwick, Leslie H. *Presidential Also-Rans and Running Mates, 1788–1996.* 2d ed. Jefferson, N.C.: McFarland, 1998.
Spalding, Gilbert R. Interview. "Full of Interest: Reminiscences of a Veteran Amusement Manager." *St. Louis Missouri Republican*, 1 Feb. 1880, p. 5.
Speaight, George. "A Note on Shakespearean Clowns." *Nineteenth Century Theatre Research* 7, no. 2 (Autumn 1979): 93–98.
———. *A History of the Circus.* London: Tantivy Press, 1980.
Stansell, Christine. *City of Women: Sex and Class in New York, 1789–1860.* New York: Knopf, 1986.
Stone, Lawrence. *Family, Sex and Marriage: England 1500–1800.* New York: Harper & Row, 1977.
Stow, Charles. "The Pioneers of the American Circus." *Theatre Magazine* (Aug. 1905): 192–194.
Stryker, William S. *Official Register of the Officers and Men in the Revolutionary War.* Baltimore: Genealogical Publ., 1967

Sturtevant, C. G. "Little Biographies of Famous American Circus Men." *White Tops* (Oct. 1928): 7.

Sylvester, Nathaniel Bartlett. *History of Saratoga County, New York, 1609–1878.* Philadelphia, 1878.

Teachout, Terry. "Beyond the Sugar Plum Fairy." *New York Times Book Review,* 3 May 1998, p. 13.

"Texas Sifting." *The New Handbook of Texas,* vol. 6. Austin: Texas State Historical Assoc., 1996.

Thayer, Stuart. "Lexicon." July 2000. Transcript to author.

———. "Mr. Lincoln, Senator Douglas and the Circus." *Bandwagon* 43, no. 3 (1999): 30–31.

———. "P. T. Barnum's Great Museum, Menagerie, Hippodrome and Traveling World's Fair: Season of 1873." *Bandwagon* 41, no. 4 (1997): 26–30.

———. "P. T. Barnum's Great Travelling Museum, Menagerie, Caravan and Hippodrome." *Bandwagon* 20, no. 4 (1976): 4–9.

———. "The Circus That Inspired the Ringlings." *Bandwagon* 40, no. 3 (1996): 23–25.

———. "The Elephant in America 1840–1860." *Bandwagon* 35, no. 5 (1991): 35–36.

———. "The History of the Concert or After-Show." *Bandwagon* 41, no. 5 (1997): 10–12.

———. "The Out-Side Shows." *Bandwagon* 36, no. 2 (1992): 24–26.

———. *Annals of the American Circus.* Vol. 1: *1793–1829.* Manchester, Mich.: Rymack, 1976.

———. *Annals of the American Circus.* Vol. 2: *1830–1847.* Seattle: Peanut Butter Press, 1986.

———. *Annals of the American Circus.* Vol. 3: *1848–1860.* Seattle: Dauven and Thayer, 1992.

———. *Traveling Showmen: The American Circus Before the Civil War.* Detroit: Astley & Ricketts, 1997.

Toll, Robert C. *Blacking Up: The Minstrel Show in Nineteenth-Century America.* London: Oxford Univ. Press, 1974.

Toole-Stott, Raymond. *Circus and Allied Arts: A World Bibliography, 1500–1957.* 4 vols. Derby, Eng.: Harpur, 1958–1971.

Towsen, John. *Clowns.* New York: Hawthorn Books, 1976.

Traber, J. Milton. "The Lives of Famous Clowns." *Billboard* (23 Dec. 1911): 5.

Trachtenberg, Alan. *The Incorporation of America: Culture and Society in the Gilded Age.* New York: Hill, 1982.

Tryon, John. *The Old Clown's History.* New York, 1872.

Turner, Andrew Jackson. "The History of Fort Winnebago." *Army Life in Wisconsin Territory.* Madison, Wisconsin 1898.

Twain, Mark. *Adventures of Huckleberry Finn.* 1884. Boston: Houghton-Riverside, 1958.

Vail, R. W. G. *Random Notes on the History of the Early American Circus.* Barre, Mass.: Barre Gazette, 1956.

[Van Orden, Wessel T. B.?] *Sketches from the Life of Dan Rice, the Shakspearian [sic] Jester and Original Clown.* Albany, N.Y., 1849. Somers (N.Y.) Historical Soc.; Tibbals.

Volk, Leonard. *History of the Douglas Monument at Chicago.* Chicago, 1880.

———. *Reminiscences.* Vol. 8. *A Catalog of the Alfred Withal Stern Collection of Lincolniana in the Library of Congress,* 1960.

Waller, George. *Saratoga: Saga of an Impious Era.* Englewood Cliffs, N.J.: Prentice, 1966.

Wallett, William F. *The Public Life of W. F. Wallett, the Queen's Jester.* John Luntley, ed. London, 1870.

Walsh, John J. *Vignettes of Old Utica.* Utica, N.Y.: Dodge Graphic Press, 1982.

Warner, Joseph. "Dan Rice, Showman." *Lansing (Mich.) Journal,* 22 Feb. 1893.

———. Interview. "A Colleague of Old Dan Rice." *Billboard* (15 April 1911): 8.

Watt, David W. "Side Lights on the Circus Business." *Bandwagon* 44, no. 5 (2000): 47.

Way, Frederick, Jr. *Way's Packet Directory, 1848–1983.* Athens: Ohio Univ. Press, 1983.

Wecter, Dixon. *Sam Clemens of Hannibal.* Boston: Houghton-Mifflin, 1952.

Welter, Barbara. "The Cult of True Womanhood: 1820–1860." *American Quarterly* 18, no. 2 (Summer 1966): 151–174.

White, Edgar. Interview. "The Oldest Living Clown." *Circus Scrap Book* 1, no. 4 (Oct. 1929): 30–37.

Whitman, Walt. "The Circus." In *New York Dissected.* Emory Holloway and Ralph Adimari, eds. New York: Rufus Rockwell Wilson, 1936.

Wiebe, Robert H. *The Opening of American Society: From the Adoption of the Constitution to the Eve of Disunion.* New York: Knopf, 1984.

Wilentz, Sean. *Chants Democratic: New York City and the Rise of the American Working Class, 1788–1850.* New York: Oxford Univ. Press, 1984.

Williams, Raymond. *Culture and Society, 1780–1950.* New York: Harper, 1966.

Wills, Garry. *Lincoln At Gettysburg: The Words That Remade America.* New York: Simon & Schuster, 1992.

Wilmeth, Don B. *The Language of American Popular Entertainment.* Westport, Conn.: Greenwood, 1981.

Wilson, H. G. *Official Route Book of the Pawnee Bill Wild West Show.* Piqua, Ohio, 1898.

Wittke, Carl. *Tambo and Bones: A History of the American Minstrel Stage.* 1930. Westport, Conn.: Greenwood Press, 1968.

Public Records

"Cholera Health Reporter." MCNY, MS. Coll., Cab. 3, Box 180.

Council Minutes. Davenport, Iowa, 30 March 1844.

Council Minutes. Lyons City (North Clinton), Iowa, 2 Aug. 1861.

Erie County Records, 1853–1902. Recorder of Deeds Office, Erie., Pa.

Historical Statistics of the United States. Washington, D.C.: Bureau of the Census, 1975.

Index of Marriages and Deaths in New York, 1788–1817. Vol. 2. Worcester, Mass.: American Antiquarian Society, 1952.

Journal of the Proceedings of the Legislative Council of the State of New Jersey. New Brunswick, 1825.

List of Vessels Chartered, Hired, Employed by the Quartermasters' Department During the Late Rebellion. National Archives, Record Group 92, Entry 1418.

Laws of Pennsylvania, 1815 (chap. 4104), supplements 1817 (chap. 4325) and 1854 (no. 629).

Marriage Records, Lavaca County, Texas, Vol. B, p. 45; Vol. C., p. 151; Vol. D, p. 177; Vol. E., p. 337.

Minutes of the District Court of Lavaca County, Vol. F, p. 135, 26 July 1875. Qtd. in letter to Leopold Morris, 3 June 1950, Boethel Archives, Friench Simpson Memorial Library, Hallettsville, Texas.

New Jersey Census, 1840, 1850, 1860.

New York City Directories, 1789 to 1846.

New York State Census, 1840, 1850, 1860.

Pittsburgh City Directories, 1837–1850. Carnegie Library of Pittsburgh.

Report of the Northwestern Sanitary Commission, Branch of the U.S. Sanitary Commission, for the Months of May and June, 1864. Chicago, 1864.

Series Y, "Voter Participation in Presidential Elections, 1824 to 1868," *Historical Statistics of the United States,* Part 2, Washington, D.C.: Bureau of the Census, 1975.

Votes and Proceedings of the Fifty Second General Assembly of the State of New Jersey, 1828.

Young v. Young, 82 Pa. Super. 492, 1924, Lexis, p. 4.

National Publications

Dramatic Mirror, 3 Mar. 1900.

Frank Leslie's Illustrated Newspaper, 11 May 1861, 406; 22 Feb. 1862, 215; 19 Mar. 1864, 403.

Harper's Weekly, Nov. 1855, 843; 4 Mar. 1865, 139; 25 Nov. 1865, 737–738.

Nation, 3 Aug. 1882, 83.

New York Clipper. 1853–1900. Cited as *Clipper.*

Police Gazette, 1 Apr. 1883, 9 May 1891.

Porter's Spirit of the Times, 4 Oct. 1856, Feb.–Apr. 1859, Dec. 1859–Feb. 1860. Cited as *Porter's Spirit.*

Spirit of the Times: A Chronicle of the Turf, Agriculture, Field Sports, Literature and the Stage. 1831–1861. Cited as *Spirit.*

Wilkes' Spirit of the Times. 1859–1861. Cited as *Wilkes' Spirit.*

[Note: William Porter started *The Spirit of the Times* in 1831, then left in 1856 to found *Porter's Spirit.* After Porter's death in 1858, George Wilkes (who had started the *Police Gazette* in 1845) took over, then left to found *Wilkes' Spirit* in 1859. All three *Spirits* were in operation as the Civil War began. In June 1861, the original *Spirit* gave up the ghost, followed by *Porter's Spirit* in December. Wilkes later claimed the mantle of the original, dropping his name from his title in 1868, and renumbering his paper in 1873 to fit the numbering of the first *Spirit.*]

Clippings

"Celebrated Showman." Obituary, Charles Noyes. *Erie Herald.* 30 Oct. 1885. CWM.
"Curiosities of Dan Rice's Great Show." Philadelphia, c. Mar. 1860. HTC.
"Dan Rice." Interview. *Chicago Tribune,* 25 Nov. 1881.
"Dan Rice." Obituary. *Dramatic Mirror,* 3 Mar. 1900.
"Dan Rice Before the Reconstruction Committee." Carthage, Ill., 10 May 1866. CWM.
"Dan Rice Celebration is Suggested by Girard Men," *Chicago Daily Tribune,* 13 Apr. 1937. Hertzberg.
"Dan Rice Farewell," *White Tops* (Dec. 1937): 30, qtg. *Hartford, Conn. Times,* 30 July 1868. CWM.
"Dan Rice's Great Show." Salem, Mass., 19 Sept. 1863. CWM.
"Dan Rice's Widow" [*sic*]. N.p., 10 Mar. 1901. Mercyhurst.
"The Docile Rhinoceros." 21 Mar. 1858. HTC.
"Du Chaillu and Dan Rice in Literature." *New York Herald,* 25 Oct. 1891.
"Famed Circus King." Obituary, John Robinson. 4 Aug. 1888. Hertzberg.
"First Showboat." Public Library of Cincinnati and Hamilton County.
"Great National Circus." Jamestown, N.Y., June 1863. Kunzog-Adams.
"The Late Mrs. Showles." Obituary. *York Dispatch,* 15 Mar. [c. 1923]. Hertzberg.
"Lives of Famous Showmen." 4 Mar. 1911. Hertzberg.
"Noted Kentucky-Born Author Recalls Thrill of First Circus." *White Tops*, May-June 1947, p. 23, rprnt. 1935 article.
"Old Dan Rice." *Chicago Times-Herald,* c. Apr. 1895. MCNY.
"Old Dan Rice." Interview. *Detroit Free Press,* 23 Feb. 1893.
"Old Dan Rice . . . of Circus Fame." Interview. Girard *Cosmopolite,* 19 Jan. 1922.
"'Old Put' Drowns." Iowa Clipping File 2: 240. State Historical Society of Iowa.
"Old Time Clown." *Boston Globe,* 19 Mar. 1907. NYPL-LC.
"Prince of the Circus Ring." Clipping, c. Feb. 1900. CWM.
"Recollections of Dan Rice." C. 1890. CWM.
"Rice for President" articles, 1867–1868. Tibbals (most reprinted, Brown 392–424).
"Romance and the American Circus." *Chicago Sunday Record-Herald,* 16 Apr. 1911.
"Special to the Indianapolis Journal." C. 1890s. HTC.
"Teacher's Institute Near Fizzle by Dan Rice's Marriage." *Girard Pa. Cosmopolite*, 11 Mar. 1955.
"What Dan Rice Recalls." c. 1891. CWM.
"When William C. Coup and Daniel Castello Came Out of the West." Hertzberg.
Show World, c. 1882. NYPL-LC.
Syracuse engagements, 8–9 June 1855 and 21 Sept. 1859. Onondaga.
Vincennes, Ind., 15 Sept. 1860. Thayer.

Newspapers by Location

[John Polacsek supplied many clippings from the Great Lakes region; Orin C. King provided those from Kansas; and Sabina Shields Freeman from Girard and Erie, Pa. Many more came from Stuart Thayer. When other evidence suggests reliability, I have quoted from Kunzog's biography or photocopies of Kunzog clippings provided by Earl Adams. Notes referring to articles from Rice!, Blue, and Mercyhurst are not listed individually here.]

Albany Argus, 1842, Nov. 1844, 1845 (Thayer), Apr. 1880.
Albany Evening Times, 12 Apr. 1880.
Ann Arbor Argus, Sept. 1864 and May 1871.
Ann Arbor Peninsular Courier, June 1862, May–June 1871.
Atchison (Kan.) Daily Champion, 11 Aug. 1869, 27–28 May 1873.
Baltimore American, 1857, 1859, Mar.–Apr. 1860, and Nov. 1871.
Baltimore Sun (cited as *Sun*), 1845–1846, Dec. 1855, Mar. 1857, 1859, Nov. 1871.
Baraboo (Wis.) Republican, 23 June 1855; 30 Aug. 1857.
Belleville (Kans.) Telescope, 29 Aug. 1878.
Bloomington (Ill.) Daily Pantagraph, July 1858. Thayer.
Blue Rapids (Kans.) Blue Valley Telegraph, 6 Sept. 1878.
Boston Herald, Aug. 1856, Dec. 1858.
Brooklyn Daily Eagle, Sept. 1857.
Buffalo Morning Express, Aug.–Sept. 1846, Sept. 1850, July 1851.
Cairo Weekly Times and Delta, 5 Dec. 1855.
Camden West Jerseyman, 24 July 1850.
Chicago Post, Sept. 1861, Dec. 1862, Oct.–Nov. 1863.
Chicago Tribune, June 1858, Sept. 1861, June 1862, Jan. 1863, 1864, Nov. 1881, Mar. 1885.
Cincinnati Daily Enquirer (cited as *Enquirer*), 1847–1865, 1875, 1885.
Clinton (Iowa) Daily Herald, 2 Sept. 1879. CWM.
Columbus (Ohio) Dispatch, 21 Dec. 1879, 2 Apr. 1883, 4 July 1883. Polacsek.
Covington Journal, 20 Aug. 1853.
Davenport (Iowa) Democrat, 4 May 1869.
Davenport (Iowa) Gazette, 28 Mar. 1844.
Decatur (Neb.) Burtonian, 18 July 1878.
Detroit Free Press, 31 May 1873. Thayer.
Eldorado (Kans.) Butler County Democrat, 5 Oct. 1882.
Erie (Pa.) Chronicle, 19 July 1853.
Erie (Pa.) Daily Dispatch, 15 Sept. 1864, 7 Feb. 1866, 2 Nov. 1865, Aug.–Nov. 1866, Jan. 1867, Jan.–Mar. 1867 (Kunzog-Adams), Oct.–Dec. 1867.
Erie (Pa.) Sunday Morning Gazette, 7 Aug. 1887.
Erie (Pa.) Weekly Gazette, 1 May 1856, 29 Aug. and 26 Sept. 1861, May 1862, 18 and 30 Apr. 1863, 9 Nov. 1865.
Essex (Mass.) Statesman, 19 Sept. 1863.
Evansville (Ind.) Daily Journal, 9 Sept. 1869, 16 May 1870. CWM.
Fond du Lac (Wis.) Daily Reporter, 31 Mar. 1883, 9 June 1885. Polacsek.

Fort Worth (Tex.) Daily Gazette, 9 June 1885.
Ft. Scott (Kan.) Daily Monitor, 24 May 1872.
Gallipolis (Ohio) Bulletin, 7 June 1876.
Galt, Ont. 25 July 1857. CWM.
Girard (Pa.) Union, 2 Nov. 1865. Lincoln Museum, Fort Wayne, Ind.
Greensburg (Pa.) Republican and Democrat, 11 Sept. 1867.
Halifax (Nova Scotia) Evening Express, 16 July 1862.
Hallettsville (Tex.) Herald, 23 Apr. 1908.
Hannibal (Mo.) Tri-Weekly Messenger, 31 Aug. 1852.
Hannibal (Mo.) Journal, 29 June 1848.
Harrisburg (Pa.) Patriot and Union, 8 Oct. 1863.
Jamestown (N.Y.) Journal, 9 May 1856, 8 July 1864.
Jersey City Daily Telegraph, 29 July 1850. Thayer.
Kenosha (Wis.) Times, June–July 1858.
Kentucky Statesman, 25 July 1854.
Keokuk (Iowa) Gate City, 7 Oct. 1881. CWM.
La Crosse (Wis.) Tri-Weekly Democrat, Aug. 1861.
Lansing (Mich.) State Journal, 28 Apr. 1955, qtg. Lansing *Semi-Weekly Republican,* 9 May 1876.
Leavenworth (Kan.) Daily Commercial, 7 Aug. 1869, 22 May 1873.
Leavenworth (Kan.) Times & Conservative, 8 Aug. 1868.
London (Ont.) Advertiser, 23 Aug. 1862.
Louisville Courier-Journal, 13 June 1887.
Lowell (Mass.) Daily Courier, July 1859, 23–24 Sept. 1863.
Lyons City (Iowa) Advocate, 27 July 1861.
Madison (Wis.) Democrat, 22 Nov. 1900.
Marietta (Ohio) Intelligencer, Oct. 1839, Aug. 1848, 18 June 1853, 8 Sept. 1858.
Marietta (Ohio) Times, 30 May 1867.
Memphis Appeal, 26 Oct., 1880, 2 Apr. 1882.
Memphis Avalanche, Nov. 1860.
Metropolis (Ill.) Promulgator, 15 Sept. 1877. Polacsek.
Mobile Register, Jan. 1848, Nov. 1852–Feb. 1853, Jan. 1872, Mar. 1881.
New Orleans Crescent (cited as *Crescent*), 1848, 1850–1856, Dec. 1860–Feb. 1861.
New Orleans Delta (cited as *Delta*), 1848, 1861.
New Orleans Picayune (cited as *Picayune*), 1848, 1861, 1865, 1872, 7 Apr. 1880, 22 Dec. 1884, 25 Dec. 1892.
New Orleans Republican, 19 Jan. 1871. Historic New Orleans Collection.
New York Daily Graphic, 12 Jan. 1888. CWM.
New York Evening Post, Jan 1823, Jan. 1848, Feb. 1858.
New York Herald, 1845–1849, Feb. 1858, Jan. 1859, Jan. 1862, Apr. 1883, June 1887, Apr.–June 1891, 23 Feb. 1900, 24 Aug. 1901.
New York Mercury, 21 Apr. 1876.
New York Morning Star, Feb. 1849.
New York Sun, Dec. 1845, 1849–1850, Jan. 1858, 14 June 1891, 23 Feb. 1900.
New York Sunday News, 3 Feb. 1884.

New York Times, 1856–1858, Jan. 1871, Aug. 1874, Dec. 1879, Feb. 1880, Apr. 1883, June 1887, Apr. 1891, 24 Feb. 1900.
New York Tribune, 27 Sept. 1850 (Onondaga), 1857–1859, May 1861, Dec. 1879, 7 Nov. 1897–Illustrated Supplement, 24 Feb. 1900.
Newport Daily News, 8 June 1856.
Norristown (Pa.) Register & Democrat, 26 Aug. 1856. CWM.
Olathe (Kans.) Mirror, 18 May 1872.
Omaha (Neb.) Republican, 11, 17–18 July 1878.
Osage Mission (Kans.) Neosho County Journal, 18 May 1872.
Oswego (N.Y.) Gazette, 17 Apr. 1883. Somers (N.Y.) Historical Society.
Parsons (Kans.) Sun, 27 Sept. 1879.
Philadelphia Bulletin, Jan. 1850, Apr. 1855, Mar. 1857, Mar. 1858, Mar 1862.
Philadelphia Inquirer, Mar. 1862.
Philadelphia North American, 28 Dec. 1900.
Philadelphia Public Ledger (cited as *Public Ledger*), Nov.–Dec. 1846, Jan.–Mar. 1847, June and Nov. 1848, Jan. 1849, Apr. 1855, Mar. 1857, Feb.–Mar. 1858.
Philadelphia Sunday Dispatch (cited as *Sunday Dispatch*), 1 Apr. 1855, Mar. 1857, Nov. 1859–Mar. 1860, Mar. 1862, June 1864.
Philadelphia United States Gazette (cited as *U.S. Gazette*), Oct. 1846–Feb. 1847.
Pittsburgh Dispatch, Nov. 1859, Jan. 1865.
Pittsburgh Gazette, 12 Oct. 1839, May 1849, June 1851, Oct. 1854, Nov. 1859, Oct. 1863, Oct.–Nov. 1867.
Pittsburgh Mercury and Democrat, 25. Aug. 1841.
Pittsburgh Mercury, 15 Aug. 1838.
Pittsburgh Daily Morning Post (cited as *Pittsburgh Post*), 1843, 1847, 1859, 1863, 1866, 1867.
Pittsburgh Union, Oct. 1857.
Portsmouth (Ohio) Times, 17 June 1876.
Quincy (Ill.) Daily Herald, 19 May 1869.
Quincy (Ill.) Whig, 20 June 1848.
Reading (Pa.) Standard, 2 Oct. 1855. CWM.
Reading (Pa.) Times, 14 Oct. 1863, 22 Apr. 1868.
Rochester Daily Democrat, Sept. 1846, Sept. 1850, July and Sept. 1851.
Rochester Daily Union, Sept. 1854, May 1856.
Rochester Union & Advertiser, May 1857, Sept. 1859, 6 Apr. 1865, 25 Apr. 1876.
Salt Lake Daily Herald, 15 July 1882.
San Antonio Light, 10 June 1885, Jan.–May and 23 Sept. 1886.
San Francisco Chronicle, Aug.–Sept. 1882.
San Francisco Daily Alta California, 29 Aug. 1882.
San Francisco Examiner, 9 Apr. 1936.
Saratoga Springs (N.Y.) Saratogian, 6 Oct. 1870.
Shreveport South-Western, 7 Mar. 1855. Thayer.
Springfield Daily Illinois Journal, 3 Oct. 1860. Thayer.
St. Louis Daily Reveille, Apr.–June and Dec. 1848.
St. Louis Missouri Republican, 1 Feb. 1880.

Steubenville, Ohio, Western Herald, 3 Aug. 1848.
Syracuse Journal, 14 July 1860 (Onondaga), 31 July 1863, 7 May 1864, 30 Mar. and 26 July 1867 (Onondaga).
Syracuse Reveille, July and Sept. 1849.
Syracuse Standard, Aug.–Sept. 1851, July–Aug. 1856, June 1857, June and Aug. 1859.
Topeka (Kans.) Daily Blade, 6 Sept. 1878.
Topeka (Kans.) Daily Capital, 24 Dec. 1879, Jan. 1880, 29 Nov. 1881.
Topeka (Kans.) Daily Commonwealth, 17–18 Aug. 1869, 5 Sept. 1878, 9 Jan. 1880.
Toronto Daily Globe, 16 July 1857.
Trenton State Gazette, 5 Sept. 1855. Thayer.
Utica (N.Y.) Daily Gazette, July 1851.
Utica, (N.Y.) Evening Telegraph, 31 Oct. 1861.
Waco (Tex.) Daily Examiner, 15 Oct. 1885.
Washington, D.C., Morning Chronicle, June 1864.
Washington, D.C., Evening Star, Feb.–Mar. 1857, Apr. 1860, Jan. 1862.
Washington, D.C., National Intelligencer, Feb. 1857, Apr. 1860.
Washington, D.C., Union, Feb. 1857, Apr. and June 1860.
West Chester (Pa.) American Republican, 2 Oct. 1855. Thayer.
Wilmington (N.C.) Commercial, 5 Feb. 1850. Thayer.
Worcester (Mass.) Aegis and Transcript, 31 Dec. 1864 and 1 Apr. 1865.
Wyandotte (Kans.) Herald, 6 June 1878.

Letters

Adams, John. Letter to Benjamin Rush, 21 June 1811. Heineman Ms. 1c, Heineman Collection, Morgan Library.
Barnum, P. T. Letter to James L. Hutchinson, 29 June 1885. In *Selected Letters of P. T. Barnum,* A. H. Saxon, ed., 263. New York: Columbia Univ. Press, 1983.
Bell, Alexander Graham. Letter to Samuel P. Langley, 15 Feb. 1902. Library of Congress, Alexander Graham Bell Papers, Series: General Correspondence, Folder: Samuel P. Langley, 1888–1904.
Greene, Fred. Letter to Mrs. Dan Rice, Philadelphia, 1 May 1858. Mercyhurst.
Rhodes, Seth C. Letter to "Librarian, Pittsburgh." 8 Feb. 1953. Carnegie Public Library.
Rice, Dan. "Dan. Rice's Letter of Acceptance," 1 Oct. 1864. Photographic copy. Author's collection.
Rice, Dan. Letter to Ben W. Austin, 16 Apr. 1889. Circus Collections, Illinois State Univ., Milner Library—Special Collections.
Rice, Dan. Letter to Bert Wurzbach, 29 July 1897. Mercyhurst.
Rice, Dan. Letter to editor, *Clipper,* 12 May 1867. HTC; copy, MCNY.
Rice, Dan. Letter to Thomas Risk, 10 Dec. 1884. Hertzberg.
Rice, Dan. Letter to W. C. Crum, 21 June 1859. Pfening.
Rice, Dan. Letters to Ebenezer Brinton, 5 Oct. and 4 Nov. 1855, and 9 Feb. 1856. CWM.

Rice, Dan. Letters to Jacob Showles, 14 Feb. 1862 and 7 Nov. 1866. MCNY.
Rice, Dan. Letters to Libbie Showles, 22 Apr. 1866 and 2 Mar. 1894. MCNY.
Rice, Dan. Letters to Morrison Foster, 17 June and 24 July 1843, 20 and 28 Sept. 1883, 26 Jan 1884. Foster Hall Collection, Univ. of Pittsburgh.
Rice, Dan. Published letter, "Won't Give It Up," 28 Aug. 1866. Author's collection.
Rice, Kate. Letter to Maggie Rice, 22 Mar. 1861. Mercyhurst.
Rice, Margaret. Letters to daughters, 12 Mar. and 15 Sept. 1859. Mercyhurst.
Sanderson, John P. Letter to Abraham Lincoln, 4 July 1862. Papers of Abraham Lincoln, Robert Todd Lincoln Collection, Library of Congress.
Woodruff, T. S. Letter to J. E. Reed, 27 Dec. 1923. York [Pa.] Historical Society.

Rice Songsters (chronological order)

[Other, apparent Rice songsters are copies of those listed. A comparison of contents in the first four songsters is available at Circus World Museum; the last two have no original Rice material.]
Dan Rice's Original Comic and Sentimental Poetic Effusions. New Orleans, 1859. Brown Univ., Buffalo Grosvenor Library.
Dan Rice's American Humorist & Shaksperian Jester. Philadelphia, 1860. Microfilm, New York Public Library.
Dan Rice's Great American Humorist Song Book. New York? 1863. NYPL-LC.
Dan Rice's Songs, Sentiments, Jests, and Stories. New York, 1865. Microfilm, Univ. of Illinois-Champaign.
Dan Rice's Song Book. n.p., 1873. Tibbals.
Dan Rice's Old Time Circus Songster. New York, c. 1882. Newberry Library, Chicago.

Handbills and Heralds

[Handbills were small advertising sheets designed to be handed out; heralds were larger handbills, often tall and thin, as much as 30" by 12".]
"Circus Blennow." Handbill, Frankfort, Germany, 17 June 1860. Thayer.
"Circus!" Herald, Grand Gulf, Miss. 21 Oct. 1848. HTC.
"Col. Joe Cushing's." Herald, Boston, 1 Feb. 1856. Ringling Museum, Sarasota.
"Col. Joe Cushing's." Herald, Boston, 8 Feb. 1856. American Antiquarian Society.
"Crucible." Herald, 27 Jan. 1851. HTC.
"D. McLaren, Sole Lessee." Herald, Philadelphia, 10 Nov. 1860. Hertzberg.
"Dan Rice & Co.'s" Herald, Evansville, 4 July 1848. HTC.
"Dan Rice and Van Orden! The Other Side of the Question!" Herald, New Orleans, 17 Jan. 1851. Hertzberg.
"Dan Rice to Adam Forepaugh." Handbill, 24 May 1879 [twentieth-century reprint]. Author's collection.
"Dan Rice's Big One Ring Show!" Herald, 17 June 1891. Tibbals.
"Dan Rice's Big One Ring Show!" Herald, Astoria, N.Y. 20 June 1891. MCNY.
"Dan Rice's Benefit." Handbill, 7 Mar. 1862. CWM.

"Dan Rice's Bulletin! Number One!" Herald, New Orleans, 24 Jan. 1851. Hertzberg; HTC.
"Dan Rice's Circus." Herald, Utica, c. Sept. 1850. HTC.
"Dan Rice's Great Show." Herald, Philadelphia, 23 Feb. 1860. American Antiquarian Society.
"Dan Rice's Great Show." Herald, Philadelphia, 10 Mar. 1860. Somers (N.Y.) Historical Society.
"Dan Rice's Great Show." Herald, Aug. 1863. MCNY.
"Dan Rice's Great Show." Herald, Portsmouth, N.H., 29 June 1859. Hertzberg.
"Dan Rice's Rail and Steamer Circus." Herald, 24 Aug. 1870. CWM.
"Dan Rice's Ultimatum." Herald, Cincinnati, 17 Apr. 1869. CWM.
"The Elephant of Siam." Herald, Philadelphia, c. Feb. 1860. American Antiquarian Society.
"Ethiopean Serenaders!" Handbill, 1845. Author's collection.
"The Great River Show." Herald, 1864. Pfening.
"Herkimer, June 1, 1875." Handbill, DeHaven. CWM.
"Lecture: Dan Rice." Handbill, Garnett, Kans., 27 Sept. 1873. Stephen Foster Memorial, Univ. of Pittsburgh.
"Niblo's Garden," Handbill [facsimile], 18 Jan. 1858. NYPL-LC.

Other Ephemera

"Circus." Pamphlet, American Sunday-School Union, 1846. Author's collection.
"Col. Dan Rice." Ledger of Rice's income, 1869. Author's collection.
"Dan Rice's Bible." Page of family records. Hazel Kibler Museum, Girard (Pa.) Historical Society.
"Dan. Rice." Credit reports, 22 June and 1 Sept. 1871; 2 July and 30 Dec. 1872; 12 July 1876, 20 Jan. and 4 June 1877. PA vol. 61, R. G. Dun & Co. Collection, Baker Library, Harvard Business School.
"Excerpts from Family Scrap Books in Possession of Mrs. Harry P. Heldt." *Genealogical Records, Shrewsbury, New Jersey, 1939.* Monmouth County Historical Association.
"In Bankruptcy." List of creditors, Dan Rice, Bankrupt, Western District of Pennsylvania, 20 Mar. 1875. Kunzog-Adams.
"John Robinson's Ten Big Shows Combined—1882." Roster, John Robinson Papers. Cincinnati Historical Society.
"Paris Pavilion Circus." Seating chart, c. 1871. MCNY.
"Traveling Season of 1849." Hw ms, 9 May 1849. Tibbals.
"Uncle Sam: A Face of the Nation." Exhibit, Aug. 1999, New-York Historical Society, Ann Weisman, curator.
Benjamin, Park. "Dan Rice, The Celebrated Shaksperian Clown." Maria Ward Brown transcript of *The New World,* 30 Oct. 1847. Tibbals.
Brown, Maria Ward. Envelope addressed to Dan Rice, 1 Apr. 1895. MCNY.
———. Poems celebrating Rice's birthdays, 1897 and 1898. Author's collection.
Bryant's Programme & Songs. New York, 1859. Author's collection.

Contract and bill of sale. 9 Aug. 1860. Typescript, Kunzog-Adams.
Contract. Dan [Rice] McLaren and Margaret Rice McLaren, 1 Aug. 1860. Mercyhurst.
Contract. Dan Rice and Margaret Rice. 29 Apr. 1859. Kunzog-Adams.
Crum Family Bible. Monmouth County Historical Society.
Dan Rice's Amphitheatre. New Orleans, 1854. New York Public Library. [Catalogued as "1853?"]
Dan Rice's Budget. Philadelphia, 1 Jan. 1860. Theater Collection, Free Library of Philadelphia.
Dan Rice's Budget. Philadelphia, 6 Feb. 1860. Princeton Univ. Library.
Dan Rice's Interlude. New Orleans, 30 Nov. 1854. MCNY.
Dan Rice's Pictorial. 1, no. 2 (Aug. 1856), Boston. Tibbals.
Dan Rice's Pictorial. 4, no. 2 (June 1857), Girard, Pa. Tibbals.
Dan Rice's Pictorial. 5, no. 1 (June 1858), Girard, Pa. Somers (N.Y.) Historical Society.
Guy Bryan, Folder 16, Bryan Obear Collection, Western Historical Manuscript Collection, Univ. of Missouri-Columbia.
Handbook of the Arena. Courier, Goodwin & Wilder Circus, 1862. Tibbals.
Inventory of Hugh Manahan. 17 Oct. 1871. New Jersey State Archives.
Minutes of the Northern New York Conference-Methodist Episcopal Church. Watertown, N.Y., 1877.
Nathans & Co.'s New Consolidated Shows, Courier, Syracuse, 25 May 1883. CWM.
Obituary, Elizabeth Showles. 19 March 1924. Author's collection.
Program, Ursuline Chapel, Cleveland. Mercyhurst, Box 1 and Account Book 2.
Programme. Advertising newspaper. 21 Jan. and 3 Feb. 1858. New York. MCNY.
Programme. Advertising newspaper. 7 Apr. 1862. New York. Scrapbook 33, Mercyhurst.
Reed, Jessie Manahan. "The Crum Family." Collections of Barbara Carver Smith, Monmouth County (N.J.) Historical Society.
Rice, Dan. "Blue." Scrapbook (dark blue cover) kept by Rice. Author's collection (photocopy, CWM).
———. "Captain Dan Rice, the Nation's Humorist, on Buchanan's Cabinet." Broadside. Salem, Mass. [1857?]. Brown Univ. Library.
———. "Dan Rice's Rochester Song No. 3." New Orleans, 1852. Tulane Univ., Louisiana Collection.
———. "Great Show" ("Dan Rice's Great Show" on cover). Ledger, 1857–1858, and scrapbook. Author's collection (photocopy, CWM).
———. "Ledger B." Ledger, Girard matters, 1860–1862. Author's collection.
———. "Ledger: Dan Rice's Own Circus." 1870. Mercyhurst.
———. "New Orleans." (Cover missing, first page: "New Orleans, Nov. 26th 1852".) Ledger, 1852 and 1856, and scrapbook. Author's collection (photocopy, CWM).
———. "Pills and Quills." Sheet music, c. 1851. Copy, MCNY. [hw "New-York Historical Society" but not found there.]
———. "Rice !" ("Dan Rice!" pasted on cover). Scrapbook kept by Rice, primarily

from 1884–1886 lecture tour. Author's collection (photocopy, CWM).
———. "The Bloomer Song." Sheet music. New Orleans, 1854. Louisiana Collection, Tulane Univ.
———. Autograph, 20 May 1863. MCNY.
———. Last Will and Testament, Dan Rice McLaren, 28 Apr. 1899, probated, 24 Apr. 1900. New Jersey State Archives.
———. Memo, "83d Regiment," c. 1895. MCNY.
Route Book, Frank A. Robbins' New Shows. 1888.
Spalding and Rogers' New Railroad Circus. N.p., 1856. New-York Historical Society.
Van Orden Vertical file. Greene County (N.Y.) Historical Society.
Van Orden, Edmund H. Statement on estate of Wessel T. B. Van Orden, 3 Sept. 1877. Greene County (N.Y.) Historical Society.
Vital Statistics file (Van Orden). Greene County (N.Y.) Historical Society.

PERMISSIONS

Frontispiece
Maria Ward Brown, *Life of Dan Rice* (Long Branch, N.J.: Author, 1901), p. 54
Title page
Missouri Historical Society, St. Louis
9 *Dan Rice's Pictorial,* 1858, Somers Historical Society, Somers, N.Y.
16 Etching by Thomas Hornor, engraved by John Hill, I. N. Phelps Stokes Collection, The New York Public Library
26 *Music is Contagious,* William Sidney Mount, 1849, The Long Island Museum of American Art, History and Carriages, Stony Brook, N.Y.
36 *Sketches from the Life of Dan Rice,* 1849, p. 8, Somers Historical Society, Somers, N.Y.
45 Center for American Music, University of Pittsburgh
52 Handbill, 1845, Author's Collection
53 Harvard Theatre Collection, The Houghton Library
55 Cover, *Comical Fellows,* London, 1863, Author's Collection
63 Detail, "Excelsior," Shelburne Museum, Shelburne, Vermont
71 Missouri Historical Society, St. Louis
73 *St. Louis Daily Reveille*, 25 May 1848, Missouri Historical Society, St. Louis
90 *Account of the Terrific and Fatal Riot,* New York, 1849, Author's Collection
99 *New York Clipper,* 17 April 1880 (William Slout)
117 P. T. Barnum, *Struggles and Triumphs,* Buffalo, N.Y., 1872. Author's Collection
122 Daguerreotype, c. 1850, Author's Collection
134 Author's Collection
139 Collection of the New York Historical Society, negative #36805
143 *Dan Rice's Pictorial,* 1858, Somers Historical Society, Somers, N.Y.
146 John C. Kunzog, *The One-Horse Show,* Jamestown, N.Y.: Author, 1962, p. 4
158 Hertzberg Circus Museum, San Antonio, Texas
171 Brown, *Life of Dan Rice,* p. 38
177 Cleveland Moffett, "How the Circus Is Put Up and Taken Down," McClure's, June 1895, Author's Collection
187 *Dan Rice's Pictorial,* 1858, Somers Historical Society, Somers, N.Y.

191 © Shelburne Museum, Shelburne, Vermont
192 *Dan Rice's Pictorial,* 1858, Somers Historical Society, Somers, N.Y.
199 John J. Jennings, *Theatrical and Circus Life,* St. Louis, 1882, p. 512
213 21 October 1856 entry, New Orleans (Rice ledger, 1856), Author's Collection
215 Brown, *Life of Dan Rice,* p. 134
220 Brown University Library
227 Circus World Museum, Baraboo, Wisconsin
232 Museum of the City of New York
247 Museum of the City of New York
258 Borough Hall, Girard, Pennsylvania, Tim Rohrbach, photographer
265 Hertzberg Circus Museum, San Antonio, Texas
273 Museum of the City of New York
277 Author's Collection
285 Bust, Hertzberg Circus Museum, San Antonio, Texas
290 General Research Division, The New York Public Library, Astor, Lenox and Tilden Foundations.
297 *Dan Rice's Pictorial,* 1858, Somers Historical Society, Somers, N.Y.
301 Author's Collection
308 Museum of the City of New York
312 Brown, *Life of Dan Rice,* p. 498
315 Author's Collection
326 Author's Collection
329 Circus World Museum, Baraboo, Wisconsin
330 Circus World Museum, Baraboo, Wisconsin
349 Photograph of original print, Author's Collection
353 Dan Rice, 1876. Circus World Museum, Baraboo, Wisconsin
363 Author's Collection
367 Brown, *Life of Dan Rice,* p. 102
372 Author's Collection
377 Jennings, *Theatrical and Circus Life,* p. 520
381 Photograph (1937), Pfening Archives, Columbus, Ohio
385 "The King of American Clowns," Isaac Greenwood, *The Circus,* New York, 1898
390 Author's Collection
394 Museum of the City of New York
397 *New York Daily Graphic,* January 12, 1888, Circus World Museum, Baraboo, Wisconsin
403 Museum of the City of New York
407 Author's Collection
414 Museum of the City of New York
415 Author's Collection

INDEX

PublicAffairs is a new nonfiction publishing house and a tribute to the standards, values, and flair of three persons who have served as mentors to countless reporters, writers, editors, and book people of all kinds, including me.

I. F. Stone, proprietor of *I. F. Stone's Weekly*, combined a commitment to the First Amendment with entrepreneurial zeal and reporting skill and became one of the great independent journalists in American history. At the age of eighty, Izzy published *The Trial of Socrates*, which was a national bestseller. He wrote the book after he taught himself ancient Greek.

Benjamin C. Bradlee was for nearly thirty years the charismatic editorial leader of *The Washington Post*. It was Ben who gave the *Post* the range and courage to pursue such historic issues as Watergate. He supported his reporters with a tenacity that made them fearless, and it is no accident that so many became authors of influential, best-selling books.

Robert L. Bernstein, the chief executive of Random House for more than a quarter century, guided one of the nation's premier publishing houses. Bob was personally responsible for many books of political dissent and argument that challenged tyranny around the globe. He is also the founder and was the longtime chair of Human Rights Watch, one of the most respected human rights organizations in the world.

. . .

For fifty years, the banner of Public Affairs Press was carried by its owner Morris B. Schnapper, who published Gandhi, Nasser, Toynbee, Truman, and about 1,500 other authors. In 1983 Schnapper was described by *The Washington Post* as "a redoubtable gadfly." His legacy will endure in the books to come.

Peter Osnos, Publisher

www.ingramcontent.com/pod-product-compliance
Ingram Content Group UK Ltd.
Pitfield, Milton Keynes, MK11 3LW, UK
UKHW041658180625
459796UK00001B/48

9 781586 482398